This book is dedicated
to a better understanding
of what happened to all of us

"There were also false prophets among the people, just as there will be false teachers among you, who will introduce destructive heresies and even deny the Master who ransomed them."

- 2 Peter 2:1

"(d) Central Intelligence Agency.

The Agency will give high and continuing priority to all activities abroad supporting the objectives of this program, e.g.,...

(b) Infiltrate individuals into foreign associations and organizations with doctrinal potential (newspapers, universities, etc.) to influence their actions and output....

(f) Exploit local divergencies, heresies or policy disagreements within opposition systems."

- Annex B to the U.S. Doctrinal Program,
PSB D-33, June 29, 1953

"It is now apparent that [Msgr. Antonino] Romeo is right and that there is...[a] world-wide movement against orthodoxy in the Church."

- Msgr. Joseph C. Fenton to Fr. Francis J. Connell,
C.Ss.R., January 23, 1961

"Clare dear: The point of this historical argument is to show that, as the institution of the state-church owed its genesis to the special structure of an historic-social situation, so also it depends for its justification on the peculiarities of this situation. Alter the situation, and the argument for the institution is undermined....How's that?"

- John Courtney Murray, SJ, to Clare Boothe Luce
February 27, 1962

"*Time* took sides. We were encouraged to take sides....*Time* reporters were reporters as well as participant-observers to influence the schemas [of Vatican II]...Murray was a member of the conspiracy."

- Robert Blair Kaiser to Author
July 2010 and July 2011

CONTENTS

PART VI

PART VII

PART VIII

PART IX

PART X

PART XI

PART XII

PART XIII

PART XIV

FOREWORD

A GLOBAL ASSAULT ON MANKIND: "THE AMERICAN PROPOSITION" AND THE DETHRONEMENT OF CHRIST THE KING

"I am not what I am." It is with these scripturally inspired words that Iago, in Shakespeare's *Othello*, openly confesses his diabolical nature and the deceptive manner in which he, as a servant of the Enemy of Mankind, carries out his nefarious works. He thereby announces himself to be the opposite of God Almighty, who, through the unfolding of Sacred History, tells us not only that He "is" but that He unchangeably is what he says He is: namely, the Father of Lights, through whose Divine Incarnate Son, Jesus Christ, comes every good and perfect gift for the redemption and sanctification of His People. But daily life demonstrates that fallen man is all too easily seduced by the devil and his minions, and even when Othello, his life in ruins, finally awakens to the truth and seeks to slay his tormentor, he finds it difficult to do so. "I bleed, sir, but not kill'd," the villain chillingly proclaims.

All of "enlightened" modernity is not what it says that it is. In its stubborn insistence upon confining man's knowledge and aspirations to the natural realm alone, it has come to trap the entire globe in the darkness of Plato's unredeemed cave, commanding its prisoners to adore the chains that bind them, as well as to reject the Platonic search for more and more of the "light" that must expand to acceptance of supernatural

Revelation and Grace under the Social Kingship of Christ if their liberation is to be secured.

The result is that modernity's claim to ensure the victory of reason, science, liberty, equality, fraternity, social order, and justice for all has succeeded only in perpetrating the most fraudulent crime against humanity in the history of the world. Its sweet language masquerades the triumph of the strongest, earth-bound, sinful wills over all that is honestly true, good, and beautiful. As a fellow wounded soldier in the early days of World War One tells Céline in his autobiographical novel, *Journey to the End of the Night*, whenever the proponents of the benefits of enlightenment gain the upper hand, their promises, in practice, amount to nothing more than the command to "pay up and march"; to pay up and march on behalf of an oligarchy that is partly ideological in its madness, partly criminal in its perversity, seriously divided in its intentions, but immensely powerful nonetheless.

What historians call the Radical Enlightenment -- the atheist, democratic vision of men like Baruch Spinoza (1632-1677) -- has never done the devil's work with long-lasting effectiveness. Most people simply find its open and clear annunciation of an anti-religious naturalist program much too unsettling to follow. It is the Moderate Enlightenment that has efficiently advanced and secured reception of the superficially sweet but deadly secularist outlook. For while also vigorously cultivating a purely earth-bound, practical, results-oriented wisdom designed to feed that "Promethean lust for material power that serves as the deepest common drive behind all modern Western cultures" (R Gawthorp, *Pietism and the Making of Eighteenth-Century Prussia*, Cambridge, 1993, p. 284), this more conservative sounding movement insists that it is actually the best friend of true religion. It claims that the natural, scientific laws that it focuses its energies on discovering are sufficient on their own to prove the existence and benevolence of a Creator God, directing men away from useless dogmatic squabbles that only feed radical atheist critiques and providing the down-to-earth improvements finally giving the one truly essential Christian principle of charitable activity for the benefit of all serious practical clout in the process. It fully expects unbounded thankfulness and blessing from religious-minded folk for offering the sole means of fending off the assault of unbelievers and generally has, in fact, received them.

These supposedly religion-friendly and scourge-of-atheist agents of the Moderate Enlightenment---who nevertheless, in their own admittedly less brutal way, drag "every good and perfect gift that comes from above, the Father of Lights" down into the realm of unredeemed and changeable nature---have historically fallen into two camps. One of these, Prussian in origin, has gone down the secularist pathway by means of open, governmental support for a non-dogmatic form of Christian Pietism that equates "charity" and carrying out the will of the Creator God with the practical successes gained by the state and its rulers for their people's earthly well-being. The other, British by birth, and closely connected with the teachings of John Locke (1632-1704), pursues its equally secularist work not from above, through the state, but from below, by means of the creation of a world of "free individuals" which, indirectly and subtly, ultimately subjects everyone to the same kind of unrelenting, naturalist, dogmatic redefinition of true religion, Christian charity, and personal well-being found in Prussia.

Unlike that small and initially rather poor Kingdom---where only two Protestant denominations, Evangelical and Reformed, had to be taught to behalf themselves in a non-dogmatic manner lest radical atheism and more powerful neighbors take advantage of their ungodly warfare to destroy religion and country simultaneously---Britain was faced with a myriad of unruly battling Christian forces that could not be brought to bay as easily. The best path to preventing any of these varied types of believers from interfering with the pragmatic, naturalist Enlightenment program through imposition of their particular militant interpretations of supernatural revelation was to hoist the banner of religious toleration, the cause of which is forever associated with Locke's name.

While seemingly befriending all those churches ready to work under the rules of the religious toleration game, the land succumbing to Locke's *modus operandi* allows so many denominations to function and command popular attention that they end by "checking and balancing" one another out of any practical social significance. Fight all they want; none of them can ever win control of the political order, which is left to be dominated by the godly "pragmatists." Moreover, as they battle on, the thoroughgoing atomistic individualism that Locke's philosophy also teaches gradually eats away at these denominations' internal unity. They become little more than private clubhouses, whose authorities, depicted as tyrannical obstacles to the complete freedom and self-perfection of their constituent believers, are totally emasculated and rendered superfluous.

Once these clubhouses and their members' "liberation" is accomplished, the formerly factionalized Christians then discover that they have actually now been reunited; reunited under the sole permissible and "truly godly" dogma; the dogma of the freedom of the practical-minded individual: a freedom accompanied by a loss of any and all understanding of the common good and a stern prohibition of renewing the historically "divisive" search to regain one. With the Social Kingship of Christ, shaped by both Revelation and Reason abandoned, the "godly society" becomes a materialist jungle ruled over by an oligarchy of the strongest, most willful, most secular-minded, and ultimately self-destructive, atomist individualists. Divided though this elite may be, it knows that its survival is dependent upon keeping its subjects ignorant of the truth that it has effectively destroyed all substantive Christian Faith; that it has dethroned Christ in the name of protecting religion.

Still, it took a much more denominationally and ethnically diverse America to provide the conditions for perfecting this indirect, British-born path to total secularization, ensuring its victory by means of the conversion of its population to a new Prussian-like civil religion: Americanism. This jealous pseudo-faith brooks no contradiction, and the cheerleader authorities of the many still nominally Christian clubhouses under its spell, along with their individual, desacralized believers, learn voluntarily and enthusiastically to enforce its stern commands. And it is to "a better understanding of what has happened to all of us" in consequence that this excellent work of David A. Wemhoff is dedicated.

"Excellent" is actually too modest a word to describe Mr. Wemhoff's achievement. "Necessary" is an infinitely more suitable one. I cannot imagine a better means of driving home to readers what, exactly, Americanism is all about, how it came to exist, and the astonishingly effective manner in which it enforces the basically liberal, Anglo-American, Moderate Enlightenment dogmatic teaching than that which is offered by this painstakingly researched and passionately written text. Two basic explanations for the author's great success in getting the message across suggest themselves to me.

The first of these is the fact that Mr. Wemhoff plunges us into his account of Americanism and its ravages during the Second World War and the post-war era: precisely when the national cult had reached its full maturity, became conscious of possessing the means to bend the rest of the world to its teaching, and demonstrated the will to do so. Hence, he introduces us not just to the underlying, seductive claim of the Moderate Enlightenment to be the practical defender of religious as well as other freedoms (something that might have seemed more plausible as the American system was still in the process of development.) He also simultaneously shows the reality to which this "last and best hope of mankind," as Lincoln called it, logically leads at the dramatic historical moment when the materialist oligarchy that had always understood the value of the American system for maintaining its power came "out of the closet" and displayed its eagerness to work together with governmental agencies gone rogue to confirm its domination and extend it globally. The two sides of the Moderate Enlightenment coin, the Sophist siren song of freedom for all and the Triumph of the Will of an elite, are thereby presented to us in all of their contradictory horror at one and the same time.

Secondly, even though Mr. Wemhoff is a lawyer by profession, and a formidable one indeed, as the meticulous construction and unanswerable solidity of his argument makes abundantly clear, his book gets the message of the meaning of Americanism across because he also has the talent of a novelist. What he offers his readers is, in many respects, a non-fictional historical novel. This is exactly what his subject demands in order to be completely and properly grasped.

Allow me to explain what I mean here in just a bit more detail. Americanism, whose cultic character is obvious to anyone with eyes to see and ears to hear, nevertheless emphatically denies that it is anything other than a successful, "pragmatic" tool for providing peace, justice, and freedom for all the diverse elements of modern "pluralist" society---religious denominations included. It is so schizophrenic that it cannot be studied purely on the rational level. The highly irrational mixture of broad-ranging messianic ideology, specific and often contradictory personal and governmental power struggles, unrelenting propaganda, and psychological terror tactics that all play their role in securing acceptance of and compliance with Americanism's cultic demands cries out for a dramatic, novelistic form of presentation to do real justice to its mad complexity. Mr. Wemhoff's "novel" brilliantly responds to this pressing need, introducing us to strong personalities fed by strange mental and materialist passions, their character development, and their arrogant exploitation of the naïve and the weak, all in the context of a gripping, cosmic battle of God, man, and demons. The psychologically deranged reality of what "has happened to all of us" thus comes to life before our eyes in all of its irrational, macabre, tragic, and ultimately blasphemous intricacy in a way that a more prosaic text could never have been capable of staging. Dostoevsky would have been proud of him.

One can see this novelistic intricacy revealed in the full title of Mr. Wemhoff's work itself: *John Courtney Murray, Time/Life, and the American Proposition: How the CIA's Doctrinal Warfare Program Changed the Catholic Church*. Here we find a priest, the influence of the media, an appeal to the national teaching, the murky activity of an espionage agency engaged in religious warfare, and the "taking of the knee" of the Mystical Body of Christ to its cultic *Diktat* all associated together with the appropriate dramatic tension. I do not think that the author will mind my altering the order in which he lists these dramatic elements so as very briefly to provide a springboard for the reader about to leap into the text that follows.

"The American Proposition" was the name given to the speech written by Fr. John Courtney Murray, S.J., the editor of *Theological Studies*, a Jesuit journal published at the Woodstock Seminary in New York State, where he was also a professor. It was delivered in Rome by Henry Robinson Luce (1898-1967), the founder of the *Time/Life* publishing empire, at the *Pro Deo* University, founded and run by a Belgian Dominican, Fr. Felix Morlion. Luce's wife Clare (1908-1987) was serving at the same time as Ambassador to Italy, and the audience included a large number of luminaries of both Church and State.

Although the actual speech itself is discussed in detail on pages 373-382, Mr. Wemhoff's entire book centers round "The American Proposition" in the broader historical sense already outlined above: namely, the most effective tool for imposing the Moderate Enlightenment vision. Once again, this "proposition" is incarnated in a dogmatic, naturalist, sectarian, political cult, worshipping the American Foundation and its Founders. While claiming that it provides the sole viable bulwark for true religion and human freedom in the modern world, the "Proposition's" real function is to protect a variegated, hopelessly materialist, deeply morally challenged, and ever more degenerate, atomistic individualist elite. In short, "The American Proposition" is Shakespeare's Iago writ large.

What is most likely to shock the *general* reader who comes to this book without any previous knowledge of the entire problem of Americanism is the ruthless and thoroughgoing *Blitzkrieg* by means of which the elite in question pursued the triumph of "The Proposition" in the postwar era. Backed by the claim that its victory was absolutely necessary to prevent the radical destruction of all freedom and justice threatened by the dominance of Soviet Marxism---and this long after it became clear that no such ascendency was a danger---that ruthless, atomistic warfare was actually aimed at subjecting America's "allies" to her own economic hegemony, destroying their substantive historical cultures in the process. Not only, as the book's title indicates, did this involve the mass media and the CIA jointly cooperating in psychological warfare to destroy the European West, but the personnel engaged in this subversion moved from government work to positions in the *Time/Life* network and back again with breathtaking ease and a sense of entitlement.

What is most likely to shock the *Catholic* reader who is similarly unenlightened regarding the *modus operandi* of "The American Proposition" is the oligarchy's recognition that its triumph depended most of all on the dismantling of the Roman Church's commitment to the anti-naturalist, anti-atomist concept of the Social Kingship of Christ and the weakening of the dogmatic defenses surrounding it. In order to demolish these, it had to gain internal Catholic support for the Lockean position, developed in the American environment as a full-fledged doctrine of religious freedom (as opposed to one of mere toleration), and an admission that this, too, was the sole possible protection for the Faith in a world threatened by atheist Communism.

It was as a "fifth columnist" working to bring the Church to "see reason" in a "pluralist environment" that the Jesuit John Courtenay Murray, the chief apologist for religious freedom as "the best possible shield for the Faith" within the Catholic world, entered into the Time/Life, CIA, "American Proposition" camp. And it was with the arguments of men like Murray, along with the unswerving monetary and propagandistic assistance provided by the Media-CIA Complex at the time of Vatican Two and afterward, that a "Pastoral Council," supposedly changing nothing in Catholic beliefs, blithely opted to become a "clubhouse" supporting the American Civil Religion, uniting Church and State dogmatically as never before in history to ensure the triumph of a naturalist, oligarchic elite. But that is a tale that the book before you has to tell.

I have not had the good fortune to meet Mr. Wemhoff, but having spent my entire academic career, in one way or another, fighting against the same enemies that he has identified so clearly in this book, there is no doubt in my mind that we are blood brothers. I would never have had the stamina to do the research he had to do to complete this work, but no matter. There is plenty of work for all of us in fighting "The American Proposition," given the fact that Iago "bleeds" but is not yet dead. There are many "mansions" in the army of those fighting to put Christ back upon his throne. Viva Cristo Rey!

Dr. John C. Rao

INTRODUCTION

Ideas have consequences, as Richard Weaver observed in 1948. Societies are ordered, organized, and operated in accordance with ideas or principles. Some of the more important principles are those that pertain to man's nature and his relation to a higher power or deity or deities, the relation of the spiritual and the material, the relation of the individual to others, the nature of the state or government, and the economic system. These principles or ideas recognize and establish a certain hierarchy of values that serve to define good and bad in a real sense for the members of that society. The society known as America and the political entity known as the United States are not exceptions to these rules.

The Declaration of Independence and the United States Constitution are two important documents that order American society and the institutions of the United States. These documents are based on and reflect a set of principles, or political philosophy, and establish something called a political economy for American society. The man perhaps most responsible for articulating or crystallizing the principles underlying and forming America was Thomas Paine (1732-1809), and he did so in *Common Sense,* which first appeared on the streets of Philadelphia on January 9, 1776. The other Founders shared his views in one form or another. Constitutional scholars, especially Gordon S. Wood in his *The*

Radicalism of the American Revolution, explain how these principles, which I call the American ideology, were unlike anything else in human history and had a quick, profound change on every society they encountered. This ideology has several main points.

First, government is evil, though a necessary evil, and society at large is good. Hence, government's powers must be limited, and its primary purpose is to protect individual rights. Second, the individual is the measure of all things, and ethnicity is either eschewed or not recognized. Third, religion is defined as worship and is a private and personal matter, while government is there to keep it that way in the name of religious liberty or religious freedom. Fourth, society is dedicated to the accumulation of material wealth and the satisfaction of worldly desires. Finally, the American ideology is universally applicable as it is the way "to begin the world over again" and serves to give birth to a "new world."

There are, and have been, several consequences to the implementation of this ideology. First, spiritual values or religious faiths do not inform the policies or laws of the government or the civil authorities. The result was the secular state, the first one in history, and that secularism was ensured with the First Amendment's "Establishment Clause." The secular state ultimately results in a secular society, for the public comes to shape the private, and the higher comes to control the lower. The secular state, or government, ultimately comes to control religion and the various religious groups, as Catholic Bishop Joseph Fessler (1813-1872), Secretary of the Vatican I Council, observed and called "heathen Caesarism." (Appendix B contains a more detailed explanation of his ideas.) This control, as this book helps show, consists largely of attempting to change doctrine or policy of the Church (and other religious groups) and influence the leadership of the religious bodies to endorse the American ideology. Second, government policies tend to favor primarily, or mainly, the powerful private interests that are also protected in the name of limited government in their efforts to shape and control the culture and, hence, society. With freedom of the press, the ability to shape thoughts, values, and perceptions lies in the hands of private parties. These private parties control society by exerting power through the various cultural engines they control (especially the press, media, and entertainment) or through the government over which they have inordinate influence. In sum, under the American ideology, private parties come to control religion either directly or through the government. Third, society becomes infused with and oriented towards material values or materialism. Italian statesman and Catholic professor Amintore Fanfani (1908-1999) explained that as materialism rises, spiritual values or faith declines, and as spiritual values or faith declines, the capitalist spirit rises. He explained that the capitalist spirit is a spirit of consumerism or a desire to acquire and enjoy an ever-growing number of things. The capitalist spirit seeks the reduction or elimination of hindrances to the spreading of that spirit, and that means the reduction of barriers to markets, the free flow of capital, and commerce. Those best situated to gain from the capitalist spirit and its increase in society are the most powerful individuals or groups in society, usually the financial interests. One of the barriers they seek to eliminate is a state-established church and a state-established religion because these things hinder their ability to pursue the accumulation of wealth and power. Hence, even greater importance is given to the concepts of religious liberty, which means the individual chooses how he or she wishes to worship, and the separation of Church and State, which means religious beliefs are not to form the basis of public policies. Other barriers targeted for elimination by the wealthy private interests are ethnicity or any other group not authorized by these elites. (Appendix A contains a more detailed explanation of Amintore Fanfani and some of his ideas key to this book.)

The American ideology is part of Liberalism or Anglo-American Liberalism. It is part and parcel of the Enlightenment. If people accept it as good, several things happen. First, they organize or reorganize their societies to be like America. Second, they accept as good American ideas, ideals, policies, and actions in the world, thereby aligning themselves with the political entity known as the United States and opening themselves to American influence. Third, they adopt the American worldview and come to look at themselves and the world itself in terms devised by the American elites. Fourth, they spread American ideas and ideals.

The Americans had been on the march for a long time, but by the 1940s, they had the motive, means, and opportunity to take their ideology around the world. To do that, they recruited, among others, the religions of the world. One of the more important religions was the Catholic Church, which has a presence in every country, if not practically in every province or town. The U.S. government, ostensibly in response to the threat posed by Soviet Communism, formalized a program of Doctrinal Warfare that aimed to establish America as good in practice and in principle in the hearts and minds of the people of the targeted societies. To that end, it relied heavily on the American Proposition, which consisted of a set of ideas devised during the early days of the Cold War by Jesuit John Courtney Murray and his good friend Henry R. Luce, media mogul and founder of Time, Inc. which had close dealings with the Central Intelligence Agency (CIA). These ideas justified as good in principle, if not as the ideal, the ideology, with its underlying political philosophy, which gave rise to the American system of social, political, and economic organization, and thereby placed power in the hands of powerful private interests.

This book discusses the creation of The American Proposition and the machinery used to deliver it. It primarily focuses on the successful American effort to get Catholics to accept as true and good the philosophy underlying American society. Some Catholics were instrumental in advancing this effort, while others opposed it. Therefore, the events in this book are largely seen through the eyes of key Catholics involved in this important struggle during the early years of the Cold War. These Catholics are mainly Clare Boothe Luce, John Courtney Murray, SJ, Francis J. Connell C.Ss.R., Msgr. Joseph C. Fenton, Msgr. George Shea, and Dr. Edward P. Lilly. There are extensive references to various government documents previously classified but now declassified. There are also extensive references to talks, writings, diaries, and correspondence of Henry R. Luce and his important aide, Charles Douglas ("C.D.") Jackson, one of the progenitors and early practitioners of political or psychological warfare. The papers and diaries of John Shaw

Billings were helpful in understanding Luce's ideas, the work of Time, Inc., and a number of other things, such as the close relationship between the Central Intelligence Agency and Time, Inc. I also benefitted from the excellent efforts of a number of authors, historians, and scholars who discuss various aspects of the Cold War period in their works.

Many are to thank for the second edition of this book coming about. First and foremost, I thank the Good Lord, His Mother, St. Dominic de Guzman, St. Pio of Pietrelcina, and others of the Church Triumphant. I thank my friends for their encouragement and continuing support for this project, and my parents' continuing support, which I know comes from beyond. I thank you in the public who showed interest in the book and purchased the book. I thank all whose assistance was invaluable in making this important and large project possible. Thank you to Adam Mitchell for your tireless work in editing this book. My thanks continue to the archivists at the following facilities I owe a great debt of gratitude for their professionalism and many courtesies: the Rockefeller Archives, Georgetown University Library, Catholic University of America Archives, the University of Notre Dame Archives, the Dwight D. Eisenhower Museum and Library, the South Caroliniana Library, Elms College, Seton Hall, Yale University, Bentley Archives of the University of Michigan. I wish to single out for special thanks Alan Delozier of Seton Hall, Graham Duncan of the South Caroliniana Library, Jane Stoeffler of the Catholic University of America, Scott Taylor of Georgetown University Library Special Collections, Christopher Abrahamson, Michelle Kopfer and Chelsea Milner of the Dwight D Eisenhower Museum and Library, and Kaaren Ray custodian of John V. Cody's papers. I wish to deeply thank the Redemptorists of Brooklyn, New York, the Archivists at the Archdiocese of Chicago, and the Baltimore Province of the Society of Jesus for their courtesy and cooperation. In particular, I wish to mention Patrick Hayes, C.Ss.R., and Carl Hoegerl, C.Ss.R. There are countless others to thank, and please forgive me for not mentioning you all by name. Finally, I wish to acknowledge and thank Fr. Francis J. Connell, C.Ss.R., whose intercession I sought and received, for understanding, clarity, strength, and patience in the completion of this work, which took the better part of seven years.

We are living today with the consequences of the past. This book attempts to make sense of the nature of America, the significance of certain events, such as the Cold War, in our lives, and the vast changes in the Catholic Church during the last fifty years. I sincerely hope this work assists in achieving a useful and correct level of understanding of these things and a better understanding of our times. The lessons in this second edition are as relevant and important as ever.

--David Wemhoff

Granger, Indiana

January 2022

SUMMARIES

PART I - HENRY ROBINSON LUCE AND THE AMERICAN CENTURY

Henry Robinson Luce was the son of a Presbyterian minister and could trace his lineage back to the American Revolution. He invented the newsmagazine with the founding of *Time*. With the mentoring of Walter Lippmann, Luce put into practice the emerging science and systemization of psychological manipulation, which used images, words, and emotions to shape, form, and influence views, ideas, and perceptions both in the United States and overseas. With his magazines, Luce came to be one of the most powerful and influential men in America and, eventually, the world. It is said that there was not a day that he did not speak of the United States Constitution, which came to represent the political manifestation of the organizing principles of American society, or in other words, the American ideology.

By 1941, the American leadership and elites had the motive, opportunity, and means to go global with the American Revolution and the American ideology. With his State of the Union Address, known as the "Four Freedoms" speech, President Franklin Delano Roosevelt declared war on the world to reshape its societies in accordance with American ideology. More than a month later, Luce wrote an article entitled "The American Century" for *Life* magazine that confirmed this and made clear the primacy of the material in American goals. The first set of enemies to be defeated was Adolph Hitler and the German National Socialists, Benito Mussolini and the Italian Fascists, and the Empire of Japan. After they were defeated, another war was waged, but not as bloody as the last.

That war was the Cold War, and it was just as global as World War II. Luce named the new enemy Soviet Communism, even before the first set of enemies went down in bloody defeat. The Soviets were presented as an implacable, powerful, cunning foe and American ideas, troops, and money were needed to resist them. This new war was fought with ideas, words, symbols, and imagery – things Luce was expert in using. The message was that America stood for freedom, and freedom led to material prosperity and personal happiness. The Soviets stood for tyranny and a collective materialism that smothered the individual. The societies of the world were told to choose America over the Soviets. The peoples of the world were being sifted or caught between two materialistic societies – the Americans and the Soviets.

PART II - CLARE BOOTHE LUCE - AMERICAN CATHOLIC

Clare Brokaw became Henry Luce's second wife in 1935. She converted to the Catholic Faith in 1946 while a Congresswoman. Fiercely independent before marrying Henry Luce, whom she affectionately called Harry, she dedicated her life to advancing his ideas and his agenda after marrying him. Clare personified the idea that Catholics could advance and prosper in American society. That, in itself, was one of Harry's ideas.

Clare understood America harmed the Church. She explained this to Bishop Fulton Sheen, the man she credited with her conversion to Catholicism. American religious liberty and disestablishment were bad and caused the Church to be corrupted. She wrote:

"Oh, do not think I do not understand how it is with the Church in America. How sweet it is to be at long last on the right side of the tracks...and to be in the religious filed, as one of my Catholic friends put it, a real-up-and-comer!...Oh could it be that the Church itself is beginning to be just a little like the rich young man...? Men I say should not spend all their novenas and so much of their life of prayer in her contemplation – not in times like these, that call for eagles, and lions and tigers of the Lord!...Ravage the world with the Truths of Christ crucified....This is a lush land of glittering corruption....No King but saints and martyrs can save us now...."[1]

Clare understood America was "inescapably pragmatic." American Catholics "spend little time trying to convert their neighbors (and are always being bawled out by their priests for this lassitude). But they make up for it by 'contributing to the missions.'" However, a Catholic was a Catholic because he or she believed it is the 'one true faith,'...."[2] The U.S. Catholic prelates were attacked and worn down by intercreedal cooperation and interreligious cooperation. The bishops became "brick and mortar" men more intent on raising money and administration than leading, teaching, and Catholicizing America. After World War II, the bishops deferred to the theologians who, like Murray, supported the American ideology and offered a way for the Church that pleased the plutocrats. The priests and prelates reported to the U.S. government on their own people. If any of them displeased the plutocrats, like Fr. Charles Coughlin, then a prelate or his representative issued a condemnation of the offender. The priests or prelates who pleased the plutocrats were assured places of honor and respect. This state of affairs was the result of decades of Catholic support for the American ideology and persists to this day. American Catholic prelates ignored Rome and expressed loyalty primarily to America and its ideas. These prelates and their flocks viewed America as teaching the Church. In 1899, Pope Leo XIII called this Americanism and condemned it as a heresy. It lived on, though, and grew stronger and more prevalent.

PART III - JOHN COURTNEY MURRAY - THEOLOGIAN FOR AMERICA

The National Conference of Christians and Jews (NCCJ) sponsored a secret meeting at a luxury hotel in midtown Manhattan in April 1948 to advance their goal of making all men brothers in America. Essential to that was to promote the American definition of religious liberty and Church-State relations, both of which were the very same liberal views condemned by the popes of the Nineteenth Century. An obstacle to this was the Catholic doctrine on Church-State relations, which condemned Liberalism.

The way around this obstacle was to liberalize or change Catholic doctrine. This meant that a justification had to be developed for Catholics to accept America, the society, and the political entity known as the U.S., as organized in accordance with Catholic principles. A Catholic theologian was needed to help in that endeavor. John Courtney Murray, SJ, editor of *Theological Studies* from Woodstock College, was there with other Jesuits and well-healed Catholics. Murray promised to provide the intellectual and doctrinal justification to change Catholic doctrine on Church-State relations and religious liberty.

Murray had the bona fides for the work. During World War II, he justified inter-creedal cooperation, a rallying cry of the American elites, Protestants, and Wall Street. He started a re-examination of Catholic teaching on Church and State relations in 1945. By the time of the Biltmore Conference, Murray showed himself as someone who could be trusted to advance the interests of the elites.

PART IV - C.D. JACKSON AND AMERICAN UNITY

"It was not in numbers but in unity, that our great strength lies," wrote American Founder Thomas Paine in *Common Sense.* Unity was found in the person of Charles Douglas Jackson ("C.D. Jackson") during the Cold War. In one person, the efforts of American media, finance and industry, and government were united in the campaign to conquer the world for American ideas and ideals. The American ideology re-ordered societies by making them individualistic and materialistic. Real power went to powerful private financial interests, all in the name of freedom, liberty under God, democracy, and other similar, ambiguous, undefined, high-sounding slogans. A limited government and disestablished churches with free exercise of religion ensured that plutocrats would shape culture and have an inordinate influence on government. Religion and government, the two traditional enemies of wealth, were weakened in the name of making things better for the common man.

C.D. Jackson proved his worth over and over. He got the American Catholics to side with the Americans against the Germans and Italians in 1941. Most importantly, he refined psychological warfare to be more powerful than the atomic bomb and directed it at the enemy, including Catholics, calling it instead "political warfare." World War II was the great testing ground for that weapon, and Americans were the real masters of this new weapon quite possibly because American society was a commercial society from the beginning. Commerce is based on a combination of emotions and natural reason, with a mixture of manipulation and emphasis on the individual. The U.S. government's intelligence agencies worked closely with Henry Luce's Time, Inc., which was America's mainstream media of the day.

PART V - MURRAY'S BASIC POSITION (JUNE 1948)

In 1946, the Catholic Theological Society of America (CTSA) came into existence largely due to the efforts of Fr. Francis J. Connell, C.Ss.R. The organization was designed to keep Catholic doctrine pure and to serve the bishops as requested. Connell saw early on the dangerous impact of American war propaganda on young Catholics returning from World War II. These young men and women held a "neo-democratic" worldview and saw the Catholic Church as incompatible with the American way of life. The CTSA was mobilized to address these and similar issues in response to requests by Catholic prelates, most notably Archbishop Richard Cushing of Boston. Despite a good beginning, the CTSA started drifting away from the guiding principles Connell set out at his inaugural talk as its first president. By late 1947, the CTSA took on a life of its own as the role of theologians started to change from that intended by the Church leadership. The theologians, and not bishops, took the lead. The topics studied were being suggested neither by the *ecclesia docens* nor in response to their needs, but out of the desires of the theologians.

During this same period, Monsignor Joseph Clifford Fenton, Connell's ally and the editor of the Catholic theological journal *American Ecclesiastical Review*, disputed *Time's* depictions of the Catholic Church and Catholic doctrine. Fenton made note of the power and influence of *Time*, noting the effectiveness of the writing. He explained that Popes Pius IX and Leo XIII condemned Liberalism as it manifested itself in Europe and America. Fenton spent some time explaining the encyclical *Longinqua Oceani* as that document by Pope Leo XIII taught that America was not the ideal of church and state relations. It was a brave position, considering that he did so after World War II, which clearly was a victory for the U.S., and at a time while American propaganda and psychological operations were being felt around the world holding America out as the model of social organization and the great hope for humanity.

Murray's paper, "The Government Repression of Heresy," was presented at the third annual CTSA convention in Chicago in late June 1948. Connell presented the paper because Murray was stricken ill. That paper set out Murray's basic position on church and state and religious liberty, and this position was the heart of the dispute between Connell and Murray. Murray's position was that the state needed only to base its actions on natural law. He first articulated this position during his support of intercredal cooperation, but at the time, he recognized the pre-eminence of the Divine Positive Law, as did Connell. Murray said the American system of social organization, with its view of separation of Church and State and religious liberty comported with the natural law, ensured societal peace, and so was approved by Catholicism. Murray maintained this basic position on church and state as well as religious liberty all throughout his disputes with Connell, Fenton, and others leading to the promulgation of *Dignitatis Humanae* at the Second Vatican Council.

Murray's paper was, in reality, a refutation of Catholic doctrine Monsignor John Ryan explained a quarter century earlier. Ryan's writings were of great concern for the Protestants, the NCCJ, and the American elites, because they threatened to upset the secular control of the monied elites over societies. Connell insisted Catholics preach to all nations, to include America, the duty of the civil authorities to recognize Christ the King. It was a dangerous proposition, given the cultural engines were preaching America as the ideal.

PART VI - THE RISE OF MURRAY (1949)

Murray was the editor of *Theological Studies,* and he used it to expound his theories of church and state. By the late summer of 1949, Murray was engaging Protestants in their own magazines about church and state. In September 1949, Henry Luce first mentioned Murray in *Time* magazine during what amounted to be a staged fight with Dean Walter Russell Bowie of the Union Theological Seminary, where Henry Luce was a trustee. It was a staged fight and one that was designed to advance the American agenda of elevating America as the ideal of social organization, or at least acceptable to Catholics. The context of these discussions was the "Red Scare," which tilted the deck in favor of the American system of social organization.

PART VII - THE AMERICANISTS VERSUS THE CATHOLICS (1950-1952)

There ensued a crucial theological debate within the Church on the issues of church and state relations, as well as religious liberty. The details of this debate have been lost to history. On the one side were the Americanists, who believed America to be good in principle if not also the ideal. They were largely led by Murray and his friend and confrere, Gustave Weigel, SJ, as well as several writers at *America* magazine. On the other side were the Catholics led by Fr. Connell, Msgr. Fenton, Msgr. George Shea, a few Italian Jesuits, and a few Spanish Jesuits who saw the Americans were seeking to canonize a political philosophy. The struggle took place in the pages of Catholic journals and the American media.

The Americanists defended as good in principle the American system of church and state relations. Essential to this were the following positions: that man can understand the natural law only with one's natural reason unaided by revelation; that the state only had an obligation to the natural law; the natural law required freedom of all religious expression and belief; the natural law did not permit or enable the state to discern the One, True Faith/Church; the natural law did not require the establishment of a state church and state religion; Catholic doctrine on Church and State relations was based on a freedom principle with which the American or Enlightenment based constitutional democracies/republics and political systems were in full accord; the constitutional democracies/republics were favorable to the Church and did not give governments the power to suppress heresy or dissenting religions; the French Revolution was different from the American Revolution; the popes of the nineteenth century in condemning Liberalism were condemning only European Liberalism. The Catholics wrote of the duty of all societies to Christ the King, regardless of the form of their government; the ability of states to recognize and establish the Catholic Church and the Catholic Faith as the One True Faith/Church; the power and duty of the state to protect and defend the Church and the Faithful; the duty of societies to conform their laws and policies to be in accord with the Divine Positive Law.

The Americanist position denied the Church and the Faith preeminence in the laws of the State, or a juridical status, claiming that it was not theologically mandated by either Church doctrine or by the Anglo-American system. To support this position, the Americanists held the limitation of the government's power, thereby weakening the ability of the civil authorities to care for the whole American society, was a good thing. To fill the vacuum, stressed was the idea the government need only follow the natural law, an equivocal concept at best, and all the people constituted the ultimate political authority. The Americanists argued the Church was free to influence the laity or the society at large that then comprised the governing institutions and affected the policies and actions of these institutions accordingly. This arrangement attenuated the power of the Church to call the governing authorities to account for their obligations to Christ the King. That attenuation was, and is, sufficient to remove the Church and the Faith from any position of real influence in society over the laws and policies of the State or even the civil rulers. The Americanists argued that the First Amendment if not the Constitution as a whole, were articles of social peace. What they meant was that tension between the state and the churches would be reduced or eliminated in favor of the government which became superior to the churches. Another tension eliminated was that between ambitious private interests and the churches who became interest groups – on the same level – with these private interests.

PART VIII - THE U.S. TARGETS ITS FRIENDS

After the Americans conquered Germany in 1945, they put in place an organization to oversee the reconstruction and re-engineering of the society. Through intense psychological manipulation, German society underwent significant changes. The Americans were impressed with that and wanted to expand these efforts to their friends.

By the early 1950s, the U.S. government undertook a program of doctrinal warfare which was "the central core of psychological war" and was designed to inculcate in the intellectuals of various world societies the idea that America was good, if not the ideal, and that American ideas on socio-political-economic matters and organization were right. Western Europe and Latin America were targeted in particular. Some of the more important societies targeted were the major religions. Murray was not the only one to see the value of using religion to advance U.S. goals. Catholic Professor and scion of a wealthy family, Edward P. Lilly, designed and implemented the Doctrinal, or Ideological, Warfare Program. He directed and coordinated the plans to infiltrate the religions of Christianity, Hinduism, Buddhism, and Islam all to further the message that America is good and consistent with the principles of the various religions. In furthering this plan, the Government utilized the perennial American approach of emphasizing practice, or practicality, over principle. Catholic priests were important assistants to the U.S. government in making all of this happen.

All of this had great significance for the Catholics. American principles inflamed Americanism. Through their efforts at re-engineering societies primarily by elevating America to be the ideal in the minds of the world, Americanism was given a boost with the Catholics in Europe and that affected the prelates who would be present in Rome. Wallace Irwin, Jr., an advisor to the Psychological Strategy Board, the U.S. government's agency responsible for coordinating psychological operations and doctrinal warfare, explained the significance of this real and important phenomenon. He wrote:

"The traditional cultural links of Latin America have been with continental Europe – France, Germany, Spain, Italy – much more than with the UK or the U.S. When Paris fell in 1940 the people of Buenos Aires wept on the streets. Thus, in cultural as well as in economic and social affairs a new orientation remains to be developed."[3]

When European Catholics – especially French, German, and Belgian – went Americanist, then the Third World went American. This was especially so with the Catholic Church.

PART IX - STALIN DIES, ROME SPEAKS, AND THE LUCAS GO TO ROME (1953)

The year 1953 was a very important year all the way around. That was the year Dwight Eisenhower became U.S. President. Within weeks, Joseph Stalin, the United States' chief bogeyman, died. It was also the year the U.S. government ramped up its political warfare efforts with the development of a doctrinal warfare program designed to make America with its unique Enlightenment and Liberal grounding, appear as the ideal in the minds of peoples around the globe. This effort became more earnest with the death of Stalin as the American leadership was concerned the Cold War may come to a premature ending.

1953 was also an important year for the Luces. Harry got Clare the job as Ambassador to Italy, a very important position because the country was strategically and economically important. Clare serving as the Ambassador to Italy also put the Luces close to the Pope, or the center of the Catholic Church, which had real power in politics, not just in Italy. The Church also had a real influence in forming societies around the globe.

The year was important for the Catholic Church in terms of the debate on church and state and religious liberty. Cardinal Ottaviani gave a talk in March in which he stated the Catholic position. This greatly distressed and angered the Americanists. In December, Pope Pius XII issued *Ci Riesce* which the Americans and Americanists claimed supported their position, while the Catholics claimed it supported theirs. These two talks revealed a dynamic that was already extant in the Church. That dynamic was to be pleasing to both, or all constituencies. Ottaviani spoke to the Catholics and the Pope spoke to the Americans and Americanists.

Murray's support at the highest levels of the Church became clear. Fellow Jesuit Robert Leiber was the Pope's confidant and supporter of Murray's efforts. This was no surprise given Leiber was both a Jesuit and an intelligence source for the Americans. Leiber had been a source of intelligence since the days of World War II and remained so during the Cold War. To this day, the CIA will not release records on him.

The CIA and Time, Inc. had a cozy and ongoing relationship. C.D. Jackson and Klaus Dohrn exemplified that relationship. C.D. had long worked with the U.S. intelligence community at the highest levels. Klaus Dohrn gathered information, or intelligence on a number of events, and he maintained contacts with prominent and influential people in the governments of Europe, most notably Germany and Italy. Perhaps most significantly, he had contacts within the Vatican itself, which provided him with vital information on the personalities, policies, and events that affected the Pope and the Catholic Church's hierarchy.

PART X - THE AMERICAN PROPOSITION (1953)

It was in Rome that Henry Luce injected The American Proposition, a doctrinal weapon that he developed along with John Courtney Murray, SJ, into the veins of the Catholic Church. This was done on November 29, 1953, in Rome, at the Pro Deo University, an institution started by Dominican Felix Morlion who received backing and support from American elites and the CIA. Pro Deo taught young Catholics, especially those in business and primarily from Latin countries, that societies should be organized along the lines of America. Pro Deo taught the American Proposition to its students, and they, in turn, went throughout the world spreading American ideas and ideals. All of this occurred with the apparent approval of the Catholic Church. The American prelates certainly approved of Pro Deo as did the Dominican order and Msgr. Giovanni Montini, later known as Pope Paul VI.

The American Proposition justified the American socio-political philosophy as good in principle. The basis of this philosophy was an adherence by societal authorities to a vague, ambiguous, and ill-defined natural law. The Declaration of Independence and the U.S. Constitution were elevated to the level of sacred documents, and freedom, whatever that meant, was the guiding light of American activities. The American Proposition was quintessential American psychological warfare and it served to advance the U.S. government's Doctrinal Warfare Program. Once target societies accepted the American Proposition as true, and American socio-political philosophy as good in principle, then that society underwent a re-organization or re-engineering that marginalized spiritual values and permitted the elevation of materialism. This was made possible by the relegation of religion to a private concern and its prohibition from informing the policies of the state. The legal principles of the Establishment Clause and the Free Exercise Clause of the U.S. Constitution implemented and protected this philosophy. At this point, then the powerful come to rule society, and the most powerful in America and similar societies are the monied elites. Acceptance of the American Proposition leads to the creation of the proper social and political environment for American capital and investment to enter societies around the globe.

In March 1953, Cardinal Ottaviani of the Holy Office of the Catholic Church gave a talk in which he laid out the Catholic doctrine on religious liberty and Church-State relations. It infuriated the Americanists and the Americans and pleased Msgr. Fenton and Fr. Connell, who could claim that Rome finally heard their pleas. The Cardinal, while not mentioning Murray by name, directly referenced his ideas and even some of his writings so as to condemn the same. Within a week of Luce's Pro Deo address, Pope Pius XII issued *Ci Riesce*. It was a nuanced talk, and it characterized the practice of the Catholic hierarchy to speak in ambiguous terms so as to be pleasing to the rank-and-file Catholics and the rich and powerful members of society. Murray and the Americanists used the address as authority for their claim Ottaviani and his views were discredited. Fenton claimed the pope was merely describing a specific situation in the world at the time in which countries were growing closer together, and the pope presented the way by which these countries should order their relations. The Catholic state was protected, and Catholic statesmen needed to coordinate with the Vatican.

Murray was emboldened, more so by his contacts with Robert Leiber, SJ, the support of the Jesuits, and the alliance with Harry and Clare Luce.

PART XI - HOT AND COLD RHETORICAL WAR (1954)

The Americanists pushed the attack in early 1954. Weigel wrote an article for *America* claiming *Ci Riesce* supported the American system of social organization as the ideal. Murray boldly attacked Cardinal Ottaviani, Msgr. Fenton and Fr. Connell in a famous speech delivered at the Catholic University of America on March 25, 1954. At Notre Dame, a noted source for research to support the U.S. Doctrinal Warfare Program, Waldemar Gurian, compiled a book from a symposium that supported American principles. Murray's thoughts were included in that book and in *Theological Studies* during this entire period.

The Catholics pushed back. Fenton explained *Ci Riesce* as an endorsement of the Catholic state as the ideal, or thesis, and that the Pope validated the principle that error has no rights. Fenton and Connell complained to Rome of Murray's actions, and he was compelled to apologize to Ottaviani. Fenton and Connell kept writing and speaking to the faithful informing them of Catholic doctrine. Part of that doctrine was the idea that the principles underlying America were a practical accommodation, not something good in principle. Fenton and Connell continued nudging Rome for a statement condemning Murray's positions. What they got was something called "Four Erroneous Propositions" that Ottaviani issued in secret. These became known as "the Secret Propositions." It was not enough, but it was consistent with the Catholic hierarchy's dualistic approach to the situation. That is, they allowed Murray and his views to circulate with the American elites while allowing Fenton and Connell to speak to the Catholic faithful in the pews. In essence, the hierarchy allowed the powerful to hear what they wanted and gave the faithful what they wanted. Two Gospels were preached.

The reason for Ottaviani's half-hearted efforts became apparent to Fenton during his many trips to Rome. One of the biggest reasons was the strong Jesuit support for Murray and divisions within Ottaviani's own office. The Cardinal's own staff was promoting Murray in a newsletter. But the greatest reason had to be the power and influence of Fr. Leiber, secretary and confident of the Pope, a known American intelligence source, who led many to believe the Pope himself supported Murray's views.

PART XII - THE AMERICANS INVENT GLOBALIZATION (1954-1955)

Henry Luce had for a long time desired something called a World Economic Plan or WEP. C.D. Jackson, while in the Eisenhower White House tried hard to get the President interested in it, but to no avail. There was too much apathy amongst administration officials, and Eisenhower himself seemed preoccupied with curtailing nuclear weapons, according to Luce.[4] "Economic power is the great peacetime weapon," Jackson wrote to Luce.[5]

So, Luce called a conference. The leaders of banking, industry, labor, intelligence, and government attended –even if it was officially only in their unofficial capacity. There, they laid out the plan to extend the power of American finance and the American dollar around the world. This necessitated the re-engineering of societies to encourage consumption or the unlimited acquisition and enjoyment of wealth. To do that, America was the antidote to a dark totalitarian Soviet Communism. If the U.S. government was not on board with the WEP, Luce still used his influential magazines to turn public opinion his way.

At about the same time, Lilly was busy devising plans and methods to harness religion to advance America as the ideal. To that end, he and others in the U.S. government realized that Stalin had some good ideas when it came to religion. Instead of fighting religion, the key was to get them to willingly carry vague ideas that the Americans could manipulate. Two of these that advanced the U.S. ideological warfare program were freedom and human dignity. These efforts stressed the individual with all his or her wants and desires, as good. And these efforts sanctified the ideas – like freedom, human dignity, limited government -- that made possible the social systems that elevated and protected the individual as the measure of all things. This, in turn, made possible the continued protection and prospering of an economic system that exploited that individual and kept real power with the wealthy.

PART XIII - A ROT IN THE CHURCH (1955-1956)

Murray kept writing and putting forth his views. He was finally censured in July 1955 and prevented by Rome from publicly writing on Church and State. The hierarchy, however, never formally and publicly repudiated his ideas. It was a half-measure at best and one that denoted a serious problem in the Church leadership. It was as though Murray was punished for personally offending Ottaviani, but not for spreading error. This gave the appearance the Catholic Church did not want to offend the Americans. Despite the failure of the hierarchy, Fenton pressed on with his work in refuting the errors set forth by Murray.

Murray's fame grew among the Americans regardless of what Rome did or did not do. Luce's magazines continued to promote him as he grew more important to Harry and the American effort at subjugating the Catholic Church. Murray supported and approved of Walter Lippmann's public philosophy, which was devoid of any endorsement of Christ and Christianity and approved of a natural law as the basis of social organization. He also assisted the Rockefellers in their efforts to discern a national purpose. Most importantly, he stood with Henry Luce who endorsed generic religious movements such as Charles Wesley Lowrey's FRASCO, a willing supporter of the U.S. government's efforts abroad in the area of ideological warfare and co-option of the religions. Despite the Rome censure, Murray still was able to create mayhem within the Catholic Church as he subverted the efforts of the National Organization for Decent Literature, or NODL.

The urgency of action was needed as the threat was immediate and real – Communism. The way to victory, as well as prosperity, was a moral way that elevated faith in the American form of government. In other words, if you joined the anti-communist crusade, you could have a good life. If you did not, then bad things would happen. The aware observer could see the elements of carrot and stick in this formulation that was repeated throughout the Cold War.

Luce and Murray set out or emphasized ideas that found their way into the Vatican II Council years later. There was a conception of modern man that included his search for truth and freedom, an undefined human dignity that came to validate every desire and wish of man, and the idea that America really was Catholic at heart. Connell's view was that Catholics could be good Americans, which meant good citizens. Murray, Luce, and the Americans presented that a Catholic could be a good American by holding American ideas.

By 1956, the Cold War was over, and the Americans knew they had won. They could not tell anyone, and they had to keep it going if the financial interests were to conquer the world. The Catholics were losing their grip. Fenton found many of the Church's leadership were no longer serious about the mission of the Church.

PART XIV - THE AMERICAN SENSE OPPORTUNITY (1956-1959)

President Eisenhower said at his second inaugural on January 20, 1957, that "The American experiment has, for generations, fired the passion and the courage of millions elsewhere seeking freedom, equality, opportunity. And the American story of material progress has helped excite the longing of all needy peoples for some satisfaction of their human wants. These hopes, that we have helped to inspire, we can help to fulfill."[6] Ike linked American-style freedom with materialism and the American system of social organization with its economics. This was great stuff for political warfare. The Rockefellers did their part by devising and advancing an idyllic image of America through the panel work of the Rockefeller Brothers Fund. Murray made a presentation in which he explained the American consensus as the heart of the American Proposition and as part of the Liberal tradition.

Luce and his people were busy promoting those who would promote America. One of them was the good-time monk Raymond Bruckberger, OP, who fancied himself a new de Tocqueville while carrying on an affair with an American woman. He and Felix Morlion, OP were part and parcel of the change that Luce and his minions observed was going on in the Church as the pontificate of Pius XII continued.

Fenton saw that materialism was gradually strangling the desire for truth and the willingness to suffer for it. The Church leadership was ossifying while the younger Catholics were more tolerant of error. Fenton was not deterred, and he wrote to define the enemy, thereby hoping to bring them out into the open to better defeat them. Fenton described the view of many Americans, to include the American Founders. The Founders, eminently practical men intent on creating a commercial society, held every religion good if they held a standard of conduct that would be conducive to business. The enemy was Liberalism, but unfortunately, Fenton could not bring himself to see that the Americans were part of that Liberalism as Murray stated to the Rockefellers.

With Pius XII's death, the Americans hoped Montini would move closer to the Papal throne, which he did. After all, he showed great openness to the Americans and supported the Pro Deo operation. Murray moved quickly to get his ideas in print. Sheed & Ward, a publisher the Luces supported, and which was decidedly Anglo-American in its orientation, was the instrument to make that happen.

PART I

HENRY ROBINSON LUCE AND THE AMERICAN CENTURY

1

HENRY ROBINSON LUCE: PRESBYTERIAN MEDIA GENIUS

Henry Robinson Luce was the man who "invented the concept of a weekly news magazine."[1] When questioned as to whether *Time* magazine was really a news magazine, Luce reportedly said, "Well, I invented the idea, so I guess I can call it anything I like."[2] Aimed at young and college-educated Americans, *Time,* like no other magazine before or since that era, convinced them to buy into a vision of the American nation so effectively by the middle of the 20th century that "his magazines would be the true voice of American life at the midcentury, what he had hoped would be the American Century, the real voice of Christian Capitalism."[3] The Italian writer and politician Amintore Fanfani remarked that in "a capitalistic system the important roles belong to the engineer and the economist, who judge means by their returns and on that basis adopt or reject them."[4] Luce was that engineer.

Luce was born April 3, 1898, in China, the son of a Presbyterian missionary. He attended Yale, where he became a member of Skull and Bones, a secret fraternity that recruited the sons of the high and mighty into a network that served the Anglo-American empire. After graduation, Skull and Bones helped Luce get his first job in journalism. Luce had ambitions at Yale to prepare for public life, to gain the upper echelons of the "Anglophilic American aristocracy," and make a lot of money to boot.[5] Luce's desire for power grew while his desire for money remained secondary, and Time, Inc., the parent company of his four magazines (*Time, Fortune, Life,* and *Sports Illustrated*), became his life.[6]

The start of World War I found Luce at Yale. With his good friend and future co-founder of *Time* magazine Britton Hadden, Luce joined the U.S. Army, where both men were commissioned lieutenants, posted to Camp Jackson, South Jackson, and in the summer of 1918, made responsible for the training of soldiers for combat in Europe. Most of these young recruits were quite different from Luce and Hadden as they were "from very small hamlets" and "had little education," with "just under 18 percent of white draftees" ever having attended high school. Arriving from their small towns across a largely rural U.S., many of these recruits had never traveled outside of their home counties, something which begat an ignorance of current affairs that "affected Luce," who proceeded to educate them about the reason for the war. He did so by giving a talk about the sinking of the *Lusitania*. "They had never heard the story," Luce remarked later, "and were on the edge of their chairs... ." After hearing the story, they "couldn't wait to get 'over there' to fix the Huns."[7]

After the war and graduation from Yale, Luce worked as a journalist before meeting up with Hadden again and forming the idea of the magazine that became *Time*. To realize that dream, they needed money, workers, and a winning idea. The $100,000 in seed money came from fellow Bonesmen and other Yale grads from wealthy families. A number of prominent Protestants like Theodore Roosevelt Jr., son of the twenty-seventh President of the United States; diplomat and Presbyterian minister Henry Van Dyke; and the presidents of Yale, Princeton, Williams, Johns Hopkins, and Columbia College, lent their names to the project. Time also drew upon the WASP elite to run the magazine. The staff and writers were drawn from recent graduates of Yale, Harvard, Princeton, Oxford, and Columbia. The editors of the new magazine admitted they would not strive for "complete neutrality on public questions," which included a "general distrust of the present tendency toward increasing interference by government."[8] Looking for the winning idea or an idea that could sell, the two came to rely on Luce's mentor, Walter Lippmann. Of Lippmann, Luce said, "No American has written more brilliantly during the last ten years on politics and government."[9]

WALTER LIPPMANN AS LUCE'S MENTOR

In 1914, Walter Lippmann became associate editor of the *New Republic.* When World War I broke out, Lippmann saw it as a "'rare opportunity' to advance democracy abroad and begin social reconstruction at home," which meant "the substitution of rational planning for the old authorities that had been discredited or destroyed by the advent of modern industrial life." The war could be used "as an efficient means of achieving intelligent control over the economic and political process."[10] Lippmann helped draft propaganda literature for the Allies during World War I, and he assisted Woodrow Wilson in drawing up the Fourteen Points.[11]

The budding science of Watsonian Behaviorism provided Lippmann with principles that could be used to govern a society. In his landmark book, *Public Opinion*, which was published in 1922, Lippmann claimed that psychologists had discovered that a "conditioned response" was "an emotion [that] is not attached merely to one idea." There "are no end of things which can arouse the emotion, and no end of things which can satisfy it," Lippmann wrote. The "whole structure of human culture is in one respect an elaboration of the stimuli and responses of which the original emotional capacities remain a fairly fixed center." Lippmann knew that mental images provoke feelings, and these, in turn, provoke a reaction. Propaganda altered the mental images, and essential to the proper and effective use of propaganda was the use of symbols that presented pictures that could educate or shape one's view of the "pseudo-environment," as sociologists termed the society. And "[p]ictures have always been the surest way of conveying an idea, and next in order, words that call up pictures in memory. But the idea conveyed is not fully our own until we have identified ourselves with some aspect of the picture." Psychoanalysis, according to Lippmann, helped one to understand "how the pseudo-environment is put together."[12]

Symbols are important in providing a stimulus that will arouse emotion. However, the symbol does not signify one thing in particular, and "it can be associated with almost anything," so therefore "it can become the common bond of common feelings." It was important to know and understand the leadership of any group. The "hierarchy, in fact, is bound together by the social leaders," which make up a "variety of personal contacts through which a circulation of standards takes place," especially among those who consider themselves "the nation."[13]

Every person holds to stereotypes concerning certain events or things that come from art, literature, moral codes, social philosophies, and political agitations.[14] One of the more important stereotypes was the "American view of Progress and Success," in which "there is a definite picture of human nature and of society." The American "kind of human nature and the kind of society . . . logically produce the kind of progress that is regarded as ideal" and "when we seek to describe or explain actually successful men, and events that have really happened, we read back into them the qualities that are presupposed in the stereotypes."[15]

The qualities constituting the American view of progress, success, human nature, and society were devised by "the older economists." These men devised a "scheme" that "consisted of various stereotypes: the capitalist who had diligently saved capital from his labor, the entrepreneur who conceived a socially useful demand and organized a factory, the workmen who freely contracted, take it or leave it, for their labor, the landlord, and the group of consumers who bought in the cheapest market those goods which by the ready use of the pleasure-pain calculus they knew would give them the most pleasure." This "model" worked because these "kind of people, which the model assumed, living in the sort of world the model assumed, invariably cooperated harmoniously in the books where the model was described."[16] According to Lippmann, shaping stereotypes was the work of those who properly organized public opinion.

Lippmann did not agree with Jefferson's view that the people can govern in a democracy. Representative government also had problems because of the "failure of self-governing people to transcend their casual experience and their prejudice....because they are compelled to act without a reliable picture of the world.....This is the primary defect of popular government."[17] Lippmann concluded that it was a mistake of democratic regimes to base the dignity of man on the "very precarious assumption, that he would exhibit that dignity instinctively in wise laws and good government." Instead, Lippmann wrote, human dignity should not be determined by this "precarious assumption" about self-government, but that one must "insist that man's dignity requires a standard of living, in which his capacities are properly exercised.... The criteria which you then apply to government are whether it is producing a certain minimum of health, of decent housing, of material necessities, of education, of freedom, of pleasures, of beauty." With this shift in emphasis, "the whole problem changes." Social control then comes to depend "upon devising standards of living and methods of audit by which the acts of public officials and industrial directors are measured."[18]

Lippmann was convinced that "representative government, either in what is ordinarily called politics or in industry, cannot be worked successfully, no matter what the basis of election, unless there is an independent, expert organization for making the unseen facts intelligible to those who have to make the decision..... My conclusion is that public opinions must be organized for the press if they are to be sound, not by the press as is the case today. This organization I conceive to be in the first instance the task of a political science that has won its proper place as formulator, in advance of real decision, instead of apologist, critic, or reporter after a decision has been made."[19] Lippmann spent the rest of his life trying to come up a "reliable picture of the world," and Luce assisted him in this important task by creating *Time* and *Life*.

THE POWER OF LUCE'S MAGAZINES

"Those Luce magazines are just too damn big," said President Harry Truman, assessing the power of the Time/Life empire. "They've got too much power over people and what they think."[20] Anyone who had ambitions, such as actor Efrem Zimbalist, Jr., recognized the power of Luce's magazines. "At that time, before the impact of television," Zimbalist wrote, "magazines were at the height of their popularity, and one towered head and shoulders above the rest: *Life*. It is impossible to overstate the influence of Henry Luce's top achiever on the conduct of American affairs."[21]

Life was "consistently named America's most 'popular' magazine," and *Time* was the "nation's most 'important'." *Time,* "the editors boasted [was] the magazine to which something like half the important people in America are turning for help in understanding the promise and the problems of our time." Luce created "new forms of information and communications at a moment in history when media were rapidly expanding." His magazines "transform[ed] the way many people experienced news and culture." *Time* was both a response to the nationalization of American culture and a contributor to that nationalization, and it played to the need to explain the ever-increasing complexity of life.[22]

Luce's magazines did something else of great importance. They created a consumer culture like never before with the effective use of advertising of consumer products like alcohol, automobiles, clothing, or jewelry. The idea was to emphasize certain lifestyles and images, and the advertisements were made visually appealing to "create impact." Society was being changed to consume more.[23] This was done by playing to the "upward aspirations" of the target audiences[24] as well as the desire for self-improvement, which for Americans is "a national conditioned reflex."[25] The advertisements were as important as the stories. Swanberg shares Hillaire Belloc's analysis of the collaboration between the media and business in *The Free Press* when he writes:

"The Timewriter created a news product slanted to draw the advertiser and *his* product. Time's extensive and admiring weekly business coverage had given it a heavy readership in the paneled offices, and the frequent canonization of businessmen on the cover had entrepreneurs at all levels yearning for similar attention. To appear on the cover was the ultimate triumph of tycoonship both in prestige and profit. Even the nonconformist Cleveland industrialist Cyrus Eaton agreed that one's portrait there was priceless 'but if it could be bought it would cost $ 20 million.'"[26]

The effectiveness of *Time* hinged on a number of important factors. First, the news was conveyed as stories so that readers could imagine themselves at the scene, and this often meant describing scenes.[27] Then, there was the stress on the "newsmaker" with a notation as to his or her physical features.[28] Luce once said, "People just aren't interesting in the mass.... It's only individuals who are exciting."[29] Being selected for the cover of *Time* came to be a very high honor for both readers and editors alike.[30] *Time* took the tone of omniscience in its accounts of events and individuals.[31] *Time's* headlines and photograph captions were designed to draw people's interest in the story or pique their interest in general.[32]

Time, Inc. was not afraid to "push the envelope." Whereas many magazines refused to touch religion, history, art, and science, Luce understood that Americans liked to complain and liked controversy, so he took that into account in his magazines.[33] The "Birth of a Baby" pictorial that *Life* ran caused a clash with the Catholics in 1937-1938. The Catholics sought to ban the issue from the newsstand, but they lost, and *Life* gained enormous readership and popularity.[34]

Catholic leaders came to know the power of the Luce media machine. For instance, Fr. Leonard Feeney's *The Point,* a copy of which found its way into the papers of Clare Boothe Luce, presented an excellent explanation of how Luce affected power over people. The article, entitled "Our Thirty-Third Degree Enemies," explained that:

"The combined circulation of the Luce publications is reported to be around seven million copies. But actually, they have many times that number of readers. *Life,* for instance, is read, or looked at, by practically everyone in America who gets his hair cut or his teeth filled. *Time,* which claims a circulation of a million and a half, is read mainly by those who fancy themselves as belonging to the social, financial, or intellectual elite.....*Fortune* has a comparatively small circulation, and is used less for control purposes than the other two....

"Luce pretends that the purpose of his magazines, particularly *Time* and *Life,* is to give unbiased, informative reports of news and events. But this is clearly not so. News for Luce is merely a vehicle to be used in conveying his messages. Every article, every picture, every squib and caption that he prints has some definite job of indoctrination to do, some point that he means for his readers to get....."[35]

The reach of *Life,* in particular, was phenomenal. It was estimated that with seven million buying the magazine every week, "the total adult readership is between four and five per copy, giving us an audience of over thirty million each week."[36] With this kind of popularity, *Time* and Luce's other magazines became the model by which journalists began measuring their craft. At the University of Minnesota's journalism school, journalism students "all wished to assiduously to mimic Time's style." An editor in Missouri wrote, "*Time* is not only a threatening competitor but a worthwhile stylebook.... For thoroughness of detail, vividness of description and a graphic simplicity of its literary style...." *Variety* noted, "Today the pattern seems to be the short, crisp, coma-studded phraseology typical of *Time*."[37] The publishing industry, according to sociologist Leo Rosen, took note, and so correspondents in Washington by the mid-1930s were reading *Time* magazine more than any other. Chain newspaper operators and owners like Frank Gannett and Lord Beaverbrook encouraged their staffs to read Time.[38] Henry Luce captured the American media.

LUCE'S IDEAS

Feeney was right – Luce's magazines spread his beliefs. Luce made that clear: "Listen," Luce explained, "I don't pretend that this is an objective magazine. It's an editorial magazine from the first page to the last and whatever comes out has to reflect my view and that's the way it is."[39] *Time*'s editors imbibed Luce's ideas from the regular conferences in the Time, Inc. offices in the Rockefeller Towers, and then publicized them to millions, thereby influencing public policy.[40]

The man who reported this conversation was an eyewitness to twenty-five years of the inner workings of the Time/Life empire. John Shaw Billings, Editorial Director of all Time, Inc. publications at the time, was then at the pinnacle of his career. He was observant, frank, and kept meticulous diaries during the years that he worked for Luce. Born and raised in South Carolina, Billings was the grandson of the great Union Doctor of the American Civil War, John Shaw Billings. He first started at *Time* as the National Affairs Editor in 1929. Billing's rise was rapid, and in 1933, he became the magazine's Managing Editor. Three years later, he became the Managing Editor of *Life*. "My job," Billings wrote, "is to pick up his [Luce's] ideas as quickly as possible – and carry them out,"[41] because, as Billings told Luce, "I believed in the same things you believed in and we traveled the same ideological road in mutual trust and harmony...."[42]

Billings explained how Luce's thoughts became the editors' thoughts: "We are an ingrown arrogant bunch at Time Inc., and behave like lords of creation.... this attitude stems from Luce."[43] According to Billings, who spent years attending editorial meetings, *Time*'s editors sat at: "a long thin table with Luce at the head, and 10 men down on each side.... Luce soon began to give 'impressions' of his trip by questions and answer. But his answers were so long they almost amounted to set speeches...I had heard all Luce's views (or read them)....[T]hinking about these 2D men around the table who constitute the top command of the company. They aren't impressive looking – they are relatively young – 40 to 45.... This scene suggested courtiers paying homage to their king – Luce on his throne and peers of the realm politely attentive to his words of wisdom."[44]

And what did Henry R. Luce believe? He believed in the American ideology or what he called "the Great Liberal Tradition." Luce believed that:

"America is the supreme embodiment of this tradition. Garibaldi wrote to Abraham Lincoln and spoke of our country as the "apostle of liberty, the harbinger of progress."... America was the great magnetic hope and example, drawing to her all who wished to make Europe at last beautiful and free.... [A] last great effort is being made to establish the liberal tradition – that is to say, political freedom and equal justice, and freedom of thought and opinion, and common decency between men and men. It is a very close battle. The odds are, so far as anyone can see, about fifty-fifty."[45]

Luce believed that the United States Constitution presented and preserved that liberal tradition.[46] As a corollary of his belief in the Constitution, Luce believed that: "Business is essentially our civilization...Business is our life."[47] The editors at Time/Life accepted this creed and the liberal theories that flowed from it. Billings described an evening gathering in January 1937 at which all the *Time* editors were present. Luce talked at length about a credo in which all of them could believe, or, in other words, a purpose for *Time* and Time, Inc. The attendees, editors, and publishers of Luce's various magazines were all in agreement that they, and *Time* in particular, had a "vast influence" on society, and they all knew that their publications would amuse, instruct, and inform. Luce said there was a right and a wrong, though just what that meant was not developed in very great detail. He said Time, Inc. believed in progress, human liberty, and freedom. Billings remarked that "it was a fruitful evening," signifying that a policy and philosophy had been forged that was to be unleashed on the world.[48]

During one luncheon editorial meeting in March 1948, the dynamic of the Cold War crystallized in Luce's mind. He told the *Life* staff that the current crisis with the Soviet Union "feels right" and that the staff "did not have the uphill emotional effort on our hands as we did in 1939." Someone then asked, "What should *Life* cover?" The answer came back quickly from one of the editors: "The Vatican's Divisions." Just as surprisingly, Luce gave the same answer. Life should cover "the Vatican," and in that coverage, it should pit American Catholics against their co-religionists in the rest of the world because "Atlee told him" that "the main base" of the Catholic Church was "U.S. Catholicism," and "it was a pity the Vatican was so far off from it...."[49] Luce knew American Catholics were far different from Catholics elsewhere in the world, especially those in Latin countries. American Catholics accepted the American ideology, which gave ultimate power to the monied elites in the name of things like freedom, free enterprise, limited government, and human rights. In a letter to Roy Alexander, the managing editor of *Time* magazine, Luce explained the basis for his editorial decision to cover "the Vatican's Divisions." There was a conflict in the Catholic Church between those who accepted American ideas and those who didn't, a group that included the rest of the faithful, most notably Latin Catholics:

"There is a left Catholicism in the simple sense of being pro-socialist – Christian Socialism. But what I suspect is more serious is a basic hostility of Latin Catholicism to Americanism in the sense of Free Enterprise, Bourgeois Democracy, etc.....[N]othing is sillier than to think of the American Catholic pro-free enterprise as typical of World Catholicism. Father M[orlion, founder of Pro-Deo University and supported by US intelligence services to advance American ideas]...would be a very strange fish in almost any other Catholic sea....Take for example Don Sturzo. He stands broadly for our idea of Democracy, Freedom, Enterprise, etc. Does he have any followers in the great Demo-Christian Party of Italy? Practically none."[50]

Luce knew the fault line in the Catholic Church. Pope Leo XIII made it clear about fifty years earlier in an apostolic letter directed to the leading prelates in the United States. That letter, entitled *Testem Benevolentiae Nostrae,* identified and condemned the notion that America knew better than the Catholic Church. The pope also condemned the idea that one's loyalty is first to America and not to Rome. The Catholics who held the condemned views became known as "Americanists," and the policies they advanced based on those views came to be known as "Americanism." This knowledge gave Luce a powerful tool to be used in turning the Vatican into a supporter of the American ideology. If Luce succeeded in converting Rome to the American ideology, the Americans would gain a worldwide ally that could spread the American ideology and thereby assist in re-ordering societies according to the goals FDR articulated in his Four Freedoms speech in January 1941. This meant promoting the primacy of material values over the spiritual and the incorporation of the world's believing peoples into the American socio-economic-cultural empire. If the year 1948 marked the dawn of the era of psychological warfare, Luce had just declared war, war on the Catholic Church.

2
THE AMERICAN CENTURY BEGINS WITH WORLD WAR II

Henry Luce's roots run deep in American history. In fact, they go all the way back to the American Revolution. Through Elihu Root, the Secretary of War for President Theodore Roosevelt, Luce "descended from the man who commanded the American Troops at Concord in 1775. This gent whose shot was heard around the world was E.R.'s [Elihu Root's] maternal grandfather."[1]

As if to show that he bore no grudges, Luce was also a great admirer of Winston Churchill at a time when the English and American establishments wanted war with Germany. Implementing what has come to be known as "the Mackinder thesis," the Anglo-American elites dedicated themselves to a long-range strategy designed to keep Germany and the Soviet Union from uniting economically and politically. This strategy sought to prevent the development of any continental power strong enough to challenge the English and the Americans. After World War I, the Anglo-American elites sought to bring Germany back as a "reactionary regime" to engage in war with the USSR.[2]

The group responsible for this policy, the Milner Group, developed in the late 1800s in reaction to the growing power of the German Empire. The founders were Cecil Rhodes of South Africa, William T. Stead, the most famous journalist of his time, and Reginald Baliol Brett (Lord Esher), who served as counselor to Queen Victoria, King Edward VII, and King George V. By 1916, the Milner Group had become the most influential foreign policy group in the foreign office, a position they would retain up to the beginning of World War II.[3]

The Group devised three major interlocking goals, which would transform the British Empire into a Commonwealth of Nations. These were, first, "the creation of a common ideology and world outlook among the peoples of the United Kingdom, the British Empire, and the United States"; second, the "creation of instruments and practices of cooperation among these various communities in order that they might pursue parallel policies"; and, third, "the creation of a federation on an imperial, Anglo-American, or world basis." By 1938, the Milner Group had been involved in policy creation and implementation for nearly eighteen years, creating first a climate of appeasement which would bring Germany into war with the Soviet Union by eliminating any obstacles to this conflict and secondly an "Oceanic bloc" which included the United States. At about the same time, attempts by forces in Germany to assassinate Hitler were stymied by the efforts of a famous Milner Group member, Neville Chamberlain, who went to Munich to make peace.[4]

The Milner Group portrayed Adolph Hitler and the German Worker's National Socialist Party as intent on "mastery of the world,"[5] something they knew was a fabrication. The Milner group collaborated with Hitler in creating a "folkish" state that needed living room to accommodate its population. In the Programme of the NSDAP dated February 24, 1920, Hitler and Anton Drexler wrote in point number 3, "We demand land and territory (colonies) to feed our people and to settle our surplus population."[6] This land and these colonies were to be in the east, according to Hitler, who never once spoke of world domination. In *Mein Kampf,* Hitler wrote that the "foreign policy of the folkish state must safeguard the existence on this planet of the race embodied in the state, by creating a healthy, viable natural relation between the nation's population and growth on the one hand and the quantity and quality of its soil on the other hand."[7] Therefore, German foreign policy was to "take up where we broke off six hundred years ago. We stop the endless

German movement to the south and west, and turn our gaze toward the land in the east.... If we speak of soil in Europe today, we can primarily have in mind only Russia and her vassal border states."[8]

According to Point 4, the German nation, as well as its political and economic system, was based on "German blood," which meant that all "non-German immigration must be prevented" (Point 8) and that the State's "primary duty [is] to provide a livelihood for its citizens" (Point 7). This involved the "nationalization of all businesses which have been formed into corporations" (Point 13), "profit sharing in large industrial enterprises" (Point 14), "the extensive development of insurance for old age" (Point 15), "the utmost consideration shall be shown to all small traders" in both retail and State orders (Point 16), and, perhaps most notably "the ruthless prosecution of those whose activities are injurious to the common interest. Common criminals, usurers, profiteers, etc., must be punished with death, whatever their creed or race" (point 18).[9] All of these ideas were anathema to the English and the Americans, who held an ideology that placed the state responsive, if not subservient, to powerful private interests.

As the 1930s drew to a close, Luce's magazines, *Time* and *Life,* began to stoke the fires of war with the Axis powers, and the famous aviator Charles Lindbergh became one of their favorite targets. Walter Lippmann was given free rein in Luce's magazines to write an "uncharacteristically dense" essay telling Americans of the dangers of Germany. The threat posed by Germany, according to Lippmann, was that once Germany came to control Europe, it would dominate the U.S. "The small American businessman," Lippman wrote, "has long complained about how difficult it is for him to survive in the competition with the large American corporation....What will he do when he has to face the competition of totalitarian monopoly organized on a continental scale?"[10] *Fortune* told Americans that the "people of the U.S. must now choose among retreat, isolation, and international leadership."[11] Luce himself said, "*Time* is prejudiced" in favor of "individual liberty" and "American leadership in the world" as he grew more certain in his beliefs.[12] Luce had a mission, and that mission was to bring about World War II.

When John Shaw Billings put together a story in *Life* on the German invasion of Poland in September 1939, Luce objected and told Billings to rewrite it in a way that would, in the words of Billings, "go overboard for the Allies" and blame Hitler for the start of the war. Billings said that he had no strong feelings either way. During the conversation, Luce mentioned what Billings called a number of "high-fallutin' ideas" such as "truth, justice, virtue" and the "need for struggle." A couple of months later, at the Publishers and Editors' Committee meeting held every Friday at noon in the Time, Inc. offices, Luce "bloviated metaphysically" about policy, claiming that he would not favor any sort of war for ideological purposes, but he was in favor of trade wars.[13]

With the start of the war, the Milner Group worked with greater fervor for a closer union with the Americans,[14] even though there was no serious threat to Britain from Germany as Hitler was being maneuvered into going into a losing war against the Soviet Union, beginning in June 1941.[15] The interests of the bellicose Americans and English were converging. Within two months of having been re-elected after a campaign in which he pledged "no more war," FDR edged toward what would become a continuous world war whose goal was the cultural, social, and economic re-engineering of the world by the Anglo-American elites to serve the interests of Anglo-American bankers. The American goals presented by FDR were the ideological and public relations tools necessary to re-engineer the world's societies, which could only come about in conjunction with a major shooting war.

On January 6, 1941, Roosevelt gave what has come to be known as "the Four Freedoms" speech:

"The first is freedom of speech and expression, everywhere in the world. The second is freedom of every person to worship God in his own way, everywhere in the world. The third is freedom from want, which, translated into world terms, means economic understandings which will secure to every nation a healthy peacetime life for its inhabitants – everywhere in the world. The fourth is freedom from fear, which, translated into world terms, means a worldwide reduction of armaments to such a point and in such a thorough fashion that no nation will be in a position to commit an act of physical aggression against any neighbor, anywhere in the world."[16]

No matter how it sounded, Roosevelt's speech, which Norman Rockwell would portray in a series of sentimental paintings, was, in reality, a declaration of world war. On the same day, the U.S. started selling ships to Britain on credit. In doing so, it went against its own decisions throughout the 1930s never to be involved with a belligerent power in the selling of arms.[17] Indeed, Congress passed a number of resolutions and laws in this regard, which became known as "Neutrality Acts." Despite that, FDR said that the U.S. must be the "great arsenal of democracy"[18] because democracy was under assault.

FDR stated repeatedly during his speech that the United States, democracy, and "American republics" were in serious and immediate danger from forces that were "aiming at domination of the whole world." At one point, he claimed that "the Nation's life is in danger." The danger came from a "new order of tyranny" that dictators sought to "create with the crash of a bomb." This new order of tyranny was at war with the "democratic way of life" either through direct military aggression or through "secret spreading of poisonous propaganda" to "destroy unity and promote discord" in peaceful countries. Democracy was under assault on four continents, by those whose resources "greatly exceeds... the sum total of the population and the resources of the whole of the Western Hemisphere many times over," FDR continued, and if the conquerors prevailed, then its dictators could not be expected to provide "international generosity, or return of true independence, or world disarmament, or freedom of expression, or freedom of religion – or even good business."[19] Prior to 1914, said FDR, the U.S. was engaged in a number of undeclared wars and two declared wars all "for the principles of peaceful commerce."[20]

Appeasement or peace with the "new order of tyranny" was unattainable, according to Roosevelt, because the "foundations of a healthy and strong democracy" demanded "equality of opportunity for youth and for others. Jobs for those who can work. Security for those who need it. The ending of special privilege for the few. The preservation of civil liberties for all. The enjoyment of the fruits of scientific progress in a wider and constantly rising standard of living." These things, FDR concluded, were the source of the "inner and abiding strength" of America's economic and political systems. Patriotism demanded the sacrifices needed to prepare for a war that would remake the world according to "four essential human freedoms" in "our own time and generation."

FDR claimed that the new world order he was planning to advance with the impending war for its fulfillment was based on "the greater conception, the moral order." Indeed, from the beginning, America had "been engaged in change—in a perpetual peaceful revolution—a revolution which goes on steadily, quietly adjusting itself to changing conditions...." The American world order involved the cooperation of "free countries, working together in a friendly, civilized society." These societies, based on freedom, were, in turn, to be based on the "supremacy of human rights everywhere," and America was always ready to support revolutionary movements "to those who struggle to gain those rights or keep them."[21] In making these comments, FDR committed the U.S. to spreading the American Revolution to every society on earth.

HENRY LUCE'S AMERICAN CENTURY

In support of FDR, Luce wrote his essay "The American Century." Luce began his editorial, which was published in *Life*'s February 17, 1941, issue, by referring to Luftwaffe attacks on England, thereby making clear in the minds of the readers that the Germans were America's enemy. This served to weaken any ethnic or social allegiance to the Fatherland that ethnic Germans living in the U.S. harbored. He kept up this dynamic when he referred disparagingly to the "hisses and roars of the Nazi Propaganda Ministry." Luce knew, though, that the Midwest was traditionally opposed to war with Germany, so he had to differentiate American Midwesterners from Germans by writing that they "are today the least provincial people in the world."[22] He then went on to put at least part of the blame for the current state of world affairs on the shoulders of Americans so that, paradoxically, he could charge Americans with the responsibility for making the world a better place. America faced the "great decisions" that war presented even though it had not actually declared war on any country by February 1941.[23] In writing "The American Century," Luce ignored the fact that the coming war was going to be fought to gain world hegemony for the "American economic system and the capitalist spirit" and instead focused on pandering to a baser form of patriotism, which portrayed America as "the most powerful and the most vital nation in the world." As a result, Americans should "accept wholeheartedly our duty and our opportunity as the most powerful and vital nation in the world and in consequence to exert upon the world the full impact of our influence, for such purposes as we see fit and by such means as we see fit."[24]

Luce explained that America cannot "impose democratic institutions on all mankind" and cannot be responsible "for the good behavior of the entire world." However, the U.S. had to "vitally affect America's environment" to prevent it from becoming "unfavorable to the growth of American life." That required making American democracy "work. . . in terms of a vital international economy and in terms of an international moral order."[25] In order to ensure "Human progress and happiness," Americans had to manage world revolution and, in so doing, "re-establish our constitutional democracy." Luce came up with four corollaries that explained Roosevelt's Four Freedoms: First, "for the first time in history," the planet is "one world, fundamentally indivisible." Second, "modern man" hated war. Third, "our world...is capable of producing all the material needs of the entire human family." Finally, the Twentieth Century must be an "American Century" if the world is to "come to life in any nobility of health and vigor."[26]

Of course, American-style economics was essential to producing the "abundant life" that would satisfy the needs of the people. According to Luce, this could only happen with "a vision of Freedom under Law. Without Freedom, there will be no abundant life. With Freedom, there can be." In the section entitled "America's vision of our world.... How it shall be created," Luce revealed the doctrinal weapons that would be used to re-engineer the world's societies. American internationalism "must be a sharing with all peoples of our Bill of Rights, our Declaration of Independence, our Constitution, our magnificent industrial products, our technical skills. It must be an internationalism of the people, by the people, and for the people." Americans were determined to advance an ideal that was meant to make "the society of men safe for freedom, growth and increasing satisfaction of all individual men." Identified with this was the "American internationalism" that included "American jazz, Hollywood movies, American slang, American machines and patented products."[27]

According to Luce, an "American Century" meant "It is for America and for America alone to determine whether a system of free economic enterprise – an economic order compatible with freedom and progress – shall or shall not prevail in this century. We know perfectly well that there is not the slightest chance of anything faintly resembling a free economic system prevailing in this country if it prevails nowhere else." America would ensure "freedom of the seas" and become a "dynamic leader of world trade" since these allowed for "the possibilities of such enormous human progress as to stagger the imagination."[28]

America had to "send out through the world its technical and artistic skills" and "undertake now to be the Good Samaritan of the entire world." But in order to ensure that the American century succeeded, Americans must keep a "vision of America as a world power" that "includes a passionate devotion to great American ideals," which are "a love of freedom, a feeling for the equality of opportunity, a tradition of self-reliance and independence and also of cooperation." These ideals will lift "the life of mankind from the level of the beasts to what the Psalmist called a little lower than the angels."

Americans inherited "justice, the love of Truth, the ideal of Charity," which are "the great principles of Western civilization." At the root of all of this was the "triumphal purpose of freedom" that wove together all the "manifold projects and magnificent purposes" that graced North America.[29] After laying out the plan for spreading the American ideology, which was to bring the world under American domination, Luce embarked upon Phase I, which meant getting America involved in the bloodiest war in human history.

3
LUCE NAMES THE NEXT BOGEYMAN

The surrender of the German Sixth Army at Stalingrad on February 1, 1943, was the beginning of the end for National Socialist Germany. That meant America needed another enemy, and soon. Luce was quick to start the search, and he found one within short order – the Union of Soviet Socialist Republics (USSR) or the Soviet Union.

"Luce cautiously began the Cold War."[1] He proceeded to rouse Americans to the Soviet danger, and he began his campaign shortly after Field Marshal van Paulus' surrender with a *Time* piece:

"The central problem was Russia...[U]nless a general and open agreement is reached soon on joint postwar policies, the Allies' present comradeship in arms may turn into a barracks brawl....Russia holds too many trumps to be finessed in the game of politics....[i]f the partners in war do not lay their cards on the table soon, there will be the devil to pay.....The peace-loving nations of the world....again showed signs of an inability to head off World War III."[2]

An entire issue of *Life* Magazine was dedicated to the USSR in March 1943. Described as being "more respectful than critical, it was yet significant in managing to swing emphasis away from the Russian as a brave warrior and ally to the Russian as a world revolutionist and postwar threat, aided by Lend-Lease and not very grateful." After the Teheran conference declaration issued in November, *Life* attacked it as being vague and questioned if it was not a "colossal fraud." *Life* wondered: "Are the Russians really dedicated to 'free lives' and the elimination of tyranny? The word 'conscience' is not exactly a Marxian word." *Life* emphasized that in the postwar era, there must be a "'world family of democratic nations' in which all peoples 'may live free lives untouched by tyranny and according to...their own consciences."[3]

Luce maintained this "propaganda drive" against the Soviets during the closing months of World War II. An article by William Bullitt in the September 4, 1944 edition of *Life* entitled "The World from Rome" gave the impression that Bullitt and *Life* were repeating the views of Pope Pius XII, whom Bullitt had met:

"[T]he Vatican should take the long view of events and strive to understand, and make understood, the deep tides that move the nations....The Italians...look beyond the end of the fighting with little hope and much fear because they are afraid that the withdrawal of American and British forces...will leave them at the mercy of the Soviet Union....The Romans... fear that in the end Moscow, in the form of Tito, will be installed on their eastern frontier....They are even more frightened by the prospect that their northern neighbor, Austria, may fall under the control of Moscow....The Romans know Hitler, and they have heard him swear that if Germany should face defeat he would pull down the pillars of Western civilization on the heads of the allies....by having Himmler turn over Germany at the moment of collapse to the Communists."[4]

In that same "editorial article," Bullitt and Luce sketched out reasons for the anti-communism crusade in terms comprehensible to Catholics: "The deepest moral issue of the modern world – the issue of man as a son of God with an immortal soul, an end in himself, against man as a chemical compound, the tool of an omnipotent state, an end in itself – may thus be fought out in Italy...."[5]

The article created an uproar, bringing condemnations from Albert Einstein, Bishop Arthur Moulton, academics at Harvard, and commentator Max Lerner. Author Lee Grant wrote, "The article...may do more harm than you or anyone else can ever measure" and "inflicted serious hurt to the cause of peace."[6]

Luce persisted. Whitaker Chambers, a former Communist and bisexual, was the man responsible for editing, if not writing, the foreign news for *Time* during this period. Under Chambers' watchful eye and quick pen, the foreign news for *Time* "became a weekly outpouring of anti-Soviet propaganda." "Ghosts on the Roof," published in the March 5, 1945 issue of *Time,* was Chambers' work written in a "Dostoievskian vein," presenting imaginary characters praising Stalin's territorial aggrandizements. At one point, the imaginary character of Tsar Nicholas II, after admiring Stalin's work, says, "I became a Marxist." [7]

The conflict with the USSR came to the fore as the fighting in Germany died down. The Soviets responded with Andrei Gromyko and Andrei Vishinsky taking rhetorical aim at Clare Boothe Luce, Henry's wife, and a congresswoman from Connecticut at the time. *The Daily Worker* and the *New Masses* headlined "Luce Plans the Next War." Indeed, "the next war" was a phrase that increasingly recurred in *Time* and *Life.*[8]

For a brief period after the cessation of fighting in September 1945, there was a period of euphoria and hope, but it was not to last. George Kennan, a Princeton graduate, and the director of the State Department's think tank, who became known as the Father of Containment, wrote his "Long Telegram" from Moscow on February 22, 1946. This gave cause for official American and British opposition to the Soviets. Soviet Communism was presented in a dramatic and dangerous light that was calculated to have a certain effect on the reading audience and the public at large. The "Long Telegram" established the shape and activities of the Soviet bogeyman against which all American governmental effort would be justified and directed and against which the American capitalists could rail while rallying the people to do their bidding. The Soviet monster described by Kennan was the same type of monster used to justify American attacks on any system not of the making or approval, of the American capitalists.

Kennan's "Long Telegram" concluded that "we have here a political force committed fanatically to the belief that with U.S. there can be no permanent *modus vivendi* that it is desirable and necessary that the internal harmony of our society be disrupted, our traditional way of life be destroyed, the international authority of our state be broken, if Soviet power is to be secure." At the heart of this Soviet mentality, Kennan saw "the party line," which "arises mainly from basic inner-Russian necessities which existed before recent war and exist today." Soviet fanaticism came from a deep-seated psychological pathology that had its roots in "traditional and instinctive Russian sense of insecurity" going back to a time before recorded history because that was a "land which had never known a friendly neighbor or indeed any tolerant equilibrium of separate powers, either internal or international."[9]

The struggle was fundamentally economic. Kennan claimed the Soviets viewed "economic conflicts of society as insoluble by peaceful means" and the "USSR still lives in antagonistic 'capitalist encirclement'." Stalin was the one responsible for stoking the flames of conflict between communism and capitalism:

"As stated by Stalin in 1927 to a delegation of American workers: 'In course of further development of international revolution there will emerge two centers of world significance: a socialist center, drawing to itself the countries which tend toward socialism, and a capitalist center, drawing to itself the countries that incline toward capitalism. Battle between these two centers for command of world economy will decide fate of capitalism and of communism in the entire world.'"[10]

The fanatical worldview of the Soviets did not blind them to sympathetic elements in the West. Kennan warned:

"It must be borne in mind that capitalist world is not all bad. In addition to hopelessly reactionary and bourgeois elements, it includes 1) certain wholly enlightened and positive elements united in acceptable communistic parties and 2) certain other elements (now described for tactical reasons as progressive or democratic) whose reactions, aspirations and activities happen to be 'objectively' favorable to interests of USSR."[11]

The Soviets were determined to use the "Democratic-progressive elements to bring pressure to bear on capitalist governments along lines agreeable to Soviet interests" in order to exploit "revolutionary upheavals within the various capitalist countries."[12]

The goal of the Soviets, according to Kennan, was to "undermine general political and strategic potential of major western powers" by disrupting "national self confidence[sic]," hamstringing "national defense," increasing "social and industrial unrest", and "stimulat[ing] all forms of disunity." People with grievances were encouraged to seek redress in a "defiant violent struggle for destruction of other elements of society," which manifested itself in the violence of the poor against the rich, black against white, young against old, and "newcomers against established residents." Communists actively worked in foreign countries for the "destruction of all forms of personal independence, economic, political or moral" because the Soviet "system can handle only individuals who have been brought into complete dependence on higher power." The Soviets were thus the enemies of Capitalism and of the American way of life because "persons who are financially independent – such as individual businessmen, estate owners, successful farmers, artisans and all those who exercise local leadership or have local prestige, such as popular local clergymen or political figures, are anathema."[13]

Kennan terrified the reader by painting a picture of seemingly omnipotent evil that could exist and act undetected. He claimed the Soviets would apply "insistent, unceasing pressure for penetration and command of key positions in administration" with an "elaborate and far flung apparatus for exertion of its influence in other countries, an apparatus of amazing flexibility and versatility, managed by people whose experience and skill in underground methods are presumably without parallel in history." The Communist Party was functioning in other countries while "many of persons who compose this category may also appear and act in unrelated public capacities, they are in reality working closely together as an underground operating directorate of world communism, a concealed Comintern tightly coordinated and directed by Moscow. It is important to remember that this inner core is actually working on underground lies, despite legality of parties with which it is associated."[14]

A "conspiratorial element has been neatly concentrated in inner circle and ordered underground" while the "rank and file...are thrust forward as bona fide internal partisans of certain political tendencies within their respective countries, genuinely innocent of conspiratorial connection with foreign states." The Communists were going to "penetrate, and...influence or dominate, as case may be, other organizations less likely to be suspected of being tools of Soviet Government...." Of course, this domination and influence by use of "penetration" could be used to take over a number of "national associations or bodies," such as "labor unions, youth leagues, women's organizations, racial societies, religious societies, social organizations, cultural groups, liberal magazines, publishing houses, etc." "[I]nternational organizations" could "be similarly penetrated through influence over various national components" with "vital importance" being "attached in this connection to international labor movement."[15]

Kennan insinuated that Communism infiltrated religious groups, and he expounded on this when he wrote that Communists could infiltrate and dominate the "Russian Orthodox Church, with its foreign branches, and through it the Eastern Orthodox Church in general." Communists could penetrate ethnic organizations such as the "Pan-Slav movement."[16]

Faced with such an enemy, the U.S. had to do several things to combat it successfully. First, Americans "must... apprehend, and recognize for what it is, the nature of the movement with which we are dealing." Second, the public must be "educated to realities of Russian situation." The American "stake in this country, even coming on heels of tremendous demonstrations of our friendship for Russian people, is remarkably small. We have here no investments to guard, no actual trade to lose, virtually no citizens to protect, few cultural contacts to preserve. Our only stake lies in what we hope rather than what we have...." Third, steps must be taken to "solve internal problems of our own society, to improve self-confidence, discipline, morale and community spirit of our own people." Fourth, America "must formulate and put forward for other nations a much more positive and constructive picture of sort of world we would like to see than we have put forward in past. It is not enough to urge people to develop political processes similar to our own....They are seeking guidance rather than responsibilities...."[17]

Kennan described the new enemy and said loyalty to America was the way to fight. The steady drumbeat for the Cold War with the Soviets intensified. In March 1946, Winston Churchill, a hero of Luce and a frequent correspondent, gave his famous "Iron Curtain" speech in Fulton, Missouri. He dramatically claimed an iron curtain of totalitarian oppression was descending across Europe. In April, Kennan was recalled to the United States and gave a number of talks about the Soviet danger. After his lecture tour, he landed at the War College and developed the doctrine of "strategic containment," published the following year under the pseudonym of "Mr. X." The "Truman Doctrine" requested funding for military aid for Greece and Turkey in response to Soviet movement in the Eastern Mediterranean. Shortly thereafter, Congress passed the "Marshall Plan" or the European Recovery Act, which granted European countries an economic stimulus ostensibly to keep them from becoming prey for the Soviets by falling into social, economic, and political anarchy. The Soviets responded in October by reviving the Cominform (Communist Information Bureau), which was soon "peddling a seductive image of the Soviet Union as the champion of world peace and the warmongering United States as its principal enemy."[18]

By late 1947, the stage was set for a world divided into two ideological camps, with the Soviets painted as a dangerous, subtle, omnipresent, horribly evil enemy. America was the shining city on the hill. It was the same fight as before: freedom versus tyranny. The fight was consistent with and advanced FDR's Four Freedoms and Luce's American Century. One either became like America, which was good, or faced dire consequences.

While still fighting the Nazis, Luce kept repeating the same rhetorical question: "Does the American nation exist for any particular purpose?" The answer, he argued, "rises in your hearts" and makes clear that "the American nation does exist for a specific purpose – in the words of the Battle Hymn: 'To make men free.'" Time, Inc.'s mission was "to explain about American journalism and in doing that we have to explain about America." That was simple because "out of the whole vocabulary of human experience to associate with America—surely it would not be hard to choose the word. For surely the word is Freedom....Without Freedom, America is untranslatable.... And therefore it seems to me that we can sum up the whole of editorial attitudes and principles in the one word Freedom." America's mission was bound up with Time, Inc.'s, and that was to assure the world that Americans "have fought, are fighting and will fight.... 'For the Freedom of All Peoples.'....We believe that the relation of the people of the U.S. with the other peoples of the world must be based on the principles of Freedom." As an editorial aside, Luce wrote: "(This can be endlessly celebrated.)"[19]

The Soviet Union, on the other hand, "'stood for nothing' and honored no principles. Soviet laws were meaningless because...they had no basis in morality or faith." American law "is written somewhere in the hearts of all men," and international law could be harnessed to "spread democracy and capitalism into a benighted world. It was a tool by which the goals of the 'American Century' might still be realized, the vehicle that allowed the United States to achieve its great mission in the world."[20]

Luce criticized Truman's approach to Communism from almost the beginning of his administration. He wrote that "the struggle between Freedom and Communism is, at bottom a moral issue... a religious issue" and that no one can say that "we can live peaceably and happily with this prodigious evil." Writing to *Time's* Paris correspondent in the late 1940s, he stated, "Communism is the most monstrous cancer which ever attacked humanity, and we shall do our best, however feeble, to combat it at all times and all places." Yet he did not seem so concerned about fighting Communism in the United States. His focus was on developing a "coherent strategy for combating global Communism" and not engaging in "witch hunt[s] for subversives in America" like those supposedly carried on by the Catholic Senator from Wisconsin, Joe McCarthy.[21]

The Soviets were depicted as a powerful foe, but the reality was far different. Research revealed the USSR was, in many ways, a paper tiger. A fast demobilization after World War II left troops in occupied countries "quite unreliable, if not rebellious." The Soviets provided no foreign aid, their economy was in shambles, and outside the USSR, the Communist parties were minority parties.[22] William Blum quoted Roger Morris, a former member of the National Security Council: "U.S. officials 'exaggerated Soviet Capabilities and intentions to such an extent,' says a subsequent study of the archives, 'that it is surprising anyone took them seriously.'" Still, there were claims of the Soviet threat being one of a worldwide conspiracy of subversion so vast and so sinister that it had to be continuously fought in every society around the globe.[23] Such gave rise to fear, a very useful tool of the masters of international banking. Any attempt to ascertain the real situation within the Soviet empire was hampered by the classification of all documents relating to American commercial dealings with the Soviets.[24]

Luce cultivated fear of a dangerous and powerful Soviet Union, justifying American involvement in every society on the earth because, without fear, there could be no Cold War. Luce told his wife, Clare, that he was a happy man because he had the opportunity to "be of service to the world" so as to "help shape 'the first global era in history.'"[25]

PART II

CLARE BOOTHE LUCE – AMERICAN CATHOLIC

4

CLARE BOOTHE LUCE – AMERICAN CATHOLIC

Clare Boothe Luce's life began humbly on April 10, 1903, in a flat belonging to Will Boothe and his second wife, Anna Clara Snyder, a former chorus girl. Named Ann Clare, she grew up in "a Bohemian atmosphere." At the age of nine, her father left her mother for another woman, but Clare's mother told her and her brother, David, that he had died. With her mother ambitious for her child, Clare was enrolled in the Cathedral School of St. Mary in Garden City, Long Island, and while there, she wrote in her diary of her desire to marry a publisher, write something to be remembered, have three children and be fluent in four languages. Two years later, she was enrolled in the prestigious school known as Castle School at Tarrytown-on-the-Hudson, where she rapidly advanced and graduated in June 1919.[1]

Clare's mother then married Dr. Albert Austin, chief of staff at the hospital, president of the Greenwich Bank and Trust Company, and Grand Master of the Greenwich Chapter of the Masonic Lodge. About that time, Clare entered business school, where she "locked herself in her room and began writing short stories" that she "furtively mailed to the magazines of the day." She also "wrote quantities of poetry."[2]

At a church service in New York in June 1922, she met George T. Brokaw, a 43-year-old playboy millionaire bachelor and clothing merchant heir, who was the object of much gossip in the New York tabloids. In August 1923, despite some apparent reservations, she married him. Her only daughter, Ann, was born in August 1924. Thereafter, the marriage deteriorated because of George's drinking, his abuse of Clare, and four miscarriages. By April 1929, Clare had enough and, with Ann, went to Nevada for a divorce. The divorce settlement assured her financial independence.[3]

Clare went looking for a job after experiencing psychoanalysis from a Dr. Feigenbaum. Conde' Nast gave Clare her first job as a writer for *Vogue* magazine. Soon, she was a part of *Vanity Fair,* where she rubbed elbows with the high society and political figures. During this time, she courted a number of eligible and not-so-eligible suitors. Clare had a serious streak, and in 1933, she presented a proposal to get the country out of the Depression. However, she realized that the corporate state was not for America and resigned from the "Blue Eagle" committee that controlled the nation's business and economic activities, saying that the plan she had helped devise "won't work if America is to remain a free country."[4]

Clare Brokaw wrote a play underwritten by her good friend, if not occasional paramour, Bernard Baruch. At the publisher's dinner party, she was seated with Henry Luce, who proceeded to act very rudely by seldom speaking with her. A year later, at a party at the Waldorf-Astoria to honor Cole Porter, Clare, and Luce met again and spoke for nearly an hour before he asked her to the lobby, where he told her, "I can't take more than five minutes. It wouldn't be good manners. I want to tell you that you are the great love of my life. And someday, I am going to marry you." They took a year getting to know each other, during which Clare was involved with rehearsing *Abide With Me,* her first full-length play. The play, which drew on her experiences in her first marriage, concerned a young woman marrying an older, alcoholic man. Henry divorced his first wife, Lila, and a few weeks later married Clare in November 1935.[5] Thus came into existence, Clare Boothe Luce.

Luce changed Clare's life. While it was a "rage for fame" that drove Claire for so many years,[6] she later explained that a fundamental shift came over her when she married Luce. Because she wanted to be a worthy partner for Luce and to bear him children,[7] she gave her life completely over to him, even abandoning her career as a playwright in order to ensure his success. She wrote for his magazines, served two terms as a Congresswoman from Connecticut, and became U.S. Ambassador to Italy.

Though Clare devoted her life to Luce and his interests, Luce always considered her more of an intellectual competitor than a supporter. In a diary entry with an imaginary marriage counselor, she wrote with a pathos that confirms the truth of her statements: "that he [Harry] never understood I was *not*_competing with him: that I was, in a profound sense, supplementary and extending his own great personality.....I was a moon in politics which shone only because of the light of his sun. I could not thrive or succeed in politics without his strong and happily given support."[8]

Clare became prominent in the public sphere. Like her husband, she wanted America to enter World War II on the side of Great Britain. In a lecture given on March 9, 1941, at Pierson College on the campus of Yale University, Clare voiced approval of war with Germany, claiming that Hitler was "an effect and not a cause" and urging the United States to "abandon forever isolationism.... I believe we should enter this war with man-power, as well as machine-power, when we have sufficient of both reasonably to assume we will win it." Clare was all for "small democracies," the "federation of Europe," and, like the Anglo-American elites, she believed in the necessity of a "union of the English-speaking nations." She stated, "An American is not a cultural or racial entity, but a two-legged legal entity and a state of mind which has heretofore been recognized as being passionately optimistic, un-class conscious, self-reliant and tolerant."[9]

In 1942, Clare ran for Congress and won. She represented Connecticut, where she and Harry owned a home in Ridgefield. In 1944, she won re-election, but in that same year, her daughter Ann died in an automobile accident, a tragedy that deeply affected her.

On February 16, 1946, while still a Congresswoman[10] and nine years after marrying Luce, Clare converted to the Catholic Faith. Clare was independently wealthy before marrying Luce, whom she affectionately called Harry, and after her conversion, she came to personify the idea Catholics could advance and prosper in American society. That in itself was one of Harry's ideas. However, Clare felt ambivalence towards being Catholic and American at the same time.

In a letter to Bishop Fulton Sheen, who she claimed was responsible for her conversion to Catholicism, Clare explained the Church was harmed by America as it implicitly supported principles such as religious liberty and disestablishment:

"Oh, do not think I do not understand how it is with the Church in America. How sweet it is to be at long last on the right side of the tracks...and to be in the religious field, as one of my Catholic friends put it, a real-up-and-comer!... Oh could it be that the Church itself is beginning to be just a little like the rich young man...? Men I say should not spend all their novenas and so much of their life of prayer in her contemplation – not in times like these, that call for eagles, and lions and tigers of the Lord!... Ravage the world with the Truths of Christ crucified.... This is a lush land of glittering corruption....No King but saints and martyrs can save us now."[11]

Clare understood America as "inescapably pragmatic." American Catholics "spend little time trying to convert their neighbors (and are always being bawled out by their priests for this lassitude). But they make up for it by 'contributing to the missions.'" However, a Catholic was a Catholic because he or she believed it was the "one true faith."[12] The U.S. Catholic prelates at least kept that aspect of Catholicism alive, but that would be attacked and worn down by inter-creedal and inter-religious cooperation. The bishops themselves adopted the American pragmatism, becoming "brick and mortar" men, thereby focusing on raising money and tending to administration. The leading and teaching were sloughed off on the theologians who turned decidedly Americanist after World War II.

These priests and bishops were also reporting to the U.S. government on their own people. If priests like Fr. Charles Coughlin displeased the American establishment, the prelates were quick to condemn. As long as priests and prelates were doing the bidding of the American elites, they were assured places of honor and respect. If they ever failed to support American efforts, such as anti-communism, they were discredited. This state of affairs was the result of decades of Catholic support for the American ideology. Catholic prelates for years had ignored Rome and expressed loyalty primarily to America and its ideas. The idea that America's role was to be a teacher to the Church was known as Americanism. It had been condemned by Pope Leo XIII in 1899, but it lived on and grew stronger and more prevalent.

Clare wrote about her conversion to Catholicism in three consecutive issues of *McCall's,* a popular magazine that appealed to the women of her day with discussions of fashion and short stories by well-known writers. The series of articles Clare wrote was entitled "The 'Real' Reason" with the subtext that this was "her personal testament." They appeared in the February, March, and April 1947 issues[13] or after she left Congress.

Clare described her Protestant upbringing as Protestant. Her mother was a lapsed Catholic, but she felt little Catholic influence in her life and was "even less subject to catholic influence than most Americans." The man responsible for introducing the Catholic influence that led to her conversion was a Jesuit priest, Fr. Edward Wiatrak of Cincinnati, who taught at a parochial school for boys. Wiatrak wrote her a letter five years earlier in which he commended her for an article she wrote about Madame Chiang Kai-Shek's war orphans and promised to remember her in his prayers. Clare replied occasionally, but his theme remained constant: "Love perfects justice, justice in which God is loved above all things, with the whole mind, heart and soul; and everything else is loved in God...."[14]

After her daughter Ann died in an automobile accident in January 1944, Wiatrak wrote to Clare, saying her death could be a blessing. Writing from New York, where he was posted at the Jesuit Mission House, Wiatrak kept in touch with her and played a "most extraordinary part" in Clare's conversion. It was Wiatrak who Clare called one night during a crisis seeking help from the Catholic Church for help and Wiatrak kept telling her that "God ought to be considered as a factor in human affairs by politicians and writers."[15]

Wiatrak also put her in touch with Monsignor Fulton Sheen, who undertook the task of educating her on the Catholic Faith, with the courses averaging fifty hours per week.[16] The culmination of Sheen's teaching, as she put it, was the Doctrine of the Divinity of Jesus Christ, a theme that she addressed in the *McCall's* articles.[17] Eventually, both Sheen and Wiatrak were replaced as guides to the Catholic faith by a "big, tall, attractive whiskey-drinking priest who wore his habit all the time."[18] That priest was the Jesuit John Courtney Murray.

An autobiographical sketch about her conversion, the *McCall's* articles contained a heavy dose of anti-Communism and the conviction that Catholics had to reject Communism. Clare had interwoven her reasons for becoming Catholic with her reasons for rejecting Communism, thereby enlisting Catholics in the American cause for the Cold War.

Clare wrote that the "personal gift of Faith by Grace and the sense of personal sin and personal responsibility are certainly two of the major reasons I became a Catholic." In promoting these ideas, the Catholic Church was unique, Clare explained, because "in this age, when the devil has at long last achieved his dearest wish – that mortals should no longer believe in his existence, we often do find that those who 'do not believe in personal sin' are likely to be the ones harshest in their judgments of their neighbor's shortcomings." The Communist, who denies the concept of "individual guilt"[19] best personified this error.

Clare made America acceptable to Catholics because "like all Americans, I am living in a Western civilization which is deeply rooted in Catholicism and is still traveling under the impetus given it by more than 1500 years of ardent Catholic belief, passionate Catholic ministry and rigorous Catholic doctrine."[20] Opposed to Catholicism were things like Freudianism and, once again, Communism.[21] Catholics could fall for Communism, as she herself had done, because "the appeal of Communism for me lay in its religious aspect." In spite of the fact that "Communism was a complete authoritarian structure,"[22] "the emotional content [was] so subtly Christian and Jewish that [it] made Communism appealing to me for a long time."[23]

Liberalism was no better because it "seemed to make room for just about everything." Liberalism was popular because it was credited with many so-called beneficial changes in society over the years, including social welfare and the abolition of slavery.[24] However, liberals were essentially atheists, like the Communists, who chastised liberals for their beliefs.[25] Liberals taught that the existence of God could not be proven, whereas the Catholic Church was able to prove God's existence and the divinity of Christ.[26]

Communism lied about the reasons for the world's problems. Clare wrote:

"I was one of those not uncommon students who read in my teens Karl Marx's *Das Capital,* religiously and was very inclined to believe that he had found the perfect blueprint for the happy society.... I was completely willing to believe until then [the Hitler-Stalin pact] that the core of the world's troubles had been created by international bankers, stockbrokers, monopolists, and industrialists who ground the faces of the poor and sent the flower of youth into battle time and time again to protect their profits." [27]

Communism blamed capitalism for all problems, yet Communism brought misery not only to "Russia, but in Poland, the Balkans, Yugoslavia and China."[28]

Communism's explanation of the human condition failed because "there exists much human suffering which cannot be traced to any economic or political causes." Communism could not "solve all the problems of life," and the Communist could "hardly claim it would solve the problem of death." The notion of personal responsibility was lost on Marxists, just as it was on Freudians. Personal responsibility requires man to face "what they hate to confess: that most of their problems are moral problems; that they do sin and are responsible for their sins to society and God."[29]

Clare wrote all this at a time when the new anti-Catholicism, as manifested in Paul Blanshard's articles in *The Nation,* was surfacing in American society. Instead of seeking Christian allies, Clare attacked Protestantism as well, explaining that if "man is not to get his ideas of God from God, that is, by revelation or grace, then he must get his ideas of God either from nature or the ideas other men have held about God. A novel combination of such ideas often results in a Protestant church." Nonetheless, she wrote, "It seems to me, today, that the differences between Christians of all denominations and unbelievers is wide and greater and more important to breach than the differences between let us say, Protestants and Catholics."[30]

After her articles appeared in *McCall's,* Clare became a sought-after speaker at Catholic forums. Her main theme was the evil of Communism and the goodness of America. Given her history as a New York socialite, the wife of the well-known and successful Henry Luce, and her conversion to Catholicism, she presented as a powerful witness.

Later, in 1947, Clare gave a talk entitled "Freedom and Catholicism." The outline sought to establish American freedom as a good that is consistent with Catholicism and a value that Catholicism has defended over the years. The great threats to this freedom came from, of course, Communism, as well as things such as secularism, worldliness, and scientism (including behaviorism, Freudianism, and Darwinism). And "individual Catholics can best help" to defend freedom by not only leading Catholic lives but by "Catholic action." Clare identified those who advance or defend freedom as "All men who believe in spiritual values and all philosophies that advance the individual dignity of man," but Christianity was the "great Defender," and the "Sermon on the Mount" and the Magnificat were instances of that defense.[31]

The theme for the Paulist Forum's 1948 Fall Lecture Series was "Can the American Way Survive?" In attempting to answer that question, Clare gave a talk entitled "Is the American Personality Neurotic?" Her talk was billed as "witty as it is wise" as she answered the questions of "What drives Americans into producing the fastest, most nervous and most nerve-wracking civilization in the world?" and "Why is the typical American less and less secure in his society, more and more restless, and anxious and unstable?" Her credentials were the "plays, books and articles" she had written, but perhaps more significantly, "her conversion has brought her a complete new insight, spiritual, metaphysical and moral, into the mainsprings of the American temperament."[32]

During the summer of 1948, Harry asked Clare to contact Randolph Churchill to ask the English novelist and former British intelligence officer Evelyn Waugh to write an article about American Catholicism. Churchill advised Clare that Waugh was not only willing to do so,[33] but he was, in fact, "very glad to enter into an arrangement with *Life* magazine, for whose general policies he has a great admiration."[34] The Waugh piece was part of Luce's Americanist ecumenism. On August 11, Billings wrote that "Luce called me in and said he wanted me to get a piece on the Jewish faith – and another on the Catholic Church in the U.S., and here was our chance to have Evelyn Waugh write the latter. It all made good sense to me: Waugh is a Catholic and a crack writer,"[35] and could presumably explain how "the Catholic Church in America... has provided world Catholicism with a new center of gravity. Its wealth is contributed generously to the Vatican. Its prestige plays a large and influential role at Rome. It is growing all the time. The importance of this shift of emphasis to American Catholicism would make an interpretive picture of the subject in LIFE most timely."[36]

5
AMERICANISM DIVIDES THE CATHOLICS

Americanism began as a battle between German and Irish immigrants over the proper relationship between Church and State. Irish prelates, like James Cardinal Gibbons and Archbishop John Ireland, who had close ties with the civic and economic leaders of the time, openly endorsed the American ideology in the last quarter of the Nineteenth Century. From America, these views spread to Italy and France, where the Americanists had allies and sympathizers among the social elites.

The reaction to Americanism was felt in Europe. The first Catholic to name and sound a warning against Americanism was Fr. Henry Tappert. At the General Convention of the German Catholics held at Cologne, Germany, on August 26, 1894, he showed how liberalism, which is the basis for the American ideology, dampened efforts at conversion, removed Christianity as the basis of public policy and helped to destroy ethnic solidarity in favor of the individual as supreme in all things. Tappert explained what would happen if the American ideology were accepted as good in principle:

"Since our enemies kept up their sorry courage to concentrate their criminal attacks on a man from the Centre, who had been highly useful to the German Catholic emigrants, you will permit me to explain our attitude towards the ecclesiastics and religio-political questions which have so prominently occupied the Catholic mind recently in the United States. Our great enemy is liberalism, the denial of the social kingdom of Christ on earth. This great heresy of our time is three-fold; first, avowed unbelief; second, social rationalism; last, but not least, an ecclesiastical liberalism which here and there blocks our way. It holds sway over certain Catholics who have inscribed on their banner: 'Union of the Church with the Age, with modern ideas, with Americanism.' Hence the extolling of modern liberties, not as a requisite for a justified tolerance, but as the ideal of political and ecclesiastical wisdom, hence the more than sparing attitude of this third kind of liberalism towards the secret societies; hence the unreasonable breaking away from sane Catholic tradition in the temperance and liquor question; hence, finally, that coquetting with a more or less general all-embracing Christianity to which a far-reaching expression was given at the Chicago religious parliament of unholy memory. From the same source originate those fulsome praises for the public schools, and that ridiculous boastfulness about Americanism, which is not ashamed to reproach foreign-born co-religionists with an attachment to the language and customs of their fathers, and brand them publicly as being opposed to the English language, and devoid of love for country."[1]

Tappert's comments began with a reference to what became known as the Cahensly Question, which involved Cardinal Gibbons' attack on the movement by German Catholic immigrants to the United States to obtain priests and bishops of the same ethnicity as their flocks. According to Tappert, Gibbons' actions amounted to the forced assimilation of Catholics into the Liberal society known as America, even if acceptance of the American ideology led to assimilation and loss of ethnic identity. Gibbons claimed that immigrant Catholics needed to share a common respect for rights, a common faith in the perpetuity of their institutions, belief in the "liberty which gave every man a chance," and "a common aspiration for a greater America" which was an example and blessing to the world.[2] The Church in America was responsible for leading Catholics "forward to that community of language, social custom and political idealism which were essential to their own welfare and the nation's safety."[3] The sentiments sounded noble and innocent enough but Gibbons' Americanism caused Catholic immigrants to accept America as good so they could materially profit, rather than working to convert it, as Archbishop John Hughes vociferously demanded in 1850.[4]

The Archangel Raphael Society, under the direction of Peter Cahensly, worked for the protection of German emigrants and became a model for other nationalities, including the Italians, Poles, and French,[5] who were interested in the spiritual welfare of their immigrants as well. In December 1890, the international congress of the Archangel Raphael Society met in Lucerne, Switzerland, and prepared a Memorial addressed to the Holy See that mentioned the Catholic Church sustained losses of more than $10,000,000. The Memorial explained this was a result of immigrants and descendants losing the faith because of many reasons, including insufficient numbers of priests versed in the language of the immigrants, lack of ethnic parishes, public schools, lack of Catholic societies based upon nationality and language, and lack of representatives of the various nationalities in the episcopate. The Memorial requested immigrants be organized into parishes and societies based on nationality, priests be appointed who could speak the language of these groups, and bishops be appointed by nationality according to population. All of this served to pass on the faith from one generation to another and maintain "harmony and concord between the different nationalities."[6]

The Memorial was prescient in explaining how souls were lost through assimilation and offered a way to bring peace between America, whose leaders long abhorred Europe, and European Catholics: "the fact that the numerous emigrants constitute a great strength, and could co-operate eminently in the expansion of the Catholic Church in the several states of America. In this way they could contribute to the moral stature of their new homeland, as well as to the stimulation of religious consciousness in the old European fatherlands."[7]

Gibbons was not sympathetic. In an interview with the *Frankfurter Zeitung,* he sided with the Americans. He said, "The Americans are striving for developing into one great nationality....This explains the propaganda for one language, the English tongue, in the Catholic Church of North America...." He went on to say that he had been pressured by the "political authorities of the United States" concerning this matter and that he and other Catholic prelates had bowed to the pressure. Gibbons, Ireland, and Archbishop John Keane of the newly formed Catholic University of America joined in attacking the Germans and Cahensly. They held that a German Church in America would not convert the Protestants and that a "Catholic Church...composed of foreigners" was viewed as a "foreign institution" and hence a "menace to the existence of the nation." Gibbons called a meeting of the Archbishops in Philadelphia to protest the demands of the Archangel Raphael Society. He stated that parishes should not exist with "distinction of nationality" and privileges should not be given any nationality.[8]

Pope Leo XIII came down on the side of the Americanists, ruling against Cahensly and the Archangel Raphael Society. In a letter dated July 4, 1891, he declared that "the existing laws for the selection of Bishops were to be observed without modification, and that no toleration could be accorded to practices which had arisen in opposition to those laws." A week later, Gibbons reported the outcome of the Cahensly Question to the President of the United States, and the President "seemed to be much pleased in receiving this information." Gibbons recorded in his journal that President Benjamin Harrison "thanked me for my denunciation of the Cahensly memorial. He said he had watched the subject with deep interest, and that he had sometimes thought of writing to me, but hesitated lest he might be interfering with church matters." [9] In a letter to Msgr. Denis O'Connell, Americanist Rector of the North American College in Italy,[10] Gibbons cited President Harrison as saying:

"I have followed the question with profound interest, and I regard it as a subject of deep importance to our country at large, one in which the American people are much concerned. I have also conversed on the subject with Mr. Tracy a member of my cabinet. Foreign and unauthorized interference with American affairs cannot be viewed with indifference....I was very much pleased with the opinion which you expressed publicly in the matter....this is no longer a missionary country like others which need missionaries from abroad. It has an authorized Hierarchy and well-established congregations. Of all men, the Bishops of the Church should be in full harmony with the political institutions and sentiments of the country."[11]

This whole episode confirmed the correctness of Bishop Josef Fessler's thesis. Fessler, the Secretary of the Vatican Council of 20 years earlier, claimed that liberal states, all of which reject an established church or religion, end up controlling religions and churches. Gibbons, who also attended that Council, had just witnessed the truth of Fessler's ideas.

POPE LEO TALKS TO THE AMERICAN PRELATES

Despite siding with them against Cahensly, Leo XIII was wary of the American episcopacy. After years of watching the Americans, in 1895, he issued *Longinqua Oceani,* which sought to correct Gibbons and other Americanists, who continued to ignore Rome's teachings as to the proper relation between Church and State. That ideal was not to be found in the United States, as the pope famously made clear in the famous paragraph 6: "It would be very erroneous to draw the conclusion that in America is to be sought the type of the most desirable status of the Church, or that it would be universally lawful or expedient for State and Church to be, as in America, dissevered and divorced."

Years earlier and after the Vatican I Council, Gibbons authored a book entitled *Faith of Our Fathers,* claiming that it was a catechism of the Catholic faith "treating thoroughly of all Catholic doctrine,"[12] but the book was notable in its omissions. In Chapters XVII and XVIII, entitled "Civil and Religious Liberty" and "Charges of Religious Persecution," respectively, he ignored the principles on which societies were to be built because these principles did not comport with the American ideology. He did not address the issue of society's duty to the Catholic Church and the Catholic Faith and held out freedom of conscience as the touchstone of the legitimacy of the state. Gibbons' emphasis, like that of the Americans, was on the rights of individuals rather than the duties of the state to God, Who was the source of all political power. The danger of Gibbons' work lay in what he did not explain and in the ambiguous terms he used.

Gibbons correctly stated the Catholic view when he said that a man "enjoys religious liberty when he possesses the free right of worshipping God according to the dictates of a right conscience, and of practicing a form of religion most in accordance with his duties to God." However, the term "right conscience" can only refer to conforming one's will and intellect to the Catholic Faith, and not to any other religion. Gibbons failed to explain this, and this omission suggested that one had a moral right to believe whatever one wanted. "The Church," he wrote, "has not only respected the conscience of the people in embracing the religion of their choice, but she has also defended their civil rights and liberties against the encroachments of temporal sovereigns."[13]

Gibbons defined civil liberty as an exemption "from the arbitrary will of others, and when he is governed by equitable laws established for the general welfare of society." He did not explain the Catholic principles by which society is to be ordered so as to ensure this general welfare, a theme the popes repeated over and over. Specifically, Gibbons made no mention of the teachings of Pius IX as contained in *Quanta Cura* and the *Syllabus.* Signaling a break with the words, if not also the spirit, of the papal teachings, Gibbons indicated he would not change the Establishment Clause nor the Free Exercise Clause. He established the position that American Catholics have held to this day: "So that if Catholics should gain the majority in a community where freedom of conscience is already secured to all by law, their very religion obliges them to respect the rights thus acquired by their fellow-citizens."[14]

In accordance with Catholic teaching, Gibbons noted that people should not be compelled against their will to "make a profession of the Christian faith." However, he never explained or defined what compulsion was, so efforts at conversion to Catholicism were hampered. His only advice was that Catholics could only engage in "endeavoring to convert men by mild persuasion." Continuing to curry acceptance with the Americans, Gibbons appealed to their long-held aversion to kings. He wrote, "the Church has ever resisted the tyranny of kings," and "distinguished representatives of the Catholic Church" played a prominent part in the American Independence. He praised the United States, and not Europe, for protecting "liberty of conscience" while preventing the state's "intermeddling with ecclesiastical affairs." He concluded that in the United States, the government did not "dictate to us what doctrines we ought to preach."[15]

In America, while the government was not granted the power to dictate what the priests "ought to preach," the opinion of the societal elites certainly did dictate what the priests could or could not say. In consonance with the American ideology, real power rested in society at large, and those with the most real power were those in the commercial class. Gibbons had a close association with these elements of society.[16] Being a bright young rising star in the Catholic Church, he could ill afford to anger these people because they had a vested interest in maintaining the American ideology with all that entailed.

Gibbons observed firsthand what the elites could do to an Episcopal career. Exhibiting qualities that were said to show he was "'destined for leadership,'" Gibbons was transferred to the Baltimore Cathedral as the secretary of Archbishop John Spalding.[17] Previously, Spalding angered the Americans after he expressed solidarity with the Confederacy. In response, the U.S. government sought to block his appointment and told the Catholic Church that Spalding was "not sufficiently in accord with the policy of repression toward the South" since he had served as a bishop in Kentucky.[18] The Vatican ignored the American protestations, and in May 1864, Spalding became Archbishop of Baltimore.[19]

Gibbons was vocal and lavish in professions of loyalty to America. He and other prelates, notably Ireland, praised the Constitution and promised that they would never seek to change it. This meant endorsing the so-called Establishment Clause, which disestablishes the Catholic Church, and any church for that matter, and prevents religious tenets, especially the Divine Positive Law, from forming the basis of public policy. Gibbons' profession of loyalty also meant never changing the Free Exercise Clause, which permits practice and adherence to any religion based on the will of the individual. Both provisions of the U.S. Constitution were condemned by papal teachings issued by a number of popes. The American prelates had the benefit of the various encyclicals written by these supreme leaders of the Catholic Church. They simply chose to ignore them or to water down Catholic teaching to please the Protestant American elites with whom they made close association.

Beginning with Pope Gregory XVI and continuing with his successors Pius IX and Leo XIII, Church doctrine on the proper organization of society was made plain. The popes issued encyclicals that condemned Liberalism, which separated the church from the state, allowed religious liberty or freedom of conscience, and permitted liberty of speech. Second, they taught the duties of the civil authorities to guard the Catholic Church and protect the Catholic Faith. Third, they explained that societies are to be based on the Gospel or Catholic teaching. Fourth, they reiterated the benefits that accrue to societies organized in accordance with Catholic teaching and the evil when that is not so. Fifth, they made clear that ideologies organizing society in accordance with just the natural law or human reason are insufficient, if not actually harmful.

Mirari Vos was promulgated in 1832 and declared that public order was destroyed when the "restraints of religion are thrown off." A dissolute liberty was perverting "sound doctrine...and errors of all kind spread boldly." Gregory XVI admonished the faithful against the love of novelty in the substance of doctrine and its expression, and against relaxing the discipline of the Church as real dangers. He quoted Pope St. Agatho from the seventh century, who said, "Nothing of the things appointed ought to be diminished; nothing changed; nothing added; but they must be preserved both as regards expression and meaning." Along with this rejection of novelty, "the discipline sanctioned by the Church must never be rejected or be branded as contrary to certain principles of natural law." Civil authorities could not interfere with Church governance and doctrine.[20]

Mirari Vos harshly condemned indifferentism, which claimed "that *it is possible to obtain the eternal salvation of the soul by the profession of any kind of religion, as long as morality is maintained.*" The pope reminded all the Faithful that "Christ Himself [said] that 'those who are not with Christ are against Him,' [fn 17: Luke 11:23] and that they disperse unhappily who do not gather with Him. Therefore 'without a doubt, they will perish forever, unless they hold the Catholic faith whole and inviolate'."[21]

Indifferentism led to "that absurd and erroneous proposition which claims that liberty of conscience must be maintained for everyone." This doctrine, which is based on "immoderate freedom of opinion, license of free speech, and desire for novelty," causes "ruin in sacred and civil affairs, though some repeat over and over again with the greatest impudence that some advantage accrues to religion from it.... When all restraints are removed by which men are kept on the narrow path of truth, their nature, which is already inclined to evil, propels them to ruin." Liberty of conscience leads to the corruption of the youth. These freedoms of opinion and license in speech, as well as desire for novelty, spread errors, and the pope, quoting St. Augustine, reminded the world that the death of the soul is "worse than freedom of error."[22]

Gregory XVI condemned the separation of Church and State: "Nor can We predict happier times for religion and government from the plans of those who desire vehemently to separate the Church from the state, and to break the mutual concord between temporal authority and the priesthood." The "lovers of liberty" wanted to destroy concord between church and state, which "always was favorable and beneficial for the sacred and civil order."[23]

Within a few months of acceding to the papacy in 1846, Pius IX issued his first encyclical, *Qui Pluribus.* Having recently experienced betrayal by the adherents of Liberalism, he condemned those who "do not preserve sound doctrine" and create false doctrines that they "spread... among ordinary people," which result in the corruption of morals, confusion, and even the overthrow of "Catholic religion and civil society." The Catholic Faith, they held, like the Church, was only a human invention. These enemies of the Church and Christianity based their views on the "power and excellence of human reason" and a "philosophy... wholly concerned with the search for truth in nature" without reference to divine revelation. Those responsible for advancing these attacks did so while appearing pious, virtuous, and wise while producing and spreading books and pamphlets that were "well-written and filled with deceit and cunning." The pretext given for this was "human progress," and it resulted in the destruction of the faith of many.[24]

Bible societies, secret societies, and others held to indifferentism and interpreted scripture without regard to the authority of the Church. Along with indifferentism, those adhering to Liberalism attacked clerical discipline, especially celibacy. To combat this, the prelates were to "foster in all men their unity with the Catholic Church, outside of which there is no salvation" and "foster their obedience towards this See of Peter." The political leaders' most important task was to protect the Church since the civil authorities received their authority from God. Priests had to undergo a religious discipline to ensure that they properly preached and lived, the Gospel and the Catholic faith.[25]

Seven months later, in the encyclical *Ubi Primum*, Pius again emphasized the need for the strict formation of priests. He wrote that those responsible for the development of priests were to guard "their holy discipline and oppose the attractions, sports, and business of the world which they have renounced; instead let them press on with unceasing prayer and the collection, teaching, and reading of heavenly things." Priests were to work for the salvation of souls by studying "heavenly things" and living lives of modesty, humility, kindliness, patience, chastity, and integrity. These holy men must renounce "the charms, pleasures, deceitfulness and vanity of all things human," study in accord with the rules of each order, and be of "one mind and one tongue and strive to maintain the unity of the Spirit in the bond of peace."[26]

As time passed, Pius saw the relation between the love of money (and power) and false doctrine. The encyclical *Quanto Conficiamur Moerore,* issued in 1863, taught that those seeking their own advantage and profit did so with no regard for their neighbor while "pitifully tearing apart and deeply disturbing minds, hearts, and souls." The Church taught all nations, and all people were bound to listen to and comply with her teachings while recognizing her authority, or else they incurred eternal damnation. All men were called to join and remain in the Church and adhere to the Catholic Faith, and if they refused to do so again, they incurred eternal damnation. The one exception was those "struggling with invincible ignorance about our most holy religion" who were "ready to obey God" and who sincerely "observed the natural law and its precepts."[27]

For nearly fifteen years, Pius IX and a number of prelates labored to produce perhaps the signature encyclical of his papacy. Entitled *A Syllabus containing the most important errors of our time, which have been condemned by our Holy Father Pius IX in Allocutions, at Consistories, in Encyclicals, and other Apostolic Letters,* this document provoked a firestorm of opposition from the leading secular powers of the day. Russia, France, and Victor Emmanuel of Italy forbade the publication of the document, and Bismarck, as well as other European statesmen, voiced public opposition to it while the Italian press was hot with criticism of it and its various theses. *The Syllabus,* its opponents claimed, was a "formal rejection of modern culture, the...declaration of war on the modern State."[28]

The Syllabus, which condemned a total of eighty theses as erroneous, went to the heart of Liberalism and the American ideology, which helped give rise to and advance Liberalism. Many of these theses were confirmed by Pius IX's successor, Leo XIII. The eighty theses were divided into ten categories. In the first category, entitled "Pantheism, Naturalism and Absolute Rationalism," Pius condemned the view that human reason alone was sufficient for finding "truth and falsehood... good and evil" and the view that human reason alone is sufficient for determining the "welfare of men and nations" as especially harmful.[29]

Section II, entitled "Moderate Rationalism," condemned the idea that human reason was on the same level as religion and that theology was just another philosophical science. The next section, "Indifferentism, Latitudinarianism," held as error that each and every man may "embrace and profess" the religion that his human reason leads him to consider as true and that Protestantism is just another form equal with the "same true Christian religion" found in the Catholic Church.[30]

Sections V ("Errors Concerning the Church and Her Rights") and VI ("Errors about Civil Society, Considered Both in Itself and In Its Relation to the Church") addressed the proper relation of the church to the state and the principles upon which societies were to be organized. It was an error for the civil authority to interfere with the governance of the church and to restrict the ecclesiastical power and authority of the Church. It was also an error to claim that the Church was to be "absolutely excluded from every care and dominion over temporal affairs." Also condemned was the proposition that the "teaching of the Catholic Church is hostile to the well-being and interests of society."[31]

Section VII, "Errors Concerning Natural and Christian Ethics," condemned the view that civil laws need not be based on divine laws or ecclesiastical authority. In Section X, proposition 77, Pius rejected the view that "it is no longer expedient that the Catholic religion should be held as the only religion of the State, to the exclusion of all other forms of worship." Pius declared as error the idea that the "Roman Pontiff can, and ought to, reconcile himself, and come to terms with progress, liberalism and modern civilization."[32]

Issued on December 8, 1864, the same day as the *Syllabus, Quanta Cura* condemned the ideas of James Madison and other founders who held religion must be separated from the state. Pius explained that the Catholic Church was good for individuals and societies and that societies needed to recognize this at their peril:

"The cause of the Catholic Church, and the salvation of souls entrusted to us by God, and the welfare of human society itself, altogether demand that we again stir up your pastoral solicitude to exterminate other evil opinions, which spring forth from the said errors as from a fountain. Which false and perverse opinions are on that ground the more to be detested, because they chiefly tend to this, that that salutary influence be impeded and (even) removed, which the Catholic Church, according to the institution and command of her Divine Author, should freely exercise even to the end of the world – not only over private individuals, but over nations, peoples, and their sovereign princes; and (tend also) to take away that mutual fellowship and concord of counsels between Church and State which has ever proved itself propitious and salutary, both for religious and civil interests."[33]

One of the chief purposes of the sovereign power of the state was to protect the Church. The "principle of 'naturalism'" hindered this requirement by teaching "the best constitution of public society and (also) civil progress altogether require that human society be conducted and governed without regard being had to religion any more than if it did not exist; or, at least, without any distinction being made between the true religion and false ones." States based on naturalism teach "against the doctrine of Scripture, of the Church, and of the Holy Fathers; they do not hesitate to assert that 'that is the best condition of civil society, in which no duty is recognized, as attached to the civil power, of restraining by enacted penalties, offenders against the Catholic religion, except so far as public peace may require.'" Instead of the doctrines of the Church, naturalist states promoted "insanity" which consisted of "liberty of conscience and worship is each man's personal right, which ought to be legally proclaimed and asserted in every righty constituted society; and that a right resides in the citizens to an absolute liberty, which should be restrained by no authority whether ecclesiastical or civil, whereby they may be able openly and publicly to manifest and declare any of their ideas whatever, either by word of mouth by the press, or in any other way."[34]

"Promising liberty whereas they are the slaves of corruption," these "wicked men" proceeded by "their deceptive opinions and most pernicious writings to raze the foundations of the Catholic religion and of civil society...." The result was to remove religion from society and to replace it with "the people's will, manifested by what is called public opinion or in some other way, constitutes a supreme law, free from all divine and human control; and that in the political order accomplished facts from the very circumstance that they are accomplished, have the force of right.'" Such a society, Pius IX wrote "can have, in truth, no other end than the purpose of obtaining and amassing wealth, and... follows no other law in its actions except the unchastened desire of ministering to its own pleasure and interests...."[35]

Societies whose purpose is the pursuit of wealth, pleasure, and personal interests target for destruction the priestly orders which are dedicated to forming men to live in accordance with the Church's approval and "Apostolic doctrine." Teaching the Faith to the Faithful was the way to blunt the attack on the Church, and Pius exhorted the prelates never to cease teaching the faith. Importantly, the prelates were to teach the proper relationship between Church and State:

"Teach that 'kingdoms rest on the foundation of the Catholic Faith;'... [N]othing is so deadly...if, believing this alone to be sufficient for us that we receive free will at our birth, we seek nothing further from the Lord; that is, if forgetting our Creator we abjure his power that we may display our freedom....And again do not fail to teach 'that the royal power was given not only for the governance of the world, but most of all for the protection of the Church;'...and that there is nothing which can be of greater advantage and glory to Princes and Kings than if, as another most wise and courageous Predecessor of ours, St. Felix, instructed the Emperor Zeno, they 'permit the Catholic Church to practise [sic] her laws, and allow no one to oppose her liberty. For it is certain that this mode of conduct is beneficial to their interests, viz., that where there is question concerning the causes of God, they study, according to His appointment to subject the royal will to Christ's Priests, not to raise it above theirs.'"[36]

Pius made clear that societies, like individuals, serve either God or Mammon. Those who rejected the correct attitude toward the Catholic Church and the Catholic Faith in informing the policies and principles of a society were bound to pursue wealth, and that led to an attack on the Church and the suffering of society at large. Because of the apparent success and prosperity of the Liberal state and the false ideas it promoted, the *Syllabus* and *Quanta Cura* fell on deaf ears in America. That, coupled with America's distance and isolation from Rome and the betrayal by their own clerical and lay leaders, further served to cut American Catholics off from the great wealth of their tradition.

Leo XIII became pope in 1878. and he continued the trend of expounding Catholic doctrine on the proper organization of society. He articulated Catholic doctrine on church and state relations, religious liberty, and the proper grounds for organizing societies so that the Catholic Church and Catholic Faith were granted positions of authority and preeminence in society. If such happened, society would benefit.

In *Inscrutabili Dei Consilio,* Leo explained the evils befalling societies were the result of withdrawing public institutions from the "wholesome control of the Church." Societies "fashioned in the mold of Christian life" are beneficent to all in that society, especially as Christianity serves to restrain "the insatiable seeking after self-interest alone." Leo observed, "A religious error is the main root of all social and political evils."[37] Societies based on error were structures of sin that resulted in misery and the propagation of evils.

About three years later, in 1881, Leo issued *Diuturnum* ("On the Origin of Civil Power"), in which he reiterated the claim that society benefits from being organized in accordance with Christianity. Failure to do so resulted in chaos, and ultimately force becomes the sole method of controlling or disciplining society. According to Catholic principles, "the right to rule is from God" and not, as philosophers claimed, "from the people." While the form of government is left up to the people, justice must be respected and that means giving all their due, including God. The civil authorities, as ministers of God, are therefore responsible for the welfare of all members of society, for "political power was not created for the advantage of any private individual" nor for the profit of those that rule. Leo noted that history showed that Christians obeyed and respected the powers of the Roman emperors, but they loved and revered Christian princes.[38]

Humanum Genus ("On Freemasonry") was published in 1884. In it, Leo XIII described the foundational beliefs of the Masons, their goal of restructuring societies so as to no longer be in accordance with the "principles of Christian wisdom," and the methods used. The Freemasons sought to organize societies according to the principles of naturalism, which claimed "human nature and human reason ought in all things to be mistress and guide." One method used included the separation of Church from State ,which meant removing the Catholic Faith as the basis of public policy and the Catholic Faith as the basis of societal organization. Another method was to constitute the State without reference to God, for the Freemasons taught there are "various forms of religion" and none "should have precedence of another." A third was to teach and organize society along the lines of the idea that "all men have the same right, and are in every respect of equal and like condition" since "each one is naturally free." Therefore, power is "held by the command or permission of the people," and rights and duties are held by "the multitude or in the governing authority when that is constituted according to the latest doctrines."[39]

Immortale Dei ("On the Christian Constitution of States"), perhaps the most significant of Leo's encyclicals, followed in November 1885. Again, Leo taught that the State is required to fulfill its duties to God in accordance with the Catholic Faith, and that includes caring for it. Leo wrote it is a "public crime to act as though there were no God" and "a sin for the State not to have care for religion as something beyond its scope, or as of no practical benefit; or out of many forms of religion to adopt that one which chimes in with the fancy; for we are bound absolutely to worship God in that way which He has shown to be His will." Society, like individuals, has a duty to God and that duty is to "cling to religion in both its reaching and practice – not such religion as they may have a preference for, but the religion which God enjoins, and which certain and most clear marks show to be the only one true religion...." Rulers have a duty to protect the Catholic Faith and the Catholic Church with the laws, especially since the eternal welfare of people is involved. It is this protection and favoring of the Catholic Faith, which is the freedom that Leo and the Church have in mind when it comes to the Church. Since the purpose, or aim, of the Church "is by far the noblest of ends," then its authority is "the most exalted of all authority," and it cannot "be looked upon as inferior to the civil power, or in any manner dependent upon it." The independence of the Church is best guarded by the civil authority and its civil sovereignty recognized.[40]

Leo enumerated and condemned the errors of the modern state and explained that beginning in the 16th century, states rejected the Gospel as a principle of organization and basis of policy and began adopting a "new conception of law which was not merely previously unknown, but was at variance" with Christianity and even the natural law. This led to the view that "all men are alike by race and nature, and so in like manner all are equal in the control of their life." Second, with the people as the source of all rights and powers, the authority of and duty to God is ignored. This took the form of rejecting a public profession of religion, refusing to inquire as to which of several religions was the true one, and permitting "equal rights to every creed so that public order may not be disturbed by any particular form of religious belief." Third, private judgment and the belief that "everyone is to be free to follow whatever religion he prefers, or none at all" reigned supreme in such societies. This supported the principle that the "judgment of each one's conscience is independent of all law" and that one may think and publish whatever one wishes. As such, the Church's role was restricted and reduced so that it may not instruct the people, and matters affecting the Church were separated from those of the State. [41]

The pope recognized the manipulative nature of the doctrine that places sovereignty in the people without reference to God. He wrote this "is doubtless a doctrine exceedingly well calculated to flatter and to inflame many passions, but which lacks all reasonable proof, and all power of insuring public safety and preserving order." The republican form of government was not a special or ideal form of government but one of many. In such modern societies, the natural is given preeminence over the supernatural, and the Church is subjected to the civil powers.[42]

In explaining the proper relation of church and state, Leo reinforced the teachings that Pius IX promulgated in the *Syllabus of Errors* and *Quanta Cura.* He wrote, "As occasion presented itself, did Pius brand publicly many false opinions which were gaining ground, and afterwards ordered them to be condensed in summary form in order that in this sea of error Catholics might have a light which they might safely follow."[43] Footnote 22 referred to both *Quanta Cura* and *The Syllabus,* and in particular, it republished propositions 19, 55, and 79 as errors opposed to the infallible teachings of the Church. Specifically, it condemned the following propositions:

"Prop. 19: The Church is not a true, perfect, and wholly independent society possessing in its own unchanging rights conferred upon it by its divine Founder; but it is for the civil power to determine what are the rights of the Church, and the limits within which it may use them.... Prop. 55. The Church must be separated from the State and the State from the Church. Prop. 79. It is unsure that the civil liberty of every form of worship, and the full power given to all of openly and publicly manifesting whatsoever opinions and thoughts, lead to the more ready corruption of the minds and morals of the people, and to the spread of the plague of religious indifference."[44]

The proper relation of Church and State must be determined by Catholic theology:

"[T]he origin of public power is to be sought for in God Himself, and not in the multitude....Again, that it is not lawful for the State, any more than for the individual, either to disregard all religious duties or to hold in equal favour different kinds of religion; that the unrestrained freedom of thinking and of openly making known one's thoughts is not inherent in the rights of citizens, and is by no means to be reckoned worthy of favour and support. In like manner it is to be understood that the Church no less than the State itself is a society perfect in its own nature and its own right, and that those who exercise sovereignty ought not so to act as to compel the Church to become subservient or subject to them, or to hamper her liberty in the management of her own affairs, or to despoil her in any way of the other privileges conferred upon her by Jesus Christ."[45]

The civil and the ecclesiastical powers are to cooperate since God has "given the charge of the human race to two powers...the one being set over divine, and the other over human, things." Each is supreme in its own sphere within fixed limits. The two must have between them "a certain orderly connection, which may be compared to the union of the soul and body in man." The rulers of the State and the pope, in exhibiting "another method of concord," should come to an understanding on various matters for the sake of peace and liberty. "Complete harmony" should exist between the State and the Church. There should be a "mutual co-ordination" in the properly ordered society in which citizens' rights are protected and delineated by "divine, by natural, and by human law." Truth and justice must secure the common good and not "delusive caprices and opinions."[46]

Leo discredited the idea that the Church was a champion of religious liberty, which placed "the various forms of divine worship on the same footing as the true religion." He stressed that rulers who "allow patiently custom or usage to be a kind of sanction for each kind of religion having its place in the State" may do so "for the sake of securing some great good or of hindering some great evil." Though the Church has been the originator, the promoter, or the guardian" of that which tends to "uphold the honour, manhood, and equal rights of individual citizens," this does not include the "exorbitant liberty" which "ends in license or in thralldom." Indeed, the liberty that the Church upholds is not the liberty that causes "contempt of the most sacred laws of God," or that would "allow men to be the slaves of error and of passion," but rather that liberty which allows for guiding citizens in wisdom and allowing for their "increased means of well-being." The Church's support of "modern research" was to prevent man from turning away from God and to encourage him to turn towards God.[47]

Catholics were called to primary loyalty to the apostolic see, and all Catholics were to be of one mind when dealing with doctrines concerning liberties because these were dangerous ideas used for evil purposes. The modern state may seem benign, Leo wrote, but the "principles on which such a government is grounded are, as We have said, of a nature which no one can approve." Catholics must conform their "life and conduct to the gospel precepts" and work to "infuse, as it were, into all the veins of the State the healthy sap and blood of Christian wisdom and virtue" while never approving blameworthy "methods of government." This did not mean Catholics had to take an active part in government as "most urgent and just reasons" could make it inexpedient to be so involved. However, if they did, "it is unlawful to follow one line of conduct in private life and another in public, respecting privately the authority of the Church, but publicly rejecting it; for it would amount to joining together good and evil, and to putting man in conflict with himself; whereas he ought always to be consistent...."[48]

Finally, in their attempt to re-Christianize civil society, Catholics must preserve unity of aim, even though methods might differ. Catholics could not reconcile the Faith with naturalism or rationalism, which is designed to eliminate Christian institutions and establish in society "the supremacy of man to the exclusion of God."[49]

Liberty was a word that Gibbons, Ireland, and other Americanists used a lot, but it did not have the same meaning Leo gave it. Leo defined the term in *Libertas.* True liberty is not license or allowing man to do whatever he desires. Since God's eternal law is the standard by which individuals and societies are to conform their conduct, then civil law is to help man "more easily conform to the prescriptions of the eternal law." The end or purpose of liberty is to bring one to God.[50]

Liberalism, he explained, promoted naturalism in morality and politics with human reason supreme while denying the existence of "any divine authority to which obedience is due." If, in essence, "every man is the law to himself," these ideas create a faulty foundation for society. The idea that the State's authority comes only from the people leads to the idea of "collective reason of the community," which leads to the "doctrine of the supremacy of the greater number," all of which is against reason.[51]

Once this occurs, then "religion as a public institution, can have no claim to exist, and...everything that belongs to religion will be treated with complete indifference." Liberals divided into two groups, with the first holding that morality is determined by unaided natural human reason alone. This is erroneous, for it limits God's authority and man's duties. The second group held that one may hold to the divine law in private, but the morality of the State was something else. However, Leo explained that the civil authorities "owe it to the commonwealth not only to provide for its external well-being and the conveniences of life but still more to consult the welfare of men's souls in the wisdom of their legislation." This meant the State errs when it endorses a freedom to profess whatever religion, or none, that one may choose, for this results in treating all religions the same. That, in turn, means that religion has no sway over civil authorities or the policies of the State. Justice and reason forbid a godless state or the adoption of a "line of action which would end in godlessness—namely to treat the various religions (as they call them) alike, and to bestow upon them promiscuously equal rights and privileges."[52]

Since public authority "exists for the welfare of those whom it governs," and though "its proximate end is to lead men to the prosperity found in this life," in doing so, it "ought not to diminish, but rather to increase, man's capability of attaining to the supreme good in which his everlasting happiness consists which ever can be attained if religion be disregarded." Therefore, "the profession of one religion is necessary in the State; that religion must be professed which alone is true and which can be recognized without difficulty, especially in Catholic States, because the marks of truth are, as it were, engraved upon it. This religion, therefore the rulers of the State must preserve and protect....with prudence and usefulness for the good of the community."[53]

The encyclical reinforced previous teachings of the popes and condemned "liberty of conscience," "liberty of speech and liberty of the press," as well as "liberty of teaching." The Church's teaching was circumscribed by the freedom that Liberalism ascribed to liberty of teaching. Such liberty does "hamper the Church in divers ways, restricting her liberty within narrowest limits." Liberalism is "utterly intolerant toward the Catholic Church, by refusing to allow her the liberty of being herself free."[54]

These and other false doctrines based on a false notion of liberty caused much misery and could only be remedied by a "restoration of sound doctrine, from which alone the preservation of order, and as a consequence, the defense of true liberty can be confidently expected." However, the Church understood there is a "great burden of human weakness" and so "while not conceding any right to anything save what is true and honest, she does not forbid public authority to tolerate what is at variance with truth and justice, for the sake of avoiding some greater evil, or obtaining or preserving some greater good." The Church does so because God Himself, in His providence, "permits evil to exist in the world, partly that greater good may not be impeded, and partly that greater evil may not ensue." Therefore, "as the authority of man is powerless to prevent every evil, it must (as St. Augustine says) overlook and leave unpunished many things which are punished by Divine Providence. But if, in such circumstances, for the sake of the common good (and this is the only legitimate reason), human law may or even should tolerate evil, it may not and should not approve or desire evil for its own sake; for evil of itself, being a privation of good, is opposed to the common welfare which every legislator is bound to desire and defend to the best of his ability." According to St. Thomas Aquinas, "human law must endeavor to imitate God, who...in allowing evil to exist in the world, 'neither wills evil to be done, nor wills it not to be done, but wills only to permit it to be done, and this is good'."[55]

The "more a State is driven to tolerate evil, the further is it from perfection," and any toleration of evil "which is dictated by political prudence should be strictly confined to the limits which its justifying cause, the public welfare, requires." If the toleration of the evil "would be injurious to the public welfare, and entail greater evils in the State, it would not be lawful; for in such case the motive of good is wanting." Likewise, the Church may acquiesce in "certain modern liberties...because she judges it expedient to permit them" but "in happier times exercise her own liberty; and, by persuasion, exhortation, and entreaty would endeavor, as she is bound, to fulfill the duty assigned to her by God of providing for the eternal salvation of mankind." The pope then got to the heart of the matter: liberty is not an end in itself, or as he put it, "the liberty which is claimed for all to do all things is not... of itself desirable, inasmuch as it is contrary to reason that error and truth should have equal rights."[56]

Leo emphasized the necessity for obedience to God in public as well as private matters.[57] Those who preach "that fatal principle of the separation of Church and State" ignore that "the two powers, though dissimilar in functions and unequal in degree, ought nevertheless to live in concord, by harmony in their action and the faithful discharge of their respective duties." The defenders of liberalism hold that there is a "duty of submitting to God... inasmuch as all nature is dependent on His will, but [they] boldly reject all laws of faith and morals which are above natural reason, but are revealed by the authority of God or who at least impudently assert that there is no reason why regard should be paid to these laws, at any rate publicly, by the State."[58] This doctrine puts the citizen in the absurd situation of respecting the Church, which the State holds in contempt.[59] According to a variation on the same view, the Church is deprived of the nature and rights of a perfect society and told "that it does not belong to her to legislate, to judge, or to punish, but only to exhort, to advise, and to rule her subjects in accordance with their own consent and will." This view perverts the very nature of a divine society and attenuates its authority as well as its office of teacher.[60]

Lastly, while some did not approve of the separation of Church and State, they "think nevertheless that the Church ought to adapt herself to the times and conform to what is required by the modern system of government." This must not occur, Leo wrote, with regard to "practices and doctrines which a perversion of morals and a warped judgment have unlawfully introduced" for "religion, truth, and justice must be ever maintained."[61]

Libertas ended with what can be termed a reservation of rights. In paragraph 43, Leo taught: "Whenever there exists, or there is reason to fear, an unjust oppression of the people on the one hand, or a deprivation of the liberty of the Church on the other, it is lawful to seek for such a change of government as will bring about due liberty of action. In such case, an excessive and vicious liberty is not sought, but only some relief, for the common welfare, in order that, while license for evil is allowed by the state, the power of doing good may not be hindered."[62] Finally a "democratic form of government" is acceptable but "if only the Catholic doctrine be maintained as to the origin and exercise of power." Leo explained that "the Church does not reject any that are fitted to procure the welfare of the subject.... they should be constituted without involving wrong to any one, and especially without violating the rights of the Church."[63]

LEO TARGETS THE AMERICANS

As mentioned earlier, Leo XIII targeted the American Catholic prelates with *Longinqua Oceani* ("Catholicism in the United States"). Leo XIII noted the Catholic Church in the U.S. had grown in numbers and physical infrastructure in the more than 100 years since the first bishopric was founded. He complimented the "virtue, the ability and the prudence of the bishops and clergy." The "main factor" driving this growth was "the ordinances and decrees of your synods, especially of those which in more recent times were convened and confirmed by the authority of the Apostolic See." The pope noted, "thanks are due to the equity of the laws which obtain in America and to the well-ordered Republic" because the Church "unopposed by the Constitution and government of your nation, fettered by no hostile legislation, protected against violence by the common laws and the impartiality of the tribunals, is free to live and act without hindrance."[64]

Leo then condemned the very things Gibbons, Ireland, and other Americanists had so frequently praised – the Constitution's Establishment Clause and Free Exercise Clause. "Yet, though all this is true," he wrote, "it would be very erroneous to draw the conclusion that in America is to be sought the type of the most desirable status of the Church, or that it would be universally lawful or expedient for State and Church to be, as in America, dissevered and divorced." Recognizing the "fecundity with which God has endowed His Church," the pope wrote that the Church in America "could bring forth more abundant fruits if, in addition to liberty, she enjoyed the favor of the laws and the patronage of the public authority."[65]

Trying to draw American Catholics nearer to the universal Church, Leo mentioned the reason for the creation of the office of the Apostolic See of an American Legation: "America occupies the same place and rights as other States, be they ever so mighty and imperial. In addition to this We had in mind to draw more closely the bonds of duty and friendship which connect you and so many thousands of Catholics with the Apostolic See."[66] The Catholic Church should "not only share in, but help to bring about" the "prospective greatness" of America, and "aid in the rapid growth of the States," something best accomplished for the benefit of the faithful, the hierarchy, and fellow citizens "by yielding a hearty submission and obedience to the Church." Liberty becomes pernicious in a "free State" unless the "precepts and laws of the Gospel" are observed, and the citizens urged to observe them.[67]

Leaders of Catholic associations must be steadfast because if they are not, their organizations can become "extremely prejudicial to the interests as well of individuals as of the community" and are therefore not beneficial.[68] Catholics "ought to prefer to associate with Catholics."[69] He condemned riots and violence as being perpetrated by "enemies of public order."[70] Catholics must be in "perfect unanimity," and bishops "are to be obeyed."[71] Writers and intellectuals must be developed who take religion for their guide and virtue for their constant companion."[72] Catholics must conduct themselves with "great circumspection and more than ordinary firmness" given that there is "familiar intercourse and intimacy between Catholics and those who are estranged from the Catholic name."[73] Leo urged Catholics to convert their fellow countrymen, many of whom were Protestant. Catholics should use "every means of persuasion to induce them to examine closely every part of the Catholic doctrine" and to provide the "force of example.".[74] "Indians and the Negroes" are a "field for cultivation" for "men of apostolic zeal" as these suffer a "long-continued unhappy lot...."[75]

Longinqua Oceani had little impact on the Americanists. Msgr. Denis J. O'Connell, Rector of the North American College in Rome and later rector of Catholic University of America in Washington, D.C., wrote a number of letters from which we may obtain an insight into the true nature of Americanism and how it was advanced by a network of Europeans and Americans.[76] It was O'Connell, coordinating his efforts with Ireland and others, who busily stoked the fires of support for "Americanism" in Germany, France, Italy, and Belgium.[77]

At the Fourth Scientific International Congress held at Freiburg in August 1897, O'Connell delivered an address entitled "Father Hecker's Americanism, What It Is And What It Is Not."[78] He said that the "American idea" was not complete but that it was not "contrary to Catholic faith."[79] In fact, the "principles of American law are nothing else than the first principles of the law of nature, as far as the authors of the Declaration of Independence were able to interpret it."[80] Hecker, he said, saw in the political aspect of Americanism "a public acknowledgment of the existence and the reign of the one, only true God" and hence a "broad basis whereon to begin among men the work of the supernatural."[81]

O'Connell distinguished ecclesiastical Americanism from political Americanism. "Ecclesiastical Americanism" dealt with peculiar relations of church and state in America and concerned the way in which "the just relations between Church and State are the expression in the concrete of the harmony that naturally exists between the two ideas incorporated in these institutions." The separation of Church and State was accepted by Hecker "because, like a pious and practical Catholic of the 19th century, looking the world around and into the future, he could find nothing that served the Church in America better."[82] Hecker accepted "political Americanism" because:

"it recognized as well, if not better than any other prevailing political system, the dominion of God and the natural dignity of man, and at the same time furnished a magnificent foundation for the work of the supernatural. He accepted it because of his great zeal for the conversion of his countrymen. Knowing their profoundly religious character, he believed their conversion to Catholic truth quite easy, but their conversion to Roman political or public law utterly impossible."[83]

Hecker held a "conviction that Roman political law was destined finally in all its traces to pass away, and the Church was to hold generations yet to come through the power of the democratic, that is to say in the general sense, the American idea."[84] O'Connell said Americanism involved "no conflict with either Catholic faith or morals." It was "nothing else than that loyal devotion that Catholics in America bear to the principles on which their government is founded, and their conscientious conviction that these principles afford Catholics favorable opportunities for promoting the glory of God, the growth of the Church, and the salvation of souls in America."[85] As O'Connell wrote late in 1897, if Americanism meant anything, it meant "modern society, modern law in contrast to the ancient law" and the "question is really the conflict of two civilizations, as Abp. Keane puts it."[86]

Americanism represented the new or modern way and not the ancient way. The Spanish-American War represented the conflict between the new and the ancient, and Msgr. O'Connell rose to the defense of the new. He wrote in one letter to the husband of Countess Sabini di Parravicino, an Americanist ally in Italy, how Archbishop Ireland was working for the "cause of peace" even though the Italian press "is opposed to America." He explained that the Italians "think the U.S. government intends annexing Cuba. Such is not the case. Nobody in

America wants Cuba and even if the Cubans requested it they would not be admitted into the Union." The war was "merely a war of humanity... Cuba will certainly be left free to govern herself.... the same for Porto [sic] Rico. I don't know what about the Philippines...." In spite of O'Connell's reassurances, the Europeans were apprehensive of the political designs of the Americans; the Europeans, in fact, "fear precisely the work you are doing: the spread of Americanism."[87]

Within weeks, O'Connell wrote to the Countess to inform her that "It seems...that now action is to be taken against Americanism, Heckerism, and Irelandism. You have helped to force a crisis, and we are not afraid of it.... They say here that while Americanism was latent and obscure, it could be ignored, but now since it is spreading, it must be met and suppressed. But I am afraid it is rather late and difficult and that they are not going to succeed...." With enthusiasm O'Connell wrote "Cuba is nothing, not worth one tenth of the money its independence will cost; but a new spirit in the Church is a great deal and worth many wars. The home of Ignatius and of the Inquisition will be stripped of its influence and the future belongs to men like John Ireland. Then under the breath of a new life, you will see your lovely and Catholic Italy enter upon a new period of greatness."[88]

LEO NAMES AMERICANISM

The Vatican responded after some deliberation. To the consternation of O'Connell and others, Leo XIII named and condemned Americanism with *Testem Benevolentiae Nostrae,* the apostolic letter by Pope Leo XIII directed to Cardinal Gibbons of the Archdiocese of Baltimore and issued on January 22, 1899.[89]

Leo defined Americanism by what it was and by what it was not. It was not "the characteristic qualities which reflect honor on the people of America, just as other nations have what is special to them. It was, however, "the above doctrines,"[90] which boiled down to one main principle: "that, in order to more easily to bring over to Catholic doctrine those who dissent from it, the Church ought to adapt herself somewhat to our advanced civilization, and relaxing her ancient rigor, show some indulgence to modern popular theories and methods...not only with regard to the rule of life, but also to the doctrines in which the *deposit of faith* is contained." The Americanist project, Leo continued, "involves a greater danger and is more hostile to Catholic doctrine and discipline, inasmuch as the followers of these novelties judge that a certain liberty ought to be introduced into the Church." The object of these errors was to allow "each one of the faithful [to] act more freely in pursuance of his own natural bent and capacity." Americanism hoped that the Church would "imitate that liberty which, though quite recently introduced, is now the law and the foundation of almost every civil community." Leo reminded the prelates he had "spoken very much at length in the Letter written to all the bishops about the constitution of States."[91]

Leo's condemnation of Americanism was a direct repudiation of statements and actions of Archbishop Ireland and Cardinal Gibbons, whose 1876 catechism, *The Faith of Our Fathers,* was condemned because it passed over the doctrines of the Faith pertaining to the duty of each society to the Church and the Faith and failed to condemn the errors of Liberalism which comprised the American ideology. Leo's condemnation was also a repudiation of Archbishop John Ireland's speech entitled "The Church and the Age," in which he struck a familiar tone lauding Cardinal Gibbons and urging the Church to grow more in harmony with the spirit of the age.[92] Leo condemned extolling "beyond measure the natural virtues as more in accordance with the ways and requirements of the present day, and [those who] consider it an advantage to be richly endowed with them, because they make a man more ready and more strenuous in action." Those who call themselves Christian should not put the natural before the supernatural virtues and attribute "to them greater power and fecundity." The supernatural virtues were primary: "Who is there who is not disturbed by passions, sometimes of a violent nature, for the persevering conquest of which, just as for the observance of the whole natural law, man must needs have some divine help?" Man needed to follow Christ as the exemplar and "they that are Christ's have crucified their flesh with the vices and concupiscenses" thereby following the evangelical virtues which are wrongly termed passive.[93]

In other words, the key to being fecund in the arena of spiritual growth and the gaining of souls for the kingdom was not to be found in activity but in conforming one's life to Christ's. But Christ's life was difficult, and He suffered and died on the cross, which alienated many people. The reason for living and advancing these errors was the mistaken view that a relaxation of the rigor of life or changing the presentation of doctrine would make it more appealing when, in fact, it would lead to the loss of the Faithful. "Far be it, then," Leo continued, "for any one to diminish or for any reason whatever to pass over anything of this divinely delivered doctrine; whosoever would do so, would rather wish to alienate Catholics from the Church than to bring over to the Church those who dissent from it."[94]

Leo's letter revealed that Americanism was a rejection of the words and spirit of St. Jerome, who, speaking to Pope St. Damasus, said, "I acknowledge no other leader than Christ, am bound in fellowship with your Holiness; that is with the chair of Peter. I know that the church was built upon him as its rock, and that whosever gathereth not with you, scattereth." Leo understood that the primacy of Christ and his Church, as well as the authority of the Holy Father, was needed to keep unity. For, as Leo XIII continued, the "true church is one, as by unity of doctrine, so by unity of government."[95] Leo knew American Catholic prelates were looking first to America and not first to Rome. These prelates believed America knew better than the Church, and so they ignored or forgot Christ's statement in Matthew 28:19-20 that they were to teach America, and not be taught by her. Catholics were divided and that fact was not lost on the American elites.

6

THE STATE OF CATHOLIC LEADERSHIP IN 1948

By the mid-1940s, Catholics in America had the illusion of possessing some social and political power. They still lived in their neighborhoods, had some political power, were largely urban, had big families, and retained a sense of identity, or at least a sense of being a little different from the Americans outside of the ethnic Catholic neighborhoods. They were growing and active and prosperous, and with the end of World War II, their population exploded by 48 percent in just a few years, including about 100,000 adult converts yearly.[1]

It looked as though America was turning Catholic. In reality, the Catholics never had a chance. The leadership sold them out by first pleasing the wealthy and successful laity, who were not about to change a system that allowed them to achieve material success. Even the prelates and priests who were not overtly Americanist were loyal first to America and not Rome.

Francis Cardinal Spellman, who was the most powerful Catholic in the United States until the election of John F. Kennedy to the Presidency, did not rise to that position by being a great theologian.[2] Worldly and ambitious, he hobnobbed with the rich and powerful and had great success, particularly in raising money.[3] Called an "astute administrator," Spellman had no qualms with asking for money from wealthy Jews and Protestants, and he got it.[4] As a result, Spellman was subject to the influence of these donors,[5] and so he served those interests even if it put him at odds with the Vatican.[6]

Spellman first exhibited where his primary loyalty lay when he volunteered to smuggle Pope Pius XI's letter entitled *Non Abbiamo Bisogno* out of Rome and then contacted all the major press agencies to publicize a Papal letter that seemed to be in conformity with American dislike of fascism.[7] Spellman served, when asked by FDR, as the military vicar of the armed forces during World War II, and when that war ended, he enlisted as an ardent anti-communist in the war against Communism known as the Cold War.[8] His efforts were in harmony with those of the American intelligence community, whether it was the OSS in the 1940s in Europe, Africa, and the Middle East during World War II or the Central Intelligence Agency in Southeast Asia during the Vietnam War.[9] He provided information to the CIA on John XXIII's successor and assisted J. Edgar Hoover and the FBI when asked.[10] At the behest of Harry Truman, he traveled to Latin America to convince the Catholics there to change their votes in the United Nations to recognize Israel, a mission that led to the deaths of millions and one which Spellman later regretted.[11]

It was well known, especially to William Buckley Jr., that Spellman was close to Henry Luce.[12] The friendship had been cemented by 1941, as evidenced by the number of handwritten notes that passed back and forth from Spellman to Luce. Luce was a WASP of the sort that Irish Catholics had always tried to emulate, but, more importantly, Luce was instrumental in helping Spellman raise money for the latter's projects. In 1946, Luce prevailed upon Winston Churchill to lend his name to a gala fundraising event that netted Spellman nearly a quarter of a million dollars – an enormous sum in those days.[13]

Luce biographer W.A. Swanberg, writing a few years after Luce's death, noted that Spellman was Luce's "good friend" and that he worked tirelessly in opposing Communism, certainly one of Luce's ardent passions. Spellman's residence in New York, Swanberg observed, was "perhaps a horizontal two hundred yards from Luce's penthouse." This proximity, as well as an ideological affinity between the two men, led Spellman to occasionally "drop in" on Luce so the two could go for "a brisk walk."[14]

Fortified by his access to powerful Americans like Luce, Spellman was not above rebelling against the Church hierarchy, as when he attempted to rehabilitate Fr. Myles Bourke, who was sanctioned by the Holy Office for making certain improper interpretations of the Gospel of St. Mathew. Bishop Bonaventure Broderick, to give another example of Spellman's penchant to intervene on the side of his Americanist friends, had been censured by the Vatican for his actions in Cuba in assisting his brother to get certain contracts. With New York as the capital of American Catholicism, Spellman's spirit infused the Catholics of America with an intense loyalty that trumped their loyalty to the Church.[15]

Spellman personified in large measure the spirit of the rest of the Catholic episcopate. The bishops were largely focused on building schools and churches, establishing and reorganizing social service agencies like Catholic Charities, professionalizing the cemetery system, and managing finances,[16] all of which took priority over, or were seen as, spreading the faith. Instead of taking their role as teachers seriously, the bishops ended up being led by the theologians[17] who were infected with the Americanist spirit.

Catholic priests and prelates regularly cooperated with the American agenda against fellow Catholics. Once a priest or prelate stopped cooperating, he found himself being demonized by his former collaborators. Bishop Bernard J. Sheil was one such example. Considered "one of the most esteemed members of the American Catholic hierarchy," Bishop Sheil founded the Catholic Youth Organization or CYO, and he became a "darling of organized labor" as well as a friend of President Roosevelt. Sheil had a "brain trust" that helped with his speeches, in which he advocated concern for such things as "social justice, democracy, racial tolerance...world order...[and] racial justice." He "espoused public housing, and urged American society to extend the blessings of democracy and equal rights to a greater portion of its citizens." Eventually, he supported the CIO, which gained him enormous respect and support in the press. [18]

Attorney William Campbell was Sheil's closest advisor. Campbell kept the CYO running, and Sheil introduced him to Cardinal Mundelein while encouraging Campbell's involvement in Democratic politics. In 1935, Harry Hopkins appointed Campbell director of the National Youth Administration in Chicago so that Campbell could start to "channel large sums of money to Catholic institutions in the form of government-salaried clerical and secretarial staff." Campbell also had contacts with Jews who contributed to Sheil's many projects. In addition to securing funding for the CYO and other Catholic groups, he gained federal recognition for the Holy Name Aeronautical School in Lockport, Illinois, another Sheil project. Campbell's good relations with Sheil and Mundelein earned him clout with the Roosevelt administration. He eventually became the district attorney for Northern Illinois and later secured a federal judgeship.[19]

When Fr. Charles Coughlin embarrassed FDR and needed to be silenced, Sheil was the first one to jump to the task. In a speech delivered in December 1938 at the request of Mundelein, Sheil said, "As an American citizen, Father Coughlin has the right to express his personal views on current events, but he is not authorized to speak for the Catholic Church, nor does he represent the doctrine or sentiments of the Church." The Catholic leadership in the U.S. willingly turned on its own to please the powerful private interests who were intent on war with Germany.[20]

Sheil fell out of favor in the late 1940s when he refused to be sufficiently anti-Communist. In a letter to Bishop John Noll of the Diocese of Fort Wayne, Sheil complained:

"I am somewhat perturbed over what I can only consider your over-emphasis of the Communist danger. Undoubtedly, Communism is a danger; I am well aware of that. Undoubtedly, it is a potent threat to everything we of the Catholic Church hold dear. Yet, I believe that your great concern over this danger and threat is out of all proportion to the strength and influence of Communism.... I have always believed that Communism is no danger in a society where justice and charity prevail. Communism, I believe, is no threat in a decent and human economic structure."[21]

Rather than simply signing on as volunteers in the anti-Communist crusade, Sheil said American Catholics "should work indefatigably to bring about a Christian economy in accordance with the magnificent teachings of our Popes. If we do this, we shall strike the greatest possible single blow to Communism....We Catholics possess the most far-reaching and radical (in the best sense of the word) plan for social reconstruction; we *must*, we are bound to put it into effect." [22]

As a result, Sheil was savaged in the media and abandoned by Cardinal Spellman, who was an ardent supporter of anti-communism. Sheil disappeared from the public scene and was retired by his bishop, Samuel Cardinal Stritch of Chicago.[23]

Some priests collaborated with the U.S. government by spying on fellow Catholics. One such example was Fr. John F. Cronin. Assisted by Spellman and Bishop John F. O'Hara, CSC, former President of the University of Notre Dame, who provided Cronin with enormous resources, Cronin spied on priests and labor leaders to determine who might be a Communist sympathizer, authored numerous reports useful to the Federal Bureau of Investigation, and tried to get various Catholic priests and bishops to agree on a "common set of social principles" that invariably supported the American agenda.[24]

Through people like J. Edgar Hoover, who recruited FBI agents from amongst the Catholics while schmoozing their leaders, the U.S. government created a sophisticated form of control and manipulation. This depended heavily on Hoover maintaining personal relationships with the bishops, paying them personal compliments, and providing whatever assistance they needed (e.g., to assist an ailing Cardinal Stritch).[25] Hoover's strategy led the bishops to believe they had friends in the government, thereby making them more pliant, responsive, and supportive of the American ideology and policies.

Hoover was not naïve. His agents spied on the bishops as well and gathered an enormous amount of data on them, which helped Hoover develop these relationships. The list of "Hoover's bishops" included John Cardinal O'Hara, President of the University of Notre Dame from 1934 to 1939; Archbishop Michael Curley of St. Augustine, Florida;

Richard Cardinal Cushing of Boston; Bishop John Noll of Fort Wayne, Indiana; Bishop Fulton J. Sheen; Spellman; and Patrick Cardinal O'Boyle. Through these and other prelates, the FBI and the elites they served gained influence over the minds of Catholics in higher education and the rank and file through publications like *Our Sunday Visitor*.[26] With the bishops' support, it was easier for the FBI, and hence the U.S. government, to get informants to spy on fellow Catholics and other segments of the population with which it had limited contact. Fr. Edward Conway, SJ, conducted information gathering and other operations on behalf of the FBI in connection with the country's atomic energy program.[27] Monsignor Charles Owen Rice performed similar work when it came to organized labor and the CIO.[28] The loyalty of the Catholic Church's leadership in the U.S. was never seriously in doubt.

7
A THEOLOGIAN IS NEEDED

In the Spring of 1948, Luce invited Billings to a lunch at Luce's Waldorf apartment with Rabbi Dr. Louis Finkelstein, head of the Jewish Theological Seminary. Billings "hustled over at 1 to meet the rabbi at the apartment door." The rabbi, who reminded Billings "of a renaissance painting of Christ on the Cross – lean ascetic face, sad brown eyes, a black beard, with protruding red lip under nose, a Hebraic accent" made a pitch to have Luce help with a project. "Religion and God should be spread to the people," said Rabbi Finkelstein. "They don't want to hear preachers on this subject but famous laymen." So, he asked, "how about getting up a committee to promote the spread of religion – and 'some American democracy.'"[1]

Luce's response was instructive, for it revealed the technique he used to promote Americanism, thereby bringing the Catholic leadership under American dominion. Billings described what happened next: "Luce reversed the field on him by arguing the people wanted to hear the truth about theology from theologians – and not laymen's personal experience with God." Finkelstein acquiesced and "got Luce to serve on his preliminary committee." Like Luce's other involvements, "it was a matter of lay sponsorship." Billings added, "Funny – but Luce has me in on many of his 'religion' activities."[2]

Luce understood the importance of theologians in advancing the American system. Even Paul Blanshard, whose book *American Freedom and Catholic Power* became the bible of anti-Catholic liberals, saw the value of Church doctrine and priests in keeping the "whole Catholic system of global discipline" together and that that system "rests fundamentally on its great army of priests." The priest had to have a lot of talents and abilities, Blanshard observed, but most importantly, he was the "agent for Roman spiritual and political goods" and "is subordinate to the hierarchy."[3] The priest lent credibility to any idea, and a priest who was a theologian was even more of an authority.

Blanshard, whose opinions reflected those of the American elites,[4] understood the role of theology in helping the Church maintain its power. According to Blanshard, "The Church's philosophy of church and state is far more important than the continued existence of a bit of acreage which has its own postage stamps and flag. In fact, the philosophy of church and state espoused by the Vatican is the most important thing in the whole Catholic system because it determines the political and social policies which the bishops and priests will pursue throughout the world."[5]

The Catholic position on the issue of Church and State meant one of three things. First, "whether on the whole the Christian faith has anything to do with political conduct of people," or in other words, whether the policies of the state were based on the Faith. Second, to what extent the ecclesiastical authorities may influence the political institutions, or in other words, the recognition of a state church. Third, to what extent the ecclesiastical structures may be subject to civil power, or in other words, whether the state could control the church.[6]

Luce showed his hand on the Church-State question early on in *Time*'s existence. When Catholic New York governor Al Smith was considering a run for president, *Time* opined: "The essential conflict that Governor Smith faces is: The Roman Catholic Church maintains that in a direct conflict between the laws of Church and State, the jurisdiction of the Church prevails."[7] The article quoted from Leo XIII's encyclical *Immortale Dei* that "'It is not lawful for the State....to disregard all religious duties or to hold in equal favor different kinds of religion,'" an assertion which contradicted the U.S. Supreme Court, which stated that our "'law is committed to the support of no dogma, the establishment of no sect.'...."[8]

Luce and *Time* practiced a number of different psychological ploys to influence their readers. One was to create "good guys" and "bad guys" in the readers' minds. Cardinal Spellman, whose life as an ambitious "church politician and organizer who in secular life might have become chairman of the Democratic National Committee," was an important "good guy" because he was sympathetic to American ideas. Spellman smuggled the Papal criticism of Fascism out of Rome in 1931, presented American ways to solve disputes in the old world, reorganized the Vatican media to be like the American media, and wrote and translated books, one of which ended up in Hollywood as the script for the MGM film called "The Risen Soldier." He served as Military Vicar to the U.S. Armed Forces, and did "much to make U.S. Catholicism more American." Spellman's connections with Pius XII prior to the latter's ascension to the Papacy were mentioned by Luce's publication. Spellman was not without faults. He complimented Franco, which "outraged many Americans," thereby supposedly starting "an ideological storm."[9]

Still, Spellman echoed Gibbons of half a century earlier. He said, "America has been, and must ever continue to be, under God, the Beacon of Liberty.... the proof that humanity can live in mutual respect based on the law of God, voiced through the conscience of man, and in mutual esteem, based on the responsibility of democratic life."[10] Reading these lines, one could conclude that America worked quite well without having the Church inform the policies of the state. When Spellman penned an Americanist prayer--"Lord, lift this mighty host that is America; Reconsecrate us in devotion to Thee...That righteousness again shall walk among the sons of men"—*Time* reprinted it, claiming that it was also the pope's prayer and that the pope had to turn to the U.S. for assistance and leadership for three urgent reasons: because the U.S. was "1) the world's most effective counterweight to the newly emergent power of Russia; 2) it was the world's greatest reservoir of food and goods to forestall the further demoralization of Europe; 3) and it was the world's greatest embodiment of the form of government which offers the Church its best milieu for survival –democracy." [11] *Time* promoted Spellman and, in doing so, subtly told Catholics in the U.S. and the world that the pope approved of America – whether it was true or not.

The bad guys, according to Luce and *Time*, were the "many European prelates" who did not like the U.S. "As a political experiment," *Time* wrote, "the U.S. has been viewed with misgivings by many European prelates ever since 1776. The strange new republic seemed based upon philosophical premises of a heretical nature and imbued with an alarming spirit of independence, not confined to temporal affairs." The European prelates "knew that Catholicism in the U.S. labored under a widespread suspicion of being an alien creed, that the Church could prosper only by doing its utmost to Americanize the immigrants and adapting its policies to those of the young democracy.... Archbishop John Ireland of St. Paul was more truculent: 'An honest ballot and social decorum will do more for God's glory and the salvation of souls than midnight flagellations or Compestellan pilgrimages.'" [12]

Time exploited the division among Catholics by claiming U.S. Catholics were supportive of America's organizational principles, especially the separation of Church and State. At the same time, the magazine sought to demoralize Catholics who held to the Catholic view of church and state relations by claiming they were in the minority. *Time* wrote that "European prelates" seemed to be in the minority, and "Though Leo's views are still repeated by a few academic theologians, they are largely ignored by the U.S. hierarchy."[13] *Time* portrayed the U.S. Catholic hierarchy as American and opposed to the views held by Latin Catholics and the Vatican hierarchy itself.

In early 1946, Pius XII decided to fill some 30 vacancies in the College of Cardinals, which had occurred over the war years. It was the first consistory since 1940, and four archbishops from the United States were to be elevated to Cardinal: Spellman of New York, Edward Mooney of Detroit, Samuel Stritch of Chicago, and John J. Glennon of St. Louis.

Insisting on traveling in coach and eschewing any special treatment, the prelates were flattered by an article in *Time,* which quoted TWA officials who described the flight of three "gleaming, four-motored planes" as "the most distinguished mass-flight of passengers across the North Atlantic in aviation history." *Time* was pandering to the American Catholic pride in their Church leaders by stressing the prelates' humility in wearing "hand me down" episcopal clothing.[14] Adulation like this blinded Catholic leaders, at least for a while, to the seriousness of the danger they faced in America.

Time always presented America as an ally for the Church, given the threat posed by the Soviets. One either supported the Americans, or one was a Communist, and the latter was bad. Luce and his editors demanded total loyalty from its American Catholic readers. One *Time* article held that the U.S. was "the world's most effective counterweight to the newly emergent power of Russia," as well as "the world's greatest embodiment of the form of government which offers the Church its best milieu for survival – democracy...." To "meet this crisis, the Vatican looks to the ideological and material support of the U.S.," and the man needed to "enlist U.S. support for the Vatican" was "the devout but uniquely American . . . character of Francis Cardinal Spellman."[15]

Months after the article that painted the U.S. prelates as good Americans, *Time* published another article asking whether Catholicism supported the First Amendment concerning freedom to worship. The article painted Spellman as a "good guy" and Pope Leo XIII as a foreign potentate and the "bad guy." Citing an article in the August 1946 edition of the "undenominational *Christian Herald*," *Time* noted that Spellman approved the following response to the question, "What is the attitude of the Catholic Church in non-Catholic countries?": "In a country like the United States, where the religious affiliations of the citizens are so numerous and so diverse...complete equality for all religions is undoubtedly the most commendable policy...." Opposed to that was the Catholic view as set forth by Pope Leo XIII, who "explained this point tersely when...he wrote: 'The Church indeed deems it unlawful to place the various forms of divine worship on the same footing.... but does not on that account condemn those rulers who, for the sake of securing some great good or of hindering some great evil patiently allow custom or usage to be a kind of sanction for each form of religion having its place in the state.'"[16]

Spellman did great work for Luce and the Americans, but he was not a theologian.

PART III

JOHN COURTNEY MURRAY – THEOLOGIAN FOR AMERICA

8

THE SECRET MEETING AT THE BILTMORE – APRIL 26, 1948

On a cool, dry, sunny Spring afternoon with hardly a breeze in the air, a group of men met in a secret conference at a luxury hotel in mid-town Manhattan to find a way to deal with what Paul Blanshard was calling the Catholic problem. The National Conference of Christians and Jews (NCCJ) was hosting an important gathering with dinner entitled "The Conference on State and Church" at the Biltmore Hotel in New York on the afternoon and evening of Monday, April 26, 1948, but the conference was not open to the public. The report of the conference, prepared by Robert A. Ashworth, was marked "Not for Publication." Ashworth wrote that the "discussion was informal, intimate and frank" and that there was "agreement that no publicity should be given to this conference."[1]

Present at the meeting were thirteen Protestant ministers, eight Catholic laymen, four Jesuit priests, three other priests, one university professor, and three Jewish rabbis, including noted civil rights champion Rabbi Maurice N. Eisendrath. The chairman of the meeting was the Protestant minister, Dr. Everett R. Clinchy, a man who had devoted his life to making all men accept the American ideology. Among the many attendees were a number of distinguished personages. There was Martin Quigley, Jr., from a well-known Catholic family, who at a young age was an author, motion picture industry executive, and former agent for the United States' World War II intelligence agency, the Office of Strategic Services (OSS). Also present was Reinhold Niebuhr, considered the most prominent Protestant theologian of the Twentieth Century. He developed the concept of Christian Realism, which held democracy, justice and power all gave America a special role. Catholic magazines were represented by Jesuit priest and founder of *America* magazine Wilfrid Parsons, SJ, and John G. Brunini, a writer for *Commonweal,* President of the Catholic Poetry Society, and organizer of the 1938 Temple of Religions for the World's Fair. And finally, presiding over the secret conference in a leadership role was Jesuit theology professor and editor of the Jesuit publication *Theological Studies,* John Courtney Murray, SJ.[2]

Murray and Niebuhr started the discussion, which focused on the decision in the *McCollum* case that had recently been decided by the Supreme Court of the United States. The court invalidated a local policy of "released time," which allowed schoolchildren to obtain religious education during the school day at public schools. Murray asked, "Is the majority decision of the Supreme Court made necessary by the Constitution?....Or is the opinion of Justice Reed more in accord with the Constitution?" Answering his own question, Murray claimed that "the secularization of education" was likely to ensue if the majority opinion stood. "The McCollum decision," Murray continued, "tends to make the child a creature of government. It strikes a blow at the rights of the parent in education...." Murray went on to say that the decision presented a "very serious danger" because "the substitute of a completely secularized myth . . . would make an idol out of democracy. Then the schools might be exploited to build up secularized democracy as an end in itself, failing to see that democracy is a means for the realization of spiritual and moral ends."[3]

The Protestants raised the possibility that there might be a middle ground between the establishment of religion and the separation of Church and State. Niebuhr largely agreed with Murray, saying that a "religion of democracy" was developing in America and that the Constitution did not require the absolute separation of Church and State. He referred, however, "to the fear of many Protestants that Roman

Catholics do not believe in the principle of the separation of Church and State but believe in the principle of establishment and said that this explains some of the movements that currently oppose the Catholic Church." Niebuhr also proposed the formation of conferences to determine principles held by Protestants and Catholics and to promote mutual understanding.[4]

The Jews were in favor of complete separation of Church and State, at least for the moment. Rabbi Eisendrath objected to the positions taken by Murray and Niebuhr, claiming that: "Jews, despite a profound concern over the possible secularization of our society, are in general support of the McCollum doctrine insofar as it relates to Released Time." While the "Jewish community recognizes the wide-spread need for religious education," it "always felt that this is the responsibility for the Synagogue rather than of the state-supported school."[5]

The second and most important topic of the meeting involved a discussion of what to do with the Catholics and their understanding of church and state relations. Reference had been made to Protestant fears in this regard earlier in the meeting. The discussion during and after the dinner was on the "statements of Roman Catholics as to the relations of Church and State in case Catholics should come to be an overwhelming majority in this country and the consequences for Protestants and others, reference being often made to statements on the subject in 'The State and the Church' by Fathers Ryan and Boland that had aroused widespread apprehension and resentment among many Protestants." The Catholics present at the secret meeting joined with the Protestants in concluding the Catholic Church's doctrine on church and state relations was a problem. A "number of Catholics expressed the view – to which there was no dissent – that the Ryan-Boland formulation was excessively rigorous; that the true doctrine of the Church on this point was susceptible of a much more liberal interpretation."[6]

Murray presented Francisco Franco's Spain as the bogeyman. He said, "We must remember two evil influences in Spanish life: a. The pagan idea that government must be a tool of the Church; b. That it is the function of the party in power to destroy the opposition party. These ideas are contrary to Catholic teaching." Both Niebuhr and Murray were asked to "form a small committee for the prolonged discussion of the issues involved in the relations of Church and State." This was in line with a larger effort to "find a group of Protestants and Catholics who could agree on the basic principles of our culture and could make public such a statement" because such a statement "might have a definite effect upon the country and upon future decisions of the Supreme Court."[7]

The conference suggested various follow-up activities. One was to hold meetings around the country to stimulate the discussion and to issue statements of their own for publication so as to affect the "climate of opinion" in the country and, therefore, influence the decisions of the Supreme Court. Another was to understand the philosophical and theological differences dividing Protestants, Catholics, and Jews and "use the same words with the same meaning in setting them forth." A third was a Statement on Church and State prepared and signed by Protestants present at the meeting, including the President of Union Theological Seminary, who was not present. That statement was prepared on June 12, 1948, and signed five days later. This statement of the Protestant position, which ultimately proved unworkable, condemned the Supreme Court's holding in *McCollum*, claiming that that decision would "greatly accelerate the trend toward the secularization of our culture." The *McCollum* decision threatened the American people's history of cooperation between Church and State, which allowed that cooperation "entered into freely by the State and Church and involving no special privilege to any Church and no threat to the religious liberty of any citizen, should be permitted."[8]

Murray agreed with the NCCJ. When it came to Church-State relations, Catholicism was the problem, not America, or as he later put it: "the Church-State problem is, in the very specific and unique sense, a Catholic problem – a Roman Catholic problem."[9] By agreeing to provide "a more liberal interpretation" of Church doctrine on church and state relations, Murray was embarking upon an enterprise that would eventually weaken one of the most important doctrines of the Catholic Church. This was certainly the position of Paul Blanshard, a rabid anti-Catholic who had written a number of articles attacking the Catholic

Church and its various doctrines in *The Nation* beginning in November 1947 and continuing into July 1948. By the time of the Biltmore Hotel secret conference, Blanshard had written critiques of the Church's doctrines on sex, reproduction, education, and how these doctrines would impact divorce, birth control, and the contents of school courses. He had also written about the Church's relationship with Fascism and the Lateran Treaty of 1929, with which Mussolini gave the Church and Catholicism pre-eminence in Italy.

In the April 17, 1948, issue of *The Nation,* just a few days before the secret conference began, Blanshard depicted Spain and the Church as the bogeymen because of their suppression of "freedom." "In this new Spain," he wrote: "the little children in all schools are told that 'Spain is a totalitarian country and its chief is His Excellency the Caudillo, Generalissimo of the Armies on land, sea and in the air, and Chief of the Government which is made up of twelve ministries.' And in the manual for religious instruction, *Nueva Repalda,* as cited by Mr. Hughes, Spanish children in all religious classes in the nation are given the following interpretation of freedom:

'Q. What are the freedoms which liberalism defends? A. Freedom of conscience, freedom of worship, and freedom of the press.

'Q. What does freedom of the press mean? A. The right to print and publish without previous censorship all kinds of opinions, however absurd and corrupting they may be.

'Q. Must the government suppress this freedom by means of censorship? A. Obviously, yes.

'Q. Why? A. Because it must prevent the deception, calumny and corruption of its subjects, which harm the general good.

'Q. Are there other pernicious freedoms? A Yes, freedom of propaganda, and freedom of assembly.

'Why are these freedoms pernicious? A. Because they serve to teach error, propagate vice, and plot against the church...'"[10]

Blanshard's views reflected those of a much larger group of people, mainly the Anglo-American Protestants whose forebears had created and who now ruled America.[11] He identified the central issue in what amounted to a war against the Catholics to subdue them so that they would accept the American ideology. In his book *American Freedom and Catholic Power,* which was based on the articles appearing in *The Nation* and newer material, Blanshard claimed that the most important issue facing Americans in their fight against the Catholics was "The Church's philosophy of church and state," which "determines the political and social policies which the bishops and priests will pursue throughout the world."[12]

The main points of contention between the Americans and the Catholics after World War II were the issues of church and state relations and religious liberty. The American view of these issues allowed real societal and political power to reside in private concerns, and it removed religion, mainly the Catholic Faith, as the basis of the laws and public policies. The Catholic view of these issues kept the moral authority of the Church and the Catholic Faith for the benefit of all members of society. Accepting the American view as good in principle had the effect of approving American political theory.

9
THE MYSTERY MAN

By the time of the Biltmore conference, Murray had gained some prominence, but he was still very much a "mystery man" and would remain one for a long time even after becoming a "giant of the Church." Robert Blair Kaiser, a former Jesuit seminarian, and *Time* reporter who covered the early days of the Vatican II Council, observed many years later Murray's private life remained a mystery, even though it was known that he was a close friend of the Luces. Kaiser said Murray frequently disappeared for days, and many did not know where he went or when he might be returning. There was even speculation he had a girlfriend.[1] Another trait of Murray's that Kaiser remembered was Murray had "great pride." Sometimes, he thought Murray "took his initials, J.C., too seriously."[2]

Murray started life in less humble surroundings than did Jesus Christ. Born Michael John Murray in Manhattan on September 12, 1904, he changed his name after entering the Jesuits. The Certificate and Record of Birth dated July 15, 1920, immediately before his entry into the Society of Jesus, revealed he was born at 437 W. 21st Street, New York, to Michael Murray, a bookkeeper aged 31, and his wife, three years his junior, Margaret. Originally from Ireland, her maiden name was Courtney. [3] According to one story about his origins, Murray was born to an

Irish Catholic mother who helped "rally" a Scottish lawyer father who had "strayed." [4]

As a young man, Michael, Jr. wanted to practice medicine and surgery, but because his family lacked the money, he joined the Society of Jesus in 1920 instead, despite the fact that he suffered from a club foot. Murray earned his bachelor's and master's degrees at Boston College and then did fieldwork in the Philippines from 1927 to 1930. After his return to the United States, he was ordained a priest at Woodstock College in 1933. Murray then underwent three years of study at the Gregorian University in Rome, after which he traveled throughout Europe. In 1937, he returned to Woodstock as a professor of theology,[5] where he taught and edited *Theological Studies* from 1941 until his death.

Other than that, there is simply very little information about Murray. A number of sources reveal he was fond of golf and whiskey and that he suffered from a heart condition for a very long time. Emmet John Hughes, the author who was supposed to pen Murray's biography but declined, relented somewhat and wrote an article eulogizing Murray. His remarks are interesting but not revealing. On Murray's desk at Woodstock "was a crudely decorated procelain [sic] beer-mug, bearing the written judgment: 'The man who fears to drink has no true soul.'" Hughes wrote, "All of his years, he reserved special respect for 12-year-old Scotch and elegant women; and while his close acquaintance with the former was far more extensive, his appreciation of both was equal." Hughes also observed that Murray, who suffered from a history of heart problems, had a large array of medication in his quarters. There was "digitalis and codeine to seconal and nitroglycerin." Murray had no art other than "a small black wood crucifix – with the figure of Christ missing." [6]

MURRAY STARTS OUT CRITICAL OF AMERICA

In an article that appeared in 1932, Murray discussed the situation in the Sixteenth Century, noting that the "Protestant menace" evoked a "lamentable lack of unity as regards the proper method" of dealing with it.[7] Eight years later, Murray had even harsher words for America in a series of talks he gave at St. Joseph's College. "Our first question must be," he began:

"What is the actual problem confronting us here today in America? What have we actually to do? It would seem that our American culture, as it exists, is actually the quintessence of all that is decadent in the culture of the Western Christian world. It would seem to be erected on the triple denial that has corrupted Western culture at its roots, the denial of metaphysical reality, of the primacy of the spiritual over the material, of the social over the individual. Hence, In view of the fact that American culture is built on the negation of all that Christianity stands for, it would seem that our first step toward the construction of a Christian culture should be the destruction of the existing one. In the presence of a Frankenstein, one does not reach for baptismal water, but for a bludgeon."[8]

Murray concluded by saying America succumbed to the temptation to make "'the individual man...an end in himself'...to the point of blasphemy." American culture is based on "profound materialism...oriented almost wholly to matter and the things of sense. It has had, in fact, one dominating ideal: the conquest of a material world, with the aid of science, a conquest that has made one promise: a more abundant life for the ordinary man and woman, the abundance being ultimately in physical comfort. It turns out one typical product: the '*homo oeconomicus*,' the business man, in a business suit, whose dreams of paradise are of a land in which there is no red ink. It has given citizens everything to live for and nothing to die for.... it has gained a continent and lost its own soul."[9]

Murray wrote that this happened because the Calvinism of the Northern States stripped the intellectual content from the philosophy of humanist democracy that originated in France and became disassociated from Christian revelation. After the loss of its intellectual basis, humanist democracy became a "moral postulate, that animated a program of economic individualism." When the moral postulate waned, humanist democracy became a mere emotion, which was the state of affairs in 1940.[10]

Around the same time, Murray commented on the need for Catholicism to inform all of our lives because, he wrote, "Catholic truth presents itself as a totality." Unfortunately, Catholics never saw it that way, and instead, they "grasped it as a more or less disconnected lot of things they had to believe...to do...." Murray insisted "upon the totality of Catholic truth and the totality of Catholic life, above all" and "its essential continuity."[11]

Murray's criticisms of America were harsh, and his insights into the Catholic creed were acute, but by the end of the 1940s, Murray was a different man largely because of his participation in the campaign for intercredal cooperation that arose during World War II. The change came abruptly after a deep personal existential crisis, which, once he weathered it, established his bona fides among the elites he had previously criticized and allowed him to address the issues of church and state in a way pleasing to Luce and the Americans.

INTERCREDAL COOPERATION

Former Catholic priest and close observer of things religious, Carlo Falconi, described the idea of intercredal cooperation, or ecumenism, as "Protestant in origin, and the Popes up to John XXIII made the great mistake of underestimating it."[12] As the Leper Priest, St. Damien de Veuster, observed in Hawai'I,[13] Protestantism always re-ordered societies to increase materialism. The ecumenical or intercredal movement was no exception to this rule. It helped Protestantism eliminate confessional barriers, thereby serving to advance the materialist, or capitalist, spirit, as professor and statesman Amintore Fanfani explained it. In time, the American monied elites realized the importance of this movement in furthering their own decidedly anti-Catholic purposes and interests.

According to Fanfani, Protestant societies promoted individual autonomy and democracy in creating societies in which everyone was to be treated as the same or equal. Individual autonomy mandated freedom of choice, and that choice had to be protected and encouraged by the state through government policies. This understanding of freedom of choice was consistent with a commercial society in which buying and selling were all-important. Freedom to choose came into being as an economic concept but soon spread to matters of politics, religion, and morality. The individual autonomy that was so characteristic of capitalistic systems allowed for the concentration of wealth or power. It was accompanied by a materialism, which in turn bred a weakening of the Catholic Faith, which holds that a man should "eschew a certain mode of action in the certainty of losing riches, but believing that they will gain a future reward in heaven."[14]

Fanfani continued:

"Let man lose this belief, and nothing remains for him, rationally speaking, but to act in a capitalistic manner. If there are no longer religious ties uniting man to man, there will be a growing number of audacious men whose sole end, in the words of Villari, is to be ahead of their fellows. Such men existed before the modern era began, and of such men it has been said that they showed "a complete lack of scruples and contempt for every moral law."[15]

American religious liberty severed unity in society. John Mackay, a Presbyterian minister and native of Scotland who became a U.S. citizen in 1941, led the Protestant effort to advance religious liberty in America after spending 20 years working to destroy Catholic solidarity in Latin America as a Protestant missionary. After studying the region, Mackay tried to unify and systematize Protestant efforts at evangelization by seeking the advice of two great American Protestant colonizers, Robert Speer (Presbyterian minister and founder of the Federal Council of Churches in 1908) and John Mott (YMCA founder). Prior to departing for South America, Mackay eagerly sought out Spanish-speaking dissidents, most notably Miguel de Unamuno of Spain, who was influential in starting the Spanish Republic in 1930.[16] Speer, who was a major proponent of the idea of religious liberty, concluded, "I should be satisfied if we could get a universal acceptance of the principle of religious liberty and toleration. This would involve no preferential policy, no exclusive or party rights, but simply give us a word of freedom in which the Truth would make its way by its own power."[17]

Speer advanced the idea of a world brotherhood that eliminated ethnic divisions, an idea also advanced by Clinchy of the NCCJ. This philosophy set out the social agenda of America's elites and was articulated in a speech Clinchy gave for the Intercollegiate YMCA of New York City in February 1918. He claimed that the current world war was the result of 1) imperfectly developed democracy, 2) nationalism as a good above the moral law, 3) the "retarding or the breaking down of the process of social evolution and human progress," 4) racial prejudice, and 5) "the resistance of national individualism to the spirit of world brotherhood and to common human interests." At the base of the speech was the idea there had to be "world wide democracy and the international spirit."[18]

Like the other Protestant missionaries, Mackay wanted to bring "sixteenth-century Reformation principles" to Latin America. Mackay arrived in Panama in 1916, ostensibly to minister to Americans in these Catholic countries, but while there, he strove to extend Protestantism. He observed that the Vatican kept its power by strengthening relations with the governments and that the Catholic Church saw Protestantism as an enemy. In keeping with the spirit of the 1910 Edinburgh Conference and the Panama Conference of 1916, he devised a strategy to counter Catholic efforts.[19] Mackay received enormous support from the Protestants, particularly the Presbyterians, who were the traditional enemies of Catholicism in his native Scotland. This support increased during the 1930s as Protestant fervor to engage in evangelization intensified. Mackay became president of the Princeton Theological Seminary in 1936, where he transposed the conflict with Catholicism to the United States, especially in the areas of social policies and the relation of church and state.[20]

In 1937, Mackay, along with John Foster Dulles, Wall Street banking lawyer and future Secretary of State, and his son, Avery, who later converted to Catholicism and became a Cardinal in the Catholic Church, attended the Oxford Conference in England to denounce Hitler in particular as a tyrant and totalitarianism in general as being incompatible with the "Christian doctrine of man." Mackay was charged at the Conference with leading the effort to increase ecumenism among the

Protestant churches and to "present Christianity to the public in a way the modern world would understand." This was part of a "living movement" with a "responsibility toward the world of nations to create a new international order." Mackay believed that "the essential oneness of the church as the Body of Christ must be gratefully acknowledged and visibly expressed, or one by one the churches will die." The Protestant church had "to rid herself from all subjugation to a prevailing culture, an economic system, a social type, or a political order" so it could become "an abiding spiritual society that shall endure through all temporal change, even though the ecclesiastical system be shattered to pieces, to an indestructible community which contains the hope and promise of a new world,...to overcome all hostile circumstances, and amid the disintegration of society around him to maintain inviolate his faith in the coming of the Kingdom of God, whose servant the Church *is,* whose servants the churches should be."[21]

At Princeton, Mackay became active in the Federal Council of Churches, which allowed him to spread the American revolutionary message from a larger stage. Dulles played a large role in this effort because he had been "greatly impressed by the fellowship that existed among delegates at the Oxford Conference." He was "interested in what the church could contribute to the world," especially since, according to Mackay, Dulles exhibited a "very, very basic concern...not merely to win a war, but to see that the country would be worthy of its tradition and also worthy of the role which it would have to play in international affairs" after World War II, which the Federal Council saw as a crusade to spread freedom around the world. Just as Dulles's help and leadership, proved instrumental in forming public opinion in support of World War II, both the Presbyterian Church and the Federal Council played influential roles in the establishment of the world order after the war.[22]

In stirring words, the Federal Council on December 30, 1941, committed Christians to participate in the war against a "manifestation of a great flood of evil that has overwhelmed nation after nation, destroying human rights and leaving men the victims of irresponsible force...." Christians' responsibility to participate in this war derived from their citizenship in a "nation, under God, that is dedicated to human freedom" and as "members of the Church in America...and...of the world-wide Church." The Christian citizens gratefully acknowledged "a priceless heritage of freedom and democratic ideals for which earlier generations struggled and sacrificed....We are resolved to defend it from the menace of rival systems from without and from degradation of abuse or neglect from within. It is our high obligation to bequeath our heritage unimpaired and strengthened unto those who follow us...."[23]

The leader of the Federal Council effort at ecumenism, which Murray endorsed, was John Foster Dulles, a Wall Street lawyer and brother of Allen Dulles, future Director of the Central Intelligence Agency. Mackay was on the Federal Council's Commission on a Just and Durable Peace, which was chaired by John Foster Dulles. In February 1943, it formulated a statement of principles for the postwar era that "would merit the support of thoughtful Christian people" and become known as the "Six Pillars of Peace." Two of the pillars called for the establishment of the United Nations. A third stated there must be an international agreement that took into account the economic and financial actions of independent and autonomous. governments. A fourth called for the control of military establishments, and a fifth for the protection of the autonomy of peoples. The sixth sought to "achieve in practice the right of every man to religious and intellectual liberty."[24]

The Anglicans and the Church of Scotland welcomed the sixth pillar enthusiastically. In the Summer of 1943, Dulles expanded his commission to include Catholic and Jewish leaders to participate in drafting a declaration on world peace. The declaration called for moral law to govern world order, the assurance of individual rights, the creation of an international peace organization, international economic cooperation, and a just social order within each state.[25]

Mackay did his part to support the war effort and to prepare Americans for a role of so-called moral leadership afterward, claiming that Protestant churches must "proclaim the enduring moral principles by which human plans are constantly to be tested." In July 1943, he organized a conference at Princeton that mobilized 61 Christian leaders to disseminate the ideas Dulles had developed as part of the Six Pillars of Peace. From that same conference came a "Christian Message on World

Order," which held that the "basic social problem of world order is that of achieving moral and spiritual community." In order to escape from "chaos and recurrent war," "social and political institutions must be brought into conformity with moral order." In November 1944, during "World Order Sunday," Dulles, who worked to generate support for the creation of the United Nations, spoke of how the "greatest obstacle to world order is the lack of any universal moral judgment about national conduct." There was a "need to safeguard peace through public opinion based on 'world-accepted definitions of right and wrong conduct.'"[26]

Given the prejudices of the organizers, it was clear that Catholics were not going to be prominent in fashioning the moral consensus of the post-war era. As part of their ecumenical efforts, Mackay joined with his friend, Methodist Bishop Bromley Oxnam, a rabid anti-Catholic and president of the Federal Council, in calling upon the "Roman Catholic Church to be a church and not to attempt to be a state and a church." The Catholic effort to participate in the peace talks was opposed by 1,600 Protestant clergy, including Mackay. The Protestants condemned the Church's Concordat with Mussolini, as did Catholic priest Don Luigi Sturzo, one of the founders of the Christian Democrats, who called it cooperation with evil.[27]

MURRAY'S CRISIS

As editor of *Theological Studies,* Murray built his bona fides as someone the Protestants and Americans could trust by writing articles supporting intercredal cooperation as early as 1942. In the following year, he represented the U.S. Catholic Bishops in drafting and promoting the "Declaration on World Peace," which was an interfaith statement of principles for postwar reconstruction.

In discussing the issue of "inter-creedal co-operation," Murray presented an approach he used repeatedly during the course of the debate on church and state in the years that followed. First of all, he set out the Catholic position. Then, he deconstructed this position after paying lip service to the principles by claiming these principles applied only to Catholics. Then, he clouded the issue by referring to various ideas from "experts" or theologians. Next, he claimed that the Catholics' primary duty was to meet a great emergency not with conversion but with social action in collaboration with non-Catholics. The practical result could only be the removal of any social and ecclesiastical restrictions that protected the flock and kept the Catholics a cohesive and effective force in a pluralistic society like America. A secondary result was the reliance on social action. Murray announced his own unique understanding of various Papal declarations or encyclicals, which he selectively quoted. Reading Murray's articles, one is left with the definite impression the Catholics were the problem, and the Protestants got it all right, whatever "it" was. Finally, in these articles, Murray stated his support for an equivocal natural law without the Divine Positive Law of Jesus Christ as a way to organize society.

In "Current Theology: Christian Co-operation," Murray wrote approvingly of British efforts at intercredal cooperation. The basis of this good effort was "a common acceptance of the natural law" that was "directed towards objectives in social, economic, and international life that are made peremptory by the natural law."[28] Murray mentioned concerns over intercredal cooperation by referring to an article by Fr. Francis J. Connell, C.Ss.R., entitled "Catholic and 'Interfaith' Groups," which appeared in *American Ecclesiastical Review*. Connell was a Redemptorist theologian with whom Murray would have many exchanges in the years to come. Connell expressed concern that Catholics were tending towards indifferentism in their reaction against a "spirit of mutual distrust and antagonism" against non-Catholics. Two principles, according to Connell, regulated the relations of Catholics with non-Catholics. The first was to strive "zealously and prudently" for the conversion of non-Catholics, and the second was that "Catholicism is the only true religion, and that its acceptance is obligatory by divine law on all mankind." Participation by Catholics in interfaith organizations and meetings was a "grave menace to the faith" of Catholics because these situations allowed for the expression of religious ideas and were directed to addressing "moral and social questions." Specific dangers included concessions by Catholics that other religions are equal to Catholicism. Also, a Catholic representative may fail to provide a "correct and complete account of the Church's teachings on the very subjects that are most likely to be brought up, such as tolerance, the relation of Church and State, [and] the scope of the Church's authority."[29]

Connell then set out four precautions that were necessary before undertaking intercredal activities. He reminded the readers the Church was likely to be called "narrow, intolerant, illiberal" when it claimed exclusivity. As a result, Catholic lay participants in dialogue had to be competent, obedient to episcopal policies, properly educated on how to take part in these meetings, and object to error.[30]

Murray, for his part, questioned the "actual effect" of the cooperative movements on Catholics. He emphasized the need for Catholics to act charitably by cooperating "with non-Catholics in the sphere of social reconstruction" so as to meet "dangers so great as to create a necessity for such co-operation." He concluded with a quote from Pius XII that "there cannot be for the Church any going back,"[31] supposedly supporting his position.

Building on that theme, Murray later claimed, "Catholic and non-Catholic have an equal stake in a just social order, and therefore an equal concern for its establishment."[32] Furthermore, Murray opined, "The Holy See desires a spiritual and interconfessional unity to be organized...for a work...which remains fundamentally a spiritual work."[33] The cooperative action was to be the work mainly of the laity. Priest-theologians were to consult with non-Catholics to determine the specifics of cooperation, such as the organization and direction of it, and also to participate in "joint public meetings of men of different creeds, held with a view to the education of the public conscience on the religious and moral implications in the present crisis."[34]

Unlike Connell's formulation, which called on priests to lead and present Catholic doctrine, Murray's formulation made priests followers of, and subservient to, the Protestants and not leaders towards truth. In a paper entitled "The Catholic, Jewish, Protestant Declaration on World Peace: An Interpretation by Rev. John Courtney Murray, SJ," Murray expressed support for the U.S. Catholic bishops who, along with the leaders of other religious groups, signed the "Declaration for World

Peace" in October 1943. He based this support on statements and allocutions from Pope Pius XII, who, Murray wrote, insisted the "primal source of modern disorder has been the decay of conscience on the part of those who govern, and a similar decay on the part of the governed." Murray noted that it was the "whole order of human life, de-Christianized and dehumanized in its spirit and its institutions, which made total war possible, and even inevitable." Needed was the "construction of a new order," which "is an immense task" and one "Catholic social action alone, for all its intrinsic resources, is simply not up to" accomplishing. Murray concluded that such a "universal undertaking for the common good" required cooperation.[35]

Fr. Paul Hanly Furfey rebutted Murray's position in the pages of *American Ecclesiastical Review* in 1944. He claimed Murray was twisting the papal teachings by reading "the encyclicals with a particular attitude of mind" to justify a certain result, such as the Catholics leading in forming some organization to engage in social reform with non-Catholics.[36] Furfey felt that the encyclicals Murray quoted did not support his position. In fact, these encyclicals actually condemned the very type of social action and organization by Catholics Murray advocated. Murray denied the accusations and used the opportunity to strengthen and refine the points he had been making all along. Murray eliminated the need to undertake conversions, writing in conclusion: "It is fantastic to suppose that effective co-operation towards making the moral law the basis of civil society must wait upon previous formal acceptance, by all men, of the magisterial and jurisdictional authority of the Church, as the one true Church." According to Murray, if the non-Catholics accepted "as true the principles that she teaches (e.g., the principles of the Pattern for Peace [the statement issued in October 1943 simultaneously by "Catholic, Protestant, and Jewish leaders"]" then "[w]e cannot ask for more than this...." Secondly, Murray approved the organization of "local organized co-operative association[s]" to express approval of statements like "Pattern for Peace." Furfey held organized activity between different religions requires Catholics to "keep silent on the full Catholic social doctrine," something he finds disastrous and lacking in any social value because "only on the basis of the full Catholic social teaching can society be saved."[37]

During the course of his work on intercredal cooperation, Murray experienced a crisis. We get a sense of that from two different sources. The first is a very strident letter about the nature of education, which he wrote to someone called Luke, in which he insisted there was an epistemological problem with philosophy instruction. "I believe," Murray wrote that "our course fails of its finality – really any finality – not because its content is speculative and academic....but because its method is dogmatic. Students don't learn; they are simply indoctrinated. And simple indoctrination does not result in a vital possession of knowledge....they never really 'feel' the questions....To conclude, the fault, dear Lucas, is not so much in our content, as in our methods, that we produce educational duds."[38]

Murray's solution was to be more human, not more Christ-like. "God demands that we be more perfectly human," wrote Murray. The bases of the

"Church's social teaching are in the order of natural morality; and today especially the Church wishes to teach the natural law as natural, and as Christian only because natural and human. Our effort has to be to get her social teaching accepted not so much because it is hers (i.e., supported by her authority), as because it is human....in all this discussion of a "Christian philosophy" we have to be careful to preserve a great historical achievement, and a great contemporary value, namely, the distinction between the orders of truth, the relative autonomy of the natural, the legitimate independence of temporal society."[39]

The new curriculum, or way of teaching, "will have to appear as a work of cold intelligence, couched in the cleanest sort of rhetoric, stripped of all the turns of phrase – colorful enough – that at times turn your 'analysis' into an attack...."[40]

The second piece of evidence showing Murray's crisis comes from a diary entry of March 23, 1943, when he wrote: "'My kingdom is not of this world.' What of my loyalty? To which kingdom? The kingdom of God is within you—Thy Kingdom come! The kingdom of my fathers. Rex Meus et Deus Meus."[41] Murray's loyalty was shifting.

CHAPTER 9

MURRAY STARTS WRITING ABOUT CHURCH AND STATE AND RELIGIOUS LIBERTY

The meeting at the Biltmore was not the first time Murray addressed the issue of church and state. Beginning in 1945 with an article that appeared in *Theological Studies*, he started publishing on the topic of religious liberty and Church-State relations. He began with "Current Theology: Freedom of Religion" (March 1945), which was a response to various statements by Presbyterian John Mackay, and proceeded with writing "Freedom of Religion. The Ethical Problem" (June 1945), and "Religious Liberty: An Inquiry" (March 1946). *America* magazine, where he served as associate editor in 1945-1946, published his articles about the same topic, including "Separation of Church and State" (December 7, 1946), "True and False Concepts: Separation of Church and State" (February 16, 1947), "The Court Upholds Religious Freedom," (March 8, 1947), and "Religious Liberty: The Concern of All" (*America,* February 7, 1948).

Murray formulated a Catholic take on the American or Protestant position on church and state, which saw religious liberty as being a positive good. In general, he did so by using Protestant concepts, twisting Papal teaching to support American ideas, and then elevating social peace or political harmony to a position as the greatest good. He also redefined Catholic terms and concepts to support American institutions. One example was the emphasis on "public order" as opposed to the common good, which was indicative that Murray adopted the position of the Federal Council and its successor, the World Council of Churches.[42] Another was to focus the church and state argument on the human individual. He was also selective in reviewing and quoting the various writings of popes from Pius VII through Pius XII, avoiding any provisions that contradicted America's organizing principles. Murray's greatest polemical achievement was making the natural law, an equivocal term at best, the basis of public policy, thereby bringing about the dethronement of Christ, all in the name of social peace. All in all, it was a stunning reversal of the positions he had taken just five years earlier.

Murray wrote his June 1945 article in *Theological Studies* with the stated "aim at conveying to our Protestant and Jewish brethren some understanding of our position," which was the position of the Americanists. In this article, Murray proposed the natural law, a vague and undefined term capable of multiple meanings, as the basis for actions by the state. He argued that the highest good and the purpose of freedom of religion was to "preserve harmony of action and mutual confidence on the political plane, in the interests of the common good" and avoid conflict. Third, Murray redefined Catholic terms, most notably the "common good," to include criteria like earthly wealth. Fourth, he minimized the differences between Catholic theology and Protestant theology to mere "disagreements in ecclesiology." Fifth, he selectively cited from *Libertas* to justify the approval of evil for political expediency, thus elevating political expediency (which got translated as "social welfare," "social peace," and the "common good") as a good or an acceptable objective in itself.[43]

Murray stressed the importance of rights for the welfare of the social and political order. "Conscience rights" were natural, moral rights and had to be protected along with a number of other rights, including the "right of personal autonomy," the "right of domestic autonomy," the "right of free association with others for religious purposes," and the "right to propagate belief in God and the precepts of morality." Murray claimed that the condemnation of Liberalism by Popes Gregory XVI, Pius IX, and Leo XIII were all directed at "European Liberalism" and did not apply to the American experiment because European Liberalism was indifferent to religion and/or rejected it.[44]

Murray endorsed the American view of religious freedom as acceptable in Catholic principle and did so in the context of discussing FDR's "Four Freedoms," claiming that "The freedom of every person to worship God in his own way everywhere in the world" was "Christian liberty...a testimony to the supreme and most rightful dominion of God over men, and to the first and highest duty that men owe to God." Christ caused a "humiliation of reason" and civil society, while "perfect and obligatory" was subordinated to the Church, which was "another perfect and obligatory society with a higher end." The natural law was no longer the complete norm of human action but had been "clarified and amplified" by the Gospel. Religious liberty consisted of "harmonizing the solution reached on the ethical plain in terms of reason and the natural law with the solution reached on the theological plain in terms of the Church and the law of the Gospel." This meant "the rights of conscience as determined by the natural law remain in their full validity under the Christian law."[45]

Murray made two other comments worthy of a brief review. First, he concurred with Monsignor John Ryan in claiming that truth will not flourish without help from the state. Murray claimed that Thomas Jefferson was a Liberal when he said, "'It is error alone which needs the support of government. Truth can stand by itself'....[W]hen error actually has the support of government, the truth has hardly a chance to survive at all, much less to influence the organization and the course of social life," and that Jefferson's statement was erroneous. Murray felt that government must "acknowledge the sovereignty of God" and that the public authorities should patronize the Catholic Faith. Government, he claimed, must "exhibit a positive patronage of religion and morality," but he claimed the natural law alone does not make clear how God is to be publicly worshipped.[46]

Murray wrote two articles that appeared in *America* starting in December 1946 in which he argued that the First Amendment was not a theological document but rather a political document based on a unique idea of the state, which is that the United States is a "lay" or "secular" state. It was also based on a unique factual premise, which was quite different from the "medieval 'one-society' theory" that held "religious unity was essentially constitutive of social unity, and that community of faith was integral to the common temporal good." In a "one-state society," religious unity "was essentially constitutive of social unity, and that community of faith was integral to the common temporal good." The state had to maintain the preservation of religious unity in order to ensure its own preservation. Because the American state was not, as Madison put it, a "'competent judge of religious truths'" and could not force the acceptance of religious truths, the American state decided to maintain "reverence for knowledge or ignorance as these are present in its citizens. It does not deny or doubt that there is a religious authority; it simply denies that it is itself a religious authority." All men, as citizens of the state regardless of their religions, were equal in "their civic liberties and in the freedom of their access to all the benefits of organized society."[47]

After the Protestant ministers used the issue of public aid to parochial schools to agitate against Catholics, Murray tried to quiet their fears by invoking Pope Pius XII, claiming that "Pius XII in his discourse to the Roman Rota, on October 6, 1946, taught that 'political, civil and social tolerance' is 'for Catholics a moral duty' as an obedience to civil law." Murray sought to allay the fears of the Protestants by explaining the meaning of the First Amendment by referring to Madison's view that there was a "constitutional 'wall' between state authority and the religious conscience." The First Amendment enabled "free communication, mutual dependence and encouragement, but respect for independent sovereignties, and no control of one by the other.... And it contains a needed warning against making the 'wall' a sort of 'iron curtain' that would deny all community of interest between Church and State." Murray saw that the wall of separation could ultimately lead to secularization of the culture and society, a reality he foresaw when he wrote a "false wall deflects all governmental aid singly and solely towards the subsidization of secularism, as the one national 'religion' and culture, whose agent of propagation is the secularized public school."[48]

Murray praised the *Everson* decision from early 1947. The ultimate issues were "the universally vital ones of religious freedom, parental rights and civic equality," and the Supreme Court got it right. He approved the Court's review of the history and purpose of the First Amendment and emphasized, "The structure of our government has, for the preservation of civil liberty, rescued the temporal institutions from religious interference. On the other hand, it has secured religious liberty from the invasion of civil authority."[49]

10
SETTING THE STAGE FOR THE STAGED FIGHT

Tension increased between Catholics and Protestants during the 1940s. Protestants expressed concern with a number of Catholic social policies (e.g., public aid to parochial schools and U.S. recognition of the Vatican). The growing Protestant missionary presence in Latin America led to Catholic demands that the Protestants withdraw from Latin America, especially Argentina. The November 1942 "Victory and Peace" statement of the Catholic hierarchy noted that the continuing Protestant missionary efforts were harming the good neighbor policy of President Roosevelt. Mackay and others accused the Catholics of hypocrisy: the Catholics took advantage of and defended a monopoly in countries where they held the majority, such as in Spain, and in places like the United States where religious liberty was the norm, Catholics took advantage of that system, too. Mackay charged Catholics with encouraging religious suppression by Latin governments.[1]

All of this was setting the stage for a fight in the American media, especially *Time,* that the Catholics could not be allowed to win. Mackay and other Protestant leaders were tied in with the Wall Street crowd through the Federal Council, later the World Council. Their goal was to discredit the Catholic view on church and state and substitute in its place the American ideology as the ideal. This would have global significance.

THE RISE OF POAU

Beginning in 1946, the Federal Council made a number of pronouncements on foreign policy, and these advanced the notion that the United States embodied the ideal socio-political organization. This effort came about in the context of trying to avoid war with the USSR In the same year, the Commission on a Just and Durable Peace adopted a draft statement on Soviet-American relations. The Commission stressed the need to avoid war and, at the same time, not compromise American principles. The way to do so was "by eliminating intolerance, which makes it impossible for conflicting beliefs to subsist and be propagated in peace." Achieving this goal, however, "made it necessary for the United States to eliminate certain prejudices and practices that," observed the Council, "unnecessarily created tensions." In addition, there would have to be cooperation at "scientific, economic, cultural, and religious levels." The final part of the statement insisted that Americans must demonstrate that: "the democratic institutions, which reflect the Christian doctrine of the sacredness of individual personality, can be made so vigorous that all peoples will want them." Concurrently, the Federal Council stressed individual liberty and liberty of conscience.[2]

Mackay's experience in Latin America, coupled with his position in the Federal Council, allowed him to advance the idea of religious liberty. At the same time, he advanced America as the ideal, thus permitting the Protestants to weaken the hold of the Vatican on Catholic societies. At Princeton, he worked to resist the efforts of Catholic bishops to convince the U.S. State Department to limit visas for Protestant missionaries to Colombia and other Latin countries.[3]

One of Mackay's most prominent targets was Franco's Spain, which became the Protestant bogeyman all throughout the 1940s and 1950s whenever the discussion on religious liberty arose. Mackay "lamented the fall of the Spanish republic." His opposition to Franco's Spain focused on the statements of Catholic prelates, such as the Archbishop of Toledo, against the republic. He claimed their statements created the conflict had resulted in so much loss of life.[4]

Another great conflict of the day for Mackay was between a united Church and totalitarianism. Ecumenism was the word given to the efforts to bring all believers in Christ into one church to serve the Lord. Given that Mackay saw Protestantism as a split within the Church of Christ, and not from the Catholic Church, and felt that the Catholics and Protestants just had two different viewpoints on what constituted the Church,[5] he argued that all Christians are in the same Church and that they should join forces against the totalitarian state, which included both Communist countries, which destroyed all Christians, and Catholic states, which kept diversity in the Church from thriving.

Mackay was affiliated with one of the more prominent anti-Catholic and pro-religious liberty associations of the day, Protestants and Other Americans United, or the POAU. Formed at a conference of leading Protestant ministers from several denominations, the POAU came into existence on October 14, 1947, for the purpose of checking "the political activity of the Catholic Hierarchy, to forestall co-operation, if not union, of this nation with the Catholic Church, to keep the Catholic Church from capturing the public schools as they had allegedly done at North College Hill in Cincinnati, to have Catholic Sisters removed from the teaching staff of public schools; to see to it that no federal or state aid would be paid even indirectly for the support of parochial school, and to have the laws in the seventeen states, which allowed public school children to receive religious instruction on released time, recalled – as well as those laws which allowed bus transportation to children attending non-public schools."[6]

The Protestants were concerned about the growth of Catholic political power. More specifically, they feared the "credit quite universally given to the Catholic Church as the one strong bulwark against Communism, the reaction of the non-Communist world to the treatment of Cardinal Mindszenty, the inclusion of so many intellectuals among converts to the Catholic faith, the crowded Catholic churches on Sunday as against the empty Protestant churches...."[7]

Mackay brought the right mix of talents to the fight against the Catholics, most notably "his direct knowledge of the practice and working theology of the Roman Catholic Church as a transnational entity," knowledge which he gleaned both during "World War II and for nearly twenty years afterwards [when] the growing ecumenical, pan-Protestant movement for world Christianity challenged the influence of the Roman Catholic Church and its hierarchy." Essential to his position was a theological argument that Protestantism was not a break from Catholicism but a break within it. Mackay launched the debate on religious liberty which might not have occurred otherwise, according to his biographer, but it was a debate "whose terms Mackay had helped to frame."[8]

BUILDING TO THE BOWIE EXCHANGE AND THE NATIONAL DEBATE

In three editorials published during November and December 1947, the *Christian Century* responded to what it called a taunt by Jesuit priest James M Gillis, who wrote that none of the Protestants had been able to define the "union of church and state," the allegedly undesirable state of affairs that is attributed to Catholic doctrine. The editorials accepted the most important principle laid out in *Everson* which was that the First Amendment applied to state and local authorities and affirmed the American principle of separation of church. Separation meant the two "are to be kept separate – completely separate – in their institutional or official functioning. The official functioning of the state must be kept separate from the official functioning of the organized church. There must be no interlocking of their respective institutional processes by law or by the administration of law. This is the constitutional basis of religious liberty." The respective functions of the two should not be "entangled" so that a "free church, side by side, with a free state" may exist, and the First Amendment was broad enough to prevent a gradual interlocking of the two spheres.[9]

The editors then ran through a list of situations that threatened the principle of separation of Church and State and found violations of the principle whenever 1) tax funds were used to provide bus transportation, free textbooks, and free lunches for parochial school pupils; 2) "released time" for religious instruction took place on public school premises; 3) as well as in the creation of an ambassadorship to the Vatican; and 4) chaplaincies for the Armed Forces. The principle was not violated with 1) prayer at the opening sessions of public events or public governmental bodies, 2) the study of religion as part of a curriculum, 3) devotional reading and prayer in public schools, and 4) vaccinations on school grounds. Additionally, the principle did not mean that "the state must be indifferent to religion; that it must be impervious to the considerations which religion may bring to bear upon its policies," nor that the "state, through its representatives, can act from religious motives... perform a religious act," nor that the state must be strictly secular, that it may not recognize the Deity."[10]

Fr. William McManus replied by issuing an editorial through the NCWC News Service dated December 22, 1947. McManus claimed that Catholics and Protestants agreed on several issues. One was that the First Amendment does not mean the "separation of religion from the state," nor did it mean the "separation of religion and politics." Another area of consensus was agreement that the "First Amendment definitely prohibits any governmental favoritism for any one particular religious sect or denomination. Exactly! Catholics agree with the Protestants, and both agree with the founding fathers." Third, "no religion is to be put under a ban by the state. No religion, on the other hand, may be given a special recognition by the state, for this obviously had the negative effect of hampering all other religions. Right again!" Finally, both Catholics and Protestants agreed the passage of legislation establishing a religion constituted giving "special recognition" to one religion by the government. McManus claimed that the Protestants had no principled stance for their position because they were silent on things like administering health services in parochial schools or devotional study of religion in public schools, which means reciting the "Protestant version of the Lord's Prayer" or reading the Protestant Bible.[11]

Murray responded to the *Christian Century* article in the March 6 and 20, 1948 editions of *America* with a personal attack on Dr. Charles Clayton Morrison, editor for thirty-nine years of the *Christian Century.*

Time called Morrison "Protestantism's gadfly," but Murray wrote he was neither an expert in Constitutional law nor an expert in Catholic teaching on church and state matters. Morrison was "devoting his declining years to a Great Cause – that of foiling, through the instrumentality of an aroused Protestantism, the plot of the Catholic hierarchy against American liberties." Murray was engaging in the very conduct he accused Morrison of undertaking, which is that "One does not indeed belittle an adversary, but one must situate him."[12]

Murray then explained the background and history of the First Amendment and the efforts to arrive at the final wording of it. Murray wrote, "The idea, as Madison had clearly expressed it, was to exclude the 'establishment' (i.e., preference by congressional law) of any one national 'religion,' to the legal exclusion and juridical inferiority of others." Murray interpreted the First Amendment to mean, "'Congress shall make no law whose effect was the legal preferment of one religion (particular articles of faith and a particular mode of worship), with consequent legal subordination of others'."[13] The First Amendment "prohibits government from using its powers in the area of 'religion' (religious belief, worship, practice); it does not prohibit it from using its powers in the area of education, to the extent of its jurisdiction in that area."[14] In criticizing the *McCollum* decision and in concluding his response to Morrison, Murray claimed that he was articulating "the basic Catholic position in this whole matter," but his response elevated the U.S. Constitution into something sacred. "Our position," he continued, "is quite simply American and it looks to the freedom of American education and the freedom of the American people to organize their education."[15]

In proposing the American Founders' view on the separation of Church and State in his response in *America,* Murray promulgated the Americanist position when it came to Church-State doctrine in the U.S. There was to be no attempt to make Catholicism the pre-eminent religion and faith of the land as mandated by the Church. Murray performed one of his rhetorical tricks in which he appeared to attack Morrison and the Protestant position but ended up endorsing the Americanist ideology condemned by Leo XIII.

All of this was consistent with positions Murray had taken weeks earlier. In his article "Religious Liberty: The Concern of All," Murray decried a January 12, 1948, POAU manifesto, which claimed that the Catholic Church "'holds and maintains a theory of the relation between church and state that is incompatible with the American ideal.'" This "theory inspires American Catholic policy," which is "plainly subversive of religious liberty as guaranteed by the Constitution." The manifesto went on to claim that the Catholic goal, advanced by Myron C. Taylor's appointment as legate to the Vatican, was for the Church to attain "a position of special privilege in relation to the State."[16]

Murray denounced the Manifesto as a "scare-technique," but he then went on to tell Catholics that they should be afraid of the Soviets and endorse the American ideology like other good Americans. To Murray, the Protestants got it right with America, and given the Soviet threat, it was time the Catholics realized as much. "Perhaps," he wrote, "we could agree to be American citizens, divided in religious faith, but united in our loyalty to the First Amendment." Catholics needed to prove to the Protestants of America that "we are the friends of its liberties, that our progress is its progress, that our power is in its service, that no man has to fear from us infringement of any of his rights." Murray emphasized, "There is a revolution going on," which "had its beginning just a century ago this January, when Marx and Engels issued the *Communist Manifesto*."[17]

Unlike the *Communist Manifesto*, the plan set in motion by the American elites was working just fine. The Protestants, with the financial interests backing them, were using the First Amendment as a club to beat the Church, yet it advanced the American ideology.

PART IV

C.D. JACKSON AND AMERICAN UNITY

11
THE CREATION OF PSYCHOLOGICAL WARFARE

Because of Communist gains during the Italian elections in the Spring of 1948, the newly formed Central Intelligence Agency, or CIA, under the leadership of James Jesus Angleton, got involved in what came to be known as covert operations by supplying disinformation damaging to the Communists to pro-Western papers.[1] At around the same time, George Kennan, author of the "Long Telegram" and a proponent of containment of the Soviet Union, began an effort to draft a plan for the "inauguration of organized political warfare." This meant the creation of a "covert political warfare operations directorate within the Government." This was especially significant given Kennan was the director of the State Department's Policy Planning Staff (PPS), which had "control of U.S. Cold War strategy."

Kennan's plan included "clandestine support of 'friendly' foreign elements, 'black' psychological warfare, and even encouragement of underground resistance in hostile states," all of which were an extension of U.S. governmental policies. Inherent in this policy was the creation of front groups, ostensibly of U.S. citizens but in reality funded secretly by the CIA. These front groups created the impression that these organizations simply came about because "of a long American tradition of voluntary association in support of 'people suffering under oppression,'" when in reality, they were part of a newly inaugurated campaign of covert political warfare, which was to be carried out around the world, even in the so-called free countries who considered themselves allies of the U.S.[2]

In June of 1948, a new agency, the Office of Special Projects (OSP), came into being as a result of NSC Directive 10/2, which superseded NSC 4-A authorizing overt operations. Citing the "vicious covert activities of the USSR, its satellite countries and Communist groups to discredit and defeat the aims and activities of the United States and other Western powers," NSC Directive 10/2 "determined that, in the interests of world peace and U.S. national security, [and] the overt foreign activities of the U.S. government must be supplemented by covert operations." [3] The OSP, which was eventually absorbed into the CIA and later renamed the Office of Policy Coordination or OPC under the direction of Frank Wisner, fulfilled its mandate to "plan and conduct covert operations."

"Understood to be all activities...which are conducted or sponsored by this Government against hostile foreign states or groups or in support of friendly foreign states or groups but which are so planned and executed that any U.S. government responsibility for them is not evident to unauthorized persons and that if uncovered the U.S. government can plausibly disclaim any responsibility for them."[4]

The OPC had the power to conduct "any covert activities related to propaganda, economic warfare; preventive direct action, including sabotage, demolition and evacuation measures; subversion against hostile states, including assistance to underground resistance movements....and support of indigenous anti-communist elements in threatened countries of the free world."[5]

After receiving his mandate, Wisner went about recruiting World War II veterans from the Office of Strategic Services to staff the new agency, which was split into five "Functional Groups" - psychological warfare, political warfare, economic warfare, preventive direct action, and 'miscellaneous' – and, in deliberate imitation of the Marshall Plan, given jurisdiction over six geographical divisions, the heads of which controlled the field staff."[6]

FORGING THE "NEW INSTRUMENT OF WAR"

America's postwar intelligence establishment had roots going back to the days shortly after FDR's "Four Freedoms" speech. Colonel William "Wild Bill" Donovan was a Catholic altar boy who fought in World War I, became a millionaire Wall Street lawyer, dabbled in politics, and conducted intelligence operations for years between the wars.[7] Donovan lobbied for, and in July 1941, was selected to lead the first central organization to "combine the functions of espionage and covert operations." He became the Coordinator of Information (COI) with the authority to oversee the existing intelligence organizations. Some of those were the Military Intelligence Division or G-2, Naval Intelligence, and the Office of Inter-American Affairs overseen by Nelson Rockefeller.[8]

Donovan was "impressed by the British method of combining... propaganda efforts with the 'unorthodox' operations of sabotage, subversion, and guerrilla warfare. Donovan had been impressed as well by the British system of intelligence and counter-intelligence....and by their ability to coordinate intelligence activities with psychological warfare and special operations."[9] During the war, FDR "welcomed the suggestion of a single agency which would serve as a clearinghouse for all intelligence, as well as an organ of counterpropaganda and a training center for what were euphemistically called 'special operations.'"[10]

By the time the COI was set up, another man who was bound to figure prominently in the Cold War, Assistant Secretary of War and powerful abettor of the WASP establishment, John McCloy, suggested to the Army the establishment of a Psychological Branch of the Military Intelligence Division and eventually became its first director. Established in June 1941, the psychological branch was created to plan for future psychological operations, but it immediately got to work in conducting psychological warfare. This included obtaining summaries of broadcasts, "completion of surveys for the Office for Coordination of Commercial and Cultural Relations and for the Council for Democracy, initiation of weekly telegram service to military missions with a brief summary of national defense progress, and purchase of copies of

Newsweek and *Life* for distribution to selected missions in Europe to counteract the pictorial propaganda of Germany."[11] The director of the Council of Democracy was Luce lieutenant and Time, Inc. executive Charles Douglas Jackson, more commonly known as C.D. Jackson.

Donovan's COI was composed of two offices. The first was Research and Analysis (R & A), which evaluated incoming intelligence under the direction of Harvard historian Dr. William Langer. The second was the Foreign Information Service (FIS), which became the psychological warfare division and was led by Robert Sherwood, a playwright and FDR confidant. The FIS "undertook to spread the gospel of democracy... and to explain the objectives of the United States throughout the world except in Latin America." The FIS broadcast propaganda on commercial shortwave stations in several languages, and after Pearl Harbor, it broadcast on more than 300 stations in Europe and Asia.[12]

According to Donovan, psychological warfare consisted of stages. The first was intelligence penetration, which involved information gathering and processing by the R & A branch, which made its research available for planning and propaganda. Donovan said propaganda was "the 'arrow of initial penetration' and believed that it would be the first phase in operations against an enemy. The next phase would be special operations in the form of sabotage and subversion, followed by commando-like raids, guerrilla actions, and behind-the-lines resistance movements. All of this represented the softening-up process prior to invasion by friendly armed forces. Donovan's visionary dream was to unify these functions in support of conventional unit operations, thereby forging 'a new instrument of war.'"[13]

In June 1942, FDR transferred the FIS to the newly created Office of War Information (OWI), which had as its first director a Columbia Broadcasting System reporter, Elmer Davis. OWI and FIS "controlled all propaganda in the United States and all 'white' propaganda – information, official or otherwise, plainly issued from a known source – outside the United States with the exception of the Western Hemisphere." Several months later, the OWI was made responsible for "conducting foreign information and overt propaganda operations."[14]

The Office of Strategic Services (OSS) was created at the same time as the OWI and placed under the Joint Chiefs of Staff, with Donovan as its director. The OSS "retained responsibility for 'black' propaganda operations, which were essentially covert activities using information issued from a concealed or falsified source to lower the enemy's morale." The Joint Psychological Warfare Committee (JPWC), which came into existence in March, was reorganized in June and also fell under the control of the JCS. In his capacity as head of the OSS, Donovan wrote the definition of psychological warfare in something called the "Basic Estimate of Psychological Warfare," which defined it as:

"the coordination and use of all means, including moral and physical, by which the end is attained—other than those of recognized military operations, but including the psychological exploitation of the result of those recognized military actions—which tend to destroy the will of the enemy to achieve victory and to damage his political or economic capacity to do so; which tend to deprive the enemy of the support, assistance or sympathy of his allies or associates or of neutrals, or to prevent his acquisition of such support, assistance, or sympathy; or which tend to create, maintain, or increase the will to victory of our own people and allies and to acquire, maintain, or to increase the support, assistance and sympathy of neutrals."[15]

The JPWC was abolished in December, and all responsibility for propaganda was handed to the OSS. Each war theater operated its own psychological warfare directorates, but this was bound to change. In March 1943, C.D. Jackson, who had been working for the OWI, asked McCloy to establish a psychological warfare department at the level of the Department of War. McCloy liked the idea and proceeded to staff and implement it by November.[16]

Donovan saw the need for a governmental intelligence agency after World War II ended. In a November 18, 1944, memorandum to FDR, Donovan wrote:

"Once our enemies are defeated the demand will be equally pressing for information that will aid us in solving the problems of peace. This will require two things: 1. That intelligence control be returned to the supervision of the President. 2. The establishment of a central authority reporting directly to you, with responsibility to frame intelligence objectives and to collect and coordinate the intelligence material required by the Executive Branch in planning and carrying out national policy and strategy."[17]

The new agency would primarily be responsible for the coordination of the collection of information "including military, economic, political and scientific, concerning the capabilities, intentions and activities of foreign nations, with particular reference to the effect such matters may have upon the national security, policies and interests of the United States...."[18]

The OSS "was the first agency of its kind in the history of the United States,"[19] and it laid the foundation for the U.S. postwar intelligence establishment.[20] This establishment was staffed by other middle-aged corporate lawyers, people like John Foster Dulles' brother Allen, and "from elite universities such as Yale (not for nothing was the OSS nicknamed 'Oh So Social')" which exhibited "a distinct predisposition toward internationalism, produced in many cases by the officers' experience of living and fighting alongside foreign partisans during the war; and a surprising amount of liberalism, even leftism, again often the result of close wartime dealings with communist-dominated resistance movements."[21]

With the end of hostilities, President Harry Truman dismantled the OSS, and the Ivy Leaguers and Wall Street lawyers returned to their jobs in American legal, economic, and media institutions, but Henry Luce had other plans.

LUCE LEADS THE WAY

From at least August 1943, Luce had been planning to bring out an international version of *Time*. Truman's decision to disband the OSS confirmed his decision. In a memorandum titled "Time Inc. Abroad," Luce laid out his plan for Time International. "Our task now," he wrote, "is to think out and to begin to establish the scheme of organization which will best serve us and our country over a relatively long period of years." The purpose of the international organization was for both profit and patriotism, though the profit may take a while to materialize. Initially, offices were to be established in the capitals of Europe.[22]

The managing editor of Time Inc. abroad was C.D. Jackson, who was to report to Luce and Roy E. Larsen. Aside from managing the foreign correspondents and foreign offices, Jackson had a public relations function. His work, Luce reminded him, would "inevitably impinge upon many complicated and frequently shifting political, economic and ideological situations."[23] Luce met with Secretary of State Byrnes on November 9 and, during the course of their meeting, voluntarily committed Time, Inc. to support a "stronger, more competent, efficient department" all over the world. In his memorandum to the Senior Editors the following day, Luce revealed he was considering using Time, Inc. as an intelligence-gathering organization.[24]

Truman eventually relented and saw the need for enhanced foreign intelligence and the centralization of collection and analysis. The Central Intelligence Group came into being in January 1946 with the appointment of Rear Admiral Sidney Souers as its first chief. The new organization proved to be inadequate to the challenge posed by the deterioration of relations between the U.S.S.R and the U.S., and in July 1947, the National Security Act created the Central Intelligence Agency (CIA) and the National Security Council (NSC). Once the CIA was given the power to perform various unspecified "other functions and duties related to intelligence affecting the national security," the stage was set for covert operations.[25]

Years later, President Truman recounted the reason for founding the CIA and his regrets at having done so. "The President," he explained, "needed at that time a central organization that would bring all the various intelligence reports we were getting in those days, and there must have been a dozen of them, maybe more, bring them all into one organization so that the President would get *one* report on what was going on in various parts of the world. Now *that* made sense, and that's why I went ahead and set up what they called the Central Intelligence Agency." Truman, however, soon realized that setting up the CIA was a mistake because "it got out of hand. Now, as nearly as I can make out, those fellows in the CIA don't just report on wars and the like, they go out and make their own, and there's nobody to keep track of what they're up to. They spend billions of dollars on stirring up trouble so they'll *have* something to report on. They've become....a government all of its own and all secret. They don't have to account to anybody...." Truman blamed this state of affairs on his successor, Dwight D. Eisenhower, who "never paid any attention to it, and it got out of hand."[26]

12
C.D. JACKSON

As Managing Editor of Time International, C.D. Jackson held one of "many senior, very senior jobs." Jackson, according to Henry Luce III, "was very close to my father.... He saw him as a troubleshooter... and expected him to get things fixed. So he depended on him a lot."[1]

A New Yorker by birth, Jackson graduated from Princeton in 1924 with a wish to follow an academic career as a French teacher. When his father died, Jackson became responsible for the family's business, C.D. Jackson & Co., a marble and stone importer. The Depression hit his business hard, and Jackson was forced to call on his old friend, Harry Luce, for a job with Time, Inc. Luce brought him on as an assistant to the president, and from there, C.D.'s career took off.[2] Luce and C.D. were "very close personal and business friends. They spent many hours discussing international affairs, and Mr. Luce would have had certain opinions that found their way into the magazine...."[3]

For nearly 33 years, C.D. served in a variety of positions at Time Inc. He was special assistant to Luce as well as general manager of *Life* magazine (1937), publisher of *Fortune* magazine in 1949, and publisher of *Life* magazine eleven years later in 1960. He took leaves of absence to get involved in public service or civic organizations, most of which dealt with issues of political warfare and psychological operations.[4] His long-time secretary, Mary McCrum, claimed that C.D. became involved in psychological warfare because of the efforts of a Mr. Halpern, an associate of William Paley, chairman of CBS.[5]

C.D. was well-suited to prosecute and conduct psychological warfare. He "had a very good sensitivity to people and situations," and he "had a good promotion and public relations sense in the finer senses of those words."[6] He took his first important job in that regard in 1940 when he became President of the Council for Democracy. The Council was supposed to "turn out young men with the knowledge and emotional drive to act as 'pro-consuls of democracy' in the course of their careers." The Council for Democracy also existed for the purpose of combating "all the nazi, fascist, communist, pacifist" anti-war groups in the United States.[7] It was as head of the Council for Democracy that C.D. earned his reputation as a propagandist.

By the following year, he and his boss, Luce, were in touch with Colonel William "Wild Bill" Donovan, who was in the process of expanding the intelligence service capabilities of the U.S. government. One of C.D.'s jobs was to keep an eye on the U.S. Catholics and recruit Catholics who could be relied on to stay in the American camp. In a memorandum dated September 23, 1941, to M. Gottfried, C.D. wrote, "As you can imagine, the U.S. Catholic Situation was an area of much interest and activity while I was at the Council [for Democracy]. One of the people that I ran into and employed is a young fellow called Philip Rodgers, an Irish Catholic on the so-called liberal side."[8] Rodgers, headquartered in New York, kept an eye on developments amongst the Catholics to see when or if the National Catholic Welfare Council (NCWC) would announce some position on war because C.D. had found an "unrealistically high percentage [of Catholics] against war."[9] Rodgers told C.D., "Many Catholics may foresee the nightmare of Hitler 'entitling himself the world scourge of Communism and Defender of the Faith,'" but, he added, to do so would be to ignore the pope.[10] Rodgers also provided valuable information about the various dynamics within the Catholic community in the United States. In a letter to C.D. dated October 14, 1941, Rodgers gave C.D. and Luce an invaluable insight into the American Catholic mind and how U.S. Catholics got information: "I am sure you will understand that I have no desire to be captious. Many thousands of Catholics must read TIME and LIFE. As a matter of fact, I am quite sure the non-denominational press is much more widely read by Catholics than are the various diocesan publications. When Catholics see what is taken for Catholic opinion in such magazines as TIME and LIFE they pay attention to it."[11]

U.S. Catholics were not particularly loyal to their own leadership. "The nearest thing we have in this country to Catholic leadership in political matters," Rodgers explained, "is the National Catholic Welfare Conference, and many Catholics do not accept even this leadership. This, I know is contrary to the opinion held by some people that Catholics react as a body when their so-called leaders speak."[12] Monsignor Fulton J. Sheen did not lead anyone, Rodgers told C.D. The one who could command the most leadership amongst Catholics was the President of Georgetown, Fr. Walsh. Bishop Hurley was one "of the most progressive and influential members of the episcopacy in America," and since he previously served in the "Vatican secretariat of State," he "can be presumed to know which way the wind blows in the Vatican."[13] Within a few months, Rodgers, with C.D.'s approval and the approval of Donovan's Office of the Coordinator of Defense Information (CDI), was allowed to conduct a "government-backed information and propaganda outfit" to work in "the Catholic field."[14]

After his stint with the Council, C.D. became a special assistant to the U.S. Ambassador to Turkey. He served with the State Department's Bureau of Economic Warfare. The same year, he was chosen to assist the OWI in North Africa, traveled with Eisenhower through North Africa and Sicily, and ended up in England, where he became Deputy Chief of the Psychological Warfare Branch, which his proposal established at the Armed Forces Headquarters. From 1944 to 1945, C.D. was the Deputy Chief of the Psychological Warfare Division of the Supreme Headquarters of the Allied Expeditionary Forces (SHAEF). There, he not only prepared the propaganda to accompany D-Day but also appraised the "reactions and ideas of liberated and conquered peoples toward the Allies in general and the U.S. in particular."[15]

Luce was also closely tied in with the intelligence agencies at the time. In August 1941, Donovan asked Archibald MacLeish, who was then the Librarian of Congress, for his assistance in outthinking the Nazis. MacLeish immediately contacted Luce to help "accomplish the difficult metamorphosis which permits a man to think as though he were someone else,"[16] thereby establishing the cozy relationship between Time, Inc. and the U.S. intelligence community, which expanded significantly with the Cold War.

13
INTELLIGENCE, MEDIA, BANKING, AND COMMUNICATION

Perhaps better than any other man of his generation, C.D. Jackson embodied all the various facets that made up the unified American effort during the Cold War. Jackson coordinated the efforts of leading members of the intelligence community with equally well-connected people in media, banking, and industry and effectively established the channels of communication that would advance the American Cold War effort. He went back and forth from his job in Time, Inc. to government service,[1] coordinating the government's intelligence agencies with media, financial, and business interests in the private sector to advance the wealth and power of the banking or monied interests. After the end of World War II, "the U.S. government's national security campaigns have usually overlapped with the commercial ambitions of major advertisers and media companies."[2] Many of America's private individuals and concerns worked with and for government intelligence agencies. Time, Inc. was the government's most important collaborator in this effort. There is no doubt that reporters and executives of Time, Inc. shared information with the CIA and often gave credentials to CIA agents.[3]

Journalism was essential in giving the impression that the policies and values of the United States were shared by all its people. Journalism also taught these values to the American people and gave credibility to the American message around the world. Unlike government propaganda issued by a state agency, journalism of the sort practiced by Time, Inc. created "the mirage of popular unanimity regarding the nation's Cold War message."[4]

As part of both the CIA and Time, Inc., Jackson was in a unique position to mobilize American elites as part of a unified campaign to win the Cold War. First of all, he knew the players, all of whom came from the same social, ethnic, and religious backgrounds. They were Protestants, Ivy-leaguers, and well-off, and, most importantly, they all knew each other. Many in the intelligence community, like Allen Dulles, Wild Bill Donovan, John Foster Dulles, Frank Wisner, and others, were Wall Street lawyers. Like Jackson's lawyer friends, the CIA agent "finds out everything he can and resorts to every means imaginable to shape the outcome."[5]

A lot of the men staffing the media and the intelligence communities served together during World War II when psychological warfare first came into being, largely through C.D.'s efforts. The "old-boy networks rooted in common wartime experiences in psychological warfare [that] extended beyond the social sciences" extended throughout the print and electronic media. The "common experience of wartime psychological warfare work became one step in a process through which various leaders in the social sciences engaged one another in tacit alliances to promote their particular interpretations of society."[6]

Time, Inc. recruited writers and editors who had served in the intelligence community. In a memorandum marked "Fortune," Billings had drawn up the names of three possible writing prospects: "Bright young men....White, 31 (Capt. Intelligence) Wise, smart. Already editing. Highly 'vulnerable.' ($ 10,000) Smith, E., 30 (Active Capt. Intelligence) Round up. Smart operator. Highly 'vulnerable' -- $ 10,000 Donovan, 36 (Lt. Co. Intelligence) Shorts, good manuscript editor – ($15,000)."[7]

Secondly, in addition to knowing the players, C.D. also knew the message, something Luce reiterated time and time again. On December 8, 1945, Luce wrote one of the clearest explanations of the political and economic system his magazines sought to advance. "We stand and have always stood for compromise," Luce told his editors and a liberal society allows for the "compromise of all purely human affairs." Four corollaries then arose from this "fundamental faith as applied to our notions about the political economy." These were 1) to preserve or conserve from the past political or economic wisdom or habit with an example being "the concept of constitutional rather than arbitrary law"; 2) "we insist therefore on the kind of society in which there will remain room for the free play of economic and social experiment"; 3) the "liberal society does not inherently present any bar" to the solution of any "practical problem of human need or welfare"; and 4) while there can be socialism in a free society, there cannot be freedom in a socialist society.[8]

Billings, while serving as the number two man at Time, Inc., set forth Luce's philosophy in a memorandum that expressed the "basic convictions of the editors":

"1. We believe in the Bill of Rights....We hope that all of these rights may be achieved by all men everywhere.

2. We believe in the Constitution of the United States....[W]e are against distortion of the Constitution; we are against violation of its spirit....

3. We believe – what must be obvious to any honest mind – that the Bill of Rights and the Constitution require the institution of private property and we denounce as balderdash the notion that 'property right' is not a 'human right.' Property is, we believe, a vitally important 'human' right.....

5. We believe that the so-called 'free enterprise' system must be the prevailing pattern of the economic life of America. We believe not only that the free enterprise system can produce a higher standard of living than any other system but, even if we did not believe that, we would be for it because we know of no other system compatible with freedom.

6. We believe in the economic sphere; we believe in the greatest good of

the greatest number. In the social sphere, we believe in giving aid to the weak.

7. We believe that the paramount interest of the United States is the extension of freedom throughout the world and we believe that the United States must be strong, militarily and diplomatically....

8. We believe that 'the work of Justice is Peace' and that Justice can do its work most notably where men are free – free to be just and to learn justice and to practice it and to accept it as a sacrament between them....."[9]

Third, Jackson felt that the Department of State, and hence the entire U.S. government, was responsible for exporting values to create the right environment for private finance. He expounded on this in memoranda to Luce and Time, Inc. staff. Once the government makes the environment safe enough, a "genuine partnership basis through private enterprise" arises to develop the resources.[10] *Time,* in a February 1955 cover story, put it succinctly: "The job of the US.... is to export principles, and then much will follow."[11] In another memo, Jackson wrote that "The State Department must be made aware of their tremendous and urgent responsibility in getting their diplomats to work forthwith on settling the appropriate capital-investment climate in various countries of the world...."[12] John Davenport, a staffer at Time, Inc., explained how institutional changes in target societies needed to make them friendly to private capital when he wrote:

"The answer surely lies not in any grandiose plan but in certain institutional factors which professional economists all too often take for granted – decent money and a functioning credit system; the relatively free pricing of goods and services; and respect for private property and the allowing of private capital to seek its own reward....What needs to be exported is not primarily dollars, but belief in a system, and if we are called old fashioned imperialists for that we shall just have to stand on it."[13]

The Americans worked together to ensure development around the world, ostensibly to combat the Soviets. C.D. wrote a "simple directive for the US" in which he stated, "After World War I the Bolsheviks did not have to be considered, and although Western Europe and the British Empire operated whenever possible in a cartel system, the overall commercial ideology was one of private enterprise. Today the ground rules are quite different. There is a Kremlin block, including the satellites, part of Germany and extending into the Far East. There are the planned economies, including the sterling area; and there is the old cartel spirit raising [sic] again in Europe."[14]

A close relationship between private interests and government was necessary, and both Jackson and Luce felt, in Jackson's words, that the "only 'viable' solution [to the Kremlin block] right now appears to be.... [A] partnership between Government and private enterprise to assist in the development of the world....[P]rivate capital will venture and assume commercial risks provided (a) it is not in competition with Government; (b) Government will arrange the necessary insurance against non-commercial hazards. Private enterprise...does not wish to undertake, besides the extraordinary risks and difficulties of doing international business today, the added risks of confiscation and nationalization...."[15]

Capital was important and "waiting to be tapped, provided allocation is worked out intelligently and without suspicion or jealousy." One country that was viewed as a "functioning entity available for development" provided there was some quid pro quo, such as the release of political prisoners and welcoming an American ambassador to the Catholic confessional state known as Spain.[16]

Fourth, C.D. Jackson knew how to communicate and achieve goals effectively, and he taught others how to do so. C.D. regularly traveled the country giving talks to a variety of professional, veteran, business, and marketing associations, as well as to military academies and colleges both in the U.S. and overseas. During the course of these talks, he explained the dynamics of the Cold War, the operation of Luce's magazines, and much about psychological warfare and political warfare. "Communications is the supreme instrument," Jackson said.

Communications, in fact, "may control the destiny of the U.S."[17] Jackson then listed eight principles governing effective communications, as used by Time, Inc., and, by implication, the U.S. government. First, "The press can accelerate an idea that is already in the public's mind, but no press lord can impose his will upon the American people.... The press can plant an idea and if the idea takes hold it can then lead that idea along, but if it overplays its hand either in implanting the idea or leading it faster than it is able to go, it's a wasted effort. It doesn't work...."[18] Second, "We've always tried to tell the story in pictures. We've done it more or less well as the years have gone on. Now we're sort of giving it another great big push. The picture has its own validity. A great picture can tell a great story...."[19] Third, there is a correct way to deal with each audience or society. C.D. explained on the CBS program "Man of the Week" that the most effective communicating was to use the target audience's media of communication and not to scream at the targets. [20]

Electronic communications were especially effective because it broke up political alliances, especially amongst Catholics. "Electronic communications," Jackson said, "is one of the reasons why the relationship of the old politicos to the new desperate immigrant has changed. No longer is the immigrant desperate. His only friend in those days was the Irish ward-heeler." When it came to rebuilding the mass communications facilities in occupied countries after World War II, the motives were not idealistic: "We found that the best way to win support in recently liberated areas was to be of help in restoring the information services to these countries. This was not as generous or as idealistic as it appeared, because by clever handling of the help and the restoration of the information series, we were frequently able to be in control, or at least to have a strong vote position...."[21]

According to Jackson, each person who hears the message and acts on it is a sign of success. "How do we know that we are getting through?" he asked. "Success is measured by one person hearing something or reading something, and then acting on the basis of that knowledge, becoming a center of radiation.... The correct yardstick is – can you ascertain positive reactions on the part of the listening audience, and equally important – can you ascertain positive reaction on the part of the communist regimes and their propaganda regimes...."[22]

Building on these comments, Jackson claimed as his fifth point that the purpose of communication was to get people to think and act a certain way. "'Propaganda that does not aim at making people act and think according to a plan of operation is poor stuff.'" It was possible to "capture an audience and to get a fast reaction when needed."[23]

Sixth, psychological warfare was a fluid practice. In a letter to William E. Daugherty of the Operations Research Office, C.D. wrote, "It is terribly hard to teach psychological warfare by the book... 'circumstances constantly arise' – which call for immediate improvisation against the background of a directive which didn't say anything in the first place."[24]

Seventh, in getting results, one should avoid telling a lie – usually. C.D. wrote, "Falsity should only be permitted in the very rare exceptions of absolutely extreme necessity or absolute certainty of success."[25] The guiding principle, in other words, was expediency and success.

Eighth, psychological manipulation had limits. C.D. wrote in one letter, "I am absolutely certain, from experience and study, that psychological warfare can only accelerate or retard a trend. It can almost never initiate or arrest. Therefore, psychological warfare, or any technique thereof, has got to be considered within the content of all the other elements at work."[26]

"Words are important," said Jackson to the American Legion at its annual convention. "What we say does have an effect. But words which do not match deeds are not persuasive. Furthermore, they can be dangerous to our interests."[27] Coupled with this preference for the term "political warfare" over "psychological warfare" in describing the method he used to influence target audiences:

"The reason I am allergic to 'psychological warfare' is that the name has mysterious clinical overtones, and has led far too many people to think that psychological warriors, by the use of either mirrors or some black magic, are able to solve foreign policy problems all by themselves. As someone who has been pretty continuously in Psychological or Political Warfare for the past fifteen years, may I say categorically that there is *no such thing* as psychological warfare per se. There are only policies and acts of Government, which can then be picked up and interpreted and communicated to the appropriate audiences...."[28]

Finally, C.D. Jackson, like Luce, a member of the Anglo-American Protestant group that founded and now ruled America and who believed deeply in the American ideology that lay at the root of America, knew who the enemies they faced in the Cold War were. This was something Archibald MacLeish, a close friend of Luce, "friend and worshipper" of Felix Frankfurter according to Billings,[29] Librarian of Congress, former writer and editor at *Fortune* from 1930 to 1938, and intelligence operative responsible for the creation of the Research and Analysis Branch of the OSS, made clear when he wrote to Luce in the early Cold War years describing a:

"great conflict between the dream of a free society on the one side and the rival authoritarianisms of political Moscow and political Rome on the other I suddenly see and feel as John Knox (to compare small things with great) might have felt it the direct and logical and essential relationship between Protestantism and individualism, Protestantism and individual freedom, Protestantism and freedom. If this is what you mean – and I dare say it is – dare say because, again I know your own beliefs – then I say Amen. But Amen as a Protestant – as a man who believes in a God Who expects much from US – who demands that we should be ourselves and bear our responsibilities first. That there must be a new world built, and that it must be the world God wants built – Yes – a thousand times Yes. But that it must be the world a Church, a priesthood, tells us to build – well, that you cannot mean. For you too hold to the hard and brdensome [sic] faith that calls upon a man to decide in his soul...."[30]

14
AN ECONOMIC EXPLANATION OF THE COLD WAR

Professor Michael Hudson explains that the post-World War II international economic "system was designed by the United States" and used "laisse faire (at least abroad)" policies to "effect a concentric world economy revolving around the United States." Currency was important to this plan.[1] In 1944, the Bretton Woods agreement established the dollar as the world's reserve currency, thus giving American banks and the United States government global power over industry, the reconstructing economies of Europe, and third-world countries with developing economies. However, there was a "huge dollar shortage" in the world, and to remedy that so that the power of money could be exercised by the banking interests, the United States had to move from the status of a country with a trade surplus to one with a trade deficit.[2]

This required building up the economies of Europe and the third world, if not also those of the Soviet bloc. In order to do that, their infrastructure had to be rebuilt or built for the first time. That both required and caused an increase in consumption and consumer demand. That increase in consumption, to the levels deemed necessary by the American planners, required a fundamental change in those societies. That fundamental change meant an alteration of the principles upon which the society was based, which in turn would allow for the creation of an economic system similar to the American system. To effect this fundamental change, the American ideology was essential. Luce, C.D. Jackson, and many other Americans in business, the media, and the government understood the relation between a society's organizing principles and its economic system, something the American Founders understood as well. In other words, political economy mattered.

The Cold War was prosecuted to strengthen the wealth, power, and influence of America's private monied interests. Spreading the American ideology was essential to make that happen. Societies that did not sufficiently allow for American-style free enterprise were targeted for change. Societies based on principles, unlike the American ideology, were targeted as well. In both cases, the reason for targeting these societies was the restriction they placed on American power and control of American money by limiting, in some way, consumption, and wealth acquisition and by giving real power to civil authorities. The major ostensible target during the Cold War was Soviet Communism, which had a centrally managed state-run economy and lacked an interest-based system of consumer and business finance. However, another major target was Catholicism and Catholic societies because these systems limited so-called "free enterprise" and gave real power to the state to control the economy for the benefit of all members of society. Both systems, the Soviet and the Catholic were authoritarian and communitarian, not individualistic and "free." Both systems were organized on principles that viewed the person and wealth differently from the Americans. Therefore, both systems drew the ire of the Americans, as Archibald MacLeish's letter to Henry Luce so clearly showed.

THE AMERICAN BUSINESS ENTERPRISE, THE WORLD'S MODEL

A *Life* magazine editorial from 1944 made the connection between societal organizing principles and economics. In "Reconversion to What? It Used to be Called 'Capitalism' By Any Name Its Basis Is the Free Market," the author wrote that: "the connection between a free market and the other freedoms of democracy is more than symbolic; it is real. The freer the market, the freer every man's choice as to what he will work at as well as what he will buy. Economic decisions are decentralized, economic power is diffused, and this makes political liberties possible."[3]

In a Strictly Confidential memorandum to Billings, Luce revealed the inner dynamic of American life, explaining that there were two great themes to American life: The first, or "the American theme," is liberty or freedom, which he defined as the ability, "to make all the money you can and 'to do as you damn please with your own'." Included in this definition of freedom was "the sense of political philosophy, of the Declaration, of the Constitution, in the sense which educated men understand." Ultimately, though, "Freedom has many meanings and it is useful to remember them all in the American sense." Americans "loath tyranny and slavery – in every form, and publicly. And the Government of the United States will never be reconciled to any form of tyranny."[4]

The second theme of American life "is building.... This theme I have described as the 'sense of Project.'" It was this theme that "requires 'initiative' or 'leadership' (individualistic virtues) but also requires, implies, and abundantly evokes the sense of co-operation. Hence, the endless voluntary group-organizations of every sort, culminating currently in this amazing phenomenon of the American corporation...." This second great American theme led to "Our major over-all project, as stated by Truman and even more eloquently by Eisenhower, [which] is to improve the economies of the world... by appropriate Government policy and by private or non-Governmental efforts...." Ultimately, there must be a World Organization that "must at least resemble the Constitution of the United States" which would work for free world trade.[5]

Luce's plan tied constitutional governments with private investment. "We must proceed with vigor toward universal agreement on basic principles of politics – on human rights and on human obligations. The means by which this is done.... is the advancement of the rule of law." The U.S. "must encourage and promote constitutional governments... the visible sign of the acceptance of the rule of law within nations. . . .

we must use economic aid primarily to promote constitutional government. The further use of economic aid and of private investment is to create a system of economic order."[6]

Billings said something similar in a directive to the *Fortune* editorial department when he wrote that the mission of that magazine was to "assist in the successful development of American Business Enterprise at home and abroad." This "American Business Enterprise" was to be a model for the world and "an outstanding example of the deepest and most precious paradox of 'free societies.'"[7]

Luce's principles influenced the U.S. government, particularly the National Security Council, which adopted the idea that economics and social organizing doctrines are interrelated. The preamble of the formerly Top Secret NSC 5501 (later NSC 5602) stated:

"The spiritual, moral and material posture of the United States of America rests upon established principles which have been asserted and defended throughout the history of the Republic. The genius, strength and promise of America are founded in the dedication of its people and government to the dignity, equality and freedom of the human being under God. These concepts and our institutions which nourish and maintain them with justice are the bulwark of our free society, and are the basis of the respect and leadership which have been accorded our nation by the peoples of the world. When they are challenged, our response must be resolute and worthy of our heritage. From this premise must derive our national will and the policies which express it. The continuing full exercise of our individual and collective responsibilities is required to realize the basic objective of our national security policies: maintaining the security of the United States and the vitality of its fundamental values and institutions."[8]

The basic objective of national security policy during the Cold War was "to preserve the security of the United States, and the fundamental values and institutions,"[9] among which the American Business Enterprise had a place of prominence. America did not allow one without the other. Luce's statement about the primary American theme is identical to Amintore Fanfani's definition of the capitalist spirit: the desire for the unrestricted accumulation and enjoyment of wealth. This spirit destroyed spiritual values in a society and reordered societies to ensure and protect capitalism's one principle: "individual economic utility," which was the "ultimate end and principle of order." Societies like this "leave the maximum autonomy to the individual." Efficiency, financial cost, and the avoidance of financial risk determine what is "just and unjust, fitting and unfitting, normal and abnormal." Capitalism needs vast, unified markets, and that means the elimination of barriers and the stimulation of consumption. The Cold War, as opposed to a hot or shooting war, was necessary at this moment in history because it allowed a "certain stability" while it was being fought and because it did not interfere with trade.[10]

American economists confirmed Fanfani's observations. American capitalism is "an individualistic system" in which cultural and religious values are not primary. One of capitalism's primary principles is the preservation of private property. Another is freedom of enterprise and of choice. The third is competition with its associated "freedom of buyers and sellers to enter or leave particular markets." The fourth is the "basic coordinating mechanism of a capitalist economy is the market or price system." The market is an "elaborate communication system through which innumerable individual free choices are recorded, summarized, and balanced against one another." The fifth is the idea that societies must be ruled by limited government because the markets, individual choices, and the rest of the capitalist system will ensure efficiency. The sixth is the extensive use of capital goods. The final principles involve specialization and the use of money, which performs a variety of purposes. Money is viewed as debt in the American capitalist system, and debt is viewed as a good for the purpose of stimulating economic growth and for the efficient and proper functioning of the system.[11]

Two consequences flowed from the principles of American capitalism. First, the banks come to control businesses. As the cash flow requirements become greater, businesses grow more dependent on borrowing, leading the banks to push for mergers and consolidations to reduce the banks' risk on their various loans.[12] Second, consolidation in finance brought about the concentration of wealth, or, as one textbook explains, "the institutions of American capitalism are permissive of the concentration of economic power and the development of oligopoly and monopoly. The relatively free, individualistic economic environment of the economy is a fertile ground for the most efficient, the most courageous, the most fortunate, or the most crafty producer to conquer rivals in an effort to become free from the regulatory powers of competition. Freedom of contract, private property, and inheritance rights have also contributed to the concentration of economic power. And, too, the business cycle has probably abetted the tendency toward monopoly."[13] John Kenneth Galbraith said essentially the same thing in *American Capitalism.*[14]

THE CATHOLIC PROBLEM

Catholicism viewed economics and, hence, societal organization differently. Catholicism recognized that man has material needs which must satisfied, but they cannot be acquired by immoral means, nor can the amount acquired exceed the need. Failure to comply with these two important rules is an offense against God. St. Thomas Aquinas wrote that "the desire of wealth is unlawful if we seek it as an ultimate end, if we seek it with too great solicitude or if we fear that, by following conscience, we shall lack necessities." Therefore, morality determines a just wage, surplus wealth is provided for the needs of one's brother, and interest is condemned. All these principles are founded on a Catholic worldview which looks to the good of human souls. The intervention of the State is looked on favorably to protect and properly orient society in accordance with the moral code, and Catholicism eschews a society "organized on an individualistic basis."[15]

Spain was the example of a Catholic state that Americans like Luce detested most. On July 19, 1936, General Emilio Mola declared martial law in Pamplona, Spain, and General Francisco Franco mobilized the Spanish Army in Morocco to march on Madrid. The Nationalists, as these forces became known, were a full-fledged cultural counterrevolutionary force. They sought a revival of Catholicism on the public level and restoration of the values and traditions of Spain, which had "lost its path by following the principles of the French Revolution and liberalism."[16]

Franco's wartime government articulated a number of very important goals and principles when it claimed that "We came for the middle class and the humble class, not the wealthy." The Nationalists did not launch their counterrevolution against Communism to "defend capitalism" but to "save the national interest of Spain," and capitalists were warned to conform and provide financial contributions. As the war raged on, the Nationalists became more powerful and more Catholic. By Spring 1938, "obligatory religious instruction was restored in public schools, crucifixes mandatorily reinstalled in all classrooms, the validity of religious marriage emphasized, and plans announced for a new religiously inspired secondary school curriculum."

Divorce was formally abolished in September 1939, and in 1941, the State re-instituted the ecclesiastical subsidy that the Republic had canceled years earlier. An agreement with the Vatican gave the Spanish state the right to nominate persons for episcopal appointments, and the Vatican did nothing to discourage support for Franco. Beginning early in the 1940s, more seminaries were built, and the number of seminarians increased while mass evangelizations occurred throughout the country. Religion again became part of public life, and the "entire year was accompanied by some form of public religious manifestation." The Ministries of Justice and Education were reserved "for ultra-Catholics so that religious norms would be brought to bear on the legal and educational systems." The state's council for scientific research had as its stated goal the "necessary reestablishment of the basic Christian unity of the sciences, destroyed in the eighteenth century"; the law of university organization stated that its "supreme guide [would be] Christian dogma and morality and the authority of sacred canons with respect to teaching," and elementary education was brought in line with the doctrine of the Catholic Church. Catholic "religious advisory agencies" were established in the ministries and state institutions.[17]

In July 1945, the Fuero de los Espanoles was promulgated, starting a number of institutional changes, including article 33, which stated that "the exercise of the rights guaranteed in this Bill of Rights may not attack the spiritual, national, and social unity of the country." Prelates served on the Council of State and the Regency Council as well as in the Cortes. After the Catholic hierarchy was integrated into the senior advisory role in state leadership, Franco said, "The perfect state is for us the Catholic state. It does not suffice for us that a people be Christian in order to fulfill the moral precepts of this order: laws are necessary to maintain its principles and correct abuses." Franco saw to it the mechanisms were put in place for the "juridical enforcement of Church norms, enforcement of Catholic standards in family law and mores, and special juridical procedure and protection for clergy accused of violating civil law."[18]

Franco's view of economics was just as Catholic. In a June 1949 speech to workers, Franco endorsed state regulation of economic life when he said, "We reject capitalism as much as Marxism." Franco promoted the "theory of Catholic state corporatism whose goal was to harmonize class conflict and carry out Catholic social principles" by improving working conditions. Franco felt that economic liberalism was inherently linked to political and cultural liberalism and that reliance on foreign investment and international commerce inevitably opened the door "to subversive foreign political and religious influences." Franco felt that the "interest of the nation, the common good and the will of the Spanish people require above all a transformation of the capitalist system, acceleration of economic progress, a more just distribution of wealth, social justice, transformation and modernization of credit, and a modernization of many basic elements of production."[19]

THE REVOLUTION OF EXPECTATIONS

Spain and other Catholic countries posed a threat to the American System that was every bit as serious as the threat posed by the Soviet Union. In order to deal with this threat, the unity of the people had to be broken and Liberalism reintroduced. Time, Inc. accomplished this by praising the American Revolution. According to C.D. Jackson, the American Revolution of 1776 is "the only revolution that has really worked for the people. The world seems to want revolution. As the greatest revolution in history, let's maintain, explain, and give them the one that works – ours."[20]

America had become a global power, and its economy was "ready to expand into markets on every continent."[21] To keep the economy booming at home for an extended period, capitalism had to be expanded, and this required the reform of economic systems around the world.[22] In reality, the "question of foreign economic policy was not the containment of communism, but rather more directly the extension and expansion of American capitalism according to its new economic power and needs. Primarily, America was committed to inhibiting and redirecting other forces and pressures of change abroad in the world among non- even anti-, Soviet states. Russia and Eastern Europe were an aspect of this problem, but the rest of the world was yet more important even in 1946...."[23]

An important problem facing the Americans early in the Cold War was the stimulation of demand or consumption, especially in Europe. Without sufficient levels of demand, American business, and hence banking, could not move into those markets, and those societies would not become exporters using the dollar as their reserve currency. In August 1949, the "father of containment" and future Director of the State Department's think tank for foreign affairs, George Kennan, stated, "It is one thing to produce; it is another thing to sell."[24] Demand in these countries was low due to a variety of factors, including the imposition of austerity measures. In a memo dated May 11, 1949, Luce wrote that "radical steps must be taken to establish orderly freedom of economic life in Europe," and this included the "development of strong constitutional regimes [and] something in the way of economic unity...." Luce believed that "the economic problem will take care of itself if you can solve the political." That meant society had to be re-engineered to prize the individual and "freedom" like America. That is why, as Luce said, the "really serious economic problem in Europe... arises from the vast discrepancy between the American scale of production and distribution and the European." Luce recognized that the European colonies had to be pacified,[25] and that meant ending unauthorized violence that interfered with trade.

The initial emphasis on Europe gradually shifted "to the decolonizing periphery, where conditions demanded new, more subtle propaganda methods."[26] This meant going into Latin America and other Catholic countries, which meant coming to grips with Catholicism as a competing economic and political system, a topic discussed in NSC-68 in early 1950. Even though NSC-68 was issued ostensibly in response to Soviet challenges, it was also designed for offensive cultural, economic, and political action elsewhere.[27]

The Marshall Plan reconstructed and integrated European economies to encourage the flow of American capital by reducing barriers and creating new markets.[28] Like other initiatives, it was designed to replicate the American experiment by creating larger markets while using a common currency. This dynamic was imposed on Europe after World War II when the European governments were too weak to object.

Second, the creation of the European Common Market served to "eliminate tariffs...permit the free flow of labor, raw materials, and money... permit capital investment without restrictions on nationality – they would thereby create a free market almost equal in population to the United States. The stimulation to business thus created would be such that the economic stability of a large portion of Europe would be thus assured, and this pragmatic step of working together would be so visible to the man in the street that it could lead at some time in the future to some kind of political union." The creation of the Common Market manifested "the advantage of Freedom."[29] National barriers ceased to be important, and people could enjoy "complete freedom of movement" to engage in the enterprises of their choosing.

Third, the destruction of business as usual on the Continent took the form of "not perpetuating ancient continental feudal business cartels." This meant adopting "market principles," which would increase the size of markets and increase income or wealth.[30]

Fourth, the implementation of American principles would stimulate consumption and create a "revolution of expectations." In a now declassified speech given at the National War College, C D Jackson explained this phenomenon: "Interestingly, this revolution of expectations all over the world has been created as much by the United States as by the USSR.....this revolution of expectations which, in simplest terms, means that hundreds of millions of people all over the world no longer consider themselves or their children doomed forever to the misery and the toil of their forefathers...."[31]

This revolution of expectations would bring about "rising incomes and rising tastes, [so that] spending will become more discretionary, more governed by taste and choice. So specialization of choice begins – no need for uniformity. The uniformity of the '50s has been simply a reflection of the blue-collar workers becoming middle class. To the worker, this was an incredible increase in opportunity and choice. Once everyone has minimum appurtenances of middle-class life, there is no distinction in being like everyone else. So pressure will come to spend money differently, to express own personality .... [The] biggest population increase in the next 10 years will be in the teenage population. They require more."[32]

Luce, Jackson, and the rest of the American elites were looking for ways to break down barriers and create new markets. The plan Luce and his minions prepared to bring this about included targeting the Catholic Church to make it more American so the Church could be used to spread the American ideology and reorder societies, making them friendly to the spread of American capital and the American political economy.

PART V

MURRAY'S BASIC POSITION (JUNE 1948)

15
TWO CATHOLIC THEOLOGIANS

True to his pledge at the Biltmore Hotel on April 26, 1948, Murray went to work on changing the Catholic Church's teachings on church and state. One prominent opportunity he had to do so was the annual meeting, set for the end of June in Chicago, of the recently created Catholic Theological Society of America (CTSA). The CTSA was constituted for the purpose of helping the prelates and fostering "the spirit of fidelity" in the "minds and hearts of candidates for the priestly office" to the "message of God as made known by the Church of Christ."[1] It came into being in 1946 largely through the efforts of Fr. Francis J. Connell, C.Ss.R., an associate professor of moral theology at the Catholic University of America.

Born in Boston on January 31, 1888, to Timothy Connell and his wife Mary nee' Sheehan, Francis came into the world the same day that St. John Bosco died. He went to Sherwin Grammar School and Boston Latin School, and after that, took and passed entrance exams for Harvard but decided to study with the Jesuits at what is now Boston College because he did not "fancy spending his life in a classroom." However, in June 1907, he changed his mind and entered the Redemptorist novitiate. Connell made his perpetual profession in 1908, attended the Redemptorist seminary in Esopus, New York, from 1910 to 1913, and was ordained a priest on June 26, 1913. During his second novitiate at Annapolis, Maryland, from 1914-1915, Praefect Fr. Francis L. Kenzel, C.Ss.R. described Connell as having a "mild and amiable" temperament and being "fluent and logical" as well as exhibiting "great energy and ambition in his work" ironically exhibiting potential as "an excellent professor." It was later, in 1915, that Connell began lecturing as a professor in dogmatic theology at Esopus, thereby starting out his career as a theologian.[2]

From 1921 to 1923, Connell studied at the Angelicum in Rome, where he earned an S.T.D. in Theology. After returning to the Redemptorist headquarters in Brooklyn for one year, Connell joined the faculty at the Esopus Seminary for 16 years as a professor. In September 1940, he began teaching at the Catholic University of America. He served as an associate professor of moral theology, and Dean for Religious Communities as well as the Dean of the School of Sacred Theology until his retirement in 1958. After retiring, Connell remained a professor emeritus and advisor to a number of Church prelates.

Connell was a prolific writer and published a number of books to including *De Sacramentis Ecclesiae* (Vol. 1)(Brussels 1934); *Morals in Politics and Professions* (Westminster, Maryland, 1947); *Fr. Connell's Catechism*; *Confraternity Catechism* (Benziger, New York 1949); *The Seven Sacraments* (Paulist Press 1951), and hundreds of articles and pamphlets, not to mention the questions and answers section of the *American Ecclesiastical Review.* He was a regular radio speaker during the Catholic Hour, Church of the Air from 1930 onwards, and he was a founding member of the Mariological Society of America. Connell received numerous awards, including the Cardinal Spellman Award for theological writings in 1947 and 1954 and the pro Ecclesia et Pontifice medal in 1954. In 1956, he began work as a consultant to the Congregation of Seminarians and Universities. Over the course of his career, Connell was involved in the formation of seven thousand priests.[3]

Connell was the "spitting of image of St Francis de Sales," who was also his patron. The likeness was perhaps not so much physical as it was spiritual because Connell was always pleasant, an extreme gentleman, never grew angry, and was a man of prayer who "prayed a lot," in addition to saying daily mass and a daily rosary. His one vice was his love of ice cream, which caused him to develop diabetes. He also enjoyed croquet, which he termed a "science," and played with regularity. The diabetes caused Connell to be very circumspect when it came to his diet, and so he disciplined himself not to eat candy or drink soda, though, according to his doctor, that did not prevent him from having an occasional shot of Scotch as he grew older. Connell was a tennis player and a daily swimmer, too, and he would enjoy a good game of pool with the seminarians and other Redemptorists.[4]

Connell invariably asked for the opinions of others, especially those of young Redemptorists, about various topics. This he often did as they walked along train tracks to West End and dinner. He typed his papers and speeches himself using two fingers and would often work until 10 p.m. at which time he would carry on telephone discussions with various priests or laymen, who called him to ask for advice or assistance on matters. Connell's work was not just as a theologian, but also he helped in local parishes every weekend "like an ordinary Redemptorist," whether he was in Washington DC or New York and Atlantic City.[5]

A great friend of Patrick O'Boyle, who was elevated to the post of Archbishop of Washington, DC, in 1947, Connell shared the money O'Boyle gave him for his vacations, as well as his time and wisdom, with students, fellow priests, and the bishops who would consult with him, whose identity he would never reveal, just as he would never reveal the identity of anyone who would consult with him. As he penned his numerous articles and books, Connell honored confidentiality and upheld the dignity of the office without any attempt to cause personal animosities.[6]

Humility marked this man, though he exhibited a little vanity about his hair. Connell wrote to present the truth as he knew it and not to prove himself right. He loved the Church and its teachings, and so he taught what the Church taught without inserting his own views into the matter and without trying to be "a pioneer" in church teachings or in developing doctrine. In spite of his humility (or perhaps because of it), Connell was not afraid to weigh in on controversial topics, including the immorality of the use of the Atomic Bomb by the Americans in 1945 on

Japan, as well as the immorality of prize-fighting, which was gaining in popularity at the time. Connell was in demand, and so he traveled to give many talks. His pastoral approach was practical and brought parishioners closer to Christ. "He gave priests something to use," said one of his confreres, and that included a set of common-sense questions and answers and a list of books to help the faithful draw closer to Christ and His Church.[7]

Connell created the CTSA to keep Catholic doctrine pure and to serve the bishops by explaining various topics. Connell and other priests saw early on the dangerous impact of American war propaganda on young Catholics returning from World War II who held a "neo-democratic" worldview and saw the Catholic Church as incompatible with the American way of life. The CTSA mobilized to address these and similar issues in response to requests by Catholic prelates, most notably Archbishop Richard Cushing of Boston. Despite a good beginning, the CTSA soon started to drift away from the guiding principles Connell set out at his inaugural talk as its first president. By late 1947, things were beginning to change as the organization took on a life of its own, addressing topics that were being suggested neither by the *ecclesia docens* nor in response to their needs but out of the desires of the theologians.

Connell somehow obtained a copy of the unpublished report of the secret meeting at the Biltmore in April 1948. He drew attention to the secret nature of that meeting with a circle, a line, and the initials "N.B." By the time the information about Murray's participation at the Biltmore conference crossed his desk, Frankie as he became known to his confreres,[8] was the most distinguished Catholic theologian in the United States during the 20th century. He was, in effect, the Catholic Theologian of America.[9] In one of the great ironies of recent Catholic history, Connell presented Murray's paper, "The Government Repression of Heresy," at the third annual CTSA convention held in Chicago at the end of June 1948 because the latter had become ill. That paper set out Murray's basic position on church and state and religious liberty, a position which never changed during the course of the dispute between Connell, Murray, and others, which lasted until the promulgation of *Dignitatis Humanae* at the Second Vatican Council.

According to Murray, the state need only base its actions on the natural law, a view Murray first articulated in the intercredal discussion at the Biltmore, but in that discussion, he at least recognized the pre-eminence of the Divine Positive Law. To Murray, the American system of church and state and the American view of religious liberty comported with the natural law because it ensured societal peace and was therefore acceptable to Catholic doctrine as being good in principle.

Murray's paper was, in reality, a refutation of Catholic doctrine, which Monsignor John Ryan articulated a quarter century earlier and Connell re-iterated. Ryan caused great concern among the Protestants and the NCCJ, as well as among the American elites. His writings threatened to upset the control that the monied elites exerted over an increasingly secular American society. Connell, writing at a time when criticism of America was more dangerous than ever, insisted that Catholics had to preach the Gospel to all nations, including America, and he reminded all of the duty of the civil authorities to recognize Christ the King.

During this same period, Monsignor Joseph Clifford Fenton, the editor of the Catholic theological journal *American Ecclesiastical Review* and Connell's ally, began disputing *Time's* accounts of the state of the Catholic Church and Catholic doctrine. Known as a humorous man with a strong will,[10] Fenton came into the world on January 16, 1906, in Springfield, Massachusetts, as the son of Michael Francis Fenton and Elizabeth nee' Clifford. After graduating from Holy Cross College in Worcester in 1926, Fenton obtained JCB, STB, and STL degrees from the University of Montreal in 1930. [11]

After his ordination in 1930, Fenton worked as a parish priest for five years, which duties did not prevent him from earning an STD in 1931 from the Angelicum in Rome, a degree which helped him to become a professor first at St. Ambrose College in Davenport, Iowa. He then became a special professor of dogmatic theology at St. Bernard's Seminary in Rochester, New York, and finally, a professor at the Catholic University of America starting in 1938 and continuing until 1963 when he became a pastor at St. Patrick's Church in Chicopee Falls, Massachusetts.[12]

Fenton became a priest because of his "personal devotion to Jesus Christ." He "loved the idea of being...an instrument of God for the salvation of souls." He loved the Holy Mother Church and believed that if people obeyed her and gave "priority to God's plan for salvation pursuing eternal goods" and "if they would follow God's unchanging truth instead of private lights," there would be no confusion, and souls could be saved. Indeed, as Fr. Edward F. Hanahoe, a former pupil of Fenton, said in his eulogy, "The Church was central in the thoughts of Monsignor Fenton" because the Church contained the "deposit of divine truth under the direction and guidance of the Holy Spirit." Fenton did not question, critique, or judge the church, but instead, he "served her lovingly" as "God's vehicle of salvation for all men."[13]

Fenton was highly decorated, and his efforts were repeatedly recognized by the Vatican. He was the counselor for the Sacred Congregation of Seminaries and Universities from 1950 to 1967, as well as the International Pontifical Marian Academy. Appointed a papal chamberlain in 1951, he helped to found the Catholic Theological Society of America in 1946 as well as the Mariological Society in 1949. He was made a domestic prelate in 1954, received the Papal medal, Pro Ecclesia et Pontifice in 1954, and in 1963, he was named a prothonotary apostolic. In 1957, Fenton was the first American to be appointed a member of the Pontifical Roman Theological Academy, and two years later, he was appointed by Pope John XXIII to serve on the Pontifical Theological Commission for the Preparation for the Second Vatican Ecumenical Council, at which he served as a *peritus* for all four sessions. Fenton wrote numerous articles and six books, and perhaps most notably for our discussion, he became editor of the *American Ecclesiastical Review* in 1944 and remained in that position until 1963. It was during his tenure as editor that the great Church and State between Murray and Connell began and continued with some ferocity until it found its grand climax when Vatican II issued *Dignitatis Humanae.*[14]

In his replies to Murray, Fenton noted the power and influence of *Time* and the effectiveness of its writing style. Fenton, like Murray, wrote that Pius IX condemned the Liberalism of Europe. Fenton also explained the relevance of Leo XIII's writings to America. Fenton claimed that the encyclical *Longinqua Oceani* taught that America was not the ideal model for church and state relations in spite of the fact that World War II had recently ended with the Americans as clear victors and in spite of the American propaganda that portrayed it as the last great hope for humanity.

Connell, Fenton, and Murray were the main actors in the Church-State debate in the United States during the 1940s and beyond. The differences in temperament were stark. Connell was a pleasant gentleman, and Fenton had an intense personality and could be irascible on occasion. In one instance, after receiving a letter from a Benedictine monk criticizing one of his articles, Fenton wrote back chastising the man for writing such a nasty note in the first communication. According to Robert Blair Kaiser, *Time*'s correspondent in Rome during Vatican II, Murray was unlike either Fenton or Connell. Kaiser described Murray as an arrogant man who grew jealous of Kaiser when Kaiser's book on the Council stole Murray's thunder, and Kaiser became the main object of the "conservatives'" ire. Murray, according to Kaiser, "was as tall as Andy Heiskell, Time, Inc.'s board chairman, carried himself like General Douglas MacArthur, and spoke with a deep, upper class New York honk. He had a tendency not to converse so much as orate, like an up-to-date reincarnation of St. Robert Bellarmine, as played by Sir John Gielgud."[15] After Kaiser's book came out, Murray was nonplussed by the shift of attention away from him to Kaiser. Murray, a proud man, saw "himself as someone above the rest of us." Kaiser was a former Jesuit seminarian, and another former Jesuit seminarian said that the culture of the Jesuits in the 1950s pandered to mamma's boys and politicians. Jesuits, this former seminarian said, "learn the art of manipulation of language, ideas, and people. That's what went wrong."[16]

16

THE CATHOLICS RESPOND

Connell sparred with Murray over intercredal cooperation in the pages of *American Ecclesiastical Review,* which Fenton edited and called by its initials, *AER*. In the same journal, Fenton and Connell took issue with *Time*'s twisting of Catholic doctrine and facts. Fenton acknowledged *Time*'s articles were "well-written" and "widely read," and he even conceded that *Time's* February 1946 article about the consistory was "manifestly favorable to the Catholic Church." *Time,* he continued, was "famed for both skilled writing and colossal distribution," but the article in question contained "several inaccurate statements about the Church's history and its present-day activity in this country." Fenton gave the editors the benefit of the doubt and ascribed the inaccuracies to the fact that "*Time,* like most news magazines, is inclined to paint with a wide brush. No one expects to find on its pages the scrupulous exactitude of a Duchesne, a Batiffol, or a Guilday."[1]

Fenton explained that while "men might be more favorably disposed towards the Church precisely by reason of the error[s]" contained in *Time*, it was still an error to state that the *ecclesia docens* did not follow the teaching of Leo XIII. *Time,* furthermore, committed a sin of omission by failing to inform its readers that the same pope condemned the relationship between Church and State in the U.S. Fenton concluded his piece by emphasizing the fact that "it is incorrect to charge the men of the apostolic college in our own country with failing to teach the truth which has been set forth by the successor of the prince of the apostles." Both the theologians and the bishops taught the "doctrine of Pope Leo on man's individual and social religious duties," and the theologians, in so doing, were acting as agents of the hierarchy.[2]

One of society's duties was to profess the Faith. That profession relates to the "place of man in civil and economic society" and requires the Faith to inform the policies of the State. The bulk of Fenton's article addressed the relationship between the Church and the state, as the term "separation of Church and State" was used in the *Time* article. Fenton denied the claim that Leo condemned the American system in *Longinqua Oceani.* However, Leo taught that the American system "did not represent the absolute ideal" and "could not be duplicated laudably in every country on earth." In those societies where there had been "a corporate profession of the Catholic faith," a move to make the Church-State relation the same as in the U.S. "would be nothing more or less than a hostile move against the government and the principles of the Church." [3] The popes clearly denounced this possibility. Because the goal and desire of the Church was always to bring everyone into the Church, the State should "not adopt an attitude of mere neutrality towards the Church," which is antithetical to the Church's "burning love for souls." Because the confessional state, and not the separation of Church and State, "renders this condition the best....It is the condition the Church works to achieve."[4]

Libertas condemned two versions of separation of Church and State, but neither of these, according to Fenton, corresponded to the American model. In the first instance, the state ignored the Catholic Church, and the Faith had no influence on governmental policies (i.e., "the State absolutely ignores the Church"). In the second instance, the state controlled the Church's internal affairs by the State (i.e., "subjects the Church to itself"). According to both *Immortale Dei* and *Mirari Vos,* those "who desire that the Church be separated from the State, and the concord between the secular and ecclesiastical authority be dissolved....live in dread of an agreement which has always been fraught with good, and advantageous alike to sacred and civil interests.'" The American system recognized the existence of religions but sought neither to rule nor to ignore them. The term "separation of Church and State" was used to keep church schools from receiving funding and a sort of integration into society at large and was not at all in keeping with the original intent of the American experiment.[5]

As the year wore on, Fenton grew more critical of *Time*'s presentation of Catholic doctrine, but he did not attribute nefarious purposes to its editorial policies. In July, *Time* published an analysis of the Catholic Church's view on church and state, as put forth in an article that appeared in the August 1946 edition of the *Christian Herald* and concluded that the Catholic Church was at odds with America:

"What is the position of the Roman Catholic Church toward other creeds? '...The very existence of any other church is opposed to the command of Christ that all men should join His one Church...' Does each American have the right to choose his religion? 'The mere fact that a person sincerely believes a certain religion to be true, gives him no genuine right to accept that religion in opposition to God's command...' Does the Roman Catholic Church ever tolerate other religions?'...Pope Leo XIII explained this point tersely when...he wrote: 'The Church indeed deems it unlawful to place the various forms of divine worship on the same footing... but does not on that account condemn those rulers who, for the sake of securing some great good or of hindering some great evil patiently allow custom or usage to be a kind of sanction for each form of religion having its place in the state.' What is the attitude of the Catholic Church in non-Catholic countries? 'In a country like the United States, where the religious affiliations of the citizens are so numerous and so diverse...complete equality for all religions is undoubtedly the most commendable policy....'" [6]

Time revealed that the Catholic responses came from a pamphlet entitled "Freedom of Worship" with Cardinal Spellman's imprimatur.[7] It was a masterful stroke designed to inflame Protestants against Catholics while further dividing Catholics and putting them on the defensive.

Fenton began his critique of the *Time* article by observing that the *Christian Herald*, as well as *Time*, presented Catholics as a threat to the First Amendment should they ever get enough power. Such an event would be against Protestant beliefs, which gave the Catholics this freedom and set up the Constitution.[8] Fenton knew the "write-up of this article in *Time*" was "[f]ar more important and dangerous" than anything contained in the *Christian Herald*, which was quoted by *Time*. The reason for this concern was twofold: *Time* had a large circulation, and it had been giving "every appearance of trying to be fair in dealing with the Catholic Church." The *Christian Herald* article contained a number of attacks on Catholic leaders such as Spellman and Clare Boothe Luce, as well as applause for an anti-Catholic "leader of the year." The article demanded the recall of Myron Taylor. All of this was after the editors professed their intent to preach and practice "tolerance" between Catholics and Protestants over the years.[9]

Time used "quotations....even more misleading than those of the magazine [from the *Christian Herald*] from which they are borrowed." *Time* asked the question: "Does each American have the right to choose his religion?" It then selectively quoted from Connell's pamphlet: "The mere fact that a person sincerely believes a certain religion to be true gives him no genuine right to accept that religion in opposition to God's command...." So, *Time* concluded that "Catholicism does not support the first article of the American Bill of Rights 'in principle.'" Fenton believed that this "regrettable confusion" was committed "apparently in good faith."[10]

Fenton explained Catholicism holds that forced conversions are unacceptable. He wrote, "[N]o man may be persecuted because of his religious beliefs." America's Founding Fathers were reacting against an established religion like the Anglican Church in England and wanted to ensure the same thing did not develop in America, especially on the national level.[11] They were not directing their efforts against Catholics because Catholicism was not an established religion in any of the colonies or states.

Fenton explained that each American "has the civil right to choose his religion," which is protected by the Free Exercise Clause, and that the

Catholic Church will not frustrate such exercise of choice. As Cardinal Manning declared in the Nineteenth Century, if "Catholics were in power tomorrow in England, not a penal law would be proposed, nor the shadow of constraint be put upon the faith of any man." Every American has the "civil right to choose a religion forbidden by God" as the "civil law makes no attempt to enforce the divine precept," which under Catholic teaching is "perfectly right and proper." However, it "is objectively and morally wrong for any American... for any human being, to disregard or to disobey a command issued by God" when it is directed to all men and brought to mankind's attention. There is a moral obligation to worship God in accordance with the Catholic Faith both in an individual and societal, or corporate, manner.[12]

Rome needed to be warned about the power of *Time* and the American media. The main problem, as Fenton explained in a letter to Msgr. Cecchetti, a member of the Curia, lay with the Catholic press in the United States, which increasingly took its cue from the powerful American press. "For your information," Fenton continued, "The great secular news-magazine 'Time,' with its millions of readers, asserted in one of its 1945 issues that the encyclicals of Pope Leo were never actually received and taught by Catholics in the United States. We took the trouble to correct that statement by an article in the Review. Now we find the same charge, coming this time from a Catholic source."[13]

THE CATHOLIC THEOLOGICAL SOCIETY OF AMERICA (CTSA)

The CTSA was a response by the Catholics to growing concerns over the purity of doctrine and the effects of American psychological manipulation from the war. After being elected the CTSA's first president, Connell told the participants at the Inaugural meeting on June 25, 1946, that CTSA's theologians were to provide "assistance...to the official teachers of the Church," when the bishops, or *ecclesia docens,* asked for it.[14] Theology, Connell continued, was the "keystone of all wisdom" because it was a "science based on divine revelation" that gives "light and direction" to the theologians. Because this science has "definitely practical bearings on everyday life," theologians must "do our part toward applying the truths with which we are familiar to the needs of the afflicted world." In doing so, theologians "must emphasize that there is only one true and authorized proponent of the message of divine revelation, the Catholic Church."[15]

About six months later, the CTSA's Committee on Current Problems met in Room 215 of Curley Hall at the Catholic University of America to draw up a list of important issues. After three hours of deliberation, the committee, led by Msgr. Edward Murray of St. John's Seminary in Brighton, Massachusetts, came up with six topics, one of which was entitled "An Authoritative Church in a Democracy."[16] The Secretary of the committee, Fr. Edmond D. Benard, explained this topic in a letter to Connell: "What Archbishop Cushing described in a letter to Msgr. Murray as the 'neo-democratic mentality of returning servicemen and the University-age generation generally' poses a challenge to Catholic apologists. It demands a careful restatement of the position that the Catholic Church can and must fill in a democratic society; and an answer to those opponents of the Church who attempt to portray it as 'incompatible with the American way of life' and 'contrary to the spirit of tolerance and the intellectual liberty of free Americans.'"[17] Commenting on another issue on the list, "The Problem of Catholic Action in the United States." Benard observed:

"There is still a great deal of confusion among American Catholics, priests and laity, concerning the forms of Catholic Action best adapted to conditions in this country, and even concerning the nature of Catholic Action. This is intensified by the fact that the classic works on the subject are of European origin and seem to be predicated on a set of enviormental [sic] circumstances and on a national mentality different from our own. Would it be possible to present a treatment of Catholic Action particularly understandable to Americans, and of a practical bent based upon the peculian [sic] problems of the American mentality and milieu?"[18]

At the CTSA's annual meeting held June 30 through July 2, 1947, at St. John's Seminary in Massachusetts, Murray presented a paper entitled "An Authoritative Church in a Democracy."[19] Murray was gaining credibility amongst Catholic theologians and the hierarchy due to his work on intercredal cooperation, religious liberty, and the relationship between church and state, all of which he saw as interrelated.[20] He also consulted with the National Catholic Welfare Council (NCWC) concerning an *amicus curiae* brief in the *Everson* case, which the United States Supreme Court decided in early 1947.

Connell spoke at the same meeting on the American rejection of theology as a true science. He blamed this on "our American emphasis on what is called practical values—which often are identified with benefits of the material order." Connell also recognized the same thing Luce and Waugh recognized – America had become ascendant in the world. Connell learned "by personal observation" during a two-month stay in Europe "how much the world depends on America at the present time. This must not be understood merely in the sense that the nations of Europe look to the United States for material resources.... We must realize that today the world looks to America for leadership in scientific matters, and that includes theology." Connell encouraged American theologians not to assume "an inferiority complex" but to take advantage of opportunities to conduct theological research, and "particularly freedom of expression," emphasizing that "We must not...yield to the mistaken notion that only Europe can produce theologians of the first rank."[21]

If there were one area in which American theologians had the potential to become theologians of first rank, it was in the area of church and state relations. In a letter dated December 16, 1947, Fr. Eugene Burke, the Secretary of the CTSA, wrote to the CTSA's president, Msgr. James O'Connell explained to the Committee on Current Problems, "problems of current importance to theology" that "ought to be placed before the members of the Society as subjects for discussion." One was "the Distinction of Church and State in the United States":

"The importance of the problem is quite obvious to the Church. It offers a constant problem not only for priests but for Catholic writers and teachers on all levels. The Committee was of the mind that it might best be treated in the following form: 1. The historical facts concerning this distinction. a. Constitutional provision and interpretation. b. The actual application of the provision in this county [sic]. 2. What are the speculative theological principles that should govern our evaluation of these facts. 3. What is the practical judgment to be made in the light of the principles and facts."[22]

Shortly thereafter, Murray reached out to Connell "to illustrate what you already know – the need of a thorough discussion of the Catholic position, in its historical evolution, in its present form, and in its possible future development. There is also the apologetic problem to call it that."[23]

Thus, the stage was set for Murray to do his work affirming America's principles of organization as compliant with Catholic doctrine.

17
"THE GOVERNMENTAL REPRESSION OF HERESY"

In the paper he delivered at the CTSA conference in 1948, Murray took aim at the writings of Msgr. John Ryan (1869-1945), a priest who had close contact with the Roosevelt administration and commanded enormous respect and influence with both Catholics and Americans. About a quarter century before the Biltmore meeting, Ryan wrote *The State and the Church,* a book that held a Nihil Obstat and an Imprimatur of Archbishop Patrick Hayes of New York, the predecessor of Cardinal Spellman, and set forth the Catholic doctrine on church and state that the Americans wanted to change.

In a chapter discussing Pope Leo XIII's *Immortale Dei,* Ryan provided an understandable and coherent explanation of key portions of this important encyclical. He began with the position that "civil laws, are, generally speaking, binding in conscience, for the simple reason that they proceed from functionaries who hold power from God, 'the Sovereign Ruler of all.' Since only God has the authority to impose moral obligation upon human beings, political rulers can enact morally obligatory ordinances only because their authority is derived from Him." The State must take an attitude towards religion. That attitude will either be an affirmative one or one of "impartial indifference." The affirmative position is either one of support or of opposition. He concluded the Federal and State governments in the United States had shown "positive friendliness towards religion" as manifested in institutions like the annual day of thanksgiving, provisioning chaplains for the armed forces, and making use of public buildings for religious matters. While it was "feeble, and inconspicuous," this was still a public profession of religion. This recognition, however, was distinct from the recognition of the true religion, which the Catholic faith demanded.[1]

"Specious neutrality" of the state towards religion was always a "policy of hostility," according to Ryan, who claimed that "Pope Leo...declares that the State must not only 'have care for religion', but recognize the *true* religion.... It is a thoroughly logical position. If the State is under moral compulsion to profess and promote religion, it is obviously obliged to profess and promote only the religion that is true...." Connected to this was the belief that: "no individual, no group of individuals, no society, no State is justified in supporting error or in according to error the same recognition as to truth."[2]

Ryan discredited the various objections to State support and promotion of Catholicism. The first error was held by those who believed "truth will by its own power speedily overcome error, and that the state should consequently assume an attitude of impartiality toward both." The second was the belief "that all forms of religion are equally good and true." The third was "that it is impossible to know which is the true" religion. Ryan explained the first is contradicted by the "persistence of a hundred errors side by side with truth for centuries." Truth could prevail over "the long run and with sufficient enlightenment...but its victory can be greatly hastened by judicious assistance from the State and, indeed, from every other kind of organized social power." The Church's victories over the rebellious Protestants during the Sixteenth and the Seventeenth Centuries were examples of state support for the true religion.[3]

To refute the second objection, Ryan explained, "It is sufficient to cite the principle of contradictions; two contradictory propositions cannot be true, any more than yes can be identified with no." The varying religious sects all contradict each other at some point, so they cannot all be valid for the obvious reason that contradictions cannot be true.[4] The third objection was erroneous because the "Church of Christ comes before men with credentials sufficient to convince all those who will deliberately examine the evidence with a will to believe." Leo XIII set forth the proofs, which are "the fulfillment of prophecies; miracles in great number; the rapid spread of the faith in the midst of enemies and in face of overwhelming obstacles; the witness of the martyrs, and the like."[5]

The conclusion was clear: the State – whether of a Catholic country or not—has an obligation under Catholic doctrine to "officially recognize the Catholic religion as the religion of the commonwealth." The State should "invite the blessing and the ceremonial participation of the Church for certain important public functions.... it should recognize and sanction the laws of the Church; and it should protect the rights of the Church, and the religious as well as the other rights of the Church's members." In Catholic states, that is those societies and political communities in which the citizens are adherents to Catholicism, and the government protects and favors the Church, the "normal relation is that of formal agreement and mutual support" which is also known as "union of Church and State." This "Union of Church and State" presents itself differently depending on whether the State or society is Catholic. Ryan distinguished between Catholic states, which supported the Church, and non-Catholic states, which still had an affirmative obligation to recognize Catholicism as the national religion, officially engage in Catholic religious activities and practices, and protect the rights of the Church and faithful.[6]

In the case of Catholic states, there is a formal agreement and mutual support union of Church and State exists. The detractors putting forth arguments against this arrangement, Ryan wrote, must be ignored because their arguments are based upon the "fallacy of the particular instance." After finding "some forms of union between Church and State working badly in some countries for certain periods of time," the detractors then "rush to the conclusion that all forms are bad, at all times, in all countries." The principle remained inviolate, and all that particular instances may show is that the principle of union between Church and State is "not necessarily dependent upon *any particular form of union that has actually been in operation."* Of course, the Middle Ages is generally cited as an example of the failure of the principle of the union of Church and State, wrote Ryan, but he refuted this claim by citing the noted German priest Fr. Joseph Pohle (1852-1922), who wrote: "'The intimate connection of both powers during the Middle Ages was only a passing and temporary phenomenon, arising neither from the essential nature of the State nor from that of the Church." The evils that arose were "excessive meddling by ecclesiastical authorities in political affairs, conflicts between the two powers which produced diminished popular respect for both" and the rise of religious hypocrisy and pietism amongst the laity as well as "spiritual torpor" amongst the clerics.[7]

Ryan emphasized that "supreme and independent authority in the spiritual realm cannot be exercised adequately unless it is recognized by the rulers of States." The Middle Ages provided numerous examples of how this authority was recognized and protected. The Papal States were a prime example of how "this independence and freedom of action were for a long time safeguarded through the Church's possession and exercise of civil sovereignty." While Pope Leo was not arguing for Church control or power over territory, he was holding forth the principle that the Church needed freedom to exercise her "spiritual and moral mission." Another way for this to happen was "adequate international recognition and guarantees."[8]

Finally, Ryan wrote the "Church is not inferior to the civil power" for the simple and logical reason that "the spiritual and eternal interests of men are certainly more important than their material and temporal interests." According to Ryan, the perennial Catholic position claimed that "the State, as well as the individual, is governed and limited by the natural law, that is by the moral law which we know by the light of reason." However, in addition to the natural law, "the State should be conformed to the law of Christian revelation, of which the guardian and interpreter is the Catholic Church."[9]

If the State acted in accordance with Catholicism, where did that put other religions in the society? Ryan met the question head-on when he asked, "Does State recognition of the Catholic religion necessarily imply that no other religion should be tolerated? Much depends upon circumstances, and much depends upon what is meant by toleration." He then proceeded to explain that one should not use physical compulsion (equated with coercion) in bringing people into the Catholic Faith. Religious practices not contrary to the natural law (e.g., "idolatry, human sacrifice, and debauchery") could be allowed and did not "necessarily imply a willful affront to the true Church nor a menace to public order or social welfare." But it was a different matter when the propagation of false doctrine amongst Catholics was involved because this is a "positive menace, to the religious welfare of true believers" and can be suppressed. This is because it is not a natural right of the propagandists if their propaganda is "harmful to the citizens and contrary to public welfare." Since rights are "merely means to rational ends," and these rational ends pertain to the human person spending eternity with God, then "no rational end is promoted by the dissemination of false doctrine," notwithstanding the argument that each person should be allowed to do what he thinks is right.[10]

Opposition to the Catholic position came from the "superficial champions of religious liberty" who denounced the position "as the essence of intolerance." Ryan explained that "error has not the same rights as truth" because the "profession and practice of error are contrary to human welfare." Therefore, if "there is only one true religion, and if its possession is the most important good in life for States as well as individuals then the public profession protection, and promotion of this religion and the legal prohibition of all direct assaults upon it, becomes one of the most obvious and fundamental duties of the State. For it is the business of the State to safeguard and promote human welfare in all departments of life." The only way error is voluntarily tolerated is by those who claim all religions are equally true or the true religion cannot be distinguished from the false.[11]

Toleration of religious sects may be allowed in certain situations, such as if, for example, various churches have already established themselves, and it is a matter of expediency to permit toleration of all sects. It may be allowed where religious liberty is made a part of the constitutions in the modern state. Referring again to Pohle, Ryan mentioned that such constitutions are binding in conscience, but these constitutions could be changed when non-Catholic sects decline. In that event, general propaganda could not be allowed to continue, and the non-Catholic sects could not be allowed to keep certain privileges that were formerly extended (e.g., tax exemption). However, Ryan said this was a remote possibility and that people should not concern themselves with this, though "some zealots and bigots will continue to attack the Church because they fear that... the United States may become overwhelmingly Catholic and may then restrict the freedom of non-Catholic denominations." Ryan concluded: "we cannot yield up the principles of eternal and unchangeable truth in order to avoid the enmity of such unreasonable persons.... they would not think us sincere. Therefore, we shall continue to profess the true principles of the relations between Church and State...."[12]

Ryan explained what would happen when Catholics took power in societies like America and, in doing so, predicted the Protestant and American attack against the Church that came in the 1940s. The proper Catholic response to these attacks was to maintain sincerity and speak truth to power. The Americans had no intention of letting Catholics come into power, so someone had to come up with a new position more amenable to those in power. That was John Courtney Murray and The American Proposition.

MURRAY'S PAPER DELIVERED IN CHICAGO

By the time of the CTSA's third annual meeting in Chicago in late June 1948, Murray had taken ill. Ironically, Francis Connell, the man who opposed Murray in the arena of intercredal cooperation and who was to be his biggest opponent in matters of church and state, was the man who presented Murray's paper. Entitled "Governmental Repression of Heresy," Murray's paper narrowly defined the issue as whether Catholic dogma or doctrine required Catholic states to suppress heresy or heterodox opinions. His conclusion, based on what he admitted was only "sketching a theory" that required more research, was in the negative. He concluded there was no duty or dogma or doctrine that required Catholic states to repress heresy, with one exception. That was if Franco's Span demonstrated Protestant religious freedom was a way by "which the allied forces inundated the helpless Spanish people with all the evils in the Anglo-Saxon world." [13]

Murray's paper did several things. First, he set the terms of the debate in such a way as to benefit the American view of social organization. The issue became the role of government at a time when authoritarianism was discredited. Second, he redefined the role of a theologian as being someone who gave meaning to papal pronouncements. The Church's real teachers now were the theologians because the theologian formulated the "principles" in papal pronouncements "in such terms that they may be asserted as constantly valid, and their organization into a coherent system that will cover all contingencies because it is dependent on none."[14] The theologian became an historian:

"All the theories of Church-state relationships cast up in the past were influenced by the facts of the problem as those facts existed at the time.... Political rulers acted, Popes acted; and then came the theologians – often politically partisan in their sympathies – to think out a theory. But their theories inevitably reflected the relativities of the time-conditioned problem that prompted the action.... [T]he Popes acted on principle, derived from faith and reason; however they always had to act, as it were, in an 'impure' context; to solve a concrete problem. Consequently, the principles motivating their action transpired through a mixed medium to the reflective theological intelligence. Consequently, too, the theories of theologians reflect both permanent principles and also the facts of a given epoch..... One must therefore consult history in this whole matter; apart from such consultation no perspective, no exact formulation of the doctrine of the Church universal in time and space, are possible. One must consequently argue from what Popes did as well as from what they said and understand what they said in the light of what they did.... Finally, all the facts of the past and all the actions of the papacy can be given their true meaning only in the light of the particular historical situation which the papacy happened to occupy, not only in relation to the civil power but more especially in relation to the whole of society at the time."[15]

As John Lamont pointed out years later, Murray ignored the fact that circumstances are under the control of Divine Providence, and "God uses this control to bring about specific contingent historical circumstances to enable the Church to arrive at and proclaim the truth."[16] Murray made clear his intentions to Clare Boothe Luce when he wrote: "Clare dear: The point of this historical argument is to show that, as the institution of the state-church owed its genesis to the special structure of an historic-social situation, so also it depends for its justification on the peculiarities of this situation. Alter the situation, and the argument for the institution is undermined...How's that?"[17]

Third, Murray, in distilling essential principles governing the relations between the Church and the State, claimed that since government was a product of the natural realm, its norm of action was the natural law. Its duty was, therefore, to ensure the freedom and the autonomy of both the Church and the state, not the dependence of the latter on the former. In answering the question, "Who had the final say?" Murray briefly examined the theory of direct power as set forth by Hugh St. Victor (1096-1141) and two theories of indirect power, one by St. Robert Bellarmine (1542-1621) and the other by John of Paris (ca. 1255-1306). The direct power theory was erroneous, according to Murray, since it violated the "autonomy of the state, in its misconception of the origin, nature, and scope of civil authority. The prince is conceived simply as *minister sacerdotii*; his political power is the direct instrument of the Church for the accomplishment of the spiritual purposes of the Church; the pope uses the prince simply as one of his 'arms.'" Bellarmine's theory of indirect power was a failure because of its "lack of logic" and because it was the same thing in reality as the direct power theory and was limited to a certain transitional period of history which included the rise of the nation-states. Bellarmine's theories had no further application to the modern day due to the passing of nation-states and the rise of constitutional states.[18]

Murray found the indirect theory of John of Paris more congenial because it "developed the concept of the state as a natural institution." The state and the Church, both from God, constitute a dyarchy whose powers "originate in different ways and for different ends, as respectively sovereign in their own sphere." The "end of the state therefore is specifically 'lay,' not religious." The Church does not teach the prince his politics.; she teaches him the law that governs politics. Since the end of the state was secular, the state cannot be used by the church "to protect her children from spiritual dangers to their faith, to punish heresy, to defend her own unity and unicity as the one Church of Christ." Protection from spiritual dangers was the job of the Church. The idea that the state could be used to suppress heresy was the result of an "historical process and not in virtue of the inherent exigencies of Catholic doctrine as such." Religious unity was not a state matter but a church matter because the "public order...is not competent positively to act in regard of all the values that are good for society; 'in regard of....religious unity —its competence is restricted to the task of guaranteeing to the proper institutions....the full freedom required for their promotion.'" Even if heretical propaganda did spiritual harm in Catholic societies, the government, "as the agent of public order" is not required to suppress the propaganda.[19] The government could only be responsible for "guaranteeing what I called the juridical statute of the Church and of assuring the juridical conditions of the Church's free and full exercise of her prophetic and pastoral office. But once it has afforded the Church this extrinsic strength, so to speak, it has stretched its arm as far as it is under any necessity...." The suppression of heresy is a "duty or function of what lies outside the sphere of its competence (which is political, not religious)" and so the Church had no right to impose such a duty or function on the government. Therefore, "a governmental right to repress heterodox religious opinions and worship enjoys no permanently valid status within the Catholic doctrine on the orderly relation of Church and state, because it is not an exigence of any of the pertinent theological or political principles."

Murray claimed Liberalism did not influence his position and wrote "no part of my argument rests on any part of the rationalist premise of Liberalism (the absolute autonomy of reason), or on its consequent false metaphysic of freedom, its individualistic....concept of 'rights', its atomistic concept of society, its concept of the juridical omnipotence of the state, or on any other element of its religious and political philosophy." Murray brushed aside the allegation that his ideas were in conflict with the tradition of the Church by writing that Catholic tradition should be distinguished from "the contingent modalities of its application, which have always been historically dependent on political conceptions, which evolve, and on social situations, which alter."[20] Separation of Church and State is not acceptable if that separation means denying or ignoring the uniqueness of the Church and at the same time refusing to recognize the existence of an "external spiritual authority that has an independent sovereignty over its subjects in all that concerns their spiritual and moral life, even as citizens or rulers." However, "civil intolerance is not the logically necessary consequence of *Libertas Ecclesiae."*[21]

Murray deconstructed papal teaching and Catholic doctrine by questioning the applicability of Papal teachings to the modern state. "Must one maintain, for instance," Murray asked, "that *Mirari Vos* or *Quanta Cura* said the last, definitive, immutable word on the political problems which the so-called 'modern liberties,' for all their aberrations and false metaphysical premises, aimed at solving?" Appealing to the spirit of his age, Murray wrote "men today are rightly sensitive to the problem of the limitation of governmental power by juridical vindication of human and civil rights." In saying such, Murray discredited Ryan equating his views with intolerance. Ryan's position scandalized the "men today" who were "rightly sensitive" to governmental power, and therefore presented a "serious obstacle to the work of the Church." Murray accused Ryan of basing his position on expediency and power, and the "sanguinary excesses of the Spanish Inquisition" for the "inhibition of the propaganda of non-Catholic sects.[22]

Murray redefined the language traditionally used in discussing Church-State relations by his novel distinction between the government and the state. The state was "the public order" or a "living action in society." The government "is not the state, but a part of the order which is the state, and a bearer of a portion of the action which is the state." Murray attacked the use of the terms thesis and hypothesis as "increasingly outweighed by its tendency to mislead, and that its categories are too facile to admit of fruitful theological and political thought." The concept of an ideal relationship of church and state was relative, depending on what the people of a society wanted the ideal to be:

"It may or may not be ideal for the Spanish people – that is their problem. But to predicate 'Catholic thesis' or 'Catholic ideal' of this particular mode of religio-political organization is, I say, at least misleading. In fact, the often-used expression, 'Catholic ideal of Church-state relationships,' is such as to create uneasiness. If it is meant that there are certain broadly but clearly defined divine intentions in the matter, manifested by reason and revelation, the assertion stands. But if it is meant that any particular form of socio-religious organization, whether of the past, present or future, constitutes the Catholic ideal, it is false."[23]

Murray rejected the clear meaning of various papal pronouncements. He admitted not conducting "an inspection of relevant papal texts." That did not stop him from stating simply that "the question is whether a secular government, denominated Catholic, is bound by any divine-positive or natural law unto the duty, and consequently empowered with a right to suppress it [heresy]. I suggest that the answer is no."[24]

CONNELL DECONSTRUCTS THE DECONSTRUCTOR

After his characteristic gentle praise for Murray's research, Connell proceeded to point out the serious errors and failings that Murray's position represented. Murray did not do his theological homework. He failed to address the doctrine of the Kingship of Jesus Christ set forth by Pius XI and by Leo XIII's encyclical *Sapientae Christianie,* which made clear that false religions may not lawfully be given the same rights as the Catholic religion. This doctrine gave the State the right to suppress heresy and false propaganda because the State was subordinate to Christ's kingly power, not because of its relationship to the Church. A state may not use the natural law to claim an exemption from its duty to follow the divine positive law. The state and society cannot merely follow the natural law; they must also adhere to the divine positive law.[25]

Taken to its logical conclusion, Murray's position led to the suppression of the Catholic faith and of the Catholic Church. It "would seem to follow that if a nation is in tranquil and unanimous possession of a false religion, and it is prudently judged by the rulers that the coming of

Catholic missionaries would be a threat to the public peace – as might well be the case, since it would stir up controversy and endanger the unity of the people – the government would have the *objective* right to prevent Catholic missionary activity."[26]

Murray's position was not only false, but it was also self-contradictory, something that became evident in the area of marriage. If, as Murray wrote, the government should recognize the Pauline privilege even though it is an exception to the natural law, then the claim of the Mormon Church to allow polygamy amongst its members had to be recognized. After all, the Mormons claimed a divine right to polygamy.[27]

Connell explained that the civil ruler's source of authority is, as Pius XI pointed out, "by the mandate and in the place of the Divine King." Such an arrangement brought "order, peace and tranquility, for there will be no longer any cause of discontent. Men will see in their king or in their rulers men like themselves... but they will not on that account refuse obedience if they see reflected in them the authority of Christ, God and Man."[28]

In an article that appeared in the *American Ecclesiastical Review* the following autumn, Connell expanded his critique of Murray's position by citing Leo XIII's *Tametsi Futura* (1900) and Pius XI's *Quas Primas* (1925), which held that "men joined in society are no less under the power of Christ than individuals." The chief positive consequence of recognizing Christ as the source of authority for the civil rulers is a peaceful and better society, as explained by Pius XI, something which Murray ignored completely.[29] Recognizing that it was unlikely "that the ideal of a Christian state is going to spread throughout the world in the near future, apart from the extraordinary intervention of Divine Providence," Connell, following Ryan, claimed that all societies, including America, had a duty to Christ the King. The current historical situation "should not prevent Catholics from proclaiming unhesitatingly the absolute necessity of a return to Christ on the part of governments as well as of individuals, if there is to be any lasting peace in the world....We must not compromise with the spirit of the times so far as to admit that the state is bound only by the natural law. We must unhesitatingly proclaim that the state cannot attain its destiny, save through Christ the King, even though that destiny is temporal, not eternal happiness."[30]

Murray borrowed the idea that the State is a natural phenomenon that need only follow the natural law from Dom Jean Leclercq, a French Benedictine who resurrected John of Paris in a 1942 article entitled "Jean de Paris et l'Ecclesiologie du XIII siècle." Leclercq cited with approval John of Paris's notion that the "civil government is purely natural in purpose and in authority," and therefore, to the state is "ascribed...a purely natural scope, subordinate only to the natural law." Leclerq and Murray supported the contention of John of Paris' *De Potestate Regia et Papali* when he wrote: "Destined by God to procure the common temporal good according to the inclination of nature, the king is bound to forbid all that is opposed to it. The norm of his actions is the natural law."[31] According to this theory, the civil ruler, even of a Catholic state, was not "bound to manifest officially any special homage to Christianity or to the Church."

Taking this position to its logical conclusion, Connell claimed that the same ruler need not respect any laws proclaimed by Christ over and above the natural law, that he could not restrict attacks on the Church, that he could not acknowledge the Catholic Church as the one, true church, and that he would have to treat heretical belief systems the same as the Catholic Church. The prince could only impose restrictions on heretical sects if their practices somehow violated the natural law through something like human sacrifice or polygamy. Murray's position jeopardized Catholic confessional states because people "could condemn the atttiude [sic] of these governments as an outmoded interpretation of the relation which should exist between Church and state, and emphatically declare that learned Catholics, particularly in the United States, disclaim it."[32]

The doctrine of Christ the King applied to all mankind and not just the baptized because, as Pius XI stated in *Quas Primas,* "men joined in society are no less under the power of Christ than individuals....Therefore, let the rulers of nations not refuse to fulfill by themselves and through their people the public duty of reverence and homage, if they wish to promote and to augment the prosperity of their country, while preserving uninjured their authority." To promote citizens' welfare, a government had to be concerned with the supernatural law of Christ in addition to the natural law. The temporal good of the people, which the government is to protect and advance, involves the practice of "supernatural virtues," which help people gain eternal life.[33]

Murray claimed there was no practical meaning to the doctrine of Christ the King, but Connell mentioned specific applications. While recognizing there are "particular circumstances of time and place" that may modify or restrict the manner or the measure of homage and obedience to Christ the King, Connell explained that Catholics should be aware that there are *per se* requirements that cannot be ignored. First, a government can adopt legislation that is based on the "moral principles laid down by the Son of God." Second, the government needs to express publicly a dependence "on God and on Jesus Christ," whether that be in a written constitution or in public religious ceremonies, or both. Indeed, not to do so is to exhibit a lack of care for religion, which, as Leo XIII wrote in *Immortale Dei,* "is a sin in the state..." Third, rulers are obliged to permit the Catholic Church to teach the Faith to the people, whether the people are baptized or not. Fourth, as Leo XIII set forth in *Immortale Dei,* the state is to promote and protect religion (that is, Catholicism) "under the credit and sanction of the laws, and neither to organize nor enact any measure that may compromise its safety." Fifth, just as the state may not compel the citizens to enter the Catholic Church or to be baptized Christian, it cannot prevent the "private exercise of false religious cults, when no harm is thereby done to the public welfare." However, public functions and activities of false religions, which could be detrimental to the Catholics' spiritual welfare, may be restricted. Finally, in the realm of marriage, the law of Christ must be respected. It is in this arena especially that the natural law cannot be at odds with Divine law or Christ's law because God is the source of both.[34]

PART VI

THE RISE OF MURRAY (1949)

18
THE RED SCARE

The Protestants and the Americanists had the Catholics at a disadvantage during the Cold War, especially in its early days from 1948 to 1954, when the Red Scare gripped the American public. During this period, the American press covered a number of high-profile events that dealt with the actual and suspected subversion of institutions of American society as well as the infiltration of the U.S. government by spies. Whittaker Chambers accused a high-ranking State Department official and Harvard lawyer, Alger Hiss, of being a Communist who handed secrets over to the Soviet Union. Hiss was convicted and sentenced to five years in prison for perjury. Klaus Fuchs, a nuclear physicist, confessed to giving the Soviets secrets from the U.S. Atomic Research Laboratory at Los Alamos, New Mexico. An electrical engineer, Julius Rosenberg, and his wife, Ethel, were convicted of spying for the Soviets and executed.

The House Un-American Activities Committee (HUAC) conducted a number of hearings into the Communist penetration of Hollywood that resulted in hundreds of writers, actors, and directors being named as Communists and blacklisted. Senator Joseph McCarthy from Wisconsin conducted much publicized Congressional inquiries into Communist subversion in universities and in the U.S. government, most notably the

State Department. Even World War II hero and author of the Marshall Plan, George C. Marshall, was accused of being pro-Communist and "part of a conspiracy so immense, an infamy so black, as to dwarf any in the history of man." J. Edgar Hoover, revered Director of the Federal Bureau of Investigation, or FBI, would declare that teachers called "Red-ucators" were "tearing down respect for agencies of government, belittling tradition and moral custom and.... creating doubts in the validity of the American way of life."[1]

On the other side of the world, China "went red" and was lost to the Communists after a ferocious and long civil war. Joseph Stalin, the Premier of the U.S.S.R, ruled like an absolute dictator and spoke of war between communism and capitalism, ratcheting up tensions. The Soviets got the Atomic Bomb in 1949, and a few months after the United States tested its Hydrogen Bomb, the Soviets tested one more advanced technologically. The Communist North Koreans, with Chinese assistance, pushed south and almost annihilated the United States military garrison on the Korean peninsula. The invasion was followed by a bloody war of attrition between Communists and the West on either side of the 38th Parallel. Stalin was building more and more prison camps. Purges in the Communist Party occurred in the U.S.S.R and in the "satellite countries." Prominent churchmen such as Josef Cardinal Mindszenty of Hungary were tried on charges of treason by the Hungarian Communists. In East Germany, workers were shot and killed, and their peaceful demonstrations were brutally suppressed upon orders of the Soviets.[2]

In the United States, "an atmosphere of fear" led many citizens and municipalities to build bomb shelters to withstand a nuclear war and to regularly practice "duck and cover" drills in the office, classroom, and home. Out of fear, members of the motion picture industry gave names to the HUAC of those suspected of disloyalty to America. After actor Ronald Reagan, as president of the Screen Actors Guild, instituted a loyalty oath, the Motion Picture Alliance for the Preservation of American Ideals, led by actor John Wayne as well as Gary Cooper, John Ford, and Clark Gable, gave the following instruction to everyone in the movie business: "Don't smear the free enterprise system...don't glorify the collective." Hollywood started turning out horror films depicting either directly or obliquely the evil of Communist subversion, as well as documentaries that promoted "good American values."[3]

Paul Blanshard's attack on the Catholic Church, which began in 1947 with articles published in *The Nation,* culminated in the publication of *American Freedom and Catholic Power* two years later. The debate between Murray and Connell over the Catholic position on the relationship between Church and state occurred at the same time and was another manifestation of the same fear-filled *Zeitgeist* that produced HUAC and horror films like "The Invasion of the Body Snatchers." That intra-Catholic debate entered a new phase in 1948 when it moved into the theological journals. Some journals advanced the Americanist position of Murray, and his friend Gustave Weigel, SJ, and others advanced the Catholic position and deconstruction of the Americanist position by the likes of Fr. Connell and Msgr. Fenton. At a time when attacking America or its founding principles could very well land one in front of a Congressional committee, or worse, anti-American sentiment had to be watered down by invoking the goodness of America and promoting its principles – such as an undefined "freedom." Doing otherwise risked losing the argument and being labeled either anti-American or un-American.

Murray used *Theological Studies,* which he edited, to expound further on his theories of church and state. By the late summer of 1949, Murray was engaging Protestant leaders in their magazines. In September of that year, Henry Luce's magazine *Time* mentioned Murray for the first time. Murray was presented as defending the Catholic position in an exchange of articles with Dean Walter Russell Bowie of the Union Theological Seminary, where Henry Luce was a trustee. It was a staged fight that was designed to advance the American agenda of elevating America as the ideal social organization. The "Red Scare" helped to make sure of that.

19
MURRAY APPEARS IN TIME

During the Summer of 1949, Robert C. Hartnett, SJ, editor of *America* and one of Murray's allies in the Church-State wars mentioned there were two views of "separation of Church and State" in an issue of *Catholic News.* The Church, according to Hartnett, was "much more interested... in having the State perform its duty of protecting and, in some more or less indirect ways, promoting religion as a social influence."[1] Murray's position as editor of *Theological Studies* prepared him for the national platform he would gain at *Time*, which allowed him to project his pro-American ideas. In an article entitled "Contemporary Orientations of Catholic Thought on Church and State in the Light of History," Murray claimed his views were supported by previous theologians like John of Paris, from whom Murray derived the idea that the state need only recognize the natural law in its policies, legislation, and actions because it is a creature of the natural law.

The U.S. Constitution continued this tradition and embodied a "concept of the state and of government that was fashioned at the dictates of practical political sense, themselves guided by a concern for justice and liberty, and illumined in their highest underlying intuitions by a belief in God and an order of natural law." The First Amendment's "guarantee of religious freedom" was related to a "rational theory of the state."

Murray held it was a "natural right" for a person to profess any or no religion. He wrote the First Amendment was consistent with Catholic doctrine, most notably the Gelasian Principle, which created a state with a "'lay' character" not competent in "the field of religion," only in the "secular and temporal" realm. [2]

Secondly, Murray distinguished the American state from the French state, claiming that Leo and other popes only condemned the French state. Murray claimed the United States Constitution created a lay state, but not a laicizing state based on the political "monism" that served as the foundation of the French regime. The First Amendment recognized the "primacy of the spiritual life of the human person, as a value supreme over any values incorporated in the state." It established a new "dyarchy" whose poles were the state and the human person instead of church and state. The American state did "not recognize on the part of any church the right to direct any authoritative intervention in its processes; to this extent it asserts its own autonomy as a political order."[3]

Third, the idea of *libertas ecclesiastica,* or freedom of the church, was the essential principle guiding all of the Church's actions in her relations with the State. This same principle led to the creation of the confessional state, which was neither a theological requirement nor doctrine. To hold otherwise "would somehow imply a denial or neglect of that 'vital law of continual adaptation' which is the law of the Church's thought and action; it would imply, in contradiction to Pius XII, that the Church somehow refuses to follow 'the providential path of history and circumstances.'"[4]

Murray argued that the United States Constitution required an evolution in Catholic thought, which made the confessional state neither a theological ideal nor a necessity. The basis for such an evolution was the concept of limited government created by the actions of the people as a whole, which did not establish a state church in law. The governmental officials who created this new system acted in accordance with the will of the people, who exercised indirect control over the government. The Church could then control the government by influencing the thoughts, consciences, and actions of the citizens who were members of the

Church. The more he argued, the more it became clear Murray was really interested in having the Church approve the American political theory.

By late summer, Murray had taken up the "religious freedom" issue in *Theological Studies.* In an article entitled "Current Theology on Religious Freedom," Murray promoted the thinking of contemporary theologians such as Fr. Jacques Leclerq and Fr. Max Pribilla, SJ, as well as Austrian nobleman Erik Kuhnelt-Leddihn, a correspondent for the British magazine *The Spectator*[5] as part of his attack on the Spanish Jesuits and *Civilta Cattolica.* Citing Leclercq, who drew a parallel between the Nazis and the Communists and Spanish Catholics, Murray claimed, "Nazism and Communism have proclaimed a doctrine of intolerance based on a dogmatic concept of the common good that allows no contradiction. At the same time the Franco victory in Spain has resulted in the reaffirmation by Spanish Catholics of the old thesis, 'thus formulating a sort of agreement in principle with the Communists.' And the confusion has been augmented by the 'disconcerting spectacle of Hitler's Germany persecuting religion within its own borders and lending its assistance to the Franco movement which presents itself as a crusade directed at the restoration of Christian principles!'"

Murray cited to Kuhnelt-Leddihn's attack on a 1948 article by F. Cavalli in *Civilta Cattolica* entitled "La condizione dei Protestani in Spagna," mentioning in a footnote that: "It is probable that nothing has been written in decades better calculated to produce in the U.S. a blind reaction of total hostility to all things Catholic than the author's ruthlessly simplifying paragraphs on the Church's 'unblushing intolerance.'" Following Kuhnelt-Leddhin's lead, Murray attacked Fr. Pablo Lopez, a Spanish Jesuit who stated Spain "is the ideal Catholic regime," and another Spanish Jesuit, Fr. E. Guerrero, who wrote approvingly of the International Catholic Conversations held at San Sebastian in September 1948. During that gathering, the teachings of the popes from Gregory XVI to Pius XII were presented as support for the thesis that "the religion-of-the-state concept still obtains, with all its implications of civil intolerance of dissenters, as the 'Catholic ideal,' though it is only realizable in a 'Catholic society.'"[6]

Like Murray, Leclercq discovered a "new principle" in Leo XIII's encyclical *Libertas,* namely "the independence of the Church in the face of political forms." Conditions should favor truth, but intolerance was a "form of social pressure," and "knowledge of truth requires an ensemble of delicate social and psychological conditions...."[7] Murray argued the problem of religious liberty could not be settled by the "facile axiom that error has no right to existence." In fact, he continued, "from this elementary generalization no conclusion can be drawn with regard to the suppression of error." Citing Kuhnelt-Leddihn, Murray argued that human beings have rights even when they are in error, an assertion he based the "law of love." By repeatedly referring to Kuhnelt-Leddihn's characterizations of the Catholic view on restricting the rights of non-Catholics in Catholic societies as nothing short of Soviet totalitarianism, Murray appealed to the prejudices of the time, as generated by both virulent anti-Communism and by Paul Blashard's attacks on the Catholic Church, which was portrayed as a crypto-fascist entity. The "Protestant and secular press in the U.S.," according to Murray, harbored the "suspicion that the 'opposition between Rome and Moscow is simply a rivalry between two absolutist and totalitarian systems.' Furthermore, the notion that there is a latent kinship between these opposing systems has been nourished by the 'Ryan-Boland thesis with regard to the 'double attitude' on the matter of religious freedom', which is supposedly basic Catholic doctrine."[8]

There were practical reasons for restricting non-Catholic religions, but the Church should hold aloft "the banner of this Freedom." Citing Pribilla, Murray argued that Proposition 77 of Pius IX's *Syllabus of Errors* did not lead to the conclusion that "a Catholic majority *must* deny the free exercise of religion to non-Catholic confessions." Coercion and hampering of "personal freedom" were to be eschewed in favor of persuasion "by objective arguments," which brought about a "more intensive apostolate."[9]

History had changed everything. The "concrete problem that confronts us is not precisely that which the Church faced in the 19th century." Nowadays, "the emergence of the threat of the totalitarian state" and the "corresponding struggling effort to validate the right of the human person to be the center, source and end of the social order demanded a re-thinking of church-state relations." [10]

Murray concluded by rejecting the view that the Spanish reading of church-state relations had either unified or protected the Spanish people. He also attacked the notion that Protestant propaganda planted "seeds of national disunity" and served "as the instrument of vile, foreign antinational influences" that functioned as "the arm of the enemies of the Church and our country." He condemned Fr. Guerrero's prescient observations that "freedom of religious propaganda would open the door to 'international Jewry and Masonry' . . . which would reduce Spanish culture to the level of the 'materialist and pagan Anglo-Saxon spirit'."[11]

Casting negative aspersions on the Spanish, Murray wrote that Spain's only claim to national unity was the Catholic faith. This unity was gained at the cost of "an armed crusade" and "preserved during the Counter-Reformation by the coercive methods of the Inquisition." According to Murray, "the fact that today national unity is imperiled, not least by weakness in religious unity" was proof that Fr. Guerrero's endorsement of coercion was invalid. Hence, the idea of a confessional state, or a state recognizing the Catholic Church as the nation's church and Catholicism as the "religion of the state," was invalid as well.[12]

In conclusion, Murray asked: "Does Spain in point of principle represent 'the ideal Catholic regime'?" Murray's answer was, of course, no. The Spanish constitutional concept of religion of the state was not "permanently and unalterably part of the Catholic thesis," nor was it "obligatory from the nature of Church and state in any 'Catholic society.'"[13] Secondly, the principle that the Spanish state could "exert. . . its coercive power even in the absence of any serious danger to religious unity" contradicted Catholic principle because "in Catholic political philosophy the action of the state was determined by the *exigences* of public order" and should be limited to "what necessarily must be done to preserve civil peace, not what possibly can be done without disturbing civic peace."[14] Murray demonstrated his willingness to betray Catholic principles.

SETTING THE STAGE

The Protestant-Catholic debate on the foundational principles of society was not just confined to the religious press. The national press, most notably *Time*, covered the discussion as well. Henry Luce wanted a certain outcome, and so the participants in the disputations had to be vetted. On the Catholic side was Murray, whose writings on intercredal cooperation and church and state met with the approval of Luce and the elites he represented. On the Protestant side was Dean Walter Russell Bowie of the Union Theological Seminary (UTS) in New York. Luce had close ties with the UTS. He became one of their trustees in 1947 after the death of his father, the Presbyterian missionary to China, Henry W. Luce.[15] Bowie joined UTS as a professor of practical theology in 1939.[16] With Henry P. Van Dusen's ascension to the presidency of UTS, Bowie was promoted to Dean of Students and served in that capacity until 1950.[17]

Van Dusen was a personal friend of Luce and a Presbyterian theologian of the inter-religious cooperation ilk who felt that the "greatest problems" can only be met by "the massed Christian strength of all churches directed unitedly [sic] upon common responsibilities."[18] Van Dusen courted Luce at a number of meetings and dinners, and Van Dusen was also responsible for putting Henry R. Luce on the Board of Directors of UTS,[19] from which position he could influence all the actors involved in changing the Church's teachings on the issue of church-state relations. Luce's involvement with UTS was reflected in the social calendars of Luce and his wife for 1947, a critical year for launching the church-state debate. One entry in that calendar indicated the Luces dined with Van Dusen and Spellman on September 30.[20]

As a result of Luce's efforts, elite Protestant theological circles opened up to Murray. As early as October 1934, Van Dusen was a member of the American Theological Society's prestigious Theological Discussion Group at Yale, whose membership included the most prominent of Protestant theologians of the day, people like Paul Tillich, Reinhold Niebuhr, and John A. Mackay.[21] A common theme in these theologians' efforts was the primacy of the American idea of separation of Church and State and the related concept of religious liberty. In a paper presented in 1937 by Harvard theologian Professor J. Seelye Bixler, the author claimed that "The real issue, says the Continental, is 'How do I stand with respect to God's will revealed in Christ?' not, as the American would put it, 'How does God stand with respect to my values?'"[22]

In April 1949, Murray submitted his own paper, entitled "Contemporary Orientations of Catholic Thought On Church and State In the Light of History," to the American Theological Society. Murray explained that the paper, which he wrote "with a view simply to clearing up my own ideas," presented a way for the Catholic Church to accept the American understanding of its separation of Church and State and its idea of religious liberty. Murray concluded that "between 'the freedom of the Church' as envisaged in the contemporary orientations of Catholic thought, and 'the freedom of the citizen, as envisaged in contemporary political realizations, there is, and need be, no conflict. This is the essential point that I wanted briefly to suggest."[23]

Murray hinted that Catholic thought or doctrine on this matter could change because changes in political theory necessitated changes in Catholic doctrine. The "political evolution," as he called it, "evolved a concept of *libertas civilis*."[24] The U.S. Constitution exemplified the "great modern fact of the lay democratic state" and gave "further nuance of development to the statement of the Church-state problem that emerged in the mighty controversy raised by Philip." John of Paris gave theological cover to King Philip of France by expounding "in the most logical fashion the philosophical, [the] natural-law concept of the state." With only natural law obligations, the way was cleared for the dethroning of Christ by eliminating the obligation of the State to Christ and His law. Both Murray and the Protestant elites who promoted his career had the same goal: the elimination of the confessional state as "the Catholic ideal," as Murray put it.[25] Murray's efforts came at a time when the conflict was escalating. With Cardinal Spellman charging Protestants with "waging a crusade of bigotry against the Roman Catholic Church,"[26] *Time* decided to join the fray.

MURRAY APPEARS IN TIME FOR THE FIRST TIME

Time sensationalized the discussion by citing Dean Bowie, a "spokesman for the Protestants," who claimed the religious and civil liberties of U.S. citizens were threatened by "the 'clearly stated Roman Catholic purpose 'to make America Catholic.'" At the root of the problem lay "certain implacable assumptions" held by Catholics, namely, the claim "to be the only church of Christ" and the even more inflammatory charge that Protestantism was a perversion.[27] Reviewing the evidence, Bowie concluded that "Roman Catholicism...is totalitarian." To counter the growing tension that arose between Protestants and Catholics because of the Catholic design to make the U.S. a Catholic state, Bowie argued for a national policy that was tantamount to the establishment of pan-Protestantism as the state religion, which he explained as believing "in the dignity of all human souls and in liberty of mind and spirit as the only guarantee of truth...." The Protestants had to resist Catholicism, or totalitarianism, even if it "covers itself with a religious garb."[28]

Bowie cited Catholic boycotts of publications as a form of censorship. He quoted an article from *La Civilta Cattolica* that *Time* cited in its June 28, 1948 edition, which stated, "The Roman Catholic Church, convinced, through its divine prerogatives, of being the only true church, must demand the rights to freedom for herself alone.... As to other religions, the Church will... require that by legitimate means they shall not be allowed to propagate false doctrine. Consequently, in a state where the majority of the people are Catholic, the Church will require that legal existence be denied to error.... The Church cannot blush for her own want of tolerance, as she asserts it in principle and applies it in practice."[29]

Murray responded in a characteristic way: by attacking the messenger, claiming there was no problem, and then surrendering the Catholic position. Bowie was "using an evasive word" when he used the word "tension" between Protestants and Catholics, according to Murray, because "Catholicism is not tense, not polarized against Protestantism." Murray then resorted to invective when he wrote that: "[E]very intelligent Catholic" would "agree that, in the contemporary spiritual state of the world, a polemic against Protestantism is practically an irrelevance." The Protestants had their own problems because Protestantism "to situate itself historically" has "to define itself. . . in terms of opposition to the Catholic Church."[30] Lest this sound too harsh to Protestant ears, Murray concluded by relinquishing any desire to convert America and bring it to its duty to serve Christ the King. "Catholic America" was "a bogeyman [that] does not exist."[31] Nor would it come into existence because Murray made clear that the Catholics were divided, Spain was the enemy, and America was safe from the Catholics.

20
PIUS XII CAUTIONS THEOLOGIANS

As 1949 wound down and Murray was given more opportunities to advance his arguments, he gained the attention of Jacques Maritain. Like Murray, this French Thomist felt the policies of the modern state could be based solely on natural law.[1] Like Murray, Maritain saw America and its form of social and political organization as the ideal.[2] In a letter dated May 1, 1950, to his good friend of many years, Charles Cardinal Journet, Maritain expressed approval of Murray's work:

"The problem is very serious here. American Catholics range from a total liberalism (in the tradition of the country) to theocratic doctrinal affirmations (learned in Rome and in the manuals of theology) that may be odious to the non-Catholic citizens. The only one attempting a synthesis is the good Jesuit Fr J. Courtney Murray, whom I quoted in my chapter."[3]

Maritain was attacked by the same Catholics Murray was battling. Fr. Pablo G. Lopez, SJ wrote an article in September 1946 entitled, "La democracia como regimen politico christiano" in which he called Maritain, according to Murray, "'este gran maestro de la tergiversacion y apostol de un morboso filantropismo ajeno a la fraternidad cristiana'(!)." Lopez was sure Maritain "has received, or will at an early date receive, the duly authorized advice and warning that his ideas are not those of the Church."[4]

Fr. Antonio Messineo, a writer for *Civilta Cattolica* and opponent of Murray's positions, explained how Maritain continued the thinking of Lamennais. Maritain rehabilitated Liberalism and secularism and made those ideas acceptable to contemporary Catholics. According to Messineo, *Civilta Cattolica* spent ten years battling the ideas that Maritain was now promoting. Maritain's opponents included the Patriarch of Venice, Angelo Cardinal Roncalli, who issued a pastoral letter condemning the errors of humanism, the secular conception of life, independence from the authority of the Church, and the naturalism from which these ideas had sprung, all of which were finding fertile soil amongst Catholics.[5]

In the vacuum left by removing the Church and Catholicism from positions of pre-eminence in society, Murray proposed the natural law, supposedly known by all, as a suitable replacement. This equivocal concept became a mainstay of American Catholic intellectuals. Early the following year, Murray authored "The Natural Law" in *Great Expressions of Human Rights,* thereby setting the tenor of Catholic thought on the matter.

Murray recognized from the beginning that the "natural-law theory does not pretend to do more than it can, which is to give a philosophical account of the moral experience of humanity and to lay down a charter of essential humanism." It alone is not enough to gain "sainthood, but only . . . manhood." Natural law prescribed the "minimum morality which must be observed by the members of a society... for a man to be reasonable and human, and for a society to be essentially civil...." The natural law could be a "dynamic of a new 'age of order.'" Its sketchiness was its advantage because it provided "the structural foundations of the political, social, and economic orders that are being most anxiously questioned." It held a "concern for the rights of the individual human person... no less than that shown in the school of individualist Liberalism with its 'law of nature' theology of rights." The "doctrine of natural law" offered a "more integral humanism, a fuller rationality, a more complete philosophy of man in his nature and history" and greater hope, especially given the prevalence of Marxism.[6]

The American Founders were influenced by Locke, and in particular by the "Lockean state of nature and law of nature. On it is based, by a process of pure postulation, the inalienability of the rights of the individual to life, liberty, and property, and the limitation of these rights solely by the equal rights of other individuals."[7] In endorsing Locke, Murray was endorsing the primacy of rights, which put real societal power in private hands, an idea that was essential to the American experiment.

MURRAY GOES TO GERMANY TO HELP JOHN MCCLOY

Murray's prestige was on the rise amongst the Catholics. In 1950, he was awarded the Cardinal Spellman Award by the Catholic Theological Society of America. At the same time, Murray was being promoted by the American establishment. In July, Luce sent to John J. McCloy, the United States High Commissioner for Germany, his approval for Murray to travel to Germany to assist the High Commissioner of that conquered country. In a letter dated July 18, 1950, McCloy responded by saying that he "will be glad to see the Reverend John Courtney Murray, S.J. when he arrives. I am glad to have your good opinion of him."[8]

During the months of July, August, and September, Murray served as a "visiting consultant" on a project that "had to do with the problem of the relationships between church and state in Germany" and, in particular, the situation in Bavaria, which was strongly Catholic. In his "Report and Recommendations Project: Church and State In Germany," which he submitted to the Chief of the Religious Affairs Branch of the Educational and Cultural Relations Division of the Office of Public Affairs of the Office of the High Commissioner, Murray found religion played an important and public role in German society. The churches were corporations of public law, and the support of the various churches was left to the various "Laender" or provinces and not the central government. Religious liberty, according to the regime that Murray helped impose on the defeated Germans, "guaranteed both freedom of faith and conscience, and also freedom of the public exercise of religion. There was to be no state church, and no state coercion in the field of religion. Moreover, there was to be complete freedom of religious association."[9]

Germany was fundamentally different from America because as a "group society," it "historically acknowledged functions and obligations with regard to religion that are foreign to American ideas." While working in Germany, Murray experienced a "strong undercurrent of resentment against Americans. The resentment has many causes. However, an important one is what many Germans judge to be an American effort to model German society on the cultural, as well as political, pattern of the United States.... In particular, there is hostility towards any American effort that seems to look towards the establishment in Germany of a system of separation of Church and State as radical and complete as the separation that exists in the United States. This is one of the cultural impacts of American occupation against which important sections of German opinion, Catholic and Protestant, would most strongly stand.... [T]here is resentment against American policies in Germany that are based on an American concept of separation of Church and State."[10]

The High Commissioner's policy was to make Germany like America. To bring this about, McCloy promoted a conception of community that violated the German view of community and religion, which is based on the idea that "community does not integrate the religious groups; rather, it is itself integrated by the religious groups....[T]he social agencies of the religious groups are genuinely community-agencies, acting in the interests of the community." The Germans were "highly critical of those American policies that seem to them to be based on a particular ideology characteristic of the United States. This ideology, they think, regards the 'secular community' as a sort of higher entity, existing above and beyond the religious groups. 'The community,' it says, is to be served directly, apart from all reference to, or alliance with, church agencies of any kind. This ideology further tends to regard 'community affairs' as a category not only distinct from, but superior to, 'church affairs.' And it is exclusively devoted to the principle of interfaith activities; these are considered to be the only activities which really 'serve the community'."[11]

The Bavarians found it "'impossible to talk to the Americans' on any profound level of understanding by reason of the absence of common religious and cultural presuppositions." This led to alienation, and in "this present moment, anything that contributes to such alienation is a source of weakness to the United States and an obstacle to its expressed designs within the world community." The important issue was whether Germany would oppose the Communists. "In the last analysis," Murray wrote, "there is only one 'German question' today: Will Germany go West or East – or 'lie down?'"[12]

To get the Germans on board for the Cold War, the American occupation forces had to appeal to "Religious forces" as "a potent factor in influencing the fateful choice towards active resistance to Soviet Communism and active alliance with the Western nations." Murray concluded religion could be harnessed for political and economic ends "If only" because "they claim and deserve attention and assistance."[13] Murray's proposal to use religion for American purposes was significant because it revealed his willingness to manipulate Catholic doctrine for political ends. More importantly, it showed Murray's willingness to use religion to advance American interests, something that was implemented on a worldwide scale by the U.S. government two years later.

After conducting numerous interviews of key personnel in Germany and attending a number of conferences and dinner parties, Murray concluded that American efforts at democratization of the society were meeting with considerable resistance, not the least of which came from German youth, who exhibited a striking apathy to the idea. Germans identified democracy with the failure of the Weimar Republic and "with bad times in general." Political freedom was synonymous with economic difficulty in the German mind. Crediting the German cynics with some truth, Murray cited their claim that "Democracy...is what we get each time we lose a war."[14]

Pursuing a program to make Germany like America, McCloy used Murray to destroy social cohesion by pushing the Germans into breaking tradition and creating a secularizing society where church and state were separate. American-style separation of Church and State appealed to the socialists, particularly the social democratic party, which "traditionally opposed the confessional school on ideological grounds." This caused fear among the Germans, who had always seen the church and the state as closely connected. The Germans, therefore, supported the Church tax because they "regard it as an important testimony on the part of the State to its appreciation of the place of religion in society and in German public life."[15] Murray tried to win the Germans to the American view of social organization, especially in matters of church and state, by promoting cultural exchange. This entailed German social, political, and religious leaders being brought to the U.S. "to create a respect for the United States."[16] In other words, personal contacts, not principles, were used to win Germans to the American causes and to restructure German society, something that remains an important strategy of the Americans.

ROME SPEAKS

On August 12, 1950, while Murray was in Europe working for McCloy, Pius XII issued *Humani Generis,* which claimed that "the principles of Christian culture" were "being attacked on all sides," which is to say, not only behind the Iron Curtain but also in the West. The heart of the attack involved ignoring the requirement that "divine revelation...be considered morally necessary so that those religious and moral truths which are not of their nature beyond the reach of reason in the present condition of the human race, may be known by all...readily with a firm certainty and with freedom from all error."[17] Natural law was just not enough because, as the pope taught, "For though, absolutely speaking, human reason by its own natural force and light can arrive at a true and certain knowledge of the one personal God, Who by His providence watches over and governs the world, and also of the natural law, which the Creator has written in our hearts, still there are not a few obstacles to prevent reason from making efficient and fruitful use of its natural ability."[18] Some of these obstacles would be "prejudice or passion or bad faith" and they would lead to refusal or resistance of the "evidence of the external proofs that are available" as well as the "impulses of actual grace."[19]

The pope condemned evolution and historical relativism, both present in some degree in Murray's thought, as erroneous and told theologians it was their "grave duty...to defend natural and supernatural truth and instill it in the hearts of men." Aware that theologians were shirking this duty, the pope criticized Catholic teachers who were "desirous of novelty" as well as those who "advocate an 'eirenism' according to which, by setting aside the questions which divide men, they aim not only at joining forces to repel the attacks of atheism, but also at reconciling things opposed to one another in the field of dogma."[20] Pope Pius condemned the efforts to "free dogma itself from terminology long established in the Church and from philosophical concepts held by Catholic teachers" so as to "satisfy modern needs," [21] another dynamic present with Murray. As a parting shot, Pius XII attacked once again those "indulging in a false 'eirenism,'" which consists in the belief "that the dissident and the erring can happily be brought back to the bosom of the Church," even "if the whole truth found in the Church is not sincerely taught to all without corruption or diminution."[22]

In the aftermath of World War II, the battle against Modernism Pope Pius X initiated at the start of the 20th century morphed into a battle between Catholics and Americanists. Murray was nonplussed by *Humani Generis*. Recognizing that it would certainly be applied to him, Murray assured Fr. McCormick of the Jesuit Generalate in Rome that "the superior general's letter on the encyclical 'will be accepted with complete loyalty, as the guide of our thinking.'"[23] In spite of his profession of loyalty, however, Murray remained undeterred in his determination to find a new formulation of the church-state issue that would be acceptable to his powerful patrons.

21
MURRAY SOUNDS ALARM BELLS

After returning from Germany, Murray sent copies of a paper entitled "The Crisis in Church-State Relationships in the U.S.A." to both Monsignor Montini (later Pope Paul VI) in the Vatican's office of the Secretary of State and to Clare Boothe Luce. In a May 4, 1951, letter marked "Confidential," Montini forwarded the paper to Cardinal Stritch of Chicago, noting the paper "discusses a question of particular importance" and asking Stritch to "examine it and... indicate any observations which you may judge opportune in this regard."[1]

In a memorandum that proffered both carrot and stick to the Church, Murray recommended adapting Catholic teaching on church-state relations to approve of the American system as a positive good as something that would both remove non-Catholic opposition to the Church and aid its evangelistic efforts. Those less enthusiastic could accuse Murray of promoting the same views prohibited by Leo XIII when warned against watering down the faith and its doctrines to be pleasing to others in *Testem Benevolentiae Nostrae* (1899), most notably, the idea that: "in order the more easily to bring over to Catholic doctrine those who dissent from it, the Church ought to adapt herself somewhat tour advanced civilization, and, relaxing her ancient rigor, show some indulgence to modern popular theories and methods." Leo XIII warned,

"Many think that this is to be understood not only with regard to the rule of life, but also to the doctrines in which the *deposit of faith* is contained. For they contend that it is opportune, in order to work in a more attractive way upon the wills of those who are not in accord with us, to pass over certain heads of doctrines, as if of lesser moment, or to so soften them that they may not have the same meaning which the Church has invariably held."[2]

Stritch's reply revealed an awareness the Church was being attacked through the church-state discussion and with the cry for "religious liberty." Stritch seemed unaware of any attempt by Murray to subvert Catholic teaching and use religion to extol the American system, as Murray had done for McCloy in Germany. In the section entitled "Some Practical Suggestions," Murray gave the strongest evidence yet that the Church was viewed as an "opposition system" by the Americans during the Cold War:

"Catholic thought on Church-State relationships ought to show a greater awareness of the American scene – its political realities and the special history and situation of the Church in America. The Church in America is a massive part of world Catholicism. And at the present moment it is called upon to share in fullest fashion the opportunities and responsibilities that have been recently thrust in increasing measure on the United States.

"All the material power, political wisdom, and spiritual strength of the United States are presently enlisted in defense of human freedom against the Communist threat. Americans in general believe that in this struggle great resources are to be drawn from the political concepts exhibited in the American Constitution, with its supporting principles. Hence, the extreme importance in the present world crisis of intelligent and firm Catholic affirmation of these concepts and these principles.

"The Catholic Church cannot with full effectiveness oppose Communism as long as it is itself regarded as being in opposition to the American political system that today stands most strongly against the spread of Communism."[3]

Per Murray, the danger to Catholicism in America was not Protestantism but rather a "newly articulate, organized, and doctrinal secularism or naturalism." The "intelligent Protestant also recognizes this naturalism as 'the enemy,' and he feels that he should make friends with the Catholic in a common struggle against it. However, he is definitely not willing to be friends with a Church that seems to him to be the political enemy of 'the American way of life,' with which Protestantism has historically identified itself...."[4]

After submitting the memorandum to Montini in April 1951, Murray asked Vincent McCormick, SJ, to keep him informed of its status. Murray wrote "that it [the memorandum] had been called to the attention of the Holy Father by Msgr. Montini himself and had been committed to the hands of 'experts.' Heaven help it, and me....If you should chance to hear any rumors or rumblings about it, I would of course be glad to be informed."[5]

PART VII

THE AMERICANISTS VERSUS THE CATHOLICS (1950-1952)

22

SHEA VERSUS MURRAY

While Murray was in Germany working for McCloy and meeting the future Pope Paul VI, Msgr. George Shea launched an attack against his positions. Shea, a diocesan priest who was also a professor of dogmatic theology at the Immaculate Conception Seminary in Darlington, New Jersey, served as the president of the Catholic Theological Society of America after a stint as Navy Chaplain during World War II.[1] One of his students described Shea as "brilliant but boring" as well as "very clear, logical, and ordered." A retiring man who "was never one to make his presence known in a group," Shea attended public events only out of a sense of duty. On one occasion, as recounted by a former student, Shea explained his presence at a dinner for a group of nuns by saying to one of his students, "I am loyal to the Archbishop, and that is why I am here." When not in the classroom, Shea retired to his quarters to think and write answers to questions that arose during the course of his work.[2]

Shea weighed into the intramural struggle between church and state with an article entitled "Catholic Doctrine and 'The Religion of the State'" published in the September 1950 edition of *American Ecclesiastical Review*. Shea attacked Murray's claim that a state religion was merely an historical incident, whereas freedom of the Church was a matter of principle or doctrine. Shea's critique threatened to bring down Murray's argument that the American system comported with the Church principle as a good. In making this claim, Murray failed to address Church doctrine on the "major obligation which natural law imposes on the State." This was the very point Murray presented in his 1945 article "Freedom of Religion: I. The Ethical Problem." Murray, according to Shea, recognized the "'major obligation which natural law imposes on the State...to acknowledge God as its author, to worship Him as He wills to be worshipped, and to subject its official life and action to His law.'" Murray also recognized that this "absolute obligation includes also the hypothetical obligation of accepting a higher belief, law, and mode of worship if God reveals them as His will.'" Shea pointed out, "On the question of the theological necessity or non-necessity of the 'religion of the state' one would like to see some explicit discussion of the possible implications" of these views. Unlike Murray, Shea claimed, "Man has an individual and social responsibility to worship as set out in Catholic doctrine. This extends to obligations of "the politically organized community, civil society as such...to profess... the true religion; to worship God in the way He wills to be worshipped."[3]

This duty to profess the true religion and to worship God is required under the natural law which includes the "duty of accepting Catholicism, its creed, code, cult. The objective duty exists for all; and where the objective duty is sufficiently known, the duty is subjective as well." In Catholic societies, it is "incumbent upon the state to be a 'Catholic state,' to declare and to treat Catholicism as 'the religion of the state.' The formal, official, and exclusive recognition and profession of Catholicism by the state in a Catholic society as its own one and only religion, in short, the establishment of Catholicism as 'the religion of the state,' seems necessarily contained in the very notion of the state's duty to accept and profess the true religion, therefore Catholicism, with its creed, code, and cult. How else could the state, qua state, in truth accept and profess Catholicism, together with its tenet that it alone is the true religion?"[4]

The "state is a moral person, able to be the subject of duties," wrote Shea. These duties are fulfilled "only through the medium of physical person[s]." Shea continued:

"Concretely, then, the state professes, exercises religion, worships God, through official acts of those placed in authority. To satisfy its religious obligations, the state must worship God not only indirectly, virtually, administratively, but also directly and formally. That is to say, not only, for example, by abstaining from whatever is contrary to divine law, not only by positive furtherance of public religion, not only by legislation, *ex motive religionis,* against perjury, public blasphemy, writings inimical to public religion and morality, etc. but also by official participation in acts of worship properly so-called...."[5]

The state had a duty to the spiritual welfare of the members of society. That meant it had to act in accordance with the Divine Positive Law or the Catholic Faith. The form of governance of the society was not significant, for as Shea wrote, "The state is a creature of God, for He is the author of man's social nature, of all authority in the state, of all the benefits the state enjoys.... Further, one perceives that, if it holds for any state, the argument holds for all... for juridical democracy and for any other new realizations in the reality of the 'state' which historical evolution has brought or may yet bring about...."[6]

Given all that, the obvious question was whether the Catholic faith could be imposed on "dissident citizens." The answer to that was negative because "reverence for the individual conscience forbids this, and the very nature of religion and of the act of faith. If these be not voluntary, they are naught." Shea's citation came from Leo XIII's *Immortale Dei,* which he quoted in a footnote: "The Church is wont to take earnest heed that no one shall be forced to embrace the Catholic faith against his will, for, as St. Augustine wisely reminds us, 'Man cannot believe otherwise than of his own free will.'" The "private external exercise" of one's religion was permissible in countries where Catholicism was "the religion of the state."[7]

Did the Catholic state have a "moral obligation . . . to restrict sects in such matters as the public profession and exercise of their false religion, in their propaganda, the spread of their heretical doctrines?" The answer was affirmative. The fact that "the mind of Pius XI that 'the religion of the state' entailed some manner of sectarian restriction, is candidly acknowledged by Fr. Murray." Shea also cited Pius XI's correspondence to Cardinal Gasparri concerning the 1929 Lateran Treaty and Concordat, in which the pope:

"forcefully insisted that it be 'clearly and loyally understood that the Catholic religion, and it alone, according to the Statute and the Treatises, is the religion of the state with the logical and juridical consequences of such a situation of constitutional law, especially with reference to propaganda'; and....that full liberty of discussion is inadmissible, since some forms of discussion can easily trick unenlightened minds and become a cloak for harmful propaganda."[8]

Murray's rejection of the theological necessity of recognizing the Catholic Church as "the religion of the state" flew in the face of the clear testimony of Leo XIII's *Humanum Genus, Immortale Dei, Libertas,* and Pope Pius X's *Vehementer nos* all of which showed the "religion of the state" was a theological necessity. The state was not just a protector "against the onslaughts of Continental Liberalism," as Murray claimed. Shea explained he was "prepared to grant that Leo XIII may have approved 'the religion of the state' for contingent reasons," but "I am not prepared to grant that he approved it for such reasons *alone.*" The state was to engage in the worship of God in accordance with the Catholic religion, to favor and protect the Catholic religion, and to engage in the public profession of that religion, regardless of the historical situation.[9]

With *Libertas,* Leo XIII taught the "profession of one religion is necessary in the State," and religion is the one "which alone is true, and which can be recognized without difficulty, especially in Catholic States, because the marks of truth are, as it were, engraved upon it....." Pius X condemned the idea that "the State should be separated from the Church is an absolutely false and most pernicious thesis." Such a view was "based on the principle that religion should be of no concern to the State," but this "does a grave injury to God," who "should be worshipped not only privately but also publicly."[10]

Finally, Shea rebutted Murray's argument that the state had neither the right nor duty to suppress heresy by "asking whether Fr. Murray has consider[ed] *all* the adverse arguments." Murray had not, and as a result, took a position inconsistent with numerous papal pronouncements. Shea reminded the bishops of their rights and duties in Canon 1381, Section 3, which gave the bishops the "right and duty of vigilance over all schools in their territory, lest anything be taught or done in these schools contrary to faith or morals."[11]

Fr. Messineo, author of "Lo Stato y la Religione," which appeared in the February 3, 1951, edition of *Civilta Cattolica,* joined Shea in attacking Murray's thesis, in particular his attempt to make toleration of different religions in a society acceptable in principle.[12] Catholics like Shea and Messineo were holding the line, and Murray was not winning over Catholic intellectuals with his arguments.

MURRAY RESPONDS TO SHEA

Responding to Shea in the May 1951 issue of *American Ecclesiastical Review,* Murray began by calling his article "superficial" and then got to the heart of the matter, claiming that the "legal establishment of Catholicism as the religion of the State need not be considered a permanent and unalterable exigence of Catholic principles governing Church-State relations." Murray claimed doctrine changed over time. Given that fact that "it would be an abdication of the theological task, if the theologian were to remain simply the literal exegete of Leo XIII, as if somehow the total doctrine and practice of Church-State relations had reached their definitive and ultimate stage of development in the Leonine *corpus.* Such a closure of development would be altogether untraditional."[13]

Murray questioned what made a society a "Catholic society," claiming, "None of the apologists are kind enough to determine the exact percentage-point at which the state-church, from being technologically non-necessary becomes necessary, and vice versa." Murray's claim that "a statistical concept is not a valid term of reference for any human law" did not stop him from counting the term "*Libertas Ecclesiae*" 81 times "in some 60 or more documents of Leo XIII." Numbers, in this instance, proved to Murray that the freedom of the church was "his [Leo XIII's] key concept, as it is the traditional one."[14]

Freedom of the Church meant the State did not control the Church so as to develop a "monism." Theologians could develop doctrine to approve of the American system in principle because "the Church can. . . regard them [other institutionalizations of Church-State relationships] as *aequo iure* valid, vital, and necessary adaptations of principle to legitimate political and social developments. . .Such a development is presented by the democratic state... in 'the liberal tradition' of the West, which has been best present, though not guarded in its purity, in the Anglo-Saxon democratic tradition."

Sounding more and more like Jacques Maritain, Murray wrote:

"The democratic form of state . . . is presently man's best, and possibly last, hope of human freedom. Secondly, this form of state presently offers to the church as a spiritual power as good a hope of freedom as she has ever had; it offers to the Church as the Christian people a means, through its free political institutions of achieving harmony between law and social organization and the demands of their Christian conscience; finally, by reason of its aspirations towards an order of personal and associational freedom, political equality, civic friendship, social justice, and cultural advancement, it offers to the church the kind of co-operation which she presently needs, and it merits in turn her co-operation in the realization of its own aspirations."[15]

Murray relegated the idea of a "state church" or a "Religion of the State" to nothing more than an adaptation of certain principles to a certain period of history. It "flourished in the era of 'confessional absolutism'" and in the "royal governments in the 'Catholic nations' of post-Reformation Europe," especially during the "monarchic restorations of the 19th century."[16] Since it is "an adaptation to a particular historical context," the state church "does not represent a permanent and unalterable exigence of Catholic principles to be realized in any and all historical situations in which there is verified the general hypothesis of a 'Catholic population.'"[17]

Murray also redefined the meaning of "profession" of the Catholic Faith. The act of making Catholicism the religion of the country was a juridical act that must be governed by social considerations. While a "common faith does indeed enter strongly into the constitution of a people, as a bond of unity and the remote inspiration of a culture...the faith does not of itself define historical destinies, or create any particular social system, or inspire any particular institutional structures of common temporal life; these are not the functions of religious faith." Once again, the crucial determinant is not the Church but rather the "shaping influence of secular history and all the forces active in it."[18] Since the "state church" was an historical contingency and Leo's pronouncements as only a criticism of Continental Liberalism, not the Anglo-American system, it was time for a "development" in Catholic theology to approve the Anglo-American system as good in principle.

Fenton, the editor of *American Ecclesiastical Review,* wrote: "It is only fair to add that he does not share Fr. Murray's views on the subject of this article."[19] He offered Murray a chance to respond to Shea, but that did not alleviate Murray's fury. Murray screeched that this "violation of editorial protocol" would not allow him to "carry on a full dress discussion on the Church-State problem in the pages of *The American Ecclesiastical Review.*" As a result, Murray's response to Shea appeared in Murray's journal, *Theological Studies.* Fenton "scorned the 'lofty lecture' of Murray's letter."[20]

SHEA CRITIQUES FURTHER

Shea closely studied Murray's article and compiled meticulous notes concerning it, although he did not publish a rebuttal article. Shea explained Murray created the problems:

"If as Murray says the Church, last bulwark of freedom, has come to be identified with oppression..., this is regrettable. But also regrettable is this, that the 'old thesis' has somehow come to be identified with oppression. And this identification of old thesis with oppression: 1) in no little part is due to well-meaning but misguided polemic of Murray et al. against old thesis; and 2) said identification has contributed to identification of church with oppression, lamented by Murray....

"Murray's tactics in his writings: to contrast abuse of old thesis, hence facts, with ideal (not stark reality of democracy....Fallacy of instituting comparison with worst side of one and best side of another....

"Murray's reply tries to make it appear that my view is simply my view... i.e., he tries to make it appear I'm alone in thinking constitutional situation of religion of state is required by state's duty to worship God. This is not so; it is held by many authors of great name; Murray himself apparently once held it (Theol. Stud. 1945)."[21]

Murray neither agreed with nor mentioned Pius X's point that the "state has to concern itself in some way with man's ultimate end." Without this, then, as Cardinal Pacelli wrote in July 1933, a "plea of separation of Church and State implies State is only concerned with man as economic units, which smacks of Marxism, etc." The most serious flaw in "Murray's theory" was that it placed the state over the church. If "the electorate [sic] wanted a law contrary to divine positive law, the action of legislators in passing it would be free even from objective, material, sinfulness...and said law would be immune to censure as immoral, contrary to divine law...." Shea concluded that liberal Catholics were the heirs of Lamennais. [22]

23
MURRAY GOES TO YALE

In the spring of 1951, Murray was asked to serve as a Visiting Professor of Philosophy at Yale University, Luce's alma mater, beginning in September. Etienne Gilson rejected an offer due to a pledge to the Medieval Institute at Toronto. "You have done work of which we know the great value on the relation of Church and State in the medieval period," wrote Charles W. Hendel, Chairman of the Department of Philosophy, in extending the offer to Murray. "What we want from you...is whatever you are yourself studying and writing about that is itself of general interest."[1]

The broad (if not vague) conditions that Yale set for his employment gave Murray a platform to espouse his ideas and an opportunity to solidify his credentials. "Actually this Yale job is not one that I myself particularly wanted," Murray wrote to fellow Americanist John Tracy Ellis, "since it carries me rather out of my own field; I cannot in any sense pretend to be a professional Philosopher. However, it seemed necessary to accept the invitation, and I shall endeavor to do no positive harm!" To Fenton, he was far more circumspect: "Personally, I did not want the job, but it was judged best that I should accept the invitation." To Provincial John J. MacMahon, SJ, Murray wrote:

"One year at Yale University would give me an experience much more valuable for the work that I want to do, especially in the field of Church-State relationship, than in teaching in a Catholic Graduate School, because it would be an opportunity to acquaint myself at first hand with opinions in this field and the attitude to the Church's doctrine entertained by non-Catholic seculars."[2]

The job at Yale paid $ 9,000 for the academic year, a large sum at the time,[3] but the prestige was more valuable. The job offer got Murray mentioned in *Time,* which stated that he was the "only Jesuit professor at any big non-Catholic university in the U.S." *Time* went on to describe the 46-year-old Murray as:

"A tall (6 ft. 4 in.), cucumber-cool intellectual who teaches theology at Woodstock (Md.) College, but is famed far beyond. Father Murray is a towering figure among U.S. Catholic scholars. A polite and learned defender of the faith, he edits the erudite quarterly, Theological Studies (he will continue to do so at Yale), and is the spearhead of a bold attempt to reconcile traditional Catholic church-state doctrine with U.S. practice....Father Murray looks forward to introducing Yalemen to Thomism: 'I want to show it is a rational philosophy, that it's acceptable intellectually not only because great intellectuals of previous ages have accepted it, but in itself as mode and body of thought. If I can't make my students see it, that's the end.' The betting at Woodstock is that Murray will make them see it."[4]

If Murray thought that by going to Yale, he could escape the controversy he had unleashed, he was mistaken. Connell would not let the church-state issue rest. In an article entitled "The Theory of the 'Lay State,'" which appeared in the July 1951 *American Ecclesiastical Review,* Connell restated Murray's position that the origin of the state's power was in the "natural moral order" which limited the "direct power" of the state. Connell said Murray argued the state had "no direct right to restrict the proselytizing activities of non-Catholic religious groups, as long as these do not disturb public order and peace," even when the "vast majority of the citizens and the rulers profess the Catholic religion." Connell pointed to Murray's statement on the matter coming from his paper delivered at the CTSA in June 1948: "The state has no empowerment from the only source from which its empowerments come (the natural law) to forbid them [individuals or groups teaching a gospel 'of their own' or of the 'true Church of Christ'], provided the tenets of their gospel are not incompatible with the order of justice and the manner of their preaching is not in prudent judgment a threat to the public peace."[5] Murray also questioned whether the encyclicals *Mirari vos* or *Quanta cura* were the last word on the "so-called 'modern liberties.'"[6]

Though Connell based his critique of Murray on direct quotes from Murray's own writings, Murray denied that he advocated the creation of a "lay state" subject to only the natural law.[7] Connell knew he was at a disadvantage as Murray's theory was one which "naturally has a strong appeal for the Catholics of our land since it is quite in harmony with the principle of 'freedom of worship,' so deeply integrated into American democracy, and with the American tenet that no particular religion has any right to special governmental favor and no citizen is to be restricted in the practice and propaganda of his religious beliefs as long as he does not thereby interfere with public order and the rights of his fellow citizens." This, however, did not change the fact that the American arrangement was an evil to be tolerated, not a good to be celebrated.

The fundamental issue was not, as Murray put it, whether civil rulers should obey Church laws but whether, as Connell put it, civil rulers should obey Christ's laws. Connell was nothing if not clear on the matter: "Civil rulers had the obligation to obey the positive law of Our Saviour in their official acts," he wrote, referring to his October 1948 article from the *American Ecclesiastical Review.* Connell was reiterating the teaching of Pope Pius XI in *Quas Primas,* which set forth the doctrine of the Kingship of Jesus Christ. This was also in accord with the teachings of Leo XIII, who wrote that the state was bound by the "law of Christ," which in "Catholic theology ordinarily includes the precepts over and above the natural law, promulgated by Our Lord as Man."

Christ was the Supreme Ruler of all, and while the state cannot be bound by some of Christ's laws (e.g., it could not receive sacraments), "civil rulers as such can be directly (and not merely through consideration for the beliefs and desires of the citizens) bound to acknowledge in the Church of Christ the authority to exercise certain functions which otherwise would belong to the state itself by natural law, and to promote in certain respects the supernatural activities of the Church." Leo taught in *Tametsi futura* (1900) all men were bound to accept the law of Christ (not only natural precepts from the ancients). Leo wrote, "the law of Christ must prevail in human association and in society so that it is the ruler and teacher, not only of private but also of public life."[8]

Because of Christ's commandment to teach all nations as contained in Matthew 28:18-20, "it is the right and the duty of the Church, independently of every civil power, to teach all nations the doctrine of the Gospel." The Catholic Church has a right to preach the "Gospel *independently of every civil power."* The Church is to announce the Gospel "to the people without hindrance. Surely this is an obligation over and above the obligations prescribed by natural law."[9]

Refuting Murray, Connell wrote that Revelation was necessary to understand the "moral (natural) law in all its details. Anyone who "tries to solve the moral problems connected with sterilization, euthanasia, contraception, etc., he will very easily go astray unless he relies on Christian revelation as proposed by the teaching authority of the Church. This involves the obligation to investigate which is the true Church. Yet, in the theory of the 'lay state' the civil ruler 'knows nothing' of the divine commission of the Church to teach all truth."[10] According to Catholic tradition, civil rulers have "the right to restrict non-Catholic propaganda and proselytizing, as an influence calculated to injure the citizens in the temporal (though supernatural) sphere." This was because the temporal is not restricted to the natural and a state's concern for the temporal welfare of its citizens "will have some concern for their supernatural happiness."[11]

After stating the Catholic position, Connell backed away from its full implications when he gave assurances "that the Catholic Church constitutes no menace to the cherished spirit of liberty so dear to all our citizens" because Catholics had "no intention or desire of modifying the system prevailing under our Constitution, the system of allowing all our citizens full liberty of conscience, complete equality of all religious denominations before the law."[12] Like Msgr. John Ryan, Connell was, in effect, promising not to work for the conversion of America. It was not a logical position, given the duties that all societies owed to the Catholic Church and to Christ's laws, and it undermined his own position and that of the Church.

The discussions over church and state revealed disagreements so fundamental that Shea suspected a coup d'état against the "older and stricter teaching on the subject" of church and state relations was afoot. Three tactics were being used: first, by proposing another theory of the state; second, by obtaining the endorsement of the apparently "ablest modern Catholic experts in the sociological and other pertinent fields"; and third, by claiming that the "teachings of the more recent Popes" support these notions. In "Orientations on Church and State" in the December 1951 *American Ecclesiastical Review,* Shea bolstered his argument by using Fr. Nell-Breuning's *Beitrage zu einem Worterbuch der Politik* to discredit Murray's "lay state" concept.[13]

Shea began by explaining Murray's new definition of the state as set out in "The Problem of the 'Religion of the State'" published in the *American Ecclesiastical Review*: destroyed the scholastics' definition of the state as a natural, perfect, and complete society identified with the body politic or political society.[14] Unlike Murray, who felt that the state was historically conditioned, Nell-Breuning claimed that it "has its foundation in human nature, whence its essence and essential meaning and purpose are withdrawn from arbitrary human decision."[15] Like Jacques Leclerq, Murray claimed that the nature of the state changed with time. According to this view: "The modern state is something essentially—and therewith also conceptually—different from the ancient state, from the medieval state or that of the 17th century.... Democracy and state are sociological, not philosophical categories, that is, they stand in the stream of time, not in the world of ideas!" [16] If, as Leclerq and Murray claimed, "the state is subject to change in its very essence," then "there can be no perennially valid formulation of what, *per se,* should be the relations between Church and state." [17]

Taking the essentialist position, Nell-Breuning accepted the Scholastic definition of a *societas naturalis, perfecta, complete* and noted it derived from human nature and hence from God, who is the Author of human nature. Therefore, the state is a "creature of God, as well as a moral person."[18] It followed then that "just as the individual human being, so too is the sate bound by God's moral law; the Church is the divinely appointed teacher and interpreter of this moral law, whose teachings and interpretations thereof are, therefore, binding on everyone, including the state – and, indeed, on principle and without exception, every state." The state is "possessed of a supernatural last end." This is an objective fact whether the state is aware of it or not, or whether the state believes it or not and the fact cannot be altered by rejection or unbelief. The Church and the State are to have relations with each other so as to "promote and assist each other, in view of the fact that they have, ultimately, a common last end." The Church "knows that it has a responsibility for the well-being of the state, a responsibility to be discharged by assistance, not by interference," and the Church's well-being is "a responsibility of the state."[19]

Nell-Breuning and Shea then concluded, "That state alone does justice to the Church, which recognizes and acknowledges the Church for what it is, the foundation of Jesus Christ, the Son of God; but such a state would be a Catholic state (*katholischer Glaubensstaat*)." Such a state was one where the citizens: "profess the Catholic faith, and whose entire activity has as its norm the moral values proper to the Catholic faith and Catholic philosophy; a state which, acknowledging the truth of the Church's claims of divine origin and mission, accepts the Church's teaching on and interpretation of the natural moral law (e.g., as regards the indissolubility of marriage, the unborn child's right to life, etc.); a state which when its undertakings and institutions require the ministrations of religion....seeks these from the Catholic Church."[20]

If citizens are not unified in the Faith, then a Catholic state is not possible. Still, the "Catholic religion is to enjoy the protection of the state and a more or less privileged position."[21] A lay state may exist if by that is meant the autonomy of the state in its own sphere, but this concept is "only half of the Catholic teaching on Church-state relations, as developed by Leo XIII; and so, by its inattention to the other and at least equally important half, it is always in danger of degenerating into a half-truth, and of gliding over into the laicism of the laicist state." The state is a moral persona and, as such, is responsible for acting in accordance with God's law, which includes the appropriate relations with the Church.[22]

Unfortunately, Shea made a rhetorical blunder when he termed Church doctrine, Nell-Breuning's writings, and those of Connell as "conservative." This could then be used to divide Catholics into two equally legitimate camps—the conservatives and their counterparts, the liberals. It was an innocent mistake, but it would have serious consequences, clouding the real issues and obscuring the real identity of the enemy.

24
THE "SUPERCILIOUS QUIBBLER" ENDS THE DISCUSSION

Murray responded to Connell in the January 1952 *American Ecclesiastical Review* by attacking Connell for something the latter did not say. Murray claimed Connell said the Church was seeking "permission" from the civil authorities, and that threatened the "principle of the freedom of the Church" because it "would imply a measure of dependence of the Church on the civil power that would be violative of the perfect independence of the Church." Murray did not address the State's duties to recognize the true religion except when he wrote, "It is the law of Christ that the Church should have direct access to all men, 'independently of every civil power.'" The "civil power does not and may not stand between the Church, as herald of the Gospel, and any of the peoples of the earth. The state is not empowered either to permit or to prohibit the preaching of the Gospel." Murray characterized Connell's position as one requiring the authorities to investigate the Church's proofs in order to "accept...and believe in the Church's divine authority." In doing this, Connell introduced an "element of rationalism into the genesis of the act of faith." This, Murray wrote, was a theological error.[1]

Murray called Connell's view of the state "a pure piece of conceptualism." Connell was arguing for "the historical spectre of the Father-King, who possessed with the nation, the *magna familia*, an authority of the same nature and scope as that of the father within the family. His subjects were only subjects, not citizens; their only duty was to obey, not to share in rule. They were the untutored multitude, both spiritually and politically immature." This view did not correspond to Murray's understanding of the American form of government, according to which the people decided "by an act of constitutional consent that the functions of civil government in regard of the supernatural blessings which are recognized as needful for their temporal happiness are to be limited to the protection of the freedom of the Church in her proper task of procuring these supernatural blessings."[2]

"Catholic theorists on Church and State" never addressed this issue because "the problem presented by a state organized according to the principles of the liberal tradition and its concept of constitutionalism and of free political institutions" developed in lands "predominantly Protestant," where the "problem of an orderly relationship between the Church and these states was not an urgent one." The struggle with "Continental Liberalism was so intense, prolonged, and bitter that it quite absorbed the energies of the Catholic thinkers." Now, "the pressure of worldwide totalitarian Communism – a threat to all that both the Church and the liberal tradition stand for"[3] demanded doctrinal development.

After misrepresenting Connell's position, Murray proceeded to attack Connell's ability and motivation. Murray claimed that Connell was one of the "unwary" and was guilty of making "injurious" claims about Murray's efforts, which were intended to "smooth the way toward a better understanding of the Catholic Church on the part of non-Catholics in America." Connell presented Murray's work as "compromising Catholic principles, or concealing them, or understating them," when Connell himself did not hold "intellectually or morally respectable" positions because he condemned the First Amendment in principle while praising it in practice. Connell, according to Murray, was a "man of the Right."[4]

CHAPTER 24

CONNELL RESPONDS

Connell responded to Murray in the same issue of the *American Ecclesiastical Review* and in the same restrained, scholarly, and humble way in which he conducted his life. Connell 1) observed Murray failed to respond to Connell's objections, 2) refuted the allegation Connell viewed the Church as subject to the state, 3) criticized Murray's fallacious logic, and 4) observed Murray engaged in personal attacks while using complicated and confusing verbiage. Connell, as did Shea in his September 1950 article, questioned whether Murray had "considered *all* the arguments" for Murray's theories and, like Shea, determined Murray had not.[5]

Dealing with Murray's claim that he was implying that the State held jurisdiction over the Church, Connell pointed out, "It is surely unfair to accuse a person of holding something *by implication,* when he *explicitly* states the contrary. Yet, that is what Fr. Murray has done in this instance. Furthermore, he avoids making any reference to my explicit statements which are directly contrary to what he ascribes to me by implication." Connell emphasized the freedom of the Church from the civil powers of society in conducting the apostolate by placing the phrase "independently of every civil power" in italics. Murray ignored this and claimed that Connell implied that the Church was juridically inferior to the State.[6] Connell had laid out his position years earlier in the October 1948 *American Ecclesiastical Review*:

"[1] The civil rulers have the obligation to permit the Catholic Church to teach its doctrines to the people, whether baptized or unbaptized. [2] In the event that the Gospel is being announced for the first time, the rulers have the right and the duty to investigate the claims of the preachers before giving positive approval. [3] Since the Church received her commission to preach directly from Christ Himself, she has the right to announce her message in non-Christian lands, whether the government consents or not. [4] However, the usual procedure of missionaries to pagan lands has been to seek governmental confirmation of their mission, when it is prudently possible to follow this procedure."[7]

In footnote 3 to his January 1952 article, "Freedom and Transcendence of the Church," Murray quoted the first two sentences above. In footnote 6, Murray quoted the fourth sentence. Murray omitted point number three in his discussion of Connell's position and then wrote that Connell "denied by implication" that it is a law of Christ that the Church should have direct access to all men, "independently of every civil power."[8] Connell invalidated Murray's claim that Connell's use of the term "permit" in connection with Catholic missionaries entering the territories of the state meant a violation of the law of Christ by subjecting the Church to the state's power. He explained "it would be clear that in my use of *permit* I had merely in mind the attitude of the government of doing nothing to hinder the activity of the Church in its divinely authorized task of preaching and ministering to the spiritual needs of the people." The *Standard Dictionary* defined "permit" as "to allow by tacit consent or by not hindering, take no steps to prevent, consent tacitly to, suffer." Webster's *International Dictionary* defined the same word as "to consent to, allow to be done, to tolerate, to put up with." The secondary meanings were different and were respectively: "to grant leave to by express consent or authorization, empower expressly, authorize" and "to grant one express license or liberty to do an act, to authorize, to give leave." Connell used the word in its primary meaning, but Murray insisted "on interpreting it in a secondary meaning and then claiming that I have enunciated (by implication) a proposition gravely derogatory to the perfect liberty which the Church received from her Divine Founder, Fr. Murray's mode of argumentation seems a bit arbitrary...." The Council of Trent emphasized the primary meaning, and even Murray's own prayers would be in regard to the primary and not the secondary meaning.[9]

Connell denied Murray's claim he was trying to subject the Church to the authority of the State when he wrote, "It is within the scope of the official duty of civil rulers to find out whether or not the Church is authorized by God to demand certain rights" which meant to "investigate the validity of its credentials."[10] Murray arrived at this conclusion by attributing to Connell a proposition he did not make and a logical conclusion that did not necessarily follow. Connell did admit that a better formulation of his position was that "The State *per se* will accept the proofs for the Church's claims and believe in the Church's divine authority."[11]

Murray's objections contained "a vital defect." Murray did not "distinguish between the preamble of faith, the motives of credibility and the judgment of credibility," which are natural, and "the truths of Faith, the motive of faith and the act of faith on the other hand," which are supernatural. Because of "his failure to make this important distinction... Fr. Murray identifies the obligation of the state to yield to the claims of the Catholic Church – which obligation I uphold – with an act of faith." Connell denied that the government "has a right to 'pass judgment on the Gospel.'" Connell meant that the "civil official has the obligation to investigate the motives of credibility of the Church" so as to pass "practical judgment" in fulfillment of an official obligation to determine whether or not "to permit the Church full freedom" in preaching the Gospel. This is different from the "supernatural act of faith," which Murray wrongly credited to Connell. He criticized Murray's suggestion that "the civil official must allow everyone who proclaims a religion to preach and minister without any investigation of his credentials" or "may not examine the proofs each has to offer for the sincere purpose of finding which is the authentic teacher." To accept this position, one must condemn public officials who seek to perform their duties towards religion.[12]

Murray's position was based on the view that if something cannot be done in a concrete situation, then Christ did not command it be done at all. Referring to the command by Christ in Matthew 28:18-20 to preach and baptize all nations, Connell wrote: "The principle proposed by Fr. Murray – that Our Lord would not lay down any absolute laws that could not be observed in all concrete situations – would fail also if applied to the unquestionable obligation imposed on the Church to preach the Gospel to all human beings. After two thousand years, it is still not possible to fulfill this precept. Similarly, the law making the reception of Baptism necessary as a means for salvation is one that cannot be observed in the case of a vast number of infants who die daily throughout the world. But the existence of such a law cannot be doubted."[13]

Therefore, there are situations or conditions that may be tolerated while the commandment or law of Jesus is being fulfilled by the work of the faithful. There are ideals that are still to be sought after even though the actual situation does not permit the fulfillment of such an ideal at the time. This latter point was made clear by Connell when he quoted Leo XIII's famous paragraph 6 of *Longingua Oceani* on church and state matters:

"The fact that Catholicity with you is in good condition, nay, is even enjoying a prosperous growth, is by all means to be attributed to the fecundity with which God has endowed His Church, in virtue of which, unless men or circumstances interfere, she spontaneously expands and propagates herself; but she would bring forth more abundant fruits if, in addition to liberty, she enjoyed the favor of the laws and the patronage of the public authority."

This quote refuted Murray's arguments limiting Leo XIII's encyclicals to only Continental Liberalism. Leo addressed the situation in America and claimed that the confessional state was the ideal for Catholic Church-State relations.[14] The American "people would do wrong by voting against governmental recognition of the true religion, just as they would do wrong if they voted that all children must attend State schools." The Church could tolerate the situation that existed in the U.S. under the provisions of the Establishment Clause but only out of a policy of practicality as enumerated by Leo XIII.[15] Connell did not concede that the American formulation of church and state relations was acceptable in principle.

Connell concluded by saying: "I do not think that Fr. Murray has given us any convincing reasons for departing from the views on the relation between Christ and the State, and the Church and the State, and on the ideal form of *Concordia* which our standard dogmatic manuals present as the commonly accepted Catholic doctrine." Connell then added the observation, shared by other theologians, that Murray's theory was difficult to understand because of "lengthy and complicated sentences, which at times furnish difficult reading." Noting Murray's many personal attacks against him and his abilities, Connell asked Murray to "give us his views simply and briefly – in two or three pages, if possible.

Then we shall be prepared to discuss more understandingly his views on Church and State."[16]

Murray never took Connell up on his offer. Instead, Murray, stating petulantly that "the cited article will not be continued in *American Ecclesiastical Review* but in *Theological Studies,"*[17] took his marbles and went home. He never again argued with Connell in print because Murray knew he could not win. Besides, with Henry Luce and *Time* magazine in his corner, Murray hardly needed *American Ecclesiastical Review*. Instead, Murray argued his position in a series of articles published between 1953 and 1955 in his journal, *Theological Studies.*[18]

MURRAY IS A SUPERCILIOUS QUIBBLER

Throughout the course of his exchange with Murray in the pages of the *American Ecclesiastical Review,* Connell received support from fellow churchmen. Fr. Tom Chapman, an observer of the Murray-Connell debate, gave his opinion in a letter to Fr. Rector R. P. Gounley. His letter encapsulated the essence of Murray's approach:

"Frankie, I think, carries off the palm in the arguments presented in the current number of the AER. Reading Murray's article brings to my mind the story told of an old shoemaker of the Middle Ages. (Stop me, if you heard it before!) The old gazebo didn't know a word of Latin; but he always made it a point to sit out in the public square with the savants during the public disputations on matters philosophical and theological. Asked one time why he did that, he said he was anxious to know who won the debates, and usually he was correct in his guess. When asked how he figured out the winner his answer was 'The loser is the first to lose his temper!' Murray made a bad impression on me when in girlish fashion he testily served notice to his readers that he isn't 'going to play in Frankie's backyard any more!' So he picks up his rubber ball and jacks, and with a swish of his skirts and a pout on his face, he runs away to the refuge of the pages of THEOLOGICAL STUDIES. (p. 28).

"Constitutionally, I am wary and even suspicious of the one who finds refuge in highfalutin language and lengthy complex sentences. And on that score, I suspect John Courtney Murray of being on the wrong side of the question. Frankie reads easier and eschews bombastic language. Perhaps the blame should be put on Murray's present environment at Yale...

"It does strike me, however, that Murray sets up 'straw' men – and knocks them down with a flourish; and that he can well be 'hoist with his own petard' – which gallantly enough Frankie didn't do. Much of Murray's argument seems to be a 'lis de verbo'....

"....as I read Murray – it occurred to me that his quarrel with Frankie is equally a quarrel with Pope Leo XIII.....Murray accuses Leo XIII of being ignorant of the set-up of Constitutional governments the world over. England was a going concern in the days of Leo XIII, and we have been doing business here for nearly two centuries....Didn't Leo XIII understand philosophically the natures of both governments? It is hard to contend that he didn't. And while the French set-up may have 'occasioned' the issuance of the Encyclicals, the philosophy and theology they expressed were intended by him to be universally applicable: that is what 'encyclical' implies....

"Reading Murray's arguments gets me all-balled-up....I ran into the same difficulties: I had to back up repeatedly to make an effort to grasp what he is saying....But I couldn't escape the suspicion that Murray himself is at times confused, mixing up 'de jure' with 'de facto'....

"It has always been my conviction that Dame Columbia [Great Britain] must consort with either Christianity or Freemasonry. Up to the present it has been with the latter....Virtually, we have in this country a 'Union' (call it a concord, an association, if one likes) of the Protestant, Masonic influences with the 'State.' Frankie's line, to me, seems to be opposed to such a domination, while John Courtney Murray's seems willing to overlook it."[19]

Fr. Joseph Deisz frequently wrote to Connell. Concerning Murray's article "On Religious Freedom" (from the September 1949 issue of *Theological Studies*), Diesz wrote that it "disgusted me as it is a manifestation of his superficiality. Why doesn't he study Church documents and the writings of authoritative teachers both ancient and modern? Of course, no authoritative serious writer can be found to uphold his errors." Deisz criticized *Time* and Fr. John Lafarge, SJ, for confusing and misrepresenting the ideas of Fr. Messineo in *Civilta Cattolica* concerning the concepts of thesis, hypothesis, and tolerance. A hypothesis could never be a thesis, and a thesis could be applied in full or in part, depending on the circumstances. Toleration meant two things. First, it allowed a lesser evil to exist, and second, it meant not compelling one to accept or reject beliefs. Deisz implored Connell to "please see to it that Fr. LaFarge's error will be brought to the attention of the Catholics.... The questions Fr. LaFarge asks in his article show the strange ignorance of this 'scholar' with regard to the duties of a Catholic state.'"[20]

In a final letter to Connell on the matter, Deisz wrote, "Fr. Murray has shown himself to be in this case a supercilious quibbler" and "sincerity, clarity, logic, charity and truth are all" on the side of Fr. Connell. Deisz noted that Murray's proposition number 6, contained in the May 1951 issue, "openly contradicts...modern papal pronouncements."[21] Deisz voiced concern that Murray was confusing Catholics by twisting Catholic doctrine: "It is clear what he attempts to prove. Hasn't he an arbitrary way of interpreting historical events and even the encyclicals? He mentions 'Immortale Dei,' which evidently destroys Fr. C. Murray's whole argumentation.... He seems to believe that democracy enjoys a special divine approbation and exemptions. The democratic Caesar seems to think Fr. C. Murray is exempt from the obligation of submission to Christ, the King." Since Fr. Murray "will not change his views and will continue to indoctrinate many to the detriment of our Faith," Deisz concluded that "the only solution" was "to stop him" by having "somebody in authority send this proposition to the Holy Office for an authoritive [sic] judgment."[22]

25
MURRAY LECTURES AT YALE

Murray had another, and perhaps better, platform from which to advance his ideas and influence the Catholics. That platform was Yale, which carried considerable prestige among the Americans and the Catholics. Murray was the first Catholic priest to hold a teaching position at Yale, and much was made of that fact, particularly when he delivered a four-part public lecture entitled "The Problem of Church and State: Some Perspectives" on the Catholic doctrine of Church and State from February 1 to 12, 1952.

In the first lecture, which was given to an audience of about 500 in the Yale Law School Auditorium on the afternoon of February 1, Murray said that the Church's insistence on "two sovereignties" limited the power of the state over the individual and "if sustained, insures [sic] man's freedom from complete domination by the state." So, when church and state clash, it is not the Church seeking power that is the cause, but rather the "opposite," because by insisting on the opposite, by the church's insistence that the sovereignty of church and state be 'distinct' the church preserves the "value of the individual and his obligations and allegiance to a higher authority than the state." By insisting on the "distinction between the things that are God's and the things that are

Caesar's," the Church prevents the state from depriving man of spiritual freedom, the ultimate freedom.[1]

The church recognizes the sovereignty of the state in temporal matters and yields to it, Murray said, but the Church is constantly resisting the efforts of the state to take control of the family, the husband-wife relationship, the parent-child relationship, and other social relationships because, according to Murray. These "come under the jurisdiction of the Divine Authority speaking through the Roman Catholic Church" and are "sacred aspects of life." State control of these endangers man's spiritual freedom.[2] Society, according to Murray, should pay "spiritual allegiance to a spiritual organization which asserts itself to be the embodiment of divine authority." Reliance on just the "individual moral conscience" will place society in a "more precarious position." According to Murray, the "conflicts throughout history between church and state have not been simply verbal arguments, but, as it were, the clash of living bodies." This is why the struggle, remaining always the same, has always been different. The Church did not "reach us in the present with entirely clean hands" because it acted like other organizations when the alternatives were unacceptable.[3]

Having established the importance of historical circumstances, Murray proceeded to attack the Catholic state by distinguishing in his February 5 lecture, "The Medieval Situation: One Society, Two Swords," between the situation in the Middle Ages and the modern era, which made the thrust of his work clear. Murray said the Gelasian Principle held "the primacy of the Spiritual, the autonomy of the temporal, and the necessary harmony between the two." The "character of the age itself influenced the expression given to the ideas," and the "question concerned simply the application of this principle in the concrete circumstances."[4] However, there was a "complicating conception" which "was the dominant one, shared by all the men at the time, which held Christendom to be 'one society,' a single commonwealth, 'one church,' with a dual administrative hierarchy that found its unit in the headship of the Roman Pontiff." Murray said the "notion of Christian entered into the definition of a citizen, and the notion of Christianity entered the definition of the city, not simply an inspiration but as a genuine intrinsic cause." This meant "Christian faith and law became the norm... and the base of the whole political order." Indeed, "supernatural justice which is the content of the Christian Gospel tended to become the content of the political order itself, and an 'object of promotion' by the temporal power." The temporal power existed within and served the Church.[5] Rulers knew "their office involved a spiritual and religious mission. In this respect the medieval concept of political power exhibits its most striking contrast with the modern notion."

However, a practical problem surfaced in the clash between Boniface VIII and Philip IV of France. In the conflict between the supporters of the papacy, the supporters of the emperor, and the "middle way," the "middle way," as expressed by St. Thomas Aquinas, won out when it claimed that the state was a "natural institution, with its own origin, purposes and processes" and autonomous at the same time. John of Paris approved of this position. The Yale news bureau concluded that "Father Murray's second lecture used the Middle Ages as a sort of case study of the interplay of doctrinal idea and historical fact in shaping the theory and practice of Church-State relationships."[6]

In his third talk, given on February 8th and entitled "Post-Reformation Europe: One Nation One Faith," Murray claimed that the idea of an international unity of all mankind was destroyed by the rise of the nation-state, which led in the Fourteenth Century to the rise of national Royal Absolutism, which "put the Church-State problem on a wholly new basis."[7]

The question then became, "What form could the Gelasian Thesis assume in these altered conditions, when the medieval Christian Commonwealth had disappeared, and when there existed only a variety of individual and independent powers? How could the distinction between Church and State be maintained, and how could harmony between them be achieved in practical fashion?" The answer was the concordat, or "contractual agreements reached between the Holy See and the national governments," which sought to achieve harmony in three ways:

"First, to obtain legal guarantees of the freedom of the Church as a spiritual authority to exercise her spiritual mission within the national kingdoms. Secondly, to insure [sic] governmental protection of Catholicism as the religion of the people – and to do this it was necessary in the circumstances to make Catholicism the religion of the State. Thirdly, to provide for conformity between the public law of the land and the law of the Church, as a means of limiting the power of government and insuring [sic] the freedom of the Christian conscience."[8]

Murray introduced historical relativism into his argument when he claimed that "the so-called 'Union of Throne and Altar' was just "another instance" of the "historical law which obliges the Church to pursue her spiritual purposes within the conditions of a particular epoch." Even within the "Union of Throne and Altar," the "Church continued to exercise her ancient function of putting a limit to the power of government." In conclusion, Murray said the "maintenance of the distinction between Church and State continued to be, even during this age when a bad political tradition prevailed, the only effective check on the absolute pretensions of the king by divine right."[9]

In his final lecture in the series, entitled "Contemporary Orientation: the Freedom of the Church and the Freedom of the People," Murray claimed that there was no "clash in principle" between the Church and the constitutional democracies of the Anglo-Saxon tradition because the Church does not oppose either the political principles or the "formal processes" by which Anglo-Saxon democracy carries out affairs of government and "organization of social life." Murray said the "Church's condemnation of the rationalist theory, on which 'the modern liberties' were first protected by the French Revolution, implied 'no condemnation of the institutions of popular rule – free speech, free association, free press and freedom of religion – as these institutions have operated in the Anglo-Saxon tradition."[10]

The French Revolution was "something entirely new" because it promoted "the secularization of power, the idea that the only duty of the State toward religion was to ignore it completely." The revolutionaries sought to exert power over the Church. The State was all-powerful, "acknowledging no higher law than its own sovereign will," and it had an "all-embracing cultural mission in society, which gives it complete control over education." Catholics stood with the "old order" or the Royalists. Leo shifted the debate away from the political one and "urged the Catholics of France to use the new methods of freedom in order to create a new order, an order whose principle would be social justice."[11]

26
CONFLICT WITH SPAIN

During a homily delivered on February 20, 1952, Pedro Cardinal Segura y Saenz of Seville exhorted the civil authorities in Spain to enforce the Spanish laws against the Protestant sects, which comprised about 20,000 people of a population of nearly 28 million.[1] The Cardinal described the growing pressure on Spain to allow the Protestants more access to the society. Interest in Spain was building in America. In 1951-1952, a number of books closely examining Spain's politics and culture were published[2] ostensibly to provide aid to the country as an ally against the alleged Soviet menace. *Time* reported on the Cardinal's pastoral in its March 17, 1952 edition, shortly after Murray ended his lectures at Yale on church and state. The American media covered the controversy as an opportunity to divide American Catholics on the church-state issue. *Time* publicized an attack on a Protestant church, which the Spanish authorities described as a "negligible, isolated incident."[3] The *Time* article quoted the Spanish Cardinal as claiming that Protestant propaganda had "considerably increased" since 1945 when the Spanish government authorized the opening of "certain Protestant churches." This propaganda, according to Cardinal Segura y Saenz, was being "tolerated to a far greater extent than is permissible in keeping with the... spirit of the charter of the Spanish people." The Cardinal criticized President Truman for expressing his lack of fondness for the "present government of Spain." [4]

The American Catholics mercilessly attacked the Cardinal, and *Time* took notice. The *Indiana Catholic and Record* published an editorial that called the remarks of Cardinal Segura "surprising" and "sure to strain the charitable efforts of Americans – Catholic as well as Protestant – to understand the Spanish mentality...." The editorial continued by conflating Catholic persecution with that of false religions:

"Cardinal Segura, Dictator Franco and others in Spain should take a look at their history books. Not only could they discover that the Protestant Revolt actually did happen and had rather considerable repercussions all over the world, but they might also notice that any persecution – short of extermination – has invariably strengthened the persecuted religion in the long run." [5]

Keeping in mind the Soviet threat, the editorial chided the Spanish claiming, that "Protestantism is the wrong dragon today. Any lances that can be spared from the anti-Communist battle had better be tossed at other targets than Protestantism." Catholicism in America was vital and full of vigor, while Catholicism in Spain was "protected and over-advertised." The editors of *Indiana Catholic and Record* wrote, "These remarks may smack of religious jingoism, but we feel it is past time for American Catholics to be relieved from the oppressive burden of our Spanish brethren. We have spent weary hours cleaning up the blood the Spaniards overzealously spilt in the Inquisition."[6]

The American press exploited Catholic division by playing up the differences between the Spanish prelates' response to the Americans, as covered in the May 12, 1952 edition of *The New York Times. Ecclesia,* a Spanish weekly, criticized *America*, run by the American Jesuits and the *Indiana Catholic and Record*, for "incurring real doctrinal errors contrary to papal encyclicals" in the editorials criticizing the Archbishop of Seville. According to *The New York Times* report:

"*Ecclesia* declared that, far from being four centuries behind the present age, Spain had clearly seen the Protestant danger before anyone else since the 16th century; that she had fought it not only with her theologians and armies but also with the Inquisition; that again, while other nations, including the United States, had granted 'full religious and political freedom,' which made communism legal, Spain took the lead in the anti-Communist fight, which is now 'fortunately' being carried on by North America, 'with ...its great resources and power.'"[7]

Ecclesia then directed its ire at the Jesuit magazine *America,* which "must conform more with theology and papal encyclicals than with political philosophy, which needs to be enlightened by theologians in such delicate matters." Describing American religious liberty as based on a "misguided conciliatory attitude toward Protestants," *Civilta Cattolica* held it smacked of indifferentism, which consisted of "juridical equality" which "is not rationally understandable unless it is assumed that all religions are good and true and that, consequently, they are equally worthy of the same treatment by the civil authorities....The results of juridical equality of cults is due only to the refusal to recognize that the Catholic religion is the only true religion and the Catholic Church the only true church."[8]

America's editor, Fr. Robert E. Hartnett, replied by claiming that there were two views on religious liberty – the Spanish and the liberal one. According to him, both views are widely accepted and acceptable to Catholics. *America* then set out, as *Ecclesia* noted, to explain how the "religious situation in the world in general imposes as an ethical duty religious freedom in Spain," but *Ecclesia* held that such an opinion contradicted papal teachings on the matter.[9]

In response to the Spanish allegation that *America* and *Indiana Catholic and Record* "incurred real doctrinal errors contrary to papal encyclicals," Hartnett relativized Catholic doctrine on the church-state issue by claiming that "just as Spanish religious journals vindicate the particular applications of Catholic teaching on Church-State relations judged best for Spain, so American Catholic journals vindicate the application judged best for the United States." He stated the "Spanish pronouncements have caused non-Catholics here to be extremely suspicious of the alleged long-range *political* aims of the Church in the United States."[10]

The *America* editorial proceeded to explain: "We feel they are entitled to know on what grounds we defend the principle of religious liberty – not as a matter of mere expediency but as compatible with the teaching of the Church. That is why we suggested that 'one can argue that in the situation of the *world at large,* religious liberty in Spain is an ethical imperative.' *Ecclesia* seems to be denying that this proposition is even *arguable.* We believe it is. That seems to be the chief point of difference between us." After arguing that religious freedom was compatible with Catholic teaching by citing a pamphlet entitled *Federal Aid to Education* that received official Church approval in early 1950, and an article in the *Catholic Encyclopedia* from 1912 by Dr. J. Pohle entitled "Toleration, and the constitution of Ireland," *America* concluded that Spain did not have religious liberty and that it should change its position.[11]

One month later, Father Shea came to the defense of the Spanish hierarchy in an article published in the May 24, 1952 edition of *The Advocate,* the official publication of the Archdiocese of Newark, when he claimed that the rights of the Protestants to practice their religion were protected by the sixth article of the Spanish Charter approved July 6, 1947, by popular referendum. The Protestants could not publicly profess their faith or have public demonstrations of their convictions, but, as the Charter stated: "No one will be disturbed for his religious beliefs or for the private exercise of his worship." Shea explained that Catholic teaching on the topic was contained in *Immortale Dei* and *Libertas.* He quoted Connell, who claimed that in a "distinctively Catholic" country ("that is, if the population is almost entirely Catholic – and the national life and institutions are permeated with the spirit of Catholicity"), "civil rulers can consider themselves justified in restricting or preventing denominational activities hostile to the Catholic religion. This does not mean that they may punish or persecute those who do not accept the Catholic faith. But they are justified in repressing written or spoken attacks on Catholicism."[12]

GUSTAVE WEIGEL, SJ, WEIGHS IN

One month after Shea's article appeared, Gustave Weigel, SJ, picked up the Americanist banner in an article entitled "The Church and the

Democratic State," which appeared in *Thought* during the Summer of 1952. In that article, he called Fenton and the Spanish defenders of the Catholic state the "static expositors" and Murray, and hence Hartnett, the "dynamic expositors."[13]

Weigel was a good friend of Murray, and his appearance on the scene while Murray went elsewhere signaled a tag-team approach repeatedly used by the Americanists. Weigel, born in January 1906 and raised in Buffalo, New York, was a fellow traveler with Murray in advancing the American view of the organization of Church and state relations. Murray met Weigel in 1930 when they began theological studies at Woodstock, and the friendship grew to "extraordinary depths of understanding and loyalty," as Murray described it years later.[14] Like Murray, Weigel liked to characterize matters in his own terms, something that became apparent with his doctoral thesis on Faustus of Riez, in which Weigel wrote, "History as it ought to have been, not as it was."[15] Weigel was at one and the same time physically large and spiritually menacing. At Vatican II, *Time's* correspondent to the Council, Robert Blair Kaiser, described him as a "cadaverous hulk, with a huge nose, baleful eyes, sparse dark hair plastered down on a mostly bald pate, and a deeply pessimistic view of life."[16]

Weigel was an ardent Americanist who was quite well-liked by the U.S. diplomatic community, which relied on his assistance while he lived and taught in Chile from 1937 to 1948 at the newly established Universidad Catolica de Chile in Santiago. During the six years he served as the Dean of the School of Theology,[17] Weigel came to know the political and social leaders of Chilean society, and he gathered a considerable amount of information about life, culture, and the Catholic Church in South America. This information was valuable to the American diplomats, especially at a time when they were preparing for world war against Germany. This information allowed the Americans to assess Latin loyalty to Fascism and the effect of Protestant sects and missionaries on Catholic societies.

In a private letter written on the eve of the Japanese attack on Pearl Harbor, Weigel wrote to Norman Armour, the U.S. Ambassador to Argentina, that the Catholic clergy, comprised mostly of Spaniards, were the real leaders of the Catholicism, which made a resurgence in the last ten years and "is a growing force" due to the "bankruptcy of the Liberal program" which took over after the "two revolutions of the 18th century." The "chaos brought about by the Liberal doctrines, today rejected by almost every philosophic school in the world," Weigel wrote, "forced men to look elsewhere for a firmer guidance." The Chileans, as a result, increasingly looked towards the Church.[18]

While the principles of Nazism violated the principles of Catholicism, and the clerics and Catholic people were generally opposed to it, the "authority and order strongly stressed by those systems are pleasant notions" to many. Some wanted "a German victory out of hatred of Great Britain." A "few isolated priests" were happy about the "Nazi attack on the Jews because these priests connect Liberalism and Free Masonry with the Jews. Spanish priests are anti-British by tradition and the position of England in the Spanish Civil War has intensified this anti-British feeling...." All of this bore directly on the United States, which was "against Nazism and Germany" and which sought to "line up solidly the South Americans with the United States."[19]

Chileans and South Americans were reluctant to join with the Americans even though they admired the U.S. They feared that "Uncle Sam will dominate him and make him a subject of American jurisdiction either overt or disguised. This he does not want under any circumstances....The basic fear.... is caused fundamentally by the realization that South America is weak while the States are strong." Weigel concluded:

"One of the forces in South America that we must win is the Catholic Church. Just what power the Catholic Church has here is a very obscure question. It is not dominant, that much is certain. Yet it is not without force, that is also certain. Through its vision it controls many of the best elements among the youth. This is an important point that must not be forgotten. The intellectual hold of Catholicism is much stronger in the younger circles than in the older groups who are in fact in power...."[20]

When it came to the Catholics and the Left, Weigel mentioned the Eucharistic Congress in Santiago earlier in the month as evidence that the two could work together despite their fundamentally different views. That was because "neither side considers itself sufficiently strong to venture a decisive battle."[21]

Chilean Catholics were suspicious of America because "America has meant Protestantism to the average South American. It has also meant Liberalism. To not a few it has meant anti-Catholicism." Many Chileans suspected American Catholicism "because while it is large, vigorous and effective, it does not use the modalities of action that South American Catholicism considers proper and necessary. The conservative South American Catholics see in this rejection of their style an implicit rejection of something Catholic. The freedom of the American clergy, which is not bound by the odious restrictions imposed on the Latin clergy shocks the older Latin Catholics."

Weigel's comments revealed his bias; his presence in South America was an experiment in the introduction of American Catholicism into Latin societies.[22] The South American belief that "America meant Protestantism of a virulent anti-Catholic type was accentuated by the itch most American Protestant Churches had of sending missionaries to the South.... Many of the missionaries were sincerely anti-Catholic and they aired their anti-Catholic ideas....The Y.M.C.A., etc. all do excellent work in the field of education and social betterment... [yet]in spite of what they say, they wish to implant Protestantism." American visitors "frequently sympathized overtly with all that the Anti-Catholic forces were doing and spoke bitterly against the Catholic activities.... Many of the things that the Liberals proposed were good things, things that we had in the United States and which we all enjoyed," but this didn't change the fact that Protestant missionaries from the United States spent money "lavishly" and conducted an aggressive proselytism that attacked Catholicism.[23]

Weigel confirmed the essence of Liberalism and Protestantism as means to reorganize society, defeat the Church,[24] and give primacy to material values when he wrote:

"Many of the things that the Liberals proposed were good things, things that we had in the United States and which we all enjoyed. Consequently the American favored them and was irked by the Catholic opposition to them. There came to him all the legends of priestcraft, clerical tyranny and oppression which formed a part of his childhood information about Catholicism. It all seemed to hang together. However, he did not see that the Liberal was basically not interested in the concrete reform he was advocating. He was interested only in one thing: the overthrow of the old spiritual concept of life and society in order to implant a materialist pattern of reality."[25]

Undeterred, Weigel made recommendations to the U.S. Ambassador about how to advance American interests and policies. First, "the American government [should] recognize the existence of Catholicism as one of the forces in South America." The U.S. government should give evidence in "all official representations" of an element "not obtrusively Catholic, but yet evidently Catholic." Weigel emphasized the importance of the media and the intellectuals when he wrote, "We must try to convince our journalists and lecturers that they must study very carefully disputed issues of a religious nature – religious explicitly or by implication – before they pontificate about them."[26]

American Catholics had a role to play in bringing about the changes Weigel favored. He stressed, "The important thing we must do is convince the American Catholics that the most effective missionary work they can do for the good of their Church and their country is here in South America." The most effective way to bring this about was through an exchange of American priests with South Americans because the "American Catholics are in the best position to furnish a strong link between the United States and South America." Involving Catholic priests from the U.S. provided the means to "realize a true Panamericanism" without the "hovering shadow of Washington."[27] In a letter dated May 4, 1942, Weigel wrote to Edward Kirchner of the Catholic University of America in Washington, D.C: "Tell the *Chronicle* that we need American priests, nuns and brothers to help in education. The mission field of the American Church is South America. This cannot be stressed too much."[28]

Stressing this point, however, eventually got Weigel expelled from Chile, something Murray felt was a great injustice, although he never said just what the injustice was. Weigel's proselytizing for the American way of life rankled his Chilean superiors, who, according to Fr. Vincent McCormick, SJ, a frequent correspondent with Murray and American Assistant of the Society of Jesus in Rome, "do not wish you to return, because they do not approve of your method or your conduct. You accepted corrections very humbly, but did not benefit by them....your religious observance was not what Superiors had a right to demand."[29]

In a letter written from Baltimore after leaving Chile and directed to St. Alberto Hurtado (1901-1952), a Chilean Jesuit priest and proponent of Catholic social teaching, Weigel gave some indication for posterity of why he became a "*persona non grata*." "My apostolate was successful," he wrote, "It was too successful because since my way of life was so different from the consecrated traditions of down there I was a temptation to our young men to depart from those holy customs."[30] Weigel indicated there was some problem with the way he conducted himself in an earlier letter to Fr. Francis McQuade, SJ, the Provincial, citing "Constant friction between myself and my environment, which with the best of will on both sides, does not diminish, but rather increases."[31] Weigel was bitter and swore vengeance:

"The point is this: was an injustice done or not? Secondly what are we going to do about this injustice? To be told that the Lord Abbot laments my absence is just silly. Not only that; it is insulting. If he regrets that I am gone, then, why in heaven's name did he send me away? He was not forced to listen to the man who runs the noviceship....You see that I am very bitter . . . . The dirty thing that was done will never be right as far as I am concerned. God in His own wisdom knows what he is doing and I have faith in Him – but only God can make good come from evil. The men who do the evil must pay even to the last centavo...."[32]

The Americans tried to keep Weigel in Chile because he was essential to their operations, had cordial relations with the U.S. Ambassador, and was "extremely active" in supporting the American initiatives. He served as the de facto American intermediator in ecclesiastical affairs, having gone on a "little mission last January" to Quito, Ecuador.[33] Cordell Hull, the Secretary of State, approved Weigel's work and designated him as the U.S. representative to the Fourth American Congress of

Teachers in Santiago, Chile, for December 26 through 31, 1943.[34] Weigel knew the significance of teachers when it came to influencing the young, who he saw as becoming more Catholic in South America. In an essay entitled "A Pedagogic Reminiscence," Weigel explained the importance of a teacher: "The young men confide in him....The pupil by right and by instinct expects to be helped by his teacher. That is why he goes to school. The teacher is fundamentally a useful thing....."[35]

America wanted to tap into that market. Claude Bowers, the U.S. Ambassador to Chile, pleaded with Weigel's Jesuit superiors:

"Father Weigel's work here, not only in the University and among the students, has been really distinguished, and he has been invaluable to the Embassy and, I think, to our country. For some years I have consulted him regularly on matters touching upon his mission and American interests. While a majority of North Americans here are not Catholics, I know no one in the American colony who is so popular or who has such prestige in the colony. He reflects credit on the United States. I had something to do with the selection of Father Weigel to deliver the oration at the great meeting of Americans on the death of President Roosevelt, and it was a brilliant performance.

"When I assure you that his withdrawal would leave a void here from the viewpoint of the Embassy and the American colony, I beg you to believe that I am not in the least exaggerating. It is the feeling of all our people here. His intimate familiarity with the conditions here, social and political, is invaluable at the present time in view of the gallant fight against communism being made in this country."[36]

It was all to no avail. Returning to the U.S., Weigel became a professor of ecclesiology at Woodstock, where he "wrote his own treatise on the Church." Murray promoted him as a "specialist in Protestant theology," and Weigel was "increasingly at the service of others to do what anybody asked him to do."[37] That meant supporting Murray's efforts in the church-state wars.

FENTON REBUTS WEIGEL, DEFENDS THE SPANISH, AND THE CONFLICT WIDENS

After Weigel's piece appeared, Fenton wrote an article placing the Spanish comments in proper context with Church teaching. Entitled "Spain and Religious Freedom" and published in the September 1952 edition of the *American Ecclesiastical Review,* the piece referred to the sixth article of the Spanish Charter. It read: "The profession and practice of the Catholic religion, which is that of the Spanish State, enjoy official protection. No one shall be molested for his religious beliefs or in the private exercise of worship. No external ceremonies or manifestations other than those of the Catholic religion shall be permitted." Fenton pointed out that forced conversions were prohibited, Cardinal Gibbons' objection that one should be "molested for his religious beliefs" was preserved, and the religious practices of different groups were allowed. The only thing prohibited was public propaganda or proselytizing by these groups.[38]

In discussing Cardinal Segura's claim that "The civil power cannot renounce its duty of defending and promoting the true religion duly known as such (the Catholic religion), and should defend it in function of the norms of this religion," Fenton criticized both the American and the Spanish view on church and state relations. His goal was to show that the Spanish model was acceptable for Catholic states and societies but that the model that prevailed in America was suitable when a Catholic state did not exist. Beginning with pronouncements from Pope Paul VI in 1790 and continuing to Pope Leo XIII in the 1880s, the Church taught that Catholic rulers of Catholic societies were responsible for protecting the Church and denying equal opportunity to non-Catholic cults.[39]

The American situation, which Fenton called "the separation of Church and State in the U.S.A.," was repeatedly approved by the American hierarchy, which recognized that the ideal was the Catholic State with a Catholic ruler defending the faith and the Church but also claimed that the "First Amendment to our Constitution solved the problem in a way that was typically American in its practical recognition of existing conditions and its evident desire to be fair to all citizens of whatever religious faith." This position was anchored in both *Immortale Dei* and in *Libertas.* The former stated, "The Church, indeed, deems it unlawful to place the various forms of divine worship on the same footing as the true religion, but does not, on that account, condemn those rulers who, for the sake of securing some great good or of hindering some great evil, allow patiently custom or usage to be a kind of sanction for each kind of religion having its place in the State." In *Libertas,* the Church "does not forbid public authority to tolerate what is at variance with truth and justice, for the sake of avoiding some greater evil, or of obtaining or preserving some greater good....but if, in such circumstances for the sake of the common good – and this is the only legitimate reason – human law may or even should tolerate evil, it may not and should not approve or desire evil for its own sake." [40]

The American position was a compromise,[41] but Hartnett and Murray were arguing that the "State should *per se* yield equal rights to all religions, as in the U.S.A." They claimed the "pronouncements of Leo XIII and of other Popes which conflict with this view...were historically conditioned by the circumstances of the times," which did not set out a "perennially valid theory of Church-State relations," which were "reducible to this: of the State the Church demands only her freedom." Therefore, the more liberal theory, that is, the American formulation, was "the ideal Church-State relationship."[42]

The Liberals had not only not proven their case given the papal pronouncements in *Longinqua Oceani,*[43] but they were arguing for a departure from the Catholic ideal in Spain because "the condition of Protestants in Spain has harmful repercussions on Catholics elsewhere in the world, especially in the USA." When Pius XII endorsed the privileged position of the Catholic Church in Spain by entering into a convention with the Spanish on June 7, 1941, he attacked Liberalism as an error to be avoided by the Christians as it was condemned by the Church. Liberalism denied the Church's supremacy, and its indirect power in mixed matters. It held that the State should be indifferent in religious matters, that the same liberty should be given to truth and to error, and that the Church should be granted the same rights as other confessions (even in Catholic countries). Tolerance can give "impetus to indifferentism, and deprives his fellow citizens of the benefit which the devotion to and love of truth offers them."[44]

The New York Times covered an exchange between Rev. Paul E Freed, a Baptist minister from Greensboro, North Carolina, and the Spanish Minister of Foreign Affairs, Alberto Martin Artajo. Freed explained that American public opinion was "so concerned about Spanish Protestants" because "the majority of Americans were Protestants and Americans believe so strongly in religious freedom," something "which is not a termorary [sic] reaction but a deep-rooted belief.'"[45]

The Spanish Foreign Minister responded by saying that "'foreign intervention' on behalf of Spanish Protestants would do more harm than good because it was viewed by the Roman Catholic population with the 'greatest distaste.'" The Spanish Constitution did not give the government of Spain the power to authorize Protestant proselytism. The majority of the Spanish people believed the "Protestant propaganda in Spain is an attempt of foreign penetration in national life, directed with political aims at the dstruction [sic] of the religious [Catholic] unity that substantially exists in Spain and that is recognized by all Spaniards." Protestants had legal channels available to them to vindicate the rights given them under Spanish law.[46]

The New York Times also ran an article in which Cardinal Segura expressed concern at the silence from the Vatican regarding the comments from *America* and *The Indiana Catholic.* Segura wrote, "This article caused spiritual harm among Catholics and therefore there is the necessity of refuting it." Both editors, Hartnett of *America* and Fr. Raymond Bosler of the *Indiana Catholic,* were unrepentant and did not withdraw their editorials. Hartnett wrote, "There is a difference of opinion among Catholic theologians regarding the compatibility of the principle of religious liberty with Catholic teaching."[47] Shea noted that Murray's ideas were gaining support in the Catholic press.[48] In contrast, Shea's ideas were rarely heard except in the classroom and an occasional article in Fenton's *American Ecclesiastical Review.*

27
CARDINAL STRITCH REJECTS MURRAY'S PLEA

In May 1952, in the midst of the Spain conflict, Cardinal Stritch decided to respond to Murray's October 1950 memorandum on the need to change Catholic teaching on church and state. Stritch disputed the phenomenon that Murray claimed to be describing and felt the outcry for "religious liberty" was really a Protestant attack on the Catholic view of the Church-State relationship. In his reply, prepared after "very careful study" of Murray's memorandum and "the articles published on the questions discussed in it by its author and the French philosopher, Jacques Maritain," Stritch wrote:

"The presentation of what the author calls 'a grave danger' which confronts the Church in the United States in my judgment is not comprehensive. All through our history, we Catholics in the United States have had to face this same attack upon the Church from non-Catholics. The point of the attack has been the same all through the years: namely, that Catholics cannot be loyal to the Constitution of the United States and at the same time loyal to their Church. The notion of religious freedom in the non-Catholic mind in the English-speaking world derives from the Protestant doctrine upholding the right of the individual to interpret for himself the Sacred Scriptures. Generally the Protestant mind and those who are not Protestants but think in the

Protestant mentality hold that the Reformation was a great emancipation of the intellect and the beginning of the day of freedoms.... The English philosopher, Locke...wrote his famous *Letters on Toleration*. He expresses in these letters the Protestant mind of his time when he excludes from his notion of toleration the Roman Catholic Church in England because of its allegiance to a foreign sovereign. It was this notion of religious tolerance which the colonists brought from England to the United States.... [T]he Protestant tradition held on in Protestant minds, and Protestants questioned the loyalty of Catholics to the Constitution, on the grounds that they could not be loyal to the grant of religious freedom and at the same time be true to their Church.... Time and time again, all through our history, we have had to face this same sort of attack on the part of our non-Catholic fellow citizens. The Protestant mind simply will not admit that there is one true Church established by our Blessed Savior." [1]

Stitch continued:

"With the coming and the spread of secularism from out of our universities, this Protestant notion of religious freedom has been reasserted. The very growth of the Church has brought about this new attack on it. The growing activity of our government in the field of human welfare has brought new clashes between the rights of the Church and the asserted rights of the State in the field of welfare and education. In our non-Catholic schools of higher learning, many of which are supported from public funds, everything is dominated by an exaggerated notion of academic freedom. In these universities there is defended the proposition that professors and students must be unfettered in making their explorations for the truth. It is true that the attack on the Church today is widespread. The leaders of this attack assert that Catholics cannot be true to our democracy and at the same time true to their Church. They quote the papal encyclicals and papal pronouncements on Church-State relationships without giving the whole of the doctrine taught by the Popes. Actually their attacks center on the question of Church-State relationships...."[2]

In articulating his beliefs about the conflict between Catholic and Protestant worldviews, Stritch conceded that Americans "will admit that Catholics today are loyal citizens, but they question the adherence of Catholics in the United States to the papal teachings on Church-State relationships," especially regarding the encyclicals of Leo XIII. The Americans ask, "'What if Catholics were a majority in the United States? Would they demand the constitutional abolition of the First Amendment? Would they be in favor of granting religious freedom to other religious groups?'"[3]

To avoid the Americans' negative reaction to Catholic teaching on Church-State doctrine, Murray argued that Catholic doctrine needed to be changed so that it could no longer be "regarded as being in opposition to the American political system." Murray argued that the Church had to assuage Protestant fears that the "Catholic Church does not fully and sincerely affirm the human and political values of a democratically organized political society... in a word, that Americanism and Catholicism are fundamentally in conflict." He conceded that "Catholic doctrine on Church-State relationships is in certain dynamic respects at variance with American constitutional principles of government. Concretely, the Catholic political ideal is considered to be inherently destructive of the institutions of freedom of religion, freedom of speech, freedom of the press, and freedom of association."[4] Murray still felt that the Church, because of the controversy, had a golden opportunity if only she would let him devise the principles for the proper adaptation of Catholic principle to American circumstances by allowing, first and foremost, the Church's position on Church-State doctrine to "develop." The Church condemned the Jacobins of the French Revolution and Continental Liberalism, but it had not taken a position on the American situation or Anglo-American Liberalism, which derived its roots from a tradition that was alien to the revolutionary Liberalism of the Continent.[5]

Stritch remained unpersuaded. His approach to the Protestant attack emphasized the truth of the Catholic position rather than a willingness to "develop" it. "A first principle in meeting this attack on the Church," he wrote, "must be that we courageously and boldly and unflinchingly state Catholic truth." Having reviewed not only Murray's memorandum but also Murray's various writings on the topic, the Cardinal expressed a hearty disagreement with Murray's position that Pope Leo XIII did not have in mind the American or Anglo-Saxon model of Church and state relations. "I cannot subscribe to this position taken by the author of the memorandum," Stritch wrote, emphasizing Murray's misreading of paragraph 6 of *Longinqua Oceani:*

"The wording of Pope Leo XII's Encyclical, *Immortale Dei,* in my judgment makes very clear the fact that he is teaching Catholic doctrine. Clearly he teaches the doctrine on the independence of the Church in the field of its own competence as an independent society. He teaches that the State in its field is an independent society. He repudiates the doctrine that the State is not subject to divine law. The Pope asserts that between these two supreme societies there must be cooperation and that in the field of 'mixed matters' the State must recognize the rights of the Church. That Pope Leo XIII was fully cognizant of conditions in the United States is evident from the letter which he wrote to the Hierarchy of the United States on January 6, 1895. This Encyclical Letter, *Longinqua Oceani Spatia,* has this passage: 'Moreover (a fact which it gives pleasure to acknowledge), thanks are due to the equity of the laws which obtain in America and to the customs of the well-ordered Republic. For the Church amongst you, unopposed by the Constitution and government of your nation, fettered by no hostile legislation, protected against violence by the common laws and the impartiality of the tribunals, is free to live and act without hindrance. Yet, though all this is true, it would be very erroneous to draw the conclusion that in America is to be sought the type of the most desirable status of the Church, or that it would be universally lawful or expedient for State and Church to be, as in America, dissevered and divorced. The fact that Catholicity with you is in good condition, nay, is even enjoying a prosperous growth, is by all means to be attributed to the fecundity with which God has endowed His Church, in virtue of which unless men or circumstances interfere, she spontaneously expands and propagates herself; but she would bring forth more abundant fruits if, in addition to liberty, she enjoyed the favor of the laws and patronage of the public authority.'"[6]

The First Amendment was, according to Stritch, an accommodation or "practical arrangement" given the presence of so many religious groups. However, "granting religious freedom to all religious groups and individuals is not a full recognition of the mandate of divine law. Moreover, in the field which the canonists call '*materia mixta*,' the rights of the Church are not always recognized."[7]

Murray argued that Catholic principles could be reconciled with the American Constitution in such a way that "the affirmation of American political principles entails no demial [sic] or diminution of traditional Catholic principles regarding the relationship between Church and State. On the contrary, only the manner of applying these principles need be different, in order that Catholic doctrine may be vitally adapted to this modern form of the democratic State." The difference was that the lay state was limited in its powers and "the people themselves bring the demands of their religious conscience to bear upon the acts and legislation of government" through "the medium of democratic institutions."[8] Stritch firmly opposed this idea arguing "any attempt to make this arrangement an objective application of Catholic doctrine in my judgment is a mistake."[9]

Stritch then articulated what he felt was the proper Catholic response to the American situation, "without detracting in any way from the teaching of the Church on Church-State relationships": "If Catholics were a majority in the United States, they would have full regard for the subjective in the consciences of their fellow citizens. Their Church would demand that they act in justice towards all. They have no right and no desire to use political influence for bringing men to the Catholic Church." That being said, the Church could not accommodate her teaching to fit historical circumstance. "What more can we say?" Stritch concluded. "We cannot give approval to the Protestant notion of religious freedom."[10]

Rather than accommodate Protestant errors, the Church should insist "rather on exposing the errors which are propagated among our citizens and prayerfully pointing out to them the authentic truth which the Church teaches." The secularism America exhibited, Stritch wrote, "is not always inimical to religion," but in articulating its essentially

Protestant principles, which is to place "religion in the domains of the private lives of individuals," it leaves people wanting more" than "something on which they can found their freedoms and their rights." That is what gives the Church a great opportunity to work for conversions.[11]

Stritch wanted to stress "the duties of the citizens in a democracy and their obligations to work for the common good, under natural and divine law," a theme set forth by Pius XII in his Christmas message. The "Church is at home in a rightly ordered democracy and ready and anxious in such a political system to shower her benefits, from which there will come a greater and greater measure of common good." One concession the Church could make was given: "In the world today the countries which are working against the powers who are fighting God and denying to men the enjoyment of their native rights are democracies, a statement of the Holy Father showing that democratic institutions are not in any way uncongenial to the Church would be helpful."[12]

28

CONNELL AND FENTON SOUND ALARM BELLS

Despite Stritch's rebuff, Murray's views continued to gain support among both religious and laity, something that became a matter of concern for Connell and Fenton. During the height of the intramural debates with Murray, Connell wrote a letter to Giuseppe Cardinal Pizzardo, the Prefect for the Congregation of Seminaries and Universities and later Secretary of the Holy Office (February 1951 to October 1959). With the letter, Connell sent the proceedings of the Third Annual Meeting of the Catholic Theological Society, including Murray's talk on the suppression of heresy by the government and Connell's own article, "Christ, the King of Civil Rulers" from the October 1948 *American Ecclesiastical Review.* Connell wrote to Pizzardo directly "instead of going through the Holy Office," underscoring his concern about "this new opinion which has won so many defenders in America during the past two years" and hoping that Pizzardo "will know the most prudent course to follow."[1]

The following summer, as Fenton was preparing for one of his many journeys to Rome, Connell asked him to persuade the Holy Office to issue a definitive doctrinal statement on church and state. Fearing that the Catholic universities had defected to the Americanist position, Connell told Fenton to "be sure to emphasize strongly the necessity of a definite statement regarding the 'lay state' theory. I doubt if theological controversy will settle the matter, however logical and strong the arguments may be that are adduced in favor of the traditional doctrine. If necessary, I believe that a declaration from the Holy Office might be desirable. The repercussions of this new idea are, I believe, very unfortunate in our land especially. I wonder if the Holy See would consider a suggestion that greater care be taken by Bishops and religious superiors to see that all that is taught in the classroom is perfectly orthodox. ....But the fact remains, that apparently some strange notions can be presented in the classroom, and no one checks on it."[2]

After his return from Rome, Fenton expressed concern about how Murray wanted to control the debate in the pages of *American Ecclesiastical Review*:

"M's letter and article came while I was gone. I have accepted the article and answered the letter. As far as I can see, M wants to control the number of the Review in which his article will appear. I had to tell him that his conditions were entirely unacceptable. He appears to be getting rather hysterical about the entire affair. I certainly shall not allow his article to run without a long and complete rejoinder from your pen. His case is much more serious than most people realize. I shall tell you more about it when you return. I do not want to give him the opportunity to say that AER refused him a chance to justify himself. Your reputation is soaring in Rome."[3]

Connell monitored the situation in the United States and kept the Church hierarchy informed about the inexorable spread of Murray's doctrines. In a letter dated February 23, 1952, to Archbishop Ameleto G. Cicognani, Apostolic Delegate to the United States, Connell mentioned a story from the February 15, 1952 edition of Washington's *Evening Star* by Associated Press writer George Cornell, tagging as enemies those in the Church holding to the Catholic viewpoint. The article misrepresented the Catholic position, something that showed that Murray's views were gaining adherents:

"Claim: If Catholics become a majority in the United States, their doctrine would compel them to suppress other faiths as false. Reply:

Some Catholic theologians do hold this restrictive thesis, on grounds that 'error has no right before truth.' Another school holds the Church should protect the liberty of all to worship as they please. In the United States the general Catholic orientation is toward the latter view. Elaborating on this subject, Msgr. Thomas J. McCarthy spokesman for the National Catholic Welfare Conference (central Catholic organization) said the restrictive idea is held mostly in "the continental school, among Italian and Spanish theologians." In this country, he said, Catholic Bishops "with uniformity accept our traditional practice. They would never favor any attempt to force the conscience of the individual, even should Catholics become a majority." "The Church is a witness for Christ,' he said. 'All it can do is persuade. It can't force."[4]

Cornell's article, Connell told Cicognani, "clearly indicates confusion of thought regarding the Catholic doctrine, a failure to perceive the distinction between the thesis and the hypothesis, with a tendency toward the opinion advocated by Father Murray. I feel that it emphasizes the growing need for an authoritative statement on this subject of Church and state from the Holy See."[5] In a response dated February 27, Cicognani recognized the concern and assured Connell that he "recently had occasion to send to the Holy See certain material on this question. I am sure that it will be seriously considered but we know that the investigation and study take time."[6] Time, however, was running out for the Catholics. Luce and his Americanist allies were preparing to take the fight directly to the headquarters of the Catholic Church, and the U.S. government had signed on to help with that effort.

PART VIII

THE U.S. TARGETS ITS FRIENDS

29
THE IMPORTANCE OF SPAIN, EDWARD P. LILLY, AND THE PSB

After the Americans conquered Germany in 1945, they put in place an organization to oversee the reconstruction and re-engineering of society. Through intense psychological manipulation, German society underwent significant changes. The Americans were so impressed with the results of social engineering in Germany that they decided to expand the scope of its operation to include their Catholic "friends." In the early part of 1950, the U.S. government expanded "the central core of psychological war" to include a program of doctrinal warfare that was designed to inculcate in the intellectuals of various world societies the idea that America was good, if not the ideal, and that American ideas on socio-political-economic matters and organization were right. In addition to targeting Western Europe and Latin America, the American psychological warfare establishment's newly created doctrinal warfare arm targeted major religions of the world.

As Catholic theologians, journalists, and editors in America and Spain were discoursing about religious liberty, the Americans were busy bringing Spain into their orbit of social, economic, and military control. An article in *The New York Times* from July 1952 reported that both the governments of the U.S. and Spain were in ongoing negotiations concerning the placement of U.S. military bases on Spanish soil. Spain wanted to be included in the Mutual Security Aid program and receive military support from the U.S. in the event of an attack by the USSR. The U.S. was offering economic assistance in addition to the use of Spanish real estate but believed Spanish demands were "unreasonable."[1]

The U.S. had long seen strategic value in Spain. A number of Joint Chiefs of Staff (JCS) resolutions revealed this strategic importance but also presented the weaknesses of the country, most notably its economy. The JCS resolutions from December 1947 to September 1951 showed an evolution in thinking about Spain. Initially, the resolutions "Hoped to replace Franco – US and UN resolution 12 Dec 46." With time, an alliance with Spain was viewed as something that "transcends political considerations."[2] A progress report detailed American improvements in Spanish transportation facilities, economic assistance, and efforts to bring Spain into the North Atlantic Treaty Organization (NATO) in return for rights to military bases.[3]

As part of this effort, the Spanish government and prelates were closely scrutinized by American intelligence. Murray was not the only one to see the value of using religion to advance American goals. The man at the center of this effort, and many more, was Dr. Edward P. Lilly, a professor of history at the Catholic University of America. Lilly was representative of the lay Catholic leadership of America, which prospered by advancing American interests. Catholic Professor and scion of a wealthy family, Edward P. Lilly, created a Doctrinal, or Ideological, Warfare Program that was designed to infiltrate Christianity, Hinduism, Buddhism, and Islam and promote the message that America was good and its ideology consistent with the principles of the world's major religions. Catholic priests were important to the U.S. government in making all of this happen.

Lilly, of "Irish stock" and from a leading Catholic family, was born in Brooklyn, New York, in 1910. He attended Brooklyn College Preparatory School and then Holy Cross College in Worcester, Massachusetts. There, he obtained an A.B. in Philosophy, History, and American Government, graduating cum laude. He then attended the Catholic University of America where he earned a Ph.D. in 1936 in American History and Political Science. From 1936 to 1939, Lilly was an Assistant Professor of History at Loyola University in Chicago, Illinois.[4]

Lilly's dissertation thesis dealt with colonial agents between the colonies and England. The thesis sparked interest in academe, and he received a scholarship in the summer of 1939 to study the matter further at Cambridge and Oxford as well as at the British Records Office. The outbreak of World War II prevented him from traveling and doing the work.[5] About this time, Joe Kennedy, father of JFK and friend of Lilly's father, wanted Lilly to tutor JFK and travel to Nazi Germany. Lilly's father was also a friend of William R. Grace, the first Catholic mayor of New York, and owner of the Norton Lilly & Company steamship line, which he eventually sold to Grace.[6] J. Peter Grace, the grandson of William R., was another pillar of Catholicism in America, as well as a business giant. Like Lilly, J. Peter Grace, who worked closely with the CIA and the entire American intelligence community, was a "firm believer" in free enterprise and the "American Way." He was a principal in CIA front organizations, like the Crusade for Family Prayer and Fr. Patrick Peyton's Family Rosary Crusade.[7]

Unable to pursue his research in England and choosing not to take Joe Kennedy up on his offer, Lilly became a Stirling Fellow in American History at Yale University from 1939 to 1940, after which he went to CUA, where he became Assistant and Associate Professor of American History, Director of Program of History of American Thought, and Director of the History Program for the Army Special Training Program.[8]

In the early part of 1944, Lilly joined the Office of War Information (OWI) as assistant to Director Elmer Davis. Davis wanted Lilly to write a history of the OWI, but Lilly wanted to "check into some of the propaganda and other news (dissemination) particularly in radio broadcasting to the Allies and to neutral peoples and to the Germans." Once Rome and Paris were occupied by U.S. forces, the OWI set up a "big propaganda organization" in each of these cities.[9] In his employment records, Lilly described his involvement with psychological warfare during World War II as being "responsible for making strictly confidential and highly classified analyses of the activities of the many bureaus and division in the Domestic and Overseas Branches of OWI and to make reports to the Director." Because he was "one of the few" who understood both the Domestic and the Overseas operations of the OWI, Lilly proposed writing a classified history of the OWI,[10] which he completed by the end of 1945.[11]

With the end of the war in sight, both Truman and Davis wanted to dissolve the OWI. As the Joint Chiefs of Staff were discussing the issue, Lilly "decided to try to persuade them to set up a psychological section." Admiral William J. Leahy liked the idea, and Lilly recounted how Leahy "called me in and said he thought that my proposal was very good and that it should be part of the Joint Chiefs of Staff's planning process."[12]

Having "convinced Admiral Leahy of [the] need for a complete history of American psychological warfare," Lilly worked for the JCS for the next six years, compiling a history that included both the military and the civilian aspects of psychological operations.[13] Lilly's "highly classified" 1,400-page history of psychological warfare during World War II was based on an "exhaustive study of the records" of the OWI, the OSS, the Department of State, the War Department, the Navy Department, the JCS, and the Coordinator of Inter-American Affairs.[14] While working on this classified history, Lilly "advised Joint Staff personnel responsible for psychological planning." These included Colonel Ivan Yeaton, Joe Dickey, the "Brown Team," and the "Joint Subsidiary Plans Division." Lilly gained his extensive knowledge of psychological warfare by interviewing returning intelligence officers, something which made him "familiar with psychological developments from 1939 to the present. The study of Psychological Operations, 1946-1951, which I made for Psychological Strategy Board, filled out my background on the national policy level on which agency developments must be based."[15]

In the autumn of 1951, Lilly was commissioned by Gordon Grey, Director of the recently formed Psychological Strategy Board (PSB), to write another history. This time he was to "prepare a brief but comprehensive background of the development of the psychological factor in National Policy from the end of World War II to the establishment of the Psychological Strategy Board by the President's directive of 4 April 1951." The project led him to a review and analysis of National Policy documents of the "highest level, consultation with policymakers on the top levels of

State Department, Central Intelligence, and the Department of Defense" as well as the Bureau of the Budget and the executive offices of the President. The resulting study was the "first all-embracive study of the development of the psychological factor in the Cold War."[16]

Lilly completed the Top-Secret document entitled "The Development of American Psychological Operations 1945-1951" on December 19, 1951. A relatively short document (95 pages) given that he had drafted histories of U.S. intelligence efforts and organizations of 400, 800, and 1,400 pages in length, this paper presented an overview of how American psychological operations were developed after World War II and how they got integrated into the Cold War. The work was valuable for a number of reasons, most notably because it revealed the influence of private industry in the development of psychological warfare. It also revealed the close collaboration between the U.S. government and private industry (primarily news, media, and entertainment) in conducting psychological warfare.[17]

Private news agencies cooperated with the government during World War II by making their overseas outlets available to the government, and also by sharing its news files with the OWI and with Nelson Rockefeller's Inter-American Affairs group. This allowed American propaganda's "uncontrolled transmission overseas as government news." Once the war ended, the private news agencies advised the government that they could no longer give them their news and that the government's Interim Information Service (IIS) was on its own. At the same time, "a few far–seeing individuals in government and in private enterprise urged the retention of some activities as necessary adjuncts to a government which had become the world power." However, two great problems existed. First, there was a question about the utility of psychological warfare, and second, there was a question on just how to measure or determine its effect.[18]

Lilly's report confirmed the belief that after the Second World War, the "major problems were: reconstruction and rehabilitation of war-torn areas and the economic and political development of the backward or colonial areas so that eventually they would be self-governing participants in the international paradise." As 1946 unfolded, government leaders increasingly believed government programs should be provided by private industry. Private industry balked at this, instead suggesting private outlets and facilities should be rented by the Government, which operated its own news and, by implication, conducted psychological operations. This view prevailed, but it created another problem —namely, how to coordinate the American message—which became more urgent once the Communists resisted the Marshall Plan. It was this "critical situation," Lilly wrote, which "awakened American officials to the necessity of our overseas information program presenting a uniform viewpoint. Whether it was issued by the Voice of America, by local USIS, by the Armed Forces Radio Service, or by American private and commercial outlets, America's story had to be uniform or Communist propaganda would exploit the differences." By the end of 1947, the need for government control of information that could "influence foreign attitudes directly by explaining American objectives and countering anti-American propaganda" led to the creation of NSC-4, "Coordination of Foreign Information Measures" in December.[19]

Domestic support for America's foreign policy objectives was important to the effort overseas. Foreign propaganda only succeeded abroad if it had first captured the mind of the American public, something Lilly made clear after the advent of NSC-68, "US Objectives and Programs for National Security," in April 1950, when he wrote, "In the political and psychological estimate of NSC-68 frequent mention was given to the psychological elements: to the power of American public opinion, to our own confidence and sense of moral direction, and to the necessity of stimulating similar feelings among our allies. If Americans increased their own confidence and moral sense, they would evoke similar strength in our Allies and other free peoples."[20]

The State Department's Campaign of Truth identified the "areas of most immediate importance and within these areas the most effective targets for psychological activities." The first area was the USSR, and the second was their satellites. The third area included two peripheral categories. These were "the immediately dangerous areas such as Eastern Germany, Iran, and Southeast Asia where existent Communist pressures could be recognized" and the areas with "longer-term problems such as India, France and Italy, where danger of Communist pressure existed but where the general trend was in support of the Free World." The last category contained the "Scandinavian countries and the Arab world, where the influential opinion had to be so prepared that these areas which were attempting to maintain neutrality in the Cold War, would be sympathetic towards the Western world if a shooting war started." Each separate area developed a "system of priorities" to present the American position. NSC-68 was then amended to encourage the development of "'a community of interest' among the governments and peoples of the Free World so that they would act in a determined manner against Communist aggression.'"[21]

By early 1951, the need to create division between the leaders of the USSR and their people became one of psychological warfare's foundational principles. To that end, "Congress was considering a series of resolutions proclaiming America's continuing friendship for the Russian people as distinct from the Kremlin. It was hoped that such official statements might develop a psychological cleavage between the Russian people and their leaders." At the same time, "influential business leaders" began demanding an organization "to push for a stronger American psychological effort to counter the apparent Russian victories in the world-wide propaganda war." Looking at the work of Radio Free Europe, President Truman issued NSC-74-/1 that authorized the Psychological Strategy Board, or PSB, which came into existence on April 4, 1951.[22]

The PSB was part of the National Security Council (NSC) and came into being to "provide guidance for the initiation of covert operations" in addition to consolidating intelligence gathering/analysis and propaganda functions at the highest levels of the government. This included the most important aspects of America's psychological or political warfare strategy and techniques.[23]

30
LILLY AND THE AMERICANS RECRUIT CATHOLICS

By the summer of 1952, Lilly was a GS-15 and a strategic planner working in the Office of Plans and Policy in the PSB. "One of a small group responsible for developing the strategic psychological plans for approval by the" PSB, Lilly focused on the "ideological and moral aspects of psychological planning" and worked to prepare not only staff studies but also on drafting plans to implement directives.[1] Psychological warfare involved both doctrinal warfare and recruiting American Catholics to re-engineer recalcitrant Catholic countries like Spain. Lilly had been watching the Spanish closely for some time, largely through reports like the one which explained that Western European countries "could not have an intimate working partnership" with Spain in economic and defense arenas because the "Spanish Government deprives the people of... fundamental basic rights of the individual."[2]

"The most desirable course of action," according to one Top Secret report that appeared during that summer, "must be designed to avoid international pressure on Spain while at the same time continuing our efforts to emphasize the need for measures of political and economic liberalization of Spain, encouraging private trade and private investment on a purely business basis and developing informal contact between Spanish and US military authorities...." These measures would bring about "evolutionary political and economic changes within Spain, which included "some moderate evolutionary steps toward democratic government" and the lessening of "repression of political expression." [3]

In the economic arena, "private business and banking arrangements should be conducted on a free and normal basis without interposing political objections or resolutions." A resolution of the "Dollar Shortage" was needed, as well as ending the "corrupt and inefficient economic administration of the regime" for there to be an "increase of private US-Spanish trade." Most Americans, it was noted, were indifferent to the effort to normalize relations with Spain. The exception to that rule was "organized labor and some Protestant groups." A principal obstacle to the normalization of relations was the Spanish view that "Spain has only to hold her own way of life and the rest of the world will fall into line." The psychological warfare establishment determined that Spain had to be opened to the world, something that could be best accomplished by telling the Spanish about the rest of the world and convincing the Spanish that the Americans wanted to "strengthen their economies and improve their standard of living." The report concluded that the most effective way of presenting America to the Spanish was through motion pictures.[4]

Portugal also ended up in the cross-hairs of the psychological warfare establishment. Because the "Roman Catholic Church...exercises strong political and social influence," Portugal was isolated from Western Europe, and it suffered from a number of "adverse factors," which included "a low living standard, a high rate of illiteracy, limited number of English-speaking citizens, and strict government censorship." The scarcity of investment capital in Portugal arose from "the low economic development level, the steady rise in population, the continuation of absentee-landlordism and the absence of any development toward a more modern social and business structure." The U.S. objectives for Portugal were similar to those for Spain: "achieve economic, political and military integration in Western Europe and coordination in North Atlantic area."[5]

In addition to the reports he was receiving, Lilly did his own research and discovered something called the Hispanidad movement, which Franco encouraged as part of an attempt to create solidarity amongst Hispanic heritage countries. Lilly dismissed the movement as not constituting a threat to Pan-Americanism.[6]

By autumn, the working draft of the PBS "Staff Study on Iberia" concluded that the Iberian Peninsula was "essential to America's long-range peace objectives," but before America could achieve its long-term goals, "IBERIA's political, social and economic conservatism [must] be tempered." That meant political changes in both Spain and Portugal, where the governments "are basically totalitarian and authoritarian, based on a close, but not completely harmonious, alliance with the army, the Catholic Church, the nobility and the industrialists."[7]

WATCHING THE CATHOLICS

A number of U.S. agencies reported on Catholic prelates and the status of the Catholic Church in various countries around the world. Their reports, for the most part, classified Secret or Top Secret, found their way to Lilly. One of the more prominent Catholic personalities was Cardinal Segura of Spain, whose honest assessments of the Protestants precipitated editorial attacks by *America* and *Indiana Catholic.* The United States Information Services (USIS) read the Cardinal's pastorals and observed that while he was "anti-Franco," he was still "very reactionary, authoritarian, etc. No salvation outside church."[8]

A PSB memorandum mentioned the American Bishops' sympathy for Catholics in China and that the National Catholic Welfare Conference encouraged prayers for "'all of those persecuted under a system of Government which is the acknowledged enemy of all those decencies which have been the special blessings of our own country,'" confirming the observations of Luce and others that American Catholics were different from Catholics in Latin countries.[9]

The PSB was also interested in the Church in Austria, especially Bishop Jachym of Vienna, who was hand-picked "by the Vatican to overshadow and eventually replace Cardinal Innitzer. His prime task at the moment is to withdraw the Church from open political action on all fronts, and instead to wage a campaign of covert influence especially on the Socialists. This campaign would be designed to win Socialist backing for Church measures, thus divorcing the Church from its traditional... alliance with the Right."[10]

The Americans sought to control the Catholic press in Austria to prevent the rise of neo-Nazism in western Austria by enlisting the support of the Catholic press "in and around Salzbourg, Linz, Innsbruck, etc...." This was not considered too difficult an undertaking because "whatever self-generated opposition exist to neo-Nazism in Western Austria today lies largely in the Catholic segment of society."[11]

In Yugoslavia, the authorities waged an anti-Catholic campaign,[12] but in Hungary, the Catholics and the Communists coexisted in a way that allowed Msgr. Imre Szabo to describe the Catholic Church in Hungary as "free and functioning normally." The PSB considered this a threat, concluding that "Since Catholics have found that they can work with Communists in Hungary, Catholics elsewhere can do the same."[13]

During the course of his work, Lilly met with a number of prelates and Catholic leaders, including the Most Rev. A. J. Muench, archbishop of Fargo and Apostolic Nuncio to West Germany. Lilly described the meeting which took place on November 6, as being on a strictly personal basis between two Americans: Meunch [sic], having desired "information, and I, having an idea on which I sought professional reaction." Lilly reported, "After emphasizing the personal nature of the meeting and the desirability of religion being a more powerful factor in check of communism, he raised the possibility of developing an inter-sectarian approach to the 1953 elections.... As a result of personal experience, he could say that inter-faith cooperation in West Germany was very extensive and very close on matters of charitable work and handling of refugees and expellees and on mutual assistance across the Iron Curtain into East Germany. However, the 1953 election is not basically an anti-communist issue."[14] As some indication of the crucial role that Germany was now to play in the anti-Communist crusade, the PBS drew attention to an article from *The New York Times* entitled "German Catholic Join War on Reds," which discussed how Catholic and Protestant hierarchy in Germany joined with the English to call on their youth to resist "Commie pressure." The bishops insisted on freedom of conscience.[15] A similar stance was taken by Cardinal Wyszjnski in Warsaw, Poland, who said, "one church objective is [to] maintain freedom [of] conscience for which he will fight 'even though it cost him his blood.'"[16]

RECRUITING CATHOLICS

Lilly, like Luce, was interested in recruiting American Catholics to advance American interests. One of Lilly's potential recruits was the Dominican Fr. Felix Morlion, OP, who proposed "using educational groups to foster anti-Communism as an aspect of a long range pro-Democratic development." Morlion was a U.S. asset and valuable to the PSB not only because he was close to the Apostolic Delegate to the U.S. but also because "he has been in touch with, and received favorable consideration from, Cardinal Stritch of Chicago Cardinal Mooney of Detroit, and Archbishop Cushing of Boston. From these men, he has received a promise that they will support the establishment of an American college at his university in Rome, and will guarantee him a minimum number of students. With this background, there is no doubt that Father Morlion is engaged in a legitimate activity." Morlion's project indicated "interesting possibilities [which] possess the advantage of the indigenous approach" while at the same time being "useful and...relatively inexpensive." Lilly concluded that the CIA should be informally queried to see what they are doing along those same lines.[17] Dr. Allen responded to Lilly through Tracy Barnes stressing, he "feels that this type of project has definite value and is the type of proposal which can be made to the 10/5 group." In addition, Allen "questioned several items in the reports prepared by Morlion, but indicated that he was going to officially present it to the 10/5 group to secure their reaction, and if possible, an evaluation of similar type of work done in 1948."[18]

Lilly attempted to recruit other priests as well, including Fr. William Gibbons, SJ, a sociology professor at Fordham. Lilly and Gibbons' "mutual friend, Ed O'Connor, told me you had recently been in Washington discussing a subject with State Department which is of major interest to my work. The possible contribution of organized religious movements to the weakening of Communist influences throughout the world is a subject in which I have long been interested."[19]

Years later, Gibbons gave a talk in St. Louis at the American Catholic Sociological Society in which he attacked the idea of large families. The size of a family, he said, should "take into account the physical and mental health of the parents, their economic condition, and the society in which they live. When you have such problems as crowding, lack of jobs and so forth, you need to retreat."[20] Gibbons was one of many Catholic intellectuals who stood ready to argue that America was better than Communism. Another was Waldemar Gurian at the University of Notre Dame.[21]

Lilly discussed the idea of using Catholics and the Catholic religion to combat Communism alongside the CIA: "Upon returning to NAME DELETED office, he raised the question of religion as a factor of ideological warfare, and he emphasized that Russian interest in religious feelings, plus the organizational strength of the Catholic Church in Europe, seemed to be overlooked in the American effort."[22] In the same month as the above meeting, Lilly discussed the same topic with Monsignor McCarthy, Director of the National Catholic Welfare Conference, to whom Lilly explained religion, as "a factor in psychological operations against communism." McCarthy, who was already a consultant for a number of government programs including Voice of America, was pessimistic about the idea of recruiting "a cooperative group of churchmen" as consultants because "there was no opposition to communism per se, but only to the Kremlin or to Soviet imperialism." The main problem lay with the government, which still hadn't "recognized the fundamental difference between democracy and communism." Until it did, the CIA would have difficulty recruiting Catholic clergy. McCarthy then came up with the names of prominent individuals who might be interested, including Reinhold Niebuhr. The only Catholic clergyman on the list was the Rev. John Courtney Murray, SJ.[23]

31
PUTTING RELIGION IN SERVICE TO THE STATE

Lilly's interest in Catholics was part of a larger plan to mobilize "moral and religious factors" to win the Cold War. In June 1951, former OSS officer and current PSB staff officer Albert P. Toner wrote a memorandum discussing the use of religion in psychological operations, which included something called "Program Guidance" for the "'Moral and Religious Factors in the USIE Program'."[1] On February 19, 1952, the PSB circulated a memo entitled "Exploitation of Basic Moral and Social Forces," which provided a proposal for the "harnessing [of] moral and social forces," which included identifying "exploitable moral and social forces with emphasis on emergent, little-known or neglected ones."[2] In the Spring of 1952, the PSB staff prepared a Top Secret draft document entitled "PSB Planning Objectives," which explained that:

"In the national interest we must make basic moral and social forces such as religion, peace-aspiration nationalism, internationalism, anti-colonialism, land hunger, racial tensions and the desire for social equality and human welfare work for us rather than against us. Where it is impracticable to harness these fundamental forces to our own national aims, we must as a minimum effort impede and where possible deny their use by the enemy. These major forces operate through the entire world and touch on all aspects of external national policy. Their consideration must therefore be both global and functional. Formal plans, policy guidance evaluations, and other staff studies that fail to deal with these factors must be considered not only incomplete, but worthless. In addition, however, we should probably produce some ad hoc plans which deal specifically with these forces."[3]

The objectives of the PSB were global in scope and involved operations on every continent to oppose Soviet Communism. The PSB was planning to develop and strengthen "conditions in the other American States which will contribute to the security and objectives of the United States and the free world, including social, economic and political improvement and the expansion of mutual defense capabilities."[4]

Tab A proposed topics for a staff study to be undertaken by the PSB: "a) The utilization of religion and other spiritual forces, b) Establishment of policy with respect to land reform, c) Review of policy decisions on the use of minority groups in psychological operations against the USSR...."[5] From this point on in the Cold War, religion was put in service to the state.

LILLY AND IKE

In a discussion with the Director of the Department of State's International Information Administration (IIA), Dr. Alfred J. McCartney, Lilly "raised the possibility of an informal approach to liberally and progressively minded church leaders in the U.S. with the hope that, as informal individual members of different Christian sects, they might be willing to form themselves into an unofficial committee to discover how they might better accomplish American premises in their regular sectarian activity. As individuals they would keep their official church leaders informed, and would, as individuals, push for official church cooperation in agreed efforts. This informal American organization would be paralleled in the overseas countries, mainly as a result of the efforts of the informal American committee. The two committees could then assist with advice, suggestions and even financial support. The American committee would likewise also be in touch with knowledgeable government officials who would not request the religious committee to do anything for the government but who would make known the government's general objective and how the activities of these groups might assist."[6]

Dr. McCartney was not optimistic, mentioning problems in interdenominational cooperation and resistance in the government to endorsing religions. "The major problem was to select the church leaders who were sufficiently farsighted to see the value of such efforts and who were sufficiently big men to undertake the responsibility of representing their churches...."[7]

Lilly, however, was undeterred by McCartney's skepticism and continued his efforts to get religious leaders' support in America's efforts in waging the Cold War. One example was Lilly's approval of the "Declaration of Faith and Call for Action" prepared by Jerome Ellison, an author from Bronxville, New York, Wallace D. Speers, a department store executive from New York City and the Chairman of the Layman's Movement for a Christian World, and John Pearson a Research executive from New Hampshire. The declaration consisted of an "An Affirmation of Faith" in which God was acknowledged to be "our Supreme Authority and Jesus Christ and the Prophets to be the revelation of His Word." The declaration insisted that "our freedoms [were] God-given" and that "God intended freedom and opportunity for all men."[8] The same declaration also called on the United States to make an "official declaration of the world-wide implications of the American Revolution of 1776 and of its religious origins" while creating "adequate means of furthering world democracy, uniting the scattered United States governmental units working hard toward this aim in a concerted national policy. Effective teaching and self-help teams could be organized and sent abroad, working openly when they could, secretly when this is impossible. Commercial and religious enterprises would be offered the opportunity to orient their overseas work to the national policy."[9]

Lilly wrote to Pearson with suggestions for corrections and changes that would make the declaration more ecumenical in scope:

"Reading that statement hurriedly, I had certain reactions with which you might be interested. I am in complete agreement with your emphasis on God as the basis of human dignity and human rights. While I am a Christian, in fact a Roman Catholic, I feel that a more practical appeal, as a counter to Communism, would result from [sic] few revisions on page 4. As individuals our acceptance of Christ, His Divinity and His Teachings, is basic to our philosophy of life but the mention of Christ in this declaration, automatically excludes Jews and Moslems from accepting it. We would not really weaken the major arguement [sic] by limiting the treatment to GOD ALMIGHTY, who can be accepted by Jew & Moslem without qualm. Our revolutionary fathers, Jefferson et alii, were deists and not fundamental Christians and hence their words better apply to the concept of GOD than they do to Christianity. Likewise, on the top of page 4, let us say that all men are our brothers. Whether they believe in God or not, they are under God the fatherland hence in the brotherhood of man, unwillingly though it may be. We do not hate the Communist; it is only the evil doctrine he possesses which can be hated. The Distinction is difficult but quite valid and definitely more appealing than distinguishing between the 'sheep and the goats.'"[10]

Lilly said the effort must "show unity and bring publicity and possibly, in unknown ways, accomplish good." He praised The National Conference of Christians and Jews as "an instrument" but suggested it "include Moslems, & if possible the Oriental groups." Lilly suggested "Letter writing between fellow religious Americans and Europeans or Asians or Africans...[to] spread the American ideal but avoid any sectarian proselytizing."[11]

Support for the use of religion as a Cold War weapon increased under President Dwight D. Eisenhower, who gave three speeches to justify the use of religion in the service of Cold War political and economic objectives: one on December 22, 1952, before the Freedom Foundation, his Inaugural on January 20, 1953, and a national broadcast by the American Legion on February 1, 1953. During his American Legion broadcast, Eisenhower claimed that "we cherish these rights so sincerely is because they are God-given. They belong to the people who have been created in His image. They belong to the lowliest among us as well as to the mightiest and the highest. That is the genius of our democracy. It is the very basis of the cause...for which so many of our fellow-citizens have died." [12]

In formulating his policies, Lilly also relied on talks from Eisenhower's Secretary of State John Foster Dulles, who told the Senate Committee on Foreign Relations that:

"The threat of Soviet communism, in my opinion, is not only the gravest threat that ever faced the United States, but the gravest threat that has ever faced what we call western civilization.... Soviet communism is atheistic in its philosophy and materialistic. It believes that human beings are nothing more than somewhat superior animals, that they have no soul, no spirit, no right to personal dignity... If you do believe in the spiritual nature of man, it is a doctrine which is utterly unacceptable and wholly irreconcilable. I do not see how, as long as Soviet communism holds those views...there can be any permanent reconciliation....between the doctrine of Soviet communism, and the doctrine of a Christian or Jewish, or, indeed, any religion, this is an irreconcilable conflict." [13]

Lilly believed these statements by Eisenhower and Dulles empowered a new form of warfare because they "indicate that moral and religious forces are expected to play a greater role in American activity vis-à-vis Soviet Communism." The feeling was mutual. "[P]rivate and religious groups have indicated a theoretical willingness to act if they are assured that such religious effort was in accord with government policy and objectives." [14]

32
DOCTRINAL WARFARE DEVELOPS

As 1952 wore on, Lilly became more deeply engaged in the development of doctrinal warfare, also known as ideological warfare, and doctrinal warfare assumed every greater significance until it was considered "the central core of psychological warfare." Ideological or doctrinal warfare involved a "planned attack against the basic hostile system conducted concurrently with a positive advocacy of basic ideas of our own system."[1] Doctrinal warfare, in other words, was a form of social engineering that involved the re-organization of the social order. Catholic Lilly was the man most responsible for developing and implementing the doctrinal warfare program[2] and turning it into a "major psychological effort by the American Government" involving both short- and long-range programs.[3]

The Top Secret document known as NSC-68 laid out the ideological parameters of the Cold War, establishing Soviet Communism as the enemy and American ideology as the ideal. Although it was implemented seven years after the end of World War II, NSC-68 was, in reality, an implementation and continuation of FDR's "Four Freedoms" speech, transposed into the context of the Cold War.

Paragraph I stated, "The Soviet Union, unlike previous aspirants to hegemony, is animated by a new fanatic faith, antithetical to our own, and seeks to impose its absolute authority over the rest of the world." The fundamental purpose of the U.S., as set out in Paragraph II, was to "maintain the essential elements of individual freedom, as set forth in the Constitution and Bill of Rights; our determination to create conditions under which our free and democratic system can live and prosper...." Paragraph IV set forth the ideological aspect of the American efforts:

"The free society values the individual as an end in himself, requiring of him only that measure of self-discipline and self-restraint which make the rights of each individual compatible with the rights of every other individual.... From this idea of freedom with responsibility derives the marvelous diversity, the deep tolerance... of the free society.... By the same token in relations between nations, the prime reliance of the free society is on the strength and appeal of its idea, and it feels no compulsion sooner or later to bring all societies into conformity with it.... The objectives of a free society are determined by its fundamental values and by the necessity for maintaining the material environment in which they flourish.....We must lead in building a successfully functioning political and economic system in the free world."[4]

The philosophy animating doctrinal warfare was perhaps best articulated by a colleague of Lilly and early collaborator on the program, Dr. Stefan T. Possony, a Professor of International Politics and advisor to the U.S. Air Force. Possony is best known as the progenitor of the idea of "Star Wars" in the early 1980s, an idea that was seized upon by President Ronald Reagan and that is claimed to have been the proverbial straw that broke the back of the Soviet Union, leading to its quick demise.

In *The Strategy of Technology*, published in 1970, Possony explained the importance of technology and the need for psychological warfare, or manipulation, to keep things stable, which is essential for investments. "The United States," he wrote, "is dedicated to a strategy of stability. We are a stabilizing rather than a disturbing power and our goal is preserving the status quo and the balance of power rather than seeking conquest and the final solution to the problems of international conflict through occupation or extermination of all opponents. In a word, the US sees the Technological War as an infinite game, one played for the sake of continuing to play, rather than for the sake of 'victory' in the narrow sense....

"The Technological War is the decisive struggle in the Protracted Conflict.... The technological War creates the resources to be employed in all other parts of the Protracted Conflict. It governs the range of strategies that can be adapted in actual or hot war. Without the proper and superior technology our strategy of deterrence would be meaningless....

"Technological War can be carried on simultaneously with any other forms of military conflict, diplomatic maneuvers, peace offensives, trade agreements, détente, and debacle. It is the source of the advanced weapons and equipment for use in all forms of warfare. It renders cold war activities credible and effective. Technological warfare combined with psychosocial operations can lead to a position of strategic dominance. . . . World War II was the last war of industrial power and mobilization, but it was also the first war of applied science.... The new technology has created weapons to be applied directly and suddenly to the national will....."[5]

Doctrinal warfare needed American technology designed to assure victory and keep all-out war from breaking out again.

CREATING THE PROGRAM

Over the Summer of 1952, Lilly promoted the development of ideological or doctrinal warfare. "PSB," he explained, "has placed great importance on this doctrinal approach. The PSB staff thought this approach was most important when it developed the original paperback in the Summer of 1952, which the Board accepted. I recall that I urged the importance of the subject upon the original panel which developed the paper which you are now responsible for coordinating."[6]

On September 11, the PSB authorized a study for a plan implementing the program to be completed by the end of April 1953. That plan needed to define terms, agree on targets, and determine the instrumentalities and tasks needed to accomplish the program. The panel complained that "The Communists have extensively used doctrinal warfare as a long-range instrument to gain influence and support in strategic areas," as opposed to the United States, which "is now doing little."[7] The early doctrinal warfare panel consisted of six members: Walter J. Stoessel of the Department of State, Thomas B. Larson also of the Department of State, Yaro J. Skalnik of the G-2 (Intelligence) of the U.S. Army, and Stefan T. Possony of the Air Force. Also on the panel were two members of the CIA whose names remain unknown to this day.[8] The panel met regularly from November until the following Summer to devise the Doctrinal Warfare Program, which eventually became known as PSB-33. The work of this panel, the coordination effected by Lilly, and the actual doctrinal warfare plan were highly classified and remained so for the most part until the early 21st century. While the panel discussed matters and traded memoranda, it also solicited and received comments from a number of persons outside of the PSB, including military officers and Harvard professors.

At the first meeting of the doctrinal warfare panel on November 14, 1952, the director of the PSB stressed the importance of the program and of psychological war in general, in addition to explaining its advantages:

"Doctrinal warfare is basically a psychological measure and definitely within the Board's authority. Doctrinal warfare is also an activity which can be extensively pushed without increasing the threats of actual warfare. The Psychological Strategy Board and the whole principle of a coordinated psychological approach can be substantiated and justified if this panel develops the powerful and useful strategic plan which I and my staff visualize it can produce on doctrinal warfare. I have great expectations that this panel will develop a plan which will clearly establish the importance of psychological considerations in the Cold War. I would like to have the panel continually keep this expectation in mind so that their horizons will be broad and their determination strong to develop the necessary plan with proper speed and completeness."[9]

Initially, the doctrinal warfare program targeted only the USSR, but the geographical scope of its mission increased with time until it came to include Soviet satellites and eventually the entire free or unaligned world. The scope of the program changed in other ways as well; from a way to defeat Soviet Communism, it grew into a way not only to spread American ideas and ideals but also to defeat any other ideological system that threatened these ideas or ideals, and at this point it began to target the same religions it viewed as allies. The stakes were high, and the enemy could include "any ideology" that challenged the American ideology with its associated form of capitalism.

"The expansion of Islam, the spread of Protestantism and the legion of adherents which Moscow has won by ideological conversion are matters of common knowledge. The history of modern treason has demonstrated that ideology provides the entering wedge for infiltration and motivates the eventual performance of treasonable acts. Any ideology can influence any other at any level. Ideological infection can no more be confined in the lower echelons than a virus be contained in one part of the human body. Nor is there any sure-fire guarantee against any ideological infection. Add to this the fact that agents, whether wittingly or unwittingly, are more often ideologically motivated than by any other factor. The importance of ideology to many aspects of the Cold War struggle appears obvious."[10]

By January 1953, the panel reached an agreement on basic terminology and the program's scope. Lilly took part in discussions about "whether doctrinal warfare was limited to opposing Stalinism" and concluded that the scope of doctrinal warfare could be expanded to "combating of ideologies hostile to American-Free World, but in order of priority, the panel could now hope only to emphasize the attack of doctrinal warfare against Stalinist Communism."[11]

At the same meeting, the panel developed a statement to the NSC expanding the role and targets of doctrinal warfare to include the positive promotion of American values:

"Panel investigations indicate that American psychological operations must not limit themselves to the defensive exploitation of the inconsistencies, contradictions and vulnerabilities of the Communist doctrine but that the positive United States-Free World ideology must be made appealing and influencing to those pro-Communist and 'fellow-traveller' [sic] elite, so that their basic motivations will be altered in our favor. The panel has prepared a progress report briefly contrasting Communist activity and American inactivity in doctrinal warfare."[12]

In another Top Secret document entitled "Annex 'A': Analysis of the Problem," the panel defined certain key terms, such as "Doctrinal (or Ideological) Warfare," which it described as a "planned attack against a basic hostile doctrinal system conducted concurrently with a positive advocacy of basic ideas of our own system. In the main, doctrinal warfare is directed at an intellectual elite, rather than the mass." Elites were defined as "those higher government officials, journalists, professors, students, and teachers, and progressive business leaders, who are interested in and who attempt to base their judgments on a philosophy or an ideology." Once doctrinal warfare was defined as "the consciously planned effort to bring this elite into contact with thought-stimulating materials which will interpret that elite's environmental ideologies into a pattern which will prepare these intellectuals to accept an ideology favorable to, or predisposing this elite towards, the ideology held by the planners of doctrinal warfare,"[13] it was clear that Catholics could just as easily be the target audience as Communists. This was especially so since the panel agreed the "target of ideological warfare is the developed mind, engaged in developing concepts and rationalizations and capable of projecting the same to others" [14] and that doctrinal systems were an "inter-related body of ideas...which explain the various aspects of life, justifies a particular type of social belief and structure, and provides a body of principles for human aspirations." [15]

A draft Top Secret document dated February 6 entitled "Statement on Doctrinal Warfare Targets" explained the relation between propaganda and doctrinal warfare. Both were components of psychological warfare. However, propaganda was directed at "large groups or the person whose change of attitude is expected to effect [sic] the leaders or decision makers." Propaganda worked through the "repetition and dogmatization of pseudo-argumentation, aims at influencing immediate behavior in terms of masses or large groups. Propaganda presupposes an emotional reaction which promotes and stimulates group action. Propaganda is aimed at large groups or the masses whose change of attitude is expected to effect [sic] the leader or the decision-maker." [16]

Doctrinal warfare, on the other hand, was not directed at "influencing mass behavior; in fact it is not immediately aimed at the masses, but at the decision-makers and their staffs." Furthermore:

"Doctrinal warfare, per se, does not attempt to convince, but certainly it develops and promotes materials which would stimulate the recipient mind to develop and to create as its own the thoughts implicit in the doctrinal material. The changed mental attitudes among the influential few are not so important as stimulants to individual action but rather as potent influences on the attitudes and mental processes of the leaders or the decision-makers. Hence, while Doctrinal Warfare may use targets and methods similar to, but not exclusive with, propaganda, it differs from propaganda in its objectives and its planned manipulation of its targets."[17]

Doctrinal Warfare, in short, targeted the "developed mind. This mind, engaged in developing concepts and rationalizations and capable of projecting the same to others, possess the ability to clarify, analyze and synthesize. The developed mind contains a store of knowledge, prejudices, opinions, pre-dispositions, and traditional use patterns of these elements. It is characterized by an active urge to present to others the conclusions of its mental processes....Doctrinal warfare will accomplish its objectives by putting into these developed minds, new facts and additional knowledge in order that their traditional mental patterns and processes will be so changed that the developed minds will be unsatisfied with their accepted ideology and will want to develop and project revised concepts more in accord with the facts which these developed minds have discovered."[18]

The PSB panel identified elite targets of doctrinal warfare by both region and religion. In areas like "the Moslem World," "Southeast Asia and

Japan," and South America, elites were always identified as including "religious leaders" or "clergy."[19]

In February 1953, C.D. Jackson, as a speechwriter for the Eisenhower campaign, was responsible for the religiously oriented speech cited above. He began serving Ike as his advisor and liaison on matters of intelligence and psychological operations. At the February 20 meeting of the PBS panel, Lilly remarked their recommendations had created a "Beautiful plan, but nobody responsible for carrying it out." The response was, "Have C.D. Jackson take care of it."[20]

33
THE DOCTRINAL WARFARE PROGRAM

A memorandum from early spring 1953 entitled "Draft National Psychological Strategy Plan for the Use of Doctrinal Warfare" emphasized the fact that doctrinal warfare could be used not only against Soviet Communism but against any other belief system that challenges "the spirit and philosophy of American and Western life." The memorandum claimed that "doctrinal warfare will remain an important and powerful means of weakening Communism and *any other doctrines hostile to the US*, and of developing simultaneously a worldwide doctrinal climate favorable to the spirit and philosophy of America and the West"[1] (my emphasis). The emphasis on the applicability to "doctrines hostile to American objectives" is not a momentary lapse; it pervades the entire document. Doctrinal warfare was designed not just to undermine Communism; it was also designed to "break down world-wide doctrinaire thought patterns which have provided a fertile intellectual basis for Communist and other doctrines hostile to American objectives."[2] Doctrinal Warfare "objectively analyzes Communism and any other doctrines hostile to American objectives." Because "American doctrinal warfare....must be looked upon as a positive contribution to the accomplishment of America's long-range objectives of a free, democratic world," it "cannot concentrate solely on the anti-Communist and anti-totalitarian aspects."[3] In a final draft of the Doctrinal Program of the United States, which was circulated to the appropriate agency heads by letter dated June 29, PSB D-33 claimed that the "Target for the U. S. Doctrinal Program" was "persons who would be interested in doctrinal matters . . . or can be influenced by, doctrinal materials," a group that was as likely to include priests as commissars.[4]

The core objectives of the Doctrinal Program were laid out in paragraph 1 of the document, known as PSB D-33. First, the program would seek to provide "permanent literature" and foster "long-term intellectual movements, which will appeal to intellectuals, including scholars and opinion-forming groups, to: (1) break down world-wide doctrinaire thought patterns which have provided an intellectual basis for Communism and other doctrines hostile to American and Free World objectives" and "(2) foster a world-wide understanding and sympathetic acceptance of the traditions and viewpoints of America and the Free World." Among the key results sought, the program was to "further general understanding and encourage acceptance for the traditions and viewpoints of the U.S. and the Free World" and "pave the way for deviations from, and schisms in, totalitarian thought patterns by stimulating intellectual curiosity and free thought on political, scientific and economic subjects."[5] America was presented as having a "fundamental characteristic...the diversity of its doctrines and philosophies." The program was to give voice to "new and stimulating ideas, even contradictory ideas" because these "have self-generative powers and are desired." Doctrinal production was not "limited to political and philosophical analyses" but included all "fields of intellectual and cultural interests from anthropology and artistic creations to sociology and scientific methodology" would "come within the gamut of the doctrinal program."[6]

In Annex C, the authors of PSB D-33 argued that doctrinal warfare grew out of the propaganda agencies of World War II and mentioned specifically "its beginnings under Office of War Information until the present has used the doctrinal approach as one method of attracting increased audiences and of influencing basic thought" and in particular included

Voice of America which "is including doctrinal aspects in its work." VOA had "developed a special ideological unit which prepares master scripts showing how current news can be doctrinally interpreted to the embarrassment of Communist doctrine" and "VOA directives urge the desks to give more and more attention to doctrinal items." It was suggested by the panel that the VOA "can and should do more than it is now doing for the Doctrinal Program" and that one such example would be to make reference to important and new doctrinal publications so as to "develop demand for books of a doctrinal character." Another tool in the doctrinal war was the International Press Service, which belonged to IIA, and which developed "an English language periodical entitled, Problems of Communism, which is definitely an important facet of a U. S. Doctrinal Program....and aimed at the same general target audiences as is proposed in this Doctrinal Program...." Notable with this periodical publication was that it emphasized articles by "named intellectual leaders" and was increasing "the number of non-American contributors to have greater audience appeal." [7]

The Doctrinal Program was viewed as something that was "long-range," had to be "continuously and consistently fostered to insure [sic]that materials which will appeal to intellectuals, including scholar and opinion-forming groups, are available in all areas," and would take time to have the "desired impact on influential groups." A needed area aside from developing studies and documentary materials critical of Communism were materials that presented "the traditions, viewpoints and concepts of America and the Free World." Indeed, the Doctrinal Program, especially in the area of the "production of materials emphasizing the various aspects of the traditions and viewpoints of American and Free World society and life should not be primarily a government responsibility. Such material is constantly being produced for the American market on an entirely free basis...."[8]

The Department of State was responsible for increasing "doctrinal materials in VOA broadcasts, particularly for publicizing and promoting interest in doctrinal matters." The Department of Defense was responsible for providing "doctrinal background" to officers and enlisted personnel in the service schools, as well as units, while speeches, technical magazines, and more would all incorporate a doctrinal aspect. The CIA's responsibilities were set forth in Annex B, a Top Secret document that was declassified in its entirety in December 2013. Of special note, the CIA was directed to:

"(a) Infiltrate individuals into foreign associations and organizations with doctrinal potential (newspapers, universities, etc.) to influence their actions and output.

(b) When appropriate stimulate through non-attributable means conferences and public forums on matters of a doctrinal nature.

(c) Interfere with the promotion and distribution of hostile doctrinal material.

(d) Create, when advisable, deviationist movements designed to split organizations promulgating hostile ideologies so long as they would not develop into a threat to U.S. security.

(e) Exploit local divergencies, heresies or policy disagreements within opposition systems."

The use of theological terms in the description of the CIA's mission statement is both striking and telling and a good indication that the program was created with Catholicism in mind as much as Communism.

The Doctrinal Program was formally accepted by the PSB on July 10, 1953, and immediately put into operation around the world.[9] The PSB, and its successor, the Operations Coordinating Board (OCB), acquired an enormous amount of power and influence in conducting and coordinating psychological operations, the heart of which was doctrinal warfare when it assumed control over the doctrinal operations of the CIA. Elmer B. Staats, appointed by Eisenhower as Executive Officer for the OCB in 1953, remarked that the "Operations Coordinating Board... had responsibility for monitoring the CIA's covert operations."[10]

34
MAKING GERMANY, WESTERN EUROPE, AND LATIN AMERICA LIKE AMERICA

As Dwight Eisenhower began his administration in January 1953, he read the first of a series of Staff Studies from the PSB that were published pursuant to draft PSB D-38, which articulated the new policy of using psychological warfare against American allies. The PSB's Top Secret document laid out the new national policy objectives, which made a "preliminary assessment of U.S. psychological capabilities in the target area," identified what it called the "limiting factors" in that area, and formulated a "meaningful psychological objective." The report claimed to identify some of the "basic psychological problems which confronted the United States in Western Europe"[1] and, more importantly, the way to remake Europe in the image of America, all in the name of fighting communism.

Psychological warfare facilitated "a much broader social shift, a shift in which modern consumer culture displaced existing social forms," which meant that societies were re-engineered to be materialist in orientation, like America. Psychological warfare strengthened a "particular social order in the United States and the world in which forceful elites necessarily rules in the interests of their vision of the greater good." This included promoting "relatively tolerant, pluralistic societies in which elite rule protected democracies from their own weaknesses – a modern form of noblesse oblige, so to speak." This meant advancing "particular interpretations of society" and "remolding attitudes among the former enemy population" – that is Germany and Japan,[2] both of whom had been economic threats to the Anglo-Americans.

SUCCESS STORY GERMANY

John J. McCloy, a Wall Street Banker and lawyer who passed between corporate and banking leadership positions and government positions throughout his career was selected as the High Commissioner charged with remaking Germany into a Western cultural and economic satrapy. As his reward, McCloy was appointed president of Chase Manhattan Bank from 1953 to 1960, "a position from which he could earn a sizeable amount of money and still influence the direction of U.S. foreign policy. The bank job not only permitted him such extracurricular activities, but actually demanded it. As he recalled later, 'The bank appealed to me as it was both a national and international institution, with broad connections in industry and banking here and abroad.'" [3]

In "1949, his assignment was the creation of a modern parliamentary state with a free-market economy."[4] To accomplish his mission, McCloy needed to change the hearts and minds of the Germans through the manipulation of their culture. One weapon in McCloy's arsenal was Hollywood, which used Germany as a "dumping ground" for its movies.[5]

Hollywood's power and that of the American media were well-known. Jewish scholar and sociologist Jacob Taubes wrote a paper on ideological warfare and sent it to Professor William Elliott at Harvard's Department of Government with the hope it might reach C.D. Jackson. Taubes explained, "Cinema and magazines are our most powerful cultural export," and the government had the right to enlist the industry in its efforts to conduct psychological warfare. The media "make America's myth," which is that America is "revolutionary in its political institutions...its social stratification...in the relation between capital and labor." [6]

C.D. Jackson remarked to Luce at one point how "a really top Hollywood producer" was "highly impressed with the power of American films abroad. He has a theory, in which I subscribe completely, that the most effective use of American films is not to design an entire picture to cope with a certain problem, but to see to it in a 'normal' picture that a certain line, aside, inflection, eyebrow movement is introduced. He told me that anytime I could give him a simple problem for a country or an area, he would find a way of dealing with it in the picture." C.D. asked Luce if he had any ideas that he wanted to be included in a film the producer was shooting later in the year.[7]

The other weapon was psychological warfare, a "tool for managing empire" that included the "ability to suppress or distort unauthorized communication among subject peoples" as "part of a strategy and culture whose premise is the rule of the strong at the expense of the weak, where coercion and manipulation pose as 'communication' and close off opportunities for other, more genuine, forms of understanding."[8] "Psychological warfare employs *any* weapon to influence the mind of the enemy. The weapons are psychological only in the *effect* they produce and not because of the nature of the weapons themselves."[9]

Germany's new American rulers conducted a number of studies to measure the effectiveness of the psychological warfare waged on the Germans. These studies document not only the methods used but also the desire of the American conquerors to shape the thoughts, opinions, values, and worldviews of the Germans. Two important areas of inquiry were the impact of American entertainment (mostly motion pictures) and the impact of American mass media, primarily Voice of America (VOA), one of the more important United States propaganda machines to the world at the time. In Report No. 119 from May 1948, it was noted that "The number of audiences within which AMZON [American Zone] Germans participated was strikingly related to attitudes toward the American way of life. Regardless of social class, the more sources of information which an AMZON German had, the more likely he was to be favorably disposed toward American policies in government or economics, ways of life, and activities...." In Report No. 184 from July

1949, about 40 percent of survey respondents in the AMZON listened to VOA "more or less regularly," VOA had the largest audience of American information programs, and VOA reached more of all segments of German society. The majority of VOA listeners considered the programs to be good. Report No. 137 from September 1948 showed that nearly two-thirds of those aged 15 to 24 in Munich attended movies and that American films were extremely popular. Report No. 188, issued one year later, revealed that 44 % of the AMZON residents believed American movies showed how American life really was.[10] In that same study, respondents were forced to choose between parents or the authorities as to who should have the final say in what children should watch.[11]

Report No. 171 from December 1952 indicated the majority of Germans interviewed saw Voice of America as a propaganda instrument of the U.S., and while 39 percent of the interviewees saw this as a good thing for Germany, the vast majority was silent on the question.[12] VOA was effective because it gave the impression of being journalism, even though, in reality, it was propaganda – something that Henry Luce pioneered with *Time*. Those who worked with VOA underwent indoctrination before being allowed to work there. The State Department regularly fed directions for stories to the VOA staff with the recurrent theme the stories were to ostensibly "promote friendliness and interest among the widest possible audience of Soviet listeners." This included stories contrasting the "dismal living conditions in the Communist regions" with the pleasant and enjoyable conditions in the U.S. The Soviet Union was portrayed as the villain and the "evil instigator of the Cold War," while "good American folk music" made the Americans appear to be anyone's good buddy. The U.S. 1952 elections were ample fodder for the VOA propagandists who presented it all as a "free and democratic system."[13]

Early in the Cold War, after the Americans saw the power and success of propaganda and psychological operations, the intelligence community poured tens of millions of dollars into efforts to expand these operations "against restless populations in Europe and the developing world, as well as against the Soviet Union and its satellites." Psychological warfare included "clandestine CIA ownership and/or subsidies of newspapers, magazines, publishing houses, and radio stations; suborning of reporters or media executives; selective financing and/or manipulation of scholars in the United States and abroad; clandestine radio broadcasting including Radio Free Europe and Radio Liberty."[14]

Anecdotal evidence, however, contradicted the success stories that the psychological warfare establishment used to increase its budgets. Propaganda was having the opposite effect on Germany's Catholic population. On April 23, 1950, after returning from his second trip to Germany, his native country since the end of the war, Dr. Georg Joseph Heiling, a Catholic from Westphalia who became a naturalized U.S. citizen in 1930, wrote to George Shuster, then considered an expert on Germany, explaining the effect that social engineering was having on his friends and relatives, who were described as "nothing else but good and devout Catholics":

"They all showed also nothing but contempt and utter distrust against the so-called 'Allied Liberators' (liberators from what?—from their property, from their possessions, from their holy and sacred rights----)....Wherever I went – and spoke with intelligent people and with all classes of people – they all told me, that they have more faith in Stalin who at least does not pretend, than in these hypocrite Western Allies, who are afraid of a united and prosperous Germany solely because of their bad conscience.....These hypocrites and degenerates want to re-educate us, but we do not need their silly education. We are an orderly, highly disciplined and cultured people and have more education, than they ever knew of and they could learn a lot from us.....The Americans have shown us nothing, they have only undermined German morale. They are talking about democracy, but they do not show democracy by their own deeds."[15]

LILLY PLANNED PSYCHOLOGICAL WARFARE AGAINST WESTERN EUROPE

A few months after finishing his Top Secret tome on the history of psychological warfare, Lilly, the American Catholic psychological warrior, was back at work devising ways to use psychological warfare against Western Europe. In a July 1, 1952 memorandum aptly entitled "Proposal for a Psychological Strategy Move against the Current Anti-American Cominform Moves in Western Europe," Lilly proposed the promotion of "freedom" by leaders in the political and religious arena as a way of turning the ideological tide. Lilly's proposal claimed that there was an "urgent need of finding effective means to renew democratic faith through a universally acceptable vision of a future society based on the development of freedom." There was a need to "initiate a more dynamic democratic movement in political and economic, in cultural, and religious circles of France, Italy, the Benelux countries, Germany, Austria, key countries of Western Europe where the anti-American sentiments have been most persistently excited...." To bring this renewal about, Lilly called for "a series of conventions for leaders in the fields of thought and action. . . starting December 1952 in Rome, Florence through January...on the subject 'Democracy of the Future.'" Lilly believed this subject would be "psychologically effective against the Communist myths of the future world....."[16]

By the fall of the same year, the PSB developed "A National Psychological Strategy Plan for the Federal Republic of Germany," designated PSB E-6, a plan that encouraged the growth of "the democratic ethos" while encouraging the integration of the FRG into Europe through informational programs and cultural exchanges.[17] PSB E-6 involved a coordinated effort between the Department of State, the Department of Defense, and the CIA. The CIA was to "develop non-attributable activities which... support, exploit, and promote political, economic, religious cultural, and other groups, such as women, labor unions, youth, veterans, etc., which are working towards approved objectives, particularly that of maximum identification of German interests with those of the European Community...." These programs were created to exploit "Europe's generally sympathetic attitude toward the United States, its sense of cultural and political identification with the West, and the reservoir of good will created by US assistance programs." It was important to encourage "indigenous pressures through official and unofficial support of private groups" which were sympathetic to U.S. policy objectives and to "concentrate to the greatest possible extent on established organizations and media and limit the use of imaginary sponsors in the Federal Republic."[18]

The point of the plan was to integrate the Federal Republic of Germany (FRG) into the rest of Western Europe. It was "essential that Germany should not again be permitted to develop political conditions or a military potential which might threaten the independence of other nations or the peace of the world." Integration of Germany was "not just in the legal sense, but in the spiritual as well." To achieve that end, the U.S. needed to build good-will and friendship towards the German people, which would give them "a sense of 'belonging'" as well as "a feeling that U.S. interests, for example, are identical with theirs, and that the structure being created in Europe today is for no one nation's benefit, nor to no one nation's detriment." To these ends, public opinion, as well as cultural, economic, military, and diplomatic events, were to be directed and employed. [19]

The European Union was the ultimate fruit of this campaign of psychological warfare. PSB-38 commissioned numerous staff studies oriented towards utilizing political warfare operations "with great vigor" to obtain support for U.S. policies encouraging "economic unification and the political federation of Europe." Political warfare involved mobilizing members of the military and economic assistance teams, members of international "opinion-forming groups," labor union representatives, business representatives, tourists, foreign nationals who visited the U.S. under government-sponsored programs, and "US citizens engaged in commercial international mass-communications." [20] Most importantly, PSB Acting Director George A. Morgan recognized controlling the indigenous media was the fastest and easiest way to achieve the psychological goals essential to the social re-engineering of Germany. The United States, Morgan wrote, had the "capability for influencing European opinion climate through (1) appropriate consultations and exchange of views, etc. with the appropriate representatives of mass-media facilities in the United Kingdom, France, Italy, Germany, the Vatican, and Spain, and (2) similar consultations and exchanges of views and, to the extent practicable, participation in and support of the information program of NATIS, the Council of Europe, OEEC, and the emerging European Political Community."[21]

The "massive intervention" by the U.S. in the domestic affairs of various countries created several "adverse factors" that needed to be considered. One Staff Study went on to state that some of the "European observers have concluded that 'most frictions are not caused by policies of the U.S. government but by ill-conceived and loud opinions spread through the media of mass communications.'" Second, there was a sense "among certain economic interests that there is little to gain and much to lose from unification of Europe." Third, there remained "neutralist attitudes" as well as hostile attitudes towards any "visible evidence of U.S. hegemony in Europe" as U.S. foreign policy was considered beneficial only to the U.S. Fourth, there was a sense of defeat and occupation that was equated with the "fear of war...still present in the minds of many Western Europeans." Fifth, the Communist party in a number of European countries stirred up sentiments against the U.S. Sixth, the U.S. trade relationships were used by "neutralist and communist propaganda" to claim that the U.S. was making Europe a satellite. Finally, stress appeared in the European colonies, given the misunderstanding of the "role of the United States in pressing for new political and economic measures."[22]

Despite these "adverse factors," the Staff Study reported that American psychological operations changed a number of attitudes, including those held by Catholic leaders and the laity. First, Europeans recognized that "the strategic initiative in the West lies inevitably with the United States," and as a result, the Europeans felt impotent in the "East-West conflict." There were also "significant European opinion groups" that believed the U.S. overestimated the military threat and under-estimated the nonmilitary threat, and so there was a reluctance to support rearmament as well as a "growing tendency in some quarters to regard the cause of anti-communism as purely American rather than a matter of utmost concern to Europeans."[23] The same Staff Study concluded that U.S. psychological operations conducted up to that point had "not succeeded in reducing the growth of anti-American sentiments." As a result, the psychological warriors concluded that they needed to try harder "in order to attain progress towards the reduction of Soviet power and influence in Europe, the reduction of Western European antagonism to the United States and its purposes should be considered a key objective of our psychological strategy." The United States needed to create a "cold war instrument" which would harness American "moral and material strength" in the world-wide struggle that would last for years "between the forces of freedom, free institutions and human dignity and the forces of total tyranny which represent Communist philosophy and strategy."[24]

In September 1953, the PSB approved "A National Psychological Strategy Program for Western Europe," a Top Secret plan for the U.S. to advance its objectives in Europe employing diplomacy, policy, economics, media, information, culture, and a host of other instruments that would tend to influence society and public opinion in favor of American objectives, such as weakening the Soviets and "strengthening the unity of the free world" and "encouragement of friendship for the United States."[25]

As part of its Methods Program, the U.S. once again "enlisted the cooperation of private agencies in providing programs for the support of approved national purposes." Coordination was to be informal. The "most influential of such agencies, the U.S. press," was not susceptible to formal coordination, according to the planners, so other means were to be used. A domestic component of the program informed Americans of the value of Western Europe and induced private organizations to support openness to Europe through "public information programs." The program relied heavily on "personal contact, persuasion and explanation" such as student exchanges, book exchanges, "cultural relations and educational programs." The "U.S. cultural debt to Europe," a sense of "common cultural and spiritual values," and a "genuine interchange of ideas with Europeans through discussion and education" were all part of the plan.[26]

As the PSB was laying the plan for making Europeans like Americans, it was reviewing new and more scientific ways to assess the effectiveness of psychological operations through something called "content analysis." The U.S. Information Agency appeared to have taken the lead in this area by encouraging the "development of standard, reliable psychometric instruments based on sound scientific theorizing as illustrated in the publication entitled 'The Illinois Associational Code for Content Analysis.'"[27]

RE-ENGINEERING LATIN AMERICA

The PSB identified Latin America as a target for psychological warfare. A Top Secret memorandum from Edmond Taylor, Assistant Director of the Office of Plans and Policy to the Acting Director of the PSB, expressed the need to consolidate support for the American ideology against other belief systems in Latin America. Taylor wrote the following recommendations for R-184, a Top Secret paper written by a Wallace Irwin, Jr. concerning policy towards Latin America:

"Make greater use of the OAS [Organization of American States] to promote, extend and fortify ideological solidarity among its members on the basis of common attachment to democratic principles, broadly interpreted.....Reasons: (1) Provides a political and psychological basis for combating Peronism, the menace of which appears to be inadequately recognized in the NSC draft....(3) Exploits the strong elements of idealism, and the addiction to abstraction and rhetoric which are characteristic of Latin American culture, in furtherance of virtually all the objectives of the paper. (4) Provides additional moral cover and justification for many US actions in support of purely national objectives. (5) Facilitates the coordination of hemispheric policies and actions with those undertaken within the framework of NATO or other free-world groupings."[28]

Under the heading of "Information and Related Activities," Taylor emphasized the need for cultural programs to bind the Latin Americans closer to the Americans. The OAS was used to create "cooperative hemispheric machinery for information and cultural programs in support of common ideals and objectives, but without committing the US to channelling [sic] a major part of its information and cultural effort through any international machinery." It was necessary to get "private US organizations and institutions in the information, cultural and educational fields to take a greater interest in Latin American affairs" because that would "convince the Latin American peoples of our sincere interest in them." The various "information and cultural programs should specifically aim at promoting, extending and fortifying ideological attachment to democratic principles, broadly interpreted and with due regard to the need to avoid creating unrest in states whose governments are friendly toward the US in foreign policy though authoritarian in domestic policy."[29]

Wallace Irwin, Jr. advised the PSB of the changing dynamics in Latin America due to free trade:

"Latin America has suffered from the world changes of the past 20 years in which a period of profitable free trade has been followed by economic upheavals which gravely threaten the 'one-crop economies' of the area. Latin American countries seek to end their 'trembling dependence' on foreign trade, which can no longer assure them prosperity or stability. These considerations have spurred the drive for industrialization, the swarming of rural populations to the cities, and the rise of a new 'middle sector' of society whose ultimate political orientation remains to be determined. The traditional order is on its way out."[30]

Part of that traditional order, per Irwin, consisted of the "cultural links of Latin America...with continental Europe – France, Germany, Spain, Italy – much more than with the UK or the U.S." These changing economic dynamics opened the door to a "new orientation" in cultural, social, and economic matters. [31]

Another analyst, Daniel N. Arsac, Jr., noted the cultural connections between Latin America and the U.S. as the reason for an absence of widespread hostility towards the U.S. These cultural connections were also a lever to be used by the Americans to their benefit by helping the Latins understand mutual economic and political interests. In a classified memorandum to C.D. Jackson, Arsac explained:

"Admittedly, the Latin American nations, proud and sensitive rebel at this relationship – note especially Argentina – and certain leaders lean toward neutralism pending the outcome of the struggle. But their more realistic and influential leaders recognize that close ties with the United States are of mutual interest. These ties will remain somewhat tense...so long as the Latin Americans feel they are neglected by us and so long as they doubt the genuineness of American interest in their political, economic and cultural advancement."[32]

According to Arsac, the "psychological problem" that needed to be solved involved convincing the Latin Americans that the North Americans were truly their friends. The U.S. government needed to facilitate friendship between the two peoples by "encouraging the already growing cultural exchanges under private auspices."[33]

PART IX

STALIN DIES, ROME SPEAKS, AND THE LUCES GO TO ROME (1953)

35
TIME, INC. AND THE CIA

On March 5, 1953, the nightmare of every American Cold Warrior became a reality. Joseph Stalin died. This posed serious problems for the Americans because it looked as if peace could break out, and if that happened, Western Europe, having no reason to fear the Soviets, might start to work with them. If that were to happen, the Americans would lose their most valuable incentive, namely, fear of Communism, and without fear of Communism as the stick that held Europe in line, the Americans could no longer engage in their efforts at reshaping societies by getting people to buy into America as the ideal, a project otherwise known as social engineering or psychological warfare. A thaw in or, worse still, the end of the Cold War threatened American efforts at worldwide colonization. America needed an enemy in order to push its agenda, and with the death of Stalin, they had lost their best salesman. Almost two years later, Stalin's successor, Premier Nikolai Bulganin, met in Geneva with President Eisenhower and the British and French prime ministers to reduce tensions. The situation was serious.

Europe wanted a "cool truce" instead of a "cold war," wrote Klaus Dohrn to Henry Luce. Dohrn was an Austrian on the payroll of both the CIA and Time, Inc. Unprecedented prosperity was just around the corner, Marxism lacked appeal, and the youth were "singularly un-revolutionary."[1] In a memorandum entitled "The End of the First Post-War Era," Dohrn wrote that Churchill's speech of May 11, 1953, about Stalin's death was "the date when European disintegration and a whittling away of the whole American position in Europe set in." The Italians were the first to reflect this change with their June 1953 elections, but the other countries were also starting to rethink their stance towards the Soviets. The Catholics were becoming more leftist in both politics and economics, seeking "new social ideas and more social action." Free enterprise was threatened. John Foster Dulles claimed that Stalin's death brought about an "agonizing reappraisal" of the thrust of American foreign policy since the end of World War II. With Communism gone, Dohrn claimed that there would be a "re-emergence of...old ills," which had led to Europe's disintegration into the disparate forces that had been submerged by the American-led anti-Communist crusade. Without Stalin to unify it under American auspices, Europe would descend into a political brawl that mirrored the real interests of the brawlers. It would turn into a free-for-all in which each party would seek to explain how it had the solution to the world's problems. Concretely, that meant "how the Catholics can beat Moscow so that Free-masonry and Liberalism won't profit from it; how the Protestants can do it so that Rome won't profit; how the Capitalists can do it so that democratic socialism won't profit; how Socialdemocrats [sic] can do it so that Wall Street and international Capitalism won't profit – and so on, in a wearying and tedious diminution of western strength."[2]

The U.S. government had to mobilize all of its assets to prevent peace from breaking out in Europe, and essential to that was closer coordination between *Time* magazine and the CIA. C.D. Jackson and Alan Grover, also a Luce confidant, were essential to making that happen, and John Shaw Billings was privy to it all.[3] In his diary, Billings described a conversation that took place during one of Time, Inc.'s regular Wednesday meetings in which Luce quoted one of Grover's CIA friends as claiming that the Russians might march west within the next two months. Shortly thereafter, the CIA demanded to see *Time*'s "whole foreign file." Roy Alexander was "dead set against" handing over the files, seeing it as "a corruption of journalism," Billings' reaction to the request was "favorable" because Time could then use Grover as a "good liaison" with the CIA.[4]

On October 23, 1950, Billings discussed the issue with Larsen, who suggested that all future CIA requests "be channeled to Grover."[5] A little over a year later, in February 1952, Billings had lunch with C.D. Jackson, who regaled the editorial staff with tales of his "successes" [Billings' quotes] behind the Iron Curtain and how "he had created 'explosive situations' in the satellite countries which could be set off in 90 days." Unfortunately, the U.S. government was in no position to "capitalize on such an explosion" as it had "no plans, no powers, for such."[6]

Jackson did such an effective job during the 1952 presidential campaign as Eisenhower's speechwriter that the newly elected president asked him to join his staff in 1953. In his diary, Billings recounted a meeting at which Jackson explained his new job:

"I took CD Jackson to Louis for lunch – the first time I've seen him since his tour of duty with the Eisenhower campaign. I found myself spilling him all sorts of secrets – Matthews' bad behavior and upcoming discharge. Clare's mean tangles with her husband, etc. Then CD opened up on his political experiences and prospects, what he wanted to talk about most. He showed me a letter from Ike thanking him profusely for his contributions to victory, a telegram from Luce suggesting he now 'cut himself some compense of satisfaction.' He was obviously well pleased with his success. Then he told me his big secret: Ike wants him as a White House assistant to coordinate all psychological warfare. Should he take it or not? I told him it was the one job he could take with a guarantee of perfect execution. We discussed the yes and no of it at length. (I'm a fine one to be urging people to do their public duty, when I do none at all myself. Well, nobody has ever ordered me to!) Back to the office – and ten minutes later in came Jackson again with news: He had just gotten a phone call from Ike HQ that the General wants a group of his top advisors to fly out to the Pacific where they would meet him on a cruiser and thrash out the Korean problem as they sailed home. Jackson was 'drafted'; so was Hughes. The others on the list were Dulles, Humphrey, Dodge, McCary, Warren, Lucius Clay – a top level outfit Jackson was pretty excited to be included in this call and spent an hour pacing up and down my office and talking about it. I was just the sympathetic listener (and secretly slightly jealous). He evidently didn't want to leave my office, but just relive the full flavor of this call. I told him about the H Bomb trouble our Washington Bureau was in. At one excited moment, I reared back in my swivel chair and fell over on the floor in a ridiculous lump. Luckily it didn't hurt me at all. Finally, CD left."[7]

Jackson also served on the President's Committee on International Information Activities (the Jackson Committee, named after the chairman William Jackson), was Special Assistant to the President for International Affairs, and worked closely with the PSB and its successor, the Operations Coordinating Board (OCB). His involvement with the OCB was to "see that the policies and acts of the U.S. government as adopted officially, as an official policy of the government, as approved by the President or the congress or the state department or whatever, were properly interpreted or conveyed abroad as necessary in order to accomplish the desired effect for this country...."[8] C.D. was to make sure the "policies of the government were correctly interpreted and 'orchestrated' abroad to maximum effect by the various departments of the government" and so he "worked directly with the heads of the government departments involved" or through the OCB.[9] He "worked very closely and met constantly" with representatives of the CIA, Treasury, State, Defense and Atomic Energy Commission as a result.[10] C.D.'s interaction with the intelligence community was extensive, and he regularly corresponded with the likes of Allen Dulles, Henry Cabot Lodge, Walter Bedell Smith, Lewis Strauss, George Kennan, Nelson Rockefeller, Walter Rostow, an economist from MIT, and representatives from Radio Free Europe, Radio Liberty, Voice of America, U.S. Information Agency, International Information Administration, Committee for Free Asia, Inc., Free World Congress, and World Veterans Federation.[11] C.D. was especially close to Allen Dulles, head of the CIA, as well as John Foster Dulles, General Walter Bedell Smith, and Frank Wisner.[12]

Jackson remained engaged in the psychological warfare machinations of the U.S. government for years after he formally left Government service, maintaining contact with Bill Jackson, Walt Rostow, Max

Milliken, Irwin Canham, Phil Reed, Sig Larmon, and Nelson Rockefeller, who, along with government operatives kept him abreast of the policies and activities of the U.S. government's intelligence agencies.[13] From his position in the Eisenhower administration, Jackson "provided direction for Eisenhower's Cold War planning," which included the administration of the Psychological Strategy Board (PSB), later known as the Operations Coordinating Board (OCB,) both of which oversaw and administered political and economic warfare. Eisenhower strongly supported Jackson, who wrote that Ike considered "political warfare 'just about the only way to win WWIII without having to fight it.... He is convinced that psychological warfare should not be the pet mystery of one or more Departments... but should be the entire posture of the entire Government to the entire world.'"[14]

After starting work for the Eisenhower administration, Jackson explained the inadequacy of the PSB as being "founded upon the misconception that 'psychological strategy' somehow exists apart from official policies and actions and can be dealt with independently by experts in this field... Except for propaganda, there are no "psychological warfare" instruments distinct from traditional instruments of policy...." Cold war" and "psychological warfare" are unfortunate terms. They do not describe the efforts of our nation and our allies to build a world of peace and freedom. . . . Because of a phoney aura of mystery which has attached itself in the concept of psychological warfare, far too many people in Government, in the press and around this country, have come to believe that when certain international problems arise, all you have to do is to turn them over to the psychological warfare experts and say, through some kind of black magic and the liberal use of mirrors, will solve them."[15]

Jackson attended another Managing Editor's lunch in December 1952 and once again regaled the staff with all sorts of insider talk, which made it perfectly clear that the CIA considered *Time* an important partner. Any doubt in this regard was removed when CIA chief Allen Dulles himself showed up for lunch. Billings described him as:

"An amiable, relaxed, almost casual man full of gossips and merry laughter – the last man you'd suspect of heading our super spy service.

He looked like a young Foxy Grandpa --- yet almost a Rotarian in outlook and manner. He began by telling us how he suffered with gout.... Then he went on to outline his philosophy of CIA – an executive agency working for Ike, not Congress. Could he predict a Soviet attack? Maybe – no guarantee. Luce was present – and Dulles outtalked him, to everybody's secret joy. Dulles gave us no real secrets, of course and just repeated the Administration line on major questions...."[16]

Having someone of Dulles's stature drop in for lunch was flattering to the staff. His visit made it clear that he wanted to pursue the relationship, but the man who was anointed to close the deal and cement the relationship was C.D. Jackson. Although nominally on Time's payroll, Jackson had developed a special relationship with the CIA. In a letter dated November 24, 1950, Grover told Billings that C.D. Jackson came to see me the other day to discuss a two months' leave after the first of the year to help the Defense Department organize their own department of psychological warfare, and I am much in favor of his doing so."[17] According to Grover's memo to Billings, Jackson was a "secret agent for Central Intelligence," even when served as head of front organizations like the National Committee for Free Europe, which claimed to be "a spontaneous movement to promote the idea of freedom, [and] to raise independent money." In his triple capacity as Time exec, freedom advocate, and spook, Jackson could mobilize people like Henry Luce, Cecil B. DeMille, and Darryl Zanuck to advance the idea of a Crusade for Freedom while at the same time lending their expertise and support to things like Radio Free Europe, which "was to become the psychological front-line of counterrevolution through seduction (the prospect of material comfort, and of American commodities, culture, and fashion) and through fear (the prospect of an enslaving, death-dealing communism)" through "music and news, skits, satires, and talks by exiled leaders." The NCFE trained cadres of young exiles to comprise the leaders of democratic groups that would appear in various homelands to fill the leadership vacuums when those countries were liberated.[18]

Radio Free Europe, according to Jackson, "cannot take a line contrary to U.S. government policy or to the beliefs of the American people reflected in the Constitution of the United States and in American institutions....Radio Free Europe aspires for Europe, to something more than a mere restoration of the prewar status....It looks forward to a liberated Europe whose leaders will strive to set up institutions that will permit all persons to live in amity and without hate....RFE is, by the nature of its support in the American people, committed to the defense and dissemination of democratic ideas. It would be useful, as well as consonant with the purposes of the American people to proceed on the assumption that the peoples we address are avid to learn about democratic institutions; that their aspirations include wide peasant proprietorship, free trade unions....freedoms of various kinds (worship, intellectual inquiry, assembly...access to higher education...."[19]

C.D. Jackson also presided over the reorganization of other governmental agencies to ensure their effective dissemination of the American message. One was the reorganization of the PSB into the OCB, which Gordon Gray, the first Director of the PSB, called a "very useful thing," especially as its membership consisted of the Under-Secretary of State, the Deputy Secretary of Defense, the Director of the CIA, the Director of the Foreign Operations Administration, and C.D. Jackson, the White House representative.[20] Another was Voice of America, which became an independent agency overseen by the U.S. Information Agency (previously the U.S. Information Service (USIS) under the State Department). As a result, VOA broadcast "straight information" so as to make it "into an effective instrument" of American psychological operations.[21]

Behind this machinery was a "new philosophy" that C.D. described: "There are no psychological warfare instruments distinct from traditional instruments of policy.....In other words, psychological warfare does not exist per se. It does not exist apart from the policies and above all the acts of government.'....The psychological warfare comes *after* the act and not before the act, which is the traditional way that had been thought of prior to this new machinery and new philosophy."[22]

As the "Special Assistant to the President with a Cold War portfolio," C.D. said he had a "responsibility to think exclusively in these terms." He explained the significance of Dulles' intelligence estimates and suggested "some of the things that might be done." In early 1954, Jackson believed that the kinks had been worked out and psychological warfare had found its way, something that inspired him with confidence: "I think we face a tremendously interesting future in psychological warfare. If there is one way to describe the year 1953, I would say it was a year in which things got unstuck." Psychological warfare survived the crisis Stalin's death brought about, allowing NATO to continue with a "united purpose" with an American "orchestration" of efforts.[23]

Jackson's success at the CIA allowed him to solidify his position at *Time*, where Luce occasionally put him in charge of what he termed "policy" questions, a position that was tantamount to boss when Luce was away. "For the next several weeks while I am in Europe," Luce directed, "Managing Editors will please refer all 'policy' questions to C.D. Jackson. He will have authority to decide same, with or without consultation with me."[24] Billings described Jackson's return "after almost a year away with Free Europe Committee" as "all oozing conscious charm and optimism and wisecracks. He is Luce's private darling. He brushed off my greetings to him to concentrate on Grover. They are rivals for Luce's favor, and oh so deliciously sweet to each other."[25]

C.D. was richly rewarded by Luce. This included valuable Time, Inc. stock, something that caused resentment among lower-paid staff members. When Jackson left the White House at the end of March 1954, Billings groused in his diary "that CD Jackson, on his return April 1 from his White House job, will spend three months in Europe surveying our foreign business operations, plus a two-month vacation. Boy, look what he gets compared to me after 25 years drudgery here!"[26]

36

ROME SPEAKS (MARCH 1953)

C.D. Jackson was not the only one who felt things came "unstuck" in 1953. The year 1953 was crucial for Catholic doctrine as well. The Church leadership publicly addressed the controversies surrounding church-state relations and religious liberty. Statements from Rome gave added confidence and support to the Catholics, but the Americanists were quick to use their substantial resources and those of their allies outside of the Church to spin the message to their advantage.

Alfredo Cardinal Ottaviani was appointed Pro-Secretary of the Supreme Congregation of the Holy Office on January 12, 1953. Less than two months later, on March 2, while Stalin lay dying from a stroke, he gave a speech at the Pontifical Lateran University in Rome to celebrate the fourteenth anniversary of the elevation of Pope Pius XII to the papacy. In attendance were the ambassadors of Ireland, France, Belgium, Portugal, Spain, Austria, Peru, Italy, and Colombia, as well as the ministers of Holland and Japan, the Venezuelan Envoy, and a number of Cardinals including Cardinals Tisserant, Micara, Pizzardo, Aloisi Masella, Piazza, Massimi, Contantni, Roncalli, Valeri, Borgongini Duca, Canali. The title of Ottaviani's talk was "Duties of the Catholic State in Regard to Religion," and he gave the talk because, as he explained several weeks later, he was "moved to do so by the great number of requests I received from writers and professors of different Institutes of Higher Studies."[1] The speech encapsulated Catholic doctrine on the matter of church/state relations and religious liberty.

Referring to "a distinguished religious" as well as to the American propaganda machine represented by Luce, Ottaviani claimed that the press was directed by "men who worship liberty far more than truth." Their efforts led to:

"The widespread confusion in the presence of which we find ourselves, the perplexities of politicians, and the enormous errors that are committed in the hybrid alliances between states and parties render it imperative that the all-important problem of the relations between Church and State should be put in unmistakable terms, that it should be treated fully, with the greatest clearness, and above all, fearlessly. Christian courage is a cardinal virtue which is called fortitude."[2]

In taking on Murray and the Americanists, Ottaviani focused on the obligations and duties of a Catholic State, but he used this opportunity to present Catholic teaching on the duties of all states to Christ and to His Church. A shortened version of the text appeared in the May 1953 edition of *American Ecclesiastical Review* and a press release issued by the National Catholic Welfare Council. Omitted in the shorter versions were the references to an ecumenical convention consisting of Protestants in August 1949, a deeper discussion of the Soviet treatment of religion, and a criticism of Protestant and American hypocrisy in their treatment of Catholicism.

The Cardinal began his talk with a simple Catholic truth: the Catholic Church and Jesus Christ are under attack now as they were in the days that He walked the earth, for His kingship is rejected by many. Referring to Luke 19:14, Ottaviani said, "Against Him the cry is raised, as it was raised long ago: 'We will not have this man to reign over us.'" The most painful thing this time around was that it largely came from Catholics who, living in "interconfessional states," should know better how the Church protects its own and should cooperate in that protection.[3]

Ottaviani refuted a number of serious errors and presented Catholic teaching on three major questions: 1) the "Catholic state and...its relative implications with reference to non-Catholic sects"; 2) the "norms of action" when presented with a Catholic country and when presented with a country in which Catholics are in the minority; and 3) the "sphere of the action and the competence of the Church."[4]

First, Ottaviani criticized those views that led to doctrinal errors. One was the rejection of the Church as a perfect society. Many viewed it as merely a juridical entity that rejected or was in conflict with its spiritual order. Therefore, in accordance with Protestant teachings on the matter, it was little more than a competing state. Ottaviani said the Church was endowed by Christ with all it needed to "carry out its mission in every State without opposition between the two societies of which He is...the Author and the Support."[5] Second, it was an error to hold the papal teachings consisted of "two elements, the one permanent, and the other transient." He rejected the view the encyclicals "reflect only historic moments of the past" as being "theoretically inadmissible." He quoted from Pius XII's *Humani Generis,* which held it error to hold "what is expounded in Encyclical Letters does not in itself demand assent."[6]

Ottaviani then addressed Church and State issues. The first one concerned the Catholic State and its relation with non-Catholics. A Catholic State was one where "the Catholic religion has been proclaimed as the religion of the State in their respective Constitutions," and this happens mostly where the country has "absolute Catholic majorities." Ottaviani recognized this was criticized by non-Catholics and considered anachronistic by Catholics advancing the erroneous view the Church can live "peacefully and in full possession of its own rights in a lay State [that is, one which does not profess the Catholic faith in its laws] even when the State is composed of Catholics." [7]

With clear reference to Murray, Ottaviani rejected the concept of the state as little more than a group of mechanical institutions. Quoting directly from Murray's piece, "The Problem of the 'Religion of the State,'" published in the May 1951 *American Ecclesiastical Review*, Ottaviani rejected Murray's argument that the state can never constitutionally recognize its duty to worship God.[8] Finally, Ottaviani rejected the idea that the only protection that the Church and the Faith need from the state is that the state guarantees their freedom.[9]

Referring to the principles of public ecclesiastical law and the various pronouncements and teachings of the popes, Ottaviani explained the duties of Catholics and the Catholic state concerning the governance of a society. First, there is the need for the social profession of the Catholic Faith. Second, there is the duty of all Catholics that legislation be inspired and informed by the Catholic Faith. Third, there is the requirement that the people's "religious patrimony" be defended.[10]

Expanding on the duties of Catholic states, Ottaviani discussed Church teaching as being applicable to all societies. He cited Leo XIII, who taught that states may not act as if God is non-existent, nor may they cast off "the care of religion." He mentioned Pius XII's encyclical *Summi Pontificatus* (1939), which explained that when a state rejects or ignores God, it gains "unlimited power of action," which is restrained only by "relative interests" or "historical exigencies." Ottaviani said that such a state will attribute to itself "absolute autonomy which belongs only to the Creator," and it will then become the "supreme end of life" as well as the "supreme norm of the moral and juridical order."[11]

Second, Ottaviani said the welfare of society required that the moral principles of the Catholic Faith infuse the State and its legislation. In a letter of October 19, 1945, for the Social Week of the Italian Catholics, Pius XII explained that the fundamental law of the State should be based on sound "religious and moral principles" along with "happy relations between Church and State."[12]

Third, the State had an obligation to protect the Church. The basis of this obligation was divine law, as explained in *Immortale Dei,* as well as the dictates of justice and reason, as explained in *Libertas.* In a clear reference to all states, *Immortale Dei* held that rulers of states "cannot choose whatever they wish" to follow, and they are obliged to follow the Catholic Faith. Leo XIII taught that any society treating all religions the same (that is, grants them all equal rights) "comes to the same thing as being atheistic." This is against reason, treats error equally with truth, and is harmful to the Church and society as division ensues.[13]

All these principles "are firm and immovable...valid in the times of Innocent III and Boniface VIII....valid in the days of Leo XIII and of Pius XII." Quoting from Pius XII's *Mystici Corporis* (1943), which quoted from Wisdom 6:4-8, and from the Christmas Message of 1942, Ottaviani said the "norms of society" were constant and unchanging from ancient days and that these "cannot be damaged by the intervention of man's genius. Men can deny them, ignore them, despise them, disobey them, but they can never abrogate them with juridical efficacy."[14]

Ottaviani addressed the issue of how the Church could maintain two norms of action: one which existed when Catholics were in the majority in a society and the other when they were not. The former called for the confessional state with a duty to protect only Catholicism, and the latter advocated a right to tolerance or "equality of cults." He explained that a multiplicity of cults is a situation that arose as a result of "free thinkers," "multiple religious professions," and the pre-eminence of private judgment. In such a situation where "the exclusiveness of its mission is not recognized," or the rights of God are ignored, the Church speaks of toleration, equality, and the rights of man. In all other situations, it speaks of God's rights, but this should not be construed as meaning that such is "a retrogression."[15] At this point, Ottaviani made reference, by way of example, to a gathering of various Protestant cults in August 1949 in Amsterdam. The sects gathered in an effort to unite, but they could not even agree on a symbol of union, nor could they agree on the Eucharistic Banquet.[16]

In response to criticism of the statement that "error has no rights," a criticism that Murray leveled in his paper entitled "Government Repression of Heresy" given at the 1948 annual meeting of the Catholic Theological Society of America, Ottaviani explained the statement was valid in that the subjects who enjoy rights are those that hold to truth. Liberal Catholics hold the same freedom for truth and error and claim the state need not give special recognition to the Faith or the Church.[17]

Ottaviani launched a bold attack against the Americans and Protestants who were critical of Spain yet silent about the Soviet treatment of religions. This was an especially powerful rhetorical move because it exposed the Americans as hypocrites. "The non-Catholics," Ottaviani explained, "would like to have unrestricted license to break up the religious unity of Catholic peoples... complain if the governments close chapels, opened without even the required authorization, or expel the so-called 'missionaries' who came into the country for purposes other than those stated in the requests for permission to enter." In such a campaign, the "Communists are among their most vigorous allies and defenders... full of zeal in helping every form of Protestant propaganda in Catholic Countries." And, "in the United States of America....there are to be found imitators of the Communists' zeal in protesting against our pretended intolerance in regard to the missionaries sent to 'evangelize' us." Ottaviani mentioned that American funding was going to promote Communism in Catholic countries.[18]

Finally, the Cardinal refuted the claim that religion and life can be separated. He boldly stated that the Gospel applies to all conduct, whether that conduct be individual, domestic, social, private, or public, and religion cannot be separated from life, nor can the Church be separated from the world. In doing so, he rejected the Americanist claim, similar to the Soviets', that religion was a private matter. The Church must always be involved in society for then it can build the foundations for the reign of Christ, as Pius XII said in his 1941 Christmas message.[19]

In a letter to Ottaviani dated April 27, 1953, Connell expressed "deep gratitude for the discourse" and wrote, "Those of us who have been upholding these views consistently are very happy to have such an explicit and definite exposition of the traditional doctrine of the Church." "I do not know, as yet," he continued, "what will be the reaction of those who have been holding the liberalistic view. I hope that they will accept the statement of Your Eminence; yet it is possible that some may still retain their erroneous notions."[20]

Connell was, of course, referring to Murray, who continued to publish articles on the issue, including a piece that came out around the same time as Ottaviani's speech in *Theological Studies* entitled "Leo XIII on Church and State: The General Structure of the Controversy." Shortly thereafter, Murray's health declined due to "extreme fatigue, rooted in a cardiac insufficiency," and he was ordered to take a rest of indefinite duration beginning in April and continuing into September. In the June

Theological Studies, Murray's article, "Leo XIII: Separation of Church and State," appeared, expressing his take on Leo XIII's encyclicals. About this time, Murray and Fenton completed an exchange in which Fenton complained of Murray trying to make him a "whipping boy" because he had criticized Weigel's *Thought* article from the previous summer as "irresponsibly vicious and mendacious." Fenton complained that an October 1952 article from *America* contained "inexcusably false charges" about him. The two men seemed to reach an agreement to "meet soon" to "clear up any misunderstandings," as Murray put it. Fenton pointed out that: "A printed charge that I misrepresented your teaching would be equally disagreeable, especially since it is completely evident that such a charge would be absolutely untrue. If, however, such a charge does appear, I shall have to face it, without rancor or bitterness."[21]

Ottaviani's speech was, without doubt, a resounding rebuke of Murray's position, but Murray had friends in high places, and these friends gave Murray hope and encouragement. Aside from Luce, one of the more important was Fr. Robert Leiber, SJ, the pope's confidant, and personal secretary. In a letter dated June 12, 1953, written in German by Leiber, Murray was given assurances that he should not fear Ottaviani because his speech "only represents the private views of the Cardinal. It has no official or semi-official character. Your Reverence would do well, in my humble opinion, at least in a personal letter to the Cardinal, to correct what he erroneously characterizes as your opinion. You would do well to leave out of this matter the personal qualities of Msgr. Fenton."[22]

In a handwritten letter dated July 7, Murray advised Clare that he had been in touch with "Roman friends" who "gave assurances about l'affaire Ottaviani = Including *l'Eminence grise,* who wrote me at great length = So my back is safe – for the moment!"[23]

"*L'Eminence grise*" was, of course, Leiber, whose letter Murray discussed in a missive to Msgr. John Tracy Ellis, written from the Luce's Ridgefield, Connecticut house, where Murray was recuperating.[24] In his letter to Ellis, Murray claimed, "The discourse by Cardinal Ottaviani in the spring may possibly precipitate something in Rome. As you doubtless know, it was a purely private utterance, possessing no official significance, either formal or informal. Moreover, I have it on the highest authority that our Holy Father was not pleased by the discourse, and did not consider that it represented the true and full mind of the Church. It is a curious thing that the views that I have tentatively put forward have been received with more sympathy in theological circles in Europe than in the United States."[25]

In another hand-written letter sent a week later, Murray complained about the U.S. bishops in general and how they handled the theme of freedom but, in the same breath, praised Cardinal Gibbons' open advocacy of Americanism:

"The curious thing is that we no longer seem to have any American Catholic bishops – like Carroll, England, Hughes, Ireland, et al. Now they are all Roman Catholic....The subject came up in a conversation I had with Msgr. Montini in Rome in 1950. He was personally sympathetic with my 'orientations,' and rather wanted his hand to be strengthened – but...."

Murray did not finish that sentence but returned again to what he felt was the perilous state of Americanism among the American bishops of his era:

"I should myself want to see the 'American tradition' which you have ably stated, enforced. But I must say that it seems to me vulnerable to our adversaries, until that time it is reinforced. I mean, it is vulnerable to its assertion, 'Spain is "the ideal", -- the U.S. Constitution is a pis-aller.' Present day thought is still cast in terms of the post-Reformation 'Catholic nation-state.' I do not indeed want the American situation canonized as 'ideal.' It would be enough if it could be defended as legitimate in principle, as standing aequo jure with the Spanish situation – each representing an important realization of principle in divergent concrete historical contexts. Are we to suppose that 30,000,000 Catholics must live perpetually in a state of hypothesis?"[26]

Around this time, as the Vatican was negotiating another concordat with Spain, another war of words broke out between Hartnett of *America* and Cardinal Segura through *Ecclesia,* all of which incensed the Americans and Protestants more. A new concordat was signed on August 27, 1953, that "permitted closer cooperation between the Church and State and a stronger governmental influence on Episcopal appointments that in the other concordats concluded since 1918."[27]

Eventually, the American press got wind of Ottaviani's talk and attacked it mercilessly. *The New York Times* quoted Glenn L. Archer, Director of Protestants and Other Americans United for Separation of Church and State (POAU), as saying: "Liberal Roman Catholic prelates have been put 'in the dog house' by a Vatican statement justifying the views of an Italian Cardinal on curbing Protestant minorities." The "Vatican statement.... expressly upholds the Spanish-Italian style of religious repression in contradistinction of the American system of religious freedom. This illiberal and opportunistic policy the Vatican now upholds as one soundly based on papal texts....This renders hollow the protestations of 'liberal' American clerics that the Roman Catholic Church supports American freedom rather than the 'through control' program which binds churches in Spain and Italy."[28]

Connell sent a copy of the article to Ottaviani with the disclaimer: "It is indeed unfortunate that there are some in our country who will not admit the traditional teaching of the Church. Doubtless there will now be a recurrence of the antagonism to the Church in our land which arises when the question is brought to the attention of the public by those who hate the Church." He then assured Ottaviani that the approved doctrine of the Church was being taught at Catholic University of America and included a copy of a paper he wrote on the topic, which was presented to the Canon Law Society of America in May.[29]

In its August 3, 1953 edition, *Time* reported Ottaviani supported "Spain's stiff-necked Archbishop of Seville, Cardinal Segura," with his "strong views on the suppression of Protestantism." A Vatican official was quoted as saying Ottaviani's speech was unexceptionable and "there was certainly nothing new in it" when Ottaviani said, "The church recognizes the necessity with which rulers in some Catholic countries may be faced of granting – because of grave reasons – a degree of tolerance to the other cults. But tolerance is not a synonym for freedom of propaganda which foments religious discord and alters the secure and unanimous possession of truth and of religious practice in countries such as Italy, Spain and others." *Time* then quoted from *American Eccle-*

siastical Review: "Now if there is any certain and indisputable truth to be found among the general principles of public ecclesiastical law it is the truth that the rulers in a state composed almost entirely of Catholics and consequently and consistently governed by Catholics, have a duty to influence the legislation of that state in a Catholic sense... to protect... the religious unity of a people who unanimously know themselves to be in secure possession of religious truth."[30]

Time presented the essence of the Catholic position in a way that was sure to divide the Catholics, claiming that the "reasoning behind Ottaviani's view is an old and deeply rutted road in Catholic polity. God, the reasoning holds, gave mankind the truth once and for all in Jesus Christ; the Roman Catholic Church was established by Christ as the single possessor of that complete truth. It is wrong, then, for the possessor of the truth, whether an individual or a group, to foster the promulgation of error, or to permit it, except for strong reasons, when it has the clear power to prevent it. Any non-Catholic religion, it argues, is error. Therefore a Catholic government of a predominantly Catholic country is morally bound to limit the freedom of such a religion."[31]

As the antidote to Ottaviani and Connell, *Time* presented the "'liberal' view" set forth by Murray, a "professor of theology at Woodstock (Md.) College," who maintained that "this antique tradition of the church presupposes an antique form of government." The article shifted to "Other Catholic liberals," who believed in accordance with a "strong human argument" that should Catholics "become the overwhelmingly predominant group in the U.S., their American principles run too deep to let them interfere with the liberties of their non-Catholic compatriots to preach what and where they would." The "old Catholic custom of alliance between church and state has in the long run done the church more harm than good, leading to the anticlericalism of such countries as France, Mexico and Communist-ridden Italy" according to "many Catholics."[32]

Time gave Murray the last word, quoting him: "His [Ottaviani's] statement was neither an official nor a semi-official utterance.... It is still entirely possible and legitimate for Catholics to doubt or dispute whether Cardinal Ottaviani's discourse represents the full, adequate and balanced doctrine of the church."[33] Murray repeated Leiber's information from June and, in doing so, aided the smooth operation of the American psychological warfare machinery.

Connell advised Ottaviani of the *Time* article and Murray's quote, noting *Time*'s influence and the growing support in its pages for Murray's views: "I am also sending Your Eminence an excerpt from *Time*, a popular American magazine in reference to Your Eminence's recent statement. I believe that it is unfortunate that Father John Courtney Murray has proposed a view on the relation of Church and State which cannot be supported by Catholic theology. The principles of theology, brought out explicitly by Pope Leo XIII, and based on the revealed doctrine that civil officials in their official capacity are obliged to acknowledge the Catholic Church as the one true Church, must be maintained. However, as the enclosed excerpt indicates, Fr. Murray seems to hold the contrary, and I presume he will continue to hold it until he is officially condemned." Mentioning Weigel's statement in a recent issue of *Theology Digest* that the traditional doctrine was static and Murray's view dynamic, Connell wrote, "I am certain that this view is gaining ground in the United States, and I fear that it will continue to grow until there is an official statement on the matter from the Holy See."[34]

In a letter dated August 7, 1953, the Father General of the Jesuits advised Murray to proceed cautiously.[35] This was passed on to Murray by Fr. Joseph F. Murphy, SJ, Rector of Woodstock College, who stated that "this is the only direct assurance he has had from Very Reverend Father General."[36] In late August, Father McCormick at the American office of the Jesuits in Rome repeated the advice and wrote Murray to "Go cautiously but with calm courage" while sending an anonymous French writing attacking liberal influences in the Church. [37] The Jesuits were looking after their own.

37
CLARE GOES TO ROME (APRIL 1953)

According to Charles Yost, an ambassador was appointed to implement U.S. foreign policy, which was often begun before the administration that appointed him took office. Yost was a career diplomat who served as U.S. Ambassador to Laos, Syria, and Morocco. He also knew the Dulles family "quite well because his [John Foster Dulles's] father was the pastor of our church in Watertown, New York and married my father and mother." Yost commented during an interview in 1978 that changes in presidential administrations did not affect U.S. foreign policy. Taken aback by Yost's answer, the interviewer asked him, "But you did not notice, as time went on, that there was any change in the fundamental assumptions behind foreign policy?" Yost replied, "No, no, I don't think so. Actually my experience has been that there's always far less change than the political campaign promises. When the new administration comes in it really has relatively little room for maneuver in matters of this kind."[1]

In April 1953, Henry Luce took a personal interest in implementing the American Cold War strategy in Europe by getting his wife Clare appointed as U.S. Ambassador to Italy.[2] During the Cold War, the goal of U.S. foreign policy was to spread American ideology. Clare's job was to do that by making changes in the Italian economy as well as through the social re-engineering of Italian society, if not also the Catholic Church so that both would come to resemble America more closely.[3] Essential to accomplishing these missions was establishing credibility with the Vatican hierarchy because the Catholic Church was important in Italy and not just as a bulwark against Communism. The Church supported the Christian Democrats (CDs), and the Americans saw both the Church and the CDs as useful for instituting American-desired "reforms" in Italian society at large. Because the U.S. did not have an ambassador to the Vatican, the Ambassador to Italy had occasion to interact with the Holy See. Because she was a successful Catholic from America, Clare had the perfect credentials to carry on psychological warfare against the Italians and the Catholics, something the Americans emphasized in a State Department dispatch when they wrote: "We are aware that according to Anglo-Saxon tradition, it is bad form to discuss anyone's religion. But still, it is impossible for anyone living in Rome not to know that Mrs. Luce is a Catholic, and that, as such, she automatically fitted into that order of civilization which has its indestructible roots in the Church of Rome."[4]

THE SITUATION IN ITALY – ECONOMICS, POLITICS, CATHOLICS, COMMUNISTS

A CIA report dated October 10, 1947, concluded that Italy "is of vital strategic importance" because "its territory constitutes a potential base of operations." America's short-term goals at the time included discrediting the Communists, who had garnered some political power in Italy and, closely allied to this goal, changing Italy's economic conditions. Politically, the Americans were somewhat sympathetic to the Christian Democratic Party (CDs), which in June 1946 received a "large plurality of seats in the Assembly." The Christian Democrats observed the CIA derived their strength "from its middle of the road position, free of either Fascist or Marxist taint, the implicit support of the Catholic Church, and its evident ability to deal on favorable terms with the Allied authorities." The Catholic Church's support was important to the CDs, and the stability of the government of Italy hinged on obtaining "adequate economic support from the United States."[5]

According to the CIA report, the Catholic Church had a marvelous organization that could be used to resist the Communists. In fact, "The Catholic Church, along with the Protestant church organizations in the Netherlands, constitutes the largest confirmed anti-Communist group in Western Europe. These religious groups are relatively secure from Communist penetration and possess closely-knit organizations. Their membership, their organizations, and their well-established chains of communication would contribute greatly to a potential underground. Their long-range outlook would provide the patience necessary to begin the organization of a permanent anti-Communist underground. This long-range outlook... in the early stages of the war... for the most part to being a good source of clandestine intelligence."[6]

The CIA saw the Church as a source of resistance to Soviet Communist occupation. If the USSR "carries out her domestic policy towards religion in the foreign areas which she is dominating (many with Catholic and other religious traditions), it will be a very long time before there is real peace in central Europe. The Catholic Church would certainly resist everywhere and muster worldwide public opinion."[7]

By 1950, the CIA no longer considered the Italian Communists as a political threat. The Agency did "not believe that the Italian Communists will be able to gain control of the Italian State in the foreseeable future"[8] because the Christian Democratic Party, led by Premier Alcide De Gasperi, won a "substantial victory" over the Communists in the 1948 elections in which the "Catholic Action, the lay arm of the Church in Italy" "powerfully supported" the CD.[9] The Christian Democrats maintained their hold on power on the Italian political scene with another victory in the June 7, 1953 elections.[10] In 1954, the CIA reiterated its earlier assessment that the Communists were no longer a political threat in Italy, concluding "that the Communists are unlikely to come to power"[11] because of the strength of a political coalition led by the Christian Democrats and the economic help the U.S. provided.[12]

Luce understood that the waning power of the Communists meant that the importance of the Catholics increased. In a memorandum to Billings, Luce wrote, "Western Europe has rejected Communism, but, of course, has as yet by no means eliminated it; the dangerous game is not finished.... Communism now has no appeal to the heart, mind or imagination of Western Europe." He made these and other observations after his trip to Europe, during which he met with and had "personal conversations" with a number of key individuals in Switzerland, England, Belgium, Holland, France, and Italy. In Italy, he spoke with a number of important personalities: Pope Pius XII, Lalli, who was the "Working Editor" of "Observatore Romano" [sic], Prime Minister Alcide de Gaspari, the U.S. Ambassador as well as ECA (i.e., Marshall Plan) officials, Don Sturzo, the Governor of Milan, and the President of the Republic of Italy, Luigi Einsudi.[13]

Catholic political parties were important throughout Europe. Equally important were their economic views, which Luce characterized as "full socially minded as the Socialists and yet they tend to favor free enterprise because they reject Statism."[14]

Luce understood the pope had real political influence: "The Pope's discourse on Monday is perhaps the clearest and most important statement he has ever made on economic and social affairs.....At least 200 words of it should be published in TIME next week." Catholics were politically important to Luce: "Europe is at least 50 percent Catholic. (That is, in so far as it is religious at all.)....Protestantism (a) is much divided, (b) expresses itself today very little politically, it having politically lost itself in the long march of liberalism and British Socialism."[15]

As to the Italian economy, the CIA observed it "is dependent on a high and stable level of foreign commerce and substantial receipts from tourism, and it is sensitive to international economic fluctuations. Italy's ability to preserve free institutions may ultimately depend upon the maintenance of a high level of international trade, and upon the reduction of restrictions on the international movement of capital and labor." As the recipients of U.S. aid, the Italians had a "substantial postwar recovery" resulting in "much...replaced and modernized, new production methods introduced, transport and marketing improved, and new products and new industries developed."[16]

The CIA concluded that Italy had economic problems, which were intensified by various "institutional weaknesses" such as:

"(a) the inefficient operations of numerous state-owned productive enterprises, which were inherited from the fascist era but never adequately reorganized; (b) large-scale state subsidization and protection of inefficient private enterprises; (c) the forced retention of excess workers on farm, factory, and government payrolls; (d) the adverse effects on the price structure and on innovation in new business initiatives resulting from monopolistic business organization and restrictive practices; and (e) an inefficient tax system...."[17]

The CIA, therefore, saw the need for "large-scale investment," which was opposed by groups fearing the generation of "inflationary pressures and dislocations which would be a greater threat to political and social stability than the failure to increase the rate of economic expansion." As a result, it was not likely that Italy would correct its economic problems during Scelba's regime or the regime of his likely successor, Amintore Fanfani, who was considered a leftist in the Christian Democratic Party.[18]

By now, it should be obvious that the Italians looked at economics differently than the Americans. Dohrn had a conversation with the Mayor of Florence, which revealed the Catholic view of American economics. In a letter to Time, Inc. executives Henry Grunwald, C.D. Jackson, and Luce, Dohrn wrote that the mayor "like most Europeans . . . doesn't believe that America's excellent experiences with free enterprise applied in any way to Europe.... America was great and rich....When I said this was exactly what Nenni had told me a few months ago, he said he wasn't arguing for socialism but for Christianity and Italian capitalists were not Christians."[19]

The Christian Democrats, the party that seemed to offer the best hope for the Americans, were far from pure when it came to espousing American capitalism. "Socialism as a dogma today in Europe," Dohrn wrote, "is so ill-defined that you find proponents of free enterprise or something amounting to that in many Western socialist parties and I am sure, among many Polish and Hungarian revolutionaries... while there are many proponents of socialism (which means planned economy if the word makes any sense) in the Christian Democratic parties of the west.... In any case, socialism and Christian democracy are nowhere a strict antithesis in the social and economic field."[20]

In addition, Catholics worried Luce because they did not seem fully committed to opposing Communism. "Does the 'Vatican' take really seriously the meance [sic] of Communism?" Luce wondered in a letter to C.D. Jackson. "A Holy See diplomat with whom I recently spoke says: 'No, not really.' There are of course some Cardinals – my friend mentioned Tisserand [sic], Constantine and Ottoviani [sic] – who do take it seriously. But most of the Cardinals and Monsignori don't...That is, they just do not think that Europe will ever really go Communism [sic]. Europe, they feel, is basically Christian, or if it isn't that, anyway Europe is basically European, which is to say that it has its own deep humanistic etc. traditions, and all these are incompatible with Communism.... This is not to say that either the Vatican or 'Europe' likes Communism even a little bit. They detest it. But for that very reason they don't fear it.... What could be simpler? Keep this in mind."[21]

Although he didn't state it in precisely those terms, Luce was concerned that the Catholics in general, and the Italians in particular, may lose their stomach for the Cold War. *Time* reported that President Giovanni Gronchi, the "Catholic advocate of the 'opening to the Left," gave a "rousing political inaugural that plainly pleased the Communists more than his own party, the Christian Democrats." *Time* reported that Gronchi, who was one of the founders of the Christian Democrats in 1943, said, "The new phase of our national life coincides with the new trends in international relations." He hinted at bringing into the Italian government Nenni's Socialists, a turn of events unheard of just a few years earlier. Later, Gronchi spoke with Amintore Fanfani, who was the party leader of the Christian Democrats, and told Fanfani, "Let's hope my election will bring about a distensione in this country, which I, as chief of state, will do my best to promote." "Distensione" meant co-existing with the Soviets and also with "fellow travelers in an old-style popular front" in Italy.[22]

Gronchi's election caused concern among Luce and the Americans, especially since it was the result of a deal between Gronchi and a wide range of Italian interests. The Big Businessmen "fat cats," Labor, and the

Communists were all part of the deal, the terms of which included no anti-communism, an international policy, and money, which came from the Americans, given to "labor and farm workers." [23]

In an assessment of the situation that he sent to C.D. Jackson, Luce launched into a discussion of the role of the Catholic Church in Italian politics, concluding that the Church would continue to be an obstacle to the introduction of an American-style democracy unless long-range efforts were undertaken to change Italian leadership so as to effect fundamental societal change. "The Italians from the Alps to Sicily," Luce wrote, "have never quite made themselves into a Nation. The Risorgimento was a glorious chapter in the march of human liberty but for various reasons including, first the unfortunate position of the Catholic Church, it never quite came off, before Mussolini. Now they start again – with the Church. The Church today is all for an Italian nation – on condition that it is also Catholic which nobody objects too much, certainly not Nenni. But the Church still doesn't understand political democracy. It understands benevolence – including benevolence to the rich. It understands socialism – and sees nothing wrong with it provided it is run by Catholics. But it doesn't understand political democracy. Do Italians? Yes, I think they do...They like liberty. (Maybe everybody does? Anyway that was my main theme in reporting on my Italian visit in 1949). But liberty is very difficult.... Circumstances are hard here – not just the economic but even more the confusion of so much contradictory tradition. There is Machiavelli and there is Mazzini. There are the Social Encyclicals – but there are also the Renaissance popes.... I have a hunch that the best in the Italian nation is not currently the most visible. Twenty years from now! Ah yes, but what now?"[24]

MADAME AMBASSADOR CLARE BOOTHE LUCE

During the period leading up to her confirmation by the Senate, Clare underwent an intense course of study and preparation, during which Murray tutored her concerning the Vatican's position on various topics and issues.[25] After she was unanimously confirmed as the United States Ambassador to Italy on March 2, 1953,[26] Clare began six weeks of intense study for the job before sailing for Italy on April 14.[27] During that time, she discussed with Luce and C.D. Jackson the issue of how to wage psychological warfare against the Italians.[28] Harry wrote a statement on Clare's behalf in the terms of John McCloy's philosophy for ambassadors, releasing it for the Western Union radio program. Clare said she would "try to do all that is expected of an ambassador in the way of formal occasions, but frankly, my chief interest will be in getting to know the Italian people, their problems, their aspirations and their way of thinking. The people of Italy want to know about America. I shall try to bring them a better understanding of our practical idealism, of our way of life, which is liberty under law."[29]

Luce and his media empire closely monitored the Italian reaction to Clare's appointment as Ambassador to shape her image and control the response. Luce, in turn, shaped public perception of this appointment by making sure his publications mentioned Clare's credentials as both an American and a Catholic.[30] Luce gave his wife high grades at the end of the first year, noting that she succeeded in getting the Scelba government to act on her urging. She also made "close acquaintances of Italian political leaders."[31]

Being married to the Ambassador to Italy gave Luce a good excuse to spend a lot of time in Rome and allowed a considerable amount of information to pass between him and his wife concerning world affairs, thereby enhancing the influence each had in their respective spheres. Clare occasionally asked Time, Inc. editors to gather information on persons of interest, such as the Konow Family, a certain Rossi-Longhi, and a Victor Emanuel.[32] C.D. Jackson regularly corresponded with Clare, and the two shared thoughts and information, perhaps most notably regarding his association with the Bilderberg meeting in 1954.[33] In any event, it was clear that Clare knew to whom she was beholden. Upon arrival in Rome, before even seeing the Papal Nuncio to Italy, Msgr. Giuseppe Fietta, on May 4, 1953, Clare dined at the Villa Taverna with Mr. and Mrs. Walter Lippmann, Harry's mentor and his wife.[34]

Clare's "initiatives followed some well-defined directives" as "an ambassador cannot autonomously decide the policy to be followed toward a host country." The aggressive policy towards Italy, which she was appointed to implement, was contained in NSC 5411. It instructed the ambassador about aiding the Italian government and private groups and showing them how to "combat Communism vigorously." According to NSC 5411, the ambassador was to prevent Italy from "falling under the domination of the Italian Communist party or of the present Italian Socialist party...To prevent Italy from falling under the domination of neo-Fascist groups.... [and to] Continue to make full use of U.S. political means and, as practical and appropriate, economic and military aid."[35] During her tenure as ambassador, Clare had carte blanche to meddle in Italian domestic affairs and to remake Italy in America's image with the full assistance of the U.S. intelligence community and other American elites. That involved teaching the Italians to conduct psychological operations against the Communists themselves under a project code-named "Demagnetize" and later renamed "Clydesdale." With "Demagnetize," the Italian government was "encouraged...to launch a political and psychological offensive" against the Communist Party.[36]

One of the first things Clare did upon assuming her duties was to condemn totalitarianism, but the way she did it caused an uproar. Introduced by CIA operative James Jesus Angleton to the Milan Chamber of Commerce on May 28, 1953,[37] Clare spoke with words that "were all honey at first, for she was able to announce a further American contribution of twenty-two million dollars to bolster the Italian economy."[38] But the honey soon turned bitter when she proceeded to warn against totalitarianism – whether on the right or on the left. "I am required in all honesty to say this," she began, "– but if – though this cannot happen – the Italian people should fall the unhappy victims of totalitarianism, totalitarianism of the right or of the left, there would follow, logically, and tragically, grave consequences for the intimate and warm cooperation we now enjoy."[39] The speech received "thunderous applause" according to Luce, but the Italian press attacked her as interfering in Italy's internal affairs. The Italian press was more perceptive than those who applauded her. In spite of (or perhaps because of) U.S. support, de Gasperi's Christian Democrats went down to defeat, and the Communists surged.[40]

Clare saw the Church as something having practical, political value, as a bulwark against Communism. In a speech she gave at the Mayflower Hotel in Washington, D.C., Clare declared that "The Church is the only effective force that cuts into the progress of Communism. Without the Church the entire country would be Communist." But she expressed misgivings about Italian participation in the effort against the Communists when she added that in Italy, "one can see the Communist mayors go to Mass to the same church where they were baptized and where they were married. The Red papers print the picture of the Pope and say that there is no incompatibility between the Church and Communism....."[41]

And so the Catholics held their noses and supported the party of their Italian co-religionists. William Colby, a Catholic from St. Paul, Minnesota, who later became CIA Director, was the second-ranking political officer in Clare's Embassy and a CIA operative. He was one of many Catholics in the CIA, and his wife Barbara, along with Clare, were members of the Women's Auxiliary of the Knights of Malta. Dual loyalty was never a problem for Colby, who "was not in thrall to Christianity, but dedicated to his country" and lived a life of "deception and manipulation" as a result. Colby's principal duty was to supply cash to the centrist Italian parties to the tune of about $ 30,000,000 per year, a large sum of money at the time. Clare supervised all of this. Assisting her was the already-mentioned James Jesus Angleton, another CIA operative and strong Zionist supporter with "unprecedented access" to Allen Dulles.[42]

A year and a half after Clare assumed her duties, the Communist Party in Italy entered a period of decline, which was due more to a rise in the standard of living than anything associated with anti-Communism initiatives being prosecuted by the Americans. Clare said the most important factor was that "every worker now has his Topolino – his little mouse Fiat – or at least a motor scooter."[43]

CHAPTER 37

IT'S THE ECONOMY

With the Communists in decline, the Americans began to focus on economic restructuring, something that entailed weakening the government's power. The Americans wanted an Italian Government that reduced barriers to international finance, and, beginning with the Marshall Plan, they pursued a policy that tried to make Europe like America by creating one vast market or European Union.[44] In a March 12, 1954 Top Secret missive to Allen Dulles, Director of the CIA, Clare claimed that the Italians' "statist" view of society and government had to be changed, something that required a change in the focus of American efforts away from the Communists. The Italian political coalition, or "Center Democracy," as she called it, that ran Italy since the end of the War was the result of U.S. aid. Its continued existence was threatened by the U.S. failure to continue the aid. In spite of that aid, Clare brought up the "equally disagreeable fact...that with the disappearance of U.S. aid from the Italian political scene we can now see clearly that the Italian State, in its economic structure is still rigidly socialist state with a closely controlled economy. Ten years after Mussolini...the Italian State has made little progress towards a free enterprise economy."[45]

Despite De Gasperi's political clout with the Christian Democrats, the "economic rulers of DeGasperi's Italy (bankers, industrialists, business men, big agriculturists, land holders, privileged classes, etc.) are pretty much the same figures who ruled Italy's economic structure under Mussolini." As a result, "no prominent leader of any political party in Italy today either wants or dares to propose changing this socialist structure – and direction, either because (a) none (except astonishing old Don Sturzo) has the vision to see how this would benefit the people, or (b) to advocate a change would be counter to his party's program, or (c) would alienate some or all of the party's backers."[46]

"A free democratic Italy," Clare wrote bitterly, "accepts without any adverse comment the concept of the socialist state." And "Every political party in Italy today is a socialist party. From the extreme right through to the extreme left, with the possible exception of the Liberals, no party shows any real intention or even desire to change the existing socialist economic machinery."[47] When it came to the Christian Democrats, there were several groups, all of which were opposed to changing the Italian economic system to resemble the American free enterprise system. The "right wing" of the CDs were beholden to the "economic rulers of IRI, ENI, AGIP and their other Milan and Turin patrons." The members of the CDs on the Left were the "'hard core' ideological CDs." They did not want to change the system because they sincerely believed in "Catholic Socialism' – the 'White Communism' of Taviani, Fanfani, Dossetti, LaPira...." The "extreme left wing CDs – Gronchi, for example," push for an opening to the economic left, and not the foreign policy left.[48]

Clare saw the "real political battle among the various parties in Italy" was not over the "reform of Mussolini's socialist state into a free enterprise state" but rather as one over the "control of the existing socialist state apparatus." The debate came down to an attempt to convince the Italian voter that "their interests not only coincide with but are best served by this desired capture."[49]

To achieve political power, a political party needed "Prestige, Power, Gold," and in Italy, there were no political figures whose "prestige is, in the patriotic, nationalist sense, politically legitimate." DeGasperi and the CDs' prestige derived "on the one hand" from "the USA a foreign source, and on the other of the Vatican a source that is not (or should not be) temporal or political." Italy's "growing awareness that while her strongest political party, the CDs, is supported by and therefore responsive to a strange triumvirate – the USA, the Papacy, and the big Italian interests, there is no other party (except the Communists) who can today hope to supplant this politically unpopular combination."[50]

There were tensions within this triumvirate. First, there was tension between the Americans and the Catholics: "The dilemma (and resultant 'immobilism') of the CD party leadership – especially De Gasperi's – is occasioned not only by the popular left wing tug within its own ranks, but by the agonizing need simultaneously to satisfy the differing demands of (a) the CD's two biggest ideological backers: The Vatican and the USA, who often do not see eye to eye on certain basic democratic questions (freedom of religion, speech, press, education – for example)."[51]

The U.S. and the Vatican faction struggled with the "Milan-Turin monopolists and industrialists who are greatly at variance on many fundamental economic questions (tax laws, land reform, oil investment in the Po – for example)." Clare related an example of this conflict concerning the CD's Mattei in Sicily, who was pursuing the interests of a company known as ENI. Mattei was "seeking to kick private oil capital out of Italy while the U.S. strives to bring private investment in. Meeting momentarily on the common ground of preserving the state socialist structure intact, the CP joins Mr. Mattei in this effort."[52]

American aid to the Christian Democrats was crucial for three reasons. These were "(a) to hide the extent to which the CDs depend on the priests as their real political activists, (b) to pacify the industrialists, who participated in aid through profits, and (c) to attract to the CDs the mass voters, who participated through housing and agrarian reform, increased employment, etc." The CDs were torn because they were based on "the essentially conflicting demands and expectations of their three backers: the Vatican, the U.S. and the Italian dirigente classes." As U.S. aid declined, problems arose. Clare believed "the matter is becoming uncomfortably clear to the electorate that the CD's only internal ideological backing comes from the Vatican, and its only internal economic backing from the ENI, IRI, and AGIP industrialists and the private monopolists, and that its external economic backer, the U.S. is 'pulling out.'" With the reduction of U.S. aid, "the dominant Italian party begins to stand revealed before the electorate for what it is – a political party led at the polls by the Papacy and economically dictated to by the same old Fascist industrialists who served and were served by....Mussolini. In short, a clerical-socialist party, controlled by renegade Fascist millionaires." De Gasperi was a failure, according to the Ambassador, because "between 1948 - 1952 he did not (with the help of U.S. aid) break the power of the industrialists over the State by moving energetically towards a free economy."[53]

Clare saw a serious fault line in Italian politics. The Christian Democrats were a "dominant clerical party, controlled by the economic right...."

The Americans saw "that given any other effective alternative, either Left or Right, Italy will vote against passing over the control of the socialist state to such a combination." The "historic fear of a clerical hegemony backed by the privileged classes (in Italy, the 'papal families' with their infinite industrial tie-ups) has always been just as real." According to Clare, on June 7, 1953, the defeat of the Christian Democrats was brought about by something called the Maggioransa law that would have "guaranteed this hegemony."[54]

Because the economic powers were breaking from the CDs, De Gasperi felt that it was necessary to have another election to allow them the opportunity to solidify their power. This concerned the Americans because the Christian Democrats had not advanced the Americans' economic agenda of restructuring the Italian economic system. It appeared that the Italian "big money can not go where it ideologically wants." The Italian industrialists did not "have to stay firmly with the CD in order to get, as before, profits via the U.S. while at the same time 'coppering' U.S. money to prevent a real reform in the government." The Italian monied interests were showing an independence of the Americans and of the Christian Democrats, and these interests were starting to go "to the right of Mr. De Gasperi (who is Mr. Center)." The Ambassador concluded that a "renewed U.S. aid program can put an ideological and financial skewer through the situation."[55]

Recognizing that the Vatican, the industrialists, and the U.S. were the power brokers in Italy, Clare presented Allen Dulles with a number of courses of action, including a proposal calling for U.S. aid to be extended to the Italian economy in greater amounts than presently planned, ostensibly to fight the Communists. To succeed, this option would have to be "extended on a firm quid pro quo, reform-and-perform-as-you-go installment-plan basis which would then secure the maximum economic and political results."[56] Clare saw potential opposition as coming from the "Milan-Turin" axis of industrialists, who "will certainly support those forces which will most quickly rally to the old Mussolini concept of the corporate economic state, which is the one that they best understand how to do business with and under." To break up this economic power through the use of the political processes,

Clare urged another option. The U.S. should support "*all* pro-west parties (including the PMM, excluding the MSI) encouraging them to meld and fuse with the CD government – i.e., the encouragement of nationalism, as being preferable to either Kremlin red, Fascist black, Royal purple, or Vatican white socialism."[57]

Clare argued against the current course of action, which was "trying to shore up the crumbling CD Coalition" without direct U.S. aid because the Milan-Turin industrialists would veto any program that did not protect their economic interests. She viewed the industrialists as an enemy only slightly less repugnant than the Communists and insisted the U.S. use the following "carrots: (a) to control as completely as possible all the democratic forces, (b) to insist that they begin to make real economic reform in the structure of the State, (c) to insist that they begin a program of anti-Communist action that will then and only then make it possible for overt aid from the U.S. to come to them." Clare proposed a program designed to weaken and destroy the economic power of the Milan-Turin industrialists in the name of fighting Communism by making U.S. aid conditional on the economic reform of Italy. Substantial U.S. aid was needed to make sure that Italy became a democracy; otherwise, it was likely that while Italy would defeat Communism, it would become either a "neo-Fascist Republican state, a Socialist monarchy, a fascist Monarchy, a Clerical-Military Dictatorship, or the first Communist Republic of western Europe."[58]

RELIGIOUS LIBERTY AS ESSENTIAL TO ITALIAN SOCIETAL RE-ENGINEERING

The Americans were interested in the interface between religion and politics, and that included interest in the pious practices of Italy's Catholics, including a weeping statue that came to be known as the Madonna Delle Lacrime of Syracuse, which attracted the attention of the Cultural Attache, George G. Fox. He sent a memo concerning the weeping of a plaster statue over the bed of a young bride, Antonina Giusto. After examination by ecclesiastical authorities, it was found that the statue did indeed weep In the course of about a month, a number of miracles were experienced by those who touched the cloth on which the tears had fallen. By October 1953, a shrine was planned, and about four million lire were pledged. The event had a powerful effect on the Italians, and it also had repercussions in the United States, where the Americans analyzed the commercial and political aspects of the miracle, noting that the Communists were using the event for their own purposes.[59]

Catholicism ordered and protected Italian society. The 1929 Concordat between the Holy See and the Italian government put the pope and Cardinals on a par with princes, who guaranteed that in "the Eternal City....the Italian government will take care to impede...whatsoever may be in opposition with its said character." The government also agreed to recognize and honor a number of Church holidays throughout the country. All of this served to give a special and undisputed place to the Catholic Church and the Faith. The Faith received even greater endorsement when the government agreed to provide religious instruction in the Catholic faith in public schools because "Catholic doctrine" was the "foundation and the crown of public instruction" in Italy.[60]

The ability of Protestants to proselytize without hindrance was an important issue for the Americans, and as their representative, Clare was quick to push religious tolerance, which, in light of history and Clare's missives to the Director of the CIA, was clearly a move to weaken the power of the Church in Italy, which in turn advanced a reorientation of society in accord with the American ideology. Shortly after arriving in Rome, Clare was faced with a situation in which Protestant evangelicals insisted that they were being discriminated against by the Italian Catholics. This was the first of many times that Clare, a Catholic, intervened with the Italian government for the purpose of advancing the religious liberty of non-Catholics.[61] This principle was, after all, a central organizing principle of America, and Harry had convinced Clare of the need to advance American-style religious liberty around the world.[62]

The fact that Murray was implicated in Clare's actions infuriated the pope. In November, McCormick wrote to Fr. Provincial McMahon that Murray had to "put down in simple, clear statements his full, present position regarding this Church-State question and to send it to me for

Father General. Sic mandatum." The reason was somewhat cryptically contained in McCormick's letter, which stated, "Read Can. 2316. If I assist a man to come to Italy for that purpose knowing that is why he is coming do I fall under the penalty? Our highest superior...thinks so, unless excused by ignorance. America might know that." McCormick's letter was sparked by Clare's efforts on behalf of the Protestants in Italy and the possibility that she violated sections 2316 and 1258 of the 1917 Code of Canon Law by defending Protestant sects.[63]

Murray went on the offensive, and in doing so, he implicated the entire leadership of the Jesuit order in his efforts. He inquired as to whether McCormick and the Father General were also suspected of heresy – if Murray was – for having encouraged Murray or if he was just an object of interest. In his November 23 letter, Murray wanted to know the attitude toward him in Rome, informing McCormick that "It would help to know whether I am speaking into a Roman climate of hostility or captivity." Murray asked point blank if he had promoted heresy in Italy in 1950 or if the McCormick letter was about something in the future.[64]

Murray sensed his views were the real reason for the Vatican's reaction to Clare's actions. "The affair of the Pentecostals from Texas," he wrote, "was at the moment in the news. And I remember telling her that she might protest arbitrary acts of violence against American citizens, but that she had no right, either as Ambassador and still less as a Catholic, to interfere with the just application of existent Italian laws. There was no mention of Canon 2316 (I carry only a limited number of canons in my head!).... One thing is certain: she never heard of Canon 2316. And I rather hope that, if there is to be a reprimand, it will be given gently preferably by the 'highest superior' himself. She is doctrinally all right in the faith, but has a woman's idea – maybe some men's idea – of positive law. Moreover... she can be stubborn and even rebellious.'"[65]

McCormick quickly advised Murray that "the Pope, who was 'almost wroth' over her [Clare's] aid to the 'dishonest and disreputable Pentecostals, himself citing the canon against her, and also resenting her failure to ask for an audience.'" McCormick assured Murray he would warn Murray "'at once and clearly' of any direct threat." McCormick quoted the Superior General and expressed his support for Murray:

"One does not know what Madrid might do next. But Rome has not expressed any fear for the orthodoxy of Fr. Murray, though not everybody in Rome, I presume, accepts his writings."[66]

It would be difficult to argue ignorance of Canon Law as an excuse for Clare's actions because she had had the opportunity and resources to investigate the wisdom of the Italian policies toward church and state and to act accordingly. Several years earlier, in 1948, Clare received from Bishop John Noll of the Diocese of Fort Wayne, Indiana, a paper entitled "The True and the False Infallibility of the Popes: A Controversial Reply to Dr. Schulte," written by Bishop Dr. Joseph Fessler, Secretary General of the Vatican Council (1869-1870) and published posthumously. The paper set out the reasons behind the Catholic position on the Church and Civil Society, and it established the proper relationship between the two societies based on their purposes or ends. Fessler held that if the Church was not established in a society, it and other religions would come to be controlled by the State, something he termed "Heathen Caesarism," [67] which precisely happened during the Cold War.

38
SPIES AND COLLABORATORS IN HIGH PLACES

The nature of an ambassador's duties is conducive to being a spy, and ambassadors are certainly valuable players in political warfare.[1] The press announcement publicizing Clare's departure from Italy in November 1956 at the end of her tour as Ambassador confirmed her role in political warfare: "Every bit of progress, in any sector of Italian life, was immediately reported to Washington by Mrs. Luce. She thus, with her invaluable work, forged even more strongly the bonds of friendship which are now so firm between Italy and the United States, and which will surely grow even stronger in the future."[2] The purpose of political warfare is "the extension of political influence or control without the necessity of recourse to warfare at all in the narrow military sense of the term."[3] To do so, Clare worked with 1,500 employees at the Palazzo Margherita, a U.S. compound. This included a contingent from the United States Information Service (later the U.S. Information Agency), certainly one of the most significant players in the psychological warfare campaign America waged around the world.[4]

Much of the spying done on Catholics in the United States was done by the FBI, with the collaboration of priests and prelates. Overseas, the spying was done by the CIA and Time, Inc., but also with the collaboration of well-placed priests. Murray and Henry Luce knew the most important agents, notably Klaus Dohrn and Robert Leiber, SJ. In this important area, Murray was closer to Henry Luce than Clare, Luce's wife.

These connections were important in monitoring activities in the Church and generally advancing the Americanist agenda, something that became clear in a letter from Murray to Clare early in her term as ambassador.[5] Murray chided Clare for not having asked for an audience with the pope, and indeed, that audience did not occur more than two years later on July 29, 1955, even though, as a private citizen, she had numerous private audiences. [6] "The Pope," Murray wrote, "is personally put out, rather hurt, that you have not asked for an audience." Murray then quoted from a "personal letter" that he received confidentially from a "friend in Rome, of the ubiquitous S.J. persuasion" in advising Clare of the pope's feelings.[7]

Murray told Clare that Pius XII was "displeased over some *demarches* you took with regard to bringing Protestant missionaries into Italy. I dunno the facts. What did you do? In any event, you ought to be prepared for this. You can easily explain your motives – that you had nothing to do with promoting the spread of heresy, violating Italian laws, etc. And if the subject were to come, you could do a good work n setting the 'nuisance' of Protestant propanganda [sic] in perspective over against the Communist 'menace.' But you know the emotional violence of Italian reaction against il Protestantesimo. It gives them an outlet for violence, and soothes their Cathcolic [sic] pride. Anyway, the rather low variety of Protestant that does missionary work in Italy – like the brethren from Texas, etf. [sic] – are no credit either to Protestantism or to America."[8]

To repair the damage her behavior caused, Murray suggested that Clare: "get in touch with my friend Klaus Dohrn (who seemingly has been taken on by Harry in some ad hoc capacity, and who may be in Rome at least he ought to be fetchable.) He is close to Fr. Robert Leiber, S.J. (Gregorian University), who is in turn close to the Pope. Let the situation be explained to H. H. [His Holiness, Pope Pius XII] by Leiber. And let him arrange an audience. The pretext could be Christmas or your return to the U.S. –it does not matter."[9]

Murray explained that Leiber, the pope's personal assistant, was an ally in the Americanist cause: "If Dohrn is not available as a go-between, you could get directly in touch with Padre Leiber. You might even use the mighty name of JCM; he is aware of my existence. He is a nice little man, with a worried manner, and enormously intelligent. He has been for years the Pope's confidant and adviser. He is also one of the few Europeans who has a sense of the U.S. church and state embroglio [sic]."[10]

This letter, which ended with Murray's characteristic "Much love....John," showed that Murray's connections in Rome went all the way to the pope. With connections like this, Murray was able to thwart Ottaviani and Connell during the Americanist insurgency that rocked the Church during the 1950s.

ROBERT LEIBER, SJ

Fr. Leiber, or "Father L.," had a long history of working with American intelligence and providing them with information about European affairs. According to an OSS report dated 18 August 1944, Leiber was a Jesuit from Bavaria who became part of the future Pope Pius XII's private staff when Cardinal Eugenio Pacelli became Papal Nuncio to Germany in 1920, after having served as nuncio to Bavaria since 1917. Leiber had been teaching in the Theological Faculty of the University of Munich and then went on to be a professor at the Vatican University or the Gregoriana. Pacelli kept Leiber as a confidant and as an aide while Pacelli was Secretary of State and then later elevated to the Papacy. In 1944, when the OSS interrogated him, Leiber was serving as "confidential secretary to the Pope, whom he sees almost daily" and was considered a "thorough anti-Nazi."[11]

From the winter of 1939-40 until September-October 1943, Leiber gave the Americans detailed information concerning the various plots against Hitler as well as the names of their leaders. His sources of information in Germany were termed "unusual" by the American interrogators, though he was not taken into the confidence of the conspirators for the July 1944 plot on Hitler's life.[12]

According to Leiber, the conspirators for the first plot were "primarily members of the German nobility" but did not have the support of the German generals even though General Halder was the leader of the plot. When the German invasion of Norway succeeded, the plot evaporated. The next conspiracy followed the German surrender at Stalingrad and was led by General Ludwig Beck. It consisted of members of all political elements of the Weimar Republic except for the "extreme Right and the extreme Left." Konrad Adenauer refused to join the conspiracy because he felt that the Nazi regime would have to lose the war before it could be overthrown. Field Marshal Manstein was to lead the German Generals on the Eastern Front in an uprising, but again, the plot failed when Manstein decided that he could indeed hold the Eastern Front, and so refused to participate in the plot. The third attempt on October 15, 1943, involved a reversal of the thinking that Manstein had exhibited. This time, the conspirators decided that if the Eastern Front could be stabilized, the plot would go forward. Since the front could not be stabilized and the Germans were in retreat in the Soviet Union, the plot failed.[13]

In an interview after the war, Leiber told American intelligence agents that he thought that German youth (10 to 30 years of age) would be lost to Catholicism without a system of state and confessional schools. He also believed that Catholics would return to the political center since that was their normal orientation.[14]

Leiber continued sharing information with American intelligence operatives like Dohrn after the war, including reports on his confidential communications with Pope Pius XII as well as the latter's private thoughts. In one instance, Leiber told Dohrn that "his boss had commented how most foreigners overestimated the ideological interests of the Italians. The same afternoon Pietro Nenni said the same thing in order to support his thesis that he was going to win away votes from the Communists. I felt like saying I'd heard the very same thing from another prominent Italian the same day....."[15] Earlier, Leiber played an important role in squelching rumors that the Vatican was going to support a second Catholic party in Italian politics.[16] Dohrn had frequent conversations with Leiber[17] on important topics, but the flow of information was a two-way street. Leiber told Dohrn what was on the pope's mind, but through Dohrn, the U.S. intelligence establishment had access to Leiber, and to this day, his records at the CIA remain classified and are not released. Leiber had influence over the pope, which gave Leiber real power in the Catholic Church.

KLAUS DOHRN

Murray had known Dohrn since at least 1952 when Dohrn was a reporter for Time, Inc. In accordance with a November 17, 1955 agreement renewing an earlier agreement with Time, Inc., Dohrn received $400 per month in return for a monthly status letter or report, which reported on three things: (a) a series of headline news items on interesting European subjects which you estimate would not normally come to the attention of our European Bureaus; (b) the Dohrn interview-of-the-month, to be reported briefly and factually, and without elaborate interpretations; (c) any interpretive material you wish to send, either on the interview or on some other subject.

Dohrn reported directly to C.D. Jackson on Time, Inc. matters[18] and was put on the CIA payroll on May 2, 1952,[19] where he stayed during much of the same time that he was also on the payroll of Time International, Inc. as a "special reporter to the editor in chief of Time Life International" with his office in Zurich, Switzerland.[20] Murray came to know Dohrn's handler, Jay Lovestone, who was tied in with American Friends of the Captive Nations,[21] another front group that was created to show American solidarity against the Communists. To be good at intelligence, one had to learn the importance of personal relationships and the importance of winning people's trust and confidence, something which would lead to other contacts, as noted by Mary Bancroft, OSS agent for Allen Dulles during World War II.[22] Dohrn's job was to travel throughout Europe and gather information from insiders and the leaders in countries like Germany, France, and Italy, and the Vatican, where he had access to "responsible and well informed advisors of the Pope."[23] In a July 2, 1952 letter, Dohrn told his handler Lovestone that he had access to "one of the most important present advisors to the Pope,"[24] someone he identified in his letter to Lovestone as "Father L."

In a letter to Clare simply dated August 30,[25] Murray introduced Dohrn and revealed his connection to Leiber, whom Murray referred to as "His Grey Eminence." In explaining his connection to Dohrn, Murray also revealed his links to the CIA and the source of much information that he obtained from Rome. The chain of information began when Leiber reported to Dohrn and continued when Dohrn reported to Lovestone at the CIA, his superiors in the Jesuits, and C.D. Jackson at Time, Inc. Murray could access critical information at any of these nodes. He could also talk directly to Henry Luce and tried to bring him into the loop through these connections as well. In the previously mentioned letter to Clare, which was probably written on August 30, 1953, Murray tried to explain his information network:

"Last Spring [1953] I tried to put a friend of mine – name of Klaus Dohrn – in touch with Harry, but it fell through on account of Harry leaving Rome ahead of schedule. Actually, Dohrn wants to see you (like half the worold [sic] in that respect). He will be in Rome from Sept. 2nd to 6th or so. Could you spare him any of your business or social time – perhaps with Harry..... Dohrn is not looking for anything. Matter of conversation with very knowledgeable man in European politics, extremely well connected all around. Basically a journalist, German origin, swam the Danube to escape Nazis from Vienna, now U.S. citizen, has done considerable confidential work for U.S. government. The only angle for you, if there is one is this: if you should ever want a confidential go-between yourself and His Gray Eminence (Robert Leiber, S.J.) and thus onward and higher, Dohrn would be the man. (I introduced them when in Rome in 1950 – remember???) (Or is it heresy and treason even to think of go-betweens with such quarters?) Dohrn has been spending some time on the Adriatic, recovering from an attack of polio. Big man, not handsome, but excellent brain and good Catholic. Might be worth a bit of time; anyway, I promised to speak for him, as my friend...."[26]

Dohrn was Murray's friend, and years later, when it appeared Dohrn might lose influence due to a change in editorial policies at *Life* magazine, Christopher Emmett appealed to Murray to prevail on Henry Luce to change the policies, thereby saving Dohrn's waning prestige.[27] Within a couple of years, largely because of Murray's efforts, Dohrn became Clare's close friend,[28] so close in fact, that, after the death of Pope Pius XII, Dohrn was lunching with Clare and Secretary of State Dulles.[29]

In a relationship that began in the late 1940s and lasted well into the 1960s, Dohrn corresponded frequently with Jay Lovestone, born Jacob Leibstein, who was himself on the CIA payroll, ostensibly working to advance and organize labor in Europe along American lines. Lovestone was a close confidant of CIA operative James Jesus Angleton, who provided significant assistance to Clare during her tenure as Ambassador to Italy[30] (while, of course, spying on Lovestone).[31]

Labor was always an area of major concern for the Americans. During World War II, the "labor factor" was viewed as the "most important factor in the psychological warfare situation in Western Europe."[32] The OSS concluded as early as July 1942 that the "industrial labor population is the largest and likeliest target for anything this country can say to affect enemy morale."[33] Indeed, the OSS concluded the *"psychological war over Europe is about...labor"*[34] and set its goals accordingly, selecting messages that could be used after the war against Germany and Italy. All these messages stressed the same free market themes, extolling "freely negotiated collective bargaining agreements," "freedom to protest to the government," "freedom to better its conditions," and "freedom to associate with international labor," all with the "net aim... to convey an impression of American industrial might, including the welfare of labor and labor support of *free* labor conditions."[35]

Lovestone was responsible for establishing collaboration between the CIA and the American Federation of Labor (AFL) beginning in late 1948 and continuing for about twenty more years. Lovestone worked with George Meany, though Meany denied the collaboration.[36] In the beginning, Lovestone received funding from the Marshall Plan, which set aside five percent of all funds for covert operations and which came into existence coincidentally (or not so coincidentally) at around the same time the CIA came into being.[37] The Cold War was good for the espionage business, and both Lovestone and his good friend Angleton played on European and American fears that "the Soviet system was bent on spreading Communism through the world and destroying America."[38] Lovestone had very strong beliefs against Communism because he had been a Communist in his younger days.[39] Angleton had a long history of working with the Vatican, which began while working with "Wild Bill" Donovan, who, as head of the OSS, developed a close rapport with Pope Pius XII during World War II.[40] By the end of the War, it was Angleton who was coordinating the most with the Vatican on intelligence matters,[41] and this provided valuable experience to Lovestone and his assets, who continued Angleton's work during the Cold War.

Lovestone focused his efforts mostly on Europe in the late 1940s and early 1950s but then shifted his field of operation to the Third World, as did the entire American anti-Communism effort. In the Third World, the AFL supported nationalist movements against the established colonial powers, which were European. In this manner, the Americans destroyed the colonial powers – those who had been their allies in World War II. An important player in that regard was the Catholic Church, and so Lovestone needed to strengthen his ties with the Church, even if he did not like Catholics and was reluctant to back Catholic unions. The reason for this partly lay in the fact that the AFL was a revolutionary outfit that sought to overthrow or weaken authoritarian regimes, whether Communist, Nazi, Fascist, Falangist, Peronist, or other. Lovestone had a free reign in his work, as revealed by the fact that he was never audited. This was revealed in the February 1967 revelations by Drew Pearson that the CIA, with Lovestone's approval, paid out about $100 million to the labor movement.[42]

PART X

THE AMERICAN PROPOSITION (1953)

39
LUCE DEPARTS TO JOIN CLARE

Henry Luce left New York in early October 1953 to join his wife in Rome. Before leaving, he wrote to the President of the United States, Dwight D. Eisenhower. His letter mentioned Emmet Hughes, who was leaving Eisenhower's staff to go back to work for Luce. Luce said Europe had reached a "turning point" that required "good reporting 'in depth' during the coming year [which] may be of real value to the cause we all aim to serve." Luce expressed regrets that he could not attend the President's dinner due to "the job I had in hand," which Luce believed the President "would have wished...to carry on with." Before returning to Rome, Luce suggested that he and Ike meet "to have a talk."[1] The fact that Luce was willing to turn down dinner with the President indicates that his mission involved more than reuniting with his wife at the Villa Taverna. He was on his way to deliver the most important speech in his life, the speech that would articulate what came to be known as the American Proposition, a doctrinal weapon.

Months earlier, the St. Benedict Center expressed trepidation at Clare's appointment as Ambassador to Italy:

"Remembering that the Masons' consuming desire is the destruction of the Church, and that the method they propose to use is secrecy and stealth, could you imagine a more favorable location, a more sinister set-up than this: for the head of the Masons to be married to a blithe, blind, and eminently successful American Catholic, to have at his disposal the most powerful journalistic enterprise in the world, and to be presently nestled, smiling and unsuspected, in the very heart of the Church, in Rome, the Eternal City?"[2]

Identifying the Luces with the Freemasons was an anachronism that provided cover for the American financial and monied elites, who stood to gain the most by subjugating the Catholic Church. These elites sought not so much to destroy the Catholic Church as to use its vast international organization to advance their aims by promoting ideas like the American ideology packaged as The American Proposition. The best way to accomplish this important goal in the Twentieth Century was to have the Catholics agree to the subjugation. To do that, it was important the Americans find Church leaders willing to open its intellectual and organizational gates to the American ideology from the inside. One of those leaders was the Belgian Dominican friar Felix Morlion, OP.

MORLION AND PRO DEO

Felix Morlion, OP, a Belgian Dominican, founded Pro Deo University. He was instrumental in creating disciples of The American Proposition, and he often explained how, in 1941, he fled the Nazis and came to the United States, where he remained until 1944. That year, he proceeded to Rome, where in November, he began the Pro Deo University. That was at least the story that he told everyone, and it was a story that Luce, C.D., and their crowd were only too happy to repeat. According to their cover story, Morlion was just a good Dominican friar dedicated to teaching and guiding the young. "Wild Bill" Donovan, the Catholic altar boy who received the Medal of Honor in World War I, worked as a Wall Street lawyer and went on to organize and head up the OSS, but told a different story about Morlion. Donovan's version is the one that best explains how it was that Morlion was so close to Luce and so supportive of the efforts to spread the American Proposition around the world, most notably by using the Catholic Church to spread the message.

Donovan recognized the importance of the Catholic Church as an "institution of immense global political importance." Donovan maintained good relations with the American hierarchy, and shortly after the liberation of Rome in July 1944, he had a papal audience with Pius XII. Donovan's direct contact with the Vatican began earlier when he evacuated Morlion from Lisbon to New York in 1941 following the German victories in Western Europe. Morlion, according to Donovan, was the "founder of a European Catholic anti-Comintern (and then anti-Nazi) intelligence service known as Pro Deo." Donovan expended "considerable expense, time, and trouble to transport Morlion from New York and establish him at the Holy See" in 1944.[3]

As a reward for his efforts, the Vatican made available to Donovan its reports from the papal nuncio in Japan concerning the effects of aerial bombardment of targets in that country. Thereafter, a steady stream of intelligence started flowing from the Vatican to the OSS, creating a relationship between the Vatican and American intelligence that only deepened with time. Around the end of the war, Donovan asked Pius XII, through his contacts, what the OSS could do for the pope. The pope asked that a papal envoy be escorted through Bavaria and Austria. According to James Jesus Angleton, that envoy was the Jesuit priest and confidant of Pius XII, Robert Leiber. The purpose of Fr. Leiber's journey was to re-establish the authority of the pope in Austria and southern Germany as a defense against Communism.[4]

According to Communist publications after the war, Morlion reorganized the Vatican intelligence service and merged it with the Jesuit "espionage network. Thereafter, the central intelligence department of the Vatican" was headed by "Janssens, a general of the Jesuit Order"; its deputy was "Montini, the acting Vatican Secretary of State" who would later become Pope Paul VI, along with Morlion who headed up the Centro d'informazione pro Deo. Branches of Vatican intelligence services existed in a number of countries, including the United States, most notably in New York, where it was headed by Cardinal Spellman. The *Guardian Weekly* reported in its February 27, 1969 edition that

Morlion approached H. L. Hunt in August 1966 to fund the Vatican anti-Communist operations in Latin America to the tune of about $ 11,000,000 per year.[5]

Morlion considered the Pro Deo University, which grew out of the Pro Deo intelligence operation, as a "joint American-European venture in the field of culture," and its doors opened in November 1944. American contributions enabled the "International 'Pro Deo' organization to start its center in Rome in November 1944 with courses and publications on the philosophy of democracy and on social methodology. They applied to European practice the solid and balanced work of the American Founding Fathers as expressed by their correspondence (1763-1776), by the Federalist papers, the Declaration of Independence, the Constitution of the U.S.A. This most realistic way of establishing a free but God-centered way of life, was soon an inspiration for the Italian and other democracies."[6]

The idea for a university dedicated to research, education, and "promotion of a broader civic unity in freedom" came about during Morlion's stay in America from 1941 to 1944. According to Morlion, "If man's dignity, and man himself, is to survive, the philosophy of Democracy under God must be applied to the newly-liberated and newly independent countries. ... European and Asiatic intellectuals, escaped from countries occupied by totalitarianism, had discovered the universal and perennial values brought into the world by the American Founding Fathers and described by George Washington as a 'flag to which all honest men can repair.'"[7]

Members of the first class at Pro Deo, who graduated in 1948, comprised a "post-fascist generation" responsible for defeating Communism not only in the April 1948 elections but in the years following. According to Morlion, Pro Deo developed courses and classes in Political Science, Management, and Labor, all in the spirit of anti-fascism, even though there still existed in Italy some "fascist laws" concerning the creation and chartering of universities. That, at least, was the situation Morlion said he faced years later. The way around this dilemma was legal maneuvering, beginning with the invocation of the 1949 Treaty of Friendship between the United States and Italy. That treaty came about after the Marshall Plan, and Morlion and others believed they could get around the Italian laws by affiliating with the American "educational membership corporation," the American Council for the International Promotion of Democracy, or CIP.[8]

The leadership of CIP constituted a who's who of the powerful in finance, the media, and U.S. intelligence. CIP was led by "American civic leaders" like "Henry Luce, Chairman; Peter Grace, President; A.M. Lederer and Paul Felix Warburg, Vice-Presidents, of the American Council for the International promotion of Democracy under God (C.I.P.)." These luminaries had, in his words:

"Rightly described this achievement as 'not only unique but trail-blazing because:' ....it is not financially supported or controlled by government or a religious body;....there is joint sponsorship by Americans and Europeans, drawing on the best aspects of both cultures; ...in its educational program and other efforts, it deliberately strives to inject into the stream of European thought and action, the American concept of economic, spiritual, political and individual freedom; ... it attempts to provide a bridge between European and American cultures; ... it is the first and only University of its kind in Europe.'"[9]

CIP came into existence in 1947 in New York, where it was incorporated under that state's law. The organizers were a group of political, civic and academic leaders, which included, most notably, Luce, Ellsworth Bunker, A. M. Lederer, Marcell Rand (President for International Affairs of the Remington-Rand Co.), Frederick Dolbeare (co-founder of the Free Europe Committee), George Schuster (President of Hunter College, and former U.S. High Commissioner to Germany), and J. D. Zellerbach (former U.S. Commissioner to Italy, President of Cross-Zellerbach).[10] Edward P. Lilly, another well-heeled American Catholic and important member of the PSB staff was monitoring Morlion, and on June 13, 1952, Lilly wrote a memorandum documenting Morlion's history:

"In September, 1944, he founded in Rome, Italy, International University Pro Deo...Of Social Realism. It is claimed that it now has 3800 students. It is claimed that this program has developed new and successful techniques for training native anti-Communist leaders. It is recognized that

Morlion is seeking money to increase his school, and he seems to be an excellent promoter. I would like to get information on the character of Morlion and particular information, and if possible evaluations, of the success of his school in Rome."[11]

Lilly, pursuant to instructions from the PSB Director, engaged Morlion in several conversations to fully assess Morlion's project, which was "to foster a greater democratic movement in Europe, and thereby counter Communism." Lilly was assured that Morlion was authorized by the "director General of the Dominican Order to undertake this current work," and he "has also come to this country with the knowledge of the Apostolic Delegate to the United States." Cardinals Stritch and Mooney gave Morlion "favorable consideration," as did Archbishop Cushing, all of whom promised him students for his endeavor in Rome. Lilly concluded by saying that Morlion was "engaged in a legitimate activity." Lilly went on to explain in a classified memorandum that the "Morlion project" had "a particular interest for PSB" because it allowed the United States government to get "its strategic objectives accomplished by native and indigenous groups." Secrecy was an important feature of all front groups because "the more successful America is in hiding the 'Made in America' label, the greater will be the possibility of the successful and permanent accomplishment of these American objectives." Beyond that front, organizations were cheaper and easier to run, especially one "which requires relatively little American output but which even if only partially successful can produce extensive returns for the American objective of weakening Communist power in Italy and in fostering the development of a free and independent government, orientated towards a Western and democratic philosophy of government."[12]

The PSB was interested in projects like Morlion's Pro Deo University because the Catholic angle suggested that:

"This type of project [could be viewed] as a moral factor in psychological operations. In developing the military defense of Western Europe....Not enough attention has yet been given to America's fostering the moral background which Europe and the United States holds in common. This background includes such generalities as the common Christian tradition, the common moral code which characterizes Western civilization, and to a more limited extent the liberal tradition or the tradition of the free man and limited governments which stand from the American, French and English political revolusions [sic], as well as from the rationalist movement of the 17th and 18th Centuries. Much of this was cleverly exploited by Franklin D. Roosevelt in such statements as the Four Freedoms, the Atlantic Charter and the idea of the United Nations. Man needs bread to live and armor to protect him but even Europeans could not live by bread alone, nor is their only thought that of the defense which will protect them. America needs to give more attention to the warp of ideas and the woof of the spirit. The PSB Staff is expecting to develop this aspect of psychological operations in the near future. There is no need, however, of delaying all actions within this field until there is a PSB-approved guidance."[13]

Morlion had an important discussion with Lilly on November 5, 1952, during which Morlion told Lilly that he approached Allen Dulles and "made a very expensive request on CIA for support of his university pro deo [sic] in Rome." As part of his request for about $900,000 to pay for the salaries of American professors, Morlion "went into extensive detail about the need of getting Americans to present practical American approaches so that a cadre of anti-communist peoples could be developed in Europe to lead the trend of Europe towards the American political theory." He then explained he was also attempting to support other efforts to promote seminars in European countries to promote the American view of political theory. Lilly's conclusion was that the PSB should analyze Morlion's ideas and "if they seemed practical, to ask the committee for France and Italy and the coordinating committee for the German plan to accept them and to secure their implementation."[14]

C.D. Jackson asked Morlion to use his institution to assist in the "spreading of the philosophy of American Business," to which Morlion assented.[15] Within a few days, Luce began his funding of Morlion's operations with a donation of about $15,000. Luce's funding efforts persisted into the mid-1960s, with contributions oftentimes amounting to about $10,000 a year, with some consisting of stock in Time, Inc.[16] Morlion kept Luce informed of the initiatives he was sponsoring in

Europe, including something called the Intercontinental Seminars and asked Luce for suggestions. When he returned to New York in late November 1952, Morlion told Luce that "we shall then be enabled to start the organization of the long-range research and teaching which is the basis for integration of American ideas into the European way of life." Morlion's visiting professors on the Intercontinental Seminars against Marxism were none other than Peter Drucker, Mortimer Adler, Robert Hutchins, and George Gallup. The seminars addressed the issues of whether economic and political competition was good for industrial societies.[17]

40

LUCE DELIVERS THE AMERICAN PROPOSITION

Henry Luce, the son of a Presbyterian missionary, put his publishing might at the service of touting the idea of America's "adherence to the moral law" and the "American Holy Alliance with God" in a 500-word document that became known as the "Ridgefield Memorandum." This document committed Time, Inc. to teaching the world about the special relationship between God and America supposedly contained in the Declaration of Independence and the Constitution.[1]

The Presbyterians had a long history of subjugating Catholics. Under King George II, the Presbyterians collaborated with the English in eradicating the Catholic presence in Scotland, particularly the Highlands. The Presbyterians and English established in its place loyalty to Protestantism, English commercial and industrial practices and theory, and the English language. After this early form of social engineering proved successful in the Highlands, it was introduced to the Mediterranean and North America.[2]

James Madison, author of the U.S. Constitution and the Bill of Rights, which includes the famous First Amendment, was himself a product of Presbyterian schooling. One of his most important tutors was the "Scottish Presbyterian minister Donald Robertson," of whom Madison later said that "all that I have been in life I owe largely to that man." Madison was also tutored by Thomas Martin, an Anglican rector and graduate of the Presbyterian College of New Jersey, and John Witherspoon, a Presbyterian minister who came to be President of the College of New Jersey. Harvard historian Sydney Ahlstrom claimed that "the religious heritage of three-fourths of the American people in 1776" was the Reformed tradition, in other words, Calvinism or Presbyterianism, which viewed Catholicism or "popery" as whereby the power of Satan established tyranny, persecution, and "arbitrary government" on earth. [3]

The Presbyterian animus against the Catholic Church continued unabated into the Twentieth Century, but now it was "American style institutions," not Calvinism, which they attempted to impose on people they encountered, with the Catholics being one of the most important targets. The new campaign of Presbyterian proselytism met enormous success because of the covert nature of how it was imposed. By stealth, the American media, which promoted crypto-Presbyterian American values to Catholics who thought of themselves as Americans, worked in tandem with the U.S. government, which by the summer of 1953 was deeply involved in promoting its Doctrinal Warfare Program. PSB D-33, the top secret government document authorizing Doctrinal Warfare, gave the CIA a number of tasks, as we have seen, not the least of which included inserting its agents into "foreign associations and organizations with doctrinal potential (newspapers, universities, etc.) to influence their actions and output." The CIA's agents were then to "create, when advisable, deviationist movements designed to split organizations promulgating hostile ideologies so long as they would not develop into a threat to U.S. security." The CIA was supposed to "Exploit local divergencies, heresies or policy disagreements within opposition systems."[4]

Luce's American Proposition was an integral part of the Doctrinal Warfare that was then being waged against the Catholic Church. Written largely by Murray, the American Proposition promoted ideas compatible with Protestantism, Calvinism, and Presbyterianism in particular, reminiscent of Thomas Paine's ideology and perfectly consistent with John Locke's political philosophy.[5] Flush with America's victory over fascism and engaged in an equally dire struggle with the Soviet Union, Luce proposed the American Proposition as America's magic formula, which could bring about a prosperous and good society in every country in the world where it was implemented. In proposing the American Proposition, Luce established a moral standard by which every society in the world was to be evaluated. It was no coincidence that Luce delivered his American Proposition speech in Rome because Luce, with Murray's help, wanted to use the Catholic Church to disseminate his message to "free" societies so these societies refashioned themselves in America's image. The Church would become a missionary for America and not for Christ, and it would preach the gospel of America, not Jesus Christ.

THE AMERICAN PROPOSITION

Luce gave his address on November 29, 1953, at the opening of the academic year at Dominican Felix Morlion's Pro Deo University. John Courtney Murray wrote the speech. In an October 28 letter to *Life* editor Jack Jessup, Luce wrote, "I send you herewith an essay by Rev. John Courtney Murray, SJ. I think you will agree it is superb. John, very kindly and very rashly, offered to write a 'rough draft of my Roman speech on the basis of a few notes which I had discussed with him.' This is the result. You will note that I have borrowed from him wholesale."[6]

Luce was so happy with Murray's essay that he wanted to share it with the world and, most especially, with the American people. "It seems to me," he wrote, "that something important ought to be done about Murray's essay. Perhaps it ought to be run in FORTUNE as a two-part piece.... It is important to tell foreigners about the American Proposition but obviously we believe it is first of all important that Americans should constantly review their Proposition...." Luce thought it could even be expanded by Murray and published in a special edition of "FORTUNE or even in LIFE for perhaps the July 4, 1954 issue, though there would have to be "a number of changes of emphasis and allusions...for an American audience"[7] because "this particular essay is directed in some details to a European Catholic audience. I don't know enough to agree with Murray on the high estate of political philosophy in the high Middle Ages – in other words, I don't agree. I do however agree with the operative effect of the natural law doctrine."[8]

Luce told Jessup he was sending a "first draft of my attempt to present the philosophical basis of the American Proposition to the Papal School of Political and Social Studies....My 'lead,' the Gettysburg Speech, and the pap about the Founding Fathers is prompted by my hunch that most of my audience, however distinguished, is not well-acquainted with the 'facts' of American history. If they have perhaps heard of the Gettysburg Speech, they have never heard it." Luce continued, "Over here one feels that the integrity of the American Proposition better make itself felt soon."[9]

After Willi Schlamm, a Time Inc. contributor and advisor, sent comments on the speech, Luce responded in a November 1, 1953 letter. Luce explained that "the main thing I felt about that, was that 'they' probably were not well-acquainted with 'what every American school boy knows.' That's why, as you'll see, I open with the Gettysburg speech and talk about the Supreme Court and the Founding Fathers and give them the national hymn." However, Luce knew he had to do more, and that is where Murray came in. "I wanted to balance this with reasonably 'professional philosophic talk – especially, e.g., about 'natural law' – so as to show a certain philosophic identity between the American Proposition and traditional Western political philosophy. At this point Father Murray's paper arrived, and I lifted heavily from it."[10]

"You may have seen the Monstrous Document I put together for Harry," Murray wrote to Clare on the same day. "He sent me a most complementary cable, which I greatly appreciated. I only hope that the thing was of some use to him. As with most things I do, it got sort of out of hand and went on and on." Murray then revealed his involvement in the push for academic freedom in universities and ended the letter with "much love...many blessings...yours always" and a word on how he spent two nights and a day at "dear old 450" (the Luce's New York apartment) where he was "Pretty lonesome, I must say. Missed you terribly. The bottle of Scotch I found in your bar was a very poor substitute!"[11]

Billings read the talk and commented on it in his diary of November 16:

"A mild summer day [Monday]....Office. Haircut at my desk. Luce is making a speech at the Vatican on 'The American Proposition'. His draft checked by Wardell, passed over my desk and I took 30 minutes off to read it. All of Luce's old familiar themes about God and the Constitution and natural law etc – but very well done – simple and eloquent. I passed it along to him in Rome, with a note praising his speech. (Still he does not write me – and I doubt if flattery will work, either)."[12]

Billings sent Luce his comments on the same day he made his diary entry, wondering whether citing the "Unitarian John Adams properly representing the serious 'Christian' as contrasted with Jefferson's Deism." As to the speech itself, Billings wrote, "It was just about the finest thing you have done. It is simple, logical and eloquent. From past experience, I knew all the themes you had used to weave it together, but in the end the result was a new and brilliant tapestry of thought." As to the Catholics, Billings thought it "eminently fair – almost too fair, Wardell seems to think." All in all, the talk would "do much to help that vague something called 'understanding of America.'"[13] "Wardell" referred to Elsa Wardell, who provided Luce with additional information on classical philosophers the American Founders read. She sent him the names of Younger Pliny, Plutarch, Livy, Tacitus, Demosthenes, and Seneca for use in his talk.[14]

On November 29, 1953, in Rome, at the Pro Deo University, an institution started by Dominican Felix Morlion, who received backing and support from American elites and the CIA, Henry Luce injected The American Proposition, a doctrinal weapon that he developed along with John Courtney Murray, SJ, into the veins of the Catholic Church. Before a crowd of thousands of expectant dignitaries, clerics, academics, and students, Luce delivered his address entitled "The American Proposition" on the opening of the academic year. Morlion described the scene:

"It was at the inauguration ceremony of the Academic year 1953...of our university. As usual there was an international panel: His Excellency De

Gasperi treating an European proposition and Ambassador Montalvo treating a Latin-American proposition. The great surprise was: The American proposition expected to be very pragmatical [sic], was sown by Mr. Henry Luce to be the most universal. The four thousand persons present discovered that American Democracy has a solid, perennial philosophy, profoundly united with the principles of living faith in God common to all authentic religious denominations. This time nobody said 'Americans are different.'"[15]

Luce began by admitting he was not Catholic, and that America was a religion: "In the form of worship in which I was brought up, it is customary for the minister to read a passage from the Holy Scriptures and to select from it a 'text.' I should like to read to you today an item of our National Scriptures which nearly every American boy and girl has learned by heart."[16] Luce then proceeded to read from Lincoln's November 1863 Gettysburg address, in which Lincoln stated the famous lines, "Fourscore and seven years ago our fathers brought forth on this continent a new nation, conceived in liberty, and dedicated to the proposition that all men are created equal." Luce emphasized that "The United States is a nation which depends for its existence on <u>a proposition</u> and that this is the unique and distinguishing fact about the United States."[17] America and its political entity, the United States, were founded on an ideology.

Union in America was achieved through the Constitution of the United States, which is preserved by the "Supreme Court of the United States," a body that Luce described as "almost sacred" because it is the "Keeper of the Ark of the Covenant." The "American Proposition is the Constitution interpreted in the light of certain first principles." While the Constitution dealt with the executive, legislative, and judicial branches of government, it provided "valuable notions of government written into this text and some profounder concepts written between the lines and beneath them." These are a "government of limited powers," the separation of powers, and the idea of a federation.[18]

The "first principles" that "inform the Constitution" are contained in the Declaration of Independence. The first is that "We hold these truths to be self-evident," though, of course, Luce "put aside the question whether the enumerated truths are really self-evident or not." The identification of certain truths was also something open for discussion, but the key point, according to Luce, was "there <u>are</u> truths" and "we <u>hold</u> them."[19]

The next principle was "the sovereignty of God over nations as well as over individual man." Closely allied to this is the idea that "there is one only source of Authority and that is God, Who is both ultimate and immanent." God is "fundamental to the American Proposition both in the sense of historical interpretation <u>and</u> in the sense of intellectual coherence <u>and</u> in the sense of dynamic present reality."[20] Luce mentioned, "George Washington, Benjamin Franklin, Alexander Hamilton, Thomas Jefferson, John Adams, James Madison. Forty or fifty men in all... [who]were the most remarkable group of men who ever came together anywhere to make or re-make a government or a nation." According to Luce, "their specialty was political philosophy," in the cause of which they "literally ransacked the pages of antiquity" studying Plato, Aristotle, Cicero, Gaius. The Founders were also "serious Christians.... They subscribed, most of them, to the Apostles Creed." Others were deists. John Adams was the "serious Christian" while Thomas Jefferson was a Deist, yet they agreed "God reigned and, directly or indirectly, ruled."[21]

The Founders were, therefore, "conscious heirs of a political tradition....the tradition of natural law." America kept the natural law tradition alive because in "reaction to the rise of absolutism, Protestant Christianity tended to substitute for natural law the revealed law of God as found in the Scriptures." Fifty years after the creation of the American Constitution, Professor Gabriel taught that the "basic postulate of the American democratic faith affirmed that God, the Creator of Man, has also created a moral law for his government and has endowed him with a conscience with which to apprehend it." Luce quoted the Third Council of Catholic Bishops that met in Baltimore in 1887 as Catholic approval of the American socio-political system: "'We consider the establishment of our country's independence, the shaping of its liberties and laws, as a work of special Providence, its framers building better than they knew, the Almighty's hand guiding them'."[22]

Luce shifted gears and started talking about freedom. After mentioning a group of Blacks who came to sing the National Anthem at the American Embassy in Rome, he said, "Freedom is holy, sacred." At the same time, and in consonance with the idea alluded to earlier in the talk that the "self-evident truths" are not so self-evident, Luce said, "There is a multitude of corollaries! In fact we may say that the whole of American life consists in a more or less conscious – and argumentative –working out of the corollaries of the American Proposition."[23]

According to Luce, "In the American Proposition, there is no vacuum. For Law pervades all." Law is not only a prohibition but a command to act in America. This was consistent with the idea of political freedom, which required "virtuous citizens" and a "dynamic sense of responsibility for achieving the good, not only in personal life but... as good citizen." Religion, irrespective of the kind, provided an "indispensable support" for the "body politic." And "Freedom of religion in the American constitutional sense, is not the freedom to exclude religion from public life.... It means the freedom to make society religious." Government works with the people by way of "formal or legal alliance" through "governmental policy."[24]

Luce proceeded to speak in "concrete detail of many, many large areas of American life," which he described as the "voluntary organized social action." He mentioned the effort of private groups to eradicate tuberculosis, and he said this demonstrated the Americans' sense of "personal civic responsibility" because it showed that government, which was "essentially inefficient," was not needed to achieve the good. Luce mentioned that Catholic education was "primarily an expression of supernatural faith" and an "heroic example of American voluntary organized action." American business life was also a "form of voluntary social action," and the "American Corporation today is a very self-conscious, socially responsible entity."[25]

Building up to the climax of his talk, Luce explained that the "function of the virtuous citizen applies to the relations between America and the world" and that good relations between the US and the rest of the world can only be established "in large part by the virtuous citizen and his purposeful voluntary associations. This follows from the very nature of the American Proposition." Americans were "missionaries, tourists, businessmen, teachers" and "strongly felt and often explored their rights and duties as citizens of the world." Americans expected only one thing from their government: "to remove the obstacles that governments have in these last bloody decades been increasingly erecting between people and people – obstacles to their free movement, information, trade, and human contact," because Americans believed that "the first function of government as they see it is not to score points of power but to open doors through which the citizen in all his multiform voluntary capacities, can go about his work in the world God gave to him and to all his fellow-creatures."[26] All Americans share "common principles, aspirations, and ideals" and the "unity of this community is strong enough to support much pluralism in religious beliefs, political opinions, and local customs." The American way of life could not be exported, but the:

"intelligent American can legitimately long for a world in which all men will think his political thoughts and talk his political language.... The language expresses the thoughts of humanity itself when it reflects on the natural and rational structure and processes of political and economic life. I mean the language of unalienable rights, constitutionalism, and the rule of law as the moral basis of government, consent and popular participation in rule and therefore limited government, separation of powers, free election, minority rights in the face of majority decision, an organic organization of the economic order with a view to its self-government under the minimum of governmental interference, a dispersal of economic power, a high degree of public prosperity achieved mainly by the principle of voluntary cooperation, etc. These are words current in America; but they are translatable into any language."

Luce stressed American ties to tradition: "Insofar as the American way of life rests upon these principles, understood in their Western traditional sense, it is exportable, but only because it is, or ought to be, indigenous everywhere."[27]

The enemy of these ideals was Soviet Communism, which Luce mentioned as one of the two great powers on earth. This enemy had to be fought not just by a "contest of arms. More importantly it was a duel of ideas. Hence, the 'complete social process' undertaken against our Enemy must involve more than military preparedness." What was needed was imbuing society with a "more positive function – this is a good American first principle. To sustain true religion, to promote education, to advance social justice, to contribute to public prosperity, to insure [sic] equal justice for all, and more than anything else, to protect fundamental human rights and freedom – these too are the functions of society. They are functions of international society...." An international juridical community could only function under the reign of law, and that was America's long-term goal. Essential to this idea of the rule of law was the idea that "the writ of natural law may run in all countries in the form of respect for human rights."[28]

After the talk, Luce directed copies of the text be given to the pro-Deo International University of Social Studies. Pro Deo taught the American Proposition to its students, and they, in turn, went throughout the world, spreading American ideas and ideals. All of this occurred with the apparent approval of the Catholic Church. The American prelates certainly approved of Pro Deo, as did the Dominican order and Msgr. Giovanni Montini, later known as Pope Paul VI. The American Proposition justified the American socio-political philosophy as good in principle. The basis of this philosophy was an adherence by societal authorities to a vague, ambiguous, and ill-defined natural law. The Declaration of Independence and the U.S. Constitution were elevated to the level of sacred documents, and freedom, whatever that meant, was the guiding light of American activities. The American Proposition was quintessential American psychological warfare, and it served to advance the U.S. government's Doctrinal Warfare Program. Once target societies accepted the American Proposition as true and American socio-political philosophy as good in principle, then that society underwent a re-organization or re-engineering that marginalized spiritual values and permitted the elevation of materialism. This was made possible by the relegation of religion to a private concern and its prohibition from informing the policies of the state. The legal principles of the Establishment Clause and the Free Exercise Clause of the U.S. Constitution implemented and protected this philosophy. At this point, then the powerful come to rule society, and the most powerful in Liberal societies like America are the monied elites. Acceptance of The American Proposition led to the creation of the proper social and political environment for American capital and investment to enter societies around the globe.

Luce sent copies of his speech to Murray and C.D. Jackson. Luce's assistant Kelly Laute was impressed, calling it "a very fine speech indeed, and I was very much impressed by his delivery of it. So restrained yet so forceful – a very different style from what we generally get over her and all the more interesting and revealing to my half-Latin, half-Nordic mentality."[29]

On March 4, 1963, at a party celebrating the birthday of Time, Inc., Luce said in no uncertain terms his publications existed to spread the American Proposition by shaping a certain understanding or view of history. By explaining "what *Time* believes" and "what *Time* stands for," Luce provided the "*inside* story of *Time,*" noting that the magazine "may often seem to be arbitrary...whimsical, even as they used to say, flippant. And yet through all the huge tapestry of 20th century history which *Time* has woven, there is a clear pattern of belief, a pattern which has become clearer and stronger with the years. *Time* believes."[30] The lack of an object in the final sentence bespoke a philosophical problem, not a grammatical lapse. A few minutes farther into his speech, Luce tried again:

"What, then, does *Time* now believe?... The whole of the American Proposition has been epitomized by *Fortune* in this formula: 'The American Proposition consists of a word, a tendency and a method. The word is liberty. The tendency is equality. The method is constitutionalism.' That is the core and essence of what *Time* believes. How well has *Time* served the American Proposition? And one way to answer that question is to ask another: How well is the United States living up to its historic faith? I give you my answer quickly: since *Time's* last birthday party, our twentieth [1943], in the midst of the first truly global war, the United States has been doing well, very well."[31]

Luce used *Time* as a powerful tool to spread the American Proposition around the globe to convince its people, as well as the Catholics, that America, with its Liberal, Enlightenment, Age of Reason foundations, was the ideal form of social organization. In a speech to the Army War College, C.D. Jackson praised the American Proposition and Pro Deo University's delivery of it as the philosophical platform from which the CIA and Time, Inc. launched its psychological warfare campaign. It was an "effective new educational activity" and "one of the few that is working and his [sic] immense potentialities. It is helping to infuse the concept of the American Proposition through young, fervent Latin American disciples instead of relying exclusively on officials from this country."[32]

41
ROME SPEAKS AGAIN (DECEMBER 1953)

One week after Luce delivered his American Proposition speech at Pro Deo University, Pope Pius XII delivered an address to the National Convention of Italian Catholic Jurists. The topic of the Convention was "The Nation and the International Community," and it came at a time in world history when the pope stated there was a "mutual drawing together...caused not only by vastly improved technological progress and by free choice but also by the....intrinsic law of development." He said there were more contacts and relations between individuals of various nations and various national governments. Communities of sovereign states had arisen, but these communities consisted of independent sovereign states, and they are not to be considered similar to the "world empires of the past or of the present, in which different racial stocks, peoples and states become fused....into a single conglomeration of states." The pope held that the conflicts of the past had been "motivated by a desire to subjugate other nations," whereas nowadays, "it is precisely the will to prevent threatening conflicts that urges men toward a supranational juridical community." He said while "utilitarian considerations...certainly carry considerable weight," other reasons were leading to this drive. The "mingling of men and different nations because of technological progress that has awakened the faith, implanted in the hearts and souls" of men had implanted in them a desire for "a higher community of men, willed by the Creator and rooted in the unity of their common origin, nature and final destiny."[1] The natural law and the positive law of each nation played a role in "establishing a community of peoples." Individual nations are no longer sovereign in that they can no longer act "arbitrarily and without regard for other states." They practice self-rule and have competence concerning that which has to be done in regard to a definite territory, but "always within the framework of international law."[2]

The pope got to the heart of the matter, namely, "the practical co-existence...of Catholic with non-Catholic states." The pope set out a rule of positive law: "Within its own territory and for its own citizens, each state will regulate religious and moral affairs by its own laws. Nevertheless, throughout the whole territory of the international community of states, the citizens of every member-state will be allowed the exercise of their own beliefs and the ethical and religious practices, insofar as these do not contravene the penal laws of the state in which they are residing." This may work where there are Christian states, non-Christian states, indifferentist states, or atheist states whether by the belief of a "great majority of citizens" or "by reason of an explicit declaration of law."[3]

Such a formulation seemed clear enough, but ambiguity crept in when the pope conceded that while "that which does not correspond to truth or to the norm of morality objectively has no right to exist, to be spread or to be activated....failure to impede this with civil laws and coercive measures can nevertheless be justified in the interests of a higher and more general good."[4] The pope then charged Catholics with a duty to "judge if this condition is verified in the concrete...by weighing the dangerous consequences that stem from toleration against those from which the community of nations will be spared, if the formula of toleration is accepted." The Catholic statesman is to be guided by the good and the judgment of the Church, which is entrusted in these matters to the Pope.[5]

The Church's divine mandate was to "bind together in religious unity the men of all races and of all times," and the juridical unity of nations, present in some degree, had a duty to "incorporate all men and all races...to bring them to the full truth and the grace of Jesus Christ." Repeating the claim that the Church cannot teach or affirm evil, he cited the eternal choice of the Church: "either incense for idols or blood for Christ" as the Church "has the duty of teaching and educating in all the inflexibility of truth and goodness, and with this absolute obligation she must remain and work among men and nations that in mental outlook are completely different from each other." And repeating the principle of toleration in "determined circumstances, toleration even in cases in which one could proceed to repression, the Church – out of regard for those who in good conscience (though erroneous, but invincibly so) are of different opinion – has been led to act and has acted with that tolerance...always for higher and more cogent motives....In such individual cases the attitude of the Church is determined by what is demanded for safeguarding and considering the *bonum commune*, on the one hand, the common good of the Church and the State in individual states, and, on the other, the common good of the universal Church, the reign of God over the whole world." The Church could not "approve complete separation of the two powers" of Church and State.[6]

Connell wrote a letter thanking the pope for his "clear exposition on the proper relations between Church and State and on religious liberty in an international federation." In the same letter, Connell informed the pope that "Recently in the United States there have been some Catholics who sought to modify the traditional teaching of the Church on this matter, with the result that many of our Catholic people have become confused and hesitant." Connell was hopeful the pope's address would bring an end to the controversy: "Now that Your Holiness has given this logical and definite statement, there is no longer any justification for uncertainty as to the true Catholic doctrine, and there is every reason to hope that those who held incorrect views will now accept the unchangeable teaching of the Church."[7] The Secretary of State took nearly three months to respond and when he did it was only to convey a cold acknowledgment of the letter and gratitude for "the sentiments of filial devotion and attachment to the Vicar of Christ."[8]

MURRAY GATHERS STRENGTH

The day after the pope gave *Ci Riesce,* Cardinal Stritch wrote Murray a letter of support, claiming that the bishops must now proceed "prudently and thoughtfully in these studies and seek the advice of competent scholars. It pleases me immensely that you are willing to help me and I want you to send me from time to time your further studies on this important question." In the same letter, Stritch referred to an October 14 talk he gave in Rome at the North American College in the presence of the pope. Stritch sounded an Americanist note when he said America is "'above everything else...a land of freemen, conscious of their rights and dignity, collaborating together in a brotherly spirit for the common good of all'."[9] Stritch referred to a conversation in Washington at a dinner Murray attended with other prelates at which Cardinal Mooney of Detroit seemed to support Murray's position. Stritch arranged another dinner in the middle of November, which Murray mentioned in a November 23, 1953 letter to McCormick. At this dinner, Stritch listened "with some sympathy" to his position on "freedom of religious propaganda" and the "religion of the state." Murray downplayed his efforts and stated, "I am not inclined to be dogmatic, but I feel that these points present real theological and political issues which have not yet been satisfactorily argued out." Murray lied to Stritch and said that Montini, not Leiber, gave him assurances that "the famous discourse of Cardinal O" was a "purely private utterance."[10]

All of this seemed to have the desired effect on Stritch, who, according to Murray, was "heartened." Murray claimed Stritch went on "to say that the *sensus fidelium* in the U.S. is definitely against the canonical thesis insofar as it asserts governmental and legal favor and protection of Catholicism and denies religious freedom as a civil right." Mooney discussed throughout the dinner the presence of "American difficulties" with the magisterial teachings on religious liberty as well as church and state relations and said, "None of us today could go as far as Gibbons went." Stritch concluded by saying "as a member of the magisterium he was obliged personally to be cautious, but that he was glad someone was attempting to cope, on the broad theological, political, and historical basis with these points, which are a genuine source of difficulty to American Catholics."[11]

The Rector of Woodstock, Joseph F. Murphy, SJ, reported to the Father General on the meeting between Murray, Stritch, and Mooney, noting that "Cardinal Mooney . . . has long approved the line of thought which Father Murray is pursuing. His purpose in staging the meeting was to have Cardinal Stritch, still scrupulous as to whether or not his statements on American Church-State relations at the dedication of the North American College, was all that it should be" and to "discuss the problem with Fr. Murray."[12]

Despite some difficulties, 1953 ended with much promise for Murray. Luce delivered his famous speech, which Murray largely wrote, "The American Proposition," at Pro Deo University on November 29. The following week, on December 6, the pope gave his *Ci Riesce* speech, which Murray presented as a victory for the Americanists, particularly himself and Hartnett. Murray labeled the pope's talk "an important disavowal of the position taken by" Ottaviani in March. The pope, according to Murray in a letter to John Tracy Ellis, "seems to accept the principle that the problem of religious freedom must receive some manner of international solution, or of solution within the context of the international community as it is presently coming into existence. I have long felt that this is one of the necessary steps in development. After the Reformation the Church accepted the fact of pluralism within the international community – that is, the distinction between 'Catholic states' and 'non-Catholic state.' But this distinction insofar as it is still at all valid is not sufficient for the present day situation."

The way forward, Murray concluded in his communications with Ellis, was to realize that "we do not or cannot now look for leadership from American bishops. Hence the only thing is, with all reverence, to do a bit of leading." Ellis seconded that thought by responding, "I agree with you that the average American bishop is so harassed by problems of administration that he has neither time nor inclination to tackle problems of high thought."[13] Murray told Ellis the way to move the ball down the field was to stress the international situation.[14] Ellis responded by informing Murray that he was assembling a number of works on Church and State relations from various Catholic authors. Fr. Joe Moody of Cathedral College, New York, was writing a popular article on Church and State in Belgium, Dr. Manoel Cardozo at the CUA was preparing a piece on Portugal as a result of the May 1940 concordat, and Ellis himself was assembling materials on the topic as it related to Ireland. "With these three cases set out in some detail," wrote Ellis, "I am hoping it may do some good to lay the ghost of the Spanish pattern on Church and State today. There is no reason for allowing our non-Catholic friends to labor under the impression that should we come into a majority in the United States they are inevitably fated to have their religious activities circumscribed as they are in Spain."[15]

Ellis thought Stritch, code-named "Chicago," would advance Murray's work, which was "All the more reason, therefore why you should bend your best efforts to blaze the trail for him."[16] Murray responded in a letter a few days later, thanking Ellis for putting together the people to do the research and writing of church and state in so many countries – it was one less thing that Murray had to do. In a conspiratorial tone, Murray wrote, "I hope to have some news from Rome, when one of my colleagues here returns next week. He has, I think, some interesting news to relate, and I shall pass it on to you." Bemoaning the lack of solidarity of the American bishops for things American, Murray wrote, "Sometimes I almost wish that Gallicanism had somehow passed over this country....The French hierarchy are always disposed to close ranks and to defend things French....." Murray relayed how some "of the French clergy, as you know, have been inclined to go a bit far in the matter of reconciling the data of modern psychology with traditional moral theology. Several books have been published, which are rather dubious in content.... The question arose whether a particular book would be condemned in France, and I have it from a friend of mine there that the French bishops will not themselves utter any condemnation. Moreover, they will be prepared to defend the freedom of the theological fraternity to investigate these difficult subjects." Expressing admiration, Murray concluded, "I cannot help but wish that a similar disposition was present here in this country."[17]

In the same letter, Murray remarked on how the Irish ambassador insisted "on the importance of lay activity" and said, "This, from an Irishman, is indeed significant." Murray recounted how when he was "young and idealistic, and when I was having much contact with university students, I had high hopes in this direction, as regards the United States." There was enormous potential in this regard, Murray believed, but "altogether too little is being made of it." The laity should be more involved in opposing Communism, especially in the Latin countries, and if "investigation into it could be pushed, I think that we might even rehabilitate the Syllabus of Pius IX."[18]

A few days before Christmas 1953, Ellis reported that "Just before the holidays I met the editor of the A.E.R. at a little Christmas party in Curley Hall and he stated that after the new year he was going to 'open his guns.' I did not ask: on whom?" Ellis also told Murray that Joseph P. Walshe, the Irish Ambassador to the Vatican, cabled holiday greetings and said he was going to "devour" Murray's latest article. According to the Ambassador, a Fr. Joseph Delos, OP, claimed that *Ci Riesce* "was a reversal of the Ottaviani thesis" of March 1953.[19] Murray took Ellis' advice and blazed a trail. With the encouragement of Leiber and Ellis, Murray was emboldened to launch an attack on Ottaviani himself.

42
HARRY, CLARE, AND JOHN

John Courtney Murray played a crucial role in Harry Luce's relationship with his wife, Clare Boothe Luce. Murray not only worked to advance Harry's plans, he kept Clare working to advance Harry's plans, and, more importantly, he also kept the two of them together, thus becoming an essential part of a very powerful trio that would make a lasting impact on the history of church-state relations in the Twentieth Century.

During the 1950s, especially during Clare's term as U.S. Ambassador to Italy, the relationship between the three of them deepened. Clare and Murray wrote letters to each other over the years, but when she went to Rome, the volume of mail increased. Many of Murray's letters to Clare remain, but most of Clare's letters to Murray have disappeared.

Murray generally wrote his letters to Clare by hand, but sometimes he typed them on Woodstock Seminary letterhead or on the stationery of the journal *Theological Studies.* Usually, he began the letters with "Clare Dear," though there was the occasional "Dear Clare." He ended most of his letters with "Love," "Devotion," and other equally personal and emotional endings. Murray always signed his letters "John," never with "Fr."

By way of contrast, Bishop Fulton Sheen, whom Clare credited as decisive in bringing her into the Church, began his letters to her in his legible and neat handwriting with "My Dear Clare" while inscribing at the top of each handwritten page "JMJ," the abbreviation for Jesus Mary Joseph. Invariably, at the start of the letter after the salutation, Sheen wrote, "God love you." All of Sheen's letters to Clare ended with "Faithfully in Christ" or "Devotedly in Christ."[1]

Murray's letters to Clare were wide-ranging and, in large measure, personal in nature, discussing affairs in the news, Murray's difficulties with the Church hierarchy in the U.S. and in the Vatican, his work for Harry, things he was doing, and, most interestingly, gossip from sources close to the pope. Murray was not afraid to voice his discontent with Europe in general and Catholic states like Italy in particular. "I think I shall leave aside the indictment of 'Catholic Italy,'" he wrote in one letter. "The same goes for the extravagances of popular piety in Latin lands, or in our own, for that matter. The thing is bothersome, as Newman found, and I, and you.... As for Rome as Rome, I think I've rather 'had' it, and the rest of Europe in the bargain. The American proposition suits me fine!"[2]

Two important letters give some insight into how Murray viewed his role as a theologian and the nature of his work. In one letter, he denigrated his own scholarship: "[A]s a pseudo sort of scholar, I have a sense of fact. Fact indeed is not particularly important. Feeling is much more important. The older I get, day by day, the more importance I attach to feeling. After all, facts are so often factitious."[3] In another, he propounded a theory which, if he had ever stated it as clearly in his theological battles, would have marked clearly as a modernist: "Clare dear: The point of this historical argument is to show that, as the institution of the state-church owed its genesis to the special structure of an historic-social situation, so also it depends for its justification on the peculiarities of this situation. Alter the situation, and the argument for the institution is undermined... How's that?"[4]

When Murray dwelt on Clare's personal traits, his letters were emotional, sentimental, and oftentimes downright flirtatious. Murray repeatedly told her how she appeared in the media, and he always expressed his concern for her welfare while expressing support for her work. Murray frequently wrote that he missed her and that he looked forward to being with her. He also repeatedly told her that he loved her. In one letter written just before he began his professorship at Yale, Murray described "thundering home....in the beloved Buick" which Harry had given him in 1951, and thinking "as I often do, of you, fondly and tenderly and concernedly... How good you are, how able, how dear, how far away...." Then, as if realizing that his fantasy was getting out of hand, Murray concluded his letter by saying, "I said lots of prayers."[5] In another letter, Murray responded to something that Clare had written by writing from his heart: "You speak of meeting a companion. That's what you met in me." He added, "Accepting you and your love doesn't mean that I don't at time feel like wringing your lovely neck – I do, and probably always shall, at times!"[6]

Clare's extant letters, mostly handwritten in her very precise handwriting with a few short typewritten notes, were invariably personal and dealt with, more often than not, her relationship with Harry. During one the most difficult periods of her marriage to Harry, when the two were facing the prospect of separation if not divorce, Clare poured out her feelings for Murray, writing that "when I can talk with you the day has meaning, it stays alive. I don't lose altitude. I can stave off melancholy and futility. Eros, filia, agape, and certain other variations hard to categorize – you have been, are all of them to me. Ooo, I've been sick for such a long time! Could you ever know how much thou art thou to me?"[7]

HARRY AND JOHN

In February 1953, Henry Luce wrote to Murray on Time, Inc. letterhead commending him on a piece entitled the "Devaluation of Intelligence." Luce went on to write, "I for one would like to see your Collected Works published as soon as possible, and leave to God whether or not it be posthumous! That is, in fact, quite serious, and I also think that as an inveterate journalist or popularizer, I ought to do something personally about getting wider currency for J.C.M.'s thinking. Meanwhile, I am most grateful to you for this manuscript. Our effort is going to press next week. I haven't seen the first draft yet, having been to Oregon and back, and I can only hope it will turn out fairly well. With all affection, Yours, Harry."[8]

Luce and his magazines could make or break people. One person they made was Evangelist Billy Graham. Graham got his big break in the evangelical world when, in the winter of 1950, Henry Luce came to hear him speak in South Carolina. Bernard Baruch sent a letter about Graham to Luce, who was so impressed by Graham that he decided that "his magazines would not only carry newsworthy articles about our work but also support us editorially."[9] Special articles in *Life* or in *Time* featured Graham and gave rise to his popularity. Throughout his career as a preacher, Graham relied on Luce for advice on how best to present himself and was given access to Luce's magazines to write his own editorials and pieces. Graham's value also lay in his "appeal and success... not only in terms as an individual, but also the national picture as of today."[10]

If Graham's trajectory was any indication of the future, by early 1953, while Clare was preparing for her ambassadorship, Murray was on his way to superstardom. Aside from giving Murray publicity, being associated with Luce opened doors to powerful Americans at the highest levels of American society, economic power, and political influence, as well as the intelligence communities of the U.S. government. A short perusal of Murray's address book reveals contact information for people like Allen Dulles, Klaus Dohrn, Philip Burnham, Arleigh Burke, John W. Gardner, Gerald Heard, Andre Helligers (Kennedy ethicist), Hans Kung, the Luces, Morris Leibman, Thomas Love (theologian who wrote a biography on Murray), the NCWC, Jaroslav Pelikan, Cyrus Vance, Bishop Ernest Primeau, Margaret Zilboorg, and of course, Yale University.[11]

In addition to granting him access to the most powerful and influential people of his age, Luce gave Murray, the Jesuit who took a vow of poverty, the trappings of wealth, too. Murray, as we have already mentioned, got Luce's Buick shortly before departing for Yale.[12] Murray regularly played golf and drank whiskey with Luce and would occasionally travel to South Carolina from Woodstock for a quick getaway where he could discuss matters with Luce. That was not all that Murray received. He was allowed the use of the Luces' New York apartment whenever he wanted. [13] Murray spent many summers in Ridgefield at their residence, visited with them in Phoenix, usually during the Christmas holidays, and, more importantly, Murray was put on an expense account by the Luces.[14] Around Christmastime, Murray generally received gifts from the Luces, and these gifts often included money.[15] He had no problems with asking Clare Luce for money for his order, his family, his high school, and the Jesuits, all of which got channeled through Woodstock and were presumably tax-deductible.[16]

In exchange for the wealth and power Luce showered on Murray, he became Luce's idea man. In the course of their long intellectual discussions, it became clear that Murray and Luce were of one mind on all important topics. John Deedy, Catholic writer, shrewd observer, and managing editor of *Commonweal* magazine, felt that Murray was an integral part of Luce's operation. Luce, according to Deedy, took "new thrusts to try on the editors" from his discussions with Murray. Murray was especially helpful in helping Luce in dealing with Catholic issues in his magazines,[17] floating "religious and social abstractions" that Luce would then "try on...the editors."[18]

Murray not only wrote for Luce, but he also functioned, in the opinion of *Time* writer Christopher Emmett, as Luce's gatekeeper. In early 1957, Emmett asked Murray to prevail upon Clare to become Honorary Chairman of the American Friends of the Captive Nations, [19] another CIA front in the American anti-communist crusade. In the same letter, Emmett asked Murray his opinion of the Saudis and of Tito, and Murray responded by agreeing that King Saud was barbaric and that since the events concerning Tito were resolved, there was no need for further inquiry.[20]

Murray also volunteered to write important addresses for the Luces. When Clare addressed the Tenth Annual Jesuit Mission Dinner at the Hotel Commodore in New York, Murray used Jesuit history to urge Catholics to fight Communism.[21] Clare's speech for Founder's Day at Georgetown gave Murray the opportunity to extol the "public philosophy" of Walter Lippmann, who, as Harry so aptly noted, "avoids any commitment to Christianity."[22]

Murray critiqued the Luces' ideas and talks, praising a talk Clare gave to the War College[23] but panning another by Harry, called "A General Remark," with 37 pages of comment. Murray was a master at psycho-logical manipulation, and the speeches he wrote were full of themes, ideas, and slogans that had an emotional impact that would justify the American socio-political-economic and cultural construct. America was all things to all people: "At the outset one basic aspect of the American Proposition must be noted: it is at once revolutionary and conservative, traditional and progressive."[24]

Finally, Murray shared his own speeches and papers with the Luces, thereby coordinating their collective efforts. Wilfrid Sheed, son of Frank Sheed and Maisie Ward, whose publishing house, Sheed & Ward, was funded and supported by the Luces and which was responsible for giving a platform for many strange voices that claimed to be Catholic, hit the nail on the head when he described Murray as "the Luces' Richelieu."[25]

It was a dubious distinction but a telling description. Armand-Jean Cardinal du Plessis de Richelieu was the 17th century French Cardinal who decided to put loyalty to France and the French King before loyalty to the Church and Christendom when Catholicism was threatened by the Thirty Years' War. As a result of his political machinations, Germany endured considerable devastation in the Protestant-Catholic wars. The Protestants survived what had been largely successful Catholic efforts to either convert their leaders or destroy Protestant military, political, and intellectual resistance. The Peace of Westphalia, signed five years after Richelieu's death, confirmed that Europe would henceforth be divided between Protestants and Catholics and marked the official end of Christendom. From that point on, the Catholics were in retreat. Wilfrid Sheed implied Murray did for Luce's America what Richelieu did for France.

PART XI

HOT AND COLD RHETORICAL WAR (1954)

43
MURRAY ATTACKS OTTAVIANI

The Americans and their allies within the Church were optimistic as 1954 opened. One week after Henry Luce delivered the American Proposition at the Pro Deo University on November 29, 1953, to hundreds of students and dignitaries, which, from all indications, was well-received, the pope issued *Ci Riesce,* which focused on the idea of an international juridical structure that appeared to be along the lines of American principles. As a result, the Americanists now felt that the pope was on their side and that they could use *Ci Riesce* to support their positions. John Tracy Ellis provided a cheery assessment of the situation in a letter to Murray dated January 8, 1954, claiming that the Papal speech was a "reversal of the Ottaviani thesis.... Matters are moving in the right direction, surely."[1]

All of this, combined with the support of the Jesuits in general and papal confidant Leiber in particular, emboldened Murray to battle Ottaviani over the meaning of *Ci Riesce.* Weigel was on one side, Fenton on the other. Also joining the fray was Edward A. Conway, SJ, who was at odds with Weigel's position but not entirely in accord with Fenton's.

In "Religious toleration in a world society," an article that appeared in the January 9, 1954 edition of *America,* Weigel argued that *Ci Riesce* applied to a new idea of a world society, one which had only been a dream before, but one which now could "effect [sic] the survival of mankind, and man's urge to survival is so great that he will adopt all means necessary thereunto...." In proposing a "juridical solution of the problem of religious disunion" based on natural law, with "friendly and cordial toleration" in the area of religion, *Ci Riesce* was advocating a "new society," one which "would not try to impose one definite religion on all men nor make such a religious uniformity a condition for the new federation" because "the function of a purely natural organization" is such that it cannot presume to become "the arbiter of what that religion must be." Since God Himself allowed a multiplicity of religions, governments should be like God in this area and follow his example by promoting tolerance rather than truth.[2]

National governments, Weigel wrote, have to practice the same tolerance as the world government because the "state is not an Hegelian idolatrous absolute but only the working instrument for society's welfare. The peace of the citizenry and their prosperity in the secular order are the state's sole purpose. Peace means a condition of freedom compatible with public order and the exigencies of living together." Weigel continued, "Moreover, for conjoint harmonious living in a concrete society conditioned by its own history and culture, it will be necessary for the state of that society to accept situations not of its own making but inherent in the evolution of the community it serves."[3]

Weigel held that Catholic states had to be tolerant because the international or world community required it. He drove this point home when he wrote: "In the new world union it cannot be the obligation of the state to deal with the theological question of religious truth. Its sole obligation will be to keep together in peace and harmony citizens who are free and responsible agents...." Weigel's claim that Pius XII had taken this position allayed the fears of "non-Catholic brethren" that the Church was involved in a "conspiracy to rob them of their right to follow conscience in their religious decisions." This position helped those "striving for world union because they will know that the great spiritual force of Catholicism is propitious to their efforts." It ended attacks on the Church that claim it has a double norm when it comes to "solving Church-State relationships." In conclusion, "The doctrine of the Pope is wholly different for he speaks of a tolerant worldwide society formed by individual sovereign states, Catholic and non-Catholic, which will govern in their own communities in accordance with the principles obtaining in the world federations."[4]

Fr. Edward Conway's article on the first part of *Ci Riesce* appeared two weeks before Weigel's, and Fenton cited it with approval. Conway wrote that the pope must have been referring to the "ideal international community, since the one he defines is nowhere concretized in the world of today." The pontiff appeared to be of the opinion that technology and human nature are "ineluctably propelling mankind toward political unity," and so he "proceeds at once [to] set up guideposts to that goal, emphasizing in the process the primacy of the natural law and 'an intrinsic law of development'...." This "Intrinsic law of development" did not mean the creation of some monolithic structure where all societies were made the same. Rather, each had the "right to existence, the right to respect from others and to one's good name, the right to one's own culture and national character, the right to develop one's self, the right to demand observance of international treaties...."[5]

Conway saw *Ci Riesce* as the third part of a trilogy that began in April 1951 with the pope's address to the members of the World Movement for World Federal Government, in which he distinguished between federalism and a "'mechanical unitarism' which destroys all differences in a monolithic, materialistic state." The second was the October 1953 talk to the International Congress of Penal Law, in which the pope "unflinchingly followed the demands of the natural law by calling not only for an international penal code but for a Court with jurisdiction reaching into individual 'sovereign' states."[6]

Fenton dealt with the moral question that Catholic leaders of Catholic States faced when presented with the hypothetical international situation that the pope described. In dealing with states that have different laws or viewpoints on religions, the pope suggested that "each state will regulate religious and moral affairs by its own laws. Nevertheless, throughout the whole territory of the community of states, the citizens of every member-state will be allowed the exercise of their own ethical and religious beliefs and practices in so far as these do not contravene the peal laws of the state in which they are residing.'" In answering the question, "Can the jurist, the statesman... and the Catholic state give their consent to such a ruling when there is a question of entering or of remaining within the community of peoples?,"[7] the Pontiff said, "'No human authority, no state, no community of states, whatever their religious character may be, can give a positive command or a positive authorization to teach or to do what would be opposed to religious truth or moral good.'" Second, occasions exist when a state can "legitimately refrain from hindering or impeding by coercive civil law or directives, what is objectively opposed to the truth and to moral good." (Naturally, this implies that the State has the power to do so and the ability to discern truth and error, all of which would cut against the teachings of Murray.) The pope rejected the view that "'religious and moral deviation ought always to be hindered whenever possible because the toleration of that deviation is immoral in itself....in its unconditioned absoluteness.'" The "supreme and ultimate standard by which the conduct of a statesman is to be measured" is therefore not the repression of moral and religious deviations. That is so because there are "higher and more general norms to which this duty must be subordinated, and these higher standards are to be found in the consideration of the purpose of the state, of the Church, and now, of the international community of sovereign states...."[8]

Should the international community order a state to do that which is objectively immoral or opposed to religious truth, then Catholics could not approve. However, Catholics could theoretically approve of a rule that allowed "these states to tolerate or not to impede some of these deviations." Fenton emphasized that the pope was addressing an imminently practical question or "an act of what St. Thomas called *prudential regnativa.*" This is the determination of what is "morally right and good in a definite situation." In reaching a decision in that regard, the Catholic statesman or jurist or State must consider the good that would be accomplished, the evil that would result from the regulation or rule, and he must consider the judgment of the Church, seeking out the counsel of the Holy See itself. This included the effect of the decision on their own nation, the Church, the Universal Church, and the entire international community. The supreme norm for Catholic and Church activities and decisions in these affairs is the "common good" of all.[9]

Concordats demonstrated the principle that agreements "express a common religious conviction" while at other times, they tolerate "certain evils and errors to which the other signer of the concordat is attached." Fenton pointed out that the pope upheld the idea of *thesis* and *hypothesis.* The pope insisted the "Church 'in principle or as a thesis...cannot approve the complete separation between the two powers [Church and state].'" The thesis "is the principle, the truth of the divine law itself. Complete separation of Church and State is opposed to the divine law, and as such, it is something to which the Catholic Church cannot give any positive approbation." The hypothesis, which is the "correlative to which the thesis is immediately referred, takes in actually existent conditions which influence the attitude of any given civil society with reference to the one true Church of Jesus Christ." A "*limited* separation of Church and State may be and sometimes is licit." Fenton noted that *Ci Riesce* reiterated the teachings of Gregory XVI against the separation of Church and State such that the concord between them should not be dissolved. The teachings of Leo XIII in *Immortale Dei* concerning the toleration by civil rulers of false religions, which through "custom or usage" permitted some religions to maintain their place in the state, were also reiterated.[10]

Fenton restated the question that *Ci Riesce* proposed: "Could a Catholic state licitly enter or remain within an international and juridical community of sovereign states which had issued a regulation that the free exercise of a religious or moral belief or practice considered legitimate in one of the member-states should not be impeded within the territory of that Catholic state by coercive state laws or directives?" *Ci Riesce,* Fenton concluded, permitted a theoretical affirmative response by the Catholic state to such a regulation. However, "in practice, it would be the duty of the men in charge of the Catholic state to investigate the good and the evil which might prudently be foreseen as consequences of the acceptance of the regulation." The good that accrued to the nation, the Church in that nation, the universal Church, and the community of nations had to be weighed with the bad, and the Holy Pontiff had to be consulted.[11]

Fenton drew from *Ci Riesce* three other principles. First, since the pope used the term "*Stato cattolica*" to refer to modern states or future states, the idea that such a conception is outmoded could not be justified. Second, the pope asserted that "'what does not correspond to the truth and to the moral standards has, objectively, no right to exist, to be taught, or to be done.' As a result we can expect that, in the future, there will be no objections raised against the teaching or the terminology of writers who hold that, in itself, error has no rights." Third, Fenton wrote that it "is certainly no longer feasible to reprove the teaching that, objectively, a complete separation of Church and State is an evil. Likewise it would appear that henceforth the legitimacy of the explanation of relations between Church and state in terms of thesis and hypothesis will be acknowledged."[12]

On February 25, Fenton, Connell, and the editorial staff of the *American Ecclesiastical Review* were bestowed the "Pro Ecclesia et Pontifice" award, instituted by Pope Leo XIII in 1888, "to those...who in a general way deserve well of the pope on account of services done for the Church and its head."[13] The award ceremony at the Catholic University of America was conducted by the Apostolic Delegate to the United States, Archbishop Amleto Giovanni Cicognani.[14]

Born in 1883 in Brisighella, Italy, Cicognani attended the seminary not far from where he grew up, was considered "a brilliant student," and by 1910 earned doctorates in theology, philosophy, and canon law, after which he assumed positions of ever greater importance and significance starting as an official in the Sacred Congregation of Sacramental Discipline, an official first class in the Sacred Consistorial Congregation, and assessor of the Sacred Congregation for the Oriental Church. [15]

Cicognani became a professor of canon law at Apollinaris College, where he authored a three-part treatise on Canon law entitled *Canon Law* and another work, *The Great Commandment of the Gospel.* His older brother Gaetano, also a priest and a prelate, was appointed Apostolic Nuncio to Peru and Spain and, in 1953, was made cardinal. Amleto

Cicognani was named Apostolic Delegate to the United States on March 17, 1933, and a month later, he was consecrated the Titular Archbishop of Laodicea in Phrygia in Santa Susanna in Rome, a church operated by the Paulists.[16]

In describing the presentation of the award, Connell told Cicognani that it "is a source of great happiness to realize that the Holy See is pleased with the theological doctrine of the American Ecclesiastical Review. We feel that this assurance of the confidence of our Sovereign Pontiff will be an inspiration to renewed efforts in behalf of the traditional doctrine of the Church." Connell also used the opportunity to express concern that "writers still claim that there are two views on the matter, the 'static view' (the traditional doctrine) and the 'dynamic view' (that of Father Murray)."

"Beyond doubt," Connell continued, "there are influences in the sphere of theology in our country today that are dangerous to orthodox Catholic doctrine. As Your Eminence is aware, this has been manifest especially in the question of the Church-State relationship. Despite the clear statement of Your Eminence last March, and the more recent statement of the Holy Father to jurists on December 6, the view proposed by Father Murray seems to be upheld by many. They pass over the clear assertion of the Sovereign Pontiff that in principle, or thesis the Church cannot approve complete separation of Church and State, and still defend the idea that the State is not bound by the divine positive law of Christ, but only by the natural law."[17]

Beneath the gratitude he expressed toward the Holy See, Connell was sending a clear message to Rome: moral theology was being corrupted. The Rev. Gerald Vann, OP, proposed changes concerning the treatment of persons involved in invalid marriages that were so radical in their departure from Catholic tradition that Archbishop Murray of St. Paul even banned the periodical containing the article in his archdiocese. Despite Murray's efforts, many of the laity read the article and "derived from it the notion that it is not very evil to live in an invalid marriage."[18] Once attractive falsehoods were given this sort of publicity, it was hard to control the damage. Connell ended his letter with the observation that "I believe Your Eminence should be acquainted with these facts, because they are surely doing harm to the faith of American Catholics."[19]

MURRAY STRIKES BACK

Encouraged by Leiber, who told him the pope had sided with him against Ottaviani, and Luce, who had the world's most powerful media machine at his disposal, Murray felt the time was ripe to discredit Ottaviani at the bishops' own university. On Thursday evening, March 25, 1954, Murray launched an attack not only on Ottaviani but also on Fenton and Connell. While there was no transcript of the talk, Murray did leave notes, and others reported on the talk.[20] One of these was Brother C. Luke Salm, a graduate student in the School of Sacred Theology, who wrote to Connell describing Murray's talk.

Murray began with a discussion of the factual background of *Ci Riesce* and the claim that Ottaviani's talk of March 1953 was unfavorably received in Rome. Ottaviani's talk upset diplomats from France, Switzerland, and Germany. The pope and many of his close advisors were also disturbed. The pope, therefore, sought to correct Ottaviani with *Ci Riesce* and to do so in such a delicate manner as to preserve the "*bona figura*" of the cardinal. The ultimate authority on this issue was the pope, a claim Murray supported by quoting his Jesuit superior from Rome, who wrote: "With the words 'only He to whom Christ has entursted [sic] the guidance of the whole Church is competent to speak in the last instance on such vital questions touching international life that is, the Roman Pontiff' exit auctoritas Eminentissimi."[21]

According to Murray, the pope corrected four errors that Ottaviani made. First, Ottaviani had a "too narrow conception of the problem." The pope recognized the "great FACT" that there is a supranational community that corresponds to the "intention of nature," and it is "from this fact that conclusions must be drawn." Second, the pope denounced Ottaviani's methodology as faulty and illustrated the correct methodology by stressing a "sense of history," which showed the "primacy of theological over juridical" and the need for a "concrete science and art of jurisprudence." Pius XII believed that the

"Church never has to fear being wrong" and that the "greatest danger is that it will become irrelevant." Institutions develop over time, and the "juridically supreme state. . .is on the way out." Because dogma took priority over law, the "full liberty of the Church to carry on her mission" was therefore superior to laws to repress heresy. Murray said that Leo XIII differed from Pius XII in that the former was a polemicist and a political moralist, whereas the latter had great jurisprudence. Pius XII could "relate principle and fact" while stressing circumstances and the "possibility of law," things that Leo apparently could not do. Laymen are able to judge the *quaestio facti* and the fact that now "toleration of evil is not due to force of circumstances" but "rather is a matter of principle of political jurisprudence, an exercise of the virtue of jurisprudence." Therefore, the pope believed that "laws that tolerate [evil] are good laws, not necessary evils based on expediency." [22]

Third, Ottaviani failed to include "all pertinent principles."[23] Fourth, and as a consequence, Ottaviani presented a false interpretation of the Catholic tradition. Juridically, "true and good have a title of right and... the false and evil have only a title of toleration." However, tradition and "a particular construct or organization of ...data" were two different things, and so Pius XII in *Ci Riesce* dismantled "a particular construct of the data of tradition, i.e. the Church-State theory of Ottaviani and his followers." Murray said that the pope opted for the legality of pluralism, with Spain representing one hypothesis and the United States another hypothesis. To the pope, "the question is not of the principle of the repression of error, but rather of its primacy. The common good is the ultimate norm in the juridical order, and not the exclusive rights of truth." Therefore, the pope rejected the duty to reject error wherever possible, as advanced by Ottaviani, and held that "it can be no valid construction of the Catholic thesis" to hold rejection of error as the ultimate norm. This suppression of error must "now be subordinated to the rank of another hypothesis," and the "possibility of repressing error is rejected as a norm, even when it could be repressed it should a [sic] times be tolerated." This is so because the "Church always tolerates the erroneous conscience," and there are "times and circumstances when the state would not even have the RIGHT to repress error."[24]

Finally, Murray said that the pope opened the way to "new lines of development" and that if legal intolerance is not the thesis, then the premise of an established religion cannot be a thesis. In the U.S., the laymen have decided the *quaestio facti* and have denied the state the right to set up an established religion. Brother Luke observed that the "audience was overwhelmingly won" over by Murray's presentation and that time was allowed time for only two or three questions. Indeed, the "guffaws of the younger element and the knowing smiles of the Professors present indicated clearly that the enemy under attack was not the distinguished Cardinal 3000 miles away but others closer at hand."[25]

THE REACTION TO MURRAY'S TALK

John Tracy Ellis, who was in the audience during Murray's talk, wrote to Murray congratulating him: "Your lecture was splendid in every way, a true university performance.... It has stirred a great deal of discussion on the campus which is all to the good...."[26] Fellow Jesuit and close acquaintance Walter Burghardt, SJ, believed that "This was a real turning point. The Argument with Rome on Church and State might have followed in any event. But this made it inevitable – and for Ottaviani, made it personal." Burghardt had no love for Fenton, calling him a "mediocre writer but vigorous talker" and "'sensational as a 16th century polemicist" for "'he loved argument.'" Nonetheless, Burghardt felt that Murray's Catholic U speech, as well as his earlier harsh treatment of Connell, who responded so meekly to his attacks in the pages of the *American Ecclesiastical Review,* were tactical blunders.[27]

In claiming that an undefined societal peace was the highest good and that it took precedence over the truth,[28] Murray was making an emotional and philosophic appeal to the American ideology. Immediately after Murray's talk, Brother Luke wrote to Dr. Giovanni Giovannini, the President of the Catholic University Chapter of the American Association of University Professors, the sponsor of Murray's talk, objecting to a "certain unfairness involved in the presentation of this disputed question." Everyone knew that Murray's views were at odds with those of professors in the School of Sacred Theology. As a result of

Murray's comments, "the vast majority of the audience left the hall convinced, not only that they understood the basic points of disagreement, but also that the views of the local professors had been thoroughly and authoritatively repudiated."[29]

In addition, Murray did not deal with "the basic point of divergence," namely, the "technical, theological, and theoretical question as to whether or not the state, ideally, has positive obligations towards the revealed law of Christ." Murray did not address this, the main issue, probably because the local theologians would gladly defend the position that it is never a good for either society or an individual to free itself or himself from the positive law of Christ. Therefore, for "Father Murray to move the thesis and hypothesis to the prudential moral question of religious tolerance or intolerance in particular circumstances renders him guilty of the very shift of which he was accusing his opponents."[30]

Brother Luke complained that the "really unfortunate aspect of the talk was the unproved assertion that the Ci Riesce 'dismantled piece by piece' the traditional construct of Cardinal Ottaviani, and, by implication, [that] of the local professors who share his view. This is as sweeping statement, fraught with serious consequences for the persons involved, and certainly demands more objective proof than was advanced last Thursday evening." Instead of conducting an analysis of the two talks (Ottaviani's in March and the pope's in December) which required "objective summary and unbiased excerpting from each," Murray gave the audience a "refutation of the premises of his own syllogized construct of the traditional view." Cardinal Ottaviani's talk was theoretical. The pope's speech dealt with an insistence on practical principles "lest diplomats and statesmen get the impression that the theoretical dogmatic thesis be considered as the unique and prior norm for practical guidance." Therefore, there was no conflict. To claim, as Murray did, that the pope attacked Ottaviani's position and dismantled it, required "strong intrinsic and/or extrinsic evidence and not mere assertion," which was all that Murray provided.[31]

To correct the situation, Brother Luke suggested that Connell be asked to present his side of the story, leaving sufficient time for a question-and-answer period. Though "not as impressive as Father Murray,"

Connell was "quite as capable of holding his audience, prsererving [sic] withal a sincere respect for his opponents."[32]

Connell sent a letter to Ottaviani on the same day, March 27, advising that Brother Luke recommended him as a speaker and that the "matter is most serious" in regard to the controversy on Church and State in the United States. He told the Cardinal that the pope's talk from December seemed to support Murray's views on Church and State and seemed to refute the cardinal's lecture given nine months earlier.[33]

Connell did nothing to hide the urgency of the situation. "Father Murray's ideas are spreading," he wrote. "In the near future a book will be published at Notre Dame University containing a chapter by Father Murray on Church and State. A few months ago a book was published in New York, also containing an article by him. His views are being widely accepted throughout America, because they are so conformable to the American idea that all religions are equally good, and that the State is bound to grant all the citizens full freedom of religious belief and worship."[34]

Connell then recounted the history of his warnings to Rome about Murray. In an August 2, 1950 letter to Cardinal Pizzardo, he provided a copy of the Catholic Theological Society of America proceedings, which included an article from Murray expounding his theory. However, Connell did not receive a response. He told Cardinal Ottaviani that he, Fenton, Shea, Dr. Martin, Msgr. Sheehy, and Dr. Rush were all upholding the "traditional doctrine of the Church on this matter." Murray's teachings on Church and State had undermined the Catholic position on marriage, including the claim that the Church has "exclusive right over the marriages of all baptized persons, independently of all rulings of the State." Using Murray's principles, many were beginning to say that the Church need not grant the Church's claim in this regard unless it was necessary for the common good.[35]

As a result of the Vatican's silence, "some are concluding that his opinion can be held by Catholics." Connell advised that "some positive statement from the Holy See is urgently needed." That statement should come from "the Holy See, sentencing him or his writings by name." The majority of Catholics would accept this statement if it were issued in the near future, but as time passed, "the theory is becoming more widely accepted, and the danger increases that there will be a widespread heresy in the United States, with perhaps many defections from the Church, if there is a condemnation." Connell concluded by advising the Cardinal that if the Church upholds Murray's teachings, he and the others would assent to them. However, he did not believe that such a thing could come to pass "without rejecting the teaching of the Church on its unique position and its immunity on certain things from civil law."[36]

Ottaviani responded quickly. In a letter dated March 31, he thanked Connell for his warning and wrote that even truth and charity have limits. It was time to act against Murray for the good of truth and Catholic doctrine.[37]

Following up on his letter to Connell, Ottaviani wrote to Cardinal Spellman the following day inquiring into Murray and his activities. Spellman responded with the assurance that he would "take up the matter which you bring to my attention with the Rector of the University." Spellman wrote he "would appreciate it if you will give more details of what Father Murray said in his lecture that was offensive to you and just what quotation he made from any address of His Holiness and what interpretations were given to the words of our Holy Father."[38]

Within a week of the Murray talk, Connell complained to the president of the AAUP chapter at CUA, Fr. Henry J. Browne, who replied, copying Archbishop O'Boyle, that "Father Murray was invited in his capacity as a world recognized theologian whose writings on the subject of his lecture to the best of my knowledge have not been censured by any official body of the Church. Even the remarks of March 25 have not been considered unfit for publication on the editorial page of the official journal of the Chancellor of the University, The Catholic Standard, in its issue of April 2, 1954." Browne explained that letting Murray speak conformed to "the essence of the concept of academic freedom in a university" because the "purpose of lectures is to afford an opportunity to hear the ideas of prominent scholars even in cases where the speaker's ideas differ from our own."[39]

Browne went on to claim that he was "not personally aware of 'unfavorable comments on...Cardinal Ottaviani,' but only on some of his teachings." Clerical and lay faculty agreed with Browne, and the "unusually strong applause of a mixed audience of 400 loyal Catholics" did not indicate there was any personal attack. Browne closed by inviting Connell to give a public lecture.[40]

Connell forwarded the letter to Ottaviani and repeated that Murray's "basic doctrine of his theory" is "that the civil governments are obliged to obey only the natural law, not the divine-positive law of Jesus Christ." He used it to point out that "His defense is that Fr. Murray's writings have not been censured by any official body of the Church. I feel sure that this idea now prevails, and that Fr. Murray's views are regarded as being approved by the Church from the very fact that there has been no official judgment regarding them. Hence, I am very glad to hear from Your Eminence that some action will be taken."[41] Ottaviani responded by again thanking Connell and noting that "It is really sad that anyone approved by the president of the C.U. AAUP can lecture in the centre of Catholic culture of the United States and express any kind of ideas. Father Brown [sic] can reply by saying they can always [sic] on for a professor who can express contrary ideas but such arguments does not stad [sic] when one deals of a subject on which the Holy See has given its directive."[42] Both men would soon learn that a private letter was no match for the forces Murray could muster.

44
MURRAY AND HESBURGH TEAM UP

Meanwhile, the University of Notre Dame and its newly elected president, Theodore Hesburgh, CSC, were drawing Murray into the fight for "academic freedom." Hesburgh wanted foundation money,[1] and the foundations, run by men opposed to Catholicism, would not give the money unless Hesburgh distanced Notre Dame from Catholicism and control by the Church. "Academic freedom" was a euphemism for the transfer of control of the Catholic university from the Church to private interests by way of the foundations and the government. Once "academic freedom," as opposed to truth or the good as determined by the Catholic Church, became the supreme arbiter of every dispute, the way was cleared to justify all sorts of human behavior and public policy as well as every attack on the authority of the Church, while putting Catholics in service to America. In a memoir written years later, Hesburgh claimed he was engaged in a struggle to determine whether "ecclesiastical authorities have control over universities that call themselves Catholic, and if so, how much control should they have and in what ways should that control be used and not used?"[2]

In order to bolster Hesburgh's credentials with the foundations, Notre Dame invited Murray to a symposium on *The Catholic Church in World*

Affairs, which led to a book by the same name that Notre Dame planned to publish through its press. The Superior General of the Holy Cross Order, Christopher O'Toole, instructed Hesburgh to keep the symposium book from reaching bookstores. Ottaviani was behind this effort but did not want anyone to know just why the book was withdrawn. O'Toole also instructed Hesburgh not to let anyone know that Ottaviani gave the order to remove the books. Hesburgh construed the order of his superior as "a frontal assault on academic freedom at Notre Dame" and "a challenge to action." In response to O'Toole's order, Hesburgh called the Notre Dame "university council together, consisting of Holy Cross priests, most of them vice presidents in the university administration. Not only were they all appalled at the idea of censorship, they all agreed that it would be ridiculous event to try to suppress the book." Perhaps more importantly, Hesburgh believed that if the book was withdrawn (it had been selected as the Catholic Book of the Month Club) then "the press would be all over me," and "we would be finished as a university, and I would be finished as its president." The outcome of following the Church on this issue was clear: "Notre Dame would lose all its credibility in the United States, and so would I."[3]

Hesburgh stalled for time with O'Toole, who, in turn, stalled for time with Ottaviani, and 6,000 copies of the book were sold, enabling the university to break even. When Fenton found a copy of the book in a bookstore, Ottaviani leaned on O'Toole, who leaned on Hesburgh, telling him to have Murray buy all the remaining copies. Hesburgh, in response to a phone call from Murray, hid the remaining 500 copies. However, shortly thereafter, O'Toole told Hesburgh and all Holy Cross religious superiors that Murray was not to either teach courses or lecture at any institutions. Hesburgh responded to that order by seeing to it that Murray received an honorary doctorate.[4]

The ecclesial situation was complicated by the fact that the book had been granted both Imprimatur and Nihil Obstat from Bishop Noll, the ordinary of the Diocese of Fort Wayne where Notre Dame was located. Ottaviani's suspicion that the book was deliberately intended as an Americanist subversion of Church teaching was strengthened by the fact that Murray's article, "On the Structure of the Church-State Problem," had pride of place as the first article in the book, something which was evident to everyone, and by the fact that Waldemar Gurian, one of the book's editors, was part of the CIA's doctrinal warfare operation, something which was not public information, either then or now.

There was nothing substantively in Murray's article that hadn't already been expressed in *Theological Studies* or in his speech at CUA. Murray's position appeared Catholic, but in reality, he presented a theory that could be used against the Catholics. He did this through a number of techniques already observed by his critics. These techniques included using undefined terms, omitting unfavorable references to papal teachings, shifting the focus or emphasis of doctrine, employing a selective historicism or relativity to Church doctrine, and raising the importance and authority of theologians.[5]

Murray's article reduced the magisterial teaching of Leo XIII to polemics and that of Pius IX to ignorant ramblings, but few seemed to notice. The primary factor or principle governing Church activities was freedom. Nazism and Communism were evils, and America was presented as the savior of the day because America provided freedom. While Murray called for more research and study, his article served a powerful purpose in working a sophisticated and subtle deconstruction of Catholic doctrine to support American ideology.

45
CAREFUL, HONEST, AND COMPETENT

In the May 1954 issue of the *American Ecclesiastical Review,* Fenton went on the offensive, calling Murray's comments "an extremely serious charge" and attacking Murray's claim that the pope rejected Ottaviani's speech as "utterly baseless and incorrect." Fenton blasted Murray's analysis: "Any careful, honest, and competent examination of the text of *Ci riesce* and that of Cardinal Ottaviani's article will show that there is absolutely no point on which these two documents contradict one another...There is no statement in either document which could in any way legitimately be interpreted as opposed to the spirit of the other."[1] Pius XII upheld the idea of a "Catholic state" in *Ci Riesce,* and he also upheld the teaching that error has no rights, points which Ottaviani made in his talk. His view that the cardinal and the pope were in accord was confirmed by the Grand Seminary or theological school of the University of Montreal in its March 1954 publication of *Le seminaire.*

Fenton pointed out that Murray's opposition to Ottaviani's position was opposition to the traditional teaching of the church. Murray was claiming a "development" of church doctrine from the days of Pius IX and Leo XIII in such a way that had Pius XII partially or totally rejecting the earlier teachings. There was no such "development" because development, in this instance, meant a break from tradition. The teaching of the current pope was in accordance with that of his predecessors.[2]

No matter how acute they were in coming up with a precise formulation of the proper relationship between church and state in Catholic theology, Connell and Fenton were losing the public relations battle because they were outgunned by *Time,* which controlled how Catholics, including Catholic writers for Catholic periodicals, thought. After *The New York Times* reported in its July 23 issue that a "high Vatican source" had commented that the teaching of Ottaviani was "neither official nor semi-official," *Time,* Fenton noted, picked up the same story in its August 3 edition even though the Holy See never corrected Ottaviani or indicated that what Ottaviani said was in error. Fenton also mentioned a "popular account" of Murray's CUA speech, which appeared in the *Denver Register* on February 28, 1954. The article implied that Murray's views were acceptable because they had never been condemned: "If we consider the fact that the Holy Father has never censured those Catholic scholars and Bishops who have argued strongly in favor of religious toleration as being perfectly consistent with Catholic teaching, I think we may conclude that they have just as much right to maintain their position, as Catholics, as have their opponents." Weigel and the "dynamic expositors" were proposing a "fresh formulation of the Catholic theory of Church and State with a view to showing that there is no antagonism between it and the American arrangement."[3]

Weigel's position effectively negated the need or justification for any missionary activity by Catholics to make societies and states Catholic. The Catholic confessional state became unrealizable and merely an historical anachronism according to the Murray and Weigel formulation. The result was the ordering of societies in accordance with the American system, which rejected Christ as Lord and eliminated the duty of men to follow Christ, His Church, and His law. This was truly dangerous stuff that promised to cause great harm to societies while benefitting the few who could manipulate the government, economics, and culture of societies. The work of Weigel and Murray was perfectly consonant with the goals and methods of the Americans during the Cold War. Paul Blanshard, according to Weigel, recognized the "*fact* of

Catholic loyalty to American democracy" and did not "deny that American Catholics do not believe that there is any opposition between their Catholic commitments and their obligations as Americans." However, the Blanshards of the world "deny...that this position is logical in the light of the authoritative Catholic doctrine on Church and State relationships."[4] The Weigel-Murray position was a direct attack on Catholic efforts to make or keep governmental policies and laws in accordance with Catholic teaching. It was an attempt to get Catholics to reject the idea that every state had an affirmative duty to the law of Christ. This would happen if the responsibility of the state to suppress error fell, for then a religion of the state could no longer be maintained. A state would only have the obligation to follow the natural law, and therefore, all religions could exist as long as that regimen was not disturbed. It was the recipe for a return to the omnipotence of the State, and it was a sure rejection of Christ. [5]

Citing Connell's 1943 pamphlet, *Freedom of Worship,* Fenton explained that Catholic toleration meant permitting a lesser evil, such as false religions, in order to either prevent a greater evil or to allow for a greater good. Catholics could never allow multiple false religions to exist with the view that such a state of affairs was a good thing in itself or that these religions have a "genuine God-given right to exist. Such a right belonged only to the one religion founded by Jesus Christ for all men." Fenton explained that "Truth is not a matter of nationality" and that the Church-State discussion did not involve the "question of accepting or rejecting a statement because it seemed more or less 'American' than its opposite."[6]

Religious toleration was a tenet of the Catholic faith. People who taught this (like Connell) in accordance with Catholic doctrine were not in danger of censure. Foreshadowing what was to come with the Ecumenical Council, still years in the future, Fenton explained that bishops are not to argue or lobby for doctrines like so much legislation, though they may propose clarifications of doctrine.[7]

In the following issue of the *American Ecclesiastical Review,* Fr. Giuseppe DiMeglio's article entitled "*Ci Riesce* and Cardinal Ottaviani's Discourse" appeared. It discredited the idea that Ottaviani's and the pope's statements were somehow at odds with each other. "Such a judgment deserves to be rejected immediately, since it is not only devoid of foundation, but also disrespectful. At the very outset, it is to be noted that these two addresses deal with two different problems," neither of which considered the other's. Cardinal Ottaviani "dealt with the *Catholic* state, and with the duties towards religion in its own *internal* order. He was not discussing the case in which that Catholic state would join, under juridical bonds, a community of states as, for example, that community of states which is the United States of America." The pope, on the other hand, discussed a situation that may arise involving a "juridical community into which 'states, remaining sovereign, freely unite'" and these states will consist of those that are Christian, non-Christian, atheist, indifferent to religion.[8]

Ottaviani's talk explained principles to guide the Catholic state, which existed when the "absolute majority" or total population was Catholic, and in that case, the rulers had a duty to "'protect against everything that would undermine...the religious unity of a people who unanimously know themselves to be in secure possession of religious truth.'" Tolerance could be practiced in such a state all the same if there were "very serious reasons for it," but that was different from allowing "'freedom to propagandize in such a way as to foment religious discord and to disturb the secure possession of truth and of religious practice in countries like Italy, Spain, and others.'"[9]

The pope's ultimate norm of action was not the repression of moral and religious error but a higher and more general norm that would tolerate evil for the sake of promoting a greater good. Such tolerance, which is a "fundamental theoretical principle," envisaged a political union and a more effective union while tolerating "at times that which it is impossible to correct but which on the other hand, must not be permitted to make a shipwreck of the community, from which a higher good is hoped for."[10] The Church could allow evil to exist for a while either to promote or at least not hinder a good. That good could be a closer union that assisted the conversion of society.

Far from disputing them, the pope confirmed the principles Ottaviani expressed concerning the "rights of religious truth." No one and no state could give a positive command contrary to religious truth and moral good as "such a command or such an authorization would have no obligatory power and would remain without effect." In considering the situation the pope presented, two essential principles had to be considered: 1) "that which does not correspond to the truth or to the norm of morality objectively has no right to exist, to be spread, or to be activated," and 2) that "failure to impede this with civil laws and coercive measures can nevertheless be justified in the interests of a higher and more general good." The Catholic statesman must consult with the Holy See to determine whether a policy of toleration had to be established.[11]

This was a far different situation than the one Murray presented to the students and faculty at CUA, where Murray claimed that the Catholic state in the modern world was bound to adopt a policy of toleration of non-Catholic religions due to the international situation. He was also thereby suggesting, if not claiming, that the common good permitted, if not positively included, the toleration of evil, even if it was for an undefined social peace.

But Fenton also made some mistakes that hurt the Catholic cause. He failed to address the central and logical point raised by Weigel and Blanshard. Given Catholic doctrine, how could Catholics keep from wanting and working to make America a Catholic confessional state by changing the U.S. laws or the Constitution to establish the Church and the Faith as the State religion? Fenton's response was to quote from Connell's pamphlet, *Freedom of Worship.* Connell wrote, "Even in a predominantly Catholic country, circumstances may render it more advisable for the government to grant non-Catholics the same measure of freedom of worship as is enjoyed by Catholics. Such a course is justifiable when it is foreseen that a policy of complete toleration will procure greater good than will repressive measures against anti-Catholic activities."[12] This response subverted the very position of Connell, Fenton, and others – the Catholic state as the ideal.

CONNELL TEACHES THE FAITHFUL AND THE HIERARCHY

Faced with a challenge they could not resolve either by intellect or will, the Catholic hierarchy adopted a dualistic response to Murray's challenge to Catholic doctrine. Fenton and Connell were allowed to communicate with the rank and file, and Murray was allowed to communicate on a national level. Fenton and Connell spoke with the faithful; Murray had the ear of the powerful. This dualism allowed the bishops to avoid causing offense.

Connell had long been in demand among Catholics as a speaker on a variety of matters concerning the Faith and the Church, and despite his advancing age, he persisted in these efforts. He was perhaps the most influential theologian among rank-and-file Catholics in the U.S. in the 1950s. "Connell's personal contact with a very large portion of the Catholic clergy and laity in this country, along with his catechetical efforts, would seem to justify the conclusion that he exercised greater influence than any other priest-educator in this country through the decade prior to the Second Vatican Council."[13]

Connell spoke to the laity on a variety of topics over the years, including, interestingly enough, the morality of psychological warfare. In the June-July 1954 issue of *Catholic Men,* in an article entitled "Radio and the Red Curtain: The Morality of Psychological Warfare," Connell evaluated the efforts of Voice of America by pointing out that American "spokesmen must adhere to the truth—not exaggerating such things as the prosperity of American life, nor exceeding the facts when Communism is denounced. The reason is that it is against the law of God to lie, even though the purpose be good. But even apart from that we do not need false propaganda."

Connell wrote that the USA was "certainly justified in penetrating the Iron Curtain in this manner, as a measure of defense. The Communistic governments are spreading lies about the United States; hence, we have the right, even against the regulations of these governments, to tell their people the truth about our land, our ideals of freedom and our desire to foster peace."[14]

Not surprisingly, Connell was often asked to speak on the topic of church and state. At St. Joseph Roman Catholic Church in Garden City, New York, he explained that a false charge leveled against Catholics in the U.S. is that they were supposedly not able to be good Americans, a charge prompted by those who "envy the success of the Catholic church." Connell explained, "Every American, Catholic or not, should have a correct idea of the relation between civil authorities and those of the church. The Church teaches that human beings are social beings made to live in society. The basic unit of society is the family. These families bend together for social welfare and thus we have the state." Additionally, "every society demands authority. In the family the father is the head of the house and in the larger social sphere, the state, there must be certain individuals empowered to make laws and see that they are carried out. All forms of government are perfectly lawful...This is only true however, as long as rulers or ruler obey the laws of God."[15]

The Church taught that "there should be some manner of union between Church and state. This union should exist because both have at heart the welfare of the people. Those who speak disparagingly of the position of the church in relation to the state in Spain and South America should look to other countries where the same applies with other religious denominations. In England there is union between the Anglican church and the government; the Lutheran church is a powerful influence in Denmark and Sweden and in Greece and Rumania the Orthodox Greek church prevails as the dominant force. Separation of Church and State does not mean that religion should be separated from the state. It means that no one particular church should be favored by the government."[16]

On January 9, 1953, in a talk on Church and State delivered at the Clerical Students' Mission Conference, Connell explained the key doctrinal principles that informed "the problem of church and state," which is a "very abstruse one with many angles." *Quas Primas* cleared up many issues and allowed a greater certainty in theological discussions, but it was still important to make distinctions. The first distinction is that of the authority of Christ (which extends to all human beings) and the authority of the Church (which extends to the baptized). Both authorities are direct – Christ in the temporal and the Church in the Spiritual. Second, in the United States, the "most feasible policy is to have separation of Church and State; but that would not necessarily mean that it is per se the best system. Hence...the thesis and the hypothesis." Third, the union of the Church and the state "does not necessarily involve any restriction on the part of the state over the propaganda of heretical sects." Connell said that "we could not say that the type of union that existed in the Middle Ages is the only type possible," but that it is essential that the state recognize all rights of the Church as regards marriage, exemption of clergy, and more. (However, in making this point, Connell inconsistently claimed that the state should allow full freedom of worship and propaganda to all.) Fourth, the government may exert jurisdiction over that which affects the public or common good, with the implication that personal conduct may impinge or affect the common or public good. Fifth, the temporal good of men "demands that they have supernatural grace and affiliation with the Church which Christ founded." Sixth, and finally, there must be a distinction between "a real (objective) right of conscience, especially the right to accept the religion founded by God for all men, and a purely subjective...right. Public authority does not have to regard this latter when the public good is at stake. The saying 'Everyone has a right to accept whatever religion his conscience dictates,' is not correct, if there is question of a real right."[17]

Connell explained, "The basis of the state's obligation to the Church is not a Church law; it is a law of God, who has decreed that all human beings, and all civil societies shall be subject to the jurisdiction of Jesus Christ. This is clearly stated by Pope Pius XI in his Encyclical on Christ the King.... Now, since the state is under the jurisdiction of Christ the king, it is bound per se to respect His kingdom and its laws. Hence, the doctrine of the ideal condition of union between Church and state, which is the traditional doctrine of the Catholic Church... It is to be noted that we do not say that any particular form of union is called for. For example union of church and state does not necessarily call for state support of the clergy...."[18]

Connell noted, "Fr. Murray's view would involve the acceptance of polygamy, divorce, etc."[19]

On Sexagesima Sunday in 1954 (February 21), Fr. Connell gave a homily entitled "Are Catholics Patriotic?" in which he discussed:

"The main argument of those who claim that Catholics are not patriotic citizens is that Catholics owe allegiance to the Pope, a foreign ruler, and hence cannot give full loyalty to the laws and government of our country. To this we answer that we obey the Pope in matters pertaining to faith and morality, but over affairs of a strictly temporal nature the Pope has no jurisdiction in our land....Indeed, our Church tells us that we must obey our civil authorities as God's representatives."[20]

Connell condemned the "argument...that if Catholics ever gained the majority of numbers in the United States they would . . . restrict the civil rights of non-Catholics" as utterly false because "as Pope Pius XII recently stated, there are occasions when Catholics may and must give complete religious toleration to non-Catholics, even when Catholics have the predominance of power in a nation. Undoubtedly, this would be the situation in the United States, even though at some future time Catholics became far more numerous than non-Catholics" and even though it is "the more desirable situation in a Catholic nation to have some union between Church and state."[21]

Pius XII's lack of clarity and the lack of further definition by Leo XIII concerning the greater evil to be avoided or the greater good to be gained in situations that justify non-repression of error created confusion and allowed an endorsement of the American situation. This dynamic became very clear in a paper that Connell prepared entitled "Propositions." In it, Connell concluded that "the present system seems the most practical, and there would be no reason to change even if we ever gained the ascendancy. Many evils would doubtless result from any repression, and besides we have our Constitution as the basis of our country."[22]

When *Look* magazine published an article entitled "Must Protestants Distrust Catholicism?" Connell notified Ottaviani of the scandal that the author of the article, *Commonweal* editor John Cogley, was causing by spreading errors. Connell quoted the offending paragraph:

"Was not Cardinal Segura expressing the Catholic position? His extreme view certainly represents a Catholic position on the Church-State question. But a Catholic view is not necessarily the Catholic view. There were many unfavorable reactions to the Cardinal's statement in the American Catholic press. More important, the Vatican's subsequent concordat with Spain incorporated the very article which Cardinal Segura criticize as 'too tolerant.' The magazine *The Priest*, which is circulated exclusively among the clergy, reprinted three editorials from Catholic publications which took lively exception to the Cardinal's outlook—with the comment that they represented the reaction of the average American priest."[23]

Noting that *Look* is "read by millions of Americans," Connell tried to explain to Ottaviani how dire the situation had become in America. "This last statement is an indication of what is happening in our land. Many priests and lay persons are accepting the view of Fr. Murray and believe that there has been a radical change in the Church-State doctrine." Connell saw that such a doctrine was leading to "the denial of the Church's immunities (including jurisdiction over the marriages of the baptized)."[24]

Connell again pleaded that "this idea will continue to spread unless there is an official statement from the Holy See emphasizing the traditional and true doctrine of the Church. It will not suffice to present this statement in general terms. It must explicitly deal with Fr. Murray's teaching, especially as expounded in the Proceedings of the Catholic Theological Society of America for the year 1948, if it is to guide aright the Catholics of the United States." The only "writers who now defend the traditional teaching on Church and State" are the theologians writing for *American Ecclesiastical Review.* Connell concluded by invoking the assistance of the recently canonized St. Pius X and the Blessed Virgin Mary, whose year it was, noting that Msgr. Fenton would soon be in Rome to discuss matters face-to-face with the Ottaviani.[25]

Murray, for his part, believed he had escaped any repercussions from the March 25 talk at CUA. In a letter to Clare, who was in Rome at the time, Murray admitted, "I was involved in trouble, now pretty well cleared up. I'll tell you about it when the chance comes (some of my 'friends' at the Catholic University delated me to Cardinals Pizzardo and Ottaviani in consequence of a lecture I gave at Catholic University on March 25. The procedure was most unfair; my Father General was drawn into it, but I had a wonderful letter from him – he is a wonderful man)." [26]

On a more serious note, Murray mentioned that "my best friend here, Fr. Weigel, came down with cancer; radical operation, resection of the colon," but he quickly reverted to the flirtatious tone that characterized most of his letters to Clare when he wrote: "Please don't relegate me to oblivion; I am never oblivious of you, but full of remembrance, each day....Love and love and love."[27]

46

FENTON DISCOVERS THE SECRET OF MURRAY'S SURVIVAL

A few weeks after Murray's love letter to Clare, Fenton disembarked in Le Havre, France, along with Cardinal Spellman and Archbishop Cicognani. This was Fenton's ninth trip to Rome in six years. During those trips, he met the most powerful and influential men in the Church. One was Msgr. Giovanni Montini, an official in the office of the Secretary of State who later became Pope Paul VI, and another was Alfredo Cardinal Ottaviani, Secretary of the Holy Office, both of whom he first met in May 1948 during his first trip to Rome. On subsequent trips, Fenton met more leaders of the Church, members of the Holy Office, like-minded churchmen, and enemies. Fenton's routine during the journeys steeled him for all these encounters and the vicious attacks he suffered afterward. The bedrock of that routine was to start each day, as he recounted in detail in his diaries, by saying Mass followed by a good breakfast.

The ninth trip was different from the others because it involved the canonization of Pope St. Pius X. Two days after the canonization, which took place on May 29, 1954, Fenton met DiMeglio, who had already joined the fight against Murray's false interpretation of *Ci Riesce*. Fenton called DiMeglio a "sharp young man" and was "delighted with his article." Fenton also met with Fr. Raymond Dulac, the editor of *La Pensee*

Catholique, and explained the difference between the Americanism controversy and the Cohensly controversy, as well as the influence of Archbishop John Ireland to him.[1]

During the following two weeks, Fenton had an opportunity to discuss the religious situation in Europe. In an entry for June 1, he wrote, "I have been astonished at the attitude of the Americans who live in Rome during the entire year. They have some queer notions on the subject of the recent doctrinal pronouncements."[2] Fenton learned that "the theological situation is very grave indeed," especially in France. "Danielou is supposed to be in trouble there this time."[3]

Fenton prepared an address tentatively scheduled to be given on Vatican radio on Saturday, June 5. The theme of the talk was the canonization of St. Pius X, which had just occurred days earlier. It was also to include a comment on the talk of Pope Pius XII, known as *Si diligis.* Pope Pius XII said that the road to Christ "yesterday as well as today and always is the Church." Pope St. Pius X made the church more "effectively suitable" to bring souls to Christ through a number of reforms to include "recasting the body of Church law" to provide for more order, certainty, and flexibility while successfully combating Modernism and improving Eucharistic Holiness.[4]

Referring to *Mystici Corporus* issued in 1943, Fenton mentioned that the Church is the Mystical Body of Christ, the Kingdom of God on earth to which St. Paul referred. "If men are going to be brought to XT [Christ] it must be in his Church" and "There is no attachment to XT [Christ] which is not an attachment to the CC [Catholic Church]." And so, Christ "wills that men should without fear or shame acknowledge before the world the faith that He has given them. He wills that men should follow the orders and the directions of those whom He has made responsible for the spiritual well-being of the flock. In the acknowledgment of that authority and in obedience to it, we find union with XT [Christ]."[5]

A few days later, Fenton penned an outline of an article on the writings of "Z," who bore a remarkable resemblance to Murray. Fenton observed that Z's articles "contain 1) dangerously erroneous teaching, 2) set forth in a confused but highly effective way. It is written in circumstances that in all probability would make it extremely powerful in France, and would tend to mislead a great many people....The basic error taught by Z consists in a contention that Catholic doctrine on concordats changes.... At the very outset we must take cognizance of the fact that this error is taught in a very confused and obscure manner which is all the more effective precisely by reason of its obscurity and confusion...."[6]

From a review of his articles, it became clear that "we have here clear evidence that for Z, what the Sovereign Pontiffs since Pope Gregory XVI have said in condemning 'the separation of the Church and State' was merely a declaration about a now outmoded 'institution' and has no reference to the life and the conditions of our time.... Objectively, then, this teaching of Z means that when the Popes, from Gregory XVI to Pius XI spoke against 'separation of Church and State,' they were expounding a doctrine which was partly true (as an expression of 'principle') and partly merely in line with the ecclesiastical temper of the times...." In sum, Murray was saying that the "teaching on 'separation of Ch. & State' was composed of 2 elements. The one an expression of Catholic principle and the other an expression of teachings or attitudes common at the time the declaration was made."[7]

Fenton provided a crucial insight into Z's way of thinking when he wrote: "But (and this is the crucial point in all of Zs teaching on this subject since the Dijon paper of 1939) the principles are nothing more or less than Z's own theses, which, taken as a group constitute a rejection of the doctrine involved in the standard manuals of ecclesiology and of public ecclesiastical law." The purpose of Z's work, Fenton opined, was to create a "theory of concordats which will be acceptable (or perhaps less completely unacceptable) to the highly vocal anti-Catholic forces of his native France. He knows that these hostile forces make use of certain statements by Pope Leo XIII in their activities against the CC. Hence, in his desire to placate these forces and to construct his new apologetics for the Church, he has been forced to think up ways to repudiate the clear statements of Leo XIII. In so doing, he has utilized a method rejected and condemned by the HF himself in his encyclical HG."[8]

Fenton understood the bad effect the Modernist deconstruction of doctrine was having on the Church. "The authority of the Roman

Church," he wrote, "is without effect for men who are willing to accept this theory of 'institutions' and to classify all the actual teaching of the magisterium as statements composed of two elements, one of which need not be taken into account by the faithful." This "effectively destroys the 'Roman' influence and nature of Catholicism in France." Murray's writings had to be condemned.[9]

The Vatican, however, seemed oblivious to Murray's growing influence in the Church. "It is difficult here in Rome," Fenton wrote, "to explain just how popular and influential a figure Z is in France. During the past spring two symposia, the one containing Z's article now under consideration, and the other published by the American Liberal Catholic periodical, *Commonweal,* both gave what can only be described as reverential treatment to Z. There is also the *Newsweek* article about Spellman which starts off with a quotation from Z."[10]

Fenton summed up Murray's method:

"Now Z is a man about 50 years old (as a matter of fact he will be 50 in September). He has a fine social presence. He speaks well. He has a certain arrogance which easily passes for culture and which seems to be the basis of his appeal. He never answers an opponent's article or argument. A well-turned phrase or a little article by one of his friends (who likewise never answer arguments or give any consideration to the traditional Catholic teachings on concordats) suffices to dispose of the arguments and the persons of his opponents. As a matter of fact, he presents his strong doctrine entirely on his own authority. We are to take Zs word for it that there are these 2 elements in papal teaching; etc. There is certainly no basis for such a statement in the teaching of the magisterium itself, and there is certainly no theological evidence of any kind adduced in support of Z's contentions."[11]

A few days later, on June 12, Fenton received disturbing information that explained why Murray was so successful at evading censure. The Jesuits were defending one of their own and Fr. Leiber was one of his main protectors. Fenton's epiphany came about fortuitously "on the piazza San Silvestri," where he "met Bob North, SJ," a man whom he considered "the best writer...for AER." Standing "at the corner of the

Vieu ales Moniti Passoli, and the Piazza Don Munzoni, on the side away from the Villa," Fenton and North "had a long talk about the Murray affair." During the discussion, Fenton brought up Murray's March 25 speech at CUA and "the bad feeling it had engendered at the University." When Fenton mentioned Leiber's letter and the influence of a certain Fordham professor, North responded by claiming that Pope Pius XII felt "that Murray was well within his rights," even though "there was nothing in North's statement to indicate that this statement was made after the Pope had heard of the March 25th affair."[12]

Instead of pressing the issue and getting into an argument with North, Fenton decided to bite his tongue and listen because what he learned from North confirmed what he had been hearing from other Jesuits, in particular Joe Lafferty, who told Fenton that the Jesuits, "especially Ed Coffey," were responsible for "spreading the report that the Pope was displeased with Ottaviani." Fenton found himself confronted with two equally repugnant alternatives: either the Jesuits were spreading "mere back stairs gossip" or, the more serious alternative, what they were saying was true based on information from Fr. Leiber, which constituted a "scandalous betrayal of trust." Eventually, Fenton settled on the latter more shocking alternative as the true state of affairs. The Jesuits were working to undermine the traditional teaching of the church on church-state relations, and they found a sympathetic ear in the pope.

"As far as I can make out at the moment, the contentions of Leiber are true, even if his statements as I explained to North, are scandalous as a betrayal of trust. Apparently, the Pope as a private theologian does approve of Murray or at least is not unsympathetic with him. But this is not a doctrine which he attempts to teach or to support, even in his capacity as a private theologian. On the other hand, the one authoritative statement which has come from him has upheld the Ottaviani thesis. There is a parallel in the case of Pius XI. According to Yele, our old rector, the old man held some weird opinions as a personal theologian. The Pius XII case seems to be a case in which the divine protection of Catholic doctrine has become for all interests and purposes, visible."[13]

In spite of the unsettling information he learned about the Jesuits, Fenton sounded hopeful while awaiting his passage to New York: "In one way the trip was much more successful than I had any reason to imagine it could be. There is a good chance that I have taken a leading part in an action which may turn out to be one of the most important in the history of the Catholic Church in the USA. There seems to be ample evidence that the big boys over there are working in the right direction. There is also a good chance, unfortunately, that their decision may be overruled. It may be that the March 25 affair was actually providential for us. Anyway, the whole business will be a major incident in history."[14]

47
FOUR SECRET ERRONEOUS PROPOSITIONS

Connell continued reporting on the deteriorating doctrinal situation in the U.S. and the growing complicity of the U.S. Catholic institutions in promoting doctrinal confusion. In a July 26 letter to Ottaviani, Connell reported on a "news bulletin from the NCWC containing portions of another article by Fr. Murray. I have underlined certain statements which I regard as ambiguous, to say the least. I am sure that the ideas of Fr. Murray will continue to spread through our country, until the Holy See takes a stand. As I have previously stated to your Eminence, I believe that the paper which Fr. Murray read at the Chicago meeting of the Catholic Theological Society of America (1948) represents the most complete presentation of his theory – that the civil government is bound only by the natural law, not by the revealed positive law of Jesus Christ. If this view of Fr. Murray is accepted, a person would have to hold that the Catholic Church has been in error for centuries."[1]

Connell concluded his letter with yet another urgent plea for a statement from the Vatican: "I trust, Your Eminence, that the Holy See will soon take action on this important matter. I am firmly convinced that the faith of millions of Catholics in the United States is in danger. I beg of Your Eminence to do all that is possible to help the Church in our country."[2]

At this point, it looked as if Fenton's and Connell's efforts were gaining traction in Rome. In August, Fr. McCormick of the American office to the Jesuit Roman Headquarters told Murray not to attack DiMeglio and that someone else, preferably not a Jesuit, was to respond to DiMeglio. This would avoid the perception the Church-State debate was a "battle against the Jesuits," even though the facts supported that perception. The real fight was between Catholics and Americanists. As some indication that the Americanists were losing ground, Murray hinted in an August 18, 1954 letter to McCormick that he had made a personal apology to Ottaviani at the instigation of the Father General of the Jesuit Order.[3]

Rome took a puzzling course of action in response. On October 28, 1954, Fenton received his copy of the Holy Office's Condemnation of Four Erroneous Propositions, entitled the "Proposizioni Dottrinali Erronee." The document, which had been sent to Fenton and Connell by the Apostolic Delegate to the United States under seal of the Holy Office, contained four statements that were deemed to be doctrinal errors:

"a) The Catholic confessional State, professing itself as such, is not an ideal to which organized political society is universally obliged. b) Full religious liberty can be considered as a valid political ideal in a truly democratic State. c) The State organized on a genuinely democratic basis must be considered to have done its duty when it has guaranteed the freedom of the Church by a general guarantee of liberty of religion. d) It is true that Leo XIII had said: '...civitates...debent eum in colendo numine morem usurpare modumque quo coli se Deus ipse demonstravit velle'[4] (Enc. Immortale Dei). Words such as these can be understood as referring to the State considered as organized on a basis other than that of the perfectly democratic State but to this latter strictly speaking are not applicable."[5]

Fenton immediately understood the consequences of this condemnation. On the day of receipt, Fenton wrote in his diary: "X must have retractions printed and added to CCIWA [*Catholic Church in World*

Affairs, the Notre Dame publication which contained Murray's essay]. Vecchio and I are to see how and when this is done. CCIWA is on sale today without corrections or retractions in Washington branch of Newman Bookshops."[6]

Fenton and Connell tried to keep Murray from speaking at Catholic institutions, where he was being described—in the *Western Michigan Catholic,* to give just one example—as "an authority on Church and State." [7] On October 30, Connell wrote to the Aquinas School of Theology in Grand Rapids, Michigan, requesting a copy of Murray's comments because "As you doubtless know, I have had a controversy with Fr. Murray on this matter. I believe his views are erroneous and been dangerous from the traditional Catholic standpoint. So I am relying on your charitable help."[8]

Rumors abounded. In a letter dated November 6, 1954, Connell informed Cicognani that "one of the priests of the University who returned from Rome last week said that it is common knowledge in Rome that Father Murray, SJ, has been ordered to retract his views. I convey this information to Your Excellency in order that you may know the source of any reports on this matter that may be circulated in our country."[9] The rumors reached Murray, who wrote Clare telling her he heard "that, of some fifty-odd propositions culled from my obscure works, some twenty-odd were condemned. Etc. If you should happen to hear any more of this effort, you can say that it is all (a). false, and (b). calumnious......"[10]

As the year 1954 came to an end, Connell reported to Ottaviani that CUA's School of Sacred Theology had more students "now than we have had for many previous years. Our students come from more than 50 dioceses of the United States and from about 35 Religious Orders." But, in spite of that good news, nothing had changed on the doctrinal front: "As far as I know Father Murray and his followers remain form [sic] in their opinions." In closing, Connell once again pleaded for a public condemnation of Murray's views: "I fear that these erroneous notions will continue to spread, unless the Holy See makes a public statement on the matter."[11]

PART XII

THE AMERICANS INVENT GLOBALIZATION (1954-1955)

48

THE PRINCETON CONFERENCE, MAY 1954

Shortly after officially leaving the Eisenhower administration, C.D. Jackson had lunch with Secretary of State John Foster Dulles, at which Dulles asked Jackson if he "had any new ideas to help in the basic struggle against Communist infiltration and encroachment." Jackson proposed the concept of a World Economic Policy for world economic growth to replace the vestigial remains of the Marshall Plan concept, which was "reconstruction and rehabilitation in response to dire emergencies."[1] Since the Soviet Union was "no more immune to certain economic laws than anyone else," economics could be used as a weapon: "a World Economic Policy by the U.S. which was in the past desirable as a <u>defensive</u> measure against further Communist encroachment, has now become the one <u>essential</u> offensive measure to roll back imperial Communism."[2]

Henry Luce advocated a World Economic Plan or WEP[3] for years before Jackson met with Dulles. Jackson, serving in the Eisenhower White House, tried hard to get the President interested in it, but to no avail. Because of the apathy among administration officials and Eisenhower's preoccupation with curtailing nuclear weapons,[4] Luce called a conference at which leaders of banking, industry, labor, intelligence, and government could lay out a plan to extend the power of American finance and the American dollar around the world. This would necessitate the re-engineering of those societies to encourage consumption and the unlimited acquisition and enjoyment of wealth. To bring that about, America was portrayed as the antidote to a dark totalitarian Soviet Communism. If, after the conference, the U.S. government was still not on board with the WEP, Luce could use his influential magazines to spread the message and turn public opinion his way.

PRINCETON 1954

C.D. Jackson presided over the unofficial and "off the record" Time, Inc. sponsored conference on the WEP at the Princeton Inn on May 15-16, 1954. The list of attendees revealed Luce's influence. There were representatives from the Department of Commerce, the Department of Treasury, the Atomic Energy Commission, the United States Information Agency, MIT, a number of banks including Chase National, various think tanks, Harvard University, the United Steelworkers, and of special note, Allen Dulles, the Director of the CIA.[5] Many of the same people from the 1952 Princeton meeting on political warfare were present at this event. These people were present in their unofficial or individual capacities.[6] The conference proposed one major theme: America had to create an environment throughout the world that assured stability, democracy, individualism, and other American principles, all of which served private capital. Once this environment was created, economic colonization would follow, of course.

Five major reports provided the basis for discussion. Taken together, these reports described "the proper relationship between foreign <u>economic</u> policy and the broader objectives of foreign policy in general" and revealed America's blueprint for ruling the world.[7] Finance was a crucial factor in implementing this rule. As Gordon Gray put it in his report: The "objective of American foreign economic policy is 'to encourage among the nations of the free world those economic conditions and relationships essential for the development of stable democratic societies willing and able to defend themselves and raise the living standards of their peoples." To bring this about, America had to set "an example in encouraging other countries to adopt the more liberal trade policies all know to be necessary if the world's payments problems are to be overcome." International cooperation, the reduction of tariffs, and the abolition of fear of competition from "cheap foreign labor" needed encouragement.[8] The elites wanted access to foreign markets, both as consumers of products produced in America and as recipients of loans, not grants, which allowed them to buy those products, thereby going into debt and becoming more dependent on the WEP.

After the five major panels presented their reports, the discussion began. Walt Rostow enumerated four interests for creating a world economic policy. The first two dealt with providing the economic base to support military forces defending against a Soviet threat. The third interest involved improving or strengthening the American economy by growing Free World economies. The fourth interest, "which is hard to state": "appeals to something quite deep and powerful in the country. It is that quite aside from our literal security interests in the world, quite aside from our literal economic interests in the world, there is, if you like, an authentic American ideological interest in the world, and it is that other societies develop not in the image of the United States, but according to some version of the humanistic tradition which is appropriate to their culture.....[W]e do have a faith that if men are making their choices without economic frustration, without social frustration and without military danger – we have a faith, and there is a lot to back us – that they will opt for societies which can live congenially with ourselves and give it an environment in which we don't become a democratic garrison...."[9]

Lest all this sound too vaguely humanitarian, participants like Arthur Flemming felt that he needed to clarify phrases like "to promote the health and growth of the free world economy." In order to be comprehensible, vague terms like growth needed to be viewed through the lens of American individualism: "What do you mean by growth?" Flemming asked, and then, answering his own question:

"If what we mean by growth is doubling the population of India and approximately increasing the national income by, say, 50 per cent, I don't think that is growth. All of you know my interest in this subject of population. I think we have to be sure that we are talking about growth in the capacity of the individual to produce more per capita, and to enjoy a greater degree of pleasure and a higher individual standard of living. I think we ought to make that unmistakably clear all through here. There is nothing good about growth as such unless it brings with it some of the benefits to the individual."[10]

Loans, not grants, were to be issued from the U.S. to help the developing countries become bigger consumers. Shorn of all the humanitarian verbiage, Luce's WEP came down to the promotion of consumerism and debt through the social re-engineering of traditional societies, like Spain, which Rostow proposed as a paradigm:

"Take the Spanish case, and it is an interesting one. There we have a major continuing military state, as near as we can see it. Bobby, aware of this, was very worried about the kind of impact we might have on the political and social setting of a place where we have a military installation.....We cannot evade the social, political and other consequences by putting bases in, and it means we may want now to begin to think about what kind of evolution is likely to take place in Spain, partly under the impact of this, and at least not to freeze into the position where our only political and economic and social view about Spain is, 'God, we have to keep it as it is now, or our military base is in danger.' It may well be that our problem in looking ahead then or twenty years is to assist Spain in making some kind of transition which would still give us our base....We cannot avoid either from our actions or other things, having the existence of these explosive and exciting examples that start people's expectations. It just means we have to back our play to make sure the thing doesn't get frustrated and go into the kind of Iranian crisis we had."[11]

Labor was no different than capital as to how they viewed the issue. The union chief, David McDonald, said, "What has made America great, people wanting things, and other people making people want things."[12] Robert Garner knew the importance of "the psychological approach so that they want" things.[13] Samuel Anderson understood that debt was essential in giving the capitalists pre-eminence, something he made clear in discussing the Middle East and oil production:

"This is an idea that came out of the conversation with Allen Dulles yesterday. I throw it out to get somebody started thinking about it. The Middle East has these perfectly enormous resources of oil....Why can't we start to dream up a scheme under which the United States would be the catalyst or would help or get into the act of forming a method by which some of these resources that don't flow with the oil, could be used for development in the Middle East. All of these sovereignties are in the Moslem [sic] world, and practically all of them find it against their religion to lend money at interest, or to receive interest or to charge interest. There must be some way around that one."[14]

According to C.D. Jackson, it was most important to get people to want to "carry the torch" for the Americans, which was a way to remake traditional societies into something desired by the American elites:

"If there has been one thing to point to as the great failure of our propaganda or psychological warfare, or whatever the hell you want to call it, abroad, it has been that we have not succeeded in generating it or in stimulating within those countries the little groups of natives who would be willing to carry the torch, and on whom we could rely just in the same way, as conversely, the Commies have found the American natives and the French natives and the English natives to carry their torch."[15]

The "story of America" had to be told while engaging small groups emotionally, according to Jackson and Garner, who then explained that more could be done when people were emotionally involved.[16] Social structures needed to change, and this involved targeting fundamental principles of social organization, such as in Italy, another Catholic country, said Rostow:

"The problem in Italy is having to work through normal diplomacy in bringing our resources an energies to bear on the key problem of the South and of the North. We have only gotten a look in on the impact on the problem in the South which is not dissimilar to that of India.....I wouldn't hinge the Italian thing on corruption. I would be more sympathetic to the Italians. I do think we have had a government which had deep political and social inhibitions on its coming to grips with its village problems...."[17]

Aid had to be tied to certain conditions. Dulles complained that with the Marshall Plan, "we ought to have made more conditions and laid down more certain conditions."[18] The discussion shifted to food and how its consumption was an important part of the American plan to keep and extend economic power. C.D. Jackson said, "Food is one of the great weapons that we have." [19] Anderson was clearer: "We will have to find some scheme, some new scheme for subsidizing the consumption of food. So what we give away represents in effect a carefully designed program to create the consumption in those places where we know it is low now and where we think we can get actual benefit out of the increased consumption for our own policy and for the position of the United States...but if they can buy more food with a subsidizing scheme consumption so that the price of the item in that country is low without breaking the international market on wheat."[20]

Stassen said that foreign countries would either have to buy food or other goods, or the U.S. would take their gold.[21] C.D. Jackson corrected one panelist who said that all of this would somehow help those around the world lead a more abundant life. C.D. said, "It isn't for a more abundant life, or something or other. It has got to do with the United States of America, and the future."[22] Jackson emphasized an increase in economic warfare as one way in which the U.S. could succeed in dominating East-West trade.[23]

As the conference wound down, the participants agreed to draft a document that called for increasing the national income of the Free World from $600 billion to $2 trillion. Part of that document should list possible roadblocks to implementing this plan.[24]

COMPENSATING FOR THE LOSS OF STALIN

The Princeton Conference, which had the support of the President,[25] took place one year after the death of Stalin, which precipitated a "general crisis in its [America's] relations to the world" due to the reduction of the "political cohesion and, therefore, the effective strength of the

Free World....over the past year." In less opaque language, the essence of the "crisis of 1954" concerned the possibility that peace might break out and bring an end to the Cold War. The absence of Stalin as bogeyman could lead "men and women throughout the Free World... to question whether the interests and objectives of the United States conform to their interests and objectives." The cold warriors feared that "without effective American leadership, the Free World is a diffuse and shapeless grouping, highly vulnerable to the unified and purposeful probing of the Soviet Bloc."[26]

The solution to this crisis was more psychological and economic warfare, or, as Eisenhower's speeches from April 16 and December 8 of the previous year indicated, "effective and constructive action" in reasserting "American purposes . . . backed by new and sustained lines of action. . . over the full spectrum of national politics, formal diplomacy, high-level statements, and our foreign military, economic, and psychological operations." Foreign economic policy played a decisive role in "recapturing the unity and sense of common purpose of the Free World alliance." While the "crisis of 1954" could not be "wholly resolved by economic means... appropriate economic action, undertaken in the right political framework, conducted on a sufficient scale, and sustained over a sufficient period may be the decisive element in its resolution."[27]

While each society was not to be molded "in our own image," that meant only that the form of economic growth be found that is "appropriate to its own traditions, values, and aspirations." This was revised to be the following: "It is the immediate purpose of the foreign economic policy of the United States to participate in a partnership with the nations and peoples of the free world designed to promote the health and growth of the free world economy. By economic growth we mean a sustained increase in production per head, which gives or promises to give a higher real income to every free world citizen.... We believe material progress to be a necessary foundation for more far reaching American aspirations for a civilization in which human dignity, freedom and respect for the individual can flourish, and in which societies based on these principles can effectively defend themselves. The concrete specifics of foreign economic policy must be related integrally to the

American dream both in our own thinking and that of the rest of the world."[28]

America provided leadership "diplomatically, militarily, economically, and ideologically." Countries such as Germany, Japan, and the UK had to be allowed sufficient markets so as to "purchase from their own resources the imports they need to support rising standards of living." Democratic societies can have a growth process that is sustained as long as "its purposes are understood and shared by the workers and peasants who must carry it through, and this demands an equitable distribution of the growing national income, as well as freedom to organize." This requires "complex and difficult changes that go deep into a society. The job must be done mainly within the country itself, on local initiative. The job takes time. But important help from outside is possible." Hence, it was recognized that there was a need for capital, science, education, and enterprise.[29]

As to capital, the conference recognized that "International private capital flows have been held up by political and psychological blocks which have perceptibly diminished although by no means disappeared. It may well be appropriate for the capital importing countries to explore now a free world code for capital movements, which incorporated these best lessons of recent experience in protecting both the national sovereignty of the recipient and the legitimate economic interests of the lender." There was also to be the transfer of "know how" and international collaboration between "universities, management associations, medical societies, and trade unions for education, research, and training...." Finally, the conference recognized that consumerism and debt were two sides of the same coin because "capital-exporting or creditor countries such as the U.S. must be willing to accept imports liberally if the debtor countries are to earn the currencies (chiefly dollars) needed to honor their debts. The U.S. has a particular responsibility in this regard in view of its two-fold positions as the largest creditor country and as leader of the free world partnership." Tariff reduction and improved currency convertibility became important.[30]

LUCE PROMOTES WEP

After the Princeton Conference, Luce's publications took his ideas and the case for a WEP to the public at large. The following month, Luce gave the following instructions to Allen Grover, Vice President of Time, Inc.: "Besides SPORT [this was in the period when *Sports Illustrated* was being born], I have one subject pressingly on my mind. That is World Economic policy. Since I seem to be almost, not quite, the only person I know who is heated up on this subject the presumption is I am somehow crazy....As Vice President in charge of me (and other problems) you must give this matter a Top Priority. Object: to quiet me down on this subject. Or join the crusade yourself. I hope the former – because God knows I don't want any more crusades....I certainly want to see Foster Dulles on this subject – and I want to be well-armed when I go."[31]

The December 13, 1954 issue of *Time* had an article entitled "New Front in the Cold War: The US Searches for a World Economic Policy," written largely by C.D. Jackson, which promoted loans from a "giant fund... made available to the have-not nations, without military or political strings, but each borrower would be expected to concentrate on those industries for which climate and resources best fitted it; there would be no 'partnership' money to set up uncompetitive prestige industries, which might require high tariff protection." Government involvement in Third World projects was to lessen, and the industries turned over to private concerns using private capital, all for private profit.[32]

Luce's magazine announced the WEP would "help the rest of the world to stand on its feet against poverty and Communism." The U.S. had more to offer "in terms of freedom, justice and plenty – than the Communists ever can." To raise living standards, the WEP satisfied Europe's need for trade while providing know-how and capital to Asia, Africa, and Latin America, especially since "one billion people in these continents are experiencing what economists call 'a revolution of expectations.'" This meant that "millions of human beings are consumed by an aching need to pull themselves up from economic servitude."[33]

John Davenport was a Yale graduate, trained economist, staff member, assistant managing editor, and Member of the Board of Editors of *Fortune* since 1937. In a "longish piece on foreign economic policy" for *Fortune,* Davenport expressed concern over the "socialistic effect" of foreign aid and proposed instead a "genuine foreign economic policy based not on a particular project such as the fund, but on common-sense principles. The essence of formulating them is to ask what in fact makes the U.S. itself tick, or more specifically how it comes about that a city like New York can survive for as much as twenty-four hours. The answer surely lies not in any grandiose plan but in certain institutional factors which professional economists all too often take for granted – decent money and a functioning credit system; the relatively free pricing of goods and services; and respect for private property and the allowing of private capital to seek its own reward. To the degree that we can help create similar conditions in the rest of the world we shall be pursuing the only kind of economic policy which will work and which will command public support."[34]

Confirming Fanfani's view in *Catholicism, Protestantism, and Capitalism,* Davenport argued that stimulating the demand for the enjoyment and accumulation of goods would "create similar conditions in the rest of the world." In a revealing summation, Davenport wrote: "Adhering to the principles of free trade and convertible and honest currencies we can, no doubt, find room for government programs to help matters along, but this at the moment seems to me to be completely secondary. What needs to be exported is not primarily dollars but belief in a system, and if we are called old-fashioned imperialists for that we shall just have to stand on it."[35]

Agreeing whole-heartedly with Davenport, C.D. Jackson wrote to Luce, Jack Jessup, and R.D. Paine, Jr. that "the State Department must be made aware of their tremendous and urgent responsibility in getting their diplomats to work forthwith on getting the appropriate capital-investment climate in various countries of the world."[36]

49
CO-OPTING RELIGION, JUST LIKE STALIN

At around the time of the Princeton Conference, Lilly was busy devising plans to harness religion to advance American interests. On March 3, 1954, Lilly wrote a memorandum to his boss, Elmer D. Staats, Director of the OCB, in which he set out the need to "intensify the use of the religious factor in Government activity implementing national security policies." The government had not done enough in using religion to support public policy, a failure he attributed to 1) the "cliché regarding Church-State relations" which "has always been a bug-a-boo to any official consideration of this effort," as well as 2) the "claim that sectarian differences and disputations would make such an effort unfruitful" and finally 3) the indifference of the planners, who did not believe such a program would result in any "world-shattering significance" any time soon.[1]

Lilly reminded Staats that both Eisenhower and Dulles "emphasized the importance of religious values which the Western world uses in countering the threat of Soviet Communism." Lilly pointed to three presidential authorizations that provided moral and spiritual initiatives in the service of government goals. One was an address from December 11, 1952, by Dulles. Another was a national broadcast by Eisenhower on February 1, 1953. A third was NSC 162/2, approved by Eisenhower on

October 30, 1953, which called for the "need for mobilizing the spiritual and moral resources necessary to meet the Soviet threat." The OCB, Lilly noted, should contribute to the "greater implementation of this paper through the more extensive coordination of member agency operations in this field." Other agencies—for example, the CIA, the State Department, and the newly formed United States Information Agency (USIA) —had undertaken efforts in the moral and spiritual fields but not enough to suit Lilly.[2]

After a region-by-region assessment of the importance of using religion to advance the American effort, Lilly proposed the creation of a working group to be located in the OCB and chaired by an "expert outside consultant" with representation from "State, CIA, Defense, USIA, FOA, and the department of Health, Education and Welfare," which would "discover and report on the actual extent" of those governmental activities that were exploiting the "religious factor overseas"; consider "possible organization, through non-governmental means, of selected leaders of individual religious groups to push for an [sic] unified and cooperative program through their church outlets abroad"; and "develop... a government-wide program which could supplement and... augment private efforts which were clearly paralleling American objectives."[3]

Shortly thereafter, the OCB developed plans to utilize religion and religious figures to advance the American ideology, ostensibly to combat Soviet Communism. A May 20 memorandum referenced Annex K of the PSB Inventory of Instrumentalities and laid out specifics of how the United States could use "religious factors" as a tool "for combating Communism." The USSR was vulnerable due to "its...opposition to religion" because:

"Religion is an established basic force which calls forth man's strongest emotions. Because of the immoral and un-Christian nature of Communism and its avowed opposition to and persecution of religions, most of the world's principal religious organizations are already allied with the sense of the free nations. Our over-all objective in seeking the use of religion as a cold war instrument should be the furtherance of world spiritual health; for the Communist threat could not exist in a spiritually healthy world."[4]

A number of actions were "already taken or underway." UNESCO was working to "promote freedom of religion among the nations of the world." The State Department encouraged the leaders and members of "individual church groups...to oppose Communist doctrine and practices." Both USIA and VOA publicized "through all available media, the Communist threat to religions and the freedom of man." A Religious Advisory Panel provided "religious support and policy guidance to the State Department's information activities."[5]

One of the most significant "Emerging Targets of Opportunity" that the OSB identified was Billy Graham, the Protestant evangelist whom Henry Luce had brought to prominence. In addition to Graham, NATO chaplains could be used to "develop a consensus that communism is the avowed enemy of religion and must be fought internally as well as externally." American missionaries reduced "anti-Western tensions arising from certain missionary groups in India," and educational exchanges coordinated by the State and USIA increased the "number of religious activists opposed to communism." The USIA's book program was essential to "reinforce doctrinal approach, particularly in the Middle East and the Far East religious groups,"[6] but more information was needed so as to determine future or appropriate actions.

Lilly and the OCB monitored the activities of the major religions. He attended the "Consultations on National Interest and International Responsibility" held at Columbia University, and after listening to the likes of Reinhold Niebuhr and Fr. Cronin of the NCWC, concluded that "this group" could make "a major contribution to the greater activity and utilization of American religious groups along lines that are favorable to American objectives."[7] The Department of State provided books and periodicals to its information centers around the world. Nearly two million books and magazines were made available. These included copies of the Bible and periodicals such as *Christian Century, Commonweal,* and *Commentary.*[8]

CHAPTER 49

RICHARD NIXON JOINS THE EFFORT

In a September 10, 1954 letter to Undersecretary of State Walter Bedell Smith, Vice President Richard Nixon recommended religious-based psychological operations (PSYOPS) as the most effective antidote to the spread of Communism in southeast Asia and suggested that "Dr. Lowry and the OCB staff can work out the details" of what eventually became a proposal for "A Spiritual Counteroffensive in Southeast Asia."[9] The Dr. Lowry to whom Nixon referred was Charles Wesley Lowry, a well-known opponent of the Catholics in the U.S. Lowry presented two papers that Nixon endorsed. Lowry argued for using "existing psychological warfare agencies" such as "USIA and economic assistance groups" to present "practical proposals regarding economic problems and political aspirations." The theme of the efforts was that "the USA was the great non-imperial power of history and a Friend of freedom in Asia, whose good faith has been proven in dealings with the Philippines." In spite of its noble goals, the government wanted to keep the real source of the operation secret, which meant employing deception and funding them as front groups:

"This operation should be as a private effort, probably with a plausible educational survey front in the first stage. Thereafter, it might...be adopted openly by the Foundation for Religious Action representing the plain Americans, who we believe, are waiting in large numbers for a practical, positive program into which they can put their concern and energy as regards Communism....."[10]

Lowry's two memoranda, "Proposal to OCB by Foundation for Religious Action" and "Spiritual Counteroffensive," presented a mutually reinforcing strategy. The use of "indigenous religious groups" in Southeast Asia "could lessen the Communist influence in Southeast Asia," he argued. These religious groups would "intensify local anti-communism," but activities in this field should be started "as a private effort and not as an official government undertaking." Buddhist leaders would be "urged to attend regional conferences on their common problems, needs and opportunities," all the while soliciting from the "local religious leaders" what they, "think should be done and how they would prefer to do it."[11]

After an initial survey, the OSB took a similar approach toward the Catholics. Private organizations were to lead the effort, and Lowry emphasized that each activity "must be developed in the area itself as contacts are made." Government policy was not directly involved, though the "OCB can find ways to insure [sic]" the continuation of a program to develop "potent anti-communist force[s]." Lowry requested that the OCB authorize a grant of money to the Foundation for Religious Action to commence and conduct this work "in the same way as its member agencies assist such enterprises as Radio Free Europe, the American Committee for the Liberation from Bolshevism, and other enterprises located in the United States."[12]

THE KREISNER PAPER

A year after the OCB started its planning to use religions, some of the religions were openly cooperating. One of the more prominent efforts was the "Statement on American Abundance and World Need," promulgated and signed by 88 religious leaders of various faiths and covered by *The New York Times*. Issued by Msgr. Luigi G. Ligutti, the Executive Director of the National Catholic Rural Life Conference, the statement was signed by a number of Catholic prelates, including Archbishop Edwin V. O'Hara, Bishop William T. Malloy, Bishop John P. Tracy, Bishop Albert R. Zuroweste, and Msgr. George G. Higgins. Jewish signatories included Rabbi Israel Goldstein, Judge Solomon Eisner, Rabbi Maurice N. Eisendrath, Dr. Samuel Bolkin, and Rabbi Philip S. Bernstein. The Protestant leaders were Ernest A. Gross, Bishop G. Bromley Oxnam, Bishop James A. Pike, Bishop Henry Knox Sherrill, and Dr. Ralph Sockman.[13]

Although ostensibly about hunger, the "Statement of American Abundance and World Need" provided carte blanche for the expansion of American capitalism through the use of food as an ideological weapon, as articulated at the Princeton Conference. In pertinent part, the Statement announced that "America's goal should be greatly expanded sharing of our material abundance, our technical skills and the dynamic spirit of a free society." International trade and monetary policies were to "facilitate and expand the international flow of goods and services." Opposed to "any form of totalitarianism," the signatories called on the American people to engage in an "all-out crusade to employ the God-given abundance of America in an expanded program of world development, human progress, and international peace."[14]

Shortly thereafter, the OCB formed a subcommittee devoted solely to monitoring, encouraging, and coordinating psychological warfare in the religious realm.[15] As one of its first acts, the subcommittee issued and reviewed a memorandum known as the "Kreisner paper on utilizing International Religious Groups." The Kreisner paper, which provided a summary examination of the status of religion around the world, began with Italy, the reality that "nearly all Italians are Catholic" and that Catholicism had created "habits of thought and social attitudes." Italy was somewhat enigmatic from the American perspective because it was unclear what effect Communist aggression would have on the Italians, given their Catholic heritage.[16]

The memorandum concluded that "religious influences at work in the contemporary world be made the subject of an exhaustive and scientific investigation in the interests of psychological warfare and of grand strategy." Chaplains were essential in that effort, but also organizations like RAND were to be tapped for their services, as well as the religious press to provide an "indication of how basic religious principles are being applied in concrete situations," particularly in Western Europe "where the religious press is particularly intelligent, alert and informed."[17]

Much was learned from Stalin, who "in reviving the patriarchate sought, apparently not without success, to convert the Church into an ancillary of the party at home and abroad." The OSB favored working with "inter-denominational and interfaith organizations, rather than particular churches, because of their greater alertness to the problem of ideological impact and because of their greater freedom of action." Some such interfaith groups were the National Conference of Christians and Jews, the World Brotherhood, and the YWCA and YMCA. The religious groups that the government favored were to promote certain messages. One would be "the affirmative answer," which meant they "should be in the front line of the effort to state the free way of life, not as a policy of selfish ease, but as a dedicated kind of life. This can be done best by the clear presentation of faith as the subsoil of freedom. The main theme should be not 'freedom for faith but 'faith for freedom.'" Secondly, the religious organizations should stress or be "well-versed" in "the ways in which the notion of each human as a child of God leads to responsibility, to equality of opportunity and to the dignity of the individual." Curiously enough, Lilly wrote that while "We can not expect full understanding of this line from our government representatives...we do have a right to expect it of the representatives of all religious groups abroad."[18]

50
IDEAS AS WEAPONS

Following the promulgation of the Top-Secret Doctrinal Warfare Program in 1953, the U.S. government became more deeply involved in using ideas as weapons. The effort received further impetus in June 1954 with the establishment of the OCB Working Group for Doctrinal Warfare. The initial members were Lilly, Leonard Horowitz, Dr. Stefan Possony (Department of Defense), Walter Radine (Department of State), Frederic O. Bundy, and Richard Humphrey (USIA). Lilly, initiator of the original program and de facto leader of the group, worried in a Top-Secret memorandum that neither the effort nor the content was adequate to the task of bringing doctrinal warfare more fully into "consonance with actual national aims and objectives."[1]

Lilly was convinced the Soviet-American struggle was "primarily ideological, with each side striving not only to hold everything now under its control, but also to sway the neutral nations of the world to take active roles" and this contest "for men's minds inevitably will continue for many years." NSC 162/2 authorized the U.S. government to "take overt and covert measures to discredit Soviet prestige and ideology as effective instruments of Soviet power and to reduce the strength of Soviet parties and other pro-Soviet elements" to "create and sustain the hope and confidence of the free world in the ability of its basic ideas and institutions, not merely to oppose the communist threat, but to provide a way of life superior to Communism." Doctrinal warfare was necessary to avoid "all-out war, prevent further Soviet aggression, and shrink the communist bloc." To counter the Soviet ideological threat, America needed "an ideology which can be used offensively, and which can express United States policy strongly and simply appears abundantly clear."[2]

America was losing the battle of the two materialisms because it had been "maneuvered into [an]...economic argument" and "branded a completely materialistic nation, as the exploiter of the world, grasping, selfish, colonialists, opposed to any change or any relief for the world economically oppressed. This is a difficult argument to counter because of the obvious fact that the United States is so disproportionately the greatest producer in the world. Thus, a condition which we should be able to exploit is, paradoxically, used against us."[3]

Worse yet, the Communists portrayed the Americans as devoid of culture. The Soviets succeeded in depicting Americans as "interested only in automobiles, electric washing machines, television, and automatic toasters, they are pictured as crude, coarse, semi-literate, gangster types....."[4] To counter this threat, America had to develop a "successful ideology" that is "completely positive...simple, forceful, direct, easily understood...." In order to succeed, the American ideology had to "inspire hope for the masses, promise of improvement in their personal and national lives, enthusiasm and fervor in its adherents, loyalty and willingness for self-sacrifice in order to advance the cause, and a will to fight." The American ideology "must be frankly revolutionary, inspiring the same enthusiasm now as successfully exploited by communism."[5]

Lilly and the doctrinal warfare working group had to return to the ideology of Thomas Paine and the American Founders to create a "long view of history," according to which the "United States is a revolutionary nation which still is in the midst of revolution.... with the shift of world power centers, America now leads a world revolution which began with the struggle of men to overthrow absolute rulers and win individual liberty." The "current revolution" had its beginnings in the

"Christian-Judaic religion which, in its very concept, recognized the dignity, worth, and right to freedom of the individual, as do most of the other major religions of the world.... This same revolution, whether violent or gentle, goes on today. America, as the leader of the Free World, leads this revolution.... America still is in the business of revolution."[6]

Acting on these recommendations, the working group issued a Preliminary Report of the Working Group on Doctrinal Warfare on July 1, 1954, a document that explained what it was and planned. The "Doctrinal Program" was "directed primarily towards the present and potential leaders of both intellectual and official life... Its purpose is to assure a thoughtful and sympathetic understanding of the institutions and principles of the Free World, and an informed rejection of communist or of other ideologies which deny the benefits of free expression and developments" with the help of private organizations such as Johns Hopkins University, the Rand Corporation, and various authors, playwrights, producers, and academics,[7] who would promote new publications through "favorable reviews in key periodicals [and] ads with crucial quotations, critical forums." Religious groups, especially those representing "International Religions: Quakers, Lutherans, Methodists, Baptists, Episcopalians, Jews, Catholics, etc." as well as professional associations, learned societies, professional societies, fraternal societies, and economic groups got drafted as well to stimulate non-governmental activity supportive of the Doctrinal, later called Ideological, Warfare program.[8]

Lilly and the working group believed that cultural programs were needed to emphasize individual freedom of opinion,[9] and that meant exploiting "existing channels to intellectual life abroad," support of "inter-cultural or other appropriate themes," and "stimulation of institution to institution relationships."[10] The "Operational Plan on the U. S. Doctrinal Program" emphasized the need to recruit "non-government groups in the doctrinal program." This meant "analyzing existing contacts, exploiting the possibility of contacts with other non-government organizations, and the development of a detailed program whereby the operating agencies and departments will intensify and coordinate their use of non-government agencies in the support of this program."[11]

"Militant Liberty" was an example of a successful doctrinal warfare operation. It was devised in November 1954 for the Joint Chiefs of Staff, which "selected indigenous people to defeat Communist subversion." The program was necessary because:

"The concept of freedom and the true worth of individual man is appreciated in the Western World; but this concept is not widely accepted or comprehended in the non-western cultures of the world. Communism is a dynamic ideology. In consequence, communist ideology can only be defeated by a stronger dynamic ideology. Therefore, the concept consists of motivating peoples everywhere to be militant in their belief in liberty. For this purpose, training must be available in the meaning of freedom, the responsibilities to freedom, and the methodology of communication and persuasion."[12]

Because of "the impact of Western culture on their ancient cultures" and the "difficult problems confronting their agrarian economies," the "underdeveloped areas of the world, particularly Asia and Africa," were "in a state of ferment and unrest...most religions of these areas have lost their appeal. Local traditional cultures have become unable to furnish an acceptable comprehension of existence in the world of today." This cultural vacuum was causing "mental and social disintegration," which "is made to order for the dynamism of the Communist creed. The unified impulse of Communism threatens to become the standard of revolt for the restless people of the underdeveloped area. The old culture ideals are to be replaced"[13] because the disintegration in the "underdeveloped world" posed a danger to the Western world, which, if not halted, would lead to "piecemeal neutralization by the threat of Soviet nuclear power." The only way to deal with this situation was "by a revitalization of Western ideals."[14]

The first objective for Militant Liberty was to "furnish the peoples of the underdeveloped areas with a new comprehension of existence, with a new dynamic idea and set of goals which will defeat Communism and support a world order in accordance with the ideals and objectives of the United States." The second was to "revitalize Western concepts of free men and to enlist the enthusiastic support of the people of the Free World Powers in the furtherance of this idea in the underdeveloped areas"[15] by arranging "to select, train and motivate indigenous leaders who will teach and inspire their people to action in accordance with the concept and ideals of freedom and the true worth of the individual man. The idea of freedom and responsibilities connected therewith when aggressively propagated, will have the dynamic appeal of a new idea in the awakening cultures of the underdeveloped agrarian areas." Militant Liberty weaponized freedom by making it "assume dynamic and constructive proportions" which "must be coupled with our other national economic, political and military programs" but "cannot supplant them."[16]

Militant Liberty required the CIA to conduct a "summary and explanation of the many complex historic culture-ideals of the people" as well as an analysis of "common stereotypes" of the economic situation, the political situation, the military situation, and the Communist party. Once these studies were completed, then the OCB would create an "ideological program for Country X" that would "be formulated for NSC approval." The Department of State, USIA, and CIA (again with OCB approval) would devise a program that would train and indoctrinate select individuals in the target country. These individuals would, in turn, target other "individuals, groups, sects, organizations," and so on for the ideological work to be supervised by the CIA, USIA, and State Department.[17]

The USIA had already gained "valuable experience" by implementing programs in Thailand and Iran and was conducting "covert operations" at that moment "in Italy."[18]

The continuing success of the program "depends in large measure on the active enthusiastic support of the American people and particularly upon the active support given by civic and social organizations to include propagation of the ideals to the overseas counterparts of local branches. Appropriate appeals to civic participation can emanate from the office of the Chief Executive." The DOD was already "considering the application of the Militant Liberty idea in relation to the Armed

Forces Reserve Program, the ROTC Program and the Troop Information and Education Program, the consolidation propaganda category of psychological warfare and certain other special programs."[19]

The conclusion of Militant Liberty was breathtaking in scope, providing nothing less than a new religion, the religion of America, which was going to furnish a "new conception of the meaning of life" to "the underdeveloped areas of the world" in a way that would circumvent the "danger of disunity and neutralism" that was currently plaguing "the Western Free World." By spreading the "true value of individual man," Militant Liberty could also "revitalize the culture ideals of western man"[20] by spreading "an informed rejection of totalitarian philosophies and practice" and "acceptance of the basic principles, values, and institutions of the Free World" through "personal and organizational contacts," covert operations and the inclusion of "as much ideological content as possible in their programs." [21]

In February 1955, the OCB published a classified "Outline Plan of Operations for the U.S. Ideological Program (D-33)," which set forth principles, objectives, and general obligations of the ideological warfare program. This included exploiting the connection between ideology and religion through grants to U.S. citizens engaged in "scholarly research activities" in "spiritual and religious studies." The government-funded exchange of scholars at the Islamic Al Azhar University in Cairo was specifically mentioned as an example of how the "best penetration of Western cultural ideas into" targeted countries took place in the cloistered atmosphere of the University." D-33 planned to coordinate "all American activities abroad, both private and governmental, including the religious endeavors of all faiths" by developing "programs to enlist the cooperation of religious leaders, religious movements, etc., of all faiths and sects therein (e.g., Christian, Jewish, Moslem, Buddhist, etc.) in promoting the objectives of the Ideological Program."[22]

American Catholics were eager to sign up for the doctrinal warfare program and spread the religion of Americanism. In a talk he gave in Sao Paolo, Brazil, in 1954 entitled "Cultural Relations Between the Old World and the New," George Shuster, President of Hunter College, claimed that the "North American is conscious...of his ability to establish a social order which, despite its need for improvement and for modification in detail, is fundamentally satisfying to the vast majority of those who live within it."[23]

Similarly, Cardinal O'Boyle urged Catholic intellectuals to join the fight against the Communists. Not everyone, however, was convinced that it was possible to fight this battle on spiritual grounds. Dr. Charles Malik felt that it was not possible because "there is little to choose between the soulless materialism of the West and the militant materialism of the (Communist) East...."[24] The Revolution of Expectations that C.D. Jackson and Henry Luce promoted was, in its nascent form, too crude to appear superior to Soviet propaganda. The doctrinal warfare program, as a result, needed someone with the sophistication of John Courtney Murray to make it appear intelligent, humane, and God-approved.

PART XIII

A ROT IN THE CHURCH (1955-1956)

51
MURRAY IS, NOT REALLY, SILENCED

In a letter dated May 19, 1955, Murray complained to Clare that his problems with the Catholic censors were creating what he called "a psychological 'block,'" which prevented him from moving on to "anything really serious. There has been no word yet about the latest long essay I sent over there for review. And I might hear tomorrow—or next November. So I hang between heaven and earth, belonging to neither sphere." Murray wrote Clare that he was "trying to write a paper on 'America's Spiritual and Moral Resources'; and I am finding it hard not to be pessimistic." In the same letter, he revealed that Dohrn and Harry supplied him with valuable information about matters of interest to the Americans in Italy. This included a report on LaPira, the mayor of Florence, and his statements against American-style capitalism and Liberalism; the political dispute between Gronchi and Scelba; the possible "*aperture a la sinistra*" by the Italians to the Communists; and the actions of John Foster Dulles and President Eisenhower towards all of these matters. He ended the letter in his usual flirtatious manner, wishing that "I had you around!" and hoping that "my little prayers . . . will find wings, if only because they are heartfelt. And I do frequently send love. ....With my new-found sense of irresponsibility I am now off to play nine holes of golf! Dearest love, carissima, and many blessings...."[1]

Murray was busy advancing the idea that "freedom of religion as a civil right can claim sanction on theological principle"[2] and steadily churning out articles in *Theological Studies* that undermined Leo XIII's teachings, including "Leo XIII on Church and State: The General Structure of the Controversy," "Leo XIII: Separation of Church and State," "Leo XIII: Two Concepts of Government." He prepared a final article on Leo XIII, which he sent off in early 1955 after informing Fr. McCormick at the Jesuit headquarters in Rome.[3]

Murray's articles consistently received positive reviews in other Catholic publications. "The Problem of Pluralism in America" appeared in *Thought* and *Commonweal* and was praised by the NCWC News Service. He claimed in the article that religious freedom and the separation of Church and State in the U.S. "benefitted the Catholic Church" and were "accepted by the nation's Catholics on principle, not as a matter of mere expediency." Murray wrote that "religious liberty and Church-State separation in this country are based on the natural law principle" that the state has no control over "certain areas of life." Catholics, Murray wrote, were "among the strongest opponents of any establishment of religion in America." Four factors made the First Amendment a "social necessity": large numbers of unchurched, large numbers of different denominations, widening religious liberty in England, and most importantly, "religious strife...was as bad for business as it was for conscience." Finally, Murray made the claim that Pius XII's *Ci Riesce* not only supported the First Amendment but also claimed that the First Amendment "is simply the legal enunciation of this Papal statement."[4]

Murray was quoted as saying much the same thing in Fordham's newspaper. The First Amendment, according to Murray, was "a social necessity at the time it was adopted," and the current situation continued "to make it a necessity." According to Murray, Pius XII's position in *Ci Riesce* was identical to the position developed by Roger Williams, a religious dissenter from Puritanism.[5] Since the First Amendment was "simply the legal enunciation of" *Ci Riesce,* it is easy to see why the Catholic conscience has always consented to the religious clauses of the Constitution. They conform to the highest criterion for all the legal rulings in this delicate matter. The criterion is moral; therefore the law that meets it is good, because it is for the common good. Therefore the consent is given to the law on grounds of moral principles."[6]

Murray sent a text of a paper further describing his positions to the Superior General in Rome for his approval "with the request that it be examined," but by January 1955, he had not heard anything. The approval of the reprint came in March 1955 after McCormick delayed the review so as not to create a stir. Murray contemplated a trip to Rome at about the same time, but McCormick discouraged him, believing that nothing good would come from it or that some would view it as Murray being summoned for punishment. In July 1955, McCormick informed Murray that the censors had decided the last of his Leonine articles could not be published but he could publish a chapter for the "Armed Forces Book" concerning Catholic contributions to the U.S. Moreover, McCormick was critical of Murray, who took "space to pay tribute to the spiritual influence of Jew and Protestant Religion...." McCormick advised Murray to abandon the Church-State issue because if not, he would be "provoking those who will not be appeased," a verdict that the Jesuit Fr. General shared. As proof, McCormick appended the verdict of one of the censors: "Textum bis ex toto perlustrato, censeo: textum prout est publici iuris fiery non posse; accusaretur auctor sine mora a suis 'amicis' in America et hic Romae apud S. offcium. Nihilominus non pauca in MS sunt perbene dicta."[7]

Later in July, even the Armed Forces article underwent a review by the censors in Rome. Murray then informed McCormick that "All the books on Church and State and on allied topics...cleared from my room, in symbol of retirement, which I expect to be permanent. When Frank Sheed returns, I shall cancel the agreement I had with him to edit and revise the articles on Church and State for a book. Fortunately, my gloomy prescience impelled me to reuse an invitation to give the Walgreen Lectures at the U. of Chicago." In a final attempt at self-defense, Murray claimed that his position was "based on the premise that civil peace, ensured by laws that are just in the circumstances, is the highest end of the political ruler." The source of American moral strength was civil peace, and Murray wrote: "I do not see that this argument raises the issue of 'indifferentism.'"[8]

MURRAY ON THE TALK CIRCUIT

The censure did not keep Murray from speaking at Catholic schools, nor did it keep him from being billed as a Catholic theologian. At the Harvard commencement on June 17, 1955, President Pusey of Harvard presented him an honorary doctorate of letters with a citation that said in part, "Son of a neighboring college, Catholic theologian and editor, the cause he serves is the relevance of Christian teaching to the whole of life." Murray was one of thirteen "leaders in government, industry, religion, education, science, and the arts" receiving honorary degrees that day...." The list included Henry Cabot Lodge, E. B. White of *The New Yorker*, as well as Robert Schuman, who led the French resistance to the Nazis and premier from 1947 to 1948.[9]

In spite of McCormick's warning, Murray kept writing. In July 1955, Rome prevented him from publicly writing about the Church and State. The hierarchy, however, never formally and publicly repudiated his ideas. It was a half-measure at best and one that denoted a serious problem in the Church leadership. It was as though Murray was punished for personally offending Ottaviani but not for spreading error. This made the appearance that the Catholic Church did not want to offend the Americans.

Murray gave a talk at St Louis University in November 1955 in which he said that Catholics had a "ministry of clarification" or a "work of discernment" to do in America. He wrote more on the topic of the role of Catholics and Catholicism in America. In "Catholics in America: A Creative Minority," he challenged Catholics to contribute something to America[10] by defending American principles like religious freedom and the separation of Church and State. He eventually succeeded not so much because of the force of his arguments but because of the backing of Henry Luce and the U.S. government. After receiving another honorary doctorate of laws at Georgetown University, Murray said that

Catholics were to reaffirm and treasure the "inner principles of free government that derive from the tradition of civility – is not this the 'magnanimous undertaking' proper to the law? And are not the men of Georgetown summoned to it by all the 'notions of public utility' that inspired John Carroll and the Founding Fathers?"[11]

Murray's fame grew regardless of what Rome did or did not do because Luce's magazines continued to promote him as he grew more important to Harry and the American effort at subjugating the Catholic Church. Murray supported and approved of Walter Lippmann's public philosophy, which was devoid of any endorsement of Christ and Christianity and approved of a natural law as the basis of social organization. He also assisted the Rockefellers in their efforts to discern a national purpose. Most importantly, he endorsed generic religious movements that Luce promoted, such as Charles Wesley Lowrey's Foundation for Religious Action in the Social Order (FRASCO), a willing supporter of the U.S. government's efforts abroad in the area of ideological warfare and co-option of the religions. Despite the Rome censure, Murray still was able to create mayhem within the Catholic Church as he subverted the efforts of the National Organization for Decent Literature, or NODL.

The threat of Communism elevated the American form of government into a secular religion that demanded unquestioned support from American Catholics, and which would provide them with a comfortable life in the bargain. One was branded disloyal for not paying homage to the American system of social organization. The carrot and stick approach characterized American efforts throughout the Cold War, and eventually, Murray's ideas found their way into the Vatican II Council years later. Vatican II, as a result, addressed a conception of man that included his search for truth and freedom and an undefined human dignity that came to validate every desire and wish of man. In the minds of many at the Council, America exemplified the best there was and ever had been. Connell taught Catholics could be good Americans despite religious freedom and the separation of Church and State, but Murray and Luce taught that a Catholic could be a good American by espousing these American ideas as ideals.

CHAPTER 51

By 1956, the Cold War was over, and the Americans knew they had won. However, they could not tell anyone, and they had to keep it going if the financial interests were to conquer the world. The Catholics were losing their grip. Fenton found that many of the Church's leadership were no longer serious about the mission of the Church.

52
LIPPMANN'S PUBLIC PHILOSOPHY

When Walter Lippmann's book *Essays in the Public Philosophy* appeared in 1955, Luce praised what he called Lippman's reminting of the phrase "public philosophy" as the antidote to the decline of power in the West and a reaffirmation of the "strength of America," which lay "in the principles by which we exist as a nation."[1] Missing from Luce's panegyric to Lippmann was any mention of the fact Lippmann specifically wrote Christianity could not be the basis of social policies.[2] Public philosophy a la Lippmann was nothing more than a religion of the State and a religion that was in service to the State, which ultimately meant service to the plutocrats. These inconvenient facts did not bother Murray or deter his enthusiasm for Lippmann's ideas because his public philosophy was completely consistent with the American Proposition. Lippmann's public philosophy supported the idea that America possesses the ideal socio-cultural-political and economic organization and that the Liberal principles underlying it are optimal for any society while at the same time being good for the Catholic Church. Murray was lavish in his praise of Lippmann, telling him:

"You may perhaps remember me from a Washington evening that we spent together at the home of our mutual friend Kronstein [Law

Professor Heinrich Kronstein]. I look back on that evening with extreme pleasure...The purpose of this note is simply to express my admiration for the achievement represented by your book. There are a number of things about which I would enjoy talking to you. And I shall not go into details here. Perhaps you will understand my feeling about the book if I say that I hope it will touch off the Great Debate issue with clarity and sober eloquence. I do not see how it can be escaped. The book simply must be read by everyone in public life, in education, and in any field where matters of public opinion are of importance."[3]

Kronstein, a law professor, fled Germany in the 1930s to found the International Law Institute at the Georgetown University Law Center in 1955. He believed closer ties between the American and European legal systems helped business and facilitated trade.[4]

Murray informed Lippmann that Clarence Faust, president of the Fund for the Advancement of Education, an entity of the Ford Foundation,[5] was interested in forming a group to discuss "the implications for education of the ideas that you have put forward." Murray wrote, "Mrs. Luce, Ambassador to Italy, made a very impressive address at an academic convocation at Georgetown last Friday, taking as her central them the concept of the public philosophy. I have asked the President of Georgetown to send you a copy,"[6] without adverting to the fact that he himself had written Clare's speech, as correspondence between Luce and his wife revealed. Murray concluded by telling Lippmann that he believed "very sincerely that you have done a great public service to the United States. It may well prove to be the most signal service that you have rendered in the course of a long and distinguished career as a writer."[7] One good turn deserved another. Lippmann acknowledged the influence of Murray's article concerning "the problem of pluralism in America" in writing his book.[8]

A closer look at Lippmann's *Essays In The Public Philosophy* shows he was arguing for a return to the paganism of the Roman Empire as the way to organize and operate America. To Lippmann, Christianity was simply not a viable alternative. Lippmann's short book was prompted, he wrote, by a "devitalization of the governing power" in "democratic states" and the dissolution of the West in general. Lippmann claimed to be a "liberal democrat," which, in his mind, gave him the authority to describe how people in democracies were hindering the government because they were emotional and unthinking in response to the issues of the day. Government officials, in turn, sought only to cater to the mentality of their constituents, and this mentality was the result of "reaction to the pictures in their heads." Returning to a theme he would repeat over the years, Lippmann wrote that "ideas have the power to organize human behavior, their efficacy can be radical." The "central and critical condition of the Western society" was that "democracies are ceasing to receive the traditions of civility in which the good society, the liberal, democratic way of life at its best, originated and developed. They are cut off from the public philosophy and the political arts which are needed to govern the liberal democratic society. They have not been initiated into its secrets, and they do not greatly care for as much of it as they are prepared to understand."[9]

Lippmann proposed the return to Roman law, which meant the *ius civile* in dealing with Roman citizens, the *ius gentium*, in dealing with commercial matters, and the *ius naturale*, which is "'the law imposed on mankind by common human nature, that is, by reason in response to human needs and instincts.' This is not, says Barker, 'a body of actual law, which can be enforced in actual courts'...but 'a way of looking at things – a spirit of 'humane interpretation' in the mind of the judge and the jurist – which may, and does, affect the law which is actually enforced, but does so without being actual law itself." The "universal rational order" was "substantial and effective" in Roman Law. Beginning in 1500 and continuing to 1800, Roman law was viewed as the "concrete expression of universal human reason." Since 1800, the West had undergone a dissolution, and it was time to return to the "public philosophy" which is known as "natural law, a name which, alas, causes great semantic confusion."[10]

The period of this dissolution corresponded with the establishment of secular states, the first being America. Christianity could not fill the void needed by the "public philosophy" because the Apostles taught something that "is not addressed to this world but to a very different one." Lippmann then pointed out the differences:

"There is, for example, the precept that we should love our enemies. It has troubled the doctors of the Church as it has the common man....St. Chrysostom says that 'it is praiseworthy to be patient under one's own wrongs, but the height of impiety to dissemble injuries done to God.' The saying disintegrates when we attempt to treat it as a specific rule of political conduct. What, then, is its wisdom? It is not the wisdom of the public world and of how to govern it. It is the wisdom of the economy of our passions, and of their education and their ordering. It does not give the rules of behavior in the actual world. It sets before men a vision of themselves transformed."[11]

The rest of Christianity was equally impractical.

"Quite evidently the ideal of non-resistance would, if literally and consistently followed, abandon the world to the predatory. Poverty, universally practiced, would sink the world in squalor and darkness. Universal celibacy would extinguish human life. All this is so obvious that, manifestly, these ideas, which we find in all high religion, cannot be treated as public rules of human conduct. They are, however, related to human conduct. For they affect the nature of man, in that the vision of ourselves transformed can modify our appetites and our passions."[12]

Lippman relegated Christianity to the celestial sphere because "they are not the practical ideals of the existential world. They are the ideals of a realm of being where men are redeemed and regenerated and the evils of the world have been outgrown. While they are on earth and belong to a human society, men cannot enter that realm. But they can be drawn toward that realm. They cannot be drawn out of the carnal world...."[13]

The public philosophy was a design to destroy any remaining vestiges of the Catholic Church, which for centuries had provided the underlying principles for society in the West. Recognizing this fact, the Rockefeller family supported various philanthropies around the world, which weakened the Catholic Church and strengthened Protestant sects, especially in Latin America. In his autobiography, David Rockefeller wrote that: "Wealthy Latin Americans had only just begun to support civil society institutions other than the Catholic Church, and convincing them to give substantial sums of money to a U.S.-based institution would be a difficult task...."[14] To help the process along, Rockefeller solicited matching funds from targeted prominent Latin Americans who aligned their interests with the Rockefellers and against the Catholic Church.[15]

53
MURRAY JOINS ANOTHER INTERCREDAL OPERATION

In the summer of 1955, Murray joined the board of the Foundation for Religious Action in the Social Order (FRASCO), an organization founded by Dr. Charles Wesley Lowry, an Episcopalian minister, and Dr. Edward L. Elson, pastor of the National Presbyterian Church. FRASCO was to be a "means of uniting the religious people of America irrespective of specific creed or denomination in a constructive program of opposition to Communism and of affirmation of the ideas of true Democracy; and of translating into practical and operational terms the concept of a spiritual and ideological counteroffensive." The strategy behind FRASCO was to seize the initiative from the Communists in waging the Cold War, and its original advisory board included luminaries like Billy Graham, Norman Vincent Peale, Herbert Hoover, Rabbi Norman Gerstenfeld, Dr. Gordon Gray, Charles Edward Wilson (chairman of GE and of W.R. Grace and Company), and Bishop Henry St. George Tucker.[1]

When FRASCO's National Advisory Council came into being, it was expanded to make room for Catholics like J. Peter Grace, Rev. Theodore Hesburgh, Fr. John F. Cronin SS, Jerome G. Kerwin, and George Shuster. The Articles of Incorporation were written by Edward Cardinal Mooney, Archbishop of Detroit since 1937, and the man instrumental in silencing the Radio Priest, Fr. Charles Coughlin, shortly after his arrival. According to Mooney, FRASCO served to unite "all people who believe in a Supreme Being into a movement having as its avowed aim and purpose the promotion of confidence of people everywhere in religious truth as the prime support of human freedom; of promoting and encouraging resistance to all attempts which may tend to destroy the confidence in religion, or which may aim at enslaving the minds of men to totalitarianism in any form; of creating an awareness of the forces bent on the destruction of religion; and of having every participant in this movement endeavor to make religious truth an effective force for the promotion of ordered freedom and the common good in every nation and in the family of nations; and employing every legitimate educational means of carrying out the aims and purposes herein enumerated."[2]

As Lowry and Rev. Banyard explained, the "major focus of FRASCO from its inception was the problem of a dynamic yet intelligent response to Communism." To accomplish this goal, FRASCO sought the assistance of Dr. Russell Kirk, the father of conservatism, to engage collegians in the issues of the day, particularly in resisting the increasing "secularization" that was going on in society.[3]

Catholics played a significant role at the first National Conference on the Spiritual Foundations of American Democracy held in November 1954 in Washington, D.C. Modern man was searching for answers to "overcome the present crisis," Dr. A. T. Mollegen of the Virginia Theological Seminar told the conference attendees on its opening day, or so the U.S. intelligence agencies were telling the world. The speakers set up a straw man known as the "modern man" to signify some sort of radically new evolution of the human character, and the rest of the conference only served to reinforce this chimera, helped along by the American Catholics in attendance, like wealthy Catholic layman and construction contractor from Philadelphia Mr. John McShain, and Archbishop Patrick O'Boyle, the ordinary for the Archdiocese of Washington, DC.[4]

President Eisenhower, the hero of World War II and the symbol of American power, told the attendees "that the most important thing in our whole theory of government was its recognition that man is worthwhile because he is born in the image of God. Fundamentally, Democracy is nothing but a spiritual conviction. All our liberty, justice, and power spring from this basic conviction. Our only challenge from within, he said, is the weakening of faith in the worthwhileness [sic] of our form of government. To this faith, however, we must add self-discipline and a fervor and strength of conviction if we are to have the maximum freedom of government and at the same time meet the challenge of Communism from without." Eisenhower praised the foundation as a "dedicated patriotic group" whose work made "the country prosper."[5]

In speaking on "The Necessity of Faith In A Living Democracy," Notre Dame's President Theodore Hesburgh, CSC, took his cue from Murray and the USIA by claiming American principles, vague and ambiguous as they may be, could bring men of good will together in a way that divisive religious principles could not. The foundation was a reason for hope, according to Hesburgh, because in it, "all of us Protestants, Catholics and Jews, have recognized a needed strength in working together as God-fearing and God-loving Americans, standing united against those who deny God.'" After Hesburgh's talk, there was a discussion that concluded "sacrifice and the restoration of faith... should be the guiding principles in the offensive against Communism as well as in approaching other problems within the social and civil order."[6]

After Murray introduced the National Commander of the American Legion, there followed a general discussion focusing on "the problem of a theological interpretation of Democracy." A number of fundamental agreements were articulated as being shared by the attendees:

"1. The religious origin and basis of Democracy in its modern form. 2. The dignity of man in virtue of his Divine creation and spiritual nature. 3. The essential conflict between a religious view of life and totalitarianism in any form. 4. The threat to religion, liberty, and high civilization presented by the rise and continuing advance of International Communism. 5. The need of a reinvigoration of our political and social institutions through the power of religious truth."[7]

Practical suggestions to implement these beliefs included a training center to carry on the work of the conference and a "re-study of the interpretation of separation of Church and State," which included schools examining religion in light of facts. This was juxtaposed with the conclusion that the "spiritual mission of the Foundation" was to be advanced to spread the influence of the conference.[8]

Luce gave money to FRASCO and asked Lowry to meet with C.D. Jackson to organize yearly conferences. In its brochure for the second yearly conference held in October 1955, the Foundation linked "our Christian religion and our competitive business system as in themselves the two most revolutionary forces in the world today. Communism and socialism, which we frequently think of as revolutionary, are, in fact, reactionary movements – leading man back to the bondage from which he has only so recently emerged. What we call 'free enterprise' or 'competitive capitalism' or 'the American way of life' ...upsets the old established order. Christianity endowed the individual with spiritual dignity; our American Constitution endowed the individual with political dignity; but it has remained for American industry to endow the individual with economic dignity.... Through spiritual pioneering one may gain a sense of fulfillment a sense of participation in the creation of a far, far better world. The future we plan for begins today."[9]

The second annual conference then came out in support of American policy, including 1) nuclear armaments control; 2) a "revival of faith in God and a fresh synthesis of faith and reason"; 3) a recognition of the existence and growing and spreading support of "human dignity...and inalienable rights"; 4) a need to assist the nations of the world "in their quest for democracy and a better life"; and 5) the call to:

"The leaders of the great religions of the world and the cultures associated with them to rise to the challenge of a global, atomic age and to labor in concert and warm friendship to bring about peace among men, unity and cooperation among nations. We issue this worldwide call, aware of the many differences of creed and worship among us, fully respectful of the rights and convictions of all men, yet fervent, in the name of God, our common Creator."[10]

One year after Murray joined FRASCO, Lowry asked him to sign an Open Letter that endorsed the American Proposition. As an inducement, Lowry informed Murray that Bishops John J. Wright and Michael J. Ready had already signed the letter, which also asked for support for Lowry's Foundation as "A spiritual offensive is long overdue against the forces that threaten the integrity of America and of all free societies. United religious action alone can launch such an offensive." Murray agreed and wrote, "I am returning the letter with my signature. I hope that you will be able to make some effective use of the document. The present moment of crisis does indeed call for whatever action we can take."[11] Later, as the American culture grew more hostile to Christianity, Lowry and Banyard hid the real issues and got the faithful to expend their resources futilely. It is a model in use to this day with other organizations involved in the so-called social and cultural issues of the day.

Lowry's actions did nothing to halt the spread of secularism, something which found expression when the Supreme Court banned prayer in public schools in the early '60s. The best he could manage in response was a private "keep prayer movement," which tacitly accepted "the current trend of the Supreme Court on religion" which "rationalized in the name of pluralism the prospect of the strangulation of the unique American middle way in religion and the state." Faced with an overt attack on the "religious" principles Eisenhower articulated in 1954, apologists for Americanism like Gustave Weigel, SJ, shifted gears and, instead of praising America, decried: "two entirely different theologies" that intermingle in our people. One has the advantage of being preferred, but the other stubbornly survives without being able to suffocate its neighbor. One is the faith of the literati, and the other, oblivious of criticism, is at home in the hearts of a large sector of our population."[12] By claiming that the "liberal intelligentsia" betrayed the religionists, Weigel laid the foundation for the great entertainment that would come to be known as the culture wars.

54
PIUS XII SPEAKS AGAIN ON CHURCH AND STATE

Pope Pius XII was not done speaking on Church and State, and when he decided to speak again, Fenton was there to cover it. The Church, Pius XII said in a talk given on September 7, 1955, to the International Congress of Historical Sciences, "possesses a sovereign right to all she needs to attain her end, even over material means." Groups claiming to be a religious society but not founded by God were "voluntary organization[s]" that were "organized for a religious purpose" and could "petition the civil authority" for recognition. Both the State and the Church are endowed by God with authority over their subjects, and they "should not ignore one another or combat one another." They are to cooperate with each other "since their activities apply to the same subject, namely to the Catholic citizen.'" Both the state and the Church have an obligation to work together for the welfare of citizens of both societies. When, the pope continued, "the laws of the state infringe upon the divine law...the Church has the moral obligation to oppose' such laws" and to pronounce these enactments as immoral.[1]

Fenton termed the talk *Vous avez voulu*, remarking that "[w]ith these words the Sovereign Pontiff expresses the Catholic teaching, traditional in the textbooks of theology and of public ecclesiastical law, on the superiority of the Church over the state. Both of these societies are sovereign and independent. They are not, however, equal." The Church, "by reason of the superiority of its commission and of its ultimate goal, is actually superior to the state."[2]

In making his case on Church and state relations, Pius XII referred to Leo XIII's encyclicals *Diuturnum, Immortale Dei,* and *Sapientia Christianae,* which claimed: "The two powers, the Church and the state, are sovereign. Their nature, and the end they seek, fix the limits within which they govern *iure proprio.* Like the state, the Church also possesses a sovereign right to all it needs, even material means, to attain its goal... " But (quoting Pope Boniface VIII) just "as the moon has no light apart from that which it receives from the sun, so no earthly power has anything except what it receives from the ecclesiastical power.... All powers...are from Christ and from us, as the Vicar of Jesus Christ." During the Middle Ages, kings and emperors were crowned by the pope or with his ecclesiastical approval and support, for "There is nothing in legitimate civil authority that does not come from Our Lord." Pius XII discussed the efforts of the Church over the years to remain independent of the civil power, and in the course of those efforts, the idea of religious liberty arose. Concerning those who were not Catholic, the pope continued:

"(1)The Church has considered and still considers the voluntary abandonment of the true faith to be a sin.... (2) The reason for the penalties inflicted on men who abandoned the true faith in past times by both the ecclesiastical and the civil authorities was the desire to prevent the breaking up of the religious and ecclesiastical unity of the West..... (3) The Church has always forbidden and will always forbid forcing people to accept the Catholic faith.... (4) The Church considers the religious convictions of non-Catholics a reason, although not always the principal reason, for tolerance."[3]

Fenton was quick to add that statement number two, "in no way constitutes a defense of the numerous inquisitions,"[4] thereby showing an American sensitivity to coercion.

The "years of conflict" the Church and state have known over the years should not blind historians to the fact that:

"From the time of Constantine the Great until the contemporary, and even the recent period, [there have been] tranquil times, often long, during which they collaborated with full understanding in the education of the same people....The Church does not hide the fact that in principle it considers this collaboration as normal, and that it regards as an ideal the unity of the people in the true religion and the unanimity of action between itself and the state.'" [5]

It is normal for the Church and the State to collaborate. When that does not happen, it is due either to the "unwillingness of a Catholic state to co-operate with the Church or the failure on the part of the majority of the people in a state to acknowledge Our Lord and His Church.[6]

Fenton concluded, "It could not be said that any Catholic state, democratic or otherwise, would be doing its duty, would be acting according to the objective norm, if its collaboration consisted only in guaranteeing the freedom of the Catholic Church by generally guaranteeing the freedom of religion." The collaboration of Church and State must be "cordial and thorough." The pope said that "the Church does not make any secret of the fact that 'it regards as an ideal the unity of the people in the true religion and the unanimity of action between itself and the state.' The ideal is the objective of the Church's prayer and work." Charity compels the Church, the Mystical Body of Christ, to this ideal, and the will of the Church is such that the State "composed of Catholics" should co-operate sincerely and effectively with the Church." However, the pope observed the trend was "'toward the multiplicity of religious confessions and concepts of life within the same national community, where Catholics are a more or less strong minority.'"[7]

The Church, however, can still flourish where Catholics are a minority and there is "no special collaboration between the state and the Catholic Church." The pope pointed to the situation in the United States as one such example where the Church flourished despite this situation. All the same, the Church should be recognized by the state. The collaboration between Church and state is not for the purpose of helping the

Church but because it is a moral right and obligation to collaborate. The traditional teaching of the Church presented by the pope "asserts that the collaboration of the state with the Church is an ideal." The pope "is speaking as the authoritative teacher of faith and morals, and not simply as one who is trying to point out conditions under which the Church can most effectively operate in a given country at a given time." Because the Church is the Kingdom of God on earth, it is, therefore, only right for all men to recognize it as such and to work with or collaborate with it.[8]

THE CTSA GOES AMERICANIST

Despite the pope's talk, the situation continued to deteriorate in America. Writing to Archbishop Cicognani, Connell enclosed a letter to the editor published in the July 31 edition of *The New York Times* from Fr. Vincent A. Brown of St. Albans, New York:

"In his excellent article 'Can Russia Really Change?' (July 24), Arnold J. Toynbee doubts whether the Roman Catholic tenet of using 'the secular arm in carrying out its mission to bring all mankind into its fold has ever been repudiated by the official custodians of the faith.' There is one eminent theologian who has done so – the Rev. John Courtney Murray SJ. And it would seem that his opinion was upheld by the Pope himself when Pius XII addressed the Union of Italian Catholic Jurists on Dec. 6, 1953, declaring that 'a higher and more general good' would justify the non-use of 'civil laws and coercive measures' in matters of faith and/or morals.'"[9]

Connell's annual Christmas letter to Ottaviani for 1955 described a "spirit of liberalism and rationalism" in the CTSA, including Modernist views in violation of Pope Pius XII's *Humani Generis.* The CTSA that Connell founded held a meeting at Woodstock the previous day, and during the conference, the attendees concluded that the Allocutions of the Holy Father did not "represent the true attitude that Catholics should have toward the ordinary magisterium of the Sovereign Pontiff." The Messianic prophecies of the Old Testament were discussed by the

CTSA, and the views expressed in that regard appeared to be condemned by Pope Pius X as Modernist.[10]

Connell reiterated his plea, asking the Holy See to issue a public statement against Murray's position. His views were carrying the day, and if the Holy See failed to act, "many in our land...will continue to uphold this view, and I fear that it will gradually spread and be accepted by many Americans." The occasion for this plea was a news release from the NCWC "containing an account of a lecture given by Fr. John Courtney Murray, SJ, at Fordham University, N.Y., several weeks ago," which claimed, "that at yet there is no certain or solid doctrine about the relation of Church and State."[11] Murray was the second speaker in the symposium that celebrated the 50th anniversary of the founding of the Fordham Law School in 1905. The symposium began on October 8, 1955, with a speech by Henry Cabot Lodge, U.S. representative to the United Nations, and concluded with a talk from Brigadier General David Sarnoff, who received an honorary doctorate.[12]

One year later, in his annual Christmas letter to Ottaviani, Connell was still pleading for action, claiming that "At the Catholic University we are striving to maintain the highest standards of ecclesiastical learning, and especially orthodoxy of doctrine. The influence of the views of some Catholics, such as Father John Courtney Murray is still strong in our land. Recently, in The Commonweal an article appeared in which he was given the highest praise. It is my earnest hope that the Holy See will one day issue a public statement on these views."[13] Within a decade of its founding by Connell, the CTSA had gone Americanist. All Connell could do was to call for help, help that never came.

55
LIFE AND MURRAY ENDORSE AMERICA

Regardless of how Rome treated Murray, Luce promoted him. Murray was a featured author in the December 26, 1955, special issue of *Life* dedicated to Christianity, which highlighted up-and-comers like Billy Graham and Murray. A full-page photo of Murray in traditional clerical garb followed by an equally flattering description of him as "one of US Catholicism's most creative and penetrating thinkers" whose "strong intellectual bent led him to the Jesuits." In the magazine, Murray attacked both the Catholic Church and Catholicism first with flattery, telling the Catholics the non-Catholics were wrong, and then, with their guard down, explaining to the Catholics why they should change, themes which would recur years later as part of the "spirit of Vatican II." These themes were the primacy of the laity; "modern man's" existence and search for truth; the existence of Catholic goodness at the heart of America, which Catholics should advance; the need for Catholics to end their separateness from the Americans all of which was coming about with the weakening of ethnic identity and the rejection of "groupism" by Catholic intellectuals; and the idea of an international community built in accordance with American principles.[1] Murray wrote that international unity was a Catholic idea, applied in the secular sense. A desire for perfectionism that places the new international community as a new Christendom should not stop Catholics from embracing this international unity, which Murray never defined other than to write "a community of nations."[2]

After dividing young Catholics from the previous generation by endorsing rude questioning and rejecting an undefined "anti-intellectualism" as equated with Catholic doctrine, Murray applied the same divide-and-conquer strategy to priests and laity. He did so by claiming that a clericalism that kept the laity from acting and exercising its competence in the secular realm was not a good thing. He stated there was a feeling amongst lay Catholics that they were wanted only as a tool of the clerics, and he argued that the freedom of the laity should not be restricted in the two important areas of journalism and education.[3] Murray's claim the laity knew better than the priests and that the young knew better than their parents came into high relief during the post-Vatican II period and was used to destroy Catholic unity.

Life used its special issue on Christianity to promote Luce's American Proposition in an editorial entitled "The American Moral Consensus." Jefferson's "'wall of separation between church and state' has grown solider with the years." Therefore, "Does the 'wall' mean that the American political system is officially agnostic and its government, as Charles Beard once called it 'secular from top to bottom?' Is religion in America a 100% private concern; or has it a public bearing? If it has, can that public bearing be defined?"[4]

The editorial defined four groups: Catholics, Protestants, Jews, and secularists, with the latter group winning after the Supreme Court decision in the *McCollum* case, which held unconstitutional a school program that allowed time for religious instruction. There had been and were battles over issues like slavery and prohibition, public aid to church school, religion in public schools, "dueling, blasphemy, atheists, lotteries, Sunday, polygamy, divorce, oaths, church property, vaccination, the Philippines, coin designs, birth control, bingo and countless other subjects." The question was whether there was an American consensus on the role of religion in America, and the editors set about "defining it by saying what it is not."[5]

The editors opined that the American Founders provided only freedom to worship: "The 'wall' was certainly not meant to be an altar. The historical record shows clearly that the authors of the Constitution were not trying to legislate against religion in America but only against favoritism to any particular church. They expected people to 'exercise' their religious freedom by worship, as did most of the founders."[6]

The religious provisions of the Constitution were a "prudent, just and extremely successful bit of legal and political wisdom, designed for a religiously pluralistic society," and these provisions were "not any kind of theological statement." The editors quoted Murray: "Father John C. Murray has called them 'Articles of Peace.'" The editors also recognized that there was a "Protestant accent to the American concept of religious freedom. Not only did Protestant sectarianism make it prudent, but Protestant enshrinement of the individual conscience made it popular." Such a design made these "Articles of Peace" broad enough to include all churches, even those of authoritarian polity." And "a long line of... Catholic thinkers have long since confirmed American Catholic attachment to the 'Articles of Peace' beyond doubt," including Fr. Hecker and Cardinal Gibbons.[7]

As proof that "there is no wall at all between religion and the American political system," the editors pointed to the comments of Alexis de Tocqueville, who opined that "the religion of Americans 'is the foremost of [their] political institutions.'" There was always an interplay between religion and the American governmental institutions. This was evident in Benjamin Franklin's comments at the Constitutional Convention that "God governs in the affairs of men," as well as in President George Washington's designation of a day of thanksgiving for the "providence of Almighty God" as well as to obey his will and secure his protection and favor. The editors believed that President Abraham Lincoln's revival of the practice of thanksgiving was further evidence. This was quite different from the French Revolution, which was hostile to religion "in general" and elevated to worship "human reason...or democracy or any other finite fact or idea."[8]

The Declaration of Independence had no reference to religion but four, all positive, to God. Man's assertion of rights, the editors opined, came about not because of man's own assertion but because they are a gift of the Creator, hence the phrase that there exist inalienable rights that come from "the laws of Nature and Of Nature's God." Paine and Jefferson both reinforced the idea that God, who gives life to children, also gives liberties to men. Jefferson wrote, "Can the liberties of a nation be thought secure when we have removed their only firm basis, a conviction in the minds of the people that their liberties are the gift of God?" And "all the secularist thinkers put together (and we have some good ones) have never succeeded in promulgating a materialistic theory of freedom which has the slightest appeal to pragmatic Americans." The nature of the "American political experiment, which in its logic and its hope, as well as in its memory, keeps reverting to God" allows for those Christians who "regard their liberty as a trove to be hugged rather than a right to be universalized." America even allowed "some self-styled materialists" who "are thoroughgoing friends of freedom."[9]

Jews, Protestants, and Catholics all echoed a hope, and thanksgiving in the "American experiment" as set forth by John Adams. Adams said the American experiment was a "'grand scheme and design in providence' for the liberation of mankind." Religion is connected with the American experiment this way: "Anyone can be a good American, but the ultimate guarantee of his freedom is in America's being a religious nation."[10]

Morality is a branch of religion, according to George Washington, and politics is a branch of morals, according to Aristotle. America is committed to this Aristotelian belief, and self-government "implies in short, that there is, or should be, a moral consensus of the American people." Each person is to be responsible in governing his private behavior because "self-government implies some agreement on the norms of responsibility, some recognition of the same abstract imperatives." The Constitution makes a connection of "our politics with eternal truth," and that connection is called "constitutionalism," which is the "element of assent and legitimacy in any form of government.... America is one of the few fortunate nations where this assent and legitimacy can be currently taken for granted." The language of the Constitution is not reverent but is "not only secular but dull, legalistic and gimpy with compromise and expediency." It must be that way "because it hides or represents something greater than itself which connects our politics with eternal truth."[11]

Delving further into the theological importance and significance of the Constitution, *Life*'s editors wrote:

"Any government, to survive, must be able to confess and correct any errors in the assumptions about man and nature on which it is based. The 18th Century American assumption about liberty, though devout toward God's authorship of it, is nevertheless optimistic about man's capacity to use it. The seats of human power have always been assailed not only by tyrants but by Utopian friends of man, not to mention blind combinations of group, class or sectional greed. But our Founding Fathers knew this. The government they designed in our Constitution was given enough power to resist these assailants but not enough to be the chief focus of their temptation. It contains, in its checks and balances and other self-limitations, a healthy dose of pessimism about the same human nature it profess to trust. It is as though the authors of this political self-limitation, who knew Montesquieu's saying that 'virtue has needs of limits,' were not only reflecting ancient wisdom, but anticipating modern theology's rediscovery of Original Sin."[12]

Emerson was of the view that American constitutionalism was a "resolve to keep our laws and institutions in harmony with" the "'constitution of the universe.'" Chief Justice John Marshall said that "principles of abstract justice" are "impressed on the mind of his creature man" by the Creator, and they "'regulate, in a great degree the rights of civilized nations.'" President Eisenhower in an August 1955 talk honoring Marshall, said, "'Our nation is ranged with those who seek attainment of human goals through a government of laws... rooted in moral law, reflecting a religious faith that man is created in the image of God.'"[13]

Lippmann's *Public Philosophy* "reasserted the connection between the American political system and the 2,000-year-old doctrine of natural law which the Declaration of Independence assumes, which modern thinkers are redefining, and without which the institutions of Western society are 'unworkable.'" The American version of natural law is contained in "Constitutionalism," which "makes our institutions work so well. As religion and human liberty are natural allies, so constitutionalism enables a human society to find its natural place between the divinely endowed individual and a divinely ordered world."[14]

Then, the editors finished with a flourish and with a doubt:

"Whether this is today the majority American view of the American system, no man can say. The moral consensus is locked in the hearts of the people alongside their religion, to which it is akin. No doubt most Americans are less religious than they should be. They then owe a vast and continuing debt to the saving remnant in their midst, who do hunger and thirst after righteousness and walk humbly before their God. They do not do this for America's sake; but without them America would be little more than a geographical expression."[15]

The response to the Christianity edition in general and Murray's article in particular was glowing. Murray had to feel some pride at having brought it all off when the Managing Editor of *Life* sent him a check and expressed appreciation of Murray's work in a letter dated January 5, 1956: "This check is for your article which is quite separate from the invaluable advice and counsel you gave us on the special issue in general. I wish also to convey personal thanks from me and from Harry to you."[16]

Murray was likewise effusive in praising the Managing Editor of *Life,* Edward Thompson, thanking him "for the generous check" and letting Thompson know that he "thought that the Christianity Issue was brilliantly successful." Indeed, the "general comment among the fraternity has been almost universally complimentary and I was glad to have had a little part in it myself." Murray let it be known he was close with Luce: "I got back last night from a week end with Harry in South Carolina. Unfortunately it was rather too cold for golf, but there were the usual high arguments."[17]

John Tracy Ellis, managing editor of *The Catholic Historical Review* at the Catholic University of America, let Murray know that his article registered a direct hit on relations between the laity and priests in the United States. Things would change, and the priests would lose control. Ellis wrote: "First let me say how much I enjoyed your article in the Christmas issue of Life. I thought it was splendid and that the emphasis was placed just right.... In the more than one hundred letters that reached me concerning the article in Thought, I detected in a considerable number a rising spirit of discontent among well-educated laymen with the traditional role in which they have been cast in the American Church by many of the clergy. The fathers, I suspect, are in for some rude awakenings in the coming years."[18]

56
AMERICA WINS THE COLD WAR

America knew it had won the Cold War when the Soviets abandoned military conquest in favor of economic competition. By 1956, the Soviets had become, at most, just another competitor in goods and services, something which troubled Secretary of State John Foster Dulles. In a letter to Luce marked "Personal and Confidential," C.D. Jackson described a meeting he had with Dulles on a Sunday afternoon in April. Dulles was upset because "it is becoming extremely difficult to maintain the ostracism" necessary to prosecute the Cold War now that "Soviet industry has reached a point where they probably can start producing consumer goods if they want to." He concluded that "We may be in very grave long-term danger because of the Soviets' new economic competition...." Dulles confided to Jackson: "Back in 1950 or '51, I spent $ 1,000 to build a bomb-proof cellar in my New York house for Janet and myself and my documents....Well, today I just would not spend that thousand dollars for that, because I don't think that is the way the struggle is shaping up any more...."[1]

Jackson, like Dulles, was concerned that the USSR might become a serious economic competitor to the West because "this new competitor, because of his economic setup which includes slave labor, does not play according to any of the rules. If an interest rate is 5%, he can offer 2%. If he takes some Egyptian cotton in payment of some arms from Czechoslovakia, he doesn't have to worry about the Liverpool Cotton Exchange when he wants to unload his cotton. And so on....."[2] The elaborate commercial and financial world hegemony established by the Americans with Bretton Woods was endangered by the "Russian competition" that threatened this monopoly.

Eventually, the Soviet Union would fail, but their failure was not necessarily due to the current administration's efforts. Luce criticized Ike for not having more "zeal" for a World Economic Policy, "law," and liberation of the Communist countries. All in all, however, the administration had done enough and used economics sufficiently well against the Soviets, who had their own internal economic problems. These problems included a struggle between what Dohrn called "political de-Stalinization" and "economic de-Stalinization," the latter of which meant a reduction in emphasis on heavy industry that took resources from consumer goods that were in demand.[3] By the mid-1950s, there was a great deal of prosperity around the whole world despite what Ike did or did not do. Still, Luce wrote, "What most of the World (certainly Europe) needs is Common Honesty, Higher Wages (not social security) for Labor, Higher Taxes on the Rich, Anti-Statism, Anti-Monopoly, Freer Trade (Outside US) etc. etc."[4]

American aid had to be in the form of "private enterprise – both business and philanthropy." For example, Luce mentioned the American colleges in the Middle East, which he called the "greatest single force for good (American style) in the Mid-East." He also mentioned the Rockefeller Hospital and Medical School in Peking, China, and the American College (Catholic Seminary) in Rome, which was the "finest building erected in Rome since the war." The latter contained a "very big chapel which is beautifully modern and religious." Luce praised the "secular American Academy," where American artists and scholars have worked and lived since 1894. He claimed credit for forecasting that America would become the "master of the Pacific Ocean" as early as 1939. The War led to a vast increase in U.S. activity around the world. Luce wrote that for "decades America has been casting the bread of capitalism and philanthropy upon the waters of humanity."[5] The mission of Time, Inc. was to get everyone on board with the pro-American effort against Soviet Communism. Neutralism, which both Luce and Jackson saw as a tool of the Soviets, was not an option. "Neutralism," Jackson wrote to Luce, "is a Soviet trump card but I doubt that it is the Ace of Spades."[6]

57
MURRAY TARGETS N.O.D.L

On May 4, 1956, Murray gave a talk in Chicago at Cardinal Stritch's request for the Thomas More Association entitled "The Question of Striking a Right Balance: Literature and Censorship." This became Chapter 7 in his famous book, *We Hold These Truths*. Murray's article touched on a familiar theme of his, which was the power of the government to act in the area of morality. Murray advanced the notion that all those cool-headed discussions between rational men could eliminate social problems without government intervention. That view prevails in large measure to this day. Civility was the highest value. Catholics then had a different view about limiting obscene literature, one which called for prohibition inspired by canon 1399 of the Code of Canon Law, which prohibited Catholics from reading books or materials that had as "their principal purpose the description, narration, or teaching of matter lascivious or obscene."[1]

Murray distinguished between prohibition and the larger idea of "social freedom," which involved "striking a right balance between freedom and restraint in society." Constraint is to provide freedom from a "host of slaveries" such as darkness, cold, and hunger, but the issue became more complicated in matters of social communication. Some literature or material could damage a person's ability to reason, but the question to Murray was, "When and under what circumstances do these influences become so corruptive that they require animadvertence by organized society itself?" After all, he wrote, the "limitation of freedom, has consequences."[2]

Limiting freedom in one area could cause freedom to expand in a second area and damage it in a third area. Also, it was not possible to know just how damaging these limits could be. Murray opined that "the social reformer whose only strength is a sense of logic may well be a menace." He cited Prohibition in the United States as an example, and he cited both Jacques Leclercq of the Catholic University of Louvain and St Augustine as claiming that "combating unhealthy sexual propaganda" could provoke worse disorders and fail to curb sexual excitement after all.[3] Murray argued against specific action by the state to curb obscenity and claimed all a society could do was proclaim the "general orientation" and hope that the populace would follow of its own accord. In the United States that was a "presumption in favor of freedom," which bespoke "a political pragmatism more enlightened than the Enlightenment ever was, because it looked to the light of experience to illuminate the prudential norms necessary to guide it in handling a concrete social reality that is vastly complicated."

Lawmakers and citizens, according to Murray, could presume that all people would make responsible use of their freedom and hence there was no need for "prior restraint" given that Americans believed in "freedom under God, a freedom that knows itself to be bound by the imperatives of the moral law." Law uses coercion, and it should be designed to "establish and maintain only that minimum of actualized morality that is necessary for the healthy functioning of the social order." Hence, even though pornography was a "corruptive social influence," Murray wrote that the laws did not have to "forbid everything that the moral law forbids." Human lawmakers "must not moralize excessively," and they are "required to be tolerant of many evils that morality condemns." This led Murray to conclude that the "net of all this is that no society should expect very much in the way of moral uplift from its censorship statutes... Particularly in the field of sexual morality the expectations are small."[4] Murray then proposed a number of rules that might lead to consensus in a complicated pluralistic society like America:

"First, within the larger pluralist society each minority group has the right to censor for its own members, if it so chooses, the content of the various media of communication, and to protect them, by means of its own choosing, from materials considered harmful according to its own standards. Second, in a pluralist society no minority group has the right to demand that government should impose a general censorship, affecting all the citizenry, upon any medium of communication, with a view to punishing the communication of materials that are judged to be harmful according to the special standards held within one group. Third, any minority group has the right to work toward the elevation of standards of public morality in the pluralist society, through the use of the methods of persuasion and pacific argument. Fourth, in a pluralist society no minority group has the right to impose its own religious or moral views on other groups, through the use of the methods of force, coercion, or violence."[5]

Informal coercion, that is, economic coercion, by voluntary associations, was unacceptable in Murray's view. Using these instruments would make the Church a "power organization" when it should use persuasion, faith, and reason. Prudence dictates, Murray argued, that Catholics must use "concrete rightness of method in the pursuit of moral aims," and prudence is an intellectual virtue or a "refinement of intelligence."[6] Catholic censors should be those who "possess professional competence in the particular field in which he is called upon to pass judgment." This norm was taken, according to Murray, from Pope Benedict XIV, and in what would become one of Murray's signature phrases, the censor in the civil realm was to give a "judgment, calm and cool, objective and unemotional." The "American Catholic community particularly needs to attend seriously to this problem of literary creation" so as to determine the good books to be read. Of course, to Murray, "society has an interest in the artist's freedom of expression which is not necessarily shared by the family," and the greatest danger was not sexual pornography but "pornography of violence."[7]

It did not take long for Catholics to figure out what Murray was up to. Bishop William Scully of Albany, New York, the chairman of the NCWC Motion Picture Committee, wrote that Murray, in giving this talk, "strikes a severe blow at the Legion of Decency." When the American representative in Rome for the Jesuit order, McCormick, advised Murray of this objection, Murray promised to meet with Scully at the bishop's conference.[8]

Murray's talk not only demoralized the Catholics but also emboldened their enemies as well. John Fischer of *Harper's* used Murray's words to attack the National Organization for Decent Literature (NODL), an advisory board to the bishops, in an article that appeared the following October.[9] When told that Stritch was distressed by Fischer's article, Murray commiserated and said that he was writing a reply to be published in *America* that would address his concerns. Murray felt that Fischer "has done a very bad job of public argument. His polemic against NODL is unjust, and his positive solution of the problem in public morality, to which NODL addresses itself, is inadequate." Second, Murray sought to "do justice to the official aims and the officially recommended methods of NODL" as these were "in accord with good Catholic principle and also in accord with good American methods of public action. According to its official literature, NODL represents the principle of voluntary reform through the cooperation of equal citizens." Finally, Murray wrote that he "felt obliged to point out that the essential idea of NODL is sometimes compromised in practice on the local level" where the lists have been used for boycott purposes when these purposes are explicitly prohibited by NODL.[10]

Murray proceeded to tell Stritch that Catholics could achieve the goal of advancing Catholic doctrine as well as "moral and social objectives" by using "public argument," setting "high value on juridical procedures," and so "represent the Catholic tradition of rationality in public discussion." The issues in the arena of censorship were complex but understandable, Murray patronizingly assured Stritch. According to Murray, obscene materials were symptomatic of "deeper ills within our society," and censorship could not correct those "profound disorders." Murray raised the Cardinal's ire with, "Finally, I think I should regret it, if the laity in the Church were to become predominantly concerned with issues of sexual morality at this present moment in American history when the basic issues confronting our country are of the intellectual order."[11]

Two days later, Stritch wrote back:

"Restricting ourselves to instructing and exhorting our own does not comprehend our full duty. I have a great deal of real sympathy for a father who refuses to allow his son to buy a 'coke' at the corner drug store, where on the newsstand obscene publications are on display. When he and other fathers in the neighborhood visit the druggist and have a serious talk on this matter, they are certainly doing a good work. When they ask their City or State Government for help, it seems to me that they are quite within what our scholars teach.... Doing our utmost to awaken our people to the larger and more fundamental problem, we must not shirk a pastoral duty for the protection of our youths and other youths.... I want to place before you this problem as a pastor of souls comes in touch with it at a time when our whole problem of juvenile delinquency is much more rooted in sex matters than some good people think."[12]

Stritch reminded Murray that NODL "is an organ of our Hierarchy," which was now aware of the tactics *Time* was using in creating division amongst the Catholics. "We knew that TIME was going to feature this article," Stritch continued, "and had reasons to believe in featuring it, it would be made to appear that there is a division of thought among us on this matter." Stritch remarked on the powerful economic interests that were aligned against any sort of legislative effort to block obscenity: "There are evidently large financial resources being used to block any attempt on the part of civil authorities to stop the exhibition and sale of these obscene publications." At the time, a New York law was being "tested on appeal." The fear was that the arguments would "center on the contention of those who hold that it is impossible in legislation to define 'obscene' without including in the definition what is not pornography and therefore rendering the legislation unconstitutional." While he ruled out boycotts or violence, Stritch reminded Murray "we cannot forget either our pastoral duty or the obligation we have to the common good."[13]

In spite of Murray's private assurances to Stritch, the publication of his promised article in *America* two weeks later only made matters worse. While approving NODL's mode of operation in general, he undercut its operation and contradicted himself when he wrote: "The history of censorship has been a history of excess. The NODL has the problem of the local zealot, operating far from the central office in Chicago, and way outside the four pages of sensible procedures sent out from it. He or she 'has the zeal of God indeed, but not according to understanding' (Romans 10:2). Such zealots are righteous, usually indignant, people. They have a cause. They want results. What they lack is St. Paul's 'understanding, which bears, he said, on 'the *way* of justification.'" And so, "the local zealot for the NODL cause assigns the primacy to the substantive over the procedural. He, or she, wants the newsstands 'cleaned up', and he, or she, in some instances doesn't greatly care how."[14]

While recognizing "the existence of a 'real national problem,'" Murray ended up agreeing with Fischer when he wrote: "He wants organizations of private right to stop campaigns of coercion. So do I." While the right to protest included boycotts, this was coercion and was incongruous "when used by citizen-groups in the interests of morality in literature or on the screen." Murray opposed NODL's "present ambiguous situation – certainly in its representation by local zealots and by the secular arm of the police." NODL's value, according to Murray, was to "represent, soberly and honestly, the principle of voluntary reform, to be accomplished on the basis of social cooperation." While claiming that Fischer failed in discussing the matter properly, Murray reserved his harshest criticism for Catholics when he wrote that Fischer's "failure is less reprehensible than that of Catholics who miss their present opportunity – and duty – to perform the instant task, which is to inject the Catholic tradition of rationality into a mass democracy that is rapidly slipping its moorings in reason."[15]

After reading his article, Msgr. Thomas Fitzgerald, the Executive Secretary of NODL, wrote to Murray expressing dismay and criticism.

"Frankly, Father," wrote Fitzgerald, "I feel that it will do a great deal of harm, because in your attempt to maintain your 'extreme center' position, you have given the opponents of NODL more material to use against it." Murray's article, Fitzgerald noted, was not factual and violated Murray's own stated attempt to avoid abhorrent "misstatements, overstatements or simplifications."[16]

Fitzgerald ended his letter by describing an incident in which a bookseller near St. Catherine of Siena Parish in the Diocese of Chicago verbally abused the pastor and others when they asked him to remove the obscene material from his shop. After enclosing some of the obscene material, Fitzgerald wanted to know if the pastor was wrong in calling for a boycott of the shop. He then brought Murray's attention to:

"The point you seem to miss entirely, Father, [which] is that we are dealing here with 'occasions of sin' for children. We are not dealing with one single publication, but with the easy availability at nominal cost, of hundreds of such publications. It is not the reading of one book that does the damage, but the forming of ideas based upon the continuous application of their minds to the available smut and violence found in the printed word of the comic book, the magazine and the pocket-size book. I would hate to stand before Christ to be judged and confess that I had had a part in scandalizing his little ones."[17]

Fitzgerald then refuted the entire premise upon which Murray had based his argument:

"I am afraid, Father, that the liberals will not be interested in your rules of public argument. They only want your words, which will bolster their campaign to discredit the efforts of voluntary groups to protect the welfare of the young. These liberals shall take your words from context; you are already the champion of their cause (I imagine you know that the Fund of the Republic is distributing your Thomas More talk throughout the country) and this article in America, properly edited, will serve their purpose well. NODL shall find its task more difficult because of it. And the sorry part of it is, it would never have been written if only you had bothered to contact us and learned the facts."[18]

Murray was nonplussed by Fitzgerald's letter and wrote a seven-page letter excoriating Fitzgerald while arrogantly and self-righteously defending himself. "Did I fail to illustrate the injustice of Mr. Fischer's attack?" Murray wondered rhetorically. "I think not. Would anything I wrote tend to render Catholics disinclined to participate in NODL's cause, or render newsdealers, et al., disinclined to lend their cooperation to the cause?...In what other ways could my article 'do great harm'?"[19]

Murray disputed Fitzgerald's characterization of both events and facts. Referring to the pastor who called the boycott, Murray wrote that it "is for the pastor of St. Catherine of Siena's Church to decide what he prudently ought to do in the hard case. But there is the further question of whether his particular mode of action ought to be generalized into a rule of action or whether it ought to be accounted the exception, which must justify itself by the hardness of the case. It was to this wider question that I addressed myself." The situation with St. Catherine's was a "hard case," Murray wrote, and hard cases make bad law, but NODL should denounce coercion like boycotts. As "a journalist," it was not his job to "sit in judgment on the pastoral decisions taken by the responsible man in such hard cases."[20]

Murray was especially annoyed at Fitzgerald's claim that he was championing the "cause of the liberals," which included discrediting the "efforts of voluntary groups to protect the welfare of the young." Murray rejected the view that writing "down certain practical conclusions, which seem to me to follow from the ensemble of the Catholic tradition, I suddenly cease to be the champion of the Catholic tradition and become the champion of the 'liberal' cause – simply because the 'liberals' also hold these practical conclusions."[21]

Murray explained that the Fund for the Republic considered both Fischer's article and Murray's for distribution by the Fund "in pursuance of its interest in civil rights," and Murray's was selected unanimously. The Fund, according to Murray, was attempting to educate "certain of the 'liberals' out of their shallow views." Murray wrote that his article had been cleared by "my own censors, by the censors of the Archdiocese of Chicago, and by the censors in the Jesuit Curia in Rome." He asked that the letter be sent by NODL to all of its branches since Fitzgerald had circulated Fitzgerald's letter to the same offices. Murray was hoping to use NODL's own system to spread disinformation. Murray promised to send the letter to Stritch, "for whose judgment and wishes I have the highest respect."[22]

If Murray was expecting support from Stritch, he must have been disappointed when he received the Cardinal's letter dated November 17. Taking personal responsibility for the censors who approved the article, Stritch then shared the bad news with Murray:

"I have talked to quite a few bishops and particularly to those who are deeply interested in this matter and are working in the Committees of our Hierarchy, both on Decent Literature and Moving Pictures. Without exception, they are of the opinion that your answer to Mr. Fischer in America was not helpful....In your answer to Mr. Fischer in America, I think that you made a demand on the NODL which was not in keeping with its competence. If in some places there has been an excess of zeal and a want of prudence, this cannot be assessed against the NODL."[23]

Six months later, Stritch wrote to Archbishop Cicognani, the Apostolic Delegate to the United States, in which he again took personal responsibility for his censors' approval of Murray's piece but went on to say that he "was considerably troubled" when he read the address himself because "the address could lead some to misinterpret our work through the National Organization for Decent Literature and the Legion of Decency." Specifically, "in some passages in Father Murray's difficult style there seems to be a criticism of N.O.D.L. based not only on insufficient knowledge but in my judgment on a wrong principle...." Stritch did not think that Murray said anything contrary to faith and morals, only that Murray's paper was "inopportune" and "there was much bad taste in it."[24]

In recounting Murray's "inadequate response to Fischer," Stritch explained that: "NODL is being taken as a target by some liberals. Recently the American Civil Liberties Union issued an attack on the NODL in many publications. We are being attacked for our stand and there is the insidious propaganda against us which would make it appear that the Catholic Church so imposes restrictions on the intellect of man that he is not free to engage in scholarly research."[25]

In the end, Stritch protected Murray, claiming that "I would much rather see a clear Statement of our Hierarchy on this subject than action on Father Murray's opinions expressed in his Chicago address."[26]

As the controversy around NODL raged, Murray received a letter from Donald J. Thorman, the Managing Editor of *The Ave Maria*, which was billed as "A weekly magazine for the Catholic home and family published by the Holy Cross Fathers," soliciting an article about the "Problem of Catholics and Conformity," a topic of "greatest importance" given the danger to the faith of Catholics by virtue of their increasing acceptance into the "institutions and associations of America." An article on this topic by someone like Murray "will perform a vital service not only for our own readers, but for all Catholics," Thorman explained. He hoped Murray agreed it was an important topic.[27]

Murray's reply was curt and negative. He declined by writing, "I am afraid I must disappoint you in the matter of the article for The Ave Maria. I do not think that I have any particular thoughts on the subject of 'Catholics and Conformity.' And I do not feel inclined to explore the subject by reason of the fact that I have other commitments. Moreover, it would not be possible for me to meet a September 15 deadline."[28] Murray's tone indicated distaste for the topic. Murray was more interested in Catholics becoming American than Catholics remaining Catholic or Americans becoming Catholic.

After his dabbling with obscenity, Murray returned to the Church-State issue. By the spring of 1957, Murray was talking to Fr. Donald Wolf, SJ, who, in the summer of 1958, wrote a piece that contained a "careful reconstruction" of Murray's ideas.[29]

58
AMERICANISM AFFLICTS THE CHURCH

Msgr. Fenton was full of optimism when he embarked upon his eleventh trip to Rome in August 1956. As he sat in his hotel in Milan, Italy, on the evening of August 12, Fenton wrote out some of the objectives for the trip. The main item on his list was finding a successor to recently deceased Bishop John Noll, ordinary of the diocese of Fort Wayne-South Bend, home of the *Sunday Visitor*, the largest circulation Catholic newspaper in the United States. In a diary entry, Fenton explained the importance of a good replacement:

"The diocese, although not particularly impressive in size, is one of the most important in the US, because of a) its predominance in the field of US Catholic journalism. The SV [*Sunday Visitor*], the diocesan organ, is one of the two most widely read Catholic newspapers in the US. It goes to thousands of parishes, and it has an immense mail circulation. If the new bishop is a man sympathetic to the ideas of M [Murray], it would be calamitous for the CC [Catholic Church] in our country. If he should be neutral, the effect would be almost as bad since the prevailing intellectual climate in the Cath. USA is one which tends toward indifferentism. B) The existence of the popular priests' magazine printed by the OSV press. C) The existence within the diocese of the Univ. of N.D. This institution is tremendously influential, and at the same time, it is

necessary influenced to a great extent by the ordinary of the diocese."
1

This was a crucial moment in Church history, and the right man had to be chosen: "The situation calls for the appointment of a man who is a theologian, loyal to genuine Catholic doctrine and personally enthusiastic in his attachment to the HS [Holy See]. The new ordinary, for the prestige of the Ch., should be a University man. He should be a writer with some reputation in literary and theological circles. The appointment should be made with a thought of the good done to M's cause by the nomination of the new A[rchbishop] for DC."[2]

One of the high points of Fenton's visit to Rome was the "interview with P. at the Supreme" because "P," Giuseppe Cardinal Pizzardo, Secretary of the Holy Office and also Prefect of the Congregation for Seminaries and Universities, seemed to be the only one who knew about what was happening with the Jesuits. Pizzardo was also one of the few who complimented Fenton for helping to identify that Americanism was afflicting the Church. "Pizzardo," according to Fenton, was "under the impression that the present evil is not modernism but something like it and worse than it. He was interested to hear that I connected both with the Testem Benevolentiae."[3]

In an entry several days after that meeting, Fenton wrote that Murray ("M.") had a close relationship with "A," who "has been the man of confidence in the office of the chief for the last six years. During that time he has also been the rector of the church and has had control of the local daily." "A" supported Murray and promoted him publicly:

"Since M started the C & S [church and state] business he has been featured in the daily as frequently as possible. This has been true even since the blow-up of March 25, 1954. Ever since that time the daily has carried statements by M on the front page in a very prominent spot. In each case the article has been worded in such a way as to make M appear as an exceptionally well-qualified Catholic theologian. During the same period M has preached the diocesan retreat for the priests and has preached at the White Mass. Thus he has received all of the prestige which the community could possibly give him. The net effect has been to make the Catholic public believe that M is a particular way the Church's man, and that his teaching has been extraordinarily successful."[4]

On the evening of September 3, Fenton dined with Fr. Coffey, a professor at the Gregorian. It was a disturbing encounter, for it revealed the purity of Catholic doctrine was endangered. Coffey "seemed convinced that all the old Catholic teaching that we received from the... Baltimore Catechism was false. He told the story that Edmund Walsh had been bawled out by Pius XI for saying that the Bolsheviks were malicious, and for speaking of mortal sin. He claimed that Ratti had said that it is practically impossible to commit a mortal sin."[5] Archbishop Carlo Confalioneri, Secretary of the Sacred Congregation of Seminaries and Universities and another powerful member of the Curia, according to Coffey, wrote an article about "the last night of Ratti. It seems that Ratti told Confalionieri that he had had a dream in which he saw the tabernacles of the Lord transferred from Europe to Africa. According to Coffey, this story is in some magazine article recently written by Confalionieri. I shall try to see Cechetti and locate the article."[6]

Fenton's dinner with Coffey dissipated the optimism that buoyed him at the beginning of the trip and left him feeling discouraged. "Coffey's table conversation," he wrote, "was extremely interesting and at the same time, discouraging. He seems to be convinced that the whole teaching of our faith must be completely changed. What his opinion comes down to is the stated or at least the implication that what has been taught as Catholic doctrine since the rise of scholasticism, or at least since the Council of Trent, was not true, and was simply a falsification of the teaching of Our Lord. He spoke continually of 'abstractions.' According to him, God Himself would seem to be an abstraction. He insisted that such realties as conscience and omnipotence were abstractions... his teaching means the abandonment of the Catholic faith. It is interesting to know that Coffey was the director of Johnny Wright's [Bishop John Wright] doctoral dissertation."[7]

Coffey mentioned the small circle that surrounded the pope. If the pope should die, Father Leiber, the Jesuit secretary of the pope, would be given three hours to get out, and Pasqualina would be given three minutes. Coffey here was referring to Sr. Pasqualina Lehnert, the German nun who headed up the Pius XII household for more than 30 years. Fenton, like many Catholics at the time, was uneasy with her presence in the Vatican. He wrote, "Coffey was telling about the pictures of Joe Malone's confirmation (the confirmation in his Jersey City Church) outside of Pasqualina's room in the Vatican. I am afraid I was unable to hide my disgust about Pasqualina and all of her doings. Last night Turner told me that he is sickened by the stories about her." To Fenton, Coffey's dualism towards Pasqualina was revolting. On one hand, he played up to her, and on the other, he feigned disgust at her. In any event, Fenton wrote, "She is a disgrace. Her control over the old man and hence over the whole set-up is a scandal."[8]

After saying his nightly office, Fenton reflected more on the evening, with his discussions with Coffey taking center stage in these reflections: "I must say that I was somewhat shocked by the attitude of Coffey. He is, incidentally, a Springfield boy. We noted that the 5 priests who were in the Roma tonight were all from Massachusetts. I have known for quite some time that a very considerable number of Catholic teachers, and men who are teachers of theology and of 'religion' were off the beam. From what Coffey said, they have strayed further from Catholic truth than I had believed. If the nonsense these people were saying (again, according to Coffey) is generally accepted in the Church, we are certainly on the way to a terrible apostasy."[9]

The faith was losing its hold on the mind of the faithful, something a young priest in charge of the Catholic radio and television corroborated. He told Fenton, "The Italian people as a whole accept the Catholic faith, not out of conviction, but out of sentiment."[10]

As his final reflection for the evening, Fenton wrote: "It is obvious that men like Coffey are in control of the Pope at the present time. Yet I am proud and privileged to be one of those called by God to combat the errors propounded by these individuals. It seems clear that I shall never obtain any promotion or real recognition from the high brows. Yet it is at a time like this that a man can realize that he is working for our crucified Divine Lord, and not for any of the instruments in the Church. It has served to strengthen my faith....It is good to be called a priest in these days."[11]

The next day, "N-R [Mario Nasalli-Rocca di Corneliano] grabbed Fenton as he was waiting for an audience with the pope "and told me to wait" because the pope, who failed to recognize Fenton's name on the list of visitors, now "wanted to see me alone." After NR ushered the other priests out, "The Pope and I were together and the only ones in the room."

Fenton began the conversation by thanking the pope for his kindness and telling him that:

"I had been privileged to write commentaries on all of his great pronouncements about the Church. I mentioned the Mystici Corporus, the Humanae Generis, the Ci riesce, the si diligis, the Magnificate Dominum, and the Vouz avez voules. I told him that I thanked God that I had been given the opportunity to work for the Church as a priest under his leadership."[12]

The pope, whom Fenton characterized as "a nice old man," was "very pleased." But when Fenton conveyed the hope "that I would have the blessing and the privilege of working under his leadership for many years," the pope responded by saying, "I am old" and then "almost ran across the room to get me some rosaries." Instead of discussing the crisis, Fenton listened to the pope tell him "that I had been very loyal, and that he liked the work I was doing," and then "left as soon as I could because I did not want to tire him. He and I were standing the whole time." The crucial moment had come and gone. Fenton's opportunity to enlist the pope in the struggle against Murray's Americanism had passed, either because he was too polite to bring it up or the pope was too old and tired to entertain it. NR "came running after" Fenton to say that the pope "was very pleased with me and very much impressed with what I had said and done."[13]

A couple of days later, at a little after eight in the morning, while Fenton was leaving his quarters, Cardinal Pizzardo's servants grabbed him and proceeded to rush him into the Cardinal's office. In a discussion that lasted about thirty minutes, Fenton told the old Cardinal that it was futile to keep the condemnation of Murray's theses a secret. "No purpose is served if this teaching is known by only two priests, both of whom are teaching at the University. In the meantime M is continually in the public eye, and is being represented as the great American theologian." Fenton stressed the need to publicly condemn Murray's theories immediately.[14] Pizzardo's response was to praise Fenton's work and then take off his red zucchetto, placing it on Fenton and "saying that this was a prophecy. He did the same thing when we got out in the anteroom where an Italian lay friend of his was waiting for him."[15] No matter how it must have pleased Fenton, who never received the red hat, Pizzardo's gesture bespoke hollow flattery as well as a lack of will to defend the faith and a lack of seriousness in dealing with modernism and Americanism that bespoke serious corruption in the Church.

PART XIV

THE AMERICANS SENSE OPPORTUNITY

(1956-1959)

59
CHANGE IS IN THE AIR

In one of his many detailed reports to Luce and the editorial board at Time, Inc., Klaus Dohrn explained the changes that were occurring in the Church by commenting on the publication of a book called *Faith to Reason* by a former Jesuit turned atheist called Proper Alfaric. *Faith to Reason* was a memoir of Alfaric's journey from faith to atheism, published in Paris by the Publications de l'Union Rationaliste in the same year as Dohrn's memo to Luce. The Swiss Jesuits, which Dohrn noted were "constitutionally non permitted," had circulated a review of the book in the Jesuit bi-monthly to a "select mailing-list," stressing the "serious motives of the apostate. . . just as much as the correctness of the form in which he separated from the Church." The book criticized the rationalistic theology of the Nineteenth Century and also noted that it would fail in terms of the psychology of today. Perhaps its greatest significance was that "a Jesuit magazine would never have treated the memories of an apostate priest like that 50 years ago just like the liberal and leftist press would not have behaved the way they did now about the visions of the Pope. This is certainly not a question of 'improved manners' but of a changed outlook in the problems themselves."[1] The Jesuits appeared to be the vanguard of these changed outlooks, something Fenton already knew.

In a detailed report that he sent to C.D. Jackson (and which ended up in Clare's files), Dohrn described the stress that the Pontificate of Pius XII had caused in the Church:

"Vatican circles have lately taken the habit of discussing this problem much more openly than used to be customary..... Officials of the Secretariat of State have been quite outspoken (in confidential conversations, of course) in saying that after this [the publication of a "vision story" about Pope Pius XII] the majority of the Cardinals would probably prefer to elect an elderly, run-of-the-mill Cardinal. They point out that great institutions sometimes need a respite and that it is not always to the good if one unusual and outspoken personality follows the other. The truth of the matter is that Pius XII has developed such a keen sense for the unusual times his pontificate has to cope with that he has been looking for unusual and extraordinary means and signs, and in the opinion of Vatican officialdom has been inclined to neglect the ordinary and the day to day administration of the Church. It is pointed out that still most of the important offices of the Vatican administration are vacant. The Pope talks about the most unusual topics and sees the most unusual people, but he seldom takes advice, and not only Cardinals of the Curia but even bishops and archbishops coming from far away for their regular canonical visits are left cooling their heels. A quieting down period of not too long a duration seems therefore to be the choice of an increasing number of Cardinals."[2]

Dohrn then forecasted with remarkable accuracy the successors to Pius XII: "The odds are for Aloisi-Masella in the first place and Roncalli of Venice in the second. After such a period of normalization usually the name of Montini is mentioned, always with a 'but not now' added."[3] The Americans knew the next two popes so that was important information.

THE "GOOD TIME MONK"

Another sign of the changing times was the rise of prominence of the Dominican priest Raymond Bruckberger, a man who came to be known as the "good-time monk" because of his penchant for vacations in

Greece and wearing American cowboy clothing. Bruckberger had been a leader of the French Resistance during World War II and was a personal confidant of the President of France, Charles DeGaulle. In 1950, he came to the United States for a visit that lasted eight years. During that time, he started a sexual relationship with an American woman named Barbara, the first of several affairs that he revealed in the waning days of his life. Bruckberger was often at odds with his superiors and admitted that "his relationship with his faith was troubled after his liaison with the American woman, one of several."[4]

Bruckberger's fame, as well as his book, *Image of America,* came about in no small measure as a result of the efforts of C.D. Jackson and Time, Inc.[5] Time, Inc. paid Bruckberger $12,500 a year and provided him with office space at 30 North Michigan Avenue to write the book,[6] which not surprisingly extolled the American system from a Catholic point of view. In a review of his book, which appeared in *The New York Times,* Arthur Schlesinger, Jr. claimed that Bruckberger was "a brave and intelligent man" who was like Alexis de Tocqueville in that he had written, "an acute and thoughtful book which will compel all its readers to deepen their own understanding of the meaning of America."[7] This was exactly what Bruckberger and the Time, Inc. crowd had in mind, as C.D. Jackson explained in an earlier memorandum to Luce:

"To refresh your memory, Heiskell and I talked to you some two years ago to advise that Father Bruckberger, extremely knowledgeable and perceptive French Dominican, had 'discovered' the United States and all that it implied for the world in general and Western Europe in particular. To oversimplify, Bruckberger thought that it was time that a new de Tocqueville wrote about America, and he believed that he could do it.

"Both Heiskell and I were intrigued with the idea, and hunched that Bruckberger might indeed pull it off. We also believed that the tactics of publishing this book were almost as important as the book itself – in other words, the book should be written in French and first published in France; only after that should there be an English translation and publication in the U.S., with possible excerpting in LIFE. You gave us an okay, and we immediately set up the operation....

"I do not think that we will get our $25,000 back in full, but that was not the purpose of the exercise. The purpose was to subsidize confidentially a contemporary de Tocqueville, and I think that while the book will not make the book-of-the-month, in Europe and particularly in France we may indeed have helped to produce a contemporary de Tocqueville."[8]

In the book *Image of America,* Bruckberger wrote that the architects of the American Revolution, while being the "political heirs of the New England Puritans...had rid themselves of prejudice and fanaticism." The American founders began "the great revolution of modern times, the only one that has essentially changed the forms of society."[9] *Time* described *Image of America* as "a kind of missionary tract for disbelieving Europeans: 'There are those who have begun to despair of the West. It is for them that I am writing...Either America is the hope of the world or it is nothing.'... What is it that the U.S. has to teach Europe? Paradoxically, says Bruckberger, it can teach Europe to be non-puritanical in its politics. Europe has consistently sacrificed man in the flesh to theory in the abstract. The French and Russian Revolutions were Procrustean; if human beings did not fit the bed of Utopia, their heads were chopped off. The American Revolution, on the other hand, assumed that the state was made for man.... that the people "have no right to deify and worship themselves."[10]

According to *Time,* Bruckberger believed that Europe "has everything to learn" from the American social and industrial revolutions, for America has "defanged and debunked the class struggle." The Americans offered a "third way" out of "Europe's venomous class-struggle impasse" because American capitalism was a marriage of capital and labor, which created "more wealth and a better life for all." *Time* concluded its review with a call to action: "Americans, Americans, return to the first seed you sowed, to that glorious Declaration of Independence....You must now help solve the social problem between proletarian and capitalist nations, and the racial problem between white and colored peoples. The West would be doomed, and you eternally shamed, if you proved incapable....of bringing that hope to the rest of the world."[11]

Jackson believed *Image of America* "will be a sensation in Europe when it is published within the next couple of months and that it will have a telling impact when it is published here in the fall. So the project has been well worthwhile."[12] Jackson was right; *Image* did become a best-seller, as Jackson explained to Peter Drucker, because Bruckberger was "a Dominican, a Priest, an artist, a theologian, an intellectual, and a Frenchman," and because he "originally came here...seriously distrusting the U.S., and prepared to dislike it...."[13]

Drucker wrote a Preface to Bruckberger's *Image of America*, describing "the essence of America" as "the primacy of the person, the live, real, three-dimensional man," realizing this meant individualism or pragmatism to Americans. The book called Americans, too, to ask a question: "Are we true to our best self today? Are we ourselves seeing the essential thing and do we even try to help others see it when they look at us.[sic]" [14]

PRO DEO AND MORE

C.D. Jackson came to see the Pro Deo operation as a significant part of the changes in the Church, which began, as he wrote to Luce in 1958, when:

"The Catholic Church looked around the world and realized that the only 'Catholic countries' in the world were backward countries. This posed a dilemma: should Church policy be such as to keep these people backward in order to have the country remain a Catholic country, or, should the Church risk losing the Catholic-ness of a country by allying itself with the forces that were at work to pull such a country out of its primitiveness."[15]

Luce and Jackson supported the Pro Deo operation because it was advancing American interests. Both men saw Pro Deo as a "foreign policy situation," not an "intelligence situation." In a letter to Allen Dulles, Jackson made this and the strategic value of the Church clear:

"If ever the worldwide organization represented by the Catholic Church was of value to the foreign policy of the United States, it is today. Not only is the Catholic Church on the side of the Protestant angels on the general subject of Communism, but the Church is also in a position of great tactical value in some of the areas that are newly opening up as a result of the confusion in the Soviet Empire. In Poland, Cardinal Wishinski; in Hungary, Cardinal Mindszenty; elsewhere, and as developments occur, there will always be some Catholic Prelate emerging from prison who will immediately occupy a highly important emotional and political position in the area."[16]

Jackson went on to assure Dulles that the Church leadership supported Pro Deo and that the CIA's continued financial support was essential to exploiting all of this:

"In Rome itself, who is interested in Pro Deo, over and above Fr. M's salesmanship? In the first place, the Pope himself, who has grasped the profound socio-religious fact that the Church in today's world must not only move forward religiously, but must also move forward socially and sociologically – the only way that it can move forward politically without being accused of interfering in politics. The Pope had the wisdom to see that by giving his blessing to this kind of operation, he could move forward internationally without getting into dogmatic problems in Vatican City.

"Besides the Pope, there is now Cardinal Siri – I gather one of the young comers and a definite candidate for the Papacy. It might turn out to be a very useful thing a few years from now to have Cardinal Siri remember how well he was supported in the Pro Deo endeavor to he has just been assigned."[17]

Jackson mentioned "Archbishop Montini [later Pope Paul VI], until recently Vatican Secretary of State, still a leading candidate for the Papacy even though he has not yet been made Cardinal" and the crucial role Montini played in founding Pro Deo: "Don't forget that it was Montini himself who originally sparked this idea."[18] Jackson emphasized the strategic value of Pro Deo to Dulles:

"Now the value of the operational link between Pro Deo and the Vatican is not a 'money's-worth-for-incidental-intelligence' value. Its value resides in two areas. One is what I would call studies-in-depth. For instance, if you and your brother could have the definitive monograph on this strange triangular operation between Warsaw, Budapest, and Rome, it should be of great value for top level U.S. foreign policy thinking. Other such situations will arise from time to time.... The other area is that as major Vatican foreign policy trends come under discussion and begin to evolve, you could be advised earlier and with greater detail and profundity than simply as a ten-line intelligence item.... The currents that ebb and flow around the Vatican, and now because of the real link to Pro Deo can be immediately and directly felt by that organization, constitute the tremendous imponderables of the world we live – imponderables which have in the past and certainly will in the future profoundly affect the minds of millions of people. They are therefore the imponderables which should also flow to you and your brother.... Even though the U.S. Government apparently does not wish to revive the Myron Taylor type operation, the top echelons in the U.S. Government should nevertheless consider it almost a must to have some kind of tie to Vatican thinking and operations. And here is a made-to-order mechanism which does not arouse any sleeping dogs."[19]

Jackson saw Morlion and Bruckberger as agents of a change in the Church's thinking. They were affecting "more high powered Vatican intellects," who were making the same "discovery" as these two priests. One such person was Cardinal Stritch of Chicago, who was selected earlier that year to lead the Society for the Propagation of the Faith headquartered in Rome. "The selection of Stritch over Spellman is, I think, quite significant, as Spellman fundamentally, liberal wisecracks and charm aside, belongs to the reactionary international group of the Church."[20] The Church was even changing its pronouncements on a number of Latin American strongmen: Peron, Rojas Finilla, Perez Jimenez, and Batista of Cuba. Perhaps the most significant indication of change in the Vatican, or "another straw in the wind," according to C.D., was "the American Jewish Committee, which thanks to Morlion has done some pretty high-powered infiltration in Rome. From them I hear that the only successful missionary work being done today in the primitive countries is Protestant and Moslem, with Catholics at the moment a rather poor third." The AJC told Jackson that "in their estimation, the Catholic Church is on the 'defensive.'"[21]

60

MURRAY AND THE ROCKEFELLERS

In the summer of 1957, Murray had a chance to explain the American Proposition to the Rockefellers when Laurance S. Rockefeller, President of the Rockefeller Brothers Fund Trustees, assembled the greatest minds of the day to produce something called *Prospect for America: The problems and opportunities confronting American democracy – in foreign policy, in military preparedness, in education, in social and economic affairs. Prospect for America* argued that America was good in principle and, therefore, ideally suited to advance the "world-wide social revolution" taking place in the mid-twentieth century. Until the end of the 1700s, the panel opined:

"Mankind accepted the view that poverty and want were no more to be questioned than illness and death.... In the late eighteenth century, the inevitability of this social order was challenged and with it the validity of the political systems that maintained it. The philosophers of the Enlightenment proclaimed the doctrine of the *political* equality of all men; the British, French, and American revolutions created institutional expressions of these beliefs. During the next century most nations of the Western world – with the notable exception of Russia – followed suit.... The advocates of political reform saw their task in sweeping away the old mercantile system and the regulation of enterprise by government charter.... Within a generation, to the original eighteenth-century postulate of political liberty was added the concept that economic liberty – in the sense of freedom from economic oppression and from extremes of want – was a necessary condition for the preservation of political liberty...."[1]

Democracy was a "powerful idea because it respects the desire of every man to share in his own rule... and must be clear to everyone everywhere that a belief in this capacity and a recognition of this desire speak to the deepest and most pervasive aspirations of modern man." In a democracy, each "individual is...the best just of the way to run his own life.... the exercise of individual judgment is itself an ultimate good of life....A considered democratic outlook, therefore, will place a special premium on the value of privacy. It will hold that there are aspects of the individual's life that no government may touch and that no public pressure may be allowed to invade. In the absence of very strong considerations to the contrary, these include the individuals' right to bring up his children as he desires, to go where he wishes, to associate with those he chooses, and to live by his own religion and philosophy, staking his destiny on the rightness of his choice...."[2]

Most importantly, the panel, which included Henry Luce as one of its members and Murray as one of its consultants, held that "there is no official creed—religious, philosophical, or scientific – that a democratic state can impose on its citizens. Each individual is free to try and win his fellows to his own views by every fair means. Truth in matters of religion, philosophy, or science cannot be determined by vote, popular pressure, or governmental fiat.... In a democracy the state is neutral with regard to religion, philosophy, or science, and citizens are free to decide for themselves where they stand in relation to the ultimate questions concerning the nature of the universe and man's place within it....." Democracy "consists in a shared allegiance to the rules by which social decisions are reached."[3]

Murray previously made contact with the Rockefellers in November 1952 through a project known as the Legal and Political Philosophy at Arden House, New York. It was a conference that brought together the preeminent, approved political thinkers of the day, including Murray,

Jacques Maritain, Robert MacIver (with whom Murray corresponded until 1954), professors from Harvard, Oxford, the University of Chicago, Princeton, and the British Ambassador to the U.S. The purpose of this conference, the first of its kind, was to "discuss the present state of political and legal philosophy and the possibilities for further research in these fields, and to discover whether fruitful opportunities exist for Foundation aid to strengthen current developments." The key question was whether "we really believe in the importance of general ideas?" The answer, according to the minutes, seemed to be a "no," and so a number of projects were suggested to "stimulate, organize, and perhaps personally direct a series of investigations and publications on topics of interest to both lawyers and social scientists" in the areas of "creating a rule of law where none exists, as in: Government of occupied territory, International relations, labor disputes" and civil liberties and federalism." [4]

Murray's work with the Rockefeller Brothers Fund began in earnest during the summer of 1956. That was when Henry Kissinger, Director of the Fund at the time, discussed with Rabbi Louis Finkelstein of both the Institute for Religious and Social Studies and the Jewish Theological Seminary of America, which was a project utilizing the services of a number of "theoreticians, drawn from a variety of disciplines and different religious and philosophical backgrounds, to work simultaneously and in parallel lines on the same problems" of applying ethics to concrete situations.[5] The following February, the Rockefellers put Murray to work on what came to be known as the Special Studies Project, which was then involved in developing the "Moral Framework of National Purpose." It was this project which brought Murray into direct contact with Nelson Rockefeller, a practitioner of covert operations.[6]

Murray's solution to the problem of "moralizing in politics" was "consensus." The point was to "erect...a moral framework within which the diversified religious and moral convictions of America cold cooperate in the reinforcement of those basic ideas that we spoke of as the first level of agreement."[7] The name of that moral framework, he told the group of luminaries the Rockefellers had assembled on that June day at the Hotel

St. Regis in New York City was The American Proposition, which needed to be implemented "itself, its underpinnings, and especially as actualized and institutionalized in all manner of policies within the international scene." The American Proposition would do three things: it would "work a discernment...work a determination and...work a decision." The American Proposition would become the ultimate criterion of action, one that would be able to determine whether a policy or action is good or bad, right or wrong in human political conduct; determine the "particular...moral quality or relevance of action of policy in given circumstances" and "enable us to decide in prima facie conflicts of duties or values, to decide on the right line of action and policy." [8]

The "American 'consensus'" provided the moral principles "that gives us our identity as a nation; it is the thing that determines our purposes; and it is the thing that lies behind all the vigor and energy of our action in history." It is "institutional in its mode of existence; it is constitutional in its contents and it is moral and religious in its origins and ultimate dynamisms"; it is also "free and rational...admits dissent....is limited both in its contents and in its efficacy."[9] Because it was "a political proposition, that is to say, that it is not a 'consensus' with regard to the economy of salvation [but] only a proposition with regard to the city of man here on earth. . . the American proposition is not in any sense Messianic."[10]

Murray's credentials as a theologian stood him in good stead with the Rockefellers, who were looking for someone, preferably a Catholic, willing to claim there was a sacredness in the temporal order of human life, which could be traced back to "the classic statement...found in the Declaration of Independence, 'We hold these truths to be self-evident. . . .'" Murray then went on to explain the truths:

"'There are truths and we hold them.' This, I think is basic to the American proposition. There are truths about the nature of man and about his origin from God. There are truths about man in his equality with his fellows. There are truths about the rule of man by man and how it is to be justified. There are truths about the panoply of rights with which man is invested by reason of his primordial sacredness. There are truths about the inherent purposes of government, and the inherent limitedness of these purposes, and these purposes are not made by men, they are found by men and found in the nature of man. Here are, therefore, certain inherent existential ends of political society....And against these ends and the measure of their achievement, all matter of political performances is to be matched. While the structure of the government is a human creation, it is based on nature, and history, and all is in the hands of God with a 'firm reliance on the protection of divine providence.'"[11]

The American Proposition "inaugurated a new political episode in the human story, in the sense that in our American proposition, the ancient truths of the sacredness of man received new political transcription in the form of a government of the people, for the people, and by the people." As a result, America became a spiritual entity, defined by its loyalty to the Christian idea of *res sacra homo.*[12] Murray, in other words, baptized the American system or consensus, which was part of the "*liberal, political tradition of the West,*" by claiming that its "central concept" was that "man is a sacredness and that there are sacredness in the political order. It says that man is made of the image of God....He can know the laws of his own nature, individual and social....he can self-determinately fulfill the order of ends that are inherent and pre-figured in his nature in his political nature....We are not talking here....about problems of private or domestic morality. We are talking about morality in its relation to national action."[13] The American consensus decrees that "*There is personal morality which is maximal, and there is social morality which is minimal*" so as to provide the "*minimal of morality which is necessary for social cooperation.*" Because it depends for its vitality and subsistence on the whole religious, moral and civilizational tradition of what we call the West," the American consensus has premises which are rooted "in the nature of man," and Murray proved this by linking America's five inherent ends to the philosophy of St. Thomas Aquinas.[14]

America needed to project all of these "universal political excellencies. . . into the international scene" as the criterion for all foreign policy and action in order to ascertain in "particular the moral quality and relevance of concrete policies and actions under given circumstances." Because there is a "relation between reality and morality, between the ideal and the given," or instance, "an economically unsound" policy "cannot be morally good." In a statement that bespoke a curious reversal of Catholic values, Murray claimed that a "policy that makes no military sense doesn't make any moral sense either." He mentioned the "revolution of rising expectations," or the "revolt of mankind against misery," as urgent in the international situation, calling for an "international constitution of an international community."[15]

In explaining the American proposition, Murray never mentioned Christ, nor did he mention man's duty to Christ and His Law, nor did he mention the Church because his entire effort was devoted to the justification—or "sanctification," as he would later put it—of the American system.

Eventually, the panel incorporated all of Murray's suggestions into its final report. In a note to Kissinger, Murray added a few caveats, urging the inclusion of "the political-moral aspect" of the American consensus, for example. He also objected to the adoption of the "Judaic-Christian ethic" as the panel's point of view because "'Judaic-Christian,' is merely a term of courtesy. The historical reality is simply the Christian ethic, which alone was politically creative."[16]

In exchange for his ideas, the Rockefellers gave Murray money[17] access to the funding offered by the elite foundations. Murray's contact with the Rockefellers allowed Georgetown University to land funding for a program entitled "An Experimental Program in Executive Education to be Undertaken Cooperatively by Georgetown University and The William A. Jump Memorial Foundation," which was meant to "enlarge the abilities" of men and women to rise in "career executive positions in the Federal Government and there exercise an important influence on the growth of democratic institutions."[18] So, he wrote a letter to Dean Rusk, the President of the Rockefeller Foundation at the time, when he asked them for money.[19] Helping the Rockefellers made one popular with Catholics in the U.S. because of the money that flowed to Catholic institutions, which seemed unconcerned about the weakening of the Catholic faith, which was the doctrinal price one had to pay in exchange for the money.

What the Rockefellers funded signaled what was important in American society. John D. Rockefeller, Jr., through the Sealantic Fund, "aided divinity schools that were interdenominational or strongly ecumenical in character."[20] Murray and others could see the proverbial writing on the wall – the powerful private interests wanted all religions to be one in America, or at least unified in not criticizing these powerful private interests.

61
FIGHTING MODERNISM AND INFERIORITY

Echoing John Tracy Ellis's indictment of Catholic intellectual inferiority, Gustave Weigel, SJ, claimed that "the general Catholic community in America does not know what scholarship is" in a piece he wrote for the University of Notre Dame's quarterly, *The Review of Politics,* a journal founded by CIA asset Waldemar Gurian. Unsurprisingly, given the CIA links shared by both publications, *Time* magazine decided to discuss this article, especially his criticism that Catholic teachers urged students "to be a sort of fifth columnist with a double duty to perform. 'He should use scholarly method to introduce into [the] sciences Catholic teachings which are really derived outside of them, and negatively he should refute, in scholarly fashion the work done by those whose findings apparently are hostile to the faith.'"[1]

"For too long," *Time* continued, citing Weigel's article: "The American Catholic has regarded himself as a member of a 'beleaguered community' constantly on the defensive. 'It is not too extreme to say that in many cases [Catholic] classes of philosophy are used to form defending debaters of Catholic positions. Philosophy is not envisaged as a personal quest for truth but rather as a predigested apologetic of religious belief. Young men, firm in their faith and lovers of debate, esteem this highly, but they escape the encounter with scholarship....Because of the general defense-mentality of the teachers for all problems, there is a marked preference for solutions given in the past.'"[2]

Weigel wrote, "'Older solutions have proved to be perfectly consonant with theological thinking. A new solution has no such guarantee'." As a result, "'New questions are preferably reduced to old ones and hence they need not be answered anew, because the old answer is already there'." Therefore, "'Instead of making the disciplines an intellectual encounter with the real as it swims into our experience, [Catholic teachers] prefer to petrify it by reducing it to a logical scheme of abstract verbalisms....'" To Weigel, "'This kind of training leads away from scholarship. The postulate of all scholarly investigation is the nagging existence of mystery. The training of not a few young Catholics makes them believe that there is no mystery. It is all objectively clear and the category schemes of the past can make it manifest. If that is so, there is nothing more to be done. It has been done already and why waste time doing it over again?'" Weigel believed the work was to get "more young Catholics into the life of true scholarship." It was "essential to woo young men and women to this vocation because...next to the contemplation of God, the contemplation of God's creation is the noblest action of man. This we must preach. This our youth must hear. Hearing, they will be attracted.'"[3]

FENTON TO ROME

Fenton's next journey to Rome was not until November 1957. By that time, Leo Pursley was Bishop of the Diocese of Fort Wayne, a fateful and disastrous state of affairs given the revolution that was brewing under the leadership of the President of the University of Notre Dame, Fr Hesburgh. Upon his arrival in Rome, Fenton dined with Ottaviani as he was wont to do. He noted that Ottaviani was "the biggest man in the Roman Church right now." Despite that, he was having problems, and one of those was the "bad treatment he was getting from magazines like Time." When Fenton suggested that he might leave *American Ecclesiastical Review* and obtain a parish, Ottaviani begged Fenton to stay: "'If you go,' he said, 'it will be the complete desarmo, the complete surrender.'" During the same dinner, Ottaviani complained about how the cardinals were being pushed away by the group running the Academy.[4]

It was becoming clear to Fenton that Rome did not want to address problems that were developing at the Catholic University of America. In reflecting on this state of affairs, Fenton wrote, "that fact that Our Lord has not called us to positions we may be expected to enjoy, but rather to a job in which we are to share His Cross. It seems to me that this factor that American Catholics as a group are prone to forget. They look on the bright side of the sacerdotal life and think of the triumphs we are supposed to gain. As a matter of fact, the true victory for Christ in this work is to be achieved in suffering and disappointment. Romeo and I are united in the thought that we shall remain faithful to Our Lord even if he is abandoned by all of those who should be loyal to Him."[5]

To make matters worse, Pizzardo was weakening. Fenton described a meeting with him: "I found that the old boy has definitely lost touch. He did not remember Sheehy's name, and after he seemed to recall Mac he asked if he was from Chicago. However I had the usual pleasant interview with him. There is evidently nothing to be hoped for from Pizzardo."[6] In talks with Ottaviani, Fenton sensed that Ottaviani was not "especially happy" about Cicognani, the Papal nuncio to the U.S.[7] Ottaviani was still talking about Murray's personal attacks years earlier at CUA. In two conversations on November 13, 1957, Ottaviani ("uncle") "seemed interested only in our old hero, the redoubtable editor of TS. He is obviously still smarting from the attack the boy made on him both in the University and in the papers. If uncle lives, the boy is definitely in for trouble."[8]

Fenton grew melancholy and realistic during the trip. He began his ruminations one day by criticizing Stanley Jaki as "one [of] these men who has used euphemisms to cover up what is, in the last analysis, a simple denial of the faith." Earlier, Fenton opined that though Jaki wrote, "a very important book...it would be unwise to accept all his conclusions." Fenton concluded, "In all, the picture here is very discouraging." Someone said, "If the Modernists were alive today, Pius XII would not condemn them. I believe that is perfectly correct. I also am convinced that the errors of Modernism are being taught today without hindrance in Catholic schools."[9]

Realizing that the enemies of Christ were gaining strength in the Church, Fenton feared a sad fate for himself, though it is clear that he also welcomed it as a way to share in the sufferings of Our Lord. He wrote: "Benigni....died in disgrace and he was punished for trying to do the very thing I have been trying to do as a professor and a writer for so many years. There can be no doubt about it. The love of the true faith and the opposition to the misstatements of Catholic teaching are not fashionable in the Church today."

Fenton saw those now known as the "Greatest Generation" were tolerant of error. He observed that "these young fellows simply do not care. They may perhaps oppose bad teaching and erroneous statements in a general sort of way. They definitely will not go out on a limb and point out any particular false statement on the subject of the faith."[10]

While Pius XII was an improvement over his predecessor, he was "not a man in the stamp of St. Pius X. It would be hard to imagine a time when the purity of the Catholic faith was so disregarded and despises as it is today." When he heard that the pope was returning from Castel Gandalfo, he described a papal address to "the butchers of Rome. It is unfortunate that he cannot find time to speak to the theologians." Instead of maintaining the faith's purity, Fenton saw that "the talk is all of lay apostolate and of missions. People are impressed with manifest results. They definitely are not satisfied with any endeavors to keep the faith in its purity." [11]

Fenton requested another audience with the pope from Ottaviani. "NR," the Domestic Prelate of His Holiness, arranged it. Two days later, Fenton had an audience with the pope, who "looked old and tired." The pope blessed his work and gave him a medal. Back at the Holy Office, Ottaviani asked about the pope. Fenton gave his report, and Ottaviani said:

"The man who is always at the Pope's side (probably NR [Mario Nasalli-Rocca di Corneliano]) had told him that the Pope had complained a couple of days ago, of being tired. Uncle's informant said that this was the first time he had ever made such an admission. I honestly think that the old boy is over-doing it. If he keeps up this pace he is not going to last very long."[12]

BACK TO ROME 1958

The following year, Fenton was awarded the Spellman Medal, and in August, he took his thirteenth trip to Rome. In New York, while preparing to depart, Fenton resolved to push hard for results. He wrote, "I think that with the help of God, this trip will be a sort of ranting binge. I have a great deal to say, even if no one but myself ever sees what I write. In the first place, I believe that I must concentrate my efforts on an insistence upon God's majesty and on Our Lord's supreme and divine dignity."

Recognizing how the media was being used to twist the minds and thinking of Catholics, he wrote: "The last statements of the weak-kneed Catholic press in the USA have shown that they still want to present the message of the Church primarily as something that will aid, or is at least compatible with 'the American way of life.' This nonsense about 'religion in a democracy' is infuriatingly stupid. Either religion is the work of giving to the true God, the Lord and Creator of Heaven and Earth, the tribute of praise and acknowledgment due to Him – or it is a farce. My October article is a halting and incipient attempt along these lines. I hope God gives me life and strength to go on with this line of thought."[13]

During his conferences with Ottaviani, Fenton made clear that his health might keep him from continuing as editor of *American Ecclesiastical Review.* Ottaviani begged Fenton to stay on and expressed his "bitterness and contempt...for...Janssens, the head of the Jebbies. He is considered as worthless for the very responsible job he holds."[14]

Fenton received another insight into the situation in America. Liberal Catholicism was materialistic and oriented towards naturalism. Fenton wrote, "liberal Catholicism bases their position on anthropomorphic, or perhaps it would be better to say, on a failure to appreciate the real majesty of God and the necessity of religion as defined and explained by St. Thomas...."[15]

By mid-1958, Cardinal Pizzardo was in physical, mental, and spiritual decline. Fenton was sorely disappointed by his meeting on August 27 with the Cardinal. "I got the idea that the old boy is overly impressed with this indifferentist philosophy of the day, and that he is actually falling for it. He is magnificently good, but fundamentally, P is a very unhappy man, or so I think." Fenton went on to speak with Archbishop Carlo Confalonieri, who was the Secretary of the Sacred Congregation for Seminaries and Universities, and he informed him of the "scandalous state of Catholic scripture studies in the USA. Without naming either King or Kennedy, I told him of King's story of the Scripture prof who did not believe that Our Lord was really crucified at all. At that Confalonieri banged the table at a great rate. He manifestly did not even realize that such shenanigans were going on. He was quite emotional in his reaction." But the bad news from America kept coming. Fenton "told him of the anti-Roman bias of the worst among the Catholic Scripture men in the USA. He learned that Cardinals Ottaviani, Pizzardo, and Raffini as well as Romeo and himself, were marked men among the progressive group in the USA. I honestly think that this talk with Confalonieri was the best service I have done the Church since I became a Counselor of the Congregation. It seemed to wake the old boy up a little bit. And anything that wakens our doughty secretary is a service to the Church. We may have some action."[16]

Earlier that same year, Connell retired and became a professor emeritus at CUA. He persisted in presenting the truth to bishops and the faithful alike wherever he was needed. With Connell retired, Fenton weakening, and a rot in the Vatican, things looked bad for the Catholics as the forces of Americanism were growing in strength and ferocity.

ATTACKING LIBERALISM

Fenton fought back by defining the enemy. He knew it was Liberalism, and while Liberalism was best manifested in the 1950s by the Americans, Fenton could not bring himself to say, "the Americans." An occasion for defining the enemies was the publication in 1958 of *The Emergence of Liberal Catholicism in America* by Dr. Robert D. Cross, a Harvard graduate. Decrying its poor scholarship, Fenton did concede that Cross addressed a movement in Catholicism that outsiders called "liberal Catholicism." To Cross, the liberals were those who went forth "with sublime confidence" to confront the non-Catholic culture, whereas the conservatives proceeded with greater caution. This classification was not an "over-simplification" as some Catholic writers suggested, but rather a "blunder," Fenton concluded. Cross argued that as a result of human effort, the Church became catholic. Fenton corrected this by referring to Vatican Council I and stating that "catholic unity" is "one of the factors by which the Church itself is recognizable as...' the bearer of a message from God.'" God Himself, as the principal cause, makes the Church catholic corrected Fenton.[17]

Fenton wrote that the real dichotomy in Catholicism was between those who were zealous in their faith versus those "whose faith was not so strong." The latter would "seek or at least accept what seemed like opportunities to shape and modify their Catholic convictions so as to bring them more into accord with the views favored in fashionable intellectual society." The "liberal Catholics" were part of a movement that had been around since at least the early nineteenth century. Its principles came from liberalism itself, which set forth the idea of the "rights of man" that inspired the French Revolution. Liberalism set out the idea that man is "considered as freed from any real and objective obligation towards God and towards Our Lord" and hence had "complete liberty to accept and to practice any religion he chose, or no religion whatsoever." The state in such a society, even if composed of Catholics, was "supposed to ignore God's sovereignty and, of course, to refuse to acknowledge the Kingship of Christ." The liberals believed the Church to be treated well if the state treated it equally with other religions. Fenton observed that with liberals "claiming the competence to deal with the true Church as with any other society, they claimed final dominion over the affairs of the Church itself. In the last analysis, the merely voluntary societies existing within the state are subject to the state's jurisdiction."[18]

Catholic thought for the last 150 years, according to Fenton, "has been dominated by the fact that elements and attitudes emanating from this philosophy of the French Revolution have entered into the teachings and the writings of many highly influential Catholics during all this period." Hence, there arose liberal Catholics and liberal Catholicism that began, according to Fenton, as a "sincere, even if unenlightened, ambition and affection for the true Church itself." The person most responsible for founding liberal Catholicism was Felicite de Lamennais and others who believed that "the interests of the Church could best and most effectively be forwarded within the framework of the liberal principles themselves." Since Catholic teaching is superior to any other belief system, Lamennais and his followers believed that freedom of speech and the denial of moral restraints would not hurt Catholicism but would allow the "superiority of Catholic truth" to be "all the more readily...apparent to the masses."

The original liberal Catholics saw the separation of Church and State as a way to give an advantage to the "Church and its message." The liberal Catholics "presupposed that all systems of religious teaching had objectively a right to be presented to the people" and that Catholicism would "win the adherence" of the people. Also, the liberal Catholics, according to Fenton, held to a belief that "all religions, and all religious teachings in general, could serve more or less effectively for the attainment of eternal salvation." This latter point was the essence of indifferentism, with Gregory XVI condemned in 1832 with *Mirari Vos,* Leo XII with *Ubi Primum* in 1828, and Pius VIII with *Traditi Humlitati Nostrae* in 1829. Fenton quoted *Mirari Vos* as he wrote that indifferentism included the view that "the eternal salvation of the soul can be attained by any kind of profession of faith, as long as a man's morals are in line with the standard of justice and honesty."[19]

From indifferentism came freedom of speech and separation of Church and State, which meant the Church would "be separated from the Kingdom" and "break off the mutual concord of the Empire with the Priesthood." This state of affairs, or "concord, which has always been favorable and salutary to both the sacred and the civil orders, is very much feared by the lovers of this most shameless liberty." Indifferentism was rejected early on in the life of the Church, Fenton wrote, and Pope Leo XII noted that many had come forward with arguments to defeat the liberal Catholic, or indifferentist, view. The Catholics know that Christ is the way to be saved and that "there is no salvation outside the Church."[20]

The original bases of liberal Catholicism were "indifferentism, false concepts of human freedom, and advocacy of a separation of Church and State," but after these were repudiated by the time of Gregory XVI, "a new set of factors entered into the composition of this system." The "most prominent...were minimism, subjectivism, and a belief in at least some transformation of the Church's dogmatic message over the course of the centuries." These latter principles were unforeseen by De Lamennais, but they were "aids required by the successors of De Lamennais in their task of continuing to teach the original principles of liberal Catholicism within the Church" after these principles were rejected. The liberals came to espouse the belief that the Church's dogma "changed over the course of the years and acquired new meanings quite different from the interpretations which the teaching Church had originally given." Fenton explained that "theological minimism was a device, employed by liberal Catholics, to make the rejection of authoritative papal teaching on any point appear to be good Catholic practice." Alternatively, it held that one need only follow the dictates of Ecumenical counsels, and it was opposed to papal infallibility. Subjectivism was "an attempt to locate the subject of indifferentism on the subjective, rather than on the objective, plane," and it was denounced by Pius IX in *Singulari quadam.* Along with all of this came the idea as set forth by the Anglican, Newman, who believed that one could believe at the same time a "universal negative proposition and a particular affirmative proposition," which contradicted the universal negative. An example was to say some may be saved outside of the Church, even though that is not true.[21]

A few months later, Fenton wrote, "Religion and Charity in Our Lady's Contribution to the Apostolate." He explained the importance of the Blessed Virgin Mary in keeping pure Catholic doctrine and explained the roles of the hierarchy or apostolate. Fenton explained that the hierarchy of the Church had the duty of "directing and instructing the people of the new covenant, and has been commissioned to persuade those who are not as yet within the true Church of the New Testament to save themselves from the perverse generation which is Satan's kingdom by entering Our Lord's Church." The hierarchy had the responsibility of "offering the sacrifice of the Mass, which is principally and preeminently the act of the Mystical Body of Jesus Christ." Around this act centered all of the operations of the hierarchy, which meant directing and caring for the spiritual welfare of the people of God who are united in the Eucharist. The work of the hierarchy was "animated and vivified throughout the exercise of the power of orders within the Church. It is enlightened by the preaching and the teaching of God's supernatural revealed message in Christ, a doctrinal work exercised either by or under the direction and the complete control of those who hold the power of jurisdiction from Our Lord Himself. It is guided by the laws and the precepts emanating from the apostolic college, and orientated towards God's glory and the salvation of souls." Fenton pointed out that the popes invoked the help of Mary to keep pure the Faith, and to fight the heresies named in a number of encyclicals. These encyclicals were *Mirari Vos, Qui Pluribus, Singulari Quadam,* and *Quanta Cura,* along with the *Syllabus of Errors.*[22]

A review of Maritain's *Reflections on America* appeared in the same issue. Written by Fr. Robert Paul Mohan, SS, it noted Maritain saw great hope in America's "economic humanism." However, the Americans had to "articulate an ideology by which the world may be informed of our [i.e., American] aspirations and ideals as well as our industrial techniques." Materialism existed in America, but Maritain discounted that as uniquely American, and he believed that the American gadgets freed people from the "servitude of matter" by reducing the "chores of everyday life." America suffered under a number of illusions. These were the "naïve acceptance of 18th century optimistic views on man and nature; the tendency to confuse external success with the development of the person spiritually and intellectually; the rejection of any concept of hierarchical values because of a vague egalitarianism; the tendency to see marriage in terms of romantic love rather than in terms of an indestructible spiritualized affection." America possessed "theoretical secularism" that "created a unique climate for the future dissemination of religious values" though not a new Christendom.[23]

62

PIUS XII DIES

At 3:52 in the morning on October 9, 1958, Pius XII died after a bout of hiccups that could not be stopped.[1] With the passing of Pius XII, the Church seemed poised for change, and, as a result, all the intelligence gathered during his papacy by Klaus Dohrn for Time, Inc. and the CIA became important and immediately relevant. Two months after the pope's death, Fenton dealt with his legacy in a December 1958 article in *American Ecclesiastical Review.* Pius XII, according to Fenton, clarified the "science of sacred theology" as it pertained to the "kingdom of God on earth." His encyclical *Mystici Corporis Christi* strengthened the teaching that the Church was necessary for salvation. Pius XII's *Humani Generis* reminded theologians that "in matters of faith and morals this sacred *magisterium* must be the proximate and universal criterion of truth for all theologians." Theologians must flee "those errors which more or less approach heresy" and rely on papal encyclicals, which were part of the ordinary teaching authority of the Church.[2] Especially important to Fenton were *Ci Riesce* (December 6, 1953) and *Si Diligis* (May 31, 1954), which appeared in response to the Church-State crisis and reminded the faithful that traditional teaching of the Church on her relationship to the state still had relevance. They also taught that "what does not correspond to the truth and to the moral standards has, objectively, no right to exist, to be taught, or to be done."

Pius XII's allocutions supported Ottaviani's statements from March 1953 and provided a way for Catholic statesmen to proceed when faced with future action of an international community because *Si diligis* did away with the notion that anyone at any time could "set himself up as a teacher of Christian doctrine within the Catholic Church." Finally, the letter on fraternal charity within the Church and within the priesthood, dated July 3, 1957, served to emphasize the need for fraternal charity between priests.[3]

Despite these great writings, the stern intellectual from a noble Roman family who was their author was gone, and no one knew what would follow. The Americans were as concerned about the future of the Church as the Catholics. Sensing an opportunity, Frederick Dolbeare, a career diplomat with ties to the American banking industry,[4] traveled to Rome in early 1957 intending to reconnoiter an upcoming consistory and ended up writing a report on his trip that ended up on C.D. Jackson's desk. The main topic of his report was Archbishop Montini and the likelihood of his elevation to the cardinalate, something he referred to as "the so-called 'Montinian question.'" The Americans were supporting Montini in spite of the fact that "many in the Papal Court, are against his appointment, and it seems that, for the moment being, they were still powerful enough to be able to obtain his candidature to the Red Hat to be postponed."[5]

Klaus Dohrn, returning to Rome as *Time*'s correspondent, wrote to Lovestone:

"If you are interested in that I think the situation is wide open. Due to the late Pope's strange reluctance to make decisions or appointments the choice of available candidates is poorer than ever in recent church history. The only candidate who really has caliber is the Armenian Cardinal Agagianian. But there seems to be a strong tendency to elect somebody presicely [sic] because he has not too much caliber and from whom a short, rather colourless pontificate can be expected, a kind of cooling-off period during which things can be brought back to order and normalcy. In this case the Italian majority in the College of Cardinals would be reestablished and the next Pope in this case would probably be Montini whom the late Pope carefully avoided to create Cardinal. Several people here think that even now he has got an outside chance to be elected although he is not Cardinal."[6]

Dohrn expressed concern that the Church could grow cold to the Americans. In a letter dated October 22, 1958, to Christopher Emmett, Dohrn wrote:

"There is much talk (or rather gossip) in Italy that the next pontificate will be more on an 'appeasement' line. Strangely enough the Russians seem to believe too and behave according....Unfortunately this might for a moment weaken Vatican-American ties (because of Galeazzi's half-brother's close relations with Cardinal Spellman and other American bishops), and there certainly will never be another Pope so close to Germany, but all the other talk about appeasement is absolute nonsense. Montini (who may be Secretary of State and in my opinion will be the next Pope but one), and Lercaro are not 'aapeasers' [sic], and Agagianian who seems to be the favorite at the moment is no 'neutralist.'"[7]

The Americans wanted Montini as the next pope. Dohrn expressed the disappointment to Lovestone when Roncalli was elected but offered hope for the next time around. In a November 2, 1958 letter, Dohrn wrote, "I still think you will get your pope next time, but the new man shows no intention to let this happen very soon in spite of the intention many of his electors no doubt had. He successfully tries to set a new style of a humorous, fatherly, down-to-earth, efficient matter-of-factness which is very good, because no one could continue on the same level and the same pitch as before."[8] These are all the qualities of an American, though Dohrn said that the "French are making a terrible noise about this being a 'French pontificate.'"[9]

The new pope had to be able to negotiate the Catholic-Protestant rift, according to Dohrn, and in making that observation, he recognized a fundamental dynamic of the Americans' reason for the Cold War:

"What I said earlier about intelligent rather than radical opposition (and how much did we experience of that on the domestic scene!) also applies to Rome. The choice wasn't the one you present. There never really was any question of Montini. The alternative would have been either Ruffini or Ottaviani. I suppose both were supported by Spellman. Both no doubt are reliably and fervently anti-Communist, but are they also intelligently so? I needn't tell you about the necessity of being open-minded about social and labor questions and social reforms but there is another angle, less apparent and important in Italy, but one where certain Italian shortcomings can have the most unfortunate consequences for countries outside Italy especially the U.S., England and Germany. I am referring to the relationship between Catholics and Protestants, certainly a pre-requisite for any intelligent and efficient fight against communism."[10]

Montini saw the possibility of collaboration with the "reformist wing of European socialism," but so did John XXIII, who would do so "without the dangers of too much influence by certain tendencies in the Vatican which, rightly or wrongly, would have been encouraged by an election of Montini at this moment."[11]

63
POPE JOHN CALLS A COUNCIL

From the day after his election to pope on October 28, 1958, John XXIII spoke about an ecumenical council. The pope bounced the idea of a council off his secretary, Msgr. Loris Capovilla, who discouraged him from undertaking it and who urged something less strenuous while putting trust in his "paternal charisma." Pope John persisted, possibly because of problems described by the cardinal electors. In November 1958, he spoke with Ernesto Cardinal Ruffini, Archbishop of Palermo, and Archbishop Giovanni Urbani (Roncalli's successor in Venice), and Bishop Girolamo Bortignon of Padua as well as a Msgr. Alfredo Cavagna. Visitors to Pope John in December and early January were being told of his idea for a council, which he termed the "Vatican council," an idea that he supposedly had since his days as a Papal Legate to Istanbul.[1]

The pope spoke with Dominico Cardinal Tardini, the Secretary of State, on January 20 about a council, and Tardini's reply, according to Pope John's own diary, was "'the most exultant surprise I could ever have expected. 'Oh! This is an idea – an enlightened and holy idea! This really comes from heaven, Holy Father. You need to cultivate, develop, and diffuse it. It will be a great blessing for the whole world.' I needed nothing more....It was as if the idea of a Council had sprung from my heart with the naturalness of a spontaneous and very sure reflection. Truly it is the Lord who has done this, and we find it marvelous to behold." Tardini recorded in his diary that "His Holiness....conceived three ideas: A Roman synod, an Ecumenical Council, and the updating of the Code of Canon Law. He wants to announce these three points to the cardinals next Sunday, after the ceremony at St. Paul's.....I said: 'For my part, I like what is new and good. Now, these three projects are excellent and the method of announcing them to the cardinals beforehand, though connected with ancient papal traditions, is appropriate and novel.'"[2]

The pope announced the council to the Cardinals on January 25, 1959, the Feast of the Conversion of St. Paul the Apostle in the Ostian Basilica. In a discourse entitled "The Festive Anniversary," John stated he came to this decision after "his personal conversations with members of the Roman Curia, the good of souls, and the urgency he felt that his pontificate correspond to the needs of the present times." After the paralysis of the late Pius XII pontificate, the Church needed to deal with the "strained situation of the Church of silence within Communist countries that had become the object of a systematic persecution aimed at its destruction. Concurrently, in the so-called free world the search for well-being carried with it the danger of a general weakening of the spiritual dimension, which could cause grave harm to the life of the Church." The way to respond to these twin threats was for the Church to conduct itself as it always had with "'ancient forms of doctrinal declarations and wise disciplinary regulations'." The situation of the day "required the discovery of new means that would yield the same effective results."[3] The *motu proprio* announcing the Council stated its name was to be "the Second Vatican Council after the place in which it would be held."[4]

The Vatican communique announcing the council identified the "Revolution of Expectations" that C.D. Jackson, Luce, and the U.S. government encouraged as the reason for the council: "As Supreme Pastor of the Church, he [Pope John XXIII] noted dangers which become more greatly menacing every day to the spiritual life of the faithful, that is, the errors which enter everywhere and the immoderate attractions of material goods, increased today more than ever with technical progress."[5] The pope hoped that the Council would extend an invitation to the "separated Communities to find unity" and "better ecclesiatical [sic] and juridical structure."[6]

In sharp contrast with the joy of Tardini, Ruffini, and Urbani, there was an ominous silence amongst many prelates after these announcements. Those who did respond did so with comments that "were largely awkward expressions of great concern over the projected Council." Of special note was Archbishop Montini of Milan, who called his "good friend Bevilacqua" to exclaim, "'Have you heard; Father?...What a hornet's nest! What a hornet's nest!'"[7]

On May 17, the pope set up a commission in preparation for the council that was forecast to commence in either 1961 or 1962.[8] The commission was to "make contact with Catholic bishops throughout the world for advice and suggestions on the planned council. The group is also to establish liaison with organs and theologians of the church and draw up a tentative agenda for the conference."[9] Tardini sent out a "circular letter to more than 2,700 bishops and heads of Sees throughout the world. The letter asked the prelates to be completely frank in making suggestions as to what topics the council should deal with." Responses came from 90% of the USA prelates, 94% from Italy, 96% from France, 98% from Spain, and 100% from Germany.[10]

The letter Tardini sent in June asked bishops, rectors, Catholic educators, and others of prominence in the Church to: "inform this Commission of those matters which seem to be most opportune for consideration by the Fathers of the Council, how they can be scientifically explored and explained, and in what practical way they can be put into operation. The subjects of research can be various: first of all dogmatic, biblical, liturgical, philosophical, moral and juridical, pastoral, social, etc. One might also deal with clerical discipline and that of the Christian people: about seminaries, schools, Catholic Action, and other things which you think benefit the Church and promote the care of souls. However, as it is evident, not all these matters nor all the questions are likely to be examined and studied by all, yet among the many you will choose only such as you believe to be not only of greater advantage to the Church but also more likely to be better and more scientifically treated by your Professors."[11]

Responding to Tardini's request, Connell prepared a three-page list of possible topics and sent the letter, written entirely in Latin, to Archbishop O'Boyle of Washington, D.C. It included eleven different points under the heading of "Res Fidei" and ten separate points under the heading of "Res Morum." One of the points Connell proposed in the "Res Fidei" section argued for the re-iteration of Catholic doctrine on the duties of states to the divine positive law, and not just the natural law. This included the recognition of the Church and its immunities by the state.[12]

Under "Res Morum," Connell presented a topic that dealt with international relations and the rights and authority of the Church in the context of international associations.[13] Connell presented additional propositions for consideration under "Res Fidei," which dealt with the authority of the pope, the need for the faithful to give assent to Papal statements, and the role of theologians.[14] Other suggestions pertained to the evil of contraception, the jurisdiction of bishops, and a definitive statement on the doctrine of just war.[15]

64
MURRAY PREPARES TO PUBLISH

Murray and the Americans were encouraged by the election of John XXIII to the chair of Peter because, as C.D. Jackson told Luce, Roncalli was not only sympathetic to the Pro Deo operation, but he was also "a good personal friend of Father Morlion's." Jackson mentioned that he got this information "through a series of 'cut outs', all with their collars on backwards," indicating that the CIA had a number of sources inside the Vatican. The bad news from these CIA cut outs was that "Tardini," someone Jackson characterized as "a mortal enemy," "might be confirmed as Secretary of State instead of Montini, who was simpatico to the Morlion operation."[1]

Emboldened by the new papacy, Murray and Luce spent the following summer getting Murray's thoughts into print and then using the Time, Inc. publicity machine to promote them. The first order of the day was finding a suitable publisher, and in the end, Luce settled on Sheed & Ward Publishers, run by Frank Sheed and his wife, Maisie Ward. According to their son Wilfred, Frank Sheed, an Australian of Irish descent, was an MI-5 agent who was sent to the United States in the 1930s "to see if he could do something about Fr. Charles E. Coughlin, the Radio Priest."[2] According to the younger Sheed's account, "Coughlin is a grubby little footnote now, but....[f]rom populist, pro-New Deal beginnings he had, by 1940, degenerated into an isolationist demagogue who blamed most of America's troubles on Jews and bankers, and there wasn't much anyone could do about him. He had his radio and he had his following, and his following could not be reached by normal means."[3]

Coughlin's message was well-received by many Catholics who, at the urging of Pius XI, opposed the spread of Communism, supporting Franco's followers in Spain, Hitler's anti-Communist efforts in Germany, and the Cristeros in Mexico.[4] Frank Sheed used subterfuge to get at Father Coughlin by insinuating himself into what Wilfrid referred to as "the relatively civilized Celtic fringe, where isolationism had nothing especially anti-Semitic about it: it was a private matter between them and the British.... If Frank had come on as a British propagandist, he would have been worthless." Knowing this, Frank created a publishing house that used his persona as "a distinguished Catholic of manifestly Irish extraction with a manifestly English wife" to disguise his MI-5 connections, which he maintained for the rest of his life.[5]

Harry and Clare Luce were big supporters of Sheed & Ward. In an exchange between the two in December 1948, Clare wrote to Harry, "Here are the Sheed and Ward papers. I'd like to put in 25,000 [dollars] if that isn't throwing money away. I mean...as the jebies say, its [sic] 'To the greater glory....' Ad major [sic] dei Gloria but not if it means a hopeless loss?"[6]

Harry responded favorably in a letter dated December 13: "To me the figures indicate that the Sheed and Ward business is a 'sound' little business. We know that its principal motivation is not 'profits' and if it ever becomes really profitable that will be 'providential.' On the other hand, it is reasonable to expect that it will not get into serious financial trouble. An investment in this business is largely an investment in Frank Sheed – in what he is able to do. I should think it would be entirely suitable for you to make an investment in him and in his unique company. My advice, then, is – go ahead."[7]

The Luces were not investing in Sheed's enterprise to make a profit but rather to promote a certain kind of Catholic writer, one who was more sympathetic to the Luces and the American Proposition than to Catholic doctrine. Wilfrid wrote Frank and Maisie "wanted a Church as sturdy as a house, and bent every effort into making Rome seem reasonable, which is much harder than selling the décor..."[8] So, "Ward ran a magazine as Sheed ran a publishing house, open to all the voices," including the voices of Modernism.[9] Wilfrid revealed, "I sometimes wondered where the Sheeds found their authors," and he went on to describe one such person, Caryll Houselander, as a "witch."[10] Wilfrid sensed something big was going on, but he couldn't figure it all out because "[t]here were connections in this whole circus that I couldn't see"[11] and "[p]eople were always staying with us for no discernible reason."[12]

The circus of activity surrounding Sheed & Ward was part of the "larger feeling that the Church was on the move, and that this office was helping it to get there in a small way. No one could have said quite *where* the Church was going: the reforms of the Second Vatican Council would have seemed much too much to hope for."[13] The Sheeds were encouraging as many divergent voices in the Church as possible, and one of the divergent voices they encouraged was Murray's. In May 1959, Murray was working with Philip Scharper, an editor at Sheed and Ward, on a book that would be "in effect, a primer of pluralism, paying special attention to the dilemmas posed to and by Catholics in a pluralistic society." Two months later, Scharper advised Murray that Sheed wanted a book that would point to "an acceptance of a pluralist society as actually existed with an effort to take soundings about problems that a Catholic meets in such a society and the service he can render it."[14]

INDEX

D

E

F

M

ABOUT THE AUTHOR

David Wemhoff received an AB in Government from the University of Notre Dame and a Juris Doctor from the University of the Pacific, McGeorge School of Law. He earned a Master of Laws (LLM) in international and comparative law from Indiana University. Mr. Wemhoff taught college-level courses at two universities in Business Law, American Government, Constitutional Law, and State and Local Government. He is a member of the Society of Catholic Social Scientists and resides in Granger, Indiana.

NOTES

SUMMARIES

1. Clare Booth Luce to Fulton Sheen, undated letter [ca. 1948], Clare Boothe Luce Papers, Box 760, Folder 15, Library of Congress, Washington, D.C.
2. Clare Boothe Luce to Simon Michael Bessie, Letter from about October-November, 1963, Clare Boothe Luce Papers, Box 56, File 13, 10-12, Library of Congress, Washington, D.C.
3. Wallace Irwin, Jr., Memorandum for Record dated April 21, 1953 Subject: Latin America – Briefing by Miron Burgin, OIR/DRA, PSB Central Files Series Box 15 Folder "PSB 091.4 Latin America," Dwight D. Eisenhower Library, Abilene, Kansas.
4. Marie McCrum, interviewed by David Horrocks on May 15, 1975, "Oral Histories," Dwight D. Eisenhower Library, Abilene, Kansas, transcript 83-84.
5. C.D. Jackson to Henry R. Luce, Memorandum dated December 21, 1955 and entitled "Components of US Foreign Policy," C.D. Jackson Papers Box 69 Log 1956(4), Dwight D. Eisenhower Library, Abilene, Kansas.
6. C.D. Jackson to Clarence B. Randall, Letter dated March 4, 1957, C.D. Jackson Papers, Box 69 Folder 1957(2), Dwight D. Eisenhower Library, Abilene, Kansas.

1. HENRY ROBINSON LUCE: PRESBYTERIAN MEDIA GENIUS

1. David Halberstam, *The Powers That Be* (Chicago, Illinois: University of Illinois Press, 2000), 47.
2. Halberstam, *The Powers That Be*, 47.
3. Halberstam, *The Powers That Be*, 46, 49.
4. Amintore Fanfani, *Catholicism, Protestantism, Capitalism* (Norfolk, Virginia: IHS Press, 2003), 61.
5. Alan Brinkley, *The Publisher: Henry Luce and His American Century* (New York: Alfred A Knopf, 2010), 76, 80.
6. Halberstam, *The Powers That Be*, 54-55.
7. James L. Baughman, *Henry R. Luce And the Rise of the American News Media* (Baltimore, Maryland: The Johns Hopkins University Press, 2001), 19-20.
8. Baughman, *Henry R. Luce And the Rise of the American News Media*, 102.
9. Brinkley, *The Publisher: Henry Luce and His American Century*, 94-98, 100, 102, 104.
10. E. Michael Jones, *Libido Dominandi: Sexual Liberation and Political Control* (South Bend, Indiana: St. Augustine's Press, 2000), 132, 151.
11. Paul Roazen, "Introduction," in *The Public Philosophy* (New Brunswick, USA: Transaction Publishers, 2003), xiv.
12. Walter Lippmann, *Public Opinion* (Radford, Virginia: Wilder Publications, 2010), 11-21, 92, 114.
13. Lippmann, *Public Opinion,* 33, 115.

14. Lippmann, *Public Opinion*, 49.
15. Lippmann, *Public Opinion*, 66-67.
16. Lippmann, *Public Opinion*, 67.
17. Lippmann, *Public Opinion*, dedication page, 197.
18. Lippmann, *Public Opinion*, 171-172.
19. Lippmann, *Public Opinion*, 22.
20. Merle Miller, *Plain Speaking: An Oral Biography of Harry S. Truman* (New York: Tess Press, 2004), 25.
21. Efrem Zimbalist, Jr., *My Dinner of Herbs* (New York: Limelight Editions, 2003), 76.
22. Brinkley, *The Publisher: Henry Luce and His American Century*, 136-137, 284, 438.
23. Daechun An, "Content Analysis of Advertising Visuals in the Magazine Advertisements: The Roaring Twenties and the Great Depression" *WJMCR* 6:3 (June 2003). http://www.scripps.ohiou.edu/wjmcr/vol06/6-3a-b.htm (accessed May 13, 2010).
24. C.D. Jackson "It's the Audience that Counts," text of talk dated December 7, 1961 to the Insurance Advertising Conference, C.D. Jackson Papers, Box 97 File "Speech Texts, 1961 (1)," Dwight D. Eisenhower Library, Abilene, Kansas.
25. C.D. Jackson, "The Editorial Policy of Life Magazine as a Taste-making Agency," text of talk dated April 19, 1956, to the Advertising Conference, University of Michigan, April 19, C.D. Jackson Papers, Box 99 File "Speech Texts 1956(5)," Dwight D. Eisenhower Library, Abilene, Kansas.
26. W. A. Swanberg, *Luce and His Empire* (New York: Scribner, 1972), 635-636.
27. Baughman, *Henry R. Luce and the Rise of the American News Media*, 43-44.
28. Baughman, *Henry R. Luce and the Rise of the American News Media*, 43, 45.
29. Brinkley, *The Publisher: Henry Luce and His American Century*, 130-131.
30. Brinkley, *The Publisher: Henry Luce and His American Century*, 131.
31. Baughman, *Henry R. Luce and the Rise of the American News Media.*, 46-47.
32. John Shaw Billings, *Oral History of Time, Inc. Part II,* dated March 4, 1966, approx. 51:45 mark, John Shaw Billings Papers, South Caroliniana Library, University of South Carolina, Columbia, South Carolina.
33. C.D. Jackson, "The Responsibilities of Magazines to Their Readers To Their Advertisers," text of talk dated October 24, 1963, to the American Marketing Association, C D Jackson Papers, Box 96 File "Speech Texts, 1963 (1)," Dwight D Eisenhower Library, Abilene, Kansas; C.D. Jackson, "Commencement Address Dickinson College Carlisle Pennsylvania June 7, 1964," text of talk dated June 7, 1964, to Dickenson College, Carlisle, Pennsylvania, C.D. Jackson Papers, Box 96 Folder "Speech Texts, 1964(1)," Dwight D. Eisenhower Library, Abilene, Kansas.
34. Brinkley, *The Publisher: Henry Luce and His American Century,* 223-224; John Shaw Billings, *Oral History of Time, Inc. Part II,* dated March 4, 1966, approx. 51:45 mark, John Shaw Billings Papers, South Caroliniana Library, University of South Carolina, Columbia, South Carolina.
35. "Our Thirty Third Degree Enemies," *The Point,* June, 1953, Clare Boothe Luce Papers Box 703 Folder 13, Library of Congress, Washington, D.C.
36. C.D. Jackson, "The Responsibilities of Magazines to Their Readers To Their Advertisers," text of talk dated October 24, 1963 to the American Marketing Association, C.D. Jackson Papers, Box 96 File "Speech Texts, 1963 (1)," Dwight D Eisenhower Library, Abilene, Kansas.
37. Halberstam, *The Powers That Be,* 59.
38. Halberstam, *The Powers That Be,* 59.

39. Halberstam, *The Powers That Be,* 62.
40. Blanche Wiesen Cook, "First Comes the Lie: CD Jackson and Political Warfare," *Radical History Review* 31(1984) : 45.
41. "The University of South Caroliniana Society Programs," 38th Annual Meeting, University of South Carolina Thursday, April 26, 1974, "The Time-Life-Fortune Papers of John Shaw Billings".
42. John Shaw Billings to Henry R. Luce, Letter dated December 29, 1954, John Shaw Billings Papers File 201, South Caroliniana Library, University of South Carolina, Columbia, South Carolina.
43. John Shaw Billings, Diary Entry for March 9, 1949, John Shaw Billings Papers, Diaries, Volume 29, South Caroliniana Library, University of South Carolina, Columbia, South Carolina.
44. John Shaw Billings, Diary Entry for May 27, 1949, John Shaw Billings Paper, Diaries, Volume 29, p. 145, South Caroliniana Library, University of South Carolina, Columbia, South Carolina.
45. Henry Luce, "The Great Liberal Tradition," *The Ideas of Henry Luce,* ed. John K Jessup (New York: Atheneum, 1969), 123-125.
46. "Nation: He Ran the Course," *Time,* March 10, 1967. http://www.time.com/time/printout/0,8816,836724,00.html (accessed December 31, 2009).
47. Brinkley, *The Publisher: Henry Luce and His American Century,* 150.
48. John Shaw Billings, *Oral History of Time, Inc. Part II,* dated March 4, 1966, approx. 39:19 mark, John Shaw Billings Papers, South Caroliniana Library, University of South Carolina, Columbia, South Carolina.
49. John Shaw Billings, Diary entry for March 10, 1948, John Shaw Billings Papers, Diaries, Volume 27, 57, South Caroliniana Library, University of South Carolina, Columbia, South Carolina.
50. Henry R. Luce to Roy Alexander, undated letter, C.D. Jackson Papers Box 70 Folder "Luce Henry & Clare 1955," Dwight D. Eisenhower Library, Abilene, Kansas.

2. THE AMERICAN CENTURY BEGINS WITH WORLD WAR II

1. Henry R Luce, "War Diary," Henry R. Luce Papers, Box 83, File 12, Library of Congress, Washington, DC.
2. Guido Preparata, *Conjuring Hitler: How Britain and America Made the Third Reich* (Ann Arbor, Michigan: Pluto Press, 2005),, xvi – xviii, 263-268.
3. Carroll Quigley, *The Anglo-American Establishment from Rhodes to Cliveden* (New York: Books in Focus, 1981), 3-7.
4. Preparata, *Conjuring Hitler,* 150, 265-266, 282, 288-289.
5. Preparata, *Conjuring Hitler,* 295.
6. "Programme of the NSDAP, 24 February 1920," http://www.hitler.org/writings/programme/ (accessed December 8, 2001).
7. Adolf Hitler, *Mein Kampf,* translated Ralph Manheim (Boston, Massachusetts: Houghton Mifflin Company, 1971), 642-643.
8. Hitler, *Mein Kampf,* 654.
9. "Programme of the NSDAP."

10. Alan Brinkley, *The Publisher: Henry Luce and His American Century* (New York: Alfred A Knopf, 2010), 246.
11. Brinkley, *The Publisher*, 246.
12. Brinkley, *The Publisher*, 243.
13. John Shaw Billings, *Oral History of Time, Inc. Part III,* dated March 4, 1966, approx. 12:00 mark and 25:21 mark, John Shaw Billings Papers, South Caroliniana Library, University of South Carolina, Columbia, South Carolina.
14. Quigley, *The Anglo American Establishment*, 295, 303.
15. Preparata, *Conjuring Hitler*, 254-261.
16. Franklin Delano Roosevelt, "Four Freedoms Speech." http://history.sandiego.edu/gen/text/us/fdr1941.html (accessed May 29, 2010).
17. Preparata, *Conjuring Hitler,* 259.
18. Preparata, *Conjuring Hitler,* 259.
19. Franklin Delano Roosevelt, "Four Freedoms Speech." http://history.sandiego.edu/gen/text/us/fdr1941.html (accessed May 29, 2010).
20. Franklin Delano Roosevelt, "Four Freedoms Speech."
21. Franklin Delano Roosevelt, "Four Freedoms Speech."
22. Henry Luce, "The American Century," *The Ideas of Henry Luce,* ed. John K Jessup (New York: Atheneum, 1969), 117, 118; Henry Luce, "The American Century," *Life,* February 17, 1941.
23. Luce, *The Ideas of Henry Luce*, 106-110.
24. Luce, *The Ideas of Henry Luce*, 110-113.
25. Luce, *The Ideas of Henry Luce*, 112-114.
26. Luce, *The Ideas of Henry Luce*, 115-116.
27. Luce, *The Ideas of Henry Luce*, 116-117.
28. Luce, *The Ideas of Henry Luce*, 118-119.
29. Luce, *The Ideas of Henry Luce*, 119-120.

3. LUCE NAMES THE NEXT BOGEYMAN

1. Swanberg, *Luce and His Empire,* 298.
2. Swanberg, *Luce and His Empire*, 299.
3. Swanberg, *Luce and His Empire*, 299-300.
4. Swanberg, *Luce and His Empire*, 306-307
5. Swanberg, *Luce and His Empire*, 303, 307-308.
6. Swanberg, *Luce and His Empire*, 308-309.
7. Swanberg, *Luce and His Empire,* 316, 325-326, 332-333.
8. Swanberg, *Luce and His Empire,* 316, 325-326, 332-333.
9. George Kennan, "George Kennan's 'Long Telegram'" George Washington University. http://www.gwu.edu/~nsarchiv/coldwar/documents/episode-1/kennan.htm (accessed July 14, 2013), Parts 2, 5.
10. Kennan, "George Kennan's 'Long Telegram," Part 1, (a).
11. Kennan, "George Kennan's 'Long Telegram," Part 1(f), and (a), (c).
12. Kennan, "George Kennan's 'Long Telegram," Part 1(f), and (a), (c).
13. Kennan, "George Kennan's 'Long Telegram," Part 4.
14. Kennan, "George Kennan's 'Long Telegram," Part 4, para. 1; Part 5
15. Kennan, "George Kennan's 'Long Telegram," Part 4, paras. 2, 3, 4.

16. Kennan, "George Kennan's 'Long Telegram," Part 4, paras. 5, 6.
17. Kennan, "George Kennan's 'Long Telegram," Part 5.
18. Wilford, *The Mighty Wurlitzer: How The CIA Played America,* 21-23.
19. Brinkley, *The Publisher: Henry Luce and His American Century,* 312.
20. Brinkley, *The Publisher: Henry Luce and His American Century,* 380.
21. Brinkley, *The Publisher: Henry Luce and His American Century,* 358-361, 366.
22. Thomas G. Paterson and Robert J. McMahon, editors, *The Origins of the Cold War, Third Edition* (Lexington, Massachusetts: D.C. Heath and Company, 1991), 206-207.
23. William Blum, *Killing Hope: US Military and CIA Interventions Since World War II* (Monroe, Maine: Common Courage Press, 1995), 6-7.
24. Antony C. Sutton, *The Best Enemy Money Can Buy* (Billings, Montana: Liberty House Press, 1986), 1-11.
25. Brinkley, *The Publisher: Henry Luce and His American Century,* 324.

4. CLARE BOOTHE LUCE – AMERICAN CATHOLIC

1. Stephen Shadegg, *Clare Boothe Luce* (New York: Simon and Schuster, 1970), 12-15, 17-24, 31.
2. Shadegg, *Clare Boothe Luce,* 27-28.
3. Shadegg, *Clare Boothe Luce,* 36-40, 42, 43-50.
4. Shadegg, *Clare Boothe Luce,* 54-69.
5. Shadegg, *Clare Boothe Luce,* 79-94.
6. Sylvia Jukes Morris, *Rage for Fame: The Ascent of Clare Boothe Luce* (New York: Random House, 1997), 4
7. Shadegg, *Clare Boothe Luce,* 94.
8. Clare Boothe Luce, "Last Resume for HRL" dated July 17, 1960, Clare Boothe Luce Papers Box 793 Folder 10, Library of Congress, Washington, D.C.
9. Clare Boothe Luce, "Credo," Clare Boothe Luce Papers Box 50 Folder 1, Library of Congress, Washington, D.C.
10. Ralph G. Martin, *Henry and Clare: An Intimate Portrait of the Luces* (New York: Putnam's Perigee Books, 1991), 260.
11. Clare Boothe Luce to Fulton Sheen, undated letter [ca. 1948], Clare Boothe Luce Papers Box 760 Folder 15, Library of Congress, Washington, D.C.
12. Clare Boothe Luce to Simon Michael Bessie, Letter from about October-November, 1963, Clare Boothe Luce Papers, Box 56, File 13, 10-12, Library of Congress, Washington, D.C.
13. Clare Boothe Luce, "The 'Real' Reason" Parts I, II, III, *McCall's* Magazine, Clare Boothe Luce Papers, Box 308 File 13, Library of Congress, Washington D.C.
14. Clare Boothe Luce, "The 'Real' Reason" Part I, *McCall's,* 3, February 1947,Clare Boothe Luce Papers Box 308 File 13, Library of Congress, Washington D.C.
15. Ibid.; Clare Boothe Luce, "The 'Real' Reason" Part III, *McCall's,* April 1947, Clare Boothe Luce Papers Box 308 File 13, p. 2, Library of Congress, Washington, D.C.
16. Ibid.; Martin, *Henry and Clare: An Intimate Portrait,* 259.
17. Clare Boothe Luce, "The 'Real' Reason" Part I, *McCall's,* February 1947, Clare Boothe Luce Papers Box 308 File 13, p. 3, Library of Congress, Washington, D.C.
18. Martin, *Henry and Clare: An Intimate Portrait,* 259.

19. Luce, "The 'Real' Reason" Part I, *McCall's,* 2.
20. Luce, "The 'Real' Reason" Part I, *McCall's,* 2.
21. Luce, "The 'Real' Reason" Part II, *McCall's,* March 1947, Clare Boothe Luce Papers Box 308 File 13, 1-3, Library of Congress, Washington, D.C..
22. Luce, "The 'Real' Reason" Part II, *McCall's,* March 1947, 3.
23. Luce, "The 'Real' Reason" Part II, *McCall's,* March 1947, 3.
24. Luce, "The 'Real' Reason" Part II, *McCall's* March 1947, 6.
25. Luce, "The 'Real' Reason" Part II, *McCall's* March 1947, 6.
26. Luce, "The 'Real' Reason" Part III, *McCall's,* April 1947, 3.
27. Luce, "The 'Real' Reason" Part II, *McCall's,* March 1947, 3.
28. Luce, "The 'Real' Reason" Part II, *McCall's,* March 1947, 3.
29. Luce, "The 'Real' Reason" Part II, *McCall's,* March 1947, 3.
30. Luce, "The 'Real' Reason" Part III, *McCall's,* April 1947, 1, 3.
31. Clare Boothe Luce, "Freedom and Catholicism (Outline)" ca. 1947, Clare Boothe Luce Papers, Box 300, Folder 43, 1, Library of Congress, Washington, D.C.
32. "Announcing The Paulist Forum's 1948 Fall Lecture Series," Clare Boothe Luce Papers. Box 703 Folder 13, Library of Congress, Washington, D.C.
33. Churchill to Clare Boothe Luce, Letter dated August 4, 1948, 1, John Shaw Billings Papers, Box II, Folder 116, South Caroliniana Library, University of South Carolina, Columbia, South Carolina.
34. Churchill to Clare Boothe Luce, Letter dated August 4, 1948, 1, John Shaw Billings Papers: Box II, Folder 116, South Caroliniana Library, University of South Carolina, Columbia, South Carolina.
35. John Shaw Billings, Diary Entry for August 11, 1948, John Shaw Billings Papers, Diaries, Volume 27, 287-288, South Caroliniana Library, University of South Carolina, Columbia, South Carolina.
36. John Shaw Billings to Waugh, Letter dated August 25, 1948, 2, John Shaw Billings Papers, Box II, Folder 116, South Caroliniana Library, University of South Carolina, Columbia, South Carolina.

5. AMERICANISM DIVIDES THE CATHOLICS

1. James H. Moynihan, *The Life of Archbishop John Ireland* (New York: Harper & Brothers, 1953), 74-75.
2. Allen Sinclair Will, *Life of James Cardinal Gibbons* (New York: John Murphy Publishers, 1911), 177-178.
3. Will, *Life of James Cardinal Gibbons* (1911), 177-178.
4. John Hassard, *Life of the Most Reverend John Hughes, D.D., First Archbishop of New York* (New York: D. Appleton and Company, 1866), 222-253, 337-340, 349-351; James M. McPherson, *Battle Cry of Freedom: The Civil War Era* (New York: Bantam Books, 1989), 132; Ray Allen Billington, *The Protestant Crusade 1800-1860: A Study of the Origins of American Nativism* (Chicago, Ilinois: Quadrangle Books, 1964), 290-292.
5. Allen Sinclair Will, *The Life of James Gibbons* (New York: EP Dutton, 1922), 498-499.
6. Will, *The Life of James Gibbons* (1922), 499-503
7. *Documents of American Catholic History,* ed. John Tracy Ellis (Milwaukee, Wisconsin: The Bruce Publishing Company, 1956), 496-499.
8. Ellis, *Documents of American Catholic History*, 510-511, 520-523.

9. Ellis, *Documents of American Catholic History*, 523-525.
10. Americanism Collection (MAMR), University of Notre Dame Archives (UNDA), University of Notre Dame, Notre Dame, Indiana; Gerald P. Fogarty, *The Vatican and the Americanist Crisis: Denis J. O'Connell American Agent In Rome 1885-1903* (Universita Gregoriana, 1974).
11. Ellis, *Documents of American Catholic History*, 523-525.
12. Will, *Life of Cardinal Gibbons* (1911), 62-69.
13. James Cardinal Gibbons, *The Faith of Our Fathers: Being a Plain Explanation and Vindication of The Church Founded by Our Lord Jesus Christ* (New York: John Murphy Company, 1905), 264, 269
14. Gibbons, *The Faith of Our Fathers*, 264, 268.
15. Gibbons, *The Faith of Our Fathers*, 265-266, 275-276, 279-282.
16. Will, *Life of James Cardinal Gibbons* (1911), 6-8, 26-27, 35-36, 45. Will wrote that Gibbons as Secretary to the Archbishop of Baltimore came into contact with "some of the most important Catholic families of the United States, pillars of the Church since the days of Leonard Calvert" and Gibbons as well as other members of the clergy had "under their spiritual care a highly cultivated element, in whose social life they mingle and from whose environment they draw a certain inspiration."
17. Will, *Life of James Cardinal Gibbons* (1911), 22.
18. Will, *Life of James Cardinal Gibbons* (1911), 22.
19. "Martin John Spalding," www.wikipedia.com (accessed July 16, 2011).
20. Pope Gregory XVI, *Mirari Vos*, paras. 5, 7, 9. www.papalencyclicals.com (accessed January 2, 2010).
21. Pope Gregory XVI, *Mirari Vos*, para. 13 (emphasis present in the original).
22. Pope Gregory XVI, *Mirari Vos*, para. 14.
23. Pope Gregory XVI, *Mirari Vos*, para. 20
24. Pope Pius IX, *Qui Pluribus*, paras. 4, 5, 7, 17. www.papalencyclicals.net (accessed April 3, 2006).
25. Pope Pius IX, *Qui Pluribus*, paras. 13-16, 20, 22-29, 34.
26. Pope Pius IX, *Ubi Primum*, paras. 7-9. www.papalencyclicals.net (accessed April 3, 2006).
27. Pope Pius IX, *Quanto Conficiamur Moerore*, paras. 7, 8, 10. www.papalencyclicals.net (accessed November 7, 2006).
28. A. Haag, "Syllabus," *In the Catholic Encyclopedia* (New York: Robert Appleton Company, 1912), from New Advent: http://www.newadent.org/cathen/14368b.htm (accessed July 11, 2011).
29. Pope Pius IX, *The Syllabus of Errors Condemned by Pius IX*. Part I, paras. 3, 4, 6. www.papalencyclicals.net/Pius09/p9syll.htm (accessed November 7, 2006).
30. Pope Pius IX, *The Syllabus of Errors Condemned by Pius IX*, Part II, para. 8; Part III, paras. 15, 18.
31. Pope Pius IX, *The Syllabus of Errors Condemned by Pius IX*, Part V, paras. 20, 27; Part VI, para. 40.
32. Pope Pius IX, *The Syllabus of Errors Condemned by Pius IX*, Part VII, paras. 56, 57; Part X, paras. 77, 80.
33. Pope Pius IX, *Quanta Cura*, para. 3. http://www.papalencyclicals.net/Pius09/p9quanta.htm (accessed November 7, 2006).
34. Pope Pius IX, *Quanta Cura*, para. 3.
35. Popc Pius IX, *Quanta Cura*, paras. 1, 4.

36. Pope Pius IX, *Quanta Cura*, paras. 4, 8.
37. Pope Leo XIII, *Inscrutabili Dei Consilio*, paras. 3, 5, 6, 15, fn 12 http://www.vatican.va/holy_father/leo_leo_xiii/encyclicals/documents/hf_1-xiii-enc-21041878... (accessed July 19, 2011).
38. Pope Leo XIII, *Diuturnum*, para. 3, 5, 7, 8, 16, 21- 24. http://www.vatican.va/holy_father/leo_xiii/encyclicals/documents/hf_1-xiii-enc-29061881... (accessed July 11, 2011).
39. Pope Leo XIII, *Humanum Genus*, paras. 8, 10, 12, 13, 22. http://www.vatican.va/holy_father/leo_xiii/encyclicals/documents/hf_1-xiii_enc_18840420... (accessed December 24, 2004).
40. Pope Leo XIII, *Immortale Dei*, paras. 1, 4, 6-10, 12. http://www.vatican.va/holy_father/leo_xiii/encyclicals/documents/hf_1-xiii_enc_01111885... (accessed July 11, 2010).
41. Pope Leo XIII, *Immortale Dei*, paras. 21 – 23, 24, 25, 26, 27, 34.
42. Pope Leo XIII, *Immortale Dei*, paras. 4, 31, 33, 36.
43. Pope Leo XIII, *Immortale Dei*, paras. 4, 31, 33, 36.
44. Pope Leo XIII, *Immortale Dei*, footnote 22.
45. Pope Leo XIII, *Immortale Dei*, para. 35.
46. Pope Leo XIII, *Immortale Dei*, paras. 13-15, 17, 18, 35.
47. Pope Leo XIII, *Immortale Dei*, paras. 35, 37, 38, 39.
48. Pope Leo XIII, *Immortale Dei*, paras. 41, 42, 43, 44, 45, 47.
49. Pope Leo XIII, *Immortale Dei*, paras. 46, 47.
50. Pope Leo XIII, *Libertas*, paras. 5 through 10. http://www.vatican.va/holy_father/leo_xiii/encyclicals/documents/hf_1-xiii_enc_20061888... (accessed December 28, 2004).
51. Pope Leo XIII, *Libertas*, paras. 9, 15.
52. Pope Leo XIII, *Libertas*, paras. 16, 17, 18, 19, 20, 21.
53. Pope Leo XIII, *Libertas*, para. 21.
54. Pope Leo XIII, *Libertas*, paras. 23-29, 35.
55. Pope Leo XIII, *Libertas*, para. 33.
56. Pope Leo XIII, *Libertas*, para. 34.
57. Pope Leo XIII, *Libertas*, paras. 36, 37.
58. Pope Leo XIII, *Libertas*, para. 38.
59. Pope Leo XIII, *Libertas*, para. 39.
60. Pope Leo XIII, *Libertas*, para. 40.
61. Pope Leo XIII, *Libertas*, para. 41.
62. Pope Leo XIII, *Libertas*, para. 43.
63. Pope Leo XIII, *Libertas*, para. 44.
64. Pope Leo XIII, *Longinqua Oceani*, paras. 5-6. http://www.vatican.va/holy_father/leo_xiii/encyclicals/documents/hf_1-xiii_enc_06011895... (accessed January 17, 2010).
65. Pope Leo XIII, *Longinqua Oceani*, para. 6.
66. Pope Leo XIII, *Longinqua Oceani*, para. 11.
67. Pope Leo XIII, *Longinqua Oceani*, paras. 13, 15.
68. Pope Leo XIII, *Longinqua Oceani*, paras. 13, 15.
69. Pope Leo XIII, *Longinqua Oceani*, para. 16.
70. Pope Leo XIII, *Longinqua Oceani*, para. 17.
71. Pope Leo XIII, *Longinqua Oceani*, para. 18.
72. Pope Leo XIII, *Longinqua Oceani*, para. 18.
73. Pope Leo XIII, *Longinqua Oceani*, para. 18.
74. Pope Leo XIII, *Longinqua Oceani*, paras. 20-21.

75. Pope Leo XIII, *Longinqua Oceani,* paras. 20-21.
76. Americanism Collection (MAMR), University of Notre Dame Archives (UNDA), University of Notre Dame, Notre Dame, Indiana.
77. Americanism Collection (MAMR), University of Notre Dame Archives (UNDA), University of Notre Dame, Notre Dame, Indiana; Gerald P. Fogarty, *The Vatican and the Americanist Crisis: Denis J. O'Connell American Agent In Rome 1885-1903* (Universita Gregoriana, 1974).
78. Moynihan, *The Life of Archbishop John Ireland,* 108-109.
79. Fogarty, *The Vatican and the Americanist Crisis: Denis J. O'Connell American Agent In Rome 1885-1903*, 265.
80. Fogarty, *The Vatican and the Americanist Crisis: Denis J. O'Connell American Agent In Rome 1885-1903*, 265.
81. Fogarty, *The Vatican and the Americanist Crisis: Denis J. O'Connell American Agent In Rome 1885-1903*, 264.
82. Fogarty, *The Vatican and the Americanist Crisis: Denis J. O'Connell American Agent In Rome 1885-1903*, 265, 267.
83. Fogarty, *The Vatican and the Americanist Crisis: Denis J. O'Connell American Agent In Rome 1885-1903*, 265, 267.
84. Fogarty, *The Vatican and the Americanist Crisis: Denis J. O'Connell American Agent In Rome 1885-1903*, 265, 267.
85. Fogarty, *The Vatican and the Americanist Crisis: Denis J. O'Connell American Agent In Rome 1885-1903*, 267-268.
86. Fogarty, *The Vatican and the Americanist Crisis: Denis J. O'Connell American Agent In Rome 1885-1903*, 275.
87. Msgr. O'Connell to Husband of Countess Sabini di Parravicino, Letter dated April 26, 1898, Americanism Collection Microfilm (hereinafter cited as MAMR), Reel 1, University of Notre Dame Archives (UNDA), Notre Dame, Indiana
88. Msgr. O'Connell to Countess Sabini di Parravicino, Letter dated June 10, 1898, MAMR 1, UNDA.
89. Pope Leo XIII, *Testem Benevolentiae Nostrae,* "True and False Americanism In Religion," in *The Great Encyclical Letters of Pope Leo XIII Plus Other Documents* (Rockford, Illinois: Tan Books and Publishers, Inc. 1995), 441.
90. Pope Leo XIII, *The Great Encyclical Letters of Pope Leo XIII Plus Other Documents*, 452.
91. Pope Leo XIII, *The Great Encyclical Letters of Pope Leo XIII Plus Other Documents*, 442 (emphasis in original), 444.
92. Will, *Life of James Cardinal Gibbons* (1911), 300-301.
93. Pope Leo XIII, *The Great Encyclical Letters of Pope Leo XIII Plus Other Documents*, 447-449.
94. Pope Leo XIII, *The Great Encyclical Letters of Pope Leo XIII Plus Other Documents*, 443.
95. Pope Leo XIII, *The Great Encyclical Letters of Pope Leo XIII Plus Other Documents*, 452.

6. THE STATE OF CATHOLIC LEADERSHIP IN 1948

1. Kevin M. Schultz, *Tri-Faith America: How Catholics and Jews Helped Postwar America to its Protestant Promise* (New York: Oxford University Press, 2011), 91.
2. John Cooney, *The American Pope: The Life and Times of Francis Cardinal Spellman* (New York: Dell Publishing, 1984), 348.

3. Cooney, *The American Pope*, 130; John Deedy, *Seven American Catholics* (Chicago, Illinois: The Thomas More Press, 1978), 73-76.
4. Deedy, *Seven American Catholics*, 82-87.
5. Deedy, *Seven American Catholics*, 77-78.
6. Deedy, *Seven American Catholics*, 68-69.
7. Deedy, *Seven American Catholics*, 72-73.
8. Cooney, *The American Pope*, 193-195.
9. Cooney, *The American Pope*, 167-170, 307-314.
10. Cooney, *The American Pope*, 351-358.
11. Benjamin Freedman, *Hidden Tyranny: A True Story* (Liberty Bell Publications), 25.
12. Cooney, *The American Pope*, 289, 350.
13. Henry R. Luce Papers, Box 2 File 29, Library of Congress, Washington, D.C.
14. W. A. Swanberg, *Luce and His Empire* (New York: Dell, 1973), 480-481, 499-500.
15. Deedy, *Seven American Catholics*, 79-82, 86-89.
16. Steven M. Avella, *This Confident Church: Catholic Leadership and Life in Chicago, 1940-1965* (Notre Dame, Indiana: University of Notre Dame Press, 1992), 3, 21-22, 71-74.
17. Avella, *This Confident Church*, 11-14.
18. Avella, *This Confident Church*, 4.
19. Avella, *This Confident Church*, 22-25.
20. Avella, *This Confident Church*, 26-29.
21. Avella, *This Confident Church*, 142-147.
22. Avella, *This Confident Church*, 142-147.
23. Avella, *This Confident Church*, 142-147.
24. Steve Rosswurm, *The FBI and the Catholic Church, 1935-1962* (Boston: University of Massachusetts Press, 2009), 133-179.
25. Avella, *This Confident Church*, 11-12.
26. Avella, *This Confident Church*, 53-96.
27. Rosswurm, *The FBI and the Catholic Church*, 180-225.
28. Rosswurm, *The FBI and the Catholic Church*, 226-273.

7. A THEOLOGIAN IS NEEDED

1. John Shaw Billings, Diary entry for May 20, 1948, John Shaw Billings Papers Diaries Volume 27, 153-54,South Caroliniana Library, University of South Carolina, Columbia, South Carolina.
2. John Shaw Billings, Diary entry for May 20, 1948, John Shaw Billings Papers Diaries Volume 27, 153-54,South Caroliniana Library, University of South Carolina, Columbia, South Carolina.
3. Paul Blanshard, *American Freedom and Catholic Power*, 34.
4. E Michael Jones, *Libido Dominandi: Sexual Liberation and Political Control*, 358.
5. Paul Blanshard, *American Freedom and Catholic Power*, 44.
6. Prof. Dondeyne "Church and State" *do-c Documentate Centrum Concile* Nr. 123 found at AND 0004.001 George Shea Papers Box 20, Monsignor William Noe Field Archives and Special Collections Center, Seton Hall University, South Orange, New Jersey
7. "National Affairs: Church v. State," *Time*, April 4, 1927. http://www.times.com/time/subscriber/printout/0,8816,722967,00.html (accessed February 25, 2012).
8. "National Affairs: Church v. State," *Time*, April 4, 1927.

9. "Religion: America in Rome," *Time,* February 25, 1946. http://www.time.com/time/subscriber/printout/0,8816,852693,00.html (accessed April 29, 2012).
10. "Religion: America in Rome," *Time,* February 25, 1946.
11. "Religion: America in Rome," *Time,* February 25, 1946.
12. "Religion: America in Rome," *Time,* February 25, 1946.
13. "Religion: America in Rome," *Time,* February 25, 1946.
14. "Religion: On the Roads to Rome," *Time* February 18, 1946. http://www.time.com/time/subscriber/printout/0,8816,792623,00.html (accessed April 29, 2012).
15. "Religion: On the Roads to Rome," *Time,* February 18, 1946.
16. "Religion: Yes & No," *Time,* July 29, 1946. http://www.times.com/time/subscriber/printout/0,8816,776965,00.htm (accessed February 25, 2012).

8. THE SECRET MEETING AT THE BILTMORE – APRIL 26, 1948

1. Minutes on Conference of Church and State April 26, 1948, Francis J Connell C.Ss.R. Papers, Redemptorist House Archives, Baltimore Province, Brooklyn, New York (hereafter cited as Minutes, Biltmore Conference).
2. Minutes, Biltmore Conference; Gary May, *Un-American Activities: The Trials of William Remington* (New York: Oxford University Press, 1994), 155-157.
3. Minutes, Biltmore Conference.
4. Minutes, Biltmore Conference.
5. Minutes, Biltmore Conference.
6. Minutes, Biltmore Conference.
7. Minutes, Biltmore Conference.
8. Minutes, Biltmore Conference; Statement on Church and State, June 17, 1948 , Francis J Connell C.Ss.R. Papers, Redemptorist House Archives, Baltimore, Province, Brooklyn New York (hereafter cited as Statement June 17, 1948).
9. Untitled text of talk by John Courtney Murray that begins with "Mr. Chairman, Ladies and Gentlemen," John Courtney Murray Papers, Box 6 File 445, Georgetown University Library, Special Collections Division, Washington, DC.
10. Paul Blanshard, "The Catholic Church and Fascism," *The Nation,* April 17, 1948, 417.
11. E Michael Jones, *Libido Dominandi: Sexual Liberation and Political Control* (South Bend, Indiana: St Augustine's Press, 2000), 358.
12. Paul Blanshard, *American Freedom and Catholic Power* (Boston, Massachusetts: The Beacon Press, 1949), 44.

9. THE MYSTERY MAN

1. Robert Blair Kaiser, interview by author, July 27, 2009.
2. Robert Blair Kaiser, *Clerical Error: A True Story* (New York: Continuum, 2003), 261.
3. Certificate and Record of birth # 41894 dated July 15, 1920.
4. "Rev. John Courtney Murray, 63, Leading Jesuit Theologian, Dies; Was Expert on Church-State Relations and on Freedom Under Religious Rules," *The New York Times* Saturday, August 19, 1967.
5. "Rev. John Courtney Murray, 63, Leading Jesuit Theologian, Dies; Was Expert on

Church-State Relations and on Freedom Under Religious Rules," *The New York Times* Saturday, August 19, 1967.

6. Emmet John Hughes, "A Man for Our Season," *John Courtney Murray Papers*: Box 28 Folder 1288, Georgetown University Library, Special Collections Division, Washington, D.C.
7. John Courtney Murray, "A Crisis in the History of Trent," *Thought* 7 (December 1932): 463-473, under "Bibliography," http://woodstock.georgetown.edu/Murray/1932.htm (accessed December 21, 2008), 464.
8. John Courtney Murray, "The Construction of a Christian Culture: I. Portrait of a Christian; II. Personality and the Community; III. The Humanism of God," abridged, and republished in *Bridging the Sacred and the Secular*, 101–123, under "Bibliography," http://woodstock.georgetown.edu/library/Murray/1940A.htm, 102 (accessed December 21, 2008), 102.
9. Murray, "The Construction of a Christian Culture," 102-103.
10. Murray, "The Construction of a Christian Culture," 103.
11. John Courtney Murray, "Necessary Adjustments to Overcoming Practical Difficulties," *Man and Modern Secularism: Essays on the Conflict of the Two Cultures*, edited by National Catholic Alumni Federation. (New York, NY: National Catholic Alumni Federation, 1940): 152–57.
12. Carlo Falconi, *Pope John and His Council: A Diary of the Second Vatican Council, September – December, 1962* (London: Weidenfeld and Nicolson, 1964), 207.
13. Jan De Volder, *The Spirit of Fr. Damien: The Leper Priest A Saint for Our Times.* (San Francisco, California: Ignatius Press, 2010), 23.
14. Fanfani, *Catholicism Protestantism and Capitalism*, 137, 143.
15. Fanfani, *Catholicism Protestantism and Capitalism*, 137, 143.
16. John Mackay Metzger, *The Hand and the Road: The Life and Times of John A. Mackay* (Louisville, Kentucky: Westminster John Knox Press, 2010), 62, 76-85, 92, 143.
17. John F. Piper, Jr. *Robert E. Speer: Prophet of the American Church* (Louisville, Kentucky: Geneva Press, 2000), 178.
18. Piper, *Robert E. Speer*, 285-286.
19. John Mackay Metzger, *The Hand and the Road: The Life and Times of John A. Mackay*, 62, 76-85, 92, 143.
20. Piper, *Robert E. Speer: Prophet of the American Church,* 263-264.
21. Piper, *Robert E. Speer: Prophet of the American Church,* 264-269.
22. Piper, *Robert E. Speer: Prophet of the American Church,* 271-272.
23. C. Gregg Singer, *The Unholy Alliance (*New Rochelle, New York: Arlington House Publishers, 1975), 130.
24. Singer, *The Unholy Alliance,* 136.
25. Singer, *The Unholy Alliance,* 137.
26. Metzger, *The Hand and the Road: The Life and Times of John A. Mackay,* 271-273.
27. Metzger, *The Hand and the Road: The Life and Times of John A. Mackay,* 273-274.
28. John Courtney Murray, "Current Theology Christian Co-operation," *Theological Studies* (September, 1942), 427-430.
29. Murray, "Current Theology Christian Co-operation," 414-416, 431.
30. Murray, "Current Theology Christian Co-operation," 414-416, 431.
31. Murray, "Current Theology Christian Co-operation," 414-416, 431.
32. John Courtney Murray, "Current Theology: Co-operation: Some Further Views,"

Theological Studies 4 (March 1943): 100-111, under "Bibliography," http://woodstock.georgetown.edu/library/murray/1943a.htm, (accessed February 12, 2012), 107-108.

33. John Courtney Murray, "Current Theology: Intercredal Co-operation: Its Theory and Its Organization," *Theological Studies* 4 (June 1943): 257-286, under "Bibliography," http://woodstock.georgetown.edu/library/murray/1943b.htm (accessed February 12, 2012), 259.
34. Murray, "Current Theology: Intercredal Co-operation: Its Theory and Its Organization," 279-281.
35. John Courtney Murray, "The Catholic, Jewish, Protestant Declaration on World Peace: An Interpretation by Rev. John Courtney Murray, SJ Editor of 'Theological Studies'," John Courtney Murray Papers, Box 6 Folder 483, Georgetown University Library, Special Collections Division, Washington, DC.
36. John Courtney Murray, "On the Problem of Co-operation: Some Clarifications," *American Ecclesiastical Review* 112 (March 1945): 194-214, under "Bibliography," http://woodstock.georgetown.edu/library/murray/1945f.htm, (accessed February 12, 2012)
37. Murray, "On the Problem of Co-operation: Some Clarifications," 209, 213-214.
38. John Courtney Murray to Luke, Letter dated March 20, 1943, John Courtney Murray Papers, Box 2 Folder 187, Georgetown University Library, Special Collections Division, Washington, D.C.
39. Murray to Luke letter dated March 20, 1943.
40. Murray to Luke letter dated March 20, 1943.
41. John Courtney Murray, Diary entry for March 23, 1943, John Courtney Murray Papers, Box 25 Folder 1210, Georgetown University Library, Special Collections Division, Washington, D.C.
42. Michael Davies, *The Second Vatican Council and Religious Liberty* (Long Prairie, Minnesota: Neumann Press, 1992), 155-157.
43. John Courtney Murray, "Freedom of Religion I. The Ethical Problem," *Theological Studies* 6 (June, 1945): 229-286, under "Bibliography," http://wodstock.georgetown.edu/library/murray/1945b.htm (accessed February 12, 2012), 229, 239-241, 244, 248-251, 263-264, 266-267, 269-272.
44. Murray, "Freedom of Religion I. The Ethical Problem," 272-283.
45. Murray, "Freedom of Religion I. The Ethical Problem," 277-278, 282-283.
46. Murray, "Freedom of Religion I. The Ethical Problem," 263-264, 282-283.
47. John Courtney Murray, "Separation of Church and State," *America,* December 7, 1946, under "Bibliography," http://woodstock.georgetown.edu/library/murray/1946e.htm (accessed February 12, 2012).
48. John Courtney Murray, "Separation of Church and State: True and False Concepts," *America,* February 15, 1947.
49. John Courtney Murray, "The Court Upholds Religious Freedom," *America,* March 8, 1947, under "Bibliography," http://woodstock.georgetown.edu/library/murray/1947b.htm (as accessed February 12, 2012).

10. SETTING THE STAGE FOR THE STAGED FIGHT

1. Metzger, *The Hand and the Road: The Life and Times of John A. Mackay,* 278, 283-285.
2. Singer, *The Unholy Alliance,* 141, 168.

3. Metzger, *The Hand and the Road: The Life and Times of John A. Mackay,* 269, 275-277, 280-285.
4. Metzger, *The Hand and the Road: The Life and Times of John A. Mackay*, 276-277.
5. Metzger, *The Hand and the Road: The Life and Times of John A. Mackay*, 275, 301-302
6. "Who's Who In the POAU?" *Our Sunday Visitor Press,* March 28, 1951, as found in the Francis J. Connell Papers of the Redemptorist Archives in Brooklyn New York, Folder marked "POAU Protestants and Other Americans ETC."
7. "Who's Who In the POAU?" 14-15
8. Metzger, *The Hand and the Road: The Life and Times of John A. Mackay,* 269, 275-277, 280-285, 301.
9. Editorials, *Christian Century,* November 19, 1947 (John Courtney Murray Papers, Box 6 Folder 498), November 26, 1947 (John Courtney Murray Papers, Box 6 Folder 488).
10. Editorials, *Christian Century,* November 26, 1947, December 10, 1947 (John Courtney Murray Papers, Box 6 Folder 488).
11. Rev. William E McManus, "Writer Says Protestant Magazine's Editorials Cloud State, Church Issue," NCWC News Service, December 22, 1947, John Courtney Murray Papers: Box 6 Folder 488, Georgetown University Library, Special Collections Division, Washington, D.C.
12. John Courtney Murray, "Dr. Morrison and the First Amendment I," *America,* March 6, 1948, 628.
13. Murray, "Dr. Morrison and the First Amendment I," 629.
14. John Courtney Murray, "Dr. Morrison and the First Amendment II," *America,* March 20, 1948, 685.
15. Murray, "Dr. Morrison and the First Amendment II," 686.
16. John Courtney Murray, "Religious Liberty: The Concern of All," *America,* February 7, 1948, under "Bibliography," http://woodstock.georgetown.edu/library/murray/1948e.htm (accessed February 12, 2012).
17. Murray, "Religious Liberty: The Concern of All."

11. THE CREATION OF PSYCHOLOGICAL WARFARE

1. Hugh Wilford, *The Mighty Wurlitzer: How the CIA Played America* (Cambridge, Massachusetts: Harvard University Press, 2008), 24.
2. Wilford, *The Mighty Wurlitzer: How the CIA Played America*, 24-26.
3. Leary, William M., ed. *The Central Intelligence Agency: History and Documents* (University, Alabama: University of Alabama Press, 1984), 131.
4. Leary, *The Central Intelligence Agency: History and Documents,* 132.
5. Wilford, *The Mighty Wurlitzer: How the CIA Played America*, 26-27.
6. Wilford, *The Mighty Wurlitzer: How the CIA Played America,* 26-27.
7. Wilford, *The Mighty Wurlitzer: How the CIA Played America* ,15-16; Alfred H. Paddock, Jr., *US Army Special Warfare: Its Origins, Psychological and Unconventional Warfare 1941-1952* (Fort Lesley J. McNair, Washington DC: National Defense University Press, 1982), 24.
8. Wilford, *The Mighty Wurlitzer*, 16; Paddock, *US Army Special Warfare,* 5.
9. Paddock, *US Army Special Warfare,* 5.
10. Paddock, *US Army Special Warfare*, 5-6.

11. Paddock, *US Army Special Warfare*, 8-9.
12. Paddock, *US Army Special Warfare*, 6.
13. Paddock, *US Army Special Warfare*, 6.
14. Paddock, *US Army Special Warfare*, 7-8.
15. Paddock, *US Army Special Warfare*, 10-11.
16. Paddock, *US Army Special Warfare*, 10-19.
17. Leary, *The Central Intelligence Agency: History and Documents*, 123.
18. Leary, *The Central Intelligence Agency: History and Documents*, 124-125.
19. Paddock, *US Army Special Warfare*, 24.
20. Wilford, *The Mighty Wurlitzer: How the CIA Played America*, 17-18.
21. Wilford, *The Mighty Wurlitzer: How the CIA Played America*, 17-19.
22. Henry R. Luce Memorandum entitled "Time, Inc., Abroad," estimated 1945, C.D. Jackson Papers, Box 70, Folder "Luce, Henry R. 1945," Dwight D Eisenhower Library, Abilene, Kansas.
23. Henry R. Luce to C.D. Jackson, Memorandum labeled "Strictly Confidential" and dated September 1, 1945, C.D. Jackson Papers Box 70 Folder "Luce, Henry R 1945," Dwight D. Eisenhower Library, Abilene, Kansas; C.D. Jackson to Henry R. Luce, "Memorandum Establishing and Explaining Time International" dated September 6, 1945, C.D. Jackson Papers Box 70 Folder "Luce Henry R. 1945," Dwight D. Eisenhower Library, Abilene, Kansas.
24. Henry R. Luce to Senior List (Editorial), Memorandum dated November 10 1945, C.D. Jackson Papers Box 70 Folder "Luce, Henry R. 1945," Dwight D. Eisenhower Library, Abilene, Kansas.
25. Wilford, *The Mighty Wurlitzer: How the CIA Played America*, 23.
26. Merle Miller, *Plain Speaking: An Oral Biography of Harry S. Truman* (New York: Tess Press, 2004),
    374.

12. C.D. JACKSON

1. Henry Luce III, interview by Mack Teasley, New York, July 26, 2000, transcript Dwight D. Eisenhower Library, Abilene, Kansas, 14-16.
2. Cook, "First Comes the Lie: C.D. Jackson and Political Warfare," 45; C.D. Jackson Chronology, C.D. Jackson Papers, Dwight D. Eisenhower Library, Abilene, Kansas.
3. Marie McCrum, interview with David Horrocks, New York, May 15, 1975, transcript Dwight D. Eisenhower Library, Abilene, Kansas, 69.
4. Cook, "First Comes the Lie: C.D. Jackson and Political Warfare," 45; C.D. Jackson Chronology, C.D. Jackson Papers, Dwight D. Eisenhower Library, Abilene, Kansas.
5. Marie McCrum, interview with David Horrocks, New York, May 15, 1975, transcript Dwight D. Eisenhower Library, Abilene, Kansas, 3-4.
6. McCrum, interview, 4.
7. Blanche Wiesen Cook, "First Comes the Lie: C.D. Jackson and Political Warfare," *Radical History Review* 31 (1984): 45-46; C.D. Jackson Chronology, C.D. Jackson Papers, Dwight D. Eisenhower Library, Abilene, Kansas.
8. C.D. Jackson to M. Gottfried, Memorandum dated September 23, 1941, C.D. Jackson Papers, Box 90, Dwight D. Eisenhower Library, Abilene, Kansas.

9. C.D. Jackson to Phil Rodgers, Memorandum dated October 18, 1941, C.D. Jackson Papers, Box 90, Dwight D. Eisenhower Library, Abilene, Kansas.
10. Phil Rodgers to C.D. Jackson, Letter dated October 14, 1941, C.D. Jackson Papers, Box 90, Dwight D. Eisenhower Library, Abilene, Kansas.
11. Rodgers to Jackson, Letter dated October 14, 1941.
12. Rodgers to Jackson, Letter dated October 14, 1941.
13. Rodgers to Jackson, Letter dated October 14, 1941.
14. Philip Rodgers to C.D. Jackson, undated letter regarding Sanford Griffith; undated handwritten note to C.D. Jackson; C.D. Jackson to Richardson Wood, memorandum dated April 10, 1942 on Time Incorporated letterhead; C.D. Jackson to Philip Rodgers, memorandum dated April 10, 1942 on Time Incorporated letterhead, C.D. Jackson Papers, Box 90, Dwight D. Eisenhower Library, Abilene, Kansas.
15. Cook, "First Comes the Lie: C.D. Jackson and Political Warfare," 45-46; Chronology, C.D. Jackson Papers at Dwight D. Eisenhower Library, Abilene, Kansas.
16. Archibald MacLeish to Henry R. Luce, letter dated August 27, 1941, Henry R. Luce Papers, Box 2 Folder 13, Library of Congress, Washington, D.C.

13. INTELLIGENCE, MEDIA, BANKING, AND COMMUNICATION

1. Kai Bird, *The Chairman John J. McCloy: The Making of the American Establishment* (New York: Simon & Schuster, 1992), 109, 411, 434.
2. Christopher Simpson, *Science of Coercion: Communication Research & Psychological Warfare 1945-1960* (New York: Oxford University Press, 1994), 3-4.
3. Wilford, *The Mighty Wurlitzer: How the CIA Played America,* 231-232.
4. Shawn J. Parry-Giles, *The Rhetorical Presidency, Propaganda, and the Cold War, 1945-1955* (Westport, Connecticut: Praeger Press, 2002), xx.
5. Burton Hersh, *The American Elite and the Origins of the CIA* (New York: Charles Scribner's Sons, 1992).
6. Simpson, *Science of Coercion,* 28-29.
7. Memorandum, undated, John Shaw Billings Papers, File 146, South Caroliniana Library, University of South Carolina, Columbia, South Carolina.
8. Henry R. Luce to Senior List, Memorandum dated December 8, 1945, C.D. Jackson Papers, Box 70 Folder "Luce, Henry R. 1945," Dwight D. Eisenhower Library, Abilene, Kansas.
9. "Preface to Time, [Work Copy]," undated Memorandum, 1-3, John Shaw Billings Papers, Folder 203, South Caroliniana Library, University of South Carolina, Columbia, South Carolina.
10. C.D. Jackson to Henry R. Luce, Memorandum dated May 29, 1956, C.D. Jackson Papers, Box 71, Folder "Luce, Henry R 1956," Dwight D. Eisenhower Library, Abilene, Kansas.
11. C.D. Jackson to John Davenport, Memorandum dated February 21, 1955, C.D. Jackson Papers, Box 39, Dwight D. Eisenhower Library, Abilene, Kansas.
12. C.D. Jackson to Ed Paine, Memorandum dated January 3, 1955, C.D. Jackson Papers, Box 39, Dwight D. Eisenhower Library, Abilene, Kansas.
13. John Davenport to C.D. Jackson, Memorandum dated December 30, 1954, C.D. Jackson Papers, Box 39, Dwight D. Eisenhower Library, Abilene, Kansas.

14. C.D. Jackson to Henry R. Luce, Memorandum dated June 29, 1949, C.D. Jackson Papers, Box 70, Folder "Luce, Henry R 1949," Dwight D. Eisenhower Library, Abilene, Kansas.
15. Jackson to Luce Memorandum dated June 29, 1949.
16. Jackson to Luce Memorandum dated June 29, 1949.
17. C.D. Jackson, notes on talk entitled "Communications and the Cold War" St. Louis Ad Club January 9, 1962, C.D. Jackson Papers, Box 97 File "Speech Texts, 1962 (4)," Dwight D. Eisenhower Library, Abilene, Kansas.
18. "Interview with C.D. Jackson on the influence of the Printed word" by the Center for the Study of Democratic Institutions, Santa Barbara, CA under a grant from the Ford Foundation, C.D. Jackson Papers, Box 97 File "Speech Texts, 1961 (3)," Dwight D. Eisenhower Library, Abilene, Kansas.
19. " Interview with C.D. Jackson on the influence of the Printed word" by the Center for the Study of Democratic Institutions, Santa Barbara, CA under a grant from the Ford Foundation, C.D. Jackson Papers, Box 97 File "Speech Texts, 1961 (3)," Dwight D. Eisenhower Library, Abilene, Kansas.
20. "Man of the Week," CBS, March 28, 1954 3:30 p.m. to 4:30 p.m., transcript, C.D. Jackson Papers, Box 99, Dwight D. Eisenhower Library, Abilene, Kansas.
21. Panel II Session 2 transcript, C.D. Jackson Papers, Box 97 File "Speech Texts, 1959 (2)," Dwight D. Eisenhower Library, Abilene, Kansas.
22. C.D. Jackson, talk on BBC News July 26, 1954, C.D. Jackson Papers, Box 100, Dwight D. Eisenhower Library, Abilene, Kansas.
23. C.D. Jackson, "What Price Intangibles?" Speech Made at the Commencement Exercises at the Harvard University Graduate School of Business Administration dated May 23, 1952, C.D. Jackson Papers, Box 101 Folder "Speech Texts, 1952(5)," Dwight D. Eisenhower Library, Abilene, Kansas.
24. C.D. Jackson to William E Daugherty, letter dated July 17, 1952, C.D. Jackson Papers, Box 110 File "War College – Washington," Dwight D. Eisenhower Library, Abilene, Kansas.
25. Jackson to Daugherty letter dated July 17, 1952.
26. C.D. Jackson to Dr. George Pettee, letter dated December 26, 1950, C.D. Jackson Papers, Box 110, Dwight D. Eisenhower Library, Abilene, Kansas.
27. C.D. Jackson, Speech before the National Security Commission & Committees of the American Legion St Louis, Missouri text dated August 28, 1953, C.D. Jackson Papers, Box 100 File "Speech Texts, 1953 (3)," Dwight D. Eisenhower Library, Abilene, Kansas.
28. C.D. Jackson, Speech before the Ohio Banker's Association text dated November 7, 1957, C.D. Jackson Papers, Box 98, Dwight D. Eisenhower Library, Abilene, Kansas. (emphasis present in original)
29. John Shaw Billings, *Oral History of Time, Inc. Part III,* dated March 4, 1966, approx. 31:40 mark, John Shaw Billings Papers: South Caroliniana Library, University of South Carolina, Columbia, South Carolina.
30. Archibald MacLeish to Henry R. Luce, Letter dated August 24, 1949, Henry R. Luce Papers, Box 2 File 13, Library of Congress, Washington, D.C.

14. AN ECONOMIC EXPLANATION OF THE COLD WAR

1. Michael Hudson, *Super Imperialism: The Origin and Fundamentals of U.S. World Dominance 2nd edition* (New York: Pluto Press, 2003), 165.
2. Anthony Santelli, "Money, Oil, Blood, Death," *Culture Wars* 32, 4 (March 2013): 17-19.
3. "Reconversion to What? It used to be called 'Capitalism.' By any Name Its Basis Is the Free Market,"
   Life, August 28, 1944.
4. Henry R. Luce to John Shaw Billings, Memorandum dated July 1, 1953, 2, 4 John Shaw Billings Papers, Folder 184, South Caroliniana Library, University of South Carolina, Columbia, South Carolina.
5. Luce to Billings, Memorandum dated July 1, 1953, 2-4.
6. Henry R. Luce, "Needed: A General Theory for US Action in World Affairs" address at the University Club New York, New York City, dated January 28, 1961, C.D. Jackson Papers, Box 71, Folder "Luce Henry R., 1961-1962," Dwight D. Eisenhower Library, Abilene, Kansas.
7. "Directive for the Editorial Development of Fortune (Preliminary Draft), 1, 23 John Shaw Billings Papers, Folder 110, South Caroliniana Library, University of South Carolina, Columbia, South Carolina.
8. Draft Revision of NSC 5501: Basic National Security Policy Top Secret [declass. 1998], undated, OCB Central File Series Box 71 Folder "Ideological Documents (6)," Dwight D. Eisenhower Library, Abilene, Kansas.
9. Ibid.; NSC 5501, dated January 7, 1955. http://webcache.googleusercontent.com/search?q=cache:fFvnujgM8hcJ:https://history.state.gov/historicaldocuments/frus1955-57v19/d6+national+security+council+5501&cd=2&hl=en&ct=clnk&gl=us (accessed February 17, 2013).
10. Fanfani, *Catholicism Protestantism and Capitalism,* 104, 115, 155.
11. Campbell R. McConnell, *Economics Principles Problems and Policies,* 9th ed. (New York: McGraw-Hill Book Company, 1984), 29, 33-38, 248, 260.
12. Richard J. Barnet and Ronald E. Muller, *Global Reach: The Power of the Multinational Corporations* (New York: Simon and Schuster, 1974), 239-241.
13. McConnell, *Economics, Principles, Problems, and Policies,* 404.
14. John Kenneth Galbraith, *American Capitalism,* rev. ed. (Boston: Houghton Mifflin Company, 1956), 35, as quoted in *Economics Principles, Problems, and Policies* by Campbell R. McConnell (9th Ed. McGraw-Hill Book Company 1984), 404.
15. Fanfani, *Catholicism Protestantism and Capitalism,* 110, 112-114, 116, 117.
16. Stanley G. Payne, *The Franco Regime 1936-1975* (Madison, Wisconsin: University of Wisconsin Press, 1987), 107-108, 119.
17. Payne, *The Franco Regime 1936-1975,* 182-183, 207, 362-366.
18. Payne, *The Franco Regime 1936-1975,* 350-351, 368-369.
19. Payne, *The Franco Regime 1936-1975,* 392-393, 470.
20. C.D. Jackson, "American industry has become a weapon instead of a whipping boy" text of talk given to "Pittsburgh," dated September, 1950, C.D. Jackson Papers, Box 101, Dwight D. Eisenhower Library, Abilene, Kansas.
21. Jeremy Isaacs and Taylor Downing, *Cold War: An Illustrated History, 1945-1991* (Boston, Massachusetts: Little Brown and Company, 1998), 24.

22. Thomas G. Paterson and Robert J. McMahon, editors, *The Origins of the Cold War*, 3rd Edition (Lexington, Massachusetts: D.C. Heath and Company, 1991), 20.
23. Paterson and McMahon, *The Origins of the Cold War*, 21.
24. Paterson and McMahon, *The Origins of the Cold War*, 244.
25. Henry R. Luce to C.D. Jackson, Memorandum dated May 11, 1949, C.D. Jackson Papers, Box 70, Folder "Luce, Henry R 1949," Dwight D. Eisenhower Library, Abilene, Kansas.
26. Wilford, *The Mighty Wurlitzer: How the CIA Played America*, 154.
27. Paterson and McMahon, *The Origins of the Cold War*, 241.
28. C.D. Jackson, "American industry has become a weapon instead of a whipping boy" text of talk given to "Pittsburgh," dated September 1950, C.D. Jackson Papers, Box 101, Dwight D. Eisenhower Library, Abilene, Kansas.
29. C.D. Jackson, "The Close of the Decade of Decision" text of talk given to the Salesmen Association of the Paper Industry, dated February 24, 1959, C.D. Jackson Papers, Box 98 File "Speech Texts, 1959(4)," Dwight D. Eisenhower Library, Abilene, Kansas.
30. C.D. Jackson, "Communication and Management in the Cold War" text of talk given at CIPM Dinner, dated January 31, 1962, C.D. Jackson Papers, Box 97, Dwight D. Eisenhower Library, Abilene, Kansas.
31. C.D. Jackson, "Social-Psychological Aspects of the World Conflict" text of talk to the National War College, dated March 24, 1959, C.D. Jackson Papers, Box 98 File "Speech Texts, 1959 (8)," Dwight D. Eisenhower Library, Abilene, Kansas.
32. Grocer's Association Panel Discussion October 28, 1959, C.D. Jackson Papers, Box 97 File "Speech Texts, 1959 (2)," Dwight D. Eisenhower Library, Abilene, Kansas.

15. TWO CATHOLIC THEOLOGIANS

1. Francis J. Connell, C.SS.R, "Address of Temporary President at Firs Session of the Inaugural Meeting of Catholic Theological Society of America," dated June 25, 1946, Catholic Theological Society of America Archives, Archive 88, Box 9, Folder 12, Catholic University of America, Washington, D.C.
2. "Connell Franciscus"; "Personnel file"; "Questionnaire for Roman Catalogue," Francis J. Connell Papers, File Connell 1 Cause for Beatification, Redemptorist House Archives, Brooklyn, New York.
3. "Connell Franciscus"; "Personnel file"; "Questionnaire for Roman Catalogue," Francis J. Connell Papers, File Connell 1 Cause for Beatification, Redemptorist House Archives, Brooklyn, New York; "Fr. Francis J. Connell, C.Ss.R.," *Who's Who in America* 31 (1960-1961), Francis J. Connell Papers, Redemptorist House Archives, Brooklyn, New York
4. Fr. Carl Hoegerl, C.Ss.R., interview by author, May 24, 2010.
5. Hoegerl interview by author.
6. Hoegerl interview by author.
7. Hoegerl interview by author.
8. Hoegerl interview by author.
9. Fr. Titus, SA, "Every Priest Is Appointed to Act for Men in Their Relationship with God," Francis J. Connell Papers, Redemptorist House Archives, Brooklyn, New York.
10. Titus, "Every Priest Is Appointed to Act for Men in Their Relationship with God."
11. Joseph A. Komonchak, "Fenton, Joseph (1906-1969)," *The Encyclopedia of American*

Catholic History, ed. Michael Glazier and Thomas J. Shelley (1997), 505-506; *Who's Who In America* Vol. 28, 1954-1955, 851.

12. Joseph A. Komonchak, "Fenton, Joseph (1906-1969)," *The Encyclopedia of American Catholic History,* ed. Michael Glazier and Thomas J. Shelley (1997), 505-506; *Who's Who In America* Vol. 28, 1954-1955, 851.
13. "Eulogy for Msgr. Fenton," *The Catholic Observer,* July 18, 1969.
14. "Eulogy for Msgr. Fenton," *The Catholic Observer*; "Funeral Mass Offered for Msgr. Fenton," *The Catholic Observer,* July 11, 1969.
15. Robert Blair Kaiser, interview by author via telephone, July 21, 2010; Robert Blair Kaiser, *Clerical Error: A True Story* (New York: Continuum, 2002), 191, 214.
16. AZ, interview by author via telephone, December 28, 2009.

16. THE CATHOLICS RESPOND

1. Joseph Clifford Fenton, "*Time* and Pope Leo," *American Ecclesiastical Review* CXIV (May, 1946): 369.
2. Fenton, "*Time* and Pope Leo," 375.
3. Fenton, "*Time* and Pope Leo," 371.
4. Fenton, "*Time* and Pope Leo," 369-371, 375.
5. Fenton, "*Time* and Pope Leo," 371-373.
6. "Religion: Yes & No," *Time,* July 29, 1946. http://www.time.com/time/subscriber/printout/0,8816,776965,00.html (accessed April 29, 2012).
7. "Religion: Yes & No," *Time,* July 29, 1946. http://www.time.com/time/subscriber/printout/0,8816,776965,00.html (accessed April 29, 2012).
8. Joseph Clifford Fenton, "The Catholic Church and Freedom of Religion," *American Ecclesiastical Review* CXV, (October 1946): 292-293.
9. Fenton, "The Catholic Church and Freedom of Religion," 295-296.
10. Fenton, "The Catholic Church and Freedom of Religion," 296-297.
11. Fenton, "The Catholic Church and Freedom of Religion," 298.
12. Fenton, "The Catholic Church and Freedom of Religion," 298-301.
13. Msgr. Joseph Fenton to Msgr. Cecchetti, letter dated February 20, 1952, Joseph Clifford Fenton Papers, Elms College, Chicopee, Massachusetts.
14. Francis J. Connell, C.SS.R, "Address of Temporary President at First Session of the Inaugural Meeting of Catholic Theological Society of America," dated June 25, 1946, Catholic Theological Society of America Archives, Archive 88, Box 9, Folder 12, Catholic University of America, Washington, D.C.
15. Connell, "Address of Temporary President at First Session of the Inaugural Meeting of Catholic Theological Society of America."
16. "Minutes of the Meetings of the Committee on Current Problems of The Catholic Theological Society of America," dated December 11, 1946, Catholic Theological Society of America Archives, Archive 88, Box 2, Folder 32, Catholic University of America, Washington, D.C.
17. Fr. Edmond D. Benard to Fr. Francis J. Connell, letter dated January 10, 1947, Catholic Theological Society of America Archives, Archive 88, Box 2, Folder 32, Catholic University of America, Washington, D.C.
18. Benard to Connell letter dated January 10, 1947.

19. "Notice for meeting of the CTSA for June 30, 1947, through July 2, 1947," Catholic Theological Society of America Archives, Archives 88, Box 9, Folder 13, Catholic University of America, Washington, D.C.
20. Donald E. Pelotte, SSS, *John Courtney Murray: Theologian in Conflict* (New York: Paulist Press, 1976), 16.
21. President's Report, Catholic Theological Society of America (Second Annual Meeting) of the CTSA for June 30, 1947 through July 2, 1947, Catholic Theological Society of America Archives, Archives 88, Box 9, Folder 13, Catholic University of America, Washington, D.C.
22. Fr. Eugene Burke to Msgr. James E. O'Connell, Letter dated December 16, 1947, Catholic Theological Society of America Archives, Archive 88, Box 2, Folder 32, Catholic University of America, Washington, D.C.
23. John Courtney Murray to Francis J. Connell, Letter dated January 14, 1948, Francis J Connell Papers, Redemptorist House Archives, Baltimore Province, Brooklyn, New York.

17. "THE GOVERNMENTAL REPRESSION OF HERESY"

1. John A. Ryan and Moorhouse F. X. Millar, *The State and the Church.* (New York: The MacMillan Company, 1930), 26-31.
2. Ryan and Millar, *The State and the Church,* 31-32.
3. Ryan and Millar, *The State and the Church,* 31-32.
4. Ryan and Millar, *The State and the Church,* 31-32.
5. Ryan and Millar, *The State and the Church*, 5, 32-33; Pope Leo XIII, *Immortale Dei* para. 7. http://www.vatican.va/holy_father/leo_xiii/encyclicals/documents/hf_l-xiii_enc_01111885... (accessed July 11, 2010).
6. Ryan and Millar, *The State and the Church*, 32-35, 37.
7. Ryan and Millar, *The State and the Church*, 32-34.
8. Ryan and Millar, *The State and the Church*, 41-42.
9. Ryan and Millar, *The State and the Church*, 39-41.
10. Ryan and Millar, *The State and the Church*, 35-36.
11. Ryan and Millar, *The State and the Church*, 36-37.
12. Ryan and Millar, *The State and the Church*, 37-39.
13. John Courtney Murray, "Governmental Repression of Heresy," in *Proceedings of the Third Annual Convention of the Catholic Theological Society of America Chicago* (Bronx, New York: Catholic Theological Society of America): 26–98, under "Bibliography," http://woodstock.georgetown.edu/library/murray/1948c.htm (accessed January 20, 2011), 97-98.
14. Murray, "Governmental Repression of Heresy," 29-34.
15. Murray, "Governmental Repression of Heresy," 35-36.
16. John Lamont, "Determining the Content and degree of Authority of Church Teachings" *The Thomist* 72 (2008): 371-407; John Lamont, "The Historical Conditioning of Church Doctrine" *The Thomist* 60 (1996): 511-535.
17. John Courtney Murray to Clare Boothe Luce, Letter dated February 27 [est. 1962], Clare Boothe Luce Papers Box 795 Folder 11, Library of Congress, Washington, D.C.
18. Murray, "Governmental Repression of Heresy," 39, 42-52.

19. Murray, "Governmental Repression of Heresy," 28-29, 52-56, 58-59, 85-86, 89-92.
20. Murray, "Governmental Repression of Heresy," 90, 93, 95-98.
21. Murray, "Governmental Repression of Heresy," 89-90, 95-96.
22. Murray, "Governmental Repression of Heresy," 26-28, 37, 85, 97-98.
23. Murray, "Governmental Repression of Heresy," 28-29, 85, 87, 97-98.
24. Murray, "Governmental Repression of Heresy," 28-29, 85, 87, 97-98.
25. Francis Connell, undated response to Murray's "Governmental Repression of Heresy," 98-100, under "Bibliography," http://woodstock.georgetown.edu/library/murray/1948c.htm (accessed January 20, 2011), 98-100.
26. Connell, undated response, 98-100.
27. Connell, undated response, 100.
28. Connell, undated response, 100.
29. Francis J. Connell, "Christ the King of Civil Rulers" *American Ecclesiastical Review* Vol. CXIX (October, 1948), 248, 253.
30. Connell, "Christ the King of Civil Rulers," 252.
31. Connell, "Christ the King of Civil Rulers," 244-246.
32. Connell, "Christ the King of Civil Rulers," 246.
33. Connell, "Christ the King of Civil Rulers," 247-248.
34. Connell, "Christ the King of Civil Rulers," 247-248.

18. THE RED SCARE

1. Jeremy Isaacs and Taylor Downing editors, *Cold War: An Illustrated History, 1945-1991* (New York: Little, Brown and Company, 1998), 107-116.
2. Isaacs and Downing, *Cold War: An Illustrated History*, 116-134.
3. Isaacs and Downing, *Cold War: An Illustrated History*, 107-116.

19. MURRAY APPEARS IN TIME

1. George W. Shea "Murrayites," AND 0004.001 George Shea Papers, Box 19, Monsignor William Noe Field Archives and Special Collections Center, Seton Hall University, South Orange, New Jersey.
2. John Courtney Murray, "Contemporary Orientations of Catholic Thought on Church and State in the Light of History," *Theological Studies* (June 1949): http://woodstock.georgetown.edu/library/Murray/1949b.htm (accessed April 24, 2012), 177-178, 185, 188-189.
3. Murray, "Contemporary Orientations of Catholic Thought on Church and State in the Light of History," 188-189.
4. Murray, "Contemporary Orientations of Catholic Thought on Church and State in the Light of History, " 229-234.
5. Murray, "Current Theology on Religious Freedom," *Theological Studies* 10 (September 1949) http://woodstock.georgetown.edu/library/Murray/1949c.htm (accessed April 24, 2012).
6. Murray, "Current Theology on Religious Freedom," 409, 414 footnote 26, 427-429.
7. Murray, "Current Theology on Religious Freedom," 410-412.
8. Murray, "Current Theology on Religious Freedom," 413-414.
9. Murray, "Current Theology on Religious Freedom," 416-420.

10. Murray, "Current Theology on Religious Freedom," 420-421.
11. Murray, "Current Theology on Religious Freedom," 429.
12. Murray, "Current Theology on Religious Freedom," 430.
13. Murray, "Current Theology on Religious Freedom," 430.
14. Murray, "Current Theology on Religious Freedom," 430-431.
15. Robert T. Handy, *A History of the Union Theological Seminary of New York* (New York: Columbia University Press, 1987), 188.
16. Handy, *A History of the Union Theological Seminary of New York,* 184.
17. Handy, *A History of the Union Theological Seminary of New York,* 222.
18. Handy, *A History of the Union Theological Seminary of New York,* 213.
19. Handy, *A History of the Union Theological Seminary of New York,* 218.
20. Clare Boothe Luce appointment calendar for 1947, Clare Boothe Luce Papers, Box 29 Folder 5, Library of Congress, Washington, D.C.
21. Theological Discussion Group (East Coast) and Membership lists, correspondence, memoranda, minutes 1933-1958, Yale Divinity School Library, Special Collections, New Haven, Connecticut.
22. J. S. Bixler, "The Problem of God: I. Three Contrasts in Contemporary Thought About God," Theological Discussion Group (East Coast) and Membership lists, correspondence, memoranda, minutes 1933-1958, Yale Divinity School Library, Special Collections, New Haven, Connecticut.
23. John Courtney Murray, "Contemporary Orientations of Catholic Thought On Church and State In the Light of History," dated April, 1949, 38, Yale Divinity School Library, Special Collections, New Haven, Connecticut.
24. Murray, "Contemporary Orientations of Catholic Thought on Church and State in the Light of History," 3-4.
25. Murray, "Contemporary Orientations of Catholic Thought on Church and State in the Light of History," 4-9.
26. Cooney, *The American Pope: The Life and Times of Francis Cardinal Spellman,* 237.
27. "Religion: Across the Gulf," *Time,* September 12, 1949. http://www.time.com/time/printout/0,8816,888629,00.html (accessed December 31, 2009).
28. "Religion: Across the Gulf," *Time.*
29. "Religion: Across the Gulf," *Time.*
30. "Religion: Across the Gulf," *Time.*
31. "Religion: Across the Gulf," *Time.*

20. PIUS XII CAUTIONS THEOLOGIANS

1. AZ, interviewed by author, December 28, 2009.
2. AZ, interviewed by author, December 28, 2009; Joseph Filipowicz, "The Sad Story of Thomism in North America," *Culture Wars* Vol. 31, 5 (April 2012): 36, 38, 41.
3. Charles Journet, *Journet Maritain Correspondence* (Paris: Editions Saint-Paul, 1996) Vol IV: 56-58. The original French: "Le problem est tres grave ici, les catholiques americains oscillant entre un total liberalism (dans la tradition du pays) et des affirmations doctrinales "theocratiques" (apprises a Rome et dans les manuels de theologie) qui reisquent de les render odieux a leurs concitoyens non catholiques. Le seul qui tente une synthese bien orientee est le Pere jesuite J. Courtney Murray, que je cite dans mon chapitre."

4. John Courtney Murray, “Current Theology on Religious Freedom,”*Theological Studies,* 10 (September 1949): 426. http://woodstock.georgetown.edu/library/Murray/1949c.htm (accessed April 24, 2012).
5. Journet, *Journet Maritain Correspondence,* 666-667.
6. John Courtney Murray, "The Natural Law," In *Great Expressions of Human Rights,* ed. Robert M. MacIver (New York: Harper), 297, 334-336. http://woodstock.georgetown.edu/library/Murray/whtt_c13_1950a.htm (accessed April 24, 2012).
7. Murray, “The Natural Law,” 302-309.
8. John J. McCloy to Henry R. Luce, Letter dated July 18, 1950, Henry R. Luce Papers: Box 2 Folder 14, Library of Congress, Washington, D.C.
9. John Courtney Murray, “Report and Recommendations Project: Church and State in Germany,” John Courtney Murray Papers: Box 6 Folder 507, Georgetown University Library, Special Collections Division, Washington, D.C.
10. Murray, “Report and Recommendations Project: Church and State in Germany.”
11. Murray, “Report and Recommendations Project: Church and State in Germany.”
12. Murray, “Report and Recommendations Project: Church and State in Germany.”
13. Murray, “Report and Recommendations Project: Church and State in Germany.”
14. Murray, “Report and Recommendations Project: Church and State in Germany.”
15. Murray, “Report and Recommendations Project: Church and State in Germany.”
16. Murray, “Report and Recommendations Project: Church and State in Germany.”
17. Pope Pius XII, *Humani Generis,* paras. 1, 2, 3. http://www.vatican.va/holy_father/pius_xii/encyclicals/documents/hf_p-xii_enc_12081950... (accessed January 18, 2010).
18. Pope Pius XII, *Humani Generis,* para. 2.
19. Pope Pius XII, *Humani Generis,* para. 4.
20. Pope Pius XII, *Humani Generis,* paras. 9, 10, 11.
21. Pope Pius XII, *Humani Generis,* paras. 14, 15.
22. Pope Pius XII, *Humani Generis,* paras. 41, 43.
23. Pope Pius XII, *Humani Generis,* paras. 34-35.

21. MURRAY SOUNDS ALARM BELLS

1. Msgr. Montini to Samuel Cardinal Stritch, Letter dated May 4, 1951, Samuel Cardinal Stritch Personal Papers, Box 4 Folder 10, Archdiocese of Chicago’s Joseph Cardinal Bernardin Archives and Records Center, 711 West Monroe Street, Chicago, Illinois.
2. Pope Leo XIII, “Testem Benevolentiae Nostrae,” *The Great Encyclical Letters of Pope Leo XIII Plus Other Documents.* (Rockford, Illinois: Tan Books and Publishers, Inc., 1995), 441-442.
3. John Courtney Murray, “The Crisis in Church-State Relationships in the U.S.A,” Samuel Cardinal Stritch Personal Papers, Box 4 Folder 10, Archdiocese of Chicago’s Joseph Cardinal Bernardin Archives and Records Center, 711 West Monroe Street, Chicago, Illinois.
4. Murray, “The Crisis in Church-State Relationships in the U.S.A.”
5. Pelotte, *John Courtney Murray: Theologian in Conflict,* 34-35.

22. SHEA VERSUS MURRAY

1. "Biographical/Historical Note," George Shea Papers, 1927-1990, AND 0004.001The Monsignor Field Archives & Special Collection Center, Seton Hall University. http://academic.shu.edu/findingaids/adn0004.001.html (accessed August 17, 2013).
2. Msgr. Francis Seymour, interviewed by author via telephone, August 28, 2013; Msgr. Francis Seymour to author, Letter dated August 28, 2013.
3. George W. Shea, "Catholic Doctrine and 'Religion of State'," *American Ecclesiastical Review*. CXXIII (September, 1950), 164-165.
4. Shea, "Catholic Doctrine and 'Religion of State'," 165-168.
5. Shea, "Catholic Doctrine and 'Religion of State'," 165-168.
6. Shea, "Catholic Doctrine and 'Religion of State'," 165-168.
7. Shea, "Catholic Doctrine and 'Religion of State'," 168.
8. Shea, "Catholic Doctrine and 'Religion of State'," 168-169.
9. Shea, "Catholic Doctrine and 'Religion of State'," 171-172.
10. Shea, "Catholic Doctrine and 'Religion of State'," 171-172.
11. Shea, "Catholic Doctrine and 'Religion of State'," 173-174.
12. Rev. Joseph Deisz to Francis J. Connell, Letter dated March 11, 1951 to Fr. Connell, Francis J. Connell Papers, Redemptorist House Archives, Baltimore Province, Brooklyn, New York.
13. John Courtney Murray, "The Problem of the 'Religion of the State'" *American Ecclesiastical Review, (*May 1951): 327, 337. http://woodstock.georgetown.edu/library/murray/1951b.htm (accessed April 21, 2012).
14. Murray, "The Problem of the 'Religion of the State'," 349-350 and footnote 3.
15. Murray, "The Problem of the 'Religion of the State'," 335-336.
16. Murray, "The Problem of the 'Religion of the State'," 333-334.
17. Murray, "The Problem of the 'Religion of the State'," 334.
18. Murray, "The Problem of the 'Religion of the State'," 344-345, 350.
19. Pelotte, *John Courtney Murray: Theologian in Conflict,* fn. 27, 62.
20. Pelotte, 35; fn. 27, 62; Murray, "The Problem of the 'Religion of the State'," fn. 34, 63.
21. George W. Shea notes from AND 0004.001 George Shea Papers: Box 19, Monsignor William Noe Field Archives and Special Collections Center, Seton Hall University, South Orange, New Jersey.
22. George W. Shea notes from AND 0004.001 George Shea Papers, Box 19, Monsignor William Noe Field Archives and Special Collections Center, Seton Hall University, South Orange, New Jersey.

23. MURRAY GOES TO YALE

1. Pelotte, *John Courtney Murray: Theologian in Conflict,* 31-33.
2. Pelotte, *John Courtney Murray: Theologian in Conflict,* 32.
3. Memorandum undated, John Courtney Murray Papers, Box 28, Folder 1251, Georgetown University Library, Special Collections Division, Washington D.C.
4. "Education: For Yale, a Thomist," *Time,* August 13, 1951. http://www.time.com/time/printout/0,8816,889191,00.html (accessed December 31, 2009).
5. Francis J. Connell, "The Theory of the 'Lay State'", *American Ecclesiastical Review* CXXV (July 1951), 7-8.

6. Connell, "The Theory of the 'Lay State'", 8-9.
7. John Courtney Murray, "For the Freedom and Transcendence of the Church," *American Ecclesiastical Review* 126 (January 1952). http://woodstock.georgetown.edu/library/Murray/1952b.htm (accessed April 21, 2012).
8. Connell, "The Theory of the 'Lay State'", 9-13.
9. Connell, "The Theory of the 'Lay State'", 11-13. (emphasis in original)
10. Connell, "The Theory of the 'Lay State'", 17.
11. Connell, "The Theory of the 'Lay State'", 17-18.
12. Connell, "The Theory of the 'Lay State'", 18.
13. George W. Shea, "Orientations on Church and State", *American Ecclesiastical Review* CXXV (December 1951), 405-406.
14. Shea, "Orientations on Church and State," 406-407.
15. Shea, "Orientations on Church and State," 407-408.
16. Shea, "Orientations on Church and State," 408-409.
17. Shea, "Orientations on Church and State," 409-410.
18. Shea, "Orientations on Church and State," 410-413.
19. Shea, "Orientations on Church and State," 413-415.
20. Shea, "Orientations on Church and State," 413-415.
21. Shea, "Orientations on Church and State," 413-415.
22. Shea, "Orientations on Church and State," 414-415.

24. THE "SUPERCILIOUS QUIBBLER" ENDS THE DISCUSSION

1. John Courtney Murray, "For the Freedom and Transcendence of the Church," *American Ecclesiastical Review* CXXVI (January, 1952), 28-33.
2. Murray, "For the Freedom and Transcendence of the Church," 33-38 and footnote 14.
3. Murray, "For the Freedom and Transcendence of the Church," 45.
4. Murray, "For the Freedom and Transcendence of the Church," 43-48 and footnote 15.
5. Francis J. Connell, "Reply to Father Murray" *American Ecclesiastical Review* CXXVI (January 1952), 49-50; Shea, "Catholic Doctrine and 'The Religion of the State'," 164-165.
6. Connell, "Reply to Father Murray," 50; cf. Francis J. Connell, "The Theory of the 'Lay State'," *American Ecclesiastical Review,* CXXV (July 1951), 13.
7. Connell, "Reply to Father Murray," 51; cf. Francis J. Connell, "Christ the King of Civil Rulers" *American Ecclesiastical Review* CXIX, 4 (October 1948), 249.
8. Connell, "Reply to Father Murray," 51; Murray, "For the Freedom and Transcendence of the Church," footnotes 3 and 6, and 29, 31.
9. Connell, "Reply to Father Murray," 51-52; Murray, "For the Freedom and Transcendence of the Church," 28.
10. Connell, "Reply to Father Murray," 53; Connell, "The Theory of the 'Lay State'," 13.
11. Connell, "Reply to Father Murray," 53; Murray, "For the Freedom and Transcendence of the Church," 33.
12. Connell, "Reply to Father Murray," 53-54; Murray, "For the Freedom and Transcendence of the Church," 31 fn.
13. Connell, "Reply to Father Murray," 54-57; cf. Murray, "For the Freedom and Transcendence of the Church," 31 fn.

14. Connell, "Reply to Father Murray," 54-57; cf. Murray, "For the Freedom and Transcendence of the Church," 31 fn.
15. Connell, "Reply to Father Murray," 57.
16. Connell, "Reply to Father Murray," 58-59.
17. Murray, "Freedom and Transcendence of the Church," fn 1.
18. These were "Leo XIII on Church and State: The General Structure of the Controversy," "Leo XIII: Separation of Church and State," "Leo XIII: Two Concepts of Government," "Leo XIII: Two Concepts of Government. II. Government and the Order of Culture," "On the Structure of the Church-State Problem."
19. Tom Chapman to R.P. Gounley, Fr. Rector, Letter dated January 31, 1952, Francis J. Connell Papers, Redemptorist House Archives, Baltimore Province, Brooklyn, New York.
20. Rev. Joseph Deisz to Francis J. Connell, Letter dated January 4, 1951, Francis J. Connell Papers, Redemptorist House Archives, Baltimore Province, Brooklyn, New York.
21. Rev. Joseph Deisz to Francis J. Connell, Letter dated January 23, 1952, Francis J. Connell Papers, Redemptorist House Archives, Baltimore Province, Brooklyn, New York.
22. Rev. Joseph Deisz to Francis J. Connell, Letter dated May 23, 1951, Francis J. Connell Papers, Redemptorist House Archives, Baltimore Province, Brooklyn, New York.

25. MURRAY LECTURES AT YALE

1. "Noted Jesuit Says Divine Authority Over Spirit of Man is Basic Premise," *New Hampshire Evening Register* February 2, 1952, as found in John Courtney Murray Papers: Box 6 Folder 443, Georgetown University Library, Special Collections Division, Washington, D.C.
2. "Noted Jesuit Says Divine Authority Over Spirit of Man in Basic Premise."
3. "Noted Jesuit Says Divine Authority Over Spirit of Man in Basic Premise."
4. Yale University News Bureau Release # 299 dated February 6, 1952, John Courtney Murray Papers, Box 6 Folder 443, Georgetown University Library, Special Collections Division, Washington, D.C.
5. Yale University News Bureau Release # 299.
6. Yale University News Bureau Release # 299.
7. Yale University News Bureau Release # 324 dated February 9, 1952, John Courtney Murray Papers, Box 6 Folder 443, Georgetown University Library, Special Collections Division, Washington, D.C.
8. Yale University News Bureau Release # 324.
9. Yale University News Bureau Release # 324.
10. Yale University News Bureau Release # 334, dated February 13, 1952, John Courtney Murray Papers: Box 6 Folder 443, Georgetown University Library, Special Collections Division, Washington, D.C.
11. Yale University News Bureau Release # 334.

26. CONFLICT WITH SPAIN

1. Joseph C. Fenton, "Spain and Religious Freedom" *American Ecclesiastical Review* CXXVII (September 1952), 161-162.

2. List of books on Spain at AND 0004.001 George Shea Papers: Box 19, Monsignor William Noe Field Archives and Special Collections Center, Seton Hall University, South Orange, New Jersey.
3. "Religion: Toleration in Seville," *Time,* March 17, 1952. http://www.time.com/time/subscriber/printout/0,8816,816,816129,00.html (accessed May 12, 2012).
4. "Religion: Toleration in Seville," *Time,* March 17, 1952. http://www.time.com/time/subscriber/printout/0,8816,816,816129,00.html (accessed May 12, 2012).
5. "Religion: Four Centuries Late," *Time,* April 7, 1952. As retrieved from the Francis J. Connell Papers, Redemptorist House Archives, Baltimore Province, Brooklyn, New York.
6. "Religion: Four Centuries Late," *Time,* April 7, 1952. As retrieved from the Francis J. Connell Papers, Redemptorist House Archives, Baltimore Province, Brooklyn, New York.
7. "Spanish Decry U.S. Catholic View; Religious Freedom Labeled 'Error'," *New York Times,* May 12, 1952. As retrieved from the Francis J. Connell Papers, Redemptorist House Archives, Baltimore Province, Brooklyn, New York.
8. "Spanish Decry US Catholic View: Religious Freedom Labeled 'Error'".
9. "Spanish Decry U.S. Catholic View; Religious Freedom Labeled 'Error'".
10. "Religious Liberty In Spain," *America,* May 24, 1952, 218.
11. "Religious Liberty In Spain."
12. Rev. George Shea, "Spain and Its Protestants," *The Advocate* Vol. 1, 22(May 24, 1952).
13. Pelotte. *John Courtney Murray: Theologian in Conflict,* 35-36.
14. John Courtney Murray, "A Memorable Man." http://woodstock.georgetown.edu/library/Murray/1967e.htm (accessed January 3, 2010).
15. Murray, "A Memorable Man."
16. Robert Blair Kaiser, *Clerical Error: A True Story* (New York: Continuum, 2003), 132.
17. "The Rev. Gustave A. Weigel SJ Papers." http://www.library.georgetown.edu/dept/speccoll/c165.htm (accessed May 15, 2012).
18. Gustave Weigel to Armour, Letter dated November 24, 1941, Gustave Weigel Papers, Box 1 Folder 61, Georgetown University Library, Special Collections Division, Washington, D.C.
19. Weigel to Armour, Letter dated November 24, 1941.
20. Weigel to Armour, Letter dated November 24, 1941.
21. Weigel to Armour, Letter dated November 24, 1941.
22. Weigel to Armour, Letter dated November 24, 1941.
23. Weigel to Armour, Letter dated November 24, 1941.
24. Gustave Weigel to Edward Kirchner, Letter dated May 4, 1942, Gustave Weigel Papers, Box 1, Folder 6, Georgetown University Library, Special Collections Division, Washington, D.C.
25. Weigel to Armour, Letter dated November 24, 1941.
26. Weigel to Armour, Letter dated November 24, 1941.
27. Weigel to Armour, Letter dated November 24, 1941.
28. Weigel to Kirchner, Letter dated May 4, 1942.
29. Vincent McCormick SJ to Gustave Weigel, Letter dated January 17, 1948, Gustave Weigel Papers, Box 1 Folder 34 , Georgetown University Library, Special Collections Division, Washington, D.C.
30. Gustave Weigel to Fr. Alberto Hurtado, Letter dated May 10, 1948, Gustave Weigel

Papers, Box 1 Folder 65, Georgetown University Library, Special Collections Division, Washington, D.C.

31. Gustave Weigel to Francis McQuade, Letter dated September 15, 1946, Gustave Weigel Papers, Box 1 Folder 63 Georgetown University Library, Special Collections Division, Washington, D.C.
32. Gustave Weigel to Fr. Alberto Hurtado, Letter dated May 10, 1948, Gustave Weigel Papers, Box 1 Folder 65, Georgetown University Library, Special Collections Division, Washington, D.C.
33. Gustave Weigel to James P. Sweeney, SJ Father Provincial, Letter dated May 4, 1944, Archives of the New York Province of the Society of Jesus.
34. Gustave Weigel Papers, Box 12, Folder 470, Georgetown University Library, Special Collections Division, Washington, D.C.
35. Gustave Weigel, "A Pedagogic Reminiscence," Archives of the New York Province of the Society of Jesus.
36. Claude G. Bowers to Msgr. Vincent L. Keelan, SJ Provincial, Letter dated March 5, 1948, Gustave Weigel Papers, Box 1, Folder 7, Georgetown University Library, Special Collections Division, Washington, D.C.
37. John Courtney Murray, "A Memorable Man."
38. Fenton, "Spain and Religious Freedom," *American Ecclesiastical Review*, 161-163.
39. Fenton, "Spain and Religious Freedom," 162-166.
40. Fenton, "Spain and Religious Freedom," 167-169.
41. Fenton, "Spain and Religious Freedom," 167-169.
42. Fenton, "Spain and Religious Freedom," 170-171.
43. Fenton, "Spain and Religious Freedom," 170-171.
44. Fenton, "Spain and Religious Freedom," 171-172.
45. Camille M Cianfarra, "US Protestants Warned by Spain: Intervention of Co-Religionists There Reacting Adversely, Baptist Minister Told," *The New York Times*, September 23, 1952, OCB Central File Series Box 71 Folder "Iberia (2)," Dwight D. Eisenhower Library, Abilene, Kansas.
46. Cianfarra, "US Protestants Warned by Spain: Intervention by Co-Religionists There Reacting Adversely, Baptist Minister Told."
47. "Spanish Cardinal Chides US Critics: Seville Churchman Says Stand of American Catholics on Protestants Is 'Strange'," *The New York Times*, October 7, 1952, OCB Central File Series Box 71 Folder "Iberia (3)," Dwight D. Eisenhower Library, Abilene, Kansas.
48. George W. Shea notes from AND 0004.001 George Shea Papers, Box 19, Monsignor William Noe Field Archives and Special Collections Center, Seton Hall University, South Orange, New Jersey.

27. CARDINAL STRITCH REJECTS MURRAY'S PLEA

1. Samuel Cardinal Stritch, "Observations on the Memorandum 'The Crisis in Church-State Relationships in the U.S.A.'" dated May 15, 1952, Samuel Cardinal Stritch Personal Papers, Box 4 Folder 10, Archdiocese of Chicago's Joseph Cardinal Bernardin Archives and Records Center, 711 West Monroe Street, Chicago, Illinois.

2. Samuel Cardinal Stritch, "Observations on the Memorandum 'The Crisis in Church-State Relationships in the U.S.A.'" dated May 15, 1952, Samuel Cardinal Stritch Personal Papers, Box 4 Folder 10, Archdiocese of Chicago's Joseph Cardinal Bernardin Archives and Records Center, 711 West Monroe Street, Chicago, Illinois.
3. Stritch, "Observations on the Memorandum 'The Crisis in Church-Structure Relationships in the U.S.A.'"
4. Murray, "The Crisis in Church-State Relationships in the U.S.A," Samuel Cardinal Stritch Personal Papers, Box 4 Folder 10, Archdiocese of Chicago's Joseph Cardinal Bernardin Archives and Records Center, 711 West Monroe Street, Chicago, Illinois.
5. Murray, "The Crisis in Church-State Relationships in the U.S.A."
6. Samuel Cardinal Stritch, "Observations on the Memorandum 'The Crisis in Church-State Relationships in the U.S.A.'", dated May 15, 1952, Samuel Cardinal Stritch Personal Papers, Box 4 Folder 10, Archdiocese of Chicago's Joseph Cardinal Bernardin Archives and Records Center, 711 West Monroe Street, Chicago, Illinois.
7. Stritch, "Observations on the Memorandum 'The Crisis in Church-State Relationships in the U.S.A.'"
8. Murray, "The Crisis in Church-State Relationships in the U.S.A."
9. Stritch, "Observations on the Memorandum 'The Crisis in Church-State Relationships in the U.S.A.'"; Murray, "The Crisis in Church-State Relationships in the U.S.A."
10. Samuel Cardinal Stritch, "Observations on the Memorandum 'The Crisis in Church-Structure Relationships in the U.S.A.'", dated May 15, 1952, Samuel Cardinal Stritch Personal Papers, Box 4 Folder 10, Archdiocese of Chicago's Joseph Cardinal Bernardin Archives and Records Center, 711 West Monroe Street, Chicago, Illinois.
11. Stritch, "Observations on the Memorandum 'The Crisis in Church-State Relationships in the U.S.A.'"
12. Stritch, "Observations on the Memorandum 'The Crisis in Church-State Relationships in the U.S.A.'"

28. CONNELL AND FENTON SOUND ALARM BELLS

1. Francis J. Connell to Giuseppe Cardinal Pizzardo, Letter dated August 1, 1950, Francis J Connell Papers, Redemptorist House Archives, Baltimore Province, Brooklyn, New York.
2. Francis J. Connell Msgr. Joseph Fenton, Letter dated June 9, 1951, Francis J. Connell Papers, Redemptorist House Archives, Baltimore Province, Brooklyn, New York.
3. Joseph Clifford Fenton Francis J. Connell, Letter dated August 29, 1951, Francis J. Connell Papers, Redemptorist House Archives, Baltimore Province, Brooklyn, New York.
4. Francis J. Connell letter to Archbishop Ameleto Cicognani, Letter dated February 23, 1952, with attachment, Francis J. Connell Papers, Redemptorist House Archives, Baltimore Province, Brooklyn, New York.
5. Connell to Cicognani letter dated February 23, 1952.
6. Archbishop Ameleto Cicognani to Francis J. Connell, Letter dated February 27, 1952, Francis J. Connell Papers, Redemptorist House Archives, Baltimore Province, Brooklyn, New York.

29. THE IMPORTANCE OF SPAIN, EDWARD P. LILLY, AND THE PSB

1. Camille M. Cianfarra, "Spain Sets High Price to US for Use of Air, Naval Bases," *New York Times,* July 29, 1952, OCB Secretariat Series Box 71 Folder "Iberia (1)," Dwight D. Eisenhower Library, Abilene, Kansas.
2. Untitled Top Secret [declassified] Document listing JCS resolutions commencing with 1821 through 1821/50, OCB Secretariat Series Box 1 Folder "Iberia (1)," Dwight D. Eisenhower Library, Abilene, Kansas.
3. NSC 72/6 Dated September 7, 1951, OCB Secretariat Series Box 1 Folder "Iberia (1)," Dwight D. Eisenhower Library, Abilene, Kansas.
4. "Background for the Attention of General Magruder," OCB Secretariat Papers Box 5 Folder "Noble Efforts," Dwight D. Eisenhower Library, Abilene, Kansas.
5. Edward P. Lilly, interviewed by Neil M. Johnson September 20, 1988, 2-3, Harry S. Truman Library and Museum. http://www.trumanlibrary.org/oralhist/lillye.htm (accessed January 29, 2013).
6. Lilly interview by Johnson, 2-4.
7. Wilford, *The Mighty Wurlitzer: How the CIA Played America,* 187-196.
8. "Background for the Attention of General Magruder," OCB Secretariat Papers, Box 5 Folder "Noble Efforts," Dwight D. Eisenhower Library, Abilene, Kansas.
9. Lilly interview by Johnson, 3.
10. Application for Federal Employment dated December 9, 1952, OCB Secretariat Series Box 5, Folder "Official Personnel Papers – PSB [Frieda Degerter and Edward P Lilly]," Dwight D. Eisenhower Library, Abilene, Kansas.
11. "Background for the Attention of General Magruder," OCB Secretariat Papers, Box 5 Folder "Noble Efforts," Dwight D. Eisenhower Library, Abilene, Kansas.
12. Lilly interview by Johnson, 6.
13. "Background for the Attention of General Magruder" DDE Archives, OCB Secretariat Series Box 5 Folder "Noble Efforts" Dwight D. Eisenhower Library, Abilene, Kansas.
14. Application for Federal Employment dated December 9, 1952, OCB Secretariat Series Box 5, Folder "Official Personnel Papers – PSB [Frieda Degerter and Edward P Lilly]," Dwight D. Eisenhower Library, Abilene, Kansas.
15. "Background for the Attention of General Magruder" DDE Archives, OCB Secretariat Series Box 5 Folder "Noble Efforts" Dwight D. Eisenhower Library, Abilene, Kansas.
16. "Background for the Attention of General Magruder."
17. Edward P. Lilly, "The Development of American Psychological Operations 1945-1951," NSC Registry Series 1947-62 Box 14 Folder "Psychological Operations, the Development 1945-1951, American," Dwight D. Eisenhower Library, Abilene, Kansas.
18. Lilly, "The Development of American Psychological Operations," 19-20.
19. Lilly, "The Development of American Psychological Operations," 21, 25, 34-35.
20. Lilly, "The Development of American Psychological Operations," 81.
21. Lilly, "The Development of American Psychological Operations," 82-84.
22. Lilly, "The Development of American Psychological Operations," 92-94.
23. Leary, *The Central Intelligence Agency,* 62-63.

30. LILLY AND THE AMERICANS RECRUIT CATHOLICS

1. "Background for the Attention of General Magruder" DDE Archives, OCB Secretariat Series Box 5 Folder "Noble Efforts" Dwight D. Eisenhower Library, Abilene, Kansas.
2. LT Healy to Edward P. Lilly, Memorandum dated July 22, 1952 Subject: Spain, OCB Central Files Series Box 71 Folder "Iberia (1)," Dwight D. Eisenhower Library, Abilene, Kansas.
3. LT Healy to Edward P. Lilly, Memorandum dated August 14, 1952 Subject: Iberian Peninsula, OCB Central File Series Box No. 71 Folder "Iberia (1)," Dwight D. Eisenhower Library, Abilene, Kansas.
4. LT Healy to Edward P. Lilly, Memorandum dated August 14, 1952 Subject: Iberian Peninsula, OCB Central File Series Box No. 71 Folder "Iberia (1)," Dwight D. Eisenhower Library, Abilene, Kansas.
5. LT Healy to Edward P. Lilly, Memorandum dated August 14, 1952 Subject: Iberian Peninsula, OCB Central File Series Box No. 71 Folder "Iberia (1)," Dwight D. Eisenhower Library, Abilene, Kansas.
6. Edward P. Lilly, Memorandum for the Record dated September 25, 1952 Subject: Memorandum of Conversation with Mr. William Dunham, Office of Western European Affairs, Dept. of State, September 23, 1952, OCB Central File Series Box 71 Folder "Iberia (2)," Dwight D. Eisenhower Library, Abilene, Kansas.
7. Working Draft of "Staff Study on Iberia" dated September 29, 1952, OCB Central File Series Box 71 Folder "Iberia (2)," Dwight D. Eisenhower Library, Abilene, Kansas.
8. USIS Country Plan – Spain - Pop. 28, 287,000 dated August 8, 1952, OCB Secretariat Series Box 71 Folder "Iberia (2)," Dwight D. Eisenhower Library, Abilene, Kansas.
9. Memorandum entitled "NCWC Admin. Board (April 1952)," OCB Secretariat Series Box 4 Folder "Moral Factor (1)," Dwight D. Eisenhower Library, Abilene, Kansas.
10. Anspacher to Edward P. Lilly, Memorandum dated September 29, 1952 Subject: Austria Secret (declassified 2006), OCB Secretariat Series Box 4 Folder "Moral Factor (2)," Dwight D. Eisenhower Library, Abilene, Kansas.
11. Anspacher to Edward P. Lilly, Memorandum dated September 29, 1952 Subject: Austria Secret (declassified 2006), OCB Secretariat Series Box 4 Folder "Moral Factor (2)," Dwight D. Eisenhower Library, Abilene, Kansas.
12. Foreign Service Despatch from the US Embassy Belgrade to the Department of State dated October 16, 1952 Confidential (declassified 1998), OCB Secretariat Series Box 4 Folder "Moral Factor (2)," Dwight D. Eisenhower Library, Abilene, Kansas.
13. Foreign Service Despatch from the US Embassy Paris to the Department of State dated October 10, 1952 Confidential (declassified 1998), OCB Secretariat Series Box 4 Folder "Moral Factor (2)," Dwight D. Eisenhower Library, Abilene, Kansas.
14. Memorandum of Conversation with Archbishop A J Meunch, Hotel Statler, November 4, 1952, OCB Secretariat Series Box 4 Folder "Moral Factor (2)," Dwight D. Eisenhower Library, Abilene, Kansas.
15. Memorandum "German Catholic Join War on Reds," OCB Secretariat Series Box 4 Folder "International Congress (2)," Dwight D. Eisenhower Library, Abilene, Kansas.
16. Incoming Telegram dated June 8, 1953 from Department of State (Warsaw) to Secretary of State Secret (declassified 1998), OCB Secretariat Series Box 4 Folder "International Congress (2)," Dwight D. Eisenhower Library, Abilene, Kansas.

17. Edward P. Lilly to Dr. Allen, Memorandum through Mr. Taylor dated July 10, 1952 Subject "The Project of Rev. F. A. Morlion, OP," OCB Secretariat Series Box 4 Folder "Moral Folder (1)," Dwight D. Eisenhower Library, Abilene, Kansas.
18. Edward P. Lilly, Memorandum for the Record dated July 14, 1952 Subject "The Morlion Project," OCB Secretariat Series Box 4 Folder "Moral Folder (1)," Dwight D. Eisenhower Library, Abilene, Kansas.
19. Edward P. Lilly to Fr. William Gibbons, SJ, Letter dated September 25, 1952, OCB Secretariat Series Box 4 File "Moral Factor (2)," Dwight D. Eisenhower Library, Abilene, Kansas.
20. "Religion: Birth Control and Catholic," *Time,* September 1, 1961. http://www.time.com/time/subscriber/article/0,33009,938765-1,00.html (accessed February 18, 2013).
21. George A. Morgan to Taylor, Letter dated September 26, 1952 Top Secret (Declassified 1997), OCB Secretariat Series Box 4 Folder "Moral Factor (2)," Dwight D. Eisenhower Library, Abilene, Kansas.
22. Edward P. Lilly, Memorandum for the record dated November 21, 1952 Subject: Conversation with NAME DELETED CIA, OCB Secretariat Series Box 2 Folder "Doctrinal Warfare (Official) (File # 1) (4)," Dwight D. Eisenhower Library, Abilene, Kansas.
23. Edward P. Lilly, Memorandum For the Record dated July 25, 1952 Subject "Conference with Monsignor McCarthy (Director, National Catholic Welfare Conference)," OCB Secretariat Series Box 4 Folder "Moral Factor (1)," Dwight D. Eisenhower Library, Abilene, Kansas.

31. PUTTING RELIGION IN SERVICE TO THE STATE

1. AP Toner to George Morgan, Letter dated April 17, 1952, OCB Secretariat Series Box 4 Folder "Moral Factor (1)," Dwight D. Eisenhower Library, Abilene, Kansas.
2. Edmond L Taylor to Mr. Barnes, Memorandum dated February 19 1952 and entitled "Exploitation of Basic Moral and Social Forces," OCB Secretariat Series Box 4 Folder "Moral Factor (1)," Dwight D. Eisenhower Library, Abilene, Kansas.
3. "PSB Planning Objectives" Top Secret [Declassified 1998] dated April 7, 1952, OCB Secretariat Series Box 3 Folder "Ideological Documents File (1)," Dwight D. Eisenhower Library, Abilene, Kansas.
4. "PSB Planning Objectives," dated April 7, 1952.
5. "PSB Planning Objectives" Top Secret [Declassified 1998] dated April 7, 1952, Tab A Proposed Work Priorities for Remainder of Calendar 1952, OCB Secretariat Series Box 3 Folder "Ideological Documents File (1)," Dwight D. Eisenhower Library, Abilene, Kansas.
6. Edward P. Lilly, Memorandum of Conversation dated November 19, 1952 Subject: "Project to Increase the Inter-denominational Cooperation of All Christian, and Possibly all Religious, Groups in Opposition to Communism" Secret (declassified 1998), OCB Secretariat Series Box 4 Folder "Moral Factor (2)," Dwight D. Eisenhower Library, Abilene, Kansas.
7. Edward P. Lilly, Memorandum of Conversation dated November 19, 1952 Subject: "Project to Increase the Inter-denominational Cooperation of All Christian, and

Possibly all Religious, Groups in Opposition to Communism" Secret (declassified 1998), OCB Secretariat Series Box 4 Folder "Moral Factor (2)," Dwight D. Eisenhower Library, Abilene, Kansas.

8. "A Declaration for Faith and A Call for Action," OCB Secretariat Series Box 4 Folder "International Congress (1)," Dwight D. Eisenhower Library, Abilene, Kansas.
9. "A Declaration for Faith and A Call for Action."
10. Edward P. Lilly to John Pearson, Letter dated September 25, 1952, OCB Secretariat Series Box 4 Folder "International Congress (1)," Dwight D. Eisenhower Library, Abilene, Kansas.
11. Lilly to Pearson Letter dated September 25, 1952.
12. Edward P. Lilly, Memorandum dated February 19, 1953 Subject " An International Conference of Religious Leaders in Berlin in late Spring or early Summer, 1953" Secret (declassified 1998), OCB Secretariat Series Box 4 Folder "International Congress (1)," Dwight D. Eisenhower Library, Abilene, Kansas.
13. Edward P. Lilly, Memorandum dated February 19, 1953 Subject " An International Conference of Religious Leaders in Berlin in late Spring or early Summer, 1953" Secret (declassified 1998), OCB Secretariat Series Box 4 Folder "International Congress (1)," Dwight D. Eisenhower Library, Abilene, Kansas.
14. Lilly, Memorandum dated February 19, 1953, Subject "An International Conference of Religious Leaders in Berlin in late Spring or early Summer, 1953."

32. DOCTRINAL WARFARE DEVELOPS

1. "Terms of Reference, Ideological Warfare Panel," OCB Secretariat Series Box 2 Folder "Doctrinal Warfare (Official) (File # 1) (4)," Dwight D. Eisenhower Library, Abilene, Kansas.
2. Shawn J. Parry-Giles, *The Rhetorical Presidency, Propaganda, and the Cold War, 1945-1955* (Westport, Connecticut: Praeger Press, 2002), 134-135.
3. Edward P. Lilly, Memorandum for all Panel Members Subject: Views Regarding Vulnerabilities dated February 20, 1953, OCB Secretariat Series Box 2 Folder "Doctrinal Warfare (Official) (File # 2) (2)," Dwight D. Eisenhower Library, Abilene, Kansas.
4. National Security Council Directive 68.
5. Stefan T. Possony, Jerry E Pournelle, Col. Francis X. Kane, ed., "The Technological War," *The Strategy of Technology.* http://baen.com/sot/sot_1.htm (accessed January 29, 2013).
6. Edward P. Lilly to George A Morgan, Memorandum dated July 29, 1953 Subject: "Suggested Comments for the Acting Director's Statement to the Doctrinal Group," PSB Central Files Series Box 15 File "PSB 091.4 Doctrinal Warfare (4)," Dwight D. Eisenhower Library, Abilene, Kansas.
7. First Progress Report of the Panel on Doctrinal Warfare dated January 9, 1953, OCB Secretariat Series Box 2 Folder "Doctrinal Warfare (Official) (File # 2) (1)," Dwight D. Eisenhower Library, Abilene, Kansas.
8. "Panel on Doctrinal Warfare," OCB Secretariat Series Box 2 Folder "Doctrinal Warfare (Official)," Dwight D. Eisenhower Library, Abilene, Kansas.
9. "Director's Introductory Statement on the Panel on Doctrinal Warfare," OCB

Secretariat Series Box 1 File "Doctrinal Warfare (Misc.) (4)," Dwight D. Eisenhower Library, Abilene, Kansas.

10. Untitled document approved for release 2001/08/27: NLE 107-001-7-1-2, OCB Secretariat Series Box 2 Folder "Doctrinal Warfare (Official) (File # 1) (1)," Dwight D. Eisenhower Library, Abilene, Kansas.
11. Edward P. Lilly, Memorandum for the Record Subject: Fifth Meeting of the Panel on Doctrinal Warfare dated January 9, 1953, OCB Secretariat Series Box 2 Folder "Doctrinal Warfare (Official) (File # 2) (1)," Dwight D. Eisenhower Library, Abilene, Kansas.
12. "Doctrinal Warfare" [Draft for inclusion in Quarterly Report to NSC] dated January 9, 1953, OCB Secretariat Series Box 2 Folder "Doctrinal Warfare (Official) (File # 2) (1)," Dwight D. Eisenhower Library, Abilene, Kansas.
13. "Annex 'A': Analysis of the Problem" Draft dated January 9, 1953, OCB Secretariat Series Box 2 Folder "Doctrinal Warfare (Official) (File # 2) (1)," Dwight D. Eisenhower Library, Abilene, Kansas.
14. "Targets of Doctrinal Warfare," undated and untitled Draft document dated January 26, 1953, OCB Secretariat Series Box 2 Folder "Doctrinal Warfare (Official) (File # 2) (2)," Dwight D. Eisenhower Library, Abilene, Kansas..
15. "Annex 'A': Analysis of the Problem" Draft dated January 9, 1953, OCB Secretariat Series Box 2 Folder "Doctrinal Warfare (Official) (File # 2) (1)," Dwight D. Eisenhower Library, Abilene, Kansas.
16. "Annex 'A': Analysis of the Problem," Draft dated January 9, 1953.
17. "Statement on Doctrinal Warfare Targets," dated February 6, 1953, OCB Secretariat Series Box 2 Folder "Doctrinal Warfare (Official) (File # 2) (2)," Dwight D. Eisenhower Library, Abilene, Kansas.
18. "Statement on Doctrinal Warfare Targets," dated February 6, 1953.
19. "Statement on Doctrinal Warfare Targets," dated February 6, 1953.
20. Panel on Doctrinal Warfare Eight Meeting February 20, 1953, OCB Secretariat Series Box 2 Folder "Doctrinal Warfare (Official) (File # 2) (2)," Dwight D. Eisenhower Library, Abilene, Kansas.

33. THE DOCTRINAL WARFARE PROGRAM

1. C.D. Jackson Papers Box 1 Folder "PSB – Miscellaneous Memos," Dwight D. Eisenhower Library, Abilene, Kansas.
2. C.D. Jackson Papers Box 1 Folder "PSB – Miscellaneous Memos," Dwight D. Eisenhower Library, Abilene, Kansas.
3. C.D. Jackson Papers, Box 1 Folder "PSB– Miscellaneous Memos," Dwight D. Eisenhower Library, Abilene, Kansas.
4. Annex A to PSB D-33 June 29, 1953, "U.S. Doctrinal Program", Psychological Strategy Board.
5. PSB D-33 June 29, 1953, "U.S. Doctrinal Program", Psychological Strategy Board.
6. PSB D-33 June 29, 1953, "U.S. Doctrinal Program", Psychological Strategy Board.
7. Annex C to PSB D-33 June 29, 1953, "U.S. Doctrinal Program", Psychological Strategy Board.
8. Annex C to PSB D-33 June 29, 1953, "U.S. Doctrinal Program", Psychological Strategy Board.

9. Edward P. Lilly to George A Morgan, Memorandum dated July 29, 1953 Subject: Suggested Comments for the Acting Director's Statement to the Doctrinal Group," PSB Central Files Box 15 File "PSB 091.4 Doctrinal Warfare (4)," Dwight D. Eisenhower Library, Abilene, Kansas.
10. Elmer B. Staats interviewed by Henry Eschwege, Werner Grosshans, Donald J. Horan and Elizabeth Poel on April 9, May 4, and May 7, 1987, v, 48, Harry S Truman Library and Museum. http://www.trumanlibrary.org/oralhist/staatse.htm (accessed December 29, 2013).

34. MAKING GERMANY, WESTERN EUROPE, AND LATIN AMERICA LIKE AMERICA

1. "Staff Study – Psychological Strategy Planning for Western Europe" January 15, 1953, PSB Central Files Series Box 17 Folder "PSB 091.4 Western Europe (1)," Dwight D. Eisenhower Library, Abilene, Kansas; Alan G Kirk to David Bruce Under Secretary of State Memorandum January 12, 1953 Subject Staff Study on Western Europe, PSB Central Files Series Box 17 Folder "PSB 091.4 Western Europe (1)," Dwight D. Eisenhower Library, Abilene, Kansas.
2. Simpson, *Science of Coercion: Communication Research & Psychological Warfare 1945-1960,* 18-21, 35.
3. Kai Bird, *The Chairman John J. McCloy: The Making of the American Establishment (*New York: Simon & Schuster, 1992), 311, 338, 391.
4. Kai Bird, *The Chairman John J. McCloy: The Making of the American Establishment (*New York: Simon & Schuster, 1992), 311, 338, 391.
5. Giles MacDonogh, *After the Reich: The Brutal History of the Allied Occupation* (New York: Basic Books, 2007), 244-249.
6. Jacob Taubes, "Notes on the Ideological Strategy of the United States Foreign Policy," and letter dated March 2, 1953, OCB Central File Series Box 71 Folder "Ideological Documents File (3)," Dwight D. Eisenhower Library, Abilene, Kansas.
7. C.D. Jackson to Henry R. Luce, Letter dated May 19, 1953, C.D. Jackson Papers, Box 70 Folder "Luce, Henry & Clare (1953)", Dwight D. Eisenhower Library, Abilene, Kansas.
8. Simpson, *Science of Coercion: Communications Research and Psychological Warfare 1945-1960,* 8.
9. Simpson, *Science of Coercion: Communications Research and Psychological Warfare 1945-1960,* 11-12.
10. Simpson, *Science of Coercion: Communications Research and Psychological Warfare 1945-1960,* 311.
11. Anna J. Merritt and Richard L. Merritt, ed., *Public Opinion in Occupied Germany: The OMGUS Surveys 1945-1949* (Urbana, Illinois: University of Illinois Press, 1970), 236, 256-257, 307-308, 311.
12. Anna J. Merritt and Richard L. Merritt, ed., *Public Opinion in Semi-sovereign Germany: The HICOG Surveys 1949-1955* (Urbana, Illinois: University of Illinois Press, 1980), 204-205.
13. Parry-Giles, *The Rhetorical Presidency, Propaganda and the Cold War, 1945-1955*, 78-80.
14. Simpson, *Science of Coercion: Communications Research and Psychological Warfare 1945-1960,* 36, 126.

15. Dr. Georg Joseph Heiling to George Shuster, Letter dated April 23, 1950, George N. Shuster Papers (CSHU) Box 6 Folder 25, University of Notre Dame Archives (UNDA), Notre Dame, Indiana 46556.
16. "Proposal for a Psychological Strategy Move against the Current Anti-American Cominform Moves in Western Europe" Submitted July 1, 1952, OCB Secretariat Series Box 4 Folder "Moral Factor (1)," Dwight D. Eisenhower Library, Abilene, Kansas.
17. "A National Psychological Strategy Plan for the Federal Republic of Germany," PSB E-6 dated November 20, 1952, NSC Registry Series Box 14 Folder "PSB Documents, Master Book of – Vol. 1 (3)," Dwight D. Eisenhower Library, Abilene, Kansas.
18. "A National Psychological Strategy Plan for the Federal Republic of Germany."
19. "A National Psychological Strategy Plan for the Federal Republic of Germany."
20. "Staff Study – Psychological Strategy Planning for Western Europe" dated January 15, 1953, PSB Central Files Series Box 17, Folder "PSB 091.4 Western Europe (1)," Dwight D. Eisenhower Library, Abilene, Kansas.
21. "Staff Study – Psychological Strategy Planning for Western Europe."
22. "Staff Study – Psychological Strategy Planning for Western Europe."
23. "Staff Study – Psychological Strategy Planning for Western Europe."
24. George A. Morgan to Admiral Kirk, Memorandum dated January 13, 1953 Subject: The Future of the Psychological Field, PSB Central Files Series Box 17 Folder "PSB 091.412 [propaganda] (1)," Dwight D. Eisenhower Library, Abilene, Kansas; Edward M O'Connor, "Some Guide Posts to the Creation and Maintenance of a 'Cold War' Instrument," PSB Central Files Series Box 17 Folder "PSB 091.412 [propaganda] (1)," Dwight D. Eisenhower Library, Abilene, Kansas.
25. "A National Psychological Strategy Program for Western Europe," PSB D-38 Dated September 22, 1953, PSB Central Files Series Box 17 Folder "PSB 091.4 Western Europe (7)," Dwight D. Eisenhower Library, Abilene, Kansas.
26. "A National Psychological Strategy Program for Western Europe."
27. William J. Morgan to Ben Gedalecia, Memorandum dated October 1, 1953 Subject: Your letter request dated 23 September 1953 for comments on 'The Illinois Associational Code for Content Analysis,'" PSB Central Files Series Box 17 Folder "PSB 091.412 [propaganda] (3)," Dwight D. Eisenhower Library, Abilene, Kansas.
28. Edmond Taylor to Acting Director of PSB, Memorandum dated February 20, 1953 Subject: Latin America – NSC Staff Assistants' Draft (Supplementary to R-184), PSB Central File Series Box 15 Folder "PSB 091.4 Latin America," Dwight D. Eisenhower Library, Abilene, Kansas.
29. Taylor to Acting Director of PSM Memorandum dated February 20, 1953.
30. Wallace Irwin, Jr., Memorandum for Record dated April 21, 1953 Subject: Latin America – Briefing by Miron Burgin, OIR/DRA, PSB Central Files Series Box 15 Folder "PSB 091.4 Latin America," Dwight D. Eisenhower Library, Abilene, Kansas.
31. Wallace Irwin, Jr., Memorandum for Record dated April 21, 1953 Subject: Latin America – Briefing by Miron Burgin, OIR/DRA, PSB Central Files Series Box 15 Folder "PSB 091.4 Latin America," Dwight D. Eisenhower Library, Abilene, Kansas.
32. Daniel N. Arsac, Jr. to Dr. Horace S. Craig, Memorandum dated August 20, 1953 Subject: Cultural Relations Between the United States and Latin America, PSB Central File Series Box 15 Folder "PSB 091.4 Latin America," Dwight D. Eisenhower Library, Abilene, Kansas.
33. Daniel N. Arsac, Jr. to Dr. Horace S. Craig, Memorandum dated August 20, 1953 Subject: Cultural Relations Between the United States and Latin America, PSB Central

File Series Box 15 Folder "PSB 091.4 Latin America," Dwight D. Eisenhower Library, Abilene, Kansas.

35. TIME, INC. AND THE CIA

1. Klaus Dohrn to Henry R. Luce, Memorandum dated May 13, 1955, C.D. Jackson Papers, Box 70 Folder "Luce Henry R & Clare 1955," Dwight D. Eisenhower Library, Abilene, Kansas.
2. Klaus Dohrn, "The End of the First Post-War Era," Memorandum dated May 13, 1955, C.D. Jackson Papers, Box 70 Folder "Luce Henry R & Clare 1955," Dwight D. Eisenhower Library, Abilene, Kansas.
3. John Shaw Billings, Diary entry March 23, 1953, John Shaw Billings Papers, Volume 35, 56, South Caroliniana Library, Columbia, South Carolina.
4. John Shaw Billings, Diary entries for August 9, 1950, John Shaw Billings Papers, Volume 31, 181, South Caroliniana Library, Columbia, South Carolina; John Shaw Billings, Diary entries for October 16, 17, 23, 1950, Vol. 31, 273-274, 281, John Shaw Billings Papers, South Caroliniana Library, Columbia, South Carolina.
5. John Shaw Billings, Diary entries for October 16, 17, 23, 1950, Vol. 31, 273-274, 281, John Shaw Billings Papers, South Caroliniana Library, Columbia, South Carolina.
6. John Shaw Billings, Diary entries for February 15, 1952, Vol. 34, 54-55, John Shaw Billings Papers, South Caroliniana Library, Columbia, South Carolina.
7. John Shaw Billings, Diary entry December 1, 1952, John Shaw Billings Papers, Volume 35, 109-111, South Caroliniana Library, Columbia, South Carolina.
8. Marie McCrum, interviewed by David Horrocks, 70-71.
9. McCrum interviewed by Horrocks, 27-28.
10. McCrum interviewed by Horrocks, 28.
11. Cook, "First Comes the Lie: C.D. Jackson and Political Warfare," 46; "Chronology," C.D. Jackson Papers, Dwight D. Eisenhower Library, Abilene, Kansas.
12. Marie McCrum, interviewed by David Horrocks, 49-50.
13. Memorandum regarding dinner at Century Club, New York, dated May 7, 1956, C.D. Jackson Papers, Box 69, Dwight D. Eisenhower Library, Abilene, Kansas.
14. Cook, "First Comes the Lie: C.D. Jackson and Political Warfare," 53-54.
15. C.D. Jackson, text of speech given to the National Security Commission & Committees of the American Legion St Louis, Missouri August 28, 1953, C.D. Jackson Papers. Box 100 File "Speech Texts, 1953 (3)," Dwight D. Eisenhower Library, Abilene, Kansas.
16. John Shaw Billings, Diary entries for October 9, 1953, Vol. 36, 193-194, John Shaw Billings Papers. South Caroliniana Library, Columbia, South Carolina.
17. Al Grover to John Shaw Billings, Letter dated November 24, 1950, John Shaw Billings Papers. Folder 151, South Caroliniana Library, University of South Carolina, Columbia, South Carolina.
18. Cook, "First Comes the Lie: C.D. Jackson and Political Warfare," 49-52.
19. "Aspects of Radio Free Europe Policy," C.D. Jackson Papers. Box 80 Folder "National Committee for a Free Europe – RFE – German Peoples," Dwight D. Eisenhower Library, Abilene, Kansas.
20. Gordon Grey, interviewed by Richard D. McKinzie June 18, 1973, 56-57, Harry S Truman Library and Museum. http://www.trumanlibrary.org/oralhist/gray/htm (accessed December 29, 2013).

21. C.D. Jackson, text of speech to the NATO Defense College dated January 11, 1954 Paris, France, C.D. Jackson Papers. Box 100 File "Speech Texts, 1954(4)," Dwight D. Eisenhower Library, Abilene, Kansas.
22. Jackson, text of speech to the NATO Defense College dated January 11, 1954.
23. Jackson, text of speech to the NATO Defense College dated January 11, 1954.
24. Henry R. Luce to Alexander, Fuerbringer, Thompson, Elson, Donovan, James, Paine, Prentice, Memorandum dated August 2, 1956, C.D. Jackson Papers. Box 71 Folder "Luce, Henry R. & Clare, 1956 (2)," Dwight D. Eisenhower Library, Abilene, Kansas.
25. John Shaw Billings, Diary entry for February 1, 1952, John Shaw Billings Papers, Volume 34, 39, South Caroliniana Library, Columbia, South Carolina.
26. John Shaw Billings, Diary entry for March 5, 1954, John Shaw Billings Papers, Volume 37. South Caroliniana Library, Columbia, South Carolina.

36. ROME SPEAKS (MARCH 1953)

1. Alfredo Cardinal Ottaviani, *Duties of the Catholic State in Regard to Religion* 2d ed., tr. Denis Fahey (Kansas City, Missouri: Angelus Press, 1993), i-iv.
2. Ottaviani, *Duties of the Catholic State in Regard to Religion.*
3. Alfredo Cardinal Ottaviani, "Church and State: Some Present Problems in the Light of the Teaching of Pope Pius XII", *American Ecclesiastical Review* CXXVIII (May, 1953), 321.
4. Ottaviani, "Church and State: Some Present Problems in the Light of the Teaching of Pope Pius XII," 321-334.
5. Ottaviani, "Church and State: Some Present Problems in the Light of the Teaching of Pope Pius XII," 321-322.
6. Ottaviani, "Church and State: Some Present Problems in the Light of the Teaching of Pope Pius XII," 323-324.
7. Ottaviani, "Church and State: Some Present Problems in the Light of the Teaching of Pope Pius XII," 324-325.
8. Ottaviani stated: "'An immediate illation from the order of ethical and theological truth to the order of constitutional law is, in principle, dialectically inadmissible.'" On page 343 of the May, 1951 issue of *American Ecclesiastical Review,* Murray wrote in his article entitled "The Problem of the 'Religion of the State'" the following: "First, an immediate illation from the order of ethical and theological truth to the order of constitutional law is, in principle, dialectically inadmissible."
9. Ottaviani, "Church and State: Some Present Problems in the Light of the Teaching of Pope Pius XII," 324-325.
10. Ottaviani, "Church and State: Some Present Problems in the Light of the Teachings of Pope Pius XII," 325-328.
11. Ottaviani, "Church and State: Some Present Problems in the Light of the Teachings of Pope Pius XII," 325-326.
12. Ottaviani, "Church and State: Some Present Problems in the Light of the Teachings of Pope Pius XII," 326-327.
13. Ottaviani, "Church and State: Some Present Problems in the Light of the Teachings of Pope Pius XII," 326-327.
14. Ottaviani, "Church and State: Some Present Problems in the Light of the Teachings of Pope Pius XII," 328-329.

15. Ottaviani, "Church and State: Some Present Problems in the Light of the Teachings of Pope Pius XII," 329-330.
16. Ottaviani, *Duties of the Catholic State in Regard to Religion,* 14-15.
17. Ottaviani, "Church and State: Some Present Problems in the Light of the Teaching of Pope Pius XII", 330-331.
18. Ottaviani, *Duties of the Catholic State in Regard to Religion,* 20-23.
19. Ottaviani, *Duties of the Catholic State in Regard to Religion,* 331-334.
20. Francis J Connell to Cardinal Ottaviani, Letter dated April 27, 1953, Francis J. Connell Papers. Redemptorist House Archives, Baltimore Province, Brooklyn, New York.
21. Pelotte, *John Courtney Murray: Theologian in Conflict,* 36.
22. Pelotte, fn 44 at 64.
23. John Courtney Murray to Clare Boothe Luce, Letter dated July 7, 1953, Clare Boothe Luce Papers. Box 795 Folder 10, Library of Congress, Washington, D.C.
24. John Courtney Murray to John Tracy Ellis, Letter dated July 13, 1953, John Courtney Murray Papers. Box 1 Folder 62, Georgetown University Library. Special Collections Division, Washington, D.C.
25. Pelotte, *John Courtney Murray: Theologian in Conflict,* 37.
26. John Courtney Murray to John Tracy Ellis, Letter dated July 20, 1953, John Courtney Murray Papers. "John Tracey Ellis" Folder, Georgetown University Library, Special Collections Division, Washington, D.C.; Pelotte, *John Courtney Murray: Theologian In Conflict,* 37-38.
27. Pelotte, *John Courtney Murray: Theologian In Conflict,* fn 57, at 66.
28. "Archer Says Vatican Denies US Freedom," *New York Times,* July 23, 1953.
29. Francis J Connell to Cardinal Ottaviani, Letter dated July 23, 1953, Francis J. Connell Papers. Redemptorist House Archives, Baltimore Province, Brooklyn, New York.
30. "Religion: Catholics and Tolerance," *Time,* August 3, 1953. http://www.time.com/time/subscriber/printout/0,8816,822913,00.html (as accessed May 19, 2012).
31. "Religion: Catholics and Tolerance," *Time,* August 3, 1953.
32. "Religion: Catholics and Tolerance," *Time,* August 3, 1953.
33. "Religion: Catholics and Tolerance," *Time,* August 3, 1953.
34. Francis J. Connell to Cardinal Ottaviani, Letter dated October 31, 1953, Francis J. Connell Papers, Redemptorist House Archives, Baltimore Province, Brooklyn, New York.
35. " *Longe abest ne P. Joannes C. Murray a Sancta Sede reprehendatur. Nihilominus passu cauto et bene ponderato prosequatur in suis studiis et investigationibus perficiendis, allorum peritorum consilio lienter audito...*"
36. Joseph F. Murphy SJ to Very Reverend Provincial John J. McMahon SJ, Letter dated December 6, 1953, John Courtney Murray Papers, Archives of the New York Province of the Society of Jesus.
37. Pelotte, *John Courtney Murray: Theologian in Conflict,* 38-39; fn 53 at 65.

37. CLARE GOES TO ROME (APRIL 1953)

1. Charles Yost, interviewed by Dr. Thomas Soapes, September 13, 1978, 1-3.
2. Brinkley, *The Publisher: Henry Luce and His American Century,* 385.
3. "The United States, Italy, and the Opening to the Left, 1953-1963," *Journal of Cold War Studies* Vol. 4 (Summer, 2002) 3:36-55.

4. Desp. No. 745 from Rome dated 20/11/1956 to Nord America 1 & 2, 2, Clare Boothe Luce Papers. Box 642 Folder 7, Library of Congress, Washington, D.C.
5. Central Intelligence Agency, "The Current Situation in Italy" dated 10 October 1947, Harry S. Truman Library Papers of Harry S. Truman President's Secretary's file. http://www.foia.cia.gov/browse_docs_full.asp (accessed May 8, 2010). 2,3.
6. Intelligence Memorandum No. 250 dated 5 April 1950; Subject: Potentialities for Anti-Soviet Underground Resistance in the Event of War in 1950. http://www.foia.cia.gov/browse_docs_full.asp (accessed May 8, 2010), Enclosure D, 12-13.
7. Whitney H. Sheperdson, Memorandum dated January 27, 1945 Subject: Harte Reports containing Memorandum from Harte to Karl Brennan dated January 4, 1945. http://www.foia.cia.gov/browse_docs_full.asp (accessed May 8, 2010), 3.
8. "Probable Developments in Italy," National Intelligence Estimate from the Central Intelligence Agency Published 31 March 1953. http://www.foia.cia.gov/browse_docs_full.asp (accessed May 8, 2010).
9. "Probable Developments in Italy."
10. "Current Intelligence Weekly," Central Intelligence Agency Office of Current Intelligence dated 5 June 1953. http//www.foia.cia.gov/browse_docs_full.asp (accessed May 8, 2010).
11. "Probable Developments in Italy," National Intelligence Estimate from the Central Intelligence Agency Published 16 November 1954. http//www.foia.cia.gov/browse_-docs_full.asp (accessed May 8, 2010).
12. "Probable Developments in Italy," 1-2.
13. Henry R. Luce to John Shaw Billings, Memorandum entitled "Luce to Billings – Personal and Confidential" dated May 11, 1949, C.D. Jackson Papers. Box 70 Folder "Luce, Henry R. 1949," Dwight D. Eisenhower Library, Abilene, Kansas.
14. Luce to Billings Memorandum dated May 11, 1949.
15. Luce to Billings Memorandum dated May 11, 1949.
16. Klaus Dohrn to C.D. Jackson, Memorandum dated April 2, 1956, 7, C.D. Jackson Papers. Box 47 "Dohrn Klaus (5)," Dwight D. Eisenhower Library, Abilene, Kansas, 7.
17. Dohrn to Jackson Memorandum dated April 2, 1956, 8.
18. Dohrn to Jackson Memorandum dated April 2, 1956, 6, 8.
19. Klaus Dohrn to Grunwald, Letter dated January 6, 1956, C.D. Jackson Papers, Box 48 Folder "Dohrn Klaus (6)," Dwight D. Eisenhower Library, Abilene, Kansas.
20. Klaus Dohrn to C.D. Jackson, Memorandum dated April 5, 1957, C.D. Jackson Papers, Box 47, Folder "Dohrn Klaus (3)," Dwight D. Eisenhower Library, Abilene, Kansas.
21. Henry R. Luce to C.D. Jackson, Letter dated May 17, 1955, C.D. Jackson Papers, Box 70 Folder "Luce, Henry R. & Clare (1955)," Dwight D. Eisenhower Library, Abilene, Kansas.
22. "Italy: Distensione," *Time* May 23, 1955. http://www.time.com/time/prntout/0,8816,891210.00.html (accessed January 2, 2011).
23. Henry R. Luce to C.D. Jackson, Letter dated May 19, 1955, C.D. Jackson Papers, Box 70 Folder "Luce, Henry R. & Clare 1955," Dwight D. Eisenhower Library, Abilene, Kansas.
24. Henry R. Luce to C.D. Jackson, Letter dated May 19, 1955, C.D. Jackson Papers, Box 70 Folder "Luce, Henry R. & Clare 1955," Dwight D. Eisenhower Library, Abilene, Kansas.
25. Clare Boothe Luce, Diary Entry dated February 16, 1953, Clare Boothe Luce Papers, Box 56 File 10, Library of Congress, Washington, D.C.
26. Alden Hatch, *Ambassador Extraordinary: Clare Boothe Luce* (New York: Henry Holt and Company, 1956), 206.

27. Hatch, *Ambassador Extraordinary: Clare Boothe Luce,* 206.
28. Clare Boothe Luce, Diary Entry dated March 13, 1953, Clare Boothe Luce Papers, Box 56 File 10, Library of Congress, Washington, D.C.
29. Kip Finch to Henry R. Luce, Memorandum dated March 26, 1953 Subject: "Mrs. Luce's Radio Statement", Clare Boothe Luce Papers, Box 634, Library of Congress, Washington, D.C.
30. Henry R. Luce to Tom Dozier, Letter dated February 7, 1953 with enclosure, Clare Boothe Luce Papers, Box 634, Library of Congress, Washington, D.C .
31. Henry R. Luce to Clare Boothe Luce, Letter dated April 5, 1954, Clare Boothe Luce Papers, Box 634, Library of Congress, Washington, D.C .
32. Allen Grover to Clare Boothe Luce, Memorandum dated May 23, 1956, Clare Boothe Luce Papers, Box 634, Library of Congress, Washington, D.C.; Clare Boothe Luce to Henry R. Luce, Memorandum dated February 14, 1956 and Allen Grover to Clare Boothe Luce, Memorandum dated February 24, 1956, Clare Boothe Luce Papers, Box 634, Library of Congress, Washington, D.C.
33. C.D. Jackson to Clare Boothe Luce, Letter dated June 24, 1954, Clare Boothe Luce Papers, Box 634, Library of Congress, Washington, D.C.
34. Clare Boothe Luce Calendar, Clare Boothe Luce Papers, Library of Congress, Washington, D.C.
35. "The United States, Italy, and the Opening to the Left," 39-40.
36. "The United States, Italy, and the Opening to the Left," 41.
37. Clare Boothe Luce, "Rome Diary 1953-1955," Clare Boothe Luce Papers, Box 641 Folder 11, Library of Congress, Washington, D.C.
38. Hatch, *Ambassador Extraordinary: Clare Boothe Luce*, 216.
39. Hatch, *Ambassador Extraordinary: Clare Boothe Luce*, 216.
40. Hatch, *Ambassador Extraordinary: Clare Boothe Luce,* 217.
41. "From L'Europeo – March 28, 1954," Clare Boothe Luce Papers, Box 634, 8, Library of Congress, Washington, D.C.
42. Randall B. Woods, *Shadow Warrior: William Egan Colby and the CIA* (New York: Basic Books, 2013), 81-88, 98-105.
43. Hatch, *Ambassador Extraordinary: Clare Boothe Luce.*, 243.
44. Jeremy Isaacs and Taylor Downing, *Cold War: An Illustrated History, 1945-1991* (Boston: Little Brown and Company, 1998), 60-61.
45. Clare Boothe Luce to Allen Dulles, Letter dated March 12, 1954, Clare Boothe Luce Papers, Box 611 File 13, Library of Congress, Washington, D.C.
46. Clare Boothe Luce to Allen Dulles, Letter dated March 12, 1954 (emphasis present in original).
47. Clare Boothe Luce to Allen Dulles, Letter dated March 12, 1954, 2.
48. Clare Boothe Luce to Allen Dulles, Letter dated March 12, 1954, 2.
49. Clare Boothe Luce to Allen Dulles, Letter dated March 12, 1954, 2 (emphasis present in original).
50. Clare Boothe Luce to Allen Dulles, Letter dated March 12, 1954, 3, 4.
51. Clare Boothe Luce to Allen Dulles, Letter dated March 12, 1954, 4.
52. Clare Boothe Luce to Allen Dulles, Letter dated March 12, 1954, 4.
53. Clare Boothe Luce to Allen Dulles, Letter dated March 12, 1954, 5, 6.
54. Clare Boothe Luce to Allen Dulles, Letter dated March 12, 1954, 5-7.
55. Clare Boothe Luce to Allen Dulles, Letter dated March 12, 1954, 5-7 (emphasis present in original).

56. Clare Boothe Luce to Allen Dulles, Letter dated March 12, 1954, 11.
57. Clare Boothe Luce to Allen Dulles, Letter dated March 12, 1954, 13-14.
58. Clare Boothe Luce to Allen Dulles, Letter dated March 12, 1954, 14-15.
59. George G. Fox to The Ambassador, Memorandum dated October 13, 1953 Subject: Madonna delle Lacrime (Syracuse), pp. 1-7, Clare Boothe Luce Papers, Box 633, Library of Congress, Washington, D.C.
60. "Lateran Pact of 1929." http://biblelight.net/treaty.htm (accessed August 27, 2013).
61. Hatch, *Ambassador Extraordinary: Clare Boothe Luce*, 234.
62. Henry R. Luce to Clare Boothe Luce, Memorandum dated April 4, 1949, Clare Boothe Luce Papers, Box 21 Folder 1, Library of Congress, Washington, D.C.
63. Pelotte, *John Courtney Murray: Theologian in Conflict,* 38-39; fn 53 at 65: "Canon 2316 reads: 'Qui quoque modo haeresis propaationem sponte et scienter iuvat, aut que communicat in divinis cum haereticis contra praescriptum can. 1258, suspectus de haeresi est.' Canon 1258 reads: '1. Haud licitum est fidelibus quovis modo active assistere seu partem habere in sacris acatholicorum. 2. Tolerari potest praesentia passive seu mere materialis, civilis officii vel hnoris causa, ob gravem rationem ab Episcopo in casu dubii probandum, in acatholicoru funeribus, nuptiis similibusque solemniis, dummodo perversionis et scandali periculum absit."
64. Pelotte, *John Courtney Murray: Theologian in Conflict,* 39.
65. Pelotte, *John Courtney Murray: Theologian in Conflict,* fn. 56 at 66.
66. Pelotte, *John Courtney Murray: Theologian in Conflict,* 40-41.
67. Dr. Joseph Fessler, Bishop of St. Polten, Austria, and Secretary General of the Vatican Council, "The True and the False Infallbility [sic] of the Popes: A Controversial Reply to Dr. Schulte," Clare Boothe Luce Papers, Box 699 Folder 3, Library of Congress, Washington, D.C.

38. SPIES AND COLLABORATORS IN HIGH PLACES

1. Paul W. Blackstock, *The Strategy of Subversion: Manipulating the Politics of Other Nations* (Chicago, Illinois: Quadrangle Books, 1964), 35.
2. Desp. No. 745 from Rome dated 20/11/1956 to North America 1 & 2, 1, Clare Boothe Luce Papers, Box 642 Folder 7, Library of Congress, Washington, D.C.
3. Blackstock, *The Strategy of Subversion: Manipulating the Politics of Other Nations,* 38.
4. Hatch, *Ambassador Extraordinary: Clare Boothe Luce,* 210.
5. The letter was dated December 2, and it was most likely of the year 1953 or the first year of Clare serving as U.S. Ambassador to Italy given that she was chastised by Murray for not seeing the Pope. Her first audience with the Pope was on July 29, 1955. The letter was found in the Clare Boothe Luce Papers, Box 795 Folder 10, Library of Congress, Washington, D.C.
6. Hatch, *Ambassador Extraordinary: Clare Boothe Luce*, 234.
7. Murray to Clare Boothe Luce, Letter dated December 2 [1953], Clare Boothe Luce Papers, Box 795 Folder 10, Library of Congress, Washington, D.C.
8. Murray to Clare Boothe Luce, Letter dated December 2 [1953].
9. Murray to Clare Boothe Luce, Letter dated December 2 [1953].
10. Murray to Clare Boothe Luce, Letter dated December 2 [1953].

11. Jurgen Heideking and Christof Mauch, ed. *American Intelligence and the German Resistance to Hitler: A Documentary History* (Boulder, Colorado: Westview Press, 1996), 278.
12. Heideking und Mauch, *American Intelligence and the German Resistance to Hitler: A Documentary History,* 279-280.
13. Heideking und Mauch, *American Intelligence and the German Resistance to Hitler: A Documentary History,* 279-280.
14. Heideking und Mauch, *American Intelligence and the German Resistance to Hitler: A Documentary History,* 280-281.
15. Klaus Dohrn to Jay Lovestone, Letter dated February 29, 1956/March 5, 1956, Jay Lovestone Papers, Box 700 Folder 14, Hoover Institution on War, Revolution, and Peace, Stanford, California.
16. Klaus Dohrn to Jay Lovestone, Letter dated July 9, 1952, Jay Lovestone Papers, Box 305 Folder "1952," Hoover Institution on War, Revolution, and Peace, Stanford, California.
17. Another source of information for Dohrn was Fr. Gustav Gundlach, also a Jesuit, who was a professor at the Gregoriana in Rome, the Pope's speechwriter, a confidant of the Pope, and a very important contact for Dohrn about whom Dohrn said "I know him well." Gundlach was a principle source of information about the Pope's concern over "Leftist Catholics" who were "violently anti-liberal and anti-modernistic" while accepting Church authority and doctrine. *See* Klaus Dohrn to Henry R. Luce, Memorandum dated April 18, 1955 and entitled "Measures against leftist Catholicism," C.D. Jackson Papers, Box 48 Folder "Dohrn, Klaus (9)," Dwight D. Eisenhower Library, Abilene, Kansas.
18. C.D. Jackson to Klaus Dohrn, Letter dated November 17 1955, C.D. Jackson Papers, "Dohrn, Klaus (8)," Dwight D. Eisenhower Library, Abilene, Kansas; C.D. Jackson to Henry R. Luce, Grunwald, Alexander, Jessup, Donovan, Davenport et al., Memorandum dated November 17, 1955, C.D. Jackson Papers, "Dohrn, Klaus (8)," Dwight D. Eisenhower Library, Abilene, Kansas.
19. Klaus Dohrn to Jay Lovestone, Letter dated May 2, 1952, Jay Lovestone Papers, Box 305 Folder "1952," Hoover Institution On War, Revolution, and Peace, Stanford, California.
20. Jay Lovestone Papers, at Hoover Institution on War, Revolution, and Peace, Stanford, California.
21. Christopher Emmett to John Courtney Murray, Letter dated January 24, 1957, Christopher Emmett Papers, Box 91 Folder "Murray," Hoover Institution on War, Revolution, and Peace, Stanford, California.
22. Mary Bancroft, *Autobiography of a Spy* (New York: William Morrow and Company, 1983), 150, 162.
23. Klaus Dohrn to Jay Lovestone, Letter dated June 19, 1952, Jay Lovestone Papers, Box 305 Folder "1952," Hoover Institution on War, Revolution, and Peace, Stanford, California.
24. Klaus Dohrn to Jay Lovestone, Letter dated July 2, 1952, Jay Lovestone Papers, Box 305 Folder "1952", Hoover Institution on War Revolution and Peace, Stanford, California.
25. Given its position in the Clare Boothe Luce Papers, at the Library of Congress, it was probably from 1953.
26. John Courtney Murray to Clare Boothe Luce, Letter dated August 30 [probably 1953], Clare Boothe Luce Papers, Box 795 Folder 10, Library of Congress, Washington, D.C.

27. Christopher Emmett to John Courtney Murray, Letter dated December 23, 1958, Christopher Emmett Papers, Box 91 Folder "Murray," Hoover Institution on War Revolution and Peace, Stanford, California.
28. Christopher Emmett to Clare Boothe Luce, Letter dated December 2, 1955, Christopher Emmett Papers, Hoover Institution on War Revolution and Peace, Stanford, California.
29. Klaus Dohrn to Christopher Emmett, Letter dated October 22, 1958, Jay Lovestone Papers, Box 450 Folder "Emmett", Hoover Institution on War, Revolution, and Peace, Stanford, California.
30. Jay Lovestone Papers, Hoover Institution on War Revolution and Peace; Ted Morgan, *A Covert Life: Jay Lovestone: Communist, Anti-Communist, Spymaster* (New York: Random House, 1999), 244-258.
31. Morgan, *A Covert Life: Jay Lovestone: Communist, Anti-Communist, Spymaster*, 265-267.
32. Heideking and Mauch, *American Intelligence and the German Resistance to Hitler: A Documentary History*, 25.
33. Heber Blankenhorn, Memorandum dated July 22, 1942, from *American Intelligence and the German Resistance to Hitler: A Documentary History* (Boulder, Colorado: Westview Press, 1996).
34. Blankenhorn, Memorandum dated July 22, 1942 (emphasis present in original)
35. Blankenhorn, Memorandum dated July 22, 1942, 29-30.
36. Morgan, *A Covert Life: Jay Lovestone: Communist, Anti-Communist, and Spymaster*, 197.
37. Morgan, *A Covert Life: Jay Lovestone: Communist, Anti-Communist, and Spymaster*, 198-199.
38. Morgan, *A Covert Life: Jay Lovestone: Communist, Anti-Communist, and Spymaster*, 253.
39. Morgan, *A Covert Life: Jay Lovestone: Communist, Anti-Communist, and Spymaster*, 281.
40. Hersh, *The Old Boys: The American Elite and the Origins of the CIA*, 178-179.
41. Hersh, *The Old Boys: The American Elite and the Origins of the CIA*, 182-183.
42. Morgan, *A Covert Life: Jay Lovestone: Communist, Anti-Communist, and Spymaster*, 191-192, 285-286, 291-292, 303-305, 338, 344.

39. LUCE DEPARTS TO JOIN CLARE

1. Henry R. Luce to Dwight D. Eisenhower, Letter dated September 25, 1953, Clare Boothe Luce Papers Box 634, Library of Congress, Washington, D.C.
2. "Our Thirty Third Degree Enemies," *The Point*, June, 1953, Clare Boothe Luce Papers Box 703, Folder 13, Library of Congress, Washington, D.C.
3. Anthony Cave Brown, *Wild Bill Donovan: The Last Hero.* (New York: Times Books, 1982), 683-684.
4. Brown, *Wild Bill Donovan: The Last Hero*, 703-704.
5. "Nazis, The Vatican, and CIA," *Covert Action Information Bulletin* 25, (Winter 1986): 30. http://www.mosquitonet.com/~prewett/caqsmom25.2.html (accessed May 4, 2012).
6. Felix A. Morlion, OP, "The American Stake in the Accreditation of the Italian Government of the International University of Social Studies 'Pro Deo' Rome," dated February 8, 1964, Henry R. Luce Papers Box 52 Folder 7, Library of Congress, Washington, D.C.

7. Felix A. Morlion OP, "The American Stake in the Accreditation of the Italian Government of the International University of Social Studies 'Pro Deo' Rome," dated February 8, 1964, Henry R. Luce Papers Box 52 Folder 7, Library of Congress, Washington, D.C.
8. Felix A. Morlion, OP, "The American Stake in the Accreditation of the Italian Government of the International University of Social Studies 'Pro Deo' Rome," dated February 8, 1964, Henry R. Luce Papers Box 52 Folder 7, Library of Congress, Washington, D.C.
9. Morlion, "The American Stake in the Accreditation of the Italian Government of the International University of Social Studies 'Pro Deo' Rome," February 8, 1964.
10. List of founding directors of CIP, Henry R. Luce Papers, Box 52 Folder 7, Library of Congress, Washington, D.C.
11. Edward P. Lilly to Charles R Norberg, Memorandum dated 13 June 1952 Subject: Information on Rev. Felix A Morlion, OP & his work in Rome, OCB Secretariat Series Files, Box 4 File "Moral Factor (1)," Dwight D. Eisenhower Library, Abilene, Kansas.
12. Edward P. Lilly to The Director, PSB Memorandum dated July 7, 1952 Subject: The project of Rev. F. A. Morlion, O.P, OCB Secretariat Series Files, Box 4 File "Moral Factor (1)," Dwight D. Eisenhower Library, Abilene, Kansas.
13. Edward P. Lilly to The Director, PSB Memorandum dated July 7, 1952 Subject: The project of Rev. F. A. Morlion, O.P, OCB Secretariat Series Files, Box 4 File "Moral Factor (1)," Dwight D. Eisenhower Library, Abilene, Kansas.
14. Edward P. Lilly, "Memorandum of Conversation with Father Morlion, 5 November 1952" dated November 5, 1952, OCB Secretariat Series Files, Box 4 File "Moral Factor (2)," Dwight D. Eisenhower Library, Abilene, Kansas.
15. Felix Morlion to C.D. Jackson, Letter dated November 8, 1952, Henry R. Luce Papers, Box 52 Folder 7, Library of Congress, Washington, D.C.
16. Henry R. Luce Papers Box 52 Folder 7, Library of Congress, Washington, D.C.
17. Felix Morlion to Henry R. Luce, Letter dated October 1952 with attached document entitled "The Urgent Program of American Ideological Challenge to Marxism in Europe Through Intercontinental Forms and Seminars 'Realism vs Utopia'," Henry R Luce Papers Box 52 Box 7, Library of Congress, Washington, D.C.

40. LUCE DELIVERS THE AMERICAN PROPOSITION

1. Swanberg, *Luce and His Empire,* 503-507.
2. Geoffrey Plank, *Rebellion and Savagery: The Jacobite Rebellion of 1745 and the Rise of the British Empire.* (Philadelphia, Pennsylvania: University of Pennsylvania Press, 2006), 113, 115, 157, 165, 182, 184
3. Mark David Hall, *Roger Sherman and the Creation of the American Republic.* (New York: Oxford University Press, 2013), 27-28, 30, 52-53.
4. Annex "B" to PSB D-33 June 29, 1953, "U.S. Doctrinal Program", Psychological Strategy Board, declassified December 19, 2013.
5. Hall, *Roger Sherman and the Creation of the American Republic,* 24, 26.
6. Henry R. Luce to Jack Jessup, Letter dated October 28, 1953, Henry R. Luce Papers, Box 75 Folder 10, Library of Congress, Washington, D.C.
7. Luce to Jessup Letter dated October 28, 1953.

8. Luce to Jessup Letter dated October 28, 1953.
9. Luce to Jessup Letter dated October 28, 1953.
10. Henry R. Luce to Willi Schlamm, Letter dated November 1, 1953, Henry R. Luce Papers, Box 75 Folder 10, Library of Congress, Washington, D.C.
11. John Courtney Murray to Clare Boothe Luce, Letter dated November 1, 1953, Clare Boothe Luce Papers, Box 795 Folder 10, Library of Congress, Washington, D.C.
12. John Shaw Billings, Diary Entry for November 16, 1953, John Shaw Billings Papers, Diaries Vol. 36, 259, South Caroliniana Library, University of South Carolina, Columbia, South Carolina.
13. John Shaw Billings to Henry R. Luce, Letter dated November 16, 1953, Henry R. Luce Papers Box 75 Folder 10, Library of Congress, Washington, D.C.
14. Elsa Wardell to Henry R. Luce, undated note, Henry R. Luce Papers, Box 75 Folder 10, Library of Congress, Washington, D.C.
15. "Address delivered by Rev. Felix A. Morlion OP President of the International University of Social Studies Pro Deo, Rome at the ceremony honoring of Henry Luce, Editor in chief of Time, Life, Fortune in New York, May 22, 1957," Henry R. Luce Papers, Box 52 Folder 7, Library of Congress, Washington , D.C.
16. Henry R. Luce, "The American Proposition," Henry R. Luce Papers, Box 75 Folder 10, Library of Congress, Washington, D.C.
17. Luce, "The American Proposition."
18. Luce, "The American Proposition."
19. Luce, "The American Proposition."
20. Luce, "The American Proposition."
21. Luce, "The American Proposition."
22. Luce, "The American Proposition."
23. Luce, "The American Proposition."
24. Luce, "The American Proposition."
25. Luce, "The American Proposition."
26. Luce, "The American Proposition."
27. Luce, "The American Proposition."
28. Luce, "The American Proposition."
29. Kelly Laute to Allen Grover, Letter dated November 30, 1953, Henry R. Luce Papers, Box 75 Folder 10, Library of Congress, Washington, D.C.
30. Henry Luce, "A Definition of *Time,*" *The Ideas of Henry Luce* ed. Jessup, 81.
31. Luce, "A Definition of *Time,*" *The Ideas of Henry Luce* ed. Jessup, 83-84.
32. C.D. Jackson Papers, Box 90 Folder "Pro Deo 1962," Dwight D. Eisenhower Library, Abilene, Kansas.

41. ROME SPEAKS AGAIN (DECEMBER 1953)

1. Pope Pius XII, *Ci Riesce.* http://www.ewtn.com/library/PAPALDOC/P12CIRI.HTM (accessed August 15, 2010).
2. Pope Pius XII, *Ci Riesce.*
3. Pope Pius XII, *Ci Riesce.*
4. Pope Pius XII, *Ci Riesce.*
5. Pope Pius XII, *Ci Riesce.*
6. Pope Pius XII, *Ci Riesce.*

7. Francis J Connell to Pope Pius XII, Letter dated December 22, 1953, Francis J. Connell Papers, Redemptorist House Archives, Baltimore Province, Brooklyn, New York.
8. Segreteria Di Stato Vatican City to Francis J. Connell, Letter dated March 18, 1954, Francis J. Connell Papers Redemptorist House Archives, Baltimore Province, Brooklyn, New York.
9. Pelotte, *John Courtney Murray: Theologian in Conflict*, fn. 54 at 65-66.
10. Pelotte, *John Courtney Murray: Theologian in Conflict*, 40.
11. Pelotte, *John Courtney Murray: Theologian in Conflict*, 40-41.
12. Pelotte, *John Courtney Murray: Theologian in Conflict*, 42-43.
13. Pelotte, *John Courtney Murray: Theologian in Conflict*, 43-44; fn. 55 at 66.
14. John Courtney Murray to John Tracy Ellis, Letter dated December 12, 1953, John Courtney Murray Papers, Box 1 Folder 62, Georgetown University Library, Special Collections Division, Washington, D.C.
15. John Tracy Ellis to John Courtney Murray, Letter dated December 16, 1953, John Courtney Murray Papers, Box 1 Folder 62, Georgetown University Library, Special Collections Division, Washington, D.C.
16. Ellis to Murray Letter dated December 16, 1953.
17. John Courtney Murray to John Tracy Ellis, Letter dated December 19, 1953, John Courtney Murray Papers, Box 1 Folder 62, Georgetown University Library, Special Collections Division, Washington, D.C.
18. Murray to Ellis Letter dated December 19, 1953.
19. John Tracy Ellis to John Courtney Murray, Letter dated January 8, 1954, John Courtney Murray Papers, Box 1 Folder 62, Georgetown University Library, Special Collections Division, Washington, D.C.

42. HARRY, CLARE, AND JOHN

1. Clare Boothe Luce Papers Box 760 File 15, Library of Congress, Washington, D.C.
2. John Courtney Murray to Clare Boothe Luce, Letter dated "Saturday, 4th", Clare Boothe Luce Papers Box 795 Folder 10, Library of Congress, Washington, D.C.
3. John Courtney Murray to Clare Boothe Luce, Letter dated "Jan. 14," Clare Boothe Luce Papers Box 766 File 11, Library of Congress, Washington, D.C.
4. John Courtney Murray to Clare Boothe Luce, Letter dated February 27 [1962], Clare Boothe Luce Papers, Box 795 File 11, Library of Congress, Washington, D.C.
5. John Courtney Murray to Clare Boothe Luce, Letter dated September 13, 1953, Clare Boothe Luce Papers, Box 795 Folder 10, Library of Congress, Washington, D.C.
6. John Courtney Murray to Clare Boothe Luce, Letter dated December 13, 1955, Clare Boothe Luce Papers, Box 795 Folder 10, Library of Congress, Washington, D.C.
7. Clare Boothe Luce to John Courtney Murray, Letter, Clare Boothe Luce Papers, Box 795 File 11, Library of Congress, Washington, D.C.
8. Henry R. Luce to John Courtney Murray, Letter dated February 23, 1953, John Courtney Murray Papers, Box 2 Folder 145, Georgetown University Library, Special Collections Division, Washington, D.C.
9. Billy Graham, *Just As I Am: The Autobiography of Billy Graham* (San Francisco: Zondervan, 1997), 162.
10. Graham, *Just As I Am: The Autobiography of Billy Graham*, 213, 220, 392-393; John D.

Rockefeller III to Henry Luce, Letter dated March 22, 1950, Henry R. Luce Papers, Box 2 File 23, Library of Congress, Washington, D.C.

11. John Courtney Murray Address Book, John Courtney Murray Papers, Georgetown University Library, Special Collections Division, Washington D.C.
12. John J. McCloy to Henry R. Luce, Letter dated July 18, 1950, Henry R. Luce Papers, Box 2, Library of Congress, Washington, D.C.; Dorothea Philip to John Courtney Murray, Letter dated April 26, 1951, John Courtney Murray Papers: Box 1 Georgetown University Library, Special Collections Division, Washington D.C.
13. John Courtney Murray to Clare Boothe Luce, letter dated "Sunday," Clare Boothe Luce Papers, Box 795 Folder 10, Library of Congress, Washington, D.C.
14. John Courtney Murray to Clare Boothe Luce, letter dated "30th", Clare Boothe Luce Papers, Box 795 Folder 10, Library of Congress, Washington, D.C.
15. John Courtney Murray to Clare Boothe Luce, letter dated "December 23," Clare Boothe Luce Papers, Box 767 File 5, Library of Congress, Washington, D.C.
16. John Courtney Murray to Clare Boothe Luce, Letter dated "January 25," Clare Boothe Luce Papers, Box 204 File 16, Library of Congress, Washington, D.C.
17. John Deedy, *Seven American Catholics* (Chicago, Illinois: The Thomas More Press, 1978), 130.
18. W. A. Swanberg, *Luce and His Empire* (New York: Dell, 1973), 599.
19. Christopher Emmett to John Courtney Murray, letter dated January 24, 1957, Christopher Emmet Papers, Box 91 Folder "Murray," Hoover Institution on Revolution War and Peace, Stanford, California.
20. Emmett to Murray Letter dated January 24, 1957; John Courtney Murray to Christopher Emmett, letter dated February 2, 1957, Christopher Emmett Papers, Box 91 Folder "Murray," Hoover Institution on Revolution War and Peace, Stanford, California.
21. Clare Boothe Luce, "St. Francis Xavier – Then and Now" an Address By Honorable Clare Boothe Luce before the Tenth Annual Jesuit Mission Dinner a the Hotel Commodore, New York City, Thursday, November 6, 1952; Clare Boothe Luce Papers, Box 685 Folder 19, p. 2, Library of Congress, Washington, D.C.
22. Marshall Berger to Roy Alexander, Telegram dated February 26, 1955, Clare Boothe Luce Papers, Box 21 File 3, Library of Congress, Washington, D.C.; Henry R. Luce to Clare Boothe Luce, Letter dated February 26, 1955, Clare Boothe Luce Papers: Box 21 File 3, Library of Congress, Washington, D.C.; Henry R. Luce to Clare Boothe Luce, letter dated March 7, 1955, Clare Boothe Luce Papers, Box 21 File 3, Library of Congress, Washington, D.C.
23. John Courtney Murray to Clare Boothe Luce, letters dated "Dec. 18" and "Sunday," Clare Boothe Luce Papers, Box 795 Folder 10, Library of Congress, Washington, D.C.
24. Henry R. Luce, "A General Remark," Henry R. Luce Papers, Box 795 File 12, Library of Congress, Washington, D.C.
25. Wilfrid Sheed, *Clare Boothe Luce* (New York: Berkley Books, 1982), 160.

43. MURRAY ATTACKS OTTAVIANI

1. Pellotte, *John Courtney Murray:Theologian in Conflict*, 44-45.
2. Gustave Weigel, "Religious toleration in a world society" *America* Vol XC, (January 9, 1954), 375.

3. Weigel, "Religious toleration in a world society," 375-376.
4. Weigel, "Religious toleration in a world society," 375-376.
5. Edward A. Conway SJ, "Pius XII on 'the community of peoples,'" *America* Vol. XC, 13 (December 26, 1953): 335-337.
6. Conway, "Pius XII on 'the community of peoples'," 337.
7. Joseph Fenton, "The Teachings of the *Ci Riesce" American Ecclesiastical Review* Vol. CXXX, (February, 1954), 114-116.
8. Fenton, "The Teachings of the *Ci Riesce,*" 115-117.
9. Fenton, "The Teachings of the *Ci Riesce,*" 116-120.
10. Fenton, "The Teachings of the *Ci Riesce,*" 120-121.
11. Fenton, "The Teachings of the *Ci Riesce,*" 121-122.
12. Fenton, "The Teachings of the *Ci Riesce,*" 122-123.
13. P. M. J. Rock, "Pontifical Decorations," *In The Catholic Encyclopedia* (New York: Robert Appleton Company, 1908). New Advent: http://www.newadvent.org/cathen/04667a.htm (accessed May 26, 2012).
14. Francis J. Connell to Alfredo Cardinal Ottaviani, Letter dated March 1, 1954, Francis J. Connell Papers, Redemptorist House Archives, Baltimore Province, Brooklyn, New York.
15. "Biographical No. 86 (Revised)" dated June 12, 1963, Francis J. Connell Papers, Redemptorist House Archives, Baltimore Province, Brooklyn, New York.
16. "Biographical No. 86 (Revised)" dated June 12, 1963, Francis J. Connell Papers, Redemptorist House Archives, Baltimore Province, Brooklyn, New York.
17. Francis J. Connell to Alfredo Cardinal Ottaviani, Letter dated March 1, 1954, Francis J. Connell Papers, Redemptorist House Archives, Baltimore Province, Brooklyn, New York.
18. Connell to Ottaviani Letter dated March 1, 1954.
19. Connell to Ottaviani Letter dated March 1, 1954.
20. Pelotte, *John Courtney Murray: Theologian in Conflict*, 46.
21. Brother Luke Salm to Fr. Connell, Letter and typewritten notes, Fr. Francis J. Connell Papers, Redemptorist House Archives Baltimore Province, Brooklyn, New York.
22. Salm to Connell Letter and typewritten notes.
23. Salm to Connell Letter and typewritten notes.
24. Salm to Connell Letter and typewritten notes.
25. Salm to Connell Letter and typewritten notes.
26. Pelotte, *John Courtney Murray: Theologian in Conflict*, 47.
27. Walter J. Burghardt, "The Confrontation with Rome", John Courtney Murray Papers, Box 2 Folder 152, Georgetown University Library, Special Collections Division, Washington, D.C.
28. Pelotte, *John Courtney Murray: Theologian in Conflict*, 46.
29. Brother Luke Salm to Dr. Giovanni Giovannini, Letter dated March 27, 1954, Francis J. Connell Papers, Redemptorist House Archives, Baltimore Province, Brooklyn, New York.
30. Salm to Giovannini Letter dated March 27, 1954.
31. Salm to Giovannini Letter dated March 27, 1954.
32. Salm to Giovannini Letter dated March 27, 1954.
33. Francis J Connell to Cardinal Ottaviani, Letter dated March 27, 1954, Francis J. Connell Papers, Redemptorist House Archives, Baltimore Province, Brooklyn, New York.

34. Connell to Ottaviani Letter dated March 27, 1954.
35. Connell to Ottaviani Letter dated March 27, 1954.
36. Connell to Ottaviani Letter dated March 27, 1954.
37. Cardinal Ottaviani to Fr. Connell, Letter dated March 31, 1954, Francis J. Connell Papers, Redemptorist House Archives, Baltimore Province, Brooklyn, New York.
38. Pelotte, *John Courtney Murray: Theologian in Conflict*, 47.
39. Henry R. Browne to Fr. Connell, Letter dated April 3, 1954, Francis J. Connell Papers, Redemptorist House Archives, Baltimore Province, Brooklyn, New York.
40. Browne to Connell Letter dated April 3, 1954.
41. Francis J. Connell to Cardinal Ottaviani, Letter dated April 7, 1954, Francis J. Connell Papers, Redemptorist House Archives, Baltimore Province, Brooklyn, New York.
42. Cardinal Ottaviani to Francis Connell, Letter dated April 14, 1954, Francis J. Connell Papers Redemptorist House Archives, Baltimore Province, Brooklyn, New York.

44. MURRAY AND HESBURGH TEAM UP

1. E Michael Jones, *Libido Dominandi: Sexual Liberation and Political Control* (South Bend, Indiana: St Augustine's Press, 2000), 413-415.
2. Theodore M. Hesburgh, *God, Country, Notre Dame: The Autobiography of Theodore M. Hesburgh,* (Notre Dame, Indiana: University of Notre Dame Press, 1999) 209.
3. Hesburgh, *God, Country, Notre Dame: The Autobiography of Theodore M. Hesburgh*, 210-211.
4. Hesburgh, *God, Country, Notre Dame: The Autobiography of Theodore M. Hesburgh*, 211-212.
5. John Courtney Murray, "On the Structure of the Church-State Problem" *The Catholic Church in World Affairs.* Waldemar Gurian and M.A. Fitzsimons, ed. (Notre Dame, Indiana: University of Notre Dame Press, 1954), 11-32.

45. CAREFUL, HONEST, AND COMPETENT

1. Joseph Clifford Fenton, "Toleration and Church-State Controversy," *American Ecclesiastical Review* CXXX (May 1954), 341.
2. Fenton, "Toleration and Church-State Controversy," 342-343.
3. Fenton, "Toleration and Church-State Controversy," 330-333, 341-342.
4. Fenton, "Toleration and Church-State Controversy," 333-334.
5. Fenton, "Toleration and Church-State Controversy," 331-337.
6. Fenton, "Toleration and Church-State Controversy," 337-339.
7. Fenton, "Toleration and Church-State Controversy," 340.
8. Guseppe DiMeglio, "*Ci Riesce* and Cardinal Ottaviani's Discourse," *American Ecclesiastical Review* CXXX (June, 1954), 384.
9. DiMeglio, "*Ci Riesce* and Cardinal Ottaviani's Discourse," 384-385.
10. DiMeglio, "*Ci Riesce* and Cardinal Ottaviani's Discourse," 385-386.
11. DiMeglio, "*Ci Riesce* and Cardinal Ottaviani's Discourse," 385-387.
12. Fenton, "Toleration and Church State Controversy", 337.
13. Smith "Selected Methodological Questions in the Fundamental Moral Theology of Francis J. Connell, C.SS.R.," Dissertation for the Degree Doctor of Sacred Theology, 315.

14. Francis Connell, "Radio and the Red Curtain: The Morality of Psychological Warfare" *Catholic Men* (June-July 1954), 6.
15. Joann Burke, "Church, State Kept Separate by Catholics, Priest Contends," Francis J. Connell Papers, Redemptorist House Archives, Baltimore Province, Brooklyn, New York.
16. Burke, "Church, State Kept Separate by Catholics, Priest Contends."
17. Francs J. Connell, "Church and State," dated January 9, 1953 for the Clerical Students' Mission Conference, Francis J. Connell Papers, Redemptorist House Archives, Baltimore Province, Brooklyn, New York.
18. Connell, "Church and State."
19. Connell, "Church and State."
20. Francis J. Connell, "Are Catholics Patriotic?" dated February 21, 1954, Francis J. Connell Papers, Redemptorist House Archives, Baltimore Province, Brooklyn, New York.
21. Connell, "Are Catholics Patriotic?"
22. Francis J. Connell, "Propositions" undated, Francis J. Connell Papers, Redemptorist House Archives, Baltimore Province, Brooklyn, New York.
23. Francis J. Connell to Cardinal Ottaviani, Letter dated May 22, 1954, Francis J. Connell Papers, Redemptorist House Archives, Baltimore Province, Brooklyn, New York.
24. Connell to Ottaviani Letter dated May 22, 1954.
25. Connell to Ottaviani Letter dated May 22, 1954.
26. John Courtney Murray to Clare Boothe Luce, Letter dated May 9, 1954, Clare Boothe Luce Papers, Box 795 Folder 10, Library of Congress, Washington, D.C.
27. Murray to Clare Boothe Luce Letter dated May 9, 1954.

46. FENTON DISCOVERS THE SECRET OF MURRAY'S SURVIVAL

1. Joseph Fenton Diaries, Entries of May 29, 31, 1954, "Ninth Trip to Rome," 3-6, Joseph Clifford Fenton Papers, Catholic University of America, Washington, D.C.
2. Joseph Fenton Diaries, Entries of June 1, 1954, "Ninth Trip to Rome," 9, Joseph Clifford Fenton Papers, Catholic University of America, Washington, D.C.
3. Joseph Fenton Diaries, Entries of June 1, 1954, "Ninth Trip to Rome," 122, Joseph Clifford Fenton Papers, Catholic University of America, Washington, D.C.
4. Joseph Fenton Diaries, Entry for "Talk for Vatican Radio," "Ninth Trip to Rome," 15-22, Joseph Clifford Fenton Papers, Catholic University of America, Washington, D.C.
5. Fenton Diaries, Entry for "Talk for Vatican Radio," 22-30.
6. Joseph Fenton Diaries, Entry of June 8, 1954, "Ninth Trip to Rome," 49-50, Joseph Clifford Fenton Papers, Catholic University of America, Washington, D.C.
7. Fenton Diaries, "Ninth Trip to Rome," 50-61.
8. Fenton Diaries, "Ninth Trip to Rome," 62-68.
9. Fenton Diaries, "Ninth Trip to Rome," 69-78.
10. Fenton Diaries, "Ninth Trip to Rome," 84-85.
11. Fenton Diaries, "Ninth Trip to Rome," 85-86.
12. Joseph Fenton Diaries, Entry of June 12, 1954, "Ninth Trip to Rome," 112-116, Joseph Clifford Fenton Papers, Catholic University of America, Washington, D.C.
13. Fenton Diaries, Entry of June 12, 1954, "Ninth Trip to Rome," 112-116.

14. Joseph Fenton Diaries, Entry of June 19, 1954, "Ninth Trip to Rome," 152-153, Joseph Clifford Fenton Papers, Catholic University of America, Washington, D.C.

47. FOUR SECRET ERRONEOUS PROPOSITIONS

1. Francis Connell to Cardinal Ottaviani, Letter dated July 26, 1954, Francis J. Connell Papers, Redemptorist House Archives, Baltimore Province, Brooklyn, New York.
2. Connell to Ottaviani Letter dated July 26, 1954.
3. Pelotte, *John Courtney Murray: Theologian in Conflict,* 49.
4. Translation: "...cities... are absolutely bound, in the worship of the Deity, to adopt that use and manner in which God himself has shown that he wills to be adored."
5. Envelope marked "Under seal of the Holy Office to Be Burned" "Proposizioni Dottinali Erronee" from Francis J. Connell Papers, Redemptorist House Archives, Baltimore Province, Brooklyn, New York.
6. Joseph Fenton, Diary entry for October 28, 1954, Vol. 3, 162-165, Joseph Clifford Fenton Papers, Catholic University of America, Washington, D.C.
7. Fenton, Diary entry for October 28, 1954, Vol. 3, 162-165.
8. Francis J. Connell to Fr. Rector, Letter dated October 30, 1954, Francis J. Connell Papers, Redemptorist House Archives, Catholic University of America, Washington, D.C.
9. Francis J. Connell to Cicognani, Letter dated November 6, 1954, Francis J. Connell Papers, Redemptorist House Archives, Catholic University of America, Washington, D.C.
10. John Courtney Murray to Clare Boothe Luce, Letter dated November 17, 1954, Clare Boothe Luce Papers Box 795 Folder 10, Library of Congress, Washington, D.C.
11. Francis J. Connell to Ottaviani, Letter dated December 17, 1954, Francis J. Connell Papers, Redemptorist House Archives, Catholic University of America, Washington, D.C.

48. THE PRINCETON CONFERENCE, MAY 1954

1. C.D. Jackson to John Foster Dulles, Letter dated December 27, 1956, C.D. Jackson Papers, Box 69 Folder 1956(4), Dwight D. Eisenhower Library, Abilene, Kansas.
2. Jackson to Dulles Letter dated December 27, 1956.
3. A document was generated in April, 1954 which was stated "The 'Truthful Vision' presented to the world the 'realistic possibility of abundance' which is 'one of the reasons why people everywhere have long since refused to accept the inevitability of poverty and misery.'" Essential to this was the convertibility of currencies and the elimination of barriers to the free flow of goods, services, and people as new markets were developed. *See,* "World Economic Policy," 1, John Shaw Billings Papers Box III, Folder 200, South Caroliniana Library, University of South Carolina, Columbia, South Carolina. Luce gave a speech in November, 1946 before the American Association of Advertising Agencies in which he laid out a similar concept saying that foreign peoples and governments "*want* what the American businessman can bring. And they like the way he brings it." All of this was meant to increase wealth abroad and reduce barriers to trade. Luce, *The Ideas of Henry Luce,* ed. Jessup, 240-255.

4. Marie McCrum, interviewed by David Horrocks on May 15, 1975, "Oral Histories," Dwight D. Eisenhower Library, Abilene, Kansas, transcript 83-84.
5. Marie McCrum, interviewed by David Horrocks on May 15, 1975, "Oral Histories," Dwight D. Eisenhower Library, Abilene, Kansas, transcript 85.
6. "Strictly Confidential – Attendees Princeton May 15-16, 1954," C.D. Jackson Papers, Box 83 Folder "Princeton Economic Conference Follow Up," Dwight D. Eisenhower Library, Abilene, Kansas. A confidential list of attendees included Samuel Anderson (Assistant Secretary of Commerce), George Baldwin (MIT Center for International Studies), Dr. Lloyd Berkner (President of Associated Universities Inc.), Richard Bissell (CIA), Robert Bowie (State Department), Dr. Arthur Burns (Chairman Council of Economic Advisers), General Robert Cutler (Special Assistant to the President), Arthur Flemming (Director of the Office of Defense Mobilization), Robert Garner (Vice President The International Bank), Dr. Gabriel Hauge (Administrative assistant to the President), John Jessup (Time, Inc.), Professor Edward S. Mason (Harvard University), David J. McDonald (President of United Steel Workers of America), Thomas McKittrick (Chase National Bank), Professor Max Millikan (President Center for International Studies, MIT), H. Chapman Rose (Assistant Secretary of the Treasury), Professor Walt Rostow (Center for International Studies), Harold E. Stassen (Director Foreign Operations Administration), Charles Stillman (Vice-President Time, Inc.), Abbot Washburn (USIA), John Mackenzie (Atomic Energy Commission), Jerry Wiesner.
7. "Five Key Reports to the Government: A Summary," dated May 13, 1954, C.D. Jackson Papers, Box 83 Folder "Princeton Economic Conf., 5/54 – Misc Correspondence, etc. (1)," Dwight D. Eisenhower Library, Abilene, Kansas. These reports were the Gray Report from November 1950; the Rockefeller Report from March 1951; the Paley Report from June, 1952; the Bell Report from February, 1953; and the Randall Report from January, 1954
8. "Five Key Reports to the Government: A Summary" with reports.
9. "Proceedings of the Off the Record Conference Held Under the Auspices of Time, Inc.," C.D. Jackson Papers, Box 83 Folder "Princeton Economic Conf., 5/54-Transcript (1)", 24-27, Dwight D. Eisenhower Library, Abilene, Kansas.
10. "Proceedings of the Off the Record Conference Held Under the Auspices of Time, Inc.," 229-230.
11. "Proceedings of the Off the Record Conference Held Under the Auspices of Time, Inc.," 245-246.
12. "Proceedings of the Off the Record Conference Held Under the Auspices of Time, Inc.," 96.
13. "Proceedings of the Off the Record Conference Held Under the Auspices of Time, Inc.," 60-62.
14. "Proceedings of the Off the Record Conference Held Under the Auspices of Time, Inc.," 239-240.
15. "Proceedings of the Off the Record Conference Held Under the Auspices of Time, Inc.,"102.
16. "Proceedings of the Off the Record Conference Held Under the Auspices of Time, Inc.," 118-119m 252-253,
17. "Proceedings of the Off the Record Conference Held Under the Auspices of Time, Inc.," 114-115.

18. "Proceedings of the Off the Record Conference Held Under the Auspices of Time, Inc.," 122.
19. "Proceedings of the Off the Record Conference Held Under the Auspices of Time, Inc.," 128.
20. "Proceedings of the Off the Record Conference Held Under the Auspices of Time, Inc.," 130-131.
21. "Proceedings of the Off the Record Conference Held Under the Auspices of Time, Inc.," 139.
22. "Proceedings of the Off the Record Conference Held Under the Auspices of Time, Inc.," 153.
23. "Proceedings of the Off the Record Conference Held Under the Auspices of Time, Inc.," 265-267.
24. "Proceedings of the Off the Record Conference Held Under the Auspices of Time, Inc.," 276-280.
25. Dwight D. Eisenhower to C.D. Jackson, Letter dated April 14, 1954, C.D. Jackson Papers Box 83 Folder "Princeton Economic Conf., 5/54—Misc. Correspondence, etc. (2)," Dwight D. Eisenhower Library, Abilene, Kansas.
26. "The Crisis of 1954," C.D. Jackson Papers Box 83 Folder "Princeton Economic Conference Follow Up," Dwight D. Eisenhower Library, Abilene, Kansas.
27. Ibid.
28. "II. What National Interests Should a Foreign Economic Policy Serve," and "Notes on Foreign Economic Policy," dated May 21, 1954, C.D. Jackson Papers Box 83 Folder "Princeton Economic Conference 5/54 Follow Up," Dwight D. Eisenhower Library, Abilene, Kansas.
29. "Notes on Foreign Economic Policy," C.D. Jackson Box 83 Folder "Princeton Economic Conference 5/54 Follow Up," Dwight D. Eisenhower Library, Abilene, Kansas.
30. "Notes on Foreign Economic Policy."
31. Marie McCrum, interviewed by David Horrocks on May 15, 1975, "Oral Histories," Dwight D. Eisenhower Library, Abilene, Kansas, transcript 84.
32. Ibid., 87-88.
33. Ibid.
34. John Davenport to C.D. Jackson, Memorandum dated December 30, 1954, C.D. Jackson Papers, Box 39, Dwight D. Eisenhower Library, Abilene, Kansas.
35. Ibid.
36. C.D. Jackson to R.D. Paine, Jr., Memorandum dated January 3, 1955, C.D. Jackson Papers, Box 39, Dwight D. Eisenhower Library, Abilene, Kansas.

49. CO-OPTING RELIGION, JUST LIKE STALIN

1. Edward P. Lilly to Elmer B. Staats, Memorandum dated March 3, 1954 Subject: "The Spiritual and Moral Factor and OCB," OCB Secretariat Series, Box 5 Folder "Moral and Religious," Dwight D. Eisenhower Library, Abilene, Kansas.
2. Lilly to Staats Memorandum dated March 3, 1954.
3. Lilly to Staats Memorandum dated March 3, 1954.
4. "Religious Factors in OCB" dated May 20, 1954, OCB Secretariat Series, Box 2 File

"OCB 000.3 [Religion](File # 1) (1) [February 1954 to January 1957]," Dwight D. Eisenhower Library, Abilene, Kansas.

5. "Religious Factors in OCB," dated May 20, 1954.
6. "Religious Factors in OCB," dated May 20, 1954.
7. Edward P. Lilly to Elmer Staats, Memorandum dated October 26, 1954 Subject: "Report on the Consultation: "National Interest and International Responsibility," OCB Secretariat Series, Box 2 File "OCB 000.3 [Religion](File # 1) (1) [February 1954 to January 1957]," Dwight D. Eisenhower Library, Abilene, Kansas.
8. "Department of State for the Press" Number 94 dated February 4, 1952, OCB Secretariat Series, Box 5 Folder "Moral and Religious (2)," Dwight D. Eisenhower Library, Abilene, Kansas.
9. Richard M. Nin to Walter Bedell Smith, Letter dated September 10, 1954, OCB Secretariat Series, Box 2 Folder "OCB (Religion)," Dwight D. Eisenhower Library, Abilene, Kansas.
10. "A Proposal: A Spiritual Counteroffensive in Southeast Asia," OCB Secretariat Series, Box 2 Folder "OCB [Religion]," Dwight D. Eisenhower Library, Abilene, Kansas.
11. "Proposal to OCB by Foundation for Religious Action," OCB Secretariat Series, Box 2 Folder "OCB [Religion]," Dwight D. Eisenhower Library, Abilene, Kansas.
12. "Proposal to OCB by Foundation for Religious Action."
13. Transcription of article "Greater Sharing is Urged on U.S: Appeal by Religious Leaders Calls for Material Help to Needy Countries" and "Statement on American Abundance and World Need," OCB Secretariat Series, Box 2 Folder "OCB 000.3 [Religion] (File # 1) (2) [February 1954-January 1957]," Dwight D. Eisenhower Library, Abilene, Kansas.
14. Transcription of article "Greater Sharing is Urged on US: Appeal by Religious Leaders Calls for Material Help to Needy Countries" and "Statement on American Abundance and World Need."
15. Memorandum of Meeting of Ideological Subcommittee on the Religious Factor held May 18, 1955, at 2:00 p.m. in OCB Conference Room, dated May 19, 1955, OCB Secretariat Series, Box 2 Folder "OCB 000.3 [Religion] (File # 1) (1) [February 1954 to January 1957]," Dwight D. Eisenhower Library, Abilene, Kansas. The initial members included Major General Charles Carpenter, a Methodist minister who was the Chief of Chaplains for the US Armed Forces, Dr. Elton Trueblood, Quaker theologian and also chaplain of Harvard and Stanford, and Lilly.
16. Memorandum of Meeting of Ideological Subcommittee on the Religious Factor 3rd Meeting 27 June 1955 1:30 p.m. Conference Room C-206 708 Jackson Place, NW, OCB Secretariat Series, Box 2 Folder "OCB 000.3 [Religion] (File #1)(2)[February 1954-January 1957]," Dwight D. Eisenhower Library, Abilene, Kansas.
17. Memorandum of Meeting of Ideological Subcommittee on the Religious Factor 3rd Meeting 27 June 1955 1:30 p.m.
18. Edward P. Lilly, "Progress Report of the Ideological Sub-Committee on the Religious Factor (Period covered May 9 to July 8, 1955)" dated July 18, 1955, OCB Secretariat Series, Box 2 Folder "OCB 000.3 [Religion](File # 1)(2) [February 1954-January 1957]," Dwight D. Eisenhower Library, Abilene, Kansas.

50. IDEAS AS WEAPONS

1. Edward P. Lilly, "Memorandum of Meeting – OCB Working Group on Doctrinal Program" dated June 15, 1954 (Secret – Declassified 1998), OCB Central Files Series, Box 70 File "OCB 091.4 Ideological Program (File # 1) (3) (December 1953 - November 1954)," Dwight D. Eisenhower Library, Abilene, Kansas.
2. Cdr. Rubinow, "Study on Ideological Strategy" Draft dated 9 June 1954 Top Secret (Declassified 1992), OCB Central Files Series, Box 70 File "OCB 091.4 Ideological Program (File # 1) (3) (December 1953 - November 1954)," Dwight D. Eisenhower Library, Abilene, Kansas.
3. Rubinow, "Study on Ideological Strategy."
4. Rubinow, "Study on Ideological Strategy."
5. Rubinow, "Study on Ideological Strategy."
6. Rubinow, "Study on Ideological Strategy."
7. "Preliminary Report of the Working Group on the Doctrinal Program," July 1, 1954 (Confidential -- declassified 1998), OCB Central Files Series, Box 70 Folder "OCB 091.4 Ideological Program (File # 1) (3) (December 1953 - November 1954)," Dwight D. Eisenhower Library, Abilene, Kansas.
8. "Outline Plan of Operations," Draft 10.20.54 (Classified Confidential declassified 1998), OCB Central Files Series, Box 70 File "OCB 091.4 Ideological Program (File # 1) (6) (December 1953 - November 1954)," Dwight D. Eisenhower Library, Abilene, Kansas.
9. "Outline Plan of Operations for the Ideological Program" Draft (Confidential declass. 1998) OCB Central Files Series Box 70 Folder "OCB 091.4 Ideological Program (File # 1) (6) (December 1953 - November 1954)," Dwight D. Eisenhower Library, Abilene, Kansas.
10. United States Information Agency, "Ideological Program," OCB Central Files Series, Box 70 Folder "OCB 091.4 Ideological Programs (File # 1) (6) (December 1953 – November 1954)," Dwight D. Eisenhower Library, Abilene, Kansas.
11. "Operational Plan on the U. S. Doctrinal Program," OCB Central Files Series, Box 70 Folder "OCB 091.4 Ideological Programs (File # 1) (4) (December 1953 – November 1954)," Dwight D. Eisenhower Library, Abilene, Kansas.
12. "Militant Liberty" (Secret, declassified 1996) November 5 1954 JSPO/JCS, OCB Central Files Series, Box 70 Folder "OCB 091.4 Ideological Programs (File # 1) (8) (December 1953 – November 1954)," Dwight D. Eisenhower Library, Abilene, Kansas.
13. "Militant Liberty."
14. "Militant Liberty."
15. "Militant Liberty."
16. "Militant Liberty."
17. "Militant Liberty."
18. "Militant Liberty."
19. "Militant Liberty."
20. "Militant Liberty."
21. BG R. W. Porter to Elmer Staats et al, Letter dated December 1, 1954 and "Outline Plan of Operations for the US Ideological Program," OCB Central Files Series Box 70 Folder "OCB 091.4 Ideological Programs (File # 2) (2) (November 1954 – November 1955)," Dwight D. Eisenhower Library, Abilene, Kansas.

22. Elmer D. Staats, "Outline Plan of Operations for the U. S. Ideological Program (D-33)" dated February 16, 1955, and Memorandum for the Operations Coordinating Board dated February 21, 1955, OCB Central File Series, Box 71 Folder "OCB 091.4 Ideological Programs [File # 2] (7) [January – May 1955]," Dwight D. Eisenhower Library, Abilene, Kansas.
23. Dr. George N. Shuster, "Cultural Relations Between the Old World and the New," OCB Central Files Series, Box 70 Folder "OCB 091.4 Ideological Programs (File # 1) (4) (December 1953 – November 1954)," Dwight D. Eisenhower Library, Abilene, Kansas.
24. "Communism and Intellectuals," *Washington Post*, January 4, 1956, as found in OCB Central File Series, Box 71 File "OCB 091.4 Ideological Programs (File # 3) (7) [June 1955 – March 1956]," Dwight D. Eisenhower Library, Abilene, Kansas.

51. MURRAY IS, NOT REALLY, SILENCED

1. John Courtney Murray to Clare Boothe Luce, Letter dated May 19, 1955, Clare Boothe Luce Papers, Box 795 Folder 10, Library of Congress, Washington, D.C.; LaPira was outspoken in that he did not see the possibility of war between the US and the USSR, *see* Klaus Dohrn to Grunwald (with copies to Henry LuceHRL and C.D. Jackson), Memorandum dated January 6, 1956, C.D. Jackson Papers, "Dohrn, Klaus (7)," Dwight D. Eisenhower Library, Abilene, Kansas.
2. "U.S. Policy of Religious Freedom In Harmony With Catholic Teaching," November 21, 1953 as found in AND 0004.001 George Shea Papers, Box 19, Monsignor William Noe Field Archives and Special Collections Center, Seton Hall University, South Orange, New Jersey
3. Pellotte, *John Courtney Murray: Theologian in Conflict*, 51.
4. "Church-State Separation in US Good for Church; First Amendment Gave New Solution to Pluralism, Theologian Says," NCWC News Service July 26, 1954 as found in AND 0004.001 George Shea Papers, Box 19, Monsignor William Noe Field Archives and Special Collections Center, Seton Hall University, South Orange, New Jersey
5. John Courtney Murray, "A Catholic Principle," Francis J. Connell Papers, Redemptorist house Archives, Baltimore Province, Brooklyn, New York.
6. Murray, "A Catholic Principle."
7. Pelotte, *John Courtney Murray: Theologian in Conflict*, 51-52.
8. Pelotte *John Courtney Murray: Theologian in Conflict*, 52-53.
9. "Jesuit Receives Honorary Degree from Harvard: Rev. John C. Murray SJ Given Doctor of Letters," Francis J. Connell Papers Redemptorist House Archives, Baltimore Province, Brooklyn, New York.
10. Pellotte, *John Courtney Murray: Theologian in Conflict*, 53-54.
11. John Courtney Murray, Draft of address at Georgetown, Clare Boothe Luce Papers, Box 795 Folder 10, Library of Congress, Washington, D.C.

52. LIPPMANN'S PUBLIC PHILOSOPHY

1. Luce, "The Public Philosophy," *The Ideas of Henry Luce*, ed. John K. Jessup, 166-167.
2. Walter Lippmann, *The Public Philosophy* (New Brunswick, USA: Transaction Publishers, 2003), 150-152.

3. John Courtney Murray to Walter Lippmann, Letter dated March 28, 1955, John Courtney Murray Papers, Box 2 Folder 139, Georgetown University Library, Special Collections Division, Washington, D.C.
4. "History and Development," International Law Institute. http://www.ili.org/about/history.html (accessed July 14, 2012).
5. "Defining Education/Clarence Faust." http://www.studyplace.org/wiki/Defining_education/Clarence_Faust (accessed July 14, 2012).
6. John Courtney Murray to Walter Lippmann, Letter dated March 28, 1955, John Courtney Murray Papers, Box 2 Folder 139, Georgetown University Library, Special Collections Division, Washington, D.C.
7. Murray to Lippmann Letter dated March 2, 1955.
8. Walter Lippmann to John Courtney Murray, Letter dated April 6, 1955, John Courtney Murray Papers, Box 2 Folder 139, Georgetown University Library, Special Collections Division, Washington, D.C..
9. Walter Lippmann, *Essays in the Public Philosophy* (Boston, Massachusetts: Little, Brown and Company, 1955), 24, 27, 92, 93, 96, 110.
10. Lippmann, *Essays in the Public Philosophy,* 101, 107-109.
11. Lippmann, *Essays in the Public Philosophy*, 150-151.
12. Lippmann, *Essays in the Public Philosophy*, 150-151.
13. Lippmann, *Essays in the Public Philosophy,* 150-151.
14. David Rockefeller, *Memoirs* (New York: Random House, 2002), 438-439.
15. Rockefeller, *Memoirs,* 438-439.

53. MURRAY JOINS ANOTHER INTERCREDAL OPERATION

1. Plans announced for National Religious Conference, Henry R. Luce Papers, Box 37 Folder 1, Library of Congress, Washington, D.C.
2. Rt. Rev. Alfred L. Banyard and Dr. Charles Wesley Lowry to Henry R. Luce, Memorandum dated May 4, 1964, and entitled "Universities Project," Henry R. Luce Papers, Box 37 Folder 2, Library of Congress, Washington, D.C.
3. Banyard and Lowry to Luce Memorandum dated May 4, 1964.
4. "Highlights First National Conference on the Spiritual Foundations of American Democracy November 8-10, 1954 Washington D.C.," John Courtney Murray Papers, Box 1 Folder 80, Georgetown University Library, Special Collections, Washington, D.C.
5. "Highlights First National Conference on the Spiritual Foundations of American Democracy November 8-10, 1954, Washington D.C."
6. "Highlights First National Conference on the Spiritual Foundations of American Democracy November 8-10, 1954, Washington D.C."
7. "Highlights First National Conference on the Spiritual Foundations of American Democracy November 8-10, 1954, Washington D.C."
8. "Highlights First National Conference on the Spiritual Foundations of American Democracy November 8-10, 1954, Washington D.C."
9. "Things you may want to remember from the second national conference on spiritual foundations" sponsored by the Foundation for Religious Action in the Social and

Civil Order, Henry R. Luce Papers, Box 37 Folder 1, Library of Congress, Washington, D.C.

10. "Things you may want to remember from the Second National Conference on Spiritual Foundations," memorandum dated October 24-26, 1955; Charles W. Lowery to Henry R. Luce, Letter of November 10, 1955; Russell Bourne to Charles A. Lowery, Letter of December 1, 1955; all documents in the Henry R. Luce Papers, Folder "Foundation for Religious Action in Social and Civil Order 1954-1955," Library of Congress, Washington, D.C.
11. Charles Wesley Lowry to John Courtney Murray, Letter dated July 17, 1956, John Courtney Murray Papers: Box 1 Folder 80, Georgetown University Library, Special Collections, Washington, D.C.; Charles Wesley Lowry to "Friend," Letter dated January 13, 1955, John Courtney Murray Papers, Box 1 Folder 80, Georgetown University Library, Special Collections, Washington, D.C.; John Courtney Murray to Charles Wesley Lowry, Letter dated July 21, 1956, John Courtney Murray Papers, Box 1 Folder 80, Georgetown University Library, Special Collections, Washington, D.C.
12. Ibid.; Charles Wesley Lowry to Henry R. Luce, Memorandum dated August 27, 1964, Henry R. Luce Papers, Box 37 Folder 2, Library of Congress, Washington, D.C.

54. PIUS XII SPEAKS AGAIN ON CHURCH AND STATE

1. Joseph Clifford Fenton, "The Holy Father's Statement on Relations Between the Church and the State," *American Ecclesiastical Review* 133 (November 1955): 323-325.
2. Fenton, "The Holy Father's Statement on Relations Between the Church and the State," 324-325.
3. Fenton, "The Holy Father's Statement on Relations Between the Church and the State," 325-328.
4. Fenton, "The Holy Father's Statement on Relations Between the Church and the State," 327-328.
5. Fenton, "The Holy Father's Statement on Relations Between the Church and the State," 328-329.
6. Fenton, "The Holy Father's Statement on Relations Between the Church and the State," 328-329.
7. Fenton, "The Holy Father's Statement on Relations Between the Church and the State," 329-330.
8. Fenton, "The Holy Father's Statement on Relations Between the Church and the State," 330-331.
9. Francis J. Connell to Cicognani, Letter dated August 1, 1955, Francis J. Connell Papers, Redemptorist House Archives, Baltimore Province, Brooklyn, New York.
10. Francis J. Connell to Alfredo Cardinal Ottaviani, Letter dated December 15, 1955, Francis J. Connell Papers, Redemptorist House Archives, Baltimore Province, Brooklyn, New York.
11. Connell to Ottaviani Letter dated December 15, 1955.
12. "Reverend John Courtney Murray Addresses Jurists, Lawyers," article found in Francis J. Connell Papers, Redemporist House Archives, Baltimore Province, Brooklyn, New York.

13. Francis J. Connell to Ottaviani, Letter dated December 10, 1956, Francis J. Connell Papers, Redemptorist House Archives, Baltimore Province, Brooklyn, New York.

55. LIFE AND MURRAY ENDORSE AMERICA

1. John Courtney Murray SJ, "Special Catholic Challenges," *Life,* December 26, 1955, 144-146.
2. Murray, "Special Catholic Challenges," *Life,* 144-146.
3. Murray, "Special Catholic Challenges," *Life,* 144-146.
4. "The American Moral Consensus," *Life,* December 26, 1955, 56.
5. "The American Moral Consensus," *Life,* 56.
6. "The American Moral Consensus," *Life,* 56.
7. "The American Moral Consensus," *Life,* 56.
8. "The American Moral Consensus," *Life,* 56.
9. "The American Moral Consensus," *Life,*56-57.
10. "The American Moral Consensus," *Life,* 57.
11. "The American Moral Consensus," *Life,* 57.
12. "The American Moral Consensus," *Life,* 57.
13. "The American Moral Consensus," *Life,* 57.
14. "The American Moral Consensus," *Life,* 57.
15. "The American Moral Consensus," *Life,* 57.
16. Edward K. Thompson to John Courtney Murray, Letter dated January 5, 1956, John Courtney Murray Papers, Box 2 Folder 140, Georgetown University Library, Special Collections Division, Washington, D.C.
17. John Courtney Murray to Edward K Thompson, Letter dated January 10, 1956, John Courtney Murray Papers, Box 2 Folder 140, Georgetown University Library, Special Collections Division, Washington, D.C.
18. John Tracy Ellis to John Courtney Murray, Letter dated January 5, 1956, John Courtney Murray Papers, Box 1 Folder 62, Georgetown Library, Special Collections Division, Washington, D.C.

56. AMERICA WINS THE COLD WAR

1. C.D. Jackson to Henry R. Luce, Letter dated April 16, 1956, C.D. Jackson Papers, Box 69 Folder 1956(2), Dwight D. Eisenhower Library, Abilene, Kansas.
2. Jackson to Luce, Letter dated April 16, 1956.
3. Klaus Dohrn Report dated August 1, 1956, C.D. Jackson Papers, Box 47 Folder "Dohrn, Klaus (4)," Dwight D. Eisenhower Library, Abilene, Kansas.
4. Henry R. Luce to C.D. Jackson, Letter dated December 7, 1955, C.D. Jackson Papers, Box 70 Folder "Luce, Henry R. & Claire 1955," Dwight D. Eisenhower Library, Abilene, Kansas.
5. Henry R. Luce to E.K. Thompson, Letters dated April 9, 1956 and April 10, 1956, C.D. Jackson Papers, Box 71 Folder "Luce, Henry R (1956)," Dwight D. Eisenhower Library, Abilene, Kansas.
6. C.D. Jackson to Henry R. Luce, Letter dated May 13, 1955, C.D. Jackson Papers, Box 71 Folder "Luce, Henry R (1955)," Dwight D. Eisenhower Library, Abilene, Kansas.

57. MURRAY TARGETS N.O.D.L

1. John Courtney Murray, *We Hold These Truths: Catholic Reflections on the American Proposition* (New York: Rowman and Littlefield Publishers, Inc., 2005), 149-153.
2. Murray, *We Hold These Truths: Catholic Reflections on the American Proposition,* 153-154.
3. Murray, *We Hold These Truths: Catholic Reflections on the American Proposition,* 154-156.
4. Murray, *We Hold These Truths: Catholic Reflections on the American Proposition,* 156-159.
5. Murray, *We Hold These Truths: Catholic Reflections on the American Proposition,* 159-160.
6. Murray, *We Hold These Truths: Catholic Reflections on the American Proposition,* 160-162.
7. Murray, *We Hold These Truths: Catholic Reflections on the American Proposition,* 162-164.
8. Pelotte, *John Courtney Murray: Theologian in Conflict,* 55.
9. John Courtney Murray, "The Bad Arguments Intelligent Men Make," *America,* November 3, 1956. http://woodstock.georgetown.edu/library/Murray/1956A.htm (as accessed June 10, 2012).
10. John Courtney Murray to Cardinal Stritch, Letter dated October 17, 1956, Samuel Cardinal Stritch Papers, Archdiocese of Chicago Joseph Cardinal Bernardin's Archives and Records Center, Chicago, IL.
11. Murray to Stritch, Letter dated October 17, 1956.
12. Samuel Cardinal Stritch to John Courtney Murray, Letter dated October 19, 1956, Samuel Cardinal Stritch Papers, Archdiocese of Chicago Joseph Cardinal Bernardin's Archives and Records Center, Chicago, IL.
13. Stritch to Murray Letter dated October 19, 1956.
14. Murray, "The Bad Arguments Intelligent Men Make."
15. Murray, "The Bad Arguments Intelligent Men Make."
16. Msgr. Thomas Fitzgerald to John Courtney Murray, undated letter, Samuel Cardinal Stritch Papers, Archdiocese of Chicago Joseph Cardinal Bernardin's Archives and Records Center, Chicago, IL.
17. Fitzgerald to Murray undated letter.
18. Fitzgerald to Murray undated letter.
19. John Courtney Murray to Fitzgerald, Letter dated November 14, 1956, Samuel Cardinal Stritch Papers, Archdiocese of Chicago Joseph Cardinal Bernardin's Archives and Records Center, Chicago, IL.
20. Murray to Fitzgerald Letter dated November 14, 1956.
21. Murray to Fitzgerald Letter dated November 14, 1956.
22. Murray to Fitzgerald Letter dated November 14, 1956.
23. Cardinal Stritch to John Courtney Murray, Letter dated November 17, 1956, Samuel Cardinal Stritch Papers, Archdiocese of Chicago Joseph Cardinal Bernardin's Archives and Records Center, Chicago, IL.
24. Cardinal Stritch to Apostolic Delegate Cicognani, Letter dated May 21, 1957, Samuel Cardinal Stritch Papers, Archdiocese of Chicago Joseph Cardinal Bernardin's Archives and Records Center, Chicago, IL.
25. Stritch to Cicognani Letter dated May 21, 1957.
26. Stritch to Cicognani Letter dated May 21, 1957.
27. Donald J. Thorman to John Courtney Murray, Letter dated August 2, 1956, John Courtney Murray Papers, Box 2 Folder 242, Georgetown University Library, Special Collections Division, Washington, D.C.

28. John Courtney Murray to Donald J. Thorman, Letter dated August 5, 1956, John Courtney Murray Papers, Box 2 Folder 242, Georgetown University Library, Special Collections Division, Washington, D.C.
29. Pelotte, *John Courtney Murray: Theologian in Conflict,* 56-57.

58. AMERICANISM AFFLICTS THE CHURCH

1. Joseph Clifford Fenton, Diary Entry for August 13, 1956, Vol. 4 12th Trip to Rome, 17-25, Joseph Clifford Fenton Papers, Catholic University of America, Washington, D.C.
2. Joseph Clifford Fenton, Diary Entry for August 13, 1956, Vol. 4 12th Trip to Rome, 17-25, Joseph Clifford Fenton Papers, Catholic University of America, Washington, D.C.
3. Joseph Clifford Fenton, Diary Entry for August 28, 1956, Vol. 4 11th Trip to Rome, 79-80 , Joseph Clifford Fenton Papers, Catholic University of America, Washington, D.C.
4. Joseph Clifford Fenton, Diary Entry for August 30, 1956, Vol. 4 11th Trip to Rome, 87-89, Joseph Clifford Fenton Papers, Catholic University of America, Washington, D.C.
5. Joseph Clifford Fenton, Diary Entry for September 3, 1956, Diaries Vol. 4 12th Trip to Rome, 105-106, Joseph Clifford Fenton Papers, Catholic University of America, Washington, D.C.
6. Fenton Diaries Vol. 4, 106-107.
7. Fenton Diaries Vol. 4, 107-108.
8. Fenton Diaries Vol. 4, 104-105.
9. Fenton Diaries Vol. 4, 109-110.
10. Fenton Diaries Vol. 4, 111.
11. Fenton Diaries Vol. 4, 110-111.
12. Joseph Clifford Fenton, Diary Entry for September 4, 1956, 120-124, Joseph Clifford Fenton Papers, Catholic University of America, Washington, D.C.
13. Joseph Clifford Fenton, Diary Entry for September 4, 1956, 120-124, Joseph Clifford Fenton Papers, Catholic University of America, Washington, D.C.
14. Joseph Clifford Fenton, Diary Entry for September 6, 1956, 128-129, Joseph Clifford Fenton Papers, Catholic University of America, Washington, D.C.
15. Fenton Diary Entry for September 6, 1956, 130.

59. CHANGE IS IN THE AIR

1. Klaus Dohrn to Henry R. Luce, Memorandum dated April 18, 1955, C.D. Jackson Papers, "Dohrn, Klaus (7)," Dwight D. Eisenhower Library, Abilene, Kansas.
2. C.D. Jackson, Memorandum dated March 30, 1956 with Letter from Klaus Dohrn dated March 30, 1956, Clare Boothe Luce Papers Box 632 Folder 6, Library of Congress, Washington, D.C.
3. Jackson Memorandum dated March 30, 1956 with Letter from Dohrn dated March 30, 1956.
4. Eric Pace, "NY Times Obituary: Raymond-Leopold Bruckberger, Priest and Author, Dies at 90" *The New York Times,* January 12, 1998. http://dominicanhisory.blogspot.com/2011/07/raymond-leopold-bruckberger-op-1907.html (accessed June 24, 2012); Douglas Johnson, "Obituary: Fr Raymond Bruckberger," *The Independent,* January 9, 1998. http://www.independent.co.uk/news/obituaries/obituary-fr-raymond-bruckberger-1137571 (accessed June 24, 2012); C.D. Jackson to John Jenkisson, Letter dated

December 3, 1958, C.D. Jackson Papers, Box 39, Dwight D. Eisenhower Library, Abilene, Kansas.

5. C.D. Jackson to Kenneth Dougan, Letter dated April 18, 1958, C.D. Jackson Papers Box 39, Dwight D. Eisenhower Library, Abilene, Kansas; W. F. McHale to CD Jackson, Letter dated June 17, 1958, C.D. Jackson Papers, Box 39, Dwight D. Eisenhower Library, Abilene, Kansas.
6. C.D. Jackson to Henry R. Luce, Memorandum dated November 17, 1957, C.D. Jackson Papers, Box 71 Folder "Luce, Henry R. 1957," Dwight D. Eisenhower Library, Abilene, Kansas.
7. Pace, "NY Times Obituary: Raymond-Leopold Bruckberger, Priest and Author, Dies at 90"; Johnson, "Obituary: Fr. Raymond Bruckberger."
8. Jackson to Luce Memorandum dated November 17, 1957.
9. Jackson to Luce Memorandum dated November 17, 1957.
10. "Books: Hope of the World," *Time,* July 13, 1959. http://www.time.com/time/subscriber/printout/0,8816,869183,00.html (accessed June 24, 2012).
11. "Books: Hope of the World," *Time,* July 13, 1959.
12. C.D. Jackson to Kenneth Dougan, Letter dated April 18, 1958, C.D. Jackson Papers, Box 39, Dwight D. Eisenhower Library, Abilene, Kansas.
13. C.D. Jackson to Peter Drucker, Letter dated December 2, 1958, C.D. Jackson Papers, Box 39, Dwight D. Eisenhower Library, Abilene, Kansas.
14. Peter Drucker to C.D. Jackson, Letter dated November 25, 1958 with attached "Preface to American Edition of Fr. Bruckberger's Book," C.D. Jackson Papers, Box 39, Dwight D. Eisenhower Library, Abilene, Kansas.
15. C.D. Jackson to Henry R. Luce, Memorandum of April 29, 1958, C.D. Jackson Papers, Box 71 Folder Henry R. Luce 1958, Dwight D. Eisenhower Library, Abilene, Kansas.
16. C. D. Jackson to Allen Dulles, Letter dated December 10, 1956, declassified December 19, 2013, Dwight D. Eisenhower Library, Abilene, Kansas.
17. Jackson to Dulles Letter dated December 10, 1956.
18. Jackson to Dulles Letter dated December 10, 1956.
19. Jackson to Dulles Letter dated December 10, 1956.
20. Jackson to Luce Memorandum dated April 29, 1958.
21. Jackson to Luce Memorandum dated April 29, 1958.

60. MURRAY AND THE ROCKEFELLERS

1. Rockefeller Panel Reports, *Prospect for America: The problems and opportunities confronting American democracy – in foreign policy, in military preparedness, in education, in social and economic affairs (*Garden City, New York: Doubleday Press, 1961), 165-166.
2. Rockefeller Panel Reports, *Prospect for America*, 395-396, 402-403.
3. Rockefeller Panel Reports, *Prospect for America*, 413.
4. Memoranda dated September 16, 1952 and November 5, 1952 entitled "Arden house," Rockefeller Brothers Fund Archives, Rockefeller Archive Center, Sleepy Hollow, NY.
5. Louis Finkelstein to Henry Kissinger, Letter dated August 9, 1956, Rockefeller Brother Fund Archives S-7, Box 48, Folder 539, Rockefeller Archive Center, Sleepy Hollow, NY.
6. Jessica Feingold to Henry Kissinger, Letter dated February 5, 1957, Rockefeller Brothers Fund S-7 Box 48 Folder 539, Rockefeller Archive Center, Sleepy Hollow, New York.

7. Transcript of McKeon comments dated June 19, 1957, Rockefeller Brothers Fund, S-7, Box 48, Folder 542, Rockefeller Archive Center, Sleepy Hollow, New York.
8. Remarks by Father John Courtney Murray Professor of Philosophy, Woodstock College Overall Panel Meeting Wednesday, June 19, 1957, Rockefeller Brothers Fund, S-7, Box 48, File 545, Rockefeller Archive Center, Sleepy Hollow, New York.
9. Remarks of Father John Courtney Murray.
10. Remarks of Father John Courtney Murray.
11. Remarks of Father John Courtney Murray.
12. Remarks of Father John Courtney Murray.
13. Remarks of Father John Courtney Murray. (emphasis supplied)
14. Remarks of Father John Courtney Murray. (emphasis supplied)
15. Remarks of Father John Courtney Murray.
16. John Courtney Murray to Henry Kissinger, Letter dated June 25, 1957, Rockefeller Brothers Fund, S-7 Box 48, Folder 545, Rockefeller Archive Center, Sleepy Hollow, New York; John Courtney Murray to Henry Kissinger, Letter dated September 24, 1957, Rockefeller Brothers Fund, S-7, Box 48, Folder 545, Rockefeller Archive Center, Sleepy Hollow, New York.
17. Funding Records, Rockefeller Brothers Foundation, Rockefeller Archive Center, Sleepy Hollow, New York.
18. Funding Records, Rockefeller Brothers Foundation.
19. John Courtney Murray to Dean Rusk, Letter dated January 7 1958, Rockefeller Brothers Foundation, Rockefeller Archive Center, Sleepy Hollow, New York.
20. John Ensor Harr and Peter J. Johnson, *The Rockefeller Century* (New York: Charles Scribner's Sons, 1988), 520-521.

61. FIGHTING MODERNISM AND INFERIORITY

1. "Education: The Absentees," *Time,* July 8, 1957. http://www.time.com/time/printout/0,8816,825113,00.html (accessed January 1, 2010).
2. "Education: The Absentees," *Time,* July 8, 1957.
3. "Education: The Absentees," *Time,* July 8, 1957.
4. Joseph Clifford Fenton, Diary Entry for November 9 1957, Vol. 4 12th Trip to Rome, 213-214, Joseph Clifford Fenton Papers, Catholic University of America, Washington, D.C.
5. Joseph Clifford Fenton, Diary Entry for November 14, 1957, Vol. 4 12th Trip to Rome, 240-241, Joseph Clifford Fenton Papers, Catholic University of America, Washington, D.C.
6. Joseph Clifford Fenton, Diary Entry for November 14, 1957, Vol. 4 12th Trip to Rome,, 235-236, Joseph Clifford Fenton Papers, Catholic University of America, Washington, D.C.
7. Joseph Clifford Fenton, Diary Entry for November 19, 1957, Vol. 4 12th Trip to Rome, 269, Joseph Clifford Fenton Papers, Catholic University of America, Washington, D.C.
8. Joseph Clifford Fenton, Diary Entry for November 13 1957, Vol. 4 12th Trip to Rome, 228, Joseph Clifford Fenton Papers, Catholic University of America, Washington, D.C.
9. Joseph Clifford Fenton, Diary Entry for November 13 and November 17, 1957, Vol. 4 12th Trip to Rome, 226, 257-258 Joseph Clifford Fenton Papers, Catholic University of America, Washington, D.C.

10. Joseph Clifford Fenton, Diary Entry for November 17 1957, Vol. 4 12th Trip to Rome, 257-259, Joseph Clifford Fenton Papers, Catholic University of America, Washington, D.C.
11. Joseph Clifford Fenton, Diary Entry for November 17 1957, Vol. 4 12th Trip to Rome, 259-261, Joseph Clifford Fenton Papers, Catholic University of America, Washington, D.C.
12. Joseph Clifford Fenton, Diary Entry for November 21, 1957, Vol. 4 12th Trip to Rome, 276-280, Joseph Clifford Fenton Papers, Catholic University of America, Washington, D.C.
13. Joseph Clifford Fenton, Diary Entry for August 5, 1958, Vol. 4 13th Trip to Rome, 292-293, Joseph Clifford Fenton Papers, Catholic University of America, Washington, D.C.
14. Joseph Clifford Fenton, Diary Entry for August 19, 1958, Vol. 4, 13th Trip to Rome, 317, Joseph Clifford Fenton Papers, Catholic University of America, Washington, D.C.
15. Joseph Clifford Fenton, Diary Entry for August 17, 1958, Vol. 4, 13th Trip to Rome, 313, Joseph Clifford Fenton Papers, Catholic University of America, Washington, D.C.
16. Joseph Clifford Fenton, Diary Entry for August 27, 1958, "My 1958 Trip to Rome and Lourdes", 22-25, Joseph Clifford Fenton Papers, Catholic University of America, Washington, D.C.
17. Joseph Clifford Fenton, "The Components of Liberal Catholicism" *American Ecclesiastical Review* 139, 1 (July 1958): 36-38.
18. Fenton, "The Components of Liberal Catholicism," 38-40.
19. Fenton, "The Components of Liberal Catholicism," 42-44.
20. Fenton, "The Components of Liberal Catholicism," 44-48.
21. Fenton, "The Components of Liberal Catholicism," 48-53.
22. Joseph Clifford Fenton, "Religion and Charity In Our Lady's Contribution to the Apostolate" *American Ecclesiastical Review* 139, 4 (October 1958): 261-266, 266-275.
23. Robert Paul Moran, SS,. "Reflections on America" *American Ecclesiastical Review* 139, 4 (October 1958): 282-283.

62. PIUS XII DIES

1. Paul I. Murphy. *La Popessa* (New York: Warner Books, 1983), 297-300.
2. Joseph Clifford Fenton, "Pope Pius XII and the Theological Treatise on the Church" *American Ecclesiastical Review* 139, 6 (December 1958): 407-414.
3. Fenton, "Pope Pius XII and the Theological Treatise on the Church," 414-418.
4. David Shavit, *The United States in Asia: An Historical Dictionary* (New York: Greenwood Press, 1990), 132.
5. "Information on an eventual consistory for the appointment of new cardinals," C.D. Jackson Papers, Box 39, Folder "Ca-Misc (1)(2)," Dwight D. Eisenhower Library, Abilene, Kansas.
6. Klaus Dohrn to Jay Lovestone, Letter dated October 15, 1958, Jay Lovestone Papers, Box 364, Folder "1958," Hoover Institution on War, Revolution and Peace, Stanford, California.
7. Klaus Dohrn to Chris Emmett, Letter dated October 22, 1958, Jay Lovestone Papers, Box 450, Folder "Emmett," Hoover Institution On War, Revolution, and Peace, Stanford, California.

8. Klaus Dohrn to Jay Lovestone, Letter dated November 2, 1958, Jay Lovestone Papers, Box 364, Folder "1958," Hoover Institution on War, Revolution and Peace, Stanford, California.
9. Dohrn to Lovestone Letter dated November 2, 1958.
10. Klaus Dohrn to Jay Lovestone, Letter dated December 10, 1958, Jay Lovestone Papers, Box 364, Folder "1958," Hoover Institution on War, Revolution and Peace, Stanford, California.
11. Dohrn to Lovestone Letter dated December 10, 1958.

63. POPE JOHN CALLS A COUNCIL

1. Mario Benigni and Goffredo Zanchi, tr. Elvira DiFabio, *John XXIII: The Official Biography* (Boston, Massachusetts: Pauline Books & Media, 2000), 291-294.
2. Benigni and Zanchi, tr. Elvira DiFabio, *John XXIII: The Official Biography,* 291-294.
3. Benigni and Zanchi, tr. Elvira DiFabio, *John XXIII: The Official Biography*, 295-296.
4. "Text of the Motu Proprio on Ecumenical Council," NCWC News Service, June 6, 1960, Francis J. Connell Papers, Redemptorist House Archives, Baltimore Province, Brooklyn, New York.
5. Aradi Zsolt, Msgr. James I. Tucek, James C. O'Neill, *Pope John XXIII: An Authoritative Biography* (New York: Farrar, Straus and Cudahy, 1959), 293-294.
6. Zsolt, Tucek, O'Neill, *Pope John XXIII: An Authoritative Biography*, 294.
7. Benigni and Zonchi, tr. Elvira DiFabio, *John XXIII: The Official Biography,* 296.
8. "Pope Picks Group to Plan Council: 12 Churchmen Will Prepare Agenda, Make Contacts for Ecumenical Meeting," *The New York Times,* May 17, 1959, at Francis J. Connell Papers, Redemptorist House Archives, Baltimore Province, Brooklyn, New York. The leader of the commission was Cardinal Tardini and it consisted of twelve prelates: "Archbishop Giuseppe Ferretto, assessor of the Vatican's Sacred Congregation of the Consistory; Archbishop Pietro Sigismondi, secretary of the Sacred Congregation for the Propagation of the Faith; Archbishop Antonio Samore, secretary for extraordinary ecclesiastical affairs at the Vatican's Secretary of State; Father Acacius Coussa, assessor for the Sacred Congregation for the Eastern Church (Lebanese); Msgr. Cesare Zerba, secretary of the Sacred Congregation of Sacramental Discipline; Msgr. Pietro Palazzini, secretary of the Sacred Congregation of the Council; Father Arcadius Larraona, secretary of Sacred Congregation of the Religious (Spaniard); Msgr. Dino Staffa, secretary of the Sacred Congregation of Seminaries and Universities; Msgr. Enrico Dante, the Pope's master of ceremonies; Father Paul Philippe, commissioner of the Supreme Sacred Congregation of the Holy Office (French), and Msgr. Pericle Felici, auditor of the Vatican Tribunal of the Sacred Rota who will be the commission's secretary
9. "Pope Picks Group to Plan Council: 12 Churchmen Will Prepare Agenda, Make Contacts for Ecumenical Meeting."
10. "Bishops of world 'exceeded all expectations' in council letter responses," NCWC News Service (Foreign), June 13, 1960, in Francis J. Connell Papers, Redemptorist House Archives, Baltimore Province, Brooklyn, New York.
11. Dominico Cardinal Tardini Letter dated June 18, 1959, Francis J. Connell Papers, Redemptorist House Archives, Baltimore Province, Brooklyn, New York.

12. "4. De relatione Ecclesiam inter et statum civilem. Recenter quidam theology proposuerunt theoriam, juxta quam rectores civiles, qua tales, non suordinantur legi divino-positivae Christi, sed tantum legi naturali, ex qua thoria sequitur statum civilem non teneri agnoscere Ecclesium Catholicam noque ejus immunitates." Translation: 4. On the relation between the Church and the Civil State. Recently there have arisen certain theologies which propose theories that civil rulers, as such are not to be subordinated to the divine positive law of Christ, but only to the natural law. From this theory it follows that the civil state does not have to recognize the Catholic Church or recognize her immunities." Francis J. Connell to Archibishop O'Boyle, Letter dated July 28, 1959, Francis J. Connell Papers, Redemptorist House Archives, Baltimore Province, Brooklyn, New York.
13. "10. De relationibus internationalibus. Ad pacem praeservandam et caritatem fevendam inter nationes, valide utiles essent declarationes auctoritativae Ecclesiae de juribus et obligatinibus nationum inter se – e.g. de jure parvarum nationum existendi et libertate fruendi, de necessitate alicujus conventus internationalis cum auctoritate dissidia componendi, etc." Translation: "10. On International Relations. For the purpose of keeping the peace and fostering charity between nations, Declarations from the authority of the Church on the rights and obligations between nations - especially the rights of small nations to exist and to enjoy their freedom, there should be an international body (conventus, congress, agreement, covenant, pact) with authority to settle disputes, and so on." Francis J Connell to Archibishop O'Boyle, Letter dated July 28, 1959, Francis J. Connell Papers, Redemptorist House Archives, Baltimore Province, Brooklyn, New York.
14. "5. De signifcatione, extesione et auctoritate magisterii ordinarii S. Pontificio. In litteris Encyclicis Humani Generis S.P. Piux XII loquitur de magisterio ordinario S. Pontificis (DB, n. 2313), asserens nonnullos non sufficienter tulem potestatem agnoscere. Plenier explicatio hujus magisterii ordinarii a Concilio apte dari posset." Translation: "5. On the significance, extension, and authority of the ordinary magisterium of the Holy Father. In the Encyclical Humani Generis, Pius XII speaks of the ordinary magisterium of the Holy Father (DB, n. 2313), asserting that some people have not sufficiently understood this power. A fuller explanation of the ordinary magisterium at the Council might be appropriate."

    "6. De infallibili magisterio S. Pontifis relate ad doctrinas non formaliter revelatas, sed cum veritatitubs formaliter revelatis intime connexas. Theologi communiter docent charisma infallibilitatis ad has etiam doctrinas extendere, utpote medium necessarium ad protegendum et rite exercendum magisterium infallibile respectu veritatum revelatuarum. Sed decisio Concilii Oecumenici hanc rem definitve solvere poterit." Translation: "6. On the Infallible Teaching of the Holy Father in relation to doctrine not formally revealed, but intimately connected to formally revealed truth. Theologians generally teach that the charism of infallibility also extends to these doctrines, as a necessary means to protect and respect the due exercise of the infallible teaching of revealed truths. A decision of an Ecumenical Council would be able to definitely resolve this point."

    7. De asseneua interno debito doctrinis a magisterio Ecclesiae docentis auctoritative sed non infallibiliter propositis. Theolgi communiter docent verum assensum internum talibus docrinis debitum esse, quem assensum religiosum vocant. Declaratio Conciliii had de re auctoritative confirmaret, et iteraret praevinus decisiones S. Sedia (E.g. DB, 1684, 2007, 2008)." Translation: "7. On the internal assent owed to

the magisterial teaching authority of the Church not infallibly proposed. Theologians commonly teach that to assent to such doctrines ought to be given, which they call religious assent. A declaration of the council might confirm this authoritatively, and follow the previous decisions of the Holy See." Francis J. Connell to Archibishop O'Boyle, Letter dated July 28, 1959, Francis J. Connell Papers, Redemptorist House Archives, Baltimore Province, Brooklyn, New York.

15. Francis J. Connell Papers, Redemptorist House Archives, Baltimore Province, Brooklyn, New York.

64. MURRAY PREPARES TO PUBLISH

1. C.D. Jackson to Henry R. Luce, Letter dated November 13, 1958, C.D. Jackson Papers, Box 71, Folder "Luce, Henry R. 1958," Dwight D. Eisenhower Library, Abilene, Kansas.
2. Wilfrid Sheed, *Frank and Maisie: A Memoir with Parents* (London, UK: Chatto & Windus, 1986), 121-122.
3. Sheed, *Frank and Maisie: A Memoir with Parents*, 122.
4. Randall B Woods, *Shadow Warrior: William Egan Colby and the CIA* (New York: Basic Books, 2013), 202-206; Richard Gid Powers, *Not Without Honor: The History of American Anticommunism* (New York: The Free Press, 1995), 132-138.
5. Sheed, *Frank and Maisie: A Memoir with Parents*, 122-123.
6. Clare Boothe Luce to Henry R. Luce, undated letter from December, 1948, Clare Boothe Luce Papers, Box 20, Folder 10, Library of Congress, Washington, D.C.
7. Henry R. Luce to Clare Boothe Luce, Letter dated December 13, 1948, Clare Boothe Luce Papers, Box 20, Folder 10, Library of Congress, Washington, D.C.
8. Sheed, *Frank and Maisie: A Memoir With Parents,* 233.
9. Sheed, *Frank and Maisie*, 249.
10. Sheed, *Frank and Maisie*, 196.
11. Sheed, *Frank and Maisie,* 196.
12. Sheed, *Frank and Maisie,* 229.
13. Sheed, *Frank and Maisie,* 217.
14. Pelotte, *John Courtney Murray: Theologian in Conflict,* 75-76, n. 11, 12, 13, at 107.